OUR OWN TIME

OUR OWN TIME

A History of American Labor and the Working Day

David R. Roediger and Philip S. Foner

Contributions in Labor Studies, Number 23

GREENWOOD PRESS
New York • Westport, Connecticut • London

Library of Congress Cataloging-in-Publication Data

Roediger, David R.
    Our own time : a history of American labor and the working day /
David R. Roediger and Philip S. Foner.
      p. cm. — (Contributions in labor studies, ISSN 0886-8239 ;
no. 23)
   Bibliography: p.
   Includes index.
   ISBN 0-313-26062-1 (lib. bdg. : alk. paper)
   1. Hours of labor—United States—History. I. Foner, Philip S.,
1910- . II. Title. III. Series.
  HD5124.R57 1989
  331.25 ′7 ′0973—dc19   87-29543

British Library Cataloguing in Publication Data is available.

Library of Congress Catalog Card Number: 87-29543
ISBN: 0-313-26062-1
ISSN: 0886-8239

First published in 1989

Greenwood Press, Inc.
88 Post Road West, Westport, Connecticut 06881

Printed in the United States of America

The paper used in this book complies with the
Permanent Paper Standard issued by the National
Information Standards Organization (Z39.48-1984).

10 9 8 7 6 5 4 3 2 1

Contents

Preface   vii

1. Time, Republicanism, and Merchant Capitalism: Consciousness of Hours before 1830   1

2. Shorter Hours and the Transformation of American Labor, 1830-1842   19

3. Mill Women and the Working Day, 1842-1850   43

4. Hours, Labor Protest, and Party Politics in the 1850s   65

5. The Civil War and the Birth of the Eight-Hour Movement   81

6. Victory, Defeat, and New Alliances, 1867-1879   101

7. Haymarket and Its Context   123

8. The Rightward Drift of the AFL and the Temporary Decline of the Hours Issue, 1887-1908   145

9. Class Conflict, Reform, and War: The Working Day from 1907 to 1918   177

10. Trade Unionism, Hours, and Workers' Control in the Postwar United States   209

11. The Great Depression, the New Deal, and Shorter Hours   243

12. The Hours Stalemate since 1939   257

Notes   279

Bibliographical Essay   365

Index   367

Preface

Since the length of the working day is itself one of the principal repressive factors imposed upon the pleasure principle by the reality principle, the reduction of the working day . . . is the first prerequisite for freedom.
(Herbert Marcuse, 1955)

In effect, the progress towards a shorter work-day and a shorter work week is a history of the labor movement itself.
(George Meany, 1956)

According to an often-repeated but possibly apocryphal account, a simple "more" was Samuel Gompers' answer when the American Federation of Labor head was asked to summarize the labor movement's goals at the 1914 hearings of the United States Commission on Industrial Relations.[1] But American labor history has turned as often on the desire of workers for less. The reduction of working hours constituted the prime demand in the class conflicts that spawned America's first industrial strike, its first citywide trade union councils, its first labor party, its first general strikes, its first organization uniting skilled and unskilled workers, its first strike by females, and its first attempts at regional and national labor organization. The length of the workdays, this study argues, has historically been the central issue raised by the American labor movement during its most dynamic periods of organization.

At least three special characteristics of the shorter-hours movement set it apart from struggles over compensation in a way that makes unedifying the tendency of many labor historians to translate the "less hours" demand as "more leisure" and to treat it as a secondary adjunct of wage disputes.[2] In its tendency to foster unity, its capacity to evoke both political and trade union struggles, and its close relationship with the question of who would control workers' lives on and off the job, the shorter-hours demand stood apart.

Reduction of hours became an explosive demand partly because of its unique capacity to unify workers across the lines of craft, race, sex, skill, age, and ethnicity. Attempts by the employing classes to divide labor could be implemented with relative ease where wage rates were concerned. The skilled and the members of favored groups could draw wages marginally higher than those of the less well placed. Members of one craft had little immediate material interest in supporting the wage demands of those performing different tasks; the less exploited might not perceive their struggles as bound up with those of the more exploited.[3] With regard to hours, the situation was different. In any one workshop or factory it was usually impractical to allow part of the work force to leave long before the rest. The hours of labor for children and adults, journeymen and apprentices, women and men, skilled and unskilled, blacks and whites,

vii

German and Irish—for all those who met at one workplace—tended to be the same. Thus the shorter working day was an issue that could mitigate, though not completely overcome, the deep racial and ethnic divisions that complicated class organization in the United States. Sometimes the industries of an entire city adopted like schedules. The observations of Joseph Weydemeyer, a nineteenth-century German-American Marxist, reflect the extent to which the hours demand of one group found an echo in others. According to Weydemeyer, the movement for a shorter day "slings a common bond round all workingmen, awakens in them a common interest, pulls down the barriers too often raised between different trades, [and] declares war against all prejudices of birth and color." Since the demand for shorter hours promised to spread employment, the jobless also had a stake in hours struggles. They might identify, for example, with Samuel Gompers's ringing assertion that "so long as there is one who seeks employment and cannot find it, the hours of labor are too long."[4]

Second, the reduction of hours has a special role in American labor history because it elicited political as well as trade union struggles. Indeed during the nineteenth century, political campaigns to shorten the working day grew from early efforts to protect women and children, to demands that governments set an example with short hours for their employees, to calls for local, state, and even federal laws limiting the maximum schedules of all workers. These campaigns did not so much alternate with trade union actions as coexist with them. Many activists worked for both legislative reform and gains through collective bargaining in a manner quite at odds with those studies that posit a sharp division between "political" and "economic" labor reformers.[5] Even after the AFL and Gompers opposed all but protective shorter hours laws, legislative struggles continued apace and with some trade union support. By the time of the Great Depression, the AFL itself was at the head of those calling for a legislated thirty-hour working week.[6]

Finally and crucially, the hours issue intimately interacted with workers' aspirations for control over the fruits of their labor and over their lives and work. Any analysis of the working day tended to pose a basic question as to how long the employee worked "for himself" (to repay wages) and how long "for his employer" (producing, in Marxist terms, surplus value). Thus David Montgomery's remark that Reconstruction era eight-hour advocates "found themselves reluctantly drawn by their own logic into challenging the very concept of private property," applies to other periods as well.[7]

Moreover, to the same extent that the reduction of hours pared down the period during which bosses exercised control on the job, it augmented the time during which workers could pursue their own interests. The writings of National Labor Union organizer Richard Trevellick capture something of the millennial hope which some labor leaders invested in the vistas opened by the promise of a working populace commanding unprecedented amounts of free time. Writing after the Civil War, Trevellick, in a florid but not atypical passage, reviewed five decades of shorter hours efforts:

> The educational advance made by the . . . laboring classes since the inaug-
> uration of the ten-hour rule of labor has been more than equal to every
> step taken . . . since John the Baptist . . . . Add two hours to the liberty
> term, and we shall increase the ratio of progress threefold . . . our country
> shall have . . . all classes of laboring men and women educated to a stan-
> dard of physical, mental, moral and social excellence that will be its own
> security against idleness, vice, degradation and misery.[8]

Here and elsewhere, shorter hours implied control of leisure, of intellect and even of political power.

It is tempting to see such demands for control over increased leisure as con-
comitant with workers' acceptance of increasingly alienated labor—as a tradeoff of control off the job for control on it. Indeed in some instances, workers and their unions countenanced (and even proposed) speedups in return for shorter hours, and in other instances, management instituted a tightening of breaks and supervision after a liberalization of hours.[9] Nonetheless, at least through 1920, shorter hours offensives generally coexisted with and reinforced struggles for control over work rather than undermining them, so much so that Montgomery is quite justified in terming reduced hours a "control" demand. Indeed, employers perceived as early as the 1830s that exercising power over when to work could go hand in hand with exercising power over how to work. Thus, the masters' appeals during the 1832 Boston ten-hour strike branded the demand as one which "strikes at the very heart of industry."[10] That protests over hours energized a unified labor movement was also connected with their relationship to control struggles. As Richard Price describes in his work on the British building trades, a standardized and shorter working day gave a common control demand to craftsmen whose other control demands were quite particularistic. Hours served sim-
ilarly as a common denominator for American control struggles. In addition, stan-
dardizing hours helped remove from lower management one source of arbitrary control over workers: the manipulation of long days, layoffs, and unfavorable shifts.[11] That the connection between control and a shorter working day was lost after 1920 is, we argue, a major factor in lack of recent labor progress in reducing working hours.

Several factors complicate the study of the shorter hours movement. As tables 1-A and 1-B indicate, progress in reducing hours has not resulted from easily summarized leaps forward, as first the ten-hour and then the eight-hour demand won universal acceptance.

Tables 1-A and 1-B[12]

Table 1-A

Average Daily Hours of Labor, 1840-1896

Year	Hours
1840	11.4
1848	11.3
1856	11.0
1864	10.8
1872	10.5
1880	10.3
1888	10.0
1896	9.9

Fulltime workers/Six-day 1840 week, Twenty-one selected industries/median.

Table 1-B

Average Weekly Hours, 1900-1972

Year	Hours
1900	59.0
1908	56.8
1916	54.9
1924	50.4
1932	38.3
1940	38.1
1948	40.0
1956	40.4
1964	40.7
1972	40.6

Fulltime workers, all manufacturing industries/median.

Lessening of hours has been gradual and piecemeal, often local and uneven. If we consider also the plethora of other influences on the length of the average workweek—Saturday work, Sunday work, the number of holidays, moonlighting, voluntary and forced overtime, the length of meals and breaks— the hours picture becomes a complex one indeed. This study has tried to do justice to that complexity by discussing both the main directions of the shorter-working-day movement and by alluding to other important factors influencing the length of labor.

The informal activities of workers add another dimension to the question of hours. In the United States, with heavy and extended immigration, generation after generation brought preindustrial habits to the workplace and limited their hours in accordance with a traditional sense of time. A host of traditions—fairs, blue Mondays, festivals, saints' days—further added to the time that workers were off their jobs, as did the simple urge to hunt or fish during certain seasons.[13]

The history of informal resistance to the time demands of employers is so long, its local and ethnic variations are so marked, and the sources illuminating it are so fugitive, that this volume cannot pretend to an exhaustive treatment of the subject. In one area, that of the very different labor system of Afro-American slavery, we do not attempt to add to the small but suggestive body of literature discussing the informal mechanisms through which the enslaved regulated their hours of labor.[14] Generally, information on the coming of industrial time-discipline and on labor's resistance to it is included as a compelling subplot in the story of the broader struggle for a shorter working day. In addition, the changes in how working people view and use leisure are included as vital, though secondary themes.

In bringing together labor and leisure, in telling the story of how workers used both formal and informal means to shape the working day and in combining our different strengths as historians, we have sought to challenge the artificial boundary between the "old" (that is, narrative and institutional) and the "new" (that is, cultural and analytical) labor history. More important, we have sought to reinterpret U.S. labor history while closing the gap recently noted by Benjamin K. Hunnicutt, who writes:

> Historians have yet to come to grips with the fact that the work week was reduced gradually but steadily for a century before the Depression and has remained stable since then. Nor have they explained why the cause of shorter hours was a crucial liberal reform from the 1830's to the 1930's, but since then it has dropped from view.[15]

The criticisms and suggestions of others have contributed immeasurably to this study. Particular thanks are due to Joel Shufro, Howard Rock, Josef Barton, David Montgomery, Herbert Aptheker, Steven Rosswurm, Charles Steffen, George Fredrickson, Milton Cantor, James Kirby Martin, Mark Lause, Franklin Rosemont, Henry Rosemont, Bruce Nelson, Al Young, Robert Wiebe, Richard Schneirov, Steven Sapolsky, Elaine Calmenson, Fred Thompson, and Robert Rodden. Mike Davis offered a particularly penetrating reading of the revised manuscript. David Roediger wishes to acknowledge long standing intellectual debts to Carolyn Odle, Ronald Harris, Margaret George, John Higginson, J. Carroll Moody, and especially to Sterling Stuckey and George Rawick. Further thanks are due to his wife, Jean M. Allman, for criticism and for comradeship, and to his sons, for forbearance. David Roediger dedicates his portion of the manuscript to his parents.

Research has been greatly facilitated by the cooperation of librarians and archivists at Northwestern University Library, Lincoln University Library, the State Historical Society of Wisconsin, University of Michigan's Labadie Collection, Pennsylvania State Library, University of Chicago, Baker Library of Harvard University, New York Public Library, Missouri Historical Society, Columbia (Illinois) Public Library, Yale University Library, Northern Illinois University

Library, Massachusetts State Archives and Library, Chicago Public Library, Washington University Library, Catholic University Library and Archives, University of Maryland Library, University of North Carolina Library and the Southern Historical Collection, Reuther Library of Wayne State University, Newark Public Library, Chicago Historical Society, Newberry Library, the Library of Congress, National Archives, and the University of Missouri Libraries at Columbia and St. Louis.

Financial support from the Northwestern University Fellowship, American Council of Learned Societies, Dissertation Year Fellowship, and Special Dissertation Research Grant aided the study. Travel funds from the American Philosophical Society were also useful as were summer grants from the University of Missouri Research Council and Newberry Library.

The nature of our collaboration on this volume requires one further comment. With the exception of chapter 11, the text has been written by David Roediger. Philip Foner, in addition to writing chapter 11, has provided voluminous research materials essential to the completion of the study.

Thanks to Patty Eggleston for expertly and patiently typing the final draft of the manuscript.

OUR OWN TIME

1

Time, Republicanism, and Merchant Capitalism: Consciousness of Hours before 1830

To industrial civilizations, few propositions seem more obvious than the idea that twelve or more hours of daily labor are too many and that workers can be expected to organize against so taxing a schedule. However, as E. P. Thompson's work on the perception of time in British history demonstrates, the notion that work should be timed and limited according to the position of the hands of a clock appeared quite foreign to preindustrial populations. In agricultural societies the rhythms of nature provided a more apt mechanism by which to regulate the term of labor. Dawn and dusk, winter and summer, planting and harvest, sun and rain, all shaped the working days of preindustrial humanity. In early America the hours of daylight bounded the day's work but left room for variation as to how those hours would be spent. Weather, season, and the nature of the work to be done made labor anything but routine, and a variety of breaks divided the day. The unit of labor was the task, not the hours, and a good working day was measured by the portion of field plowed or the number of rows harvested. Hiring of labor, even in the agricultural setting, quickened the employer's interest in how much work could be performed in a set period of time, but measurements remained impressionistic. Only later, with the expansion of markets and with increased demand for goods by merchant capitalists, did the employer conceive of work less in terms of tasks than of time spent in the orderly pursuit of routinized production. Still later, to use Thompson's phrasing, as workers "accepted the categories of their employers and learned to fight back within them," the possibility of struggle for shorter hours emerged.[1]

This chapter explores those factors that gave rise to a "time" rather than a "task" orientation toward work in America and laid the basis for the mass shorter-hours movement that emerged in the second quarter of the nineteenth century. While following Thompson in stressing changes at the workplace in accounting for the rise of struggles over the length of labor, this chapter argues that the United States presents a different case from Thompson's Britain. Specifi-

1

cally, the American movement gathered force in very small artisan shops embedded in a merchant capitalist economy, while, according to Thompson, British labor's combativeness over hours must be traced to the "transition to industrial capitalism" and to mechanization in industry. The predominance of bakers, house carpenters, shipwrights, and painters in the early American movement serves to point up how poorly the specifics of Thompson's model apply on the Atlantic's other shore, in that these trades did not experience especially rapid technological and mechanical change in the early nineteenth century.[2] The occurrence, for example, of a general strike for the ten-hour day in Philadelphia in 1835 calls into question any direct link between large-scale development of industrial capitalism and shorter-hours movement. As late as 1850 the mean number of workers in that city's manufacturing workplaces was ten and the median number only four.[3]

In the American context it was not so much the rise of factory production, nor even the use of machinery, that first precipitated new attitudes toward time. Instead, subtle and often small reorganizations, subdivisions, and speedups of production were crucial. Nor did working people merely react to objective alterations in the labor process. Many viewed each change through a prism of republican ideology which suspected increases in supervision and cherished both customary rights on the job and the ideal of an independent craftsman. Energized by the American Revolution, some workers came to regard long hours as a roadblock to their full participation in political affairs and began to make a distinction between working time and time for civic duty, even before they differentiated between labor and leisure.

Colonial America was heir to an especially long-standing British concern over the hours of labor on the part of both guilds and government. As early as 1321 the London Weavers' Guild approved "ordinances" to cut their hours of labor. Five other crafts in the same city ordered that "no one of the said trade shall work on Saturday after Noon has been rung out" and forbade further labor "until Monday morning following" in a series of work rules passed between 1344 and 1389.[4] These early successes, linked to the extreme labor shortages associated with the Black Death, helped provoke the "Statutes of Labourers," a series of laws that set less favorable scales of pay and hours for day laborers and artisans. These laws, the first of which was passed in 1350, typically specified a fourteen-or fifteen-hour day in the warmer months with three hours set aside for meals and rest. The winter working day stretched from 5 A.M. until dark and allowed less meal time. A preamble to the 1495 statute complains that laborers "waste much part of their day . . . in late coming unto their work, early departing there from, long sitting at their [meals], and long time of sleeping after noon," and thus indicates that one goal of the laws was to increase working hours. In 1563 British labor law was systematized, but not significantly altered, in the "Statute of Artificers," a code that influenced the American colonies. The number of holidays providing respite from labor in premodern Britain—as many as 165 annually—rapidly dwindled, especially under Puritan rule, reaching a nadir in 1647 with the abolition of Easter and Christmas. But the codification of Sabbath-keeping somewhat mitigated this loss of leisure.[5]

With the rising incidence of wage labor and mechanization, collective actions over hours grew in Britain. Between 1718 and 1734 London wheelwrights struck on three occasions to reduce their hours of work. By 1720 journeymen tailors had begun a shorter-hours campaign, which was to involve members of that craft in eight collective protests in four English towns over the next half century. In 1760 weavers in Wigan and cabinetmakers in Manchester and in Liverpool struck "to reduce the number of hours they have always worked." London cabinetmakers imitated their Manchester-Liverpool fellows during the next year. In the years immediately before the American Revolution, journeymen hatters in London won a reduction in hours. The eighteenth-century British efforts to reduce the hours of work were neither quickly nor universally successful. A 1734 pamphlet breaks down the working hours of 118 London trades as follows: thirteen from 6 A.M. to 6 P.M.; three from 7 to 7; sixty-one from 6 to 8; thirty-nine from 6 to 9; and two from 5 to 9. But the trend was toward a ten-hour day in most artisan trades in Britain as the eighteenth century proceeded—a trend not applicable in the colonies, however.[6]

The regular working hours for laborers and craftsmen in colonial America generally extended from sunrise to sunset at least six days per week. The actual hours of labor were less than this arduous schedule might suggest because meals, morning and afternoon rest periods, and other customary pauses broke up the working day. In accordance with the "Statute of Artificers," with which some colonial workers were familiar, the day included three hours for meals and rest in summer and two and one-half hours for food and breaks during the colder months. In theory, sunrise to sunset labor would indicate a fourteen-hour day in the summer and an eleven-hour winter working day, but custom made an average of just over ten hours nearer the norm. Even thus mitigated, more than twelve hours of actual labor were required on the year's hottest and longest days.[7]

In some colonies laws also regulated the hours of work, but the bearing of these laws on actual practice is problematic, and the earliest legal codes are sometimes misleading indices as to the prevailing work schedules. One might despair, for example, that any progress toward shortening hours has been made in 350 years after reading Virginia Governor Thomas Gates's 1621 order on labor. Gates required settlers in his colony to work from 6 to 10 A.M. and again in the afternoon from 2 until 4—a six-hour day! Similarly, the 1641 laws of Hingham, Massachusetts, included a statute regulating "the prices of labourers' wages and commodities" which contained a provision that would not apply to American labor generally for three centuries. "They are," the law stated, "to work eight hours a day." The picture was hardly as bright as the laws imply, however. Richard B. Morris suggests that the latter law applied only to field teams (who may have done other work part of the day) and that Hingham's craftsmen worked far longer hours.[8]

Later colonial legislation on the hours of labor conformed more closely to the pattern of a sunrise-to-sunset working day. Seventeenth century laws in Connecticut and Massachusetts set either ten or twelve hours "besides repast" as a summer workday and termed eight or nine hours, exclusive of meals, "a full dayes worke" in the winter.[9] A wage bill proposed to the Massachusetts legislature in 1670 is of interest in that it set a laborer's summer schedule of work at "10 hours in the daye besides repast" and specified that daily wages for the months from October until April would be less than 65 percent of the summer amount. In Pennsylvania a 1682 law required laborers and servants to work the "whole day, the Master or Dame allowing time for food and rest." From the early days, that colony and others apparently continued the English custom of using bells to announce the day's start and finish as well as the rest periods for workers.[10]

Indeed, a strong Protestant, and often specifically Puritan, heritage combined with racism and with mercantilist strictures against idleness to elevate work bells and steady labor to a significantly more exalted position than would be the norm in a preindustrial society. It is true that the most successful colonists, particularly those who employed labor, exhibited the most admiration for persistence and punctuality. But such values were also extant in the larger settler population. As the work of William Cronin and especially of Edmund Morgan suggests, the encounter with Indians led white migrants to emphasize their own devotion to settled agriculture and steady work, in order to differentiate themselves from the indigenous people they encountered, fought, and often dispossessed. Indeed, one justification for such dispossession was the notion that whites could more efficiently husband the New World's resources than could allegedly "lazy Indians." The desire of whites to distance themselves from black slaves and to justify slavery also reinforced self-images of the white population as comparatively hardworking, though in the invidious comparisons with both red and black, whites clearly described their own perceptions, not reality.[11] Moreover, in the early stages of settlement much of society probably also came to fear that idleness could endanger its already precarious existence and to appreciate, in the absence of clocks and watches, the bells that called citizens to work and roughly subdivided the day. In New York City in 1733, for example, the Fort Bell had its clapper replaced, much to the delight of at least one of the city's artisans who promised that the clapper "will produce a great Reformation . . . we shall breakfast, dine and sup, according to Rule and Compass, and know how to square our work as in the days of our Forefathers."

Since most colonial artisans worked for themselves or looked forward to a speedy rise to doing so, the labor being disciplined and the rewards of that labor were the artisan's own. Benjamin Franklin, later the hero of many artisans, spoke for more than the mercantile elite of colonial society when he advised in 1751, "our time is reduced to a Standard, and the Bullion of the Day minted out into Hours, the Industrious few know how to employ every Piece of Time to a real Advantage . . . he that is prodigal of his Hours is . . . a Squanderer of Money." Colonial society, clearly preindustrial, was for a variety of reasons committed both to steady work and to monetary gain. A rudimentary notion that "time is money" even existed in some quarters. However, and critically, the methods of production outside the slave South still relied largely on the farmer and on the self-paced independent artisan. Though cultural sanctions favored diligent labor, that diligence was measured more by the completion of tasks at a certain level of quality than by clocks or even bells.[12]

Neither the British heritage nor the concern over hours engendered by the exigencies of settlement gave rise to anything resembling a shorter hours movement in the colonies. Because of its variety and its punctuation by many breaks and because it conformed to the "natural" work cycles and to the religious presentiments of an overwhelmingly agricultural and Protestant society, the sunrise-to-sunset working day excited small protest. Indeed, the only important recorded action taken by workers in the American colonies on the issue was that by Boston barbers, who reduced their work week when they proposed in the *New England Courant* of December 7, 1724, that "no one of their Faculty should shave or dress Wiggs on Sunday mornings for the future." In 1788 this reduction of hours was either reestablished or extended when the same city's barbers and "Peruke Makers" entered into a written agreement "not to carry on their Business in their Shops or in private Houses on the Lord's Day as the practice appears to them not only contrary to the Law of God & the Land, but to be highly offensive to the sober inhabitants." Religion and the desire for shorter hours also came together in a more minor way in colonial protests over working on Christmas. By 1725 most American colonies had completed the development of Sabbatarian legislation which, with near uniformity but by no means total effectiveness, banned Sunday labor. But, as Winton Solberg has observed, Puritan-influenced Sabbath legislation was meant to enforce the injunction "Sixe dayes shalt thou laboure," with a day of rest and replenishment. It did not challenge, and indeed reinforced, long hours the rest of the week.[13]

The American Revolution helped to speed a series of changes that would undermine the notion that the hours of daylight constituted the "natural" parameters of the working day. Among the revolutionary and early republican elite, interest in the question of time came from at least two sources. On the one hand, many patriot leaders, typified by Thomas Jefferson, Benjamin Franklin, and the Philadelphia scientist and statesman David Rittenhouse, nurtured a fascination for both more-or-less practical mechanics and the sureties of Newtonian physics. These converged in a fascination with clocks. While, as Garry Wills has put it, earlier eighteenth-century clockmakers had accomplished "the linking of human measure, in clock and calendar, to the measured universe [by showing] phases of the moon and days of the month on their clockfaces," Rittenhouse's 1767 clock designed for Drexel Institute "created an astronomical face-design that included six dials—one registering 'the equation of time'." Rittenhouse followed this creation with an even more ambitious astronomical clock and model of the universe, which he called the "orrery." Jefferson could suggest but one improvement: *planetarium Americanum*, not orrery, should be its name.[14]

The second source of concern with time among the founding fathers lay in fears that idleness would undermine republican virtues. According to Jefferson, "Idleness begets ennui, ennui hypochondria and that a diseased body." Mixing biological, political, and mechanical metaphors, and recalling their own criticisms of idleness and corruption in British society, many leaders seized on Dr. Benjamin Rush's image of "republican machines" as the industrial ideal to be created among the citizens of the new nation.[15] In some cases, of course, those preaching discipline were employers of labor but more than a rationalization of habits designed to increase productivity was involved. At issue was the internalization of the bourgeois value of self-denial and husbanding this value in a quest for mobility to master artisan status, as well as a sense of revolutionary duty. Franklin, for example, regimented his own time as strictly as that of his employees and appears to have opposed alcohol breaks and Saint Mondays both as a journeyman printer and later as an employer. His injunction "Lose no time; be always employ'd in something useful; cut off all unnecessary actions" was as much a personal credo as a management technique. Moreover, a concern with steady work habits did not necessarily mean advocacy of laboring every waking moment. Franklin, for example, worked an eight-hour day as a master printer and reputedly proposed a four-hour day as a future possibility.[16]

With the beginning of revolutionary combat, the gap between those hiring labor and those hired widened in some crafts, especially in response to the increase in demand for military supplies. The rising need put a premium on quantity rather than quality with the result that in some instances the small shop, presided over by the craftsmen-entrepreneur and manned by a few journeymen and apprentices, began to give way to a larger unit with more factory-like methods of production. Morris identifies the Revolution and its wake as a period during which the "transition from custom work to wholesale order work, and the concentration of workers in certain expanding industries served to bring about . . . more distinct class stratifications." He adds that "inexpert workmen" came to compete with the multiskilled journeymen as merchant capitalists contracted to fill orders and "pitted master against master" by opting to do business with those who produced most cheaply.[17]

Nor was the transformation confined to the sphere of production. At least as important were the changes in outlook and growth of confidence of those artisans and laborers who came to see themselves as the backbone of the Revolution and the repositories of republican virtues. Though the upper classes feared for the fate of cities in which "the lowest Mechanicks discuss upon the most important points of Government with the Utmost Freedom," they could hardly reverse the trend. As Eric Foner points out in his recent studies of the relationship between the artisan community and the radicalism of Tom Paine, in Philadelphia alone, "hundreds, indeed thousands, of men were brought into organized political life for the first time." And the initiates included not just masters but a broad spectrum of "poorer artisans, journeymen, apprentices and laborers" organized in the militia. These artisans and occasionally unskilled revolutionaries pressed their demands for political participation without property qualifications and their claims for an important part in the new republican order. "The mob," commented New York's conservative Gouverneur Morris, "begin to think and reason."[18]

A reasonable corollary to the desire of working people to participate in republican government was that they ought to have time to do so. Of what good was independence if laborers had no time to enjoy its blessings? What was the benefit of universal suffrage, for which some continued to struggle, if the worker had not the knowledge to make wise use of the ballot? In 1784 "An Old Mechanic" stressed the tension between long hours and republicanism in a manner which would remain common in protests made decades later. Writing in the *Philadelphia Independent Gazetteer*, he affirmed that his fellows "have exactly the same right as any class of men whatever," but complained, "they have barely sufficient time to acquaint themselves with the true interests of our country." At about the same time New York City building tradesmen appear to have undertaken the first sporadic disputes "concerning a day's work" in United States history. For some, at least, the seamless quality of time, in which work, family, and leisure activities coexisted so closely as to be hardly distinguishable, was supplemented by a separate and new category which might be called "citizenship time." The banner of the clock and watchmakers, carried in the July 4, 1788, Philadelphia celebration of the U.S. Constitution, proclaimed "Time Rules All Things."[19] So important a commodity would soon be fought over.

If the "old mechanic" survived seven years, he could have witnessed the efforts of a group of Philadelphia carpenters who tried to remedy the problem of long hours. Especially incensed by their employers' practice of paying a flat daily wage for the long summer shift and resorting to piece rates during short winter days, the carpenters mounted America's first ten-hour-day strike in May 1791. Though brief and apparently unsuccessful, the strike action of the journeymen deserves attention because it anticipated the very form that the demand for the ten-hour day was to take through the 1850s. The strikers' promise that "a Day's Work, *amongst us*, shall be deemed to commence at six o'clock in the morning and terminate at six in the evening of each day," with two hours for meals, became the formula for the ten-hour movement of the nineteenth century.[20] It was to be more than three decades before the "From six to six!" cry grew very loud. Further changes in the economy would occur before the revolutionary promise of a laboring class with time for self-education and political participation could find expression in a mass movement of labor. When such a movement did develop, the republican distinction between time to work and time to participate in government continued to be vital.

At the end of the eighteenth century and throughout the first quarter of the nineteenth century, changes in the production process gathered momentum. Mass production became more common, especially in the textile industry where the factory system first took hold. By 1790 Samuel Slater and David Wilkinson had constructed the first Arkwright spinning machinery to be successfully operated in the United States. A year later several machines, tended by children and powered by water, produced yarn in Slater's Pawtucket, Rhode Island, mill. In 1816 the Boston Manufacturing Company centralized all the processes in the manufacture of cotton cloth under one roof in a Waltham, Massachusetts, factory. Once established, factory-based production in the textile industry quickly spread through Massachusetts, New Hampshire, Rhode Island, Maine, and Pennsylvania. But the factory system remained far from being a dominant mode of production. As late as 1831, fewer than 67,000 of America's approximately thirteen million citizens engaged in factory-based production of cotton textiles, and in most cases they labored in mills employing thirty or fewer laborers.[21] But however modest its proportions, the factory system had a significant impact both on the lives of its workers and on the psyches of a much larger number of craftsmen for whom the factory gate became a symbol of the threats to their ideal of independent, diversified artisan and yeoman production.

Outside the textile industry, in those crafts not quickly reorganized along the lines of factory production, substantial changes in the productive process were also occurring. These crafts bore the stamp of an increasingly powerful merchant capitalist group. As improved canal and turnpike transportation opened new markets, the merchant capitalist bought raw materials, found a producer to manufacture them into finished goods, and secured buyers for their sale. The master craftsman who owned a workshop became little more than a labor contractor. His profit was the difference between the price he received from the merchant capitalist and the wages he paid to his workmen. As David T. Saposs has observed, the masters thus could gain only from changes in "wages and work" and of necessity embarked on a search for new methods of production which, especially as they increased division of labor, laid the basis for timed work. "They organized their workmen into teams," according to Saposs, "with the work subdivided in order to lessen dependence on skill and to increase speed of output. They played the less skilled against the more skilled . . . and reduced wages while enhancing exertion." The presence of the merchant capitalist, he continued, "intensifie[d] . . . the antagonism between 'capital and labor'. . . by forcing the separation of functions and classes a step further than it had been forced."[22] The rhythms of an agricultural society, timed, as Ralph Waldo Emerson put it, "to Nature, and not to city watches," were for many fast-fading memories.[23]

Those workshops influenced by the activities of merchant capitalists were similarly productive of a heightened consciousness of the hours of labor. Indeed, the workshops and not the factories would generate most early agitation over hours. In order to increase his profits and to compete for the orders of the merchant capitalists, the master often, while maintaining the traditional sunrise-to-sunset working day, eliminated part of the time customarily allotted for meals, drink, and rest. Furthermore, since wages of the workers who were paid by the piece often fell (at the same time that prices for goods rose), they were required to work a longer day for the same pay. In 1806 a skilled shoemaker testified, "I could only make eight dollars and a half a week and I worked from five in the morning till twelve or one at night." John Bradford, a New York City bookbinder and poet, indicated in verses from 1813 that journeymen of his trade also had to work by candlelight well into the evening during the five coldest months. In increasingly bastardized crafts, poorer "masters" pushed themselves longer and longer hours, sometimes for smaller and smaller returns.[24]

By divorcing skilled from unskilled work, the factories and the reorganized workshops paved the way for the introduction of cheaply rewarded female, child, and convict labor in low-skill jobs. These additions to the work force heightened sensitivity to the issue of hours. By 1820 Alexander Hamilton's prediction that the rising manufacturing establishments would find the labor of women and children "more useful, and the latter more early useful than they would otherwise be," was confirmed. In that year as many as half the workers in many factories were boys and girls who had not reached their eleventh birthday.[25] The entry of significant numbers of women and children into the labor market contributed to increasing consciousness of the hours of labor in at least two ways. By adding to the pool of unskilled workers, women and children made possible a fuller division of labor on lines of skill. As early as 1799, for example, Baltimore's journeymen tailors complained that their wages plummeted and their work became less diversified after the hiring of women workers who did "most of the easy work at half the price." In such trades the skilled artisan's day was increasingly given over to the continued performance of tasks requiring dexterity and concentration. Again, a speedup had taken place within the confines of the traditional sunup-to-sundown working day.[26] Furthermore, the proliferation of female, and particularly of child laborers led to calls for the regulation of hours in order to protect those disenfranchised and allegedly weaker workers who were not adult males. Indeed, the first major government investigation of working hours, a report to the Massachusetts legislature in 1825, concerned the schedules of children in factories and revealed that the typical twelve-hour day rendered the education of the children impossible.[27]

For those craftsmen who experienced some worsening of conditions at the workplace, a sense of lost independence probably stung as badly as any specific grievance. To those brought up in the countryside, the city's routinized labor, paced either by machines or, more often, by an increasingly observant boss, likely jarred against memories of the more varied, seasonal, and self-supervised rural tasks of youth, even if hours were roughly the same. For those whose backgrounds featured long familiarity with craft labor, the slightest speedup, the shortening of a break, the failure to allow drinking on the job, a slowing in the mobility from journeyman to master, the subdivision of the productive process—any of these—signaled a long step backward from the ideal existence of an independent craftsman. The journeymen measured their situation not simply against that of yesterday but also against the agrarian virtues posited by Jeffersonianism and the independent life styles of artisan-heroes like Franklin and Paine.[28]

Ultimately, the issue of hours would provide a common denominator around which workers from various crafts and in various cities could discuss their fears and register their protests against the myriad of particularistic, local, and subtle grievances that accompanied changes in methods of production. A transitional stage, during which individual crafts slowly became cognizant of the fact that the hours of labor were subject to change, would first intervene.

With such pronounced changes in the productive process, and in consciousness, eroding the status of the traditional sunup-to-sundown working day—and with the proliferation of cheap wooden clocks in common usage—it is hardly surprising that workers and their young trade unions turned to the regulation of hours. The earliest reflections of labor's increasing consciousness of the hours question was the simple awareness of the number of hours in a working day. As early as 1805, New York City carpenters and masons no longer relied on the course of the sun to determine the length of their toil. Instead they worked under a wage list that specified a ten-hour day in summer and nine hours of daily labor in winter.[29] Even in trades in which piece rates prevailed, the awareness of time increased. By 1809 a proposed wage agreement for New York City compositors specified an eleven-hour day, but the provision was not included in the final agreement. Philadelphia pressmen sought a ten-hour day in an 1816 wage list. Baltimore cordwainers struck over wages in 1811, but their appeal to the public challenged, "Let any candid man that has the least spark of generosity in him say if $8.50 . . . per week is too much wages for a mechanic who labors 14 hours each day." Some workers had begun to adopt a "time orientation" toward their labor.[30]

The initial nineteenth century protests over hours of work were informal ones designed to resist incursions on the customary schedule of the working day. In 1817, for example, a Medford, Massachusetts, shipbuilder won a brief struggle with his employees. The builder, Thatcher Magoun, had decided to discontinue the practice of supplying rum to the laborers at specific times. One account of the event described what lay behind the seemingly trivial conflict: "These two periods for drink were really periods of rest, and were called luncheon times, the men having an opportunity to eat as well as drink, and Mr. Magoun's no-rum movement meant no luncheon time and was practically an increase in the working time." Six years later, Lynn, Massachusetts, carpenters likewise rose to the defense of their dram breaks. As late as 1839, some Philadelphia laborers accepted, in lieu of a wage increase, a boost in whiskey rations. The one and a half pints given out daily were administered in nine "doses" spread throughout the day.[31]

Breaks were also at issue in the first major American strike involving both men and women, a defensive 1824 walkout of weavers in a Pawtucket, Rhode Island, mill designed to forestall the employer's attempt to add an hour to the working day by cutting the "time allowed at the several meals." By coupling this action with a wage cut directed only at female weavers, the owners hoped to divide the work force by sex. However, the hours issue laid the basis for a unified strike, which was partially successful.

In 1828 young mill operatives in Paterson, New Jersey, struck to prevent a moving back of the dinner hour from noon to 1 P.M. "The children would not stand for it," said one observer, "for fear if they assented to this, the next thing would be to deprive them of eating at all." The ten-hour demand probably first found expression among factory workers during the course of this bitter dispute, which was also marked by the first recorded use of the militia against American strikers. Pronouncing themselves "determined to resist the unworthy efforts of the mechanics," who struck in solidarity with the operatives, the employers vowed to "teach the children the necessity of civility and obedience." After firing strike leaders, the owners acceded on the timing of lunch, but not on the ten-hour issue.[32]

In the 1820s, as unions gathered force after the intense economic crisis of 1819, formal movements for shorter hours began to crop up sporadically. The bakers, whose incredibly arduous schedule ranged up to 115 working hours per week as late as 1834, led the way in 1821 by calling a New York City mass meeting at which the subject of eliminating Sunday labor in their trade was discussed.[33] The next year in Philadelphia, newspapers reported that "the journeymen millwrights and machine workers . . . met at a tavern, and passed resolutions that ten hours labor was enough for one day."[34]

By 1825 some laborers were ready to mount aggressive struggles for shorter hours. One of Thompson's observations regarding Britain applies to the United States as well: "as the new time-discipline is imposed, so the workers begin to fight, not against time, but about it."[35] In America, spurred on by a desire for the time to train themselves for full republican citizenship, working people proved quick to discern the radical implications of the new attitudes toward time and work. The influence of merchant capital had, by 1825, helped to shape new patterns of labor—patterns that gave rise, in some workers' minds, to a sharpening distinction between that part of the day their bosses controlled and that which was their own.

During the next five years in Philadelphia, Boston, and New York City—that is in the centers of merchant capitalism and artisan republicanism—aggressive ten-hour movements formed. Boston carpenters started the ball rolling in 1825. For several months they discussed the "impropriety of working so many hours during the longest days in summer, for a day's work," and the need for a system "whereby every mechanic might be expected to work the exact specified time for his employer and yet have some leisure time to regulate his affairs." On April 12, 800 carpenters gathered at Concert Hall to hear several "animated addresses" condemning "their present mode of despotic servitude." About 500 voted for a strike "to . . . establish a day's work to ten hours."[36]

The response of the employers was speedy. More than any other Jacksonian issue, the hours issue drew a line between masters and journeymen. Boston master carpenters passed resolutions voicing, "surprise and regret that a large number of those who are employed as journeymen . . . have entered into a combination for the purpose of altering the time of commencing and terminating their daily labor from that which has been customary from time immemorial."[37] The masters sought to set journeymen against apprentices. They warned that the "numerous and pernicious evils" of the ten-hour day would eventually damage the journeymen who struck because "all Journeymen of good character and of skill, may expect very soon to become masters, and like us the employers of others." Perhaps, as Paul Johnson's work on Rochester suggests, part of the anxiety on the part of employers regarding journeymen's and apprentices' leisure stemmed from the early nineteenth-century collapse of the "household economy" in which masters and subordinates had long lived and labored side by side and in which masters acted out of a sense of religious stewardship in supervising household members. Even the journeymen, feared the Boston masters, would succumb to "many temptations and improvident practices" with so much leisure at their disposal.[38] In a final resolution, the masters promised "no alteration" in the length of the day and pledged to refuse employment to ten-hour agitators.[39]

On April 21 Boston merchant capitalists met to throw their weight behind the resolutions of the master carpenters. The merchant capitalists wrote with rich, if unconscious, irony. After castigating the carpenters for using methods which would "give an artificial and unnatural turn to business, and tend to convert all its branches into Monopolies," the merchants demonstrated that trade unions were not needed to usher in financial oligarchy in Boston. The merchant capitalists vowed "to suspend, if necessary, building altogether" for an entire season. Another resolution promised "not to employ such Journeymen, or any other Master Carpenter who shall yield to their pretensions." Having raised these formidable sticks against the strikers, the merchant capitalists also held out some carrots by offering bribes to strike leaders willing to defect. A young journeyman who held out till the end lamented, "One fainted, one after another, till our fabric fell." The words of John R. Commons provide an even more apt epitaph for the strike: "Defeated, not by the master carpenters but, by the employers of the masters, the capitalists and merchants."[40]

That the Boston merchant capitalists responded so forcefully is understandable in terms of their grasp of the crucial issues involved in the strike. Like the masters, they deplored the "idleness and vice" said to be engendered by the ten-hour system, but the merchant capitalists further feared that "discontent and insubordination" at the workplace would be a by-product of the shorter hours struggles. Their resolutions also complained that the journeymen would raise "the value of labor by abridging its duration" if the strike was successful. That is, they foresaw that a shorter day would make labor scarcer and therefore more expensive. Most important, the merchant capitalists realized the capacity of the hours demand to mushroom, capturing the support of many crafts. "If the confederacy should be countenanced by the community," cautioned their resolutions, "it must . . . extend to and embrace all the Working Classes in every department of Town and Country, thereby effecting a most injurious change in all modes of business." Mainly because of the exertions of the merchant capitalists, such a wave of shorter hours solidarity never materialized in Boston in 1825. The Boston agitation disintegrated quickly, though it may have been instrumental in spawning a shorter-hours meeting with delegates from five states in Providence in December 1825.[41] Two years later in Philadelphia the pattern would be different.

In Philadelphia artisan intellectual activity preceded strike action to win the ten-hour day. William Heighton, a young English immigrant writing under the unassuming pseudonym of "An Unlettered Mechanic," invigorated the labor movement with a series of addresses also printed as pamphlets.[42] As a cordwainer, Heighton practiced a trade in which piece rates muted the hours question. But his addresses fed Philadelphia's shorter hours agitation by producing telling arguments against the traditional working day. Influenced by Ricardian socialists, Heighton held that labor created value and briefly anticipated the Marxist theory of surplus value, arguing that laborers produce a value equivalent to their wages in a part of the working day and capitalists exact a surplus by requiring further labor after that point.[43] He held that "those who are toiling day after day, spending their strength and wasting their health in the production of wealth, are doomed . . . to poverty" so long as society is split into "two classes, viz.—the working or productive class and the non-productive class."[44]

Heighton pitched his arguments broadly in suggesting that education and labor action could save an imperiled republic. As the last great heroes of the revolutionary generation passed from the scene, he recalled the "august and venerated" men who had written that "all men are created equal; that they are endowed with certain inalienable rights, that among these are life, liberty and the pursuit of happiness." However, he added, "those equal rights which were at that time asserted, and purchased with blood and treasure, are not enjoyed . . . by a majority of American citizens."[45]

To rectify the prevailing injustices, Heighton proposed self-education as "one of the best means of meliorating our condition" and founded a workers' library where regular discussions took place. He projected a citywide labor organization of all trades and a labor party, but all of these hopes hinged upon education.[46] And education, of course, was in turn predicated upon the acquisition of enough leisure to pursue knowledge. As the historian Leonard Bernstein observes, the ten-hour plank came to be perceived as the precondition necessary to win further gains. Workers waged the "fight for sufficient leisure to attain the knowledge necessary to put universal suffrage to use."[47]

Alongside these sweeping arguments stood appeals to the immediate interests of those artisans experiencing deteriorating conditions of work and irregularity of employment due to the introduction of new methods of production and new technology. Heighton accepted advances in production, lauding the "power in nature calculated to confer unlimited blessings on the human race; calculated to *increase* the enjoyments . . . while it *lessens* the labours of man! . . . to confer . . . an abundance of leisure to follow after intellectual pursuit . . . the POWER OF INVENTION." He saw the problem not in machinery but in the "influence of commercial competition" which caused inventions to increase the misery of labor. If it were properly used, Heighton predicted that technology could lead to not just one but a series of reductions in the hours of labor. Hours could decrease from twelve to ten to eight to six and further "until the development and progress of science have reduced human labour to its lowest terms."[48]

The ideas of Heighton, first expressed to a large audience in April 1827, doubtless influenced Philadelphia's journeymen carpenters, who struck for a ten-hour day in the summer of that year. No longer content to suffer "under a grievous and slave-like system of labor . . . injurious alike to the community and the workmen," the carpenters resolved that "ten hours industriously employed are sufficient for a day's labour." They contended, in the high revolutionary style of Heighton, that "all men have a just right, derived from their Creator, to have sufficient time in each day for the cultivation of the mind and for self-improvement." In addition, the journeymen deplored the effect of long hours on health.[49]

As in Boston, a group of master carpenters convened to denounce the journeymen's society for tending "to subvert the good order." The masters agreed to refuse work to ten-hour men and insisted that "the whole time of the workmen" had to be used in order to maintain wages. Their resolutions also featured an appeal for the cooperation of the merchant capitalists.[50]

The journeymen decided to strike in an attempt to force the masters to bargain with their representatives, but there is no evidence that a delegation from the masters ever negotiated with the journeymen's twelve-man strike committee. Although 600 carpenters struck for at least ten days, the sunrise-to-sunset work day survived. That the masters advertised extensively for out-of-town strikebreakers may have been instrumental in bringing journeymen back to work, although at least some of the strikers probably remained out long enough for individual masters to accede to the ten-hour demand.[51]

Though at best a partial success, the 1827 strike was important. While on strike, the journeymen connected long hours with wintertime unemployment. They argued that the masters maligned the ten-hour day because it would "make a journeyman of nearly as much value in the winter as in the summer." Under the ten-hour system, work would have averaged nine and one-half hours in winter and only a half-hour more in summer. The employer would no longer be in a position to benefit greatly from "employing a man during the summer and . . . discharging him in the winter."[52]

More significantly, the 1827 strike produced some first glimmers of labor unity across craft lines. The house painters and glaziers met during the strike, probably to support the carpenters and to seek the ten-hour day in their own trades. Journeymen bricklayers resolved "that ten hours be considered as a day's work" and pledged support to a newspaper, the *Journeymen Mechanics' Advocate*, whose title promised even broader cross-craft cooperation.[53] A few months after the strike's beginning, this impulse toward solidarity found expression in the formation of the first American city central labor organization, the Mechanics' Union of Trade Associations. Journeymen from as many as fifteen crafts, including the carpenters, painters, typographers, cordwainers, and glaziers, joined forces in the union.[54]

The "Preamble" of the Mechanics' Union, probably penned by Heighton, illustrates the large extent to which Helen Sumner was correct in attributing this "first union of all organized workmen in any city" to ferment arising from the ten-hour movement. Amidst the preamble's repeated references to the injustice of "incessant toil" is a long and ringing question which brings together themes prominent in shorter-hours agitation:

Is it equitable that we should waste the energies of our minds and bodies, and be placed in a situation of such unceasing exertion and servility as must necessarily . . . render the benefits of our liberal institutions to us inaccessible and useless, in order that the products of our labor may be accumulated by a few . . . to overawe the meagre multitude and fright away that shadow of freedom which still lingers among us?

The constitution which follows the preamble stresses the development of a large and unified strike fund to support approved "stand-outs" for either "wages or hours."[55]

In 1828 both the political resolve and the treasury of the young Mechanics' Union were tested by shorter hours struggles. That spring the *Mechanics' Free Press* promised that "thousands yet unborn will reap the advantages should the labourer succeed" in winning a shorter day. The same article issued a pioneer call for political action by labor for shorter hours, recommending that the city council be petitioned to enact a law "making ten hours to constitute the standard day's work." By May, the Mechanics' Union had proposed to its constituent societies that labor should nominate candidates for the city council and the state legislature. After enthusiastic responses from the carpenters, the cordwainers, the hatters, and other trades, the Mechanics' Union initiated the Working Men's party, which fielded a slate of candidates in the fall elections. As William Sullivan observes concerning the origins of this first American labor party, "The demand for the ten-hour day was the immediate issue which sent the workingmen into politics."[56]

As they considered the political fight for shorter hours, Philadelphia's building tradesmen launched trade union actions designed to win the ten-hour day. Following their 1827 strike, the carpenters worked the shorter winter days and saved for the summertime to come. An early 1828 circular addressed to the masters brimmed with confidence: "a great number [of us] will have the hours without a word." Sustained also by the strike fund of the Mechanics' Union, the journeymen faced down threats to import scabs or hire large numbers of boy apprentices. Remembering the "good old motto, 'United we stand, divided we fall'," the carpenters (and the bricklayers who joined them) won nearly complete victory by June.[57]

The resourcefulness and dynamism displayed by Philadelphia's skilled workers in 1827 and 1828 does, as one scholar suggests, signal "a sharp turning point in the history of labor in the United States." Nonetheless, on both the economic and political fronts, the advances made by the mechanics were tenuous. The carpenters, for example, appear to have been forced to return to sunup-to-sundown labor within a few seasons. Meanwhile, other trades de-emphasized labor organization in favor of political action. The Mechanics' Union quickly lost eleven of its fifteen member societies and, in November of 1829, disbanded.[58] Until the general strike of 1835, trade union action for shorter hours remained less than effectual in Philadelphia.

The Working Men's party, though it began auspiciously, also proved unable to deliver shorter hours. While no 1828 candidates running solely on its ticket received as much as 10 percent of the vote, a score of candidates who combined Working Men's party affiliation with the backing of Jacksonian Democracy did triumph. The congressional candidates of both major parties felt constrained to admit "the justice of the working people's attempts to lessen the established hours of labor." Both major parties prominently displayed the slogan "From Six to Six".[59]

Although successful at injecting the hours question into politics (and with it the complementary issue of equal education), the Working Men's party secured no legislation on the issue; nor did it have more than limited objectives in this area. It is unlikely that many of the party's supporters or leaders conceived of a state power strong enough to enforce ten-hour laws in Philadelphia's many workshops or to supercede the power of individual contracts. In demanding that politicians endorse the principle of the shorter day, the laborers probably sought only a guideline that would provide a standard for city employees and would stand as an example buttressing the tradesmen's position in contractual negotiations with their employers.[60] Such a strategy was workable only if trade unions remained strong. In any case, the party's campaigns stressed the hours issue less as union organization dwindled. After slightly increasing its vote totals and winning some of its demands, the experiment in labor politics collapsed in 1831—a victim of inability to win a solid base of voters outside the major parties and of failure to consolidate a statewide organization.[61]

That Philadelphia and Boston hosted the first major shorter-hours movements is instructive, as is the leadership of skilled workers from the building trades in both instances. Both these two large cities boasted a large artisan community with a rich history of participation in both the Revolution and in republican politics. Oscar Handlin's description of Boston's early nineteenth-century artisans as a "large group, eminently respectable, hitherto prosperous, and always influential in the community," applied to Philadelphia as well. However, as the century entered its second quarter, the artisans' preindustrial work patterns came under increasing attack. Fairs, days off, long meals, and social drinking during the day gave place to a rhythm of work and a discipline set by machinery and by the demands of masters pressured by merchant capitalists. As Commons points out, the impact of the latter group was particularly large and early in the building trades in cities, like Boston and Philadelphia, whose fast physical growth channeled merchant capital into construction.[62] In other trades, machinery and production for regional markets also brought periodic gluts causing economic dislocation for artisans. Meanwhile a large part of the manufactured goods came to be consumed by a growing middle class whose prestige and standard of life increased at the expense of the skilled worker.[63]

Artisan responses to these changed conditions varied. Although pure types were rare and individuals changed in response to changes in the strength of the economy and the labor movement, three different responses may be described for purposes of analysis. Some craftsmen reacted by redoubling their commitment to a preindustrial life-style. Their drinking, absenteeism, and tardiness was grievous to manufacturers and reformers alike. Others, sometimes termed loyalists, accepted the new demands for discipline at the workplace and combined temperance with a sober Protestant morality that could feed the anti-immigrant hysteria of nativism. But a third avenue was also open. Many skilled workers internalized the new discipline but never accepted their employers' right to limitless power. These journeymen, whom Paul Faler has termed "rebel mechanics," used the discipline they acquired to mount increasingly effective struggles against the encroachments of capital. The rebel mechanics, confident of their ability to order their own work and their own leisure, became passionately concerned about hours of work. When they organized for a ten-hour day, such rebel mechanics could hope, at least episodically, to attract support from those who valued leisure for traditional, preindustrial reasons, and even from loyalists who could at times be reached through arguments stressing leisure for family, religion, and self-improvement.[64]

In New York City, a third booming metropolis with a strong tradition of political action by craftsmen, the circumstances differed from those that spawned the

Boston and Philadelphia agitations. For reasons still unclear, the ten-hour movement prevailed in a minority of New York City trades, possibly from as early as 1805.[65] In April of 1829 employers intimated that longer hours would soon be required in these crafts. Their plans to require eleven hours of work met with a vigorous protest from skilled workers—a protest that gave rise to America's second labor party. Under the leadership of the radical land reformer, Thomas Skidmore, trade unionists convened to consider responses to the employer offensive. Skidmore, a machinist, joined representatives of sundry crafts at the April 23 meeting. Once again building tradesmen were most active in the hours agitation.[66] The unionists, who cited the threat of massive unemployment posed by an increase in hours, held that "ten hours . . . is as much as an employer ought to receive . . . [from] any artisan, mechanic or labourer." Their resolutions also hinted that the "displeasure of a just community" could lead to the confiscation of property from those who tried to "exact excessive toil."[67]

A second meeting, on April 28, occasioned much excitement. It filled the meeting hall and a pair of nearby streets with 5,000 to 6,000 people. Again a ten-hour resolution was passed, this time supplemented with a promise to publish, "in the public papers," the names of employers and employees who broke the ten-hour rule. The craftsmen also inaugurated a strike fund and appointed a Committee of Fifty to coordinate strategy. These vigorous responses caused the employers to refrain from further mention of increased hours, but the Committee of Fifty continued to meet regularly, and, prior to the fall elections, called a mass meeting to discuss labor's role in the voting. Out of this mobilization came the New York Working Men's party. That this party contained its share of maneuverers from the pro-Jackson faction of New York's Republican (Democratic) party and that it quickly splintered into three squabbling parts does not vitiate Walter Hugins's reminder that New York's first venture in labor politics owed its "initial impetus" to a "protest against unemployment and a defense of the ten-hour day."[68] There and elsewhere, in defending and extending the ten-hour system, a labor movement had begun to take shape.

2

Shorter Hours and the Transformation of American Labor, 1830-1842

One American historian has posed the central question of the history of labor during the Age of Jackson with special force:

What new circumstances made craftsmen in every major city . . . expand their concern beyond the limits of their own trades, create Trades' Unions as new institutions to fuse the efforts of the several crafts [and] undertake unprecedented united action with unskilled laborers, giving rise to something worthy of the name labor movement?[1]

The following chapter argues that increasing attention to the hours issue was the key element in the transformation of labor's consciousness and organization during this period. The ten-hour demand divided journeymen from masters and proved particularly contagious, spreading from craft to craft, from city to city, from skilled to unskilled. Moreover, labor developed a powerful and broad series of arguments for the reduction of hours. The hours issue came to symbolize health, education, steady employment, and political participation. As a young nation contemplated the deaths of the last of its revolutionary heroes and confronted increasing domestic disorders, organized tradesmen came to see the shortening of the workday as a step toward reviving the Republic and to seek the ten-hour day using both trade union and political means.[2]

The importance of the hours question in these formative years of modern trade unionism can hardly be overstated. As Helen L. Sumner points out, "The most frequent cause of complaint among working people [during the Age of Jackson] was the lack of leisure." The list of major American strikes between 1833 and 1837, as prepared by E. B. Mittleman, enumerates 172 "turn-outs" of which thirty-one revolved around the issue of hours. Of the 131 strikes concerning wages, twenty-seven were purely defensive reactions to wage cuts. At least eight more were responses by trades (such as cordwaining and cigarmaking) which operated on piece rates but whose workers wanted raises commensurate with those of other trades that had won the ten-hour day. Hours, using these figures, figured in well over 25 percent of the labor offensives during those years.[3]

Local and state studies present more striking evidence. Anita Gorochow's work on Baltimore labor during the Jackson era points to "tremendous agitation" on the hours issue, holding that strikes in Baltimore more often involved time than money. For Boston, Edward Pessen concludes that the "long working day . . . [was] undoubtedly the issue which aroused the most immediate and direct concern of all . . . workers." William Sullivan's study of Philadelphia finds the hours issue similarly dominant there. The same author's broader monograph on Pennsylvania labor lists the cause of fifty-eight separate strikes between 1827 and 1835. Of these, twenty-five demanded shorter hours while twenty-one centered on wages.[4] The strike statistics still understate the relationship between hours and the maturation of trade unionism. The demand for a shorter day, by giving common cause to workers from various cities and various crafts, gave rise to innovative and broad forms of labor organization, including city central, regional, and national unions.

Employers helped to ensure that the hours issue would sharply emerge by attempting to extract labor beyond that given in the traditional working day. In 1831 in Taunton, Massachusetts, sixty machinists were forced to strike in order to continue to leave work at sundown. Employers wanted to continue operations until 7:30 P.M. during the winter.[5] A more common complaint was that bosses "shaved" time by manipulating clocks. Employers, whose bells or clocks often set the time for the whole town, apparently abused their monopoly regularly. One report on a Rhode Island factory complained that there were "about 20 or 25 minutes added [to the thirteen-and-one-half-hour day]" because what the workers called "factory time" lagged "behind the true solar time."[6] Master craftsmen could be as devious. In the shipyards, another favorite spot for the investment of merchant capital, one shipwright observed that "sun up" was construed as "the first glance the bosses could catch at a sunbeam gilding the tallest spire in sight." Since no steeples were near the yard where this artisan labored, "the bosses used to catch their matin sunbeam from the vane of the 170-foot Liberty pole." The tradesmen's republican sensibilities were thus doubly offended.[7]

The response of the laborers to the employer's abuse of his control over the time of day was sometimes direct. In Pawtucket, operatives and artisans joined in what Gary Kulik has called a "community alliance against the mill owners" by raising $500 to build a town clock in 1828. No longer, they promised, would "the clock . . . be figured to suit the owner." By 1832 the city apparently operated on solar time again.[8] In New York's shipyards, carpenters and caulkers erected a "Mechanics' Bell" which served the same purpose as Pawtucket's clock. The first bell, built in 1831, insured that the gains journeymen made in a series of 1830s strikes over hours and the length of meals, would be observed. The bell became a symbol of the shorter-hours struggle and was recast in 1844 as the "Ten-Hour Bell." By 1887 it rang out the hours of a nine-hour day. That same year, the labor activist George McNeill wrote, "As the 'Liberty Bell' rang out the proclamation of liberty from monarchical control, so the 'Mechanics' Bell' proclaimed the liberty of leisure for the sons of toil."[9]

Like the public timepiece, the public school became a bone of contention in the struggle over hours. Although recent scholarship has illuminated the role of bourgeois ideology in seeking to reorder society and discipline labor through educational reform, the passion for learning among members of the early labor movement must not be minimized.[10] Equal education was, as Mittelman puts it, "the first and foremost political demand" of most early labor organizations.[11] New York's pro-Jackson *Daily Sentinel* was only one of several papers that appealed to a working class readership by heading the list of "WORKING MEN'S MEASURES" on its masthead with "EQUAL UNIVERSAL EDUCATION." Workers, especially skilled tradesmen, started their own "mechanics" libraries and institutes while simultaneously campaigning for public facilities that would educate all children.[12]

On the one hand, labor's enthusiasm for public schools reflected a concern over a serious crisis in American education, which left as many as 1,250,000 children illiterate. An aspect of this crisis was the tendency for masters, straining after increased production, to neglect the schooling of youths (often journeymen's children) apprenticed to them. Children in factories fared still worse.[13] On the other hand, the commitment of craftsmen to republican education drew upon a strong strain of gnosticism inside the labor movement. Utopian socialists, workingmen's institute leaders, and union militants alike proclaimed the potential of an enlightened working class as the refrain "knowledge is power" echoed through the movement.[14]

The issue of education intertwined with that of hours. As the Philadelphia events had demonstrated, agitation for an educated populace presupposed adequate free time for self-cultivation. Subsequent reformers followed Heighton in linking learning with leisure. They punctuated their appeals for equal education of children with repeated references to the "unreasonable hours" which consigned adult laborers to the ranks of the "ignorant, dependent, depraved and degraded."[15] The 1830 Independence Day toast of one Jacksonian Democrat captured the high hopes of the craftsmen: "May the day soon come when in the point of literary acquirements, the poorest peasant shall stand on a level with his more wealthy neighbors."[16]

In Philadelphia, where one "Unlettered Mechanic" had shaken the city, the *National Gazette* responded to the prospect of training a whole class of educated tradesmen with fear and trepidation. Its editors merged the issues of universal equal education and shorter hours, denying the possibility of either. Replying directly to the Jacksonian toast, they warned: "The 'peasant' must labour during those hours of the day which his wealthy neighbor can give to abstract culture . . . ; the mechanic cannot abandon the operation of his trade for general studies; if he should . . . langour, decay, poverty [and] discontent would soon be visible among all classes."[17]

The prevalence of child labor further connected the issues of hours and education. If confined for long hours in factories or workshops, children could not avail themselves of whatever educational opportunities did exist. In Providence the Association of Workingmen coupled ten-hour agitation with measures designed to provide for the education of young workers. In 1830 "Many Operatives" in Philadelphia made the same point in a letter to the *Mechanics' Free Press*. Citing the long hours in cotton factories, the operatives doubted that one child laborer in six had found sufficient time to learn to read or write his or her name.[18] Several subsequent reports on child labor by committees of trade unionists uniformly deplored the gruelling work schedules in the factories and the effects of long hours on education. From Pennsylvania and New England came additional references to "employers' threats, that if [parents] take one [child] from their employ . . . a short time for school," the entire family would be fired.[19]

The sardonic comments of Frances Wright captured the impact of overwork upon childhood education and indicated that apprentices as well as factory children were victims. In 1829 she observed to a Philadelphia audience:

In your manufacturing districts you have worked children twelve hours a day . . . . What leisure or what spirit may [the] children find for visiting a school, although the same should be open to them from sunrise to sunset? Or what leisure have usually the children of your most thriving mechanics, after their strength is sufficiently developed to spin, sew, weave, or wield a tool?

Wright wittily concluded, "to build school houses now-a-days is something like building churches. When you have them, you need some measure to ensure their being occupied."[20]

Though significant, the bell tower and the school did not replace the picket line as the main rallying point in the shorter-hours struggles of the early 1830s. When Pittsburgh carpenters struck for the ten-hour day in 1831, their masters alleged that the 200 to 300 striking journeymen were promoting the "subversion of society" as well as "temptations, prodigality and dissipation." As the strike continued, the employers resorted to more formal charges, having the journeymen indicted for conspiracy. The ten-hour men won an acquittal in a jury trial, but after ten weeks their strike ended in failure. Only a few masters gave in to the ten-hour demand. When a renewal of the strike proved equally unsuccessful in the summer of 1832, some of the journeymen opted for contracting their own work cooperatively, probably on a ten-hour basis. In Cincinnati 250 carpenters also struck without success for the ten-hour day in 1831.[21]

In 1831 New York City's ship carpenters and caulkers fought early campaigns to shorten hours, and at least seventy Buffalo tradesmen pledged "to work no more than ten hours for a day's work," during July of that year. These actions further heightened the consciousness of the hours issue among those New York trades which had not yet won the shorter day. Appealing to the "example of the Buffalo Working Men," the *Daily Sentinel* advised, "If the tailoresses of [New York City] could reduce their hours from fourteen or fifteen to ten, their wages would increase." The scope of the agitation is indicated by the *Advocate*'s mention of the initial recorded instance of a shorter-hours protest by a white-collar worker; "A Druggist's Clerk" wrote to the editor to object to his 125-hour work week.[22]

As the labor force in a large center of the import trade, New York City workers were among the first to encounter new arguments against a reduction in hours. The employers held that the ten-hour day hurt American labor by enabling "foreigners [to] compete with us to every advantage and undersell us." Others held out the threat that immigrant labor would replace the ten-hour men. The *Working Man's Advocate* at first simply implored, "Are we to slave thirteen or fourteen hours a day, because the Manchester spinner or the Birmingham blacksmith, so slaves?" However, the journeymen, many of whom were themselves British immigrants, soon argued that shorter hours were needed on both sides of the Atlantic and took inspiration from the struggles of English workers. By 1834 the *New England Artisan* was asking, "If the working men of Great Britain have the daring hardihood to declare that they will work but eight hours . . . , how should the comparatively free . . . American working citizen feel?"[23] Those who labored in American workshops and factories came to stress that the pace and the duration of their jobs exceeded that required in Britain.[24]

In 1832 shorter hours agitation spread quickly in and outside of New England, gaining a foothold in smaller cities and bringing with it new strategies on both sides. Laboring men in Lowell, Rochester, Fall River, South Boston, Wheeler's Point, and Taunton, Massachusetts, as well as in Bath, Maine, Providence, Rhode Island, and as far away as Louisville, Kentucky; Detroit, and Utica, New York, acted to secure the ten-hour system, often with some success.[25] The largest ten-hour strikes erupted in Boston and New Bedford, Massachusetts. Both of these strikes featured participation by ship carpenters and caulkers, whose work often necessitated cramped, uncomfortable positions. The New Bedford strike was large and bitter, involving over 500 workers. Illustrative of the popular support enjoyed by the ten-hour men was the practice of having strike meetings announced by the town crier. Comparing themselves to "the illustrious sages of '76, struggling to throw off oppression," the operatives signed a "constitution" limiting labor to ten hours. The employers displayed equally high passion with one declaring, "Before I will employ a ten-hour man my ships shall rot at the wharves—my half-finished buildings shall totally decay." The resulting stand-off brought the ten-hour day to some New Bedford tradesmen, while others "resumed their labors on the old system" after a six-week strike. If New Bedford and the earlier Pawtucket example are typical, in smaller towns and cities the community threw its weight behind the strikers more than in larger urban areas.

That those who possessed capital in the smaller cities were often outsiders and that journeymen there may have been especially active in civic affairs may help to explain this support.[26]

Boston journeymen hoped to show sufficient moderation in order to win their masters away from the merchant capitalists and to the ten-hour system. Having approved a ten-hour strike in late March 1832, the house carpenters called a general meeting of masters and journeymen, "for the purpose of adopting a uniform system . . . to govern the hours of labor, and if possible to unite the interests of the employer and the employed." The carpenters were joined in their strike by Boston's shipwrights, caulkers, masons, painters, slaters, and sailmakers, as well as by tradesmen in Charlestown and South Boston, and by those working on the Boston and Roxbury Mill Dam. But in no trade did significant numbers of masters stand with their journeymen.[27] On May 15, leading Boston merchant capitalists met to denounce "the folly and caprice of a few journeymen mechanics . . . , who are now idle two or three of the most valuable hours of the day." The "merchants and ship-owners" pledged to blacklist all ten-hour journeymen and to deny "work to any master- mechanic who shall employ them." The journeymen involved in ship construction and repair issued a conciliatory response in which they promised to work odd hours during emergencies but held to the idea that overtime should be paid after ten hours. Shortly thereafter, as the merchant capitalists raised a $20,000 fund to break the strike, every master in the Boston area assented to a pact agreeing "to abide by and to support the resolutions of the Merchants." The masters then advertised for strikebreakers at wages about double the prevailing rates.[28]

The strike lost its force under the twin assaults of merchant and master. On July 20 the merchants wrote to the masters that "it being understood that the journeymen [ship] carpenters and caulkers have abandoned their combination to control the hours of Labour," lunch breaks might be extended to two hours (rather than one) for the next six weeks. The "extreme warmth of the weather" and "fear of Pestilence [specifically cholera]" ostensibly motivated the merchants in their beneficence.[29] Seth Luther, New England carpenter and rebel mechanic *par excellence*, heaped scorn on this lordly "Cholera Ukase." Luther maintained that the workers had begun to take the extended break weeks before the edict. Luther also held that several Boston crafts won shorter hours in 1832. Although there is evidence of scattered success in newspaper accounts, this was at best temporary. Helen Sumner is correct in terming the strike generally unsuccessful.[30] While Luther may have overstated the achievements of the 1832 Boston strikes, he accurately diagnosed their limitations and analyzed the forces arrayed against them. In the wake of the strikes Luther, delivered his "Address to the Working-Men of New England" throughout Massachusetts, Maine, and New Hampshire before it became a popular pamphlet. Holding up British industry as a negative example, Luther urged all "friends of 'Humanity'" to push for reduced hours. He perceived the way in which the shorter hours struggles of skilled craftsmen were bound up with those of factory operatives. In Boston and Providence, he wrote, the merchants, "who are also largely concerned in manufacturing," especially attacked the ten-hour movement for fear that "if hours are reduced . . . , [the] 'help' in the mills will hear of it and it will make them uneasy." Luther looked to the day when "mechanics and labourers" would match their employers' unity. Calling on skilled and unskilled laborers to "form a *front*," he foresaw victory over those who demanded long hours—those who stood for "oppression and tyranny at home."[31]

In 1832 and 1833 the initial hints of such solidarity on hours between skilled and unskilled workers appeared. Even before the 1832 strikes, the New England Association of Farmers, Mechanics, and Other Working Men met and framed a constitution. Born out of a meeting of ten-hour advocates in Providence, the New England Association made labor unity and shorter hours its founding principles. Its appeal for the participation of "other working men," in particular those in "manufacturing villages", signaled the first American effort to bring factory hands, common laborers, and skilled craftsmen together in one labor organization. This maiden attempt at organization along the lines of industrial unionism centered on the ten-hour day. Its constitution required all members "except practical farmers" to "labor no more than ten hours for one day," unless paid overtime. March 20, 1832, was set as the date for the inauguration of the system.[32]

Not surprisingly, employers disdained the association's plans for a voluntary transition to the ten-hour system. The strikes of 1832 were in large part the attempts of association backers to enforce through trade union action what voluntarism could not achieve. The plan to expel all those who worked more than ten hours evaporated, and the association raised a strike fund to aid those who held out. After it became obvious that its funds were overmatched by those of the merchants, the association turned to political action. Its memorials to legislative bodies helped to keep the issues of shorter hours and child labor alive, but the promise of recruiting factory workers went unfulfilled. A New Haven delegate to the association's 1833 convention did not help matters much by declaring that factory workers were "already sold to the oppressor."[33]

However, by 1833 other developments indicated that some of the unskilled had begun to embrace the shorter-hours demand even as strikes for the ten-hour day ebbed among journeymen. That same year, a relative handful of Boston building tradesmen pursued the issue along with a larger number of Washington, D.C., carpenters. The latter group, after registering a protest against the "custom that bound them to stand at their benches from fifteen to seventeen hours" during summer days, apparently won the ten-hour day and went on to initiate a city central in the nation's capital. In Baltimore, where as many as seventeen trades held coordinated meetings to discuss the ten-hour movement, a strong city central emerged. The eight or more unions that struck for shorter hours in that city in 1833 made only ephemeral gains, however. Even the machinists, metal workers, and iron founders, whose political pressure elicited a statement of support from the city's Democratic mayor, failed to triumph.[34] No other city recorded major shorter-hours strikes by craftsmen.

Meanwhile, stirrings among the unskilled were beginning. In Exeter, New Hampshire, factory women staged a militant 1833 turn-out to protest their employer's practice of tacking thirty extra minutes on to the day by cheating on time. The victory of the strikers brought promises that "the foreman's watch [would] be regulated." In Philadelphia, where a city central was reforming around demands for "a system of General Education—the ten-hour system of labor—and wages adequate to the labor done," factory operatives and skilled weavers were active in advancing those demands. Not only did textile workers from the industrial suburb of Manayunk inspire the original 1833 joint meetings of Philadelphia tradesmen, but the Schuylkill Falls, the Blockley, and Haverford trade societies were among the first to join forces with the new citywide union. Commons describes these societies as being made up "doubtless of factory operatives." As the 1833 appeal addressed by "The Working People of Manayunk to the Public" makes clear, the hours of labor constituted a central concern of the factory hands, who advanced arguments frequently made by craftsmen. Complaining of the long days with "never a refreshing breeze to cool us," the Manayunk workers expressed fears for their "health, . . . appetite and strength." They further protested that their children would be "reared in total ignorance" until "a reasonable time for labor [was] established."[35]

In 1834, during a brief but sharp economic downturn, strikes for shorter hours were rare although agitation around the issue was not. Rochester's journeymen carpenters did turn out for the ten-hour day, and in New York City the Baker's Trades' Union Society, 300 strong, struck for both more wages and shorter hours. The bakers' demands illustrate the uneven character of the campaign to cut hours. At a time when most journeymen pushed for the 60-hour week, and when factory operatives labored 75 to 90 hours per week, the bakers complained of a schedule which required up to 115 hours of weekly work. The protests of the journeymen bakers concentrated on the issue of Sunday toil and appealed to the logic of the city's Sabbatarian movement. Linking freedom of religion with shorter hours, the bakers resolved "that no sponge be ready before 8 o'clock on the Sabbath evening." The trade agreements ending the dispute did give many journeymen a Sunday respite.[36]

Boston Trades' Union joined the proliferating number of city centrals in March 1834. Even in the wake of 1832's failed attempt to enlist Boston masters in support of the ten-hour cause, some of the new citywide union's organizers continued, in contrast to organizers in other cities, to envision a labor movement embracing employer and employed. Possibly because of such hopes the divisive question of hours found no place in the circular that announced the formation of the city central. However, from the outset, the city central's leadership fell to outspoken advocates of the shorter working day. Dr. Charles Douglas, former leader of the New England Association, convened the group's first meeting. Seth Luther, representing the house carpenters, addressed the gathering and won office as secretary of the citywide body. Since both Luther and Douglas already enjoyed national reputations as ten-hour advocates, the issue was unlikely to stay long submerged.[37]

Indeed the city central had met for only a few months when Frederick Robinson delivered a strong call for shorter hours in his speech at a union-sponsored Independence Day celebration. Robinson, later active in the Massachusetts legislature as a Jacksonian Democrat, maintained that the work formerly accomplished in a twelve-hour shift had been reduced to a task requiring little more than a half an hour in some trades, and predicted that overproduction would make depressions "as regular . . . as . . . the seasons" if the duration of daily labor was not limited. The speaker charged his audience with the responsibility for using their political power to ameliorate the schedules of female factory workers through "direct legislation" to establish a *six-hour* day for female and child laborers.[38]

Douglas pursued a still more aggressive course by bringing the struggle straight before the factory hands. His 1834 remarks to "a large number of females" from the Lowell mills stressed "the necessity of the working class doing all in their power to improve their present condition." "The first and most important step in this path," Douglas insisted, was the winning of "immediate measures to diminish . . . the hours of labor so as to afford . . . ample time for mental improvement and for healthful exercise." He argued that "eight hours a day was time enough" for anyone to work. A final Douglas thrust resonated with the religious revivalism then overspreading Massachusetts, reviling those employers who demanded more than eight hours of daily labor as having chosen "to disregard the requirements of the Deity" by destroying the health of their workers.[39]

Indeed, Douglas's religious defense of shorter hours, and those arguments borrowed by the New York City bakers from the Sabbatarians, are illustrative of the manner in which ideas normally thought to be bulwarks of the status quo came to be reshaped by ten-hour advocates. Luther, Douglas, and others also gave a radical twist to religious conviction in a way that exemplified German philosopher Max Horkheimer's assertion that "again and again in history, ideas have cast off their swaddling clothes and struck out against the social systems that bore them." Revivalist faith, for all its inculcating of habits conducive to productivity under a capitalist order, came also to be a part of the arsenal of the ten-hour movement. Luther's writings demonstrate the variety of ways that religious ideas could be used to attack capitalist power. Most obvious are his Old Testament jeremiads that shout, "Ye cannot serve God and Mammon!" On other occasions religion and natural rights merge, with those who require long hours seen as sinning as much against Jefferson as against God. Most subtle, as Louis Hartz has observed, is the "curious boomerang effect" by which the merchant capitalists, who trumpeted the spiritual value of "capitalist virtues" like "temperance, prudence and gain," came to be blamed for undermining those very virtues through long working hours. Thus, according to Luther, the employer shouldered the blame for such ills as drunkenness, dissipation, and prostitution.[40]

In late August 1834, when six of the nation's city centrals sent representatives to form America's first national labor organization, Douglas pressured the convention of the National Trades' Union (NTU) to take a firm stand on the reduction of hours. Early in their proceedings the NTU delegates voted to "prepare a statement on the best means to . . . ensure the reduction [of] hours of labor." That statement largely sidestepped the issue by reporting that "the number of hours to constitute a day's labor" merited "no recommendation from this Convention." The committee drafting the statement doubted that it was possible to fix a "general rule for all portions of the country" and advised that the "separate trades can regulate this business with less risk of discontent."[41]

Another NTU resolution did "view with serious alarm the deplorable condition of the . . . children employed in the cotton and woolen manufactories . . . , and the many privations . . . arising from . . . the enormous length of . . . a day's labor," but it stopped short of an explicit call for shorter hours. Only after Douglas's speech at the "Discussion on the Conditions of Females in Manufacturing Establishments" did the NTU convention of 1834 enter vigorous debate on what role a national labor organization could play in the fight to secure a shorter workday for adult, as well as child, laborers.[42]

Douglas's remarks, and the debate they sparked, are miscast by the dominant tradition in American labor historiography. The Commons school (though not Commons himself) deprecated the NTU as "never . . . more than an agitational and advisory convention" and eagerly found in the organization the beginnings of "the controversy . . . between 'economic' and 'political' action." From the latter preoccupation it proved but a short leap to the view that Douglas, incorrectly identified as "the only delegate not a wageearner," spoke for political action while other delegates opted for a strategy relying more purely on trade union activity.[43] Such a formulation obscures the large area of agreement among delegates that some attention to politics was both necessary and desirable. The convention, for example, took stands on such political matters as equal education and distribution of public lands and resolved that workers should, "regain and maintain, by correct legislation, what they have lost by inattention to their own interests."[44]

At one point in the proceedings delegates did vote to substitute the word "intellectual" for "political" in a resolution mandating the drafting of a statement regarding the "social, civil and political condition of the laboring classes." However, this change stemmed not from an animus toward political action but from the feeling that "political" would be perceived as implying support for one or the other of the two major parties, or as requiring the immediate creation of a labor party and thus prove divisive. Indeed, when Douglas held that workers should pursue their own political goals while realizing that they "belonged to no party" and should support only *"workeyism,"* the Newark delegate who had led the opposition to the term "political" allowed that he *agreed* with Douglas but continued to fear that the term would be misunderstood. And when Philadelphia's John Ferral introduced the motion to replace "political" with "intellectual," Ferral added that he was nonetheless sure that "the working classes would never . . . remedy the evils . . . they were suffering until they carried their grievances to the polls."[45]

The stir that greeted Douglas's address thus came less from opposition to political action in general than from the reaction of delegates to the bold political course charted by Douglas. The *Artisan*'s editor mapped out a strategy that, while not new to Boston labor leaders (nor to Rhode Islanders, in whose state Luther had first lobbied for a ten-hour law) must have struck representatives from other areas as novel and extreme. Douglas maintained that legislation to protect and educate child laborers was by itself of little use unless extended to cover adult women workers. Douglas proposed that labor should push the legislatures to limit the hours of work which a factory owner could legally require with a strong law under which the "men of high percentage" would be "forced to shut their mills at a regular hour." That NTU delegates did not embrace Douglas's proposal is not surprising. Clashing with both the Whiggish commitment to private property and the Jeffersonian-Jacksonian predilection for limited government, Douglas's plan for enforceable shorter-hours legislation for adult (though only female) laborers was several years in capturing the imagination of trade unionists and several decades in winning over lawmakers.[46]

The response to Douglas's remarks at the NTU convention nonetheless serves as a barometer of the attitudes of Jacksonian labor leaders toward shorter-hours legislation. According to E. B. Mittelman of the Commons group, Douglas had hardly yielded the floor when New York City carpenter Robert Townsend "again raised the political spectre." Actually Townsend, consecutively active in the Workingmen's, Anti-Masonic, Whig, and Equal Rights parties, was among the most politically inclined of the delegates. He had been the main defender of the use of the term "political" earlier in the convention and evidently still smarted from losing that debate. After agreeing with Douglas that legislation to reduce hours fell "legitimately with the bounds of our labor," he could not resist a jab at those delegates who shied away from avowing political intentions. He warned that securing such legislation would require more political resolve and unity than the convention had yet displayed. While cynical, Townsend's comments opposed neither Douglas's proposal nor political action in general. David Scott, a New York tailor, spoke more directly in favor of Douglas's plan, adding that he felt that the NTU was not "debarred from all political action" and that it remained possible to pursue shorter hours legislation and avoid partisan squabbling.[47]

The arguments of those who opposed putting the NTU on record as backing a campaign for laws to reduce the length of the adult woman's working day were largely as political and sometimes as radical as those of Douglas. John Commerford, another New Yorker and a representative of the Chair Makers' Society, held that such a campaign "could not at this time be safely entered upon" because factory owners could not grant concessions and still remain competitive with European capitalists. Commerford, active in the Equal Rights party, blamed the tariff and Henry Clay's "American System" for allowing the factories to establish themselves initially.[48] John Ferral agreed that the NTU "could not act as a Convention" on the hours matter and successfully argued the position that the individual delegates should be instructed to fight against "a system which fastens slavery upon future generations." Ferral, a Philadelphia handloom weaver, described the threat in words strikingly similar to those later used by the famed traveler Alexis de Tocqueville.[49] He predicted that factory production could beneficially continue only if "The people . . . control it," and envisioned "the entire reformation of the system." Like other participants in this significant debate, Ferral called for anything but narrow trade union action.[50]

Details can obscure the overriding importance of the eventful 1834 shorter-hours discussion, however. Most vital and magnificent was the very participation of the nation's brightest rebel mechanics (minus Luther) in a session which probed the question of working hours and the ways to lessen them. The network of communication forged between these labor leaders provided a medium through which they continued to share ideas. During the next year their eager exchange of information on the ten-hour campaigns in various cities provided a key ingredient in spreading these struggles.

Again in 1835 Boston carpenters tested the ten-hour waters, this time in league with masons and stonecutters. Late April joint meetings of the three crafts bared tensions between journeymen and masters. The influence of the masters held sway in the mild committee report which supposed that the shorter day might be won on a voluntary basis if individual journeymen persuaded their bosses that the system was efficacious. But the journeymen, preferring bolder concerted action, rejected the committee report and began a strike in early May.[51] They quickly issued a "Ten-Hour Circular" which gathered the arguments supporting a shorter day and served notice that journeymen were to lead the agitation. A committee of three produced the circular, but if style and biting satire are the tests, Seth Luther did the bulk of the writing. The withering but controlled comments on masters who opposed cutting hours were, for example, vintage Luther:

> We would not be too severe on our employers, they are slaves to the Capitalists, as we are to them. "The power behind" their throne is greater than the throne itself. But we cannot bear to be the servant of servants and slaves to oppression, let the source be where it may.[52]

Such rhetoric expresses not just its authors' ire but also a serious attempt to modify the prevailing Jacksonian and republican view of class as a distinction between all "producers" (including masters) and "capitalists," by emphasizing that the "producing" masters sided with merchant capitalists on the hours issue. At the same time, however, it must be acknowledged that the ten-hour issue, in naturally drawing on a republican heritage, justified itself in terms of community more often than of class and, especially in Boston, cherished the notion of orderly work and orderly leisure in a united community of masters and journeymen.

Few antebellum documents match the "Ten-Hour Circular" in class consciousness, intelligence, eloquence, or influence. Defining the contest as one between "Money and Labor," its authors claimed "by the blood of [their] fathers, shed . . . in the War of the Revolution, the rights of American Freeman." They contended that workers had "duties to perform as American Citizens" and could therefore not afford "to dispose of more than Ten Hours for a day's work." Long hours were linked to mental and physical debilitation. They were defined as an offense against both God and natural rights. Especially acerbic was the "Ten-Hour Circular"'s reply to the bosses' standard objection that the shorter day would lead laborers into "Drunkenness and Debauchery": "they employ us . . . during the longest and hottest days, and in short days hundreds of us remain idle for want of work . . . . When the long days again appear, our guardians set us to work as they say 'to keep us from getting drunk.'[53] The "Ten-Hour Circular" became the rallying point for a long Boston strike. The strikers had walked the picket line for two months when the journeymen housewrights joined their ranks "almost to a man," injecting vigor into the struggle by parading through the city's upper-class districts singing the *Marseillaise*.[54] By October, nonetheless, the Boston Trades' Union had collapsed. The long unsuccessful strike had not only taxed the financial resources of Boston's young city central but had also shattered the master-journeyman unity that had served as the central union's organizational principle.[55] Late November saw the journeymen back on the job, working a ten-hour day enforced not by contract but by the length of late autumn sunshine.[56]

Ironically, Boston did prove an effective exporter of the ten-hour idea. From New England to the Carolinas, the "Ten-Hour Circular" aroused local discussion and action around the demand.[57] The earliest such connection took place when the document reached Philadelphia. Luther forwarded a copy of the circular to John Ferral shortly after it had been drafted. Ferral, after consulting with William English, decided that the Philadelphia unions should reprint the circular. The intention was to use the circular to gather support for the Boston strike. Ferral later wrote that the "effect was electric" when the reprint became available in Philadelphia. "The Circular," he recalled, "became the absorbing topic of conversation" among Philadelphia laborers. It spurred not just a feeling of solidarity with the Boston tradesmen but also a desire to end dawn-to-dusk labor in Philadelphia.[58] This desire, which first found expression among the unskilled, raced from craft to craft and culminated in America's first general strike. Even before the "Ten-Hour Circular" had appeared in Philadelphia, the coal heavers on the city's Schuylkill River had walked off their jobs demanding higher wages and a ten-hour day. At least 300 of the largely Irish heavers struck in May and patrolled the docks to prevent goods from moving. The probusiness *Niles' Register* stigmatized the strike leaders as "chiefly freshly imported *foreigners*—who despise and defy the law." The *Philadelphia Gazette* stressed images of fearsome pickets "commanded by a man with a drawn sword."[59] But organized craftsmen refused to be swayed by appeals to ethnic hatred and expressed esteem for the unskilled Irish and their conduct of the strike. The *National Trades' Union* newspaper praised the dockworkers for holding firm "against the tremendous power of wealth and avarice" and for pressing the ten-hour demand.[60] Imitation proved a more effectual form of flattery when the Philadelphia craftsmen themselves struck for the ten-hour day.

Fired by the "Ten-Hour Circular," the handloom weavers and makers of ladies' shoes began to conceive of their own strikes over piece rates as campaigns to win enough wages to be able to limit their labor to ten hours daily. The cordwainers connected their plight with that of the heavers. Displaying, as Ferral put it, "that sympathy of feeling, which pervades all intelligent working men," some 700 cordwainers marched to the docks to symbolically join the forces of the skilled and unskilled in early June. The resulting mass meeting featured speeches calling for a ten-hour day in all trades. The carpenters, who soon joined the strikers, marched behind banners which read "From 6 to 6."[61]

Mass meetings, sometimes held in the appropriate confines of Independence Square, became a regular occurrence. "Each day," according to Ferral, "added thousands" to the ranks of the ten-hour advocates. Bricklayers, plasterers, masons, and hod carriers quickly followed the carpenters to the picket line and smiths, sheet iron workers, lamp makers, plumbers, painters, and leather dressers were not far behind. Cigar makers, saddlers, and printers soon took up the same argument of the weavers and cordwainers, an argument common in small-scale, bastardized, piece-working crafts—that piece rates in their trades should rise so that only ten hours of daily labor would be required to maintain prestrike wages. Bakers demanded an end to Saturday night and Sunday labor.[62] Within ten days the strike wave was general, with the *Saturday Evening Post* listing some twenty trades on strike. The editors of the local *Gazette* fretted that the "times are completely out of joint," and warned that the "streets and squares are crowded with an idle population . . . ." French traveler Michel Chevalier observed, "The militia looks on; the sheriff stands with folded arms."[63]

The processions of strikers, though not violent, did have an exuberant flavor of class-conscious pageantry. The burgeoning crowds enjoyed the music of fifes and drums and held aloft banners demanding not only "From 6 to 6" but "Liberty, Equality and the Rights of Man." A contingent of 500 sailors brandished the banner "Grog or death," indicating that some "traditionalists" could rally to the ten-hour cause. The mass of marching craftsmen carried their tools.

One of the largest such processions paraded to the public works, where city employees left their job to join the march.[64]

In the face of the public workers' walkout and the receipt of petitions signed by "many thousand citizens," the Whig-dominated Common Council passed the nation's first ten-hour law on June 4. The law, which applied only to city workers, conformed to the "6 to 6" formula desired by the strikers, and maintained previous daily wages. In the manufacturing suburb of Southwark, the town council granted public workers a ten-hour day and raised pay from eighty-seven and a half cents per day to one dollar. On June 6 Ferral chaired a meeting of doctors, merchants, lawyers, politicians, and workers, supporting the ten-hour demand. This group backed shorter hours as necessary for "physical comfort, moral improvement and social happiness" and organized a boycott of scab coal. The pro-Jackson *Pennsylvanian* agreed that, "Politically it is of immense importance that a change should be effected. Our institutions place all power in the hands of the very men who are now . . . debarred from . . . that cultivation which alone can render them capable of wielding their tremendous strength."[65]

With the example of the ten-hour day set by law, with large sections of the community behind the demand, and with the general strike solidly successful, even antilabor forces began to approve concessions. *Niles' Register* allowed that ten hours was probably a long enough working day, at least for those exposed to the sun, and even the *Journal of Commerce* softened its opposition.[66] Within a few days individual employers capitulated and Ferral could proudly write Luther to "proclaim the triumph of our bloodless revolution." The 1835 events, coordinated by the city's General Trades' Union, had, as Michael Feldberg observes, "welded various elements of the Philadelphia working classes into a single, self-conscious working class."[67] Although the result of an alliance between dockworkers and artisans, the strike also came to involve white collar and factory workers. In the midst of the strike wave, the *United States Gazette* announced a projected June 8 meeting of "the salesmen and clerks of the city and county of Philadelphia . . . for the purpose of gaining time for a summer recreation." No extant record indicates what took place at that meeting. The Commons group cites further demands for early closings by retail clerks two weeks later. However, a later study shows that these appeals came from the store owners rather than from their clerks and persuasively argues that retailers, especially in the grocery business, led campaigns for a uniform closing "at early candlelight" because they wished to limit their own hours at the store and to regulate late-night competition. This later study adds, though, that "since even the threat of a clerks' strike must have been a shock to retailers in 1835, its possible effects should not be discounted." The agreements of several merchants to close at either 8 or 9 P.M. five days per week lasted but a short while before longer hours again prevailed. Two years later a movement led by the clerks themselves again raised the issue of early closings.[68]

Factory workers in the industrial suburb of Manayunk also contracted the shorter-hours fever in the summer of 1835. As Ferral informed Luther on June 22, "the oppressed females, and children employed in cotton mills in Manayunk, (those brutalizing emporiums of human misery) have caught the spark of freedom's fire and are now on strike for hours." The women and children won an agreement that their "day's service shall close at a somewhat earlier hour," but the settlement probably fell short of the ten-hour day.[69]

With the "Ten-Hour Circular" and the example of Philadelphia before them, skilled workers in many areas agitated for the shorter day in the summer of 1835. As far south as Baltimore, carpenters, millwrights, and bricklayers repeated the united efforts they had first attempted two years before. According to some evidence, employers there granted the ten-hour day to all the city's mechanics. In New York City ship carpenters and sail makers walked off their jobs to protest the length of work, and the former group gained the ten-hour day.[70] Smaller communities also witnessed action around the issue as the new system took effect after strikes in New Brunswick, New Jersey; Albany, Batavia, and Seneca Falls, New York; Salem, Massachusetts; and Hartford, Connecticut. The journeymen artisans working outdoors in Newark, the mechanics in Paterson, New Jersey, and many tradesmen in Troy and Schenectady, New York, appear to have achieved the reduction without a strike.[71]

Hartford typified the smaller cities in that public opinion was a major factor in deciding the issue there. The striking journeymen stressed the benefits to society when "every freeman had time to be devoted . . . to the acquiring of information." The masters countered the attack by branding trade unions as "subversive of the very first principles of the social compact." Members of the employers' association formed by the masters resolved that they "would never enter into any such combinations" even as they met to break the strike. But in Hartford, as in most of the other smaller cities, the masters' posture was defensive. Even the employers' association supposed that the "interest of both Master Mechanics and Journeymen" would be served by adopting a "definite number of hours for a day's labor." Ten-hour advocates carried the day in Hartford and in most of the other smaller cities.[72]

For skilled craftsmen 1835 marked a turning point in the ten-hour struggle. For the first time journeymen in many urban areas won major changes in work schedules. Nevertheless, the assessment of the Commons group regarding progress made in reducing hours during that year needs some revision. According to their study, "At the close of . . . 1835, excluding Boston, . . . ten hours became the standard day's work for most . . . city mechanics." Several caveats are necessary in order to reflect the uneven nature of the success of the ten-hour movement. Boston did not stand alone as a stronghold of sunrise-to-sunset labor. Washington, D.C., for example, joined many cities in the West and South and some in the East, in adhering to the older standard.[73] In Newark, New Jersey, some indoor mechanics continued to work longer hours, and even in New York City some still failed to share in the "Six-to-Six" schedule that building tradesmen there had long enjoyed. Those working in sweated trades and those paid by piece rate typically worked longer hours. Government works also constituted an important exception to the shorter hours trend.[74]

Among the unskilled 1835 constituted no turning point, although it did feature heightening activity around the issue of hours. In Philadelphia the class conscious solidarity of Schuylkill's unskilled heavers and the city's skilled journeymen energized a movement that ultimately also came to involve factory hands. Unskilled railroad builders in nearby Norristown also successfully struck to reduce their daily hours to ten. Throughout the period numerous wildcat strikes among laborers in the transport industry defended the traditional practices of taking breaks for drinking and smoking. Some such laborers, especially in Massachusetts, also struck for a shorter day. But only at Norristown, where the example of Philadelphia was strong and community pressure especially intense, did the ten-hour demand materialize among railroad laborers.[75]

Among factory workers outside Philadelphia, only a remarkable group of Paterson, New Jersey, children raised the issue of the length of the working day in 1835. Child laborers, many of them female, began the Paterson fight by striking on the eve of Independence Day. Their demands centered on a reduction of daily labor from thirteen and one-half hours to eleven hours during the week, and to nine on Saturdays. The youths protested against the fines used to enforce work-discipline, the withholding of wages, and the store-order system. Many of the children likely had journeymen fathers and knew of the successful ten-hour campaign of Paterson craftsmen during the same summer. The parents and others aided the children in late July by organizing the "Paterson Association for the Protection of the Working Classes." Through the association, a "vigilance committee" formed to maintain an orderly, effective strike and to gather support. After employers refused to bargain with representatives of the Association, the work stoppage spread to twenty mills and came to involve 2,000 workers. Substantial monetary support came from skilled workers in New York City and in Newark, New Jersey, with tradesmen in the latter city also sending an investigating committee to Paterson. The republican investigators found that the cotton mills "would be more congenial to the climate of [the] autocrat of all the Russias, than [to] this 'land of the free and home of the brave'."[76]

Such unity of the skilled and unskilled helped to sustain the strike for upwards of two months. The compromise settlement sent most of the strikers back to work on twelve-hour shifts, except on Saturdays when a nine-hour regimen was implemented. Those who held out for the eleven-hour demand met defeat and employers blacklisted the children of association leaders.[77] Nonetheless, the strike, which added a dozen hours to each worker's weekly leisure, must have been counted a success by the children initiating it.

With so many centers of ten-hour agitation having already secured the shorter day, the number of such strikes over hours predictably plummeted in the last five years of the decade. A few did press to extend the gains that had been made. In

1836, for example, the editors of the *National Laborer* declared, "we believe that eight hours is a just . . . number . . . for any man to work."[78] But a more common strategy among trade unionists was to press for higher wages in the wake of the hours victories. The reduction of summertime labor from over twelve hours per day to just ten hours amounted to a large drop in the labor supply (measured in man-hours). This put craftsmen in good position to win higher pay and to keep pace with the rampant inflation which had sent food prices up by a third over their 1833 levels.[79] Thus 1836 witnessed a rash of strikes over wages. "In most instances," according to Mittelman, "the employers allowed the increase as soon as it was demanded . . . , in others after but a brief strike." The connection of the previous year's cuts in working time with the winning of wage increases led one labor paper to advise, "Let them [workers] reduce their hours of labor, and their compensation will . . . inevitably be increased." Some unionists and reformers may have envisioned a steady spiral of gains in terms of hours and of wages—indeed a few predicted a four-hour day—but such hopes were dashed by the depression of 1837 and by the subsequent weakening of union organization.[80]

Even so, the ten-hour movement did not disappear after 1835 nor even after 1837. Strikes continued at a reduced level. In 1836 ten-hour offensives took place among day laborers, ship carpenters, and cotton spinners in Philadelphia; spinners and weavers in Rockdale, Pennsylvania; factory operatives in Pittsburgh; building tradesmen in Lockport, New York; and mechanics in Waterford, New York. Boston's house carpenters may also have made another brief attempt, while ship carpenters there began to win a ten-hour day on repair work. Cordwainers in New York City, Philadelphia, and Washington, D.C., struck for an increase in piece rates designed to cut their working time to ten hours per day, as did Philadelphia's saddlers.[81] Also, in 1836, employers provoked defensive work stoppages by Baltimore's masons, Philadelphia's leather dressers, and Paterson's carpenters by reneging on ten-hour agreements.[82]

Even after the depression of 1837, strikes over hours were not entirely absent. It took time for both the ten-hour idea and the devastating effects of the economic crisis to reach cities in the West. In 1837 carpenters in both Pittsburgh and Saint Louis organized for the shorter day. In the latter city various trade societies made the ten-hour day general among journeymen in some trades in the summer of 1838, either by striking or by threatening to do so. The leading student of this chapter in Saint Louis history concludes, "it was job control and especially the ten-hour day that became the driving force of the labor movement." As in Philadelphia, a protracted battle to keep and extend the ten-hour day ensued and cooperation among as many as twenty-three trades developed along with a briefly influential labor party.[83]

Many employers saw the depression years as an opportune time to dismantle trade unions, and some glimpsed the chance to roll back the ten-hour system specifically. Even before the economic downturn, masters strengthened their employers' associations and probusiness newspapers decried the effects of the ten-hour day. With the advent of the depression came a scramble for jobs and a weakening of trade unions. In New York City alone an estimated 50,000 could not find work in 1837; 6,000 building tradesmen in that city sought employment. New York's *Journal of Commerce* reflected the opinions of employers who saw that the competition for work could be used as a lever to increase hours. The widely quoted *Journal* maintained, "Now is the time to deliver mechanics . . . from . . . the Union . . . . The rules of the Unions as to hours, pay and everything else ought to be broken up." The ten-hour system drew special attention as "one of the worst deformities of their [the unions'] deformed code."[84]

Some employers acted on such logic and attempted to extend hours during the depression. One such attempt directed against railway laborers in Bordentown, New Jersey, gave rise to an 1837 strike there. In Saint Louis the employers acted after an 1839 report from the city's Master Builders' Association. Complaining that the ten-hour system spawned "habits of idleness, if not of dissipation," the master builders refused to employ workers except on the longer schedule. Employers in other crafts followed suit with the result that journeymen carpenters and members of other trades struck successfully in 1839 to defend the ten-hour day they had won just a year before.[85]

Nonetheless, such depression incursions on the ten-hour system were quite scattered. Employers cut wages far more frequently than they augmented working time. With markets glutted and unemployment high, adding hours made little immediate sense. The surplus of labor and of goods made it more in the employers' interest to trim costs through wage reductions. An increase in working hours would also have further swelled the ranks of the increasingly militant unemployed.[86] At the same time, the choice of the employers to concentrate on cutting pay indicated that the ten-hour idea had become entrenched among laborers and accepted by the population. The ability of the shorter day to weather the depression testified to the maturity and appeal of the ten-hour movement.[87]

More direct evidence of the resilience of the ten-hour forces is found in their ability to build strong political pressure for a shorter day. At both the state and national levels labor and its allies applied such pressure. Just as Boston and Philadelphia had been the most active centers of strikes over hours, so too did Massachusetts and Pennsylvania witness the most dynamic political action at the state level. In 1836 the lower house of the legislature of Massachusetts empowered a committee to consider "whether any, and what, provision ought to be made for the better education of children employed in manufactures." Chaired by James G. Carter, a newly elected school reformer with a long-established interest in the welfare of factory children, the committee produced a mild report with copious evidence of the existence of a large class of working youths who received no schooling at all. The report moved the lawmakers to pass a statute that forbade employers from hiring a child under fifteen in any manufacturing corporation unless the child had studied under a qualified teacher for at least three months during the previous year. This law lacked provisions for enforcement and did not interfere with the employer's prerogative of running factories on as long a shift as he pleased. However, it was America's first child labor law and an important precedent for Massachusetts's 1842 legislation limiting factory labor to ten hours daily for youths under twelve.[88]

In Massachusetts and elsewhere labor increasingly forced state political leaders to take a position on the hours of adult as well as child laborers. Norwich, Connecticut, trade unionists drafted a memorial that petitioned the legislature of their state to adopt "The Ten-Hour System in . . . Cotton and Woollen Manufactories," the first call by an American labor organization for government action to limit the hours of adult workers in private industry. By 1840 Governor Marcus Morton of Massachusetts appealed to Charlestown, Massachusetts, workers with a letter assuring them of "his entire approbation of Ten-Hour System." The governor of New Jersey apparently proposed shorter hours legislation in 1841.[89]

The question of the length of the working day received its most sustained airing in the Pennsylvania Senate in 1837 and 1838. A committee of that body conducted the first government investigation considering together the hours of child and adult laborers, and heard testimony for six weeks in Philadelphia, Manayunk, and Pittsburgh. The hearings drew the participation of working people from across the state. Reports from Philadelphia on child labor documented youngesters whose fourteen-hour days consisted of repeatedly carrying boxes on their heads up four flights of stairs. Immigrants from both England and Ireland maintained that they worked longer and harder in the New World than they had in the Old. Physicians contributed testimony concerning the ill effects of long hours. The committee, though not the Senate, concluded that not only would the shorter day be "necessary for the preservation of child laborers' health," but that "ten hours of labor per day is as much as the majority of adults can perform without ultimate injury."[90]

These state actions coexisted with efforts to make the federal government set an example by granting the ten-hour day to manual workers in its employ. Laborers raised the call for the rapid adoption of the new system in those cities where some craftsmen in private industry had secured the ten-hour day. Early in 1835 mechanics from the New York City-Brooklyn area directed an appeal "praying for a reduction of the hours of labor on public works" to the secretary of the navy, who dismissed the petition. At least some Philadelphia shipyards had granted the ten-hour demand in early 1834. In 1835 laborers at the government yard began to call for the new schedule to apply to their work.[91]

Refusal of many Philadelphia shipwrights to continue to work for the navy under the old system prompted the commandant of the local yard to write John Rodgers, the head of the national Board of Navy Commissioners, to complain of the difficulty of enforcing sunup-to-sundown labor. Rodgers's advice, to offer slightly longer summertime breaks, pleased neither the commandant nor his employees. Working through the NTU's Philadelphia Committee on Correspondence, the ten-hour advocates directed a letter to the secretary of the navy. By August the secretary admitted that "10 hours of labor in a Navy yard should *upon an average* be considered a day's work," but his underscored words signaled a new plan, still unsatisfactory to the laborers. The secretary devised an elaborate schedule making up for the short duration of winter sunlight by adding hours in the summer, to produce a yearly norm of about ten hours per day. This new arrangement took effect in all navy yards by October and left employees toiling nearly twelve hours daily throughout June and July.[92]

At its 1835 convention the NTU registered its dissatisfaction with the failure of naval administrators to respond to ten-hour appeals. The convention approved a resolution to draft a memorial petitioning Congress to remove the power to set hours from the hands of the "petty tyrants" at the Board of Navy Commissioners and to institute the ten-hour system on all government works. The memorial marshaled the standard shorter-hours arguments of citizenship, health, self-improvement, and time for family life, and added the pragmatic consideration that, since the government required longer hours but paid the same wages as private industry, it would attract the worst workers. The convention forwarded the memorial to Ely Moore, a former NTU chairman serving as a U.S. congressman from a working-class New York district. Moore unenthusiastically introduced the document to the House, but members of both the Democratic and Whig parties dismissed it by early 1836 on the grounds that Congress could not interfere in labor relations.[93]

That summer the shipwrights, joiners, and other workers in the Philadelphia navy yard chose to combine direct action with political pressure on the executive branch. Large public meetings punctuated their extended strike against the government yards. By early August the success of the agitation caused the government to offer higher wages for long days. The laborers held to the ten-hour principle and refused to return to work. Their appeals for aid from "every friend of human rights and human improvement" elicited further support among the working people of the city.[94] Especially after attempts by the courts and the city government to break the union of the day laborers, again striking on Schuylkill docks, large crowds turned out to show their solidarity with those on strike. On August 22, at one strike support rally, thousands came together in Independence Square to hear speeches by Ferral and other leaders of the previous year's general strike. The gathering, described as a "town meeting" or a "great meeting of the workingmen" backed the government workers by appointing a committee to draft a letter calling upon President Andrew Jackson to intervene on the laborers' behalf.[95]

The Philadelphians posted their letter on August 29; on August 31 the president ordered his secretary of the navy to grant the ten-hour day in the Philadelphia yards; on September 3 the new schedule took effect. Never have either the mails or the wheels of government moved at such a pace. The president obviously had made his decision before receiving the Philadelphia memorial. As early as June the local commandant had advised federal officials to accede to the ten-hour demand in Philadelphia. Jackson may also have followed the events in that city through the press or through reports from political advisors and may have known, after August 22, that a petition from Philadelphia workers was forthcoming. A less impressive petition from Baltimore had apparently already arrived. This knowledge would help explain the president's ability to, as his secretary of the navy put it, "anticipate the wishes" of the Philadelphia petitioners.[96]

Praise for the order dimmed after the scope of the directive became clear. Only those government works in cities where the ten-hour day had already been obtained in private industry adopted the new system. Thus, according to an NTU report from 1836, only yards in Pennsylvania, Maryland, and New York operated on the ten-hour system, while in Brooklyn and "the District of Columbia, Gosport, Norfolk, and throughout the southern states, 12 to 14 hours are still claimed by the government." This practice conflicted with the NTU's 1835 recommendation to Congress and with the expectations of trade unionists that government action would spread the ten-hour movement by setting a national example on which the Philadelphia memorial had spoken fully. Similarly, the NTU expressed its hopes that government policy would set "an example [to] be speedily felt and followed, and ten hours for a day will thus in spirit become the law of the land." The piecemeal order of 1836 failed to provide such a symbolic yardstick, and the NTU promised further lobbying to elicit additional executive action.[97]

On March 31, 1840, President Martin Van Buren did issue a broadly applicable executive order granting the ten-hour day to all those government employees engaged in manual labor. His timing and motivation remain at issue. George McNeill, writing in the nineteenth century, credited the labor movement with "organization and agitation . . . of such magnitude as to warrant" Van Buren's proclamation. The historian Mary Beard later wrote that the president acted "after a spirited threat of political action on the part of organized labor." More recent scholarship has objected that since the NTU had not existed for three years prior to the order and since the depression had weakened local unions, Van Buren must have acted to win election year votes, rather than because of pressure from labor.[98] Evidence of political agitation involving working people in statewide political campaigns for shorter hours, as presented above, gives some continued credence to the views of Beard and McNeill. At least it seems likely that labor and its allies kept the issue enough alive for the President to know that his order would be warmly received.[99]

Whatever its motivation, Van Buren's proclamation thrilled shorter hours advocates. The executive order itself provided that all those "whether laborers or mechanics," employed at government works would "be required to work only the number of hours prescribed by the ten-hour system." Van Buren also made it clear that "no corresponding reduction in wages" ought to occur.[100] The order failed to include white-collar employees, but that was of small consequence since most federal offices opened just eight hours daily in winter and ten in summer under an 1836 federal law. A poignant passage in the diary of Michael Shiner, a free black worker in the Washington Navy Yard, captured the way in which Van Buren's order endeared him to many workers. Some years after 1840, Shiner wrote, "the Working Classes of people of the United States, Mechanic and labourers ought to never forget the Hon ex President Van Buren for the ten hour sistom . . . his name ought to be Recorded in every Working Man heart."[101]

Van Buren's order capped a decade and a half of intense activity surrounding the ten-hour issue. This activity centered among rebel mechanics drawn from the ranks of journeymen craftsmen, but came to involve some unskilled workers. Throughout the Jackson Era the issue of hours energized the trade union movement, lending it the kind of unity which could undergird the efforts of young trade unions joined together in class-conscious protests. Because it divided those who made the rules regarding hours from those who worked under them, the shorter hours demand differentiated between masters and journeymen, and quickened the formation of unions which excluded employers and based themselves on the demands of wage laborers.[102] Because it so captured the imagination and aspirations of journeymen for full intellectual, political, and family life, and so clashed with the employer's desire for complete control over production, the ten-hour struggle evoked passionate commitment on both sides. Shorter hours were the focal point of the Jacksonian labor movement.

Indeed, it is only after the hours issue is placed in the center that the broader picture of the relationship of labor activism to Jacksonian America becomes more clear. The commitment of so many egalitarian, working artisans to educational reforms (which modern scholars label "bourgeois") best makes sense in terms of the intricate connection made by journeymen between education, self-improvement, republicanism, and the right of labor to limit hours and to exercise intelligent control over its own time. Similarly, the perception of the hours movement as a central one recasts our view of the 1830s labor movement's relation to politics. Where hours are concerned, it is impossible to identify a "political" and an "economic" wing of the trade unions. It was virtually axiomatic that some political agitation should take place around the issue even if tactical proposals varied.[103]

Still more broadly, the sudden spread of new attitudes toward time and of shorter-hours protests constituted one aspect of the rapid social change which characterized Jacksonian America. Insofar as they illuminate the pace of such change, the reminiscences of an anonymous New York shipwright serve to compress the experiences of the whole ten-hour movement and of a fast-moving society. The ship carpenter recalled swift changes during the 1830s:

Mechanical mankind had labored from sunrise to sunset . . . so long that, at the beginning of my apprenticeship, New York Mechanics . . . had no idea of a briefer term of labor; and one night, when some premature philosopher . . . preached *ten hours* to eight or nine hundred of us . . . we laughed at his absurd theories, ourselves convinced that the advent of the ten-hour system was ten times more remote than that of the millennium. Shortly thereafter these very workers struck for the ten-hour day.[104]

The same striking change in consciousness was repeated in workshops throughout the 1830s. In the 1840s it would recur among women inside the factory gate.

3

Mill Women and the Working Day,
1842-1850

In July 1844, S. C. Hewitt, a mechanic and itinerant organizer for the Fall River Mechanics' Association, began a series of New England speeches by acquainting a Pawtucket rally with the virtues of the ten-hour system. Hewitt's enthusiasm over the reception he received was tempered by his concern about the absence of women in his audience. He worried that the language of the handbill publicizing the meeting might have been to blame. Defending to himself his choice of wording, Hewitt explained in his journal, "In calling upon the working men, I certainly supposed the women would feel themselves [included], inasmuch as the 'woman is of the man' and not the man of the women." Hewitt also observed that "women work harder than males" and should be expected to play a large role in ten-hour agitation. Later at a factory village near Woonsocket, Hewitt drew an encouraging crowd of women and punned, "I was honored by the attendance of a *fair* number of the FAIR. These *fair* ones would be fairer still if the present *un*-fair system of labor were superseded."[1]

Partly as a result of Hewitt's tour, a regional labor organization, the New England Workingmen's Association, took shape that fall. At its first convention the association promised to admit female labor groups on equal terms. Already women industrial workers constituted the leading edge of many local labor movements. By 1846 they participated so fully in the Workingmen's Association that the organization's name no longer seemed apropos. The group, rechristened the Labor Reform League, seldom failed to address its appeals explicitly to "workingmen and women."[2]

The experiences of Hewitt and of the regional association typify broader trends in the labor movement of the 1840s. Organizing mainly around the ten-hour demand, labor groups proved egalitarian in practice as well as in language.[3] A burst of self-activity on the part of the "factory girls" of New England and the Middle Atlantic states transformed a movement previously based on the participation of journeymen. Because the women textile workers sought the shorter day principally through petitioning state legislatures, a special kind of cooperation between the sexes developed. Disenfranchised women carried petition drives forward. But they necessarily appealed to male voters to back up their political demands. This chapter examines the relations of the sexes in the ten-hour movement of the 1840s and the circumstances under which factory women came to raise the ten-hour banner. It examines why the middle and later years of the decade witnessed such feverish activity by females before the movement ebbed at decade's end.

Substantial continuity was maintained between the artisan-based shorter-hours movement of the 1830s and the renascent movement of the early 1840s. As trade unions bounced back from the Panic of 1837, familiar names made familiar arguments for the ten-hour day. Charles Douglas, John Ferral, and Seth Luther reemerged in the new struggles. Male artisans were most influential in reviving the movement to reduce hours. The first stirrings actually predated the depression's end. Heartened by President Martin Van Buren's 1840 directive on hours, many workers in private shipyards began to agitate for a ten-hour day or less. Results varied but, by 1842, the Mystic, Connecticut, yards ran on ten-and-one-half hour shifts, and the ten-hour system held tenuous sway in Bath, Maine's, shipbuilding industry. At the Massachusetts Navy Yard in Charlestown, carpenters and caulkers doing repair work on old ships—work which often required the assumption of cramped positions—won the eight-hour day in 1842 with joiners following suit three years later.[4]

Other evidence also indicates that the ten-hour movement of the early 1840s depended on the support of male journeymen. The earliest ten-hour petitions received by the Massachusetts legislature came, in 1842 and 1843, mainly from cities such as Fall River, Mansfield, New Bedford, Newburyport, and Taunton, which more often possessed a heritage of craft-based ten-hour struggles than a large female factory population. The small 1843 petition from the textile center of Lowell bore mostly male signatures. The Ten-Hour Republican Association, which gave the early petition drives a semblance of cohesion, consisted of skilled mechanics. As late as 1844 Fall River remained the hub of the regional movement, sending out an organizer (Hewitt) and publishing an aptly-titled paper, *The Mechanic.*[5] The Fall River Mechanics' Association did value the aid of its auxilliary, the Ladies' Mechanic Association, but the women apparently were organized as the relatives of journeymen rather than as workers themselves.[6]

Popular culture of the period reflected artisan enthusiasm for reducing the working day. Shorter-hours meetings featured a plethora of songs that expressed the feelings of the craftsmen. In "Six to Six," for example, racist humor cloaked the comparison of the hours of journeymen with the schedule assumed to have been worked by slaves: "The niggers have their tasks, and when done they may spree it, But the jers [journeymen] they were asked to stick to work as long as they could see it." More typical was the republicanism of "The All-Day System," a song that predicted that "The old all-day system, the ruinous system, Affrighted will flee from Columbia's shore."[7]

In Elihu Burritt, a blacksmith who ranked among America's finest scholars and who found time to master a dozen languages, the mechanics found a hero. Burritt symbolized the enlightened working population that might emerge if hours were cut to ten or even less. At an Independence Day celebration in 1844, one Fall River activist admitted the practicality of calling for the ten-hour system as an immediate demand but reminded his listeners that "The learned Blacksmith [Burritt] of this State pursues the following order: eight hours of manual labor, eight for intellectual improvement and eight for rest."[8]

That the journeymen should have sustained so active an interest in ten-hour agitation even after the gains of the 1830s is not surprising. In many areas, particularly southern ones, sunrise-to-sunset labor survived for skilled as well as for unskilled labor. For instance, in 1847, journeymen house carpenters in the growing community of Nashville, Tennessee, reiterated the arguments made by their craft brothers in Philadelphia two decades before: "We need . . . recreation. It is estimated by political economists that five hours labor per day . . . would be sufficient for support of the human race . . . . We have minds and they must be improved. We are lovers of our country and must have time . . . to study its interests." A year later Rochester, New York, journeymen still fought for the ten-hour system.[9]

In New England the ten-hour cause had progressed unevenly. Long hours applied to some journeymen and many mill workers. Believing that the sight of a "[working] man of the village . . . at leisure" might tempt factory workers away from steady labor, the textile capitalists fought against the ten-hour demand in workshops as well as in mills. In Boston, home of the textile industry's elite, well-financed campaigns countered each ten-hour offensive. Journeymen there still mounted efforts to win the shorter day as late as 1859.[10] In mill towns a large number of skilled male workers labored as machinists tending factory equipment, and in production tasks like tentering, carpet weaving, and mule-spinning. Even in those large mills that opted for a maximum of female labor, males constituted about a seventh of the work force.[11] The males brought substantial skills and craft pride to the factories but had to work roughly the same shifts as the female hands and sometimes had to labor on Sundays as well.[12] Mill owners also profited by long hours in workshops of the factory community because they were then not disadvantaged in the market for skilled male labor. Conversely, mechanics had an interest in extending hours agitation into the mills.

If the artisan movement for a shorter day showed continuity between the 1830s and 1840s, the response of the factory population shifted sharply. Aside from previously discussed outbreaks in Pawtucket (1824), Paterson (1828), Exeter (1833), Philadelphia-Rockdale (1835 and 1836), and again in Paterson (1835), before 1840 few operatives challenged the long hours worked in the mills by undertaking formal labor protests. Only the latter two concerted actions definitely posed the ten-hour demand. Those changes in factory production and in the work force that underlay the rising combativeness over hours were subtle and various. The most common explanation for the factory women's mounting militancy regarding hours is that the congenial early mills, run to the paternal specification of the group of Boston merchant capitalists, changed under the pressures of competition in the 1840s. According to this view, a new generation of factory owners forgot the social responsibility of the 1820s and 1830s and made factory work distasteful. There are threads of truth in such an analysis, but on the whole it does not wash. As Helen Sumner, historian of women workers, observed long ago, "no 'golden era' ever really existed in the textile factories of this country."[13]

In some respects the early years were the worst. Samuel Slater's Pawtucket mill constituted a prototype imitated by the overwhelming majority of textile factories built in the first quarter of the century. These mills, in which child labor was rife, were of the "Rhode Island" or "family" type. Each employed a small work force, usually fewer than 35 persons. The personnel consisted of families, often of dispossessed farm families.[14] Long hours prevailed—probably over 70 hours weekly, with at least some mills institutionalizing overtime pay after 72 hours per week. Some owners operated on Sundays, and some required as many as sixteen hours of daily toil.[15]

After 1814 Francis Lowell's Waltham plant served as a model for a second type of factory organization and as the source of the myth of a "Golden Age" of textile production. Waltham-type mills, which thrived in northern Massachusetts, New Hampshire, and Maine, contrasted with the family type mills. They featured greater capitalization, corporate ownership, management by salaried agents, and a largely adult and female labor force lodged in company boardinghouses. In choosing to employ young women from New England farms, the owners bolstered the image of Waltham-type factories which benefited by comparison to those English and smaller American mills using large amounts of child labor. The brief tenure of factory women in the jobs and habits of deference learned by women in the patriarchal countryside combined to promise high production without a permanent proletariat and without degradation. Paeans to factories of the Waltham variety became virtual set pieces for travelers writing of New England. By 1832 as many American women labored in mills built along the lines of Waltham as did in family-system factories.[16]

However, the decisions of Lowell, his associates in the Boston Manufacturing Company, and other capitalists to tap the "well-educated and virtuous" New England farm women as a labor pool stemmed from economic calculation and created no ideal conditions of work. As Howard Gitelman argues, the transition to adult female in the work force resulted from the combination of the availability of a supply of cheap labor and of a technology that achieved high productivity using semiskilled labor and supplanted skilled, independent male mulespinners.[17] Similarly, the supervision by "moral police"—as the supervisors of boardinghouses and the overseers of work were called—had a pragmatic edge in that they encouraged farmers to allow their daughters to enter the factories.[18] However benevolently the employers looked after the moral welfare of the women, management differentiated little between profitable control at work and guardianship during leisure:

> All persons in the employ of the Company, are required to attend assidu-
> ously to their various duties, or labor, . . . to aspire to the utmost efficiency
> in the work or business they may engage to perform, and to evince on all
> occasions, in their deportment and conversation, a laudable regard for tem-
> perance, virtue, and their moral and social obligations . . . . No persons can
> be employed . . . whose known habits are . . . dissolute, indolent, dishon-
> est, or intemperate, or who habitually absent themselves from public
> worship.[19]

Conditions of work were far from ideal in the Waltham-type factories during the pre-1840 years. Investigations, travelers' accounts, and reminiscences agree that the working day averaged between twelve and thirteen hours during the late 1820s and 1830s.[20] Summer days must have seemed especially confining to the former farm girls who now had little or no time for outdoor activities during day-light hours, save on Sundays. Some factories compounded this deprivation by nailing windows shut to regulate changes in humidity and prevent the breaking of threads. Such grievances may have been very much in the minds of factory girls who sang in 1836:

> Oh! Isn't it a pity
> that such a pretty girl as I
> Should be sent to the factory to pine away and die?
> Oh! I cannot be a slave
> I will not be a slave
> For I'm so fond of liberty
> That I cannot be a slave.[21]

Rushed meals provided but a slight break from the confinement in the noisy factories. Even at Lowell, showcase of the factory cities, workers had but 30 min-utes to walk from work to boardinghouse, eat breakfast or dinner, and return to work. Some employers "shaved" even this time by manipulating clocks during meals. Such haste caused Seth Luther to quip, in 1832, that the "light and cheer-ful step" of the girls betrayed necessity, not good health. In spite of glittering accounts to the contrary, the situation of the early factory women was not so golden as to lead to an unconcern over the length of the working day.[22]

Other, less sweeping, reasons for the quiescence of the early factory women regarding hours therefore merit attention. The early mills, especially of the family type, did not require utterly alienating labor. In the smaller mills, turning out a diverse line of goods, tasks varied. Workers, especially adult males, could some-times switch from job to job during the day. Craft skills were at times prized, especially in carpet production. In the 1830s even in the Waltham-type factories, as many as two women in five worked in pairs or in small groups and could trade tasks or even leave the job entirely for short periods. The pace of work allowed for talking and reading on the job.[23]

In the few large factories outside the textile industry, workers sometimes retained fantastic options as to how they would organize time and tasks. The federal armory at Harpers Ferry stands as an extreme example of an antebellum plant in which highly skilled workers largely supervised themselves. As Merritt Roe Smith's study indicates, the employees at that gun-producing factory commanded scarce skills and managed to work as few as five hours daily during the 1830s. The factory opened at dawn and closed at dusk, but workers came and went at will, working just enough to produce a fixed quantity of goods. When, in 1842, government managers instituted the ten-hour system prescribed by Van Buren's 1840 directive, the armorers mounted a "clock strike" *against* the new system. Harpers Ferry, part factory and part government pork-barrel project, hardly typifies manufacturing establishments of the antebellum period. Nonetheless, the behavior of the armory's craftsmen does illuminate the relationship between closely supervised, highly specialized labor and the desire to codify and limit hours. To the extent that early textile mills (and mines) allowed for varied, self-paced work, they forestalled shorter-hours demands.[24]

The composition of the labor force in pre-1840 textile factories also militated against ten-hour agitation. Family-system mill workers sometimes had few choices and little social power. Landless and often indebted, they depended, for their incomes, on the mill in which they worked. Their lives centered around company houses and company stores. The favorite reaction to harsh conditions in a family-system mill was to move to another, where hours often were as long and labor as unrewarding.[25]

In the early Waltham-system mills, migration also represented the most common response to lengthy schedules and tightening discipline. The factory women, most of whom hailed from areas relatively near the mill during the period prior to 1840, could return to farms for a respite or for good. Many eased the transition to the long periods of confinement required by factory life by departing for short stretches, especially during summers and berry-picking seasons.[26] These excursions often had the overseer's sanction because they restored lost vigor and, if the women persuaded neighbors to return to the factory with them, provided a means to recruit new labor. Others, perhaps as many as 10 percent of the workers in some mills, punctuated their factory labor with terms of schoolteaching in the countryside.[27] Such time away from the factory made grievances over time seem less urgent. In a sense, the preindustrial work pattern of bouts of intense labor followed by rest was being reproduced in the industrial centers.

The records of the Hamilton Company Mills in Lowell during 1826 and 1827 suggest that many women resisted the demands of factory discipline, but did so informally and individually. If the knowledge that nearby farms awaited their return emboldened them, it also helped to create a pattern of protest that management could divert by isolating and firing the offenders. Among the 107 firings charted by the Hamilton Company were the following dismissals, which must have drained the mill of many of its most militant workers:

6 were discharged for misconduct
5 were discharged for mutiny
3 were discharged for disobedience to orders
1 was discharged for impudence to the overseer
1 was discharged for levity
1 would not do her duty
5 were discharged for lying, misrepresentation, or circulating false stories
1 was discharged for captiousness
1 ran away
1 was hysterical . . . [and]
1 had written after her name emphatically "regularly discharged *forever*"[28]

The nearby farm and the short tenure in the early mills made it possible for many of the women to see their wage-working years as temporary sojourns designed mainly to acquire cash as quickly as possible.[29] Such factors tended to focus formal protests on wages rather than conditions and hours.

By the mid-1840s the composition of the labor force and the nature of the work process had changed in ways causing a sharp increase in ten-hour protest. Several historians have held that the major change was the transition to a more "permanent working class," which had a much lower rate of turnover than that of the pre-1840 period. The fugitive figures regarding rates of persistence among workers in the larger textile factories do not permit so large a generalization. In 1826 and 1827 the Hamilton Company showed a replacement rate (discharges/total number of hands) of about 35 percent. By 1845 rates varied from 25 percent to 50 percent and, as late as 1853, the Pepperrell Mills had 100 percent replacement rates. The Boott Corporation Mill Number 2 figures from 1841 show an average persistence rate of 4.8 years, according to an overseer's estimate. The 1845 figures in Lowell Mills, roughly computed at 4.5 years or "between four and five years" are hardly different enough to account for the emergence of a ten-hour movement. To complicate matters further, Dr. Josiah Curtis's medical study of Lowell, which included brief terminations of employment in calculating persistence, found that the average tenure in the mills, from 1840 through 1849, was but nine months.[30]

Changes in the work force were subtle and complex but telling. One vital transition involved the recruitment of labor from greater distances. By 1845 only 12 percent of the operatives studied in a survey of eight Massachusetts mills hailed from that state. Whether the recruitment of women from far away stemmed from a labor shortage or from a desire to stabilize the labor force and render it less able to count on local resources is of little consequence here. Vital instead was the rising incidence of protest against recruiting agents who drove, as the labor press put it, "a 'long, low black' wagon . . . we term 'a slaver'" into fara-way areas to recruit labor, often under false pretenses.[31] Another effect of more far-flung recruitment was to make the operatives less able to take brief trips home to escape the rigors of factory life.

Moreover, while turnover remained high in any given factory, higher levels of agricultural debt helped assure that many women would remain in some wage-earning occupation on a more-or-less permanent basis. Caroline Ware's state-ment that "All evidence agrees that need was not the chief motive that brought girls to the mills," may apply well to the 1820s and early 1830s, but not to the 1840s.[32] Mary Alice Feldblum's recent research suggests as much, and, although Thomas Dublin has given us grounds to think labor literature exaggerated the poverty of the operatives, agricultural misery surely sent some women into the mills. Labor literature of the 1840s stressed that most women did not work for pin money or to send a brother to college. The *Voice of Industry* described work-ers in New England textile factories as "a large share of poverty's daughters whose fathers do not possess one foot of land." Other accounts related that in Pittsburgh, the nation's most militant center of textile labor organization, "the 'law' ha[d] made the parents of these poor [factory] girls landless, and thrown them in the factory stock-yards, homeless, destitute and dependent." Even Har-riet Farley, editor of the proemployer *Lowell Offering*, accounted for ill health in the mills by referring to part of the factory population as "too poor because par-ents, children or other relatives may be dependent on their wages for support." Workers who complained that "The whip which brings us to Lowell is NECES-SITY," were not apt to consider their wage-earning careers as voluntary and temporary.[33] Women workers looked to the farm past with longing but lived amidst factory conditions. Their poetry mixed agricultural rhythms with indus-trial ones but left little doubt as to which governed their existence. "The Factory Bell" juxtaposed solar and factory time, especially in its first and its final stanzas:

> Loud the morning bell a ringing,
> Up, up sleepers, haste away;
> Yonder sits the redbreast singing,
> But to list we must not stay.
> Sol behind the hills descended,
> Upward throws his ruby light;
> Ding, dong ding—our toil is ended,
> Joyous bell, good night, good night.[34]

The presence of a core of women who remained in the mills for a long time came to have a quantitative impact transcending the numerical size of the group. The 20 to 25 percent of the textile workers in large factories who were females with three or more years of seniority constituted, according to historian Ray Gin-ger, "the best prospects for trade unionism in a cotton mill." This stable section of the working class provided leadership in the ten-hour movement. Of the six women testifying on behalf of the ten-hour petition from Lowell at the 1845 Massachusetts House of Representatives hearings on the factories, for example, one had nearly three years of seniority, one four, one five, and two over eight years. The more senior workers commanded respect, had learned time-discipline, often owned watches, and had witnessed enough incremental changes in the work process to mount an impressive critique of trends in capitalist production.[35]

Speedup of production proved the most galling grievance developing over the years. The most direct of such speedups was the increase of working hours. According to Norman Ware, corporations added to hours "year after year, week after week, minute by minute." The best estimates of historians hold that about fifteen minutes were added to the working day between 1829 and 1841.[36] During the 1840s efforts to augment the length of labor continued. Sarah Bagley, leader of the Lowell Female Labor Reform Association, reported, in 1845, on factories seeking to add two hours to the daily schedule. Other complaints hinged on the shaving of time which resulted in adding from five to thirty minutes to the working day through the manipulation of clocks and bells.[37] Modern observers must exercise imagination to perceive the importance attached to even a fifteen-minute increase in working time. Operatives of the 1840s did not see the speedup as a tiny increase in working time but as a substantial *decrease* in the small amount of *leisure* time at a factory worker's disposal.[38]

Part of the increase in working time during the 1840s came from use of artificial lighting for night work. Such illumination violated the "natural" work patterns of operatives familiar with agricultural labor and posed hazards to health and safety. During the period from September 20 until March 20, most large mills "lighted up," often before dawn and again after dark. A Peterboro, New Hampshire, resolution reflected the workers' perception:

> *Resolved*, That although the evening and the morning is spoken of in Scripture . . . no mention is made of an evening in the morning. We therefore conclude that the practice of lighting up in the morning and thereby making two evenings in every twenty-four hours is not only oppressive but unscriptural.[39]

The *Factory Girl's Garland* also objected, writing "we trust the girls . . . will rise up against this outrageous custom."[40]

"Lighting up" drew further criticism because the many lamps raised the temperatures, the level of pollution, and the risk of fire. Josiah Curtis's 1849 report to the American Medical Association, for example, described a typical factory room as having "fifty solar lamps . . . which assist not only in impairing the confined air but also in raising the temperature frequently to 90F." Small whale oil lamps supplemented the larger gas and oil-fueled devices so that, according to the 1845 testimony of one Massachusetts woman, as many as sixty-one large and

293 small lamps burned together to illuminate a single work room containing 150 employees.[41]

The bells and parades marking the start and end of the "lighting up" period expressed and ritualized the operatives' opposition to the practice. The ceremony in March featured a festive atmosphere in which workers "decorate[d] their large hanging lamps with flowers, and form[ed] garlands of every ingenious description." At one Rhode Island celebration in 1845, laborers chanted "Liberation" in support of the freeing of the leaders of the Dorr Rebellion and to greet their own relative freedom. At the start of the period of artificial lighting there was little to celebrate and, on at least one occasion—in 1846 at Nashua, New Hampshire—factory women struck to protest.[42]

Other speedups involved tighter supervision and a faster pace of work. Most factory rules and schedules specified details by the 1840s and 1850s, even to the extent of strictures such as "In all cases the first stroke of the bell is considered as marking the time."[43] Talking on the job, reading at work, and raising potted flowers in the mills came under attack. Some women did smuggle printed pages into the factory after books were banned, but even these pages, including Bible passages, were confiscated by overseers whose zeal was encouraged by premium bonuses for productivity.[44]

Speedups and new technology also meant that the women came to tend more looms. In the late 1820s New England factories, like those in Britain, generally assigned a pair of looms to each operative. By the 1840s, no fewer than three, and sometimes four looms per person were typical. The speed of individual looms, measured in "beats per minute" (an index expressive of how rhythms of the mill derived from the machine) was varied to achieve optimal production.[45] Workers transferred to newly built mills felt the impact of changes keenly, reporting that the new factories were "vastly more laborious" than the old.[46]

Speedups might not have generated so large a ten-hour movement had piece rates not dropped with increases in production. To women new to the mills, piece rates likely appeared as a reasonable kind of remuneration. Payment according to production meshed with the tradition of task orientation toward work that was common on farms.[47] Or so it seemed. But as the women witnessed one reduction of rates after another, it became clear that their wages were not tied to production. Wages stayed about the same, and sometimes fell, even as productivity rose by 100 percent. The labor press saw the logic of piece rates as "the increased work being done by labor and the profit going to capital," and offered a new definition of "operative" as a "person who . . . generally earns three times as much as she receives." Strikes over piece rates, such as the turnouts in Lowell in 1842 and in Chicopee in 1843, often preceded ten-hour campaigns.[48]

In 1845 even the procorporation *Lowell Offering* took an uncharacteristic and critical "Second Peep at Factory Life." Two characters in the *Offering*'s story exchange thoughts on piece rates and work:

"This cutting down wages is not what they cry it up to be. I wonder how they'd like to work as hard as we do, digging and drudging day after day, from morning to night, and then, every two or three years, have their wages reduced . . . ."

"And besides this, who ever heard of such a thing as their being raised again?" says the first speaker. "I confess that I never did so long as I've worked in the mills and that's been ten years."[49]

Previous accounts have detailed the struggles of factory women and their male allies to win the ten-hour day.[50] What follows adds to those but slightly. The emphasis here is on the way in which the campaigns of the 1840s reflect themes that run throughout the history of the shorter-hours movement. Most noteworthy among these themes are the sense of solidarity evidenced by workers of different sexes and of various levels of skill, and the willingness to experiment with political and economic strategies in pursuit of the ten-hour goal. Also compelling is the way in which women recast the arguments for a shorter working day, developing their own criticisms of the impact of long hours on health, intellect, and political participation. By 1844, the year during which male mechanics and reformers organized the New England Working Men's Association, stirrings among female workers became apparent, although no strong organization had emerged to give shape to ten-hour agitation among women. The first association meeting attracted 207 delegates from over a score of New England and New York cities and towns but apparently no females attended, even among the large Lowell delegation. The convention, which featured an articulate sprinkling of utopian socialists, such as L. W. Ryckman and George Ripley, and land reformers (particularly George Henry Evans and Alvan Bovay), subordinated the ten-hour issue to that of "Freedom and Public Lands." But delegates did vote to "memorialize . . . the legislatures to pass a law that shall prohibit any corporation from employing a person more than ten-hours per day." They also invited "Female Labor Reform Associations" to join their ranks with equal "right, privileges and obligations." This action may have reflected the knowledge that in some cities factory women had begun to secure signatures for ten-hour petitions. In any event, the petitions which circulated in late 1844 and early 1845 included large numbers of female signers for the first time. Half of Andover's 500 signers were female while in Lowell women comprised 75 percent of the more than 1,100 petitioners.[51]

The first of the local New England Female Labor Reform Associations met at Lowell in January 1845 with only two members in addition to its thirteen officers. By April the group counted 304 members, and just two months later it reported that between 400 and 500 women had enrolled.[52] Lowell women initiated or attended organization meetings in other mill towns including Fall River, Massachusetts, and Dover and Nashua, New Hampshire. In Manchester, New Hampshire, the pace of growth rivaled that of Lowell. Over 1,000 Manchester operatives, two thirds of them women, attended a December 1845 organization meeting with speakers from Lowell. Sixty members founded the Manchester Labor Reform Association that night, and by the end of the next summer, the group had grown five fold.[53]

Growth hinged on able, intelligent leadership, a vigorous press, and an effective intervention into politics. Sarah Bagley played a key role in the press and politics while typifying the best qualities of the pioneer women labor leaders. A weaver, Bagley came to the mills from New Hampshire possessed of a common school education and a passion for knowledge. She participated in female literary study groups known as the Lowell Improvement Circles, contributed articles to the first issues of the *Lowell Offering*, frequented public lectures, supervised a night school, and generally qualified as a leader among the "culture-crazy girls" of the mills.[54] Such educated factory women, one of whom Harriet Hanson Robinson remembered as having come to the factories from Maine "for the express purpose of getting books," had long drawn the praise of management as particularly diligent workers.[55] With Bagley and others, the chickens came home to roost. The zeal and skill of some of the educated women operatives found application in campaigns designed to shorten working hours. A commitment to learning came to include a commitment to ending the factory schedules which, as domestic reformer Catharine Beecher put it, made factory women snatch an education during "hours which should have been given to sleep."[56]

Bagley's turn from the genteel self-improvement and sisterhood of the reading circle to the militant self-improvement and sisterhood of the ten-hour movement was cemented by her break from the *Lowell Offering*. During its early days the *Offering* printed Bagley's prose, which concentrated on praising the virtue and initiative of women workers more than on extolling the factory system. After the *Offering* attracted the financial support of the owners, who saw the journal as literary proof against the charge that factory labor was degrading, the magazine came to the overt defense of the corporations. In 1842 its ownership transferred from a local clergyman who mildly opposed long hours to the promanagement Whig editor and politician William Schouler. Harriet Farley and Harriet Curtis, a pair of declassed daughters of old New England families, assumed editorial responsibilities for the monthly. Even in an expanded format, they failed to find room for Bagley's increasingly critical articles.[57]

The *Offering* gave Curtis and Farley a forum to declare their belief that no descent to working-class status had taken place among those ladies who "temporarily" did factory work. In return, the editors avoided discussion of issues such as wages and conditions on the ground that "these depend on [factors] over which we have not control." Veiled protests, which hinted that a nine-, eight-, or even six-hour day ought to prevail, sometimes appeared, but Bagley's indictments of the length and nature of factory labor did not. A chasm had opened between Bagley's approach to labor problems and the pieties of the *Offering*. Farley's own ten-hour strategy best revealed that gulf: "I dislike heartily the long-hour system . . . but I have a joyful faith in the corporations. . . . I have no doubt that in their own good time, they will introduce the ten-hour system; and will not this be a noble deed?"[58]

Excluded from the *Offering*, Bagley devoted her talents to the *Voice of Industry*, a Massachusetts weekly endorsed by the New England Working Men's Association. During the summer of 1845 the *Voice* instituted an autonomous "Female Department" which functioned "under the immediate supervision of the Lowell Female Labor Reform Association." Bagley and Huldah Stone ran the department and, after the *Voice* moved its offices to Lowell, Bagley edited the paper briefly. Her tenure established her as the first female labor editor in the United States and oriented the *Voice* even more toward women readers. Eventually Lowell females assumed ownership of the paper.[59]

Under both Bagley and a male editor, W. F. Young, the *Voice* concentrated its agitation on uniting men and women around the ten-hour demand. The paper repeatedly castigated the *Offering* for its refusal to favor ten-hour legislation.[60] The *Voice* also served to spread the ten-hour message to smaller textile centers. Its agents in several states announced the regional scope of the movement and the paper became a clearinghouse circulating petitions and reporting on ten-hour struggles from New England to Pennsylvania.[61]

Political pressure at the state level, a tactic developed by male mechanics in the early 1840s, remained the favorite strategy of ten-hour advocates after large numbers of factory women entered the campaign, but the women brought new dimensions to the statewide petition drives. Not only did the female activity lead to larger numbers of petition signatures, but by drawing women into political participation, it raised feminist issues alongside labor issues. Historians have argued that the antislavery petition drives of the 1830s and 1840s assumed special significance to women because they represented a way to participate in the political arena when other avenues were closed; this observation applies as well to the factory petitioners.[62] Mill women, acting on their own behalf and living in a community of females, were arguably more politicized and sensitized to sexual oppression by their experiences in the petition drives than were their antislavery sisters. Although few of the working women made a quick transition into the middle-class women's suffrage movement, they did raise vital issues, such as equal pay for equal work, suffrage, and the rights of women to free speech, while demonstrating the potential political power of women by influencing elections even without the franchise.[63]

The actions of state and local governments during the petition campaigns took factory women more deeply into politics. In Manchester the largely female Labor Reform Association battled with the mayor and aldermen throughout much of 1846 and 1847 over the denial of rental of the city hall for a ten-hour rally. The women won the right to use the hall but not before they wondered whether "monarchical government" prevailed in their city.[64]

The Massachusetts legislature ignored the ten-hour petitions it received in 1845 on the grounds than many of the signers were female. The House committee investigating labor conditions hoped that reticence among women might provide reasons to avoid holding hearings on the hours issue. Writing the organizers of the petition drives, the committee suggested that "as the greater part of the petitioners are females, it will be necessary for them to make the defence, or we shall be under the necessity of laying it [the petition] aside." The women defied a taboo on female public speaking and declared themselves "in readiness to defend the petitions." Bagley led six women in testifying before the committee. Her defense of the right of women to speak suggests the extent to which the petition drives politicized the workers on sexual as well as on labor matters:

> For the last half a century, it has been deemed a violation of woman's-sphere to appear before the public as a speaker; but when our rights are trampled upon and we appeal in vain to our legislators, what are we to do . . . ? Shall not our voice be heard . . . , shall it be to the daughters of New England that they have not political rights?[65]

The hearings and subsequent committee reports and legislation provided fresh opportunities to organize ten-hour support. The Massachusetts legislature had given a prominent forum to Bagley and other activists who raised the question of the impact of long hours on health. The biggest 1845 petition contended that workers were "toiling from thirteen to fourteen hours per day, confined in unhealthy apartments, exposed to poisonous contagion of air [and] debarred from proper exercise." Further complaints held that "time for mental discipline and Mastication [was] cruelly limited," and the petition blamed long hours for the "pain, disease . . . privation [and] premature grave" of many workers.[66] The committee report absolved the companies of blame, but admitted that the quality of air and length of breaks were not adequate.[67]

So unsympathetic were the 1845 House and 1846 Senate reports that their authors became the objects of contempt of the organized women. The 1845 document, produced by a committee chaired by *Lowell Courier* editor William Schouler, gathered a small amount of data from procorporation sources before declaring the health of the mill workers to be "good." The report also declared that in Massachusetts labor was "on equality with capital and indeed controls it," that the fact that British operatives worked less hours than Americans was of no consequence, that a Massachusetts ten-hour law would "close the gate of every mill in the State," and that any abridgement of hours would entail a reduction in wages. The conclusion of the 1845 document hoped for an amelioration of the long-hours system with "the progressive improvement in art and science, . . . a less love for money and more ardent love for social happiness" but added "the remedy is not with us."[68] Even the *Offering* commented on the lack of respect shown the petitioners; the *Voice* branded the report a collection of lies, which systematically misrepresented the testimony of witnesses. When the Senate committee published its findings the next year, its conclusions differed little from those of the House, and Bagley dismissed the document mockingly as a "capital report."[69]

The reaction of the Female Labor Associations to the 1845 committee hearings included an intensified commitment to political action. The 2,139 signatures on the Massachusetts petitions presented in 1845 had not represented an especially impressive total. Even in Lowell, where 1,151 women and men in a town of 25,000 signed, the *Offering* could note that "the petitioners [were] but a very small proportion of the whole number of laborers." By 1846 the petitioners numbered over 10,000 statewide, including the 4,000-5,000 names which followed Bagley's on the huge petition from Lowell. The latter figure, perhaps a third of the city's women mill workers, is particularly noteworthy given the discrimination by management against any who circulated petitions on company premises.[70]

The Lowell labor reformers also initiated a campaign against William Schouler's reelection to the legislature. Branding the Whig committee chairman as "a corporation . . . tool," the Female Labor Reform Association pledged "to keep him in the 'city of spindles,' . . . and not trouble Boston folks with him." The male voters responded to the agitation, and Schouler lost for the only time in his political career. However, in 1846 Lowell's representative also failed to support the operatives' demand energetically, and after that year the ten-hour forces were unable to bring their case before the Massachusetts legislature's committee again until the 1850s.[71]

In New Hampshire and Pennsylvania, mill laborers combined political pressure with a more frequent recourse to strikes and won passage of some ten-hour laws, albeit ineffective ones. Centered in Nashua and Manchester, the New Hampshire movement began at the close of 1845. By the summer of 1846 ten-hour petitions circulated by the Reform Associations received a hearing before the New Hampshire legislature. But the legislators received the bill with little more sympathy than had those of Massachusetts. In New Hampshire Daniel Clark of Manchester filled Schouler's role as the chief spokesman against the operatives. Clark, terming the petition organizers "lazy Devils," feared that, if workers received an hour's break at dinner, they would begin "wandering about the town, and singing and dancing about the mills." Like Schouler, he drew the wrath of the Labor Reform Association, especially in Manchester where the organized women dreamed, "Should we be allowed to vote next year, Daniel will surely be kept at home."[72]

Lacking the vote, the women considered other tactics. Their leader, Mehitabel Eastman, intimated strongly that strike action would be necessary. Eastman, who like Bagley was an eight-year veteran of mill labor and a fine public speaker, asked "What can the operatives do to . . . reduce the hours of labor?" She answered: "What cannot the operatives do?' Our oppressors well know our strength. Ask the capitalist, if you please, what the operatives have done for him. Then he will ask what cannot we do for ourselves."[73]

In 1846 the beginning of Nashua's "lighting up" period of night work coincided with a meeting of the New England Workingmen's Association in that city. The association, now largely female, heard Eastman speak, passed ten-hour and antiblacklist resolutions, and voted to change its name to the Labor Reform League. The week's real drama came on Wednesday evening when about two-thirds of the Nashua Corporation's women workers, along with some from the Jackson Corporation, refused to work after dark. The overseers locked the factory gates and confined the women in the mill yard until the evening bell rang. Nearly a thousand persons surrounded the gate. The crowd included male machinists whose signs read "No lighting up." A constable's attempts to read the riot act went unheeded beneath the chants of the assembled workers. The strike did not carry its demand, but few of the strikers lost their jobs and male mechanics won a concession in the form of shorter hours with reduced pay.[74]

In 1847 the New Hampshire legislature passed the nation's first ten-hour law, but strikes and protests nonetheless followed as its inefficacy became clear. The statute enjoyed both Whig and Democratic support. One section forbade employers from working minors (under fifteen) for more than ten hours and provided a mechanism for enforcement. The other section, which set ten hours as "a day's work" immediately undercut its own force by adding "unless otherwise agreed by the parties" and prescribing no penalties for violation. The *Voice of Industry* headed its article on the act with "ALL HAIL NEW HAMPSHIRE," and managed to show enthusiasm even as it predicted that corporations might "institute their own rules relative to hours of labor and denominate them 'special contracts'" to circumvent the law. Horace Greeley's *Tribune* was franker, finding the law "a very poor affair" and a "milk-and-water enactment."[75]

Even before the passage of the law, employers had submitted contracts to mill workers that required acceptance of hours "as long as the mills run." After the passage of the law, such contracts were pushed by fraud and force. So deceptive were the practices in securing signatures that Harriet Putnam, a Labor Reform Association leader, signed a long-hours contract. In the weeks immediately before the law was to take effect, both sides quickened the pace of activity. The operatives relied upon petitions and on mass meetings of men and women who resolved that "after the 15th of September next we will not work more than the legal number of hours," and offered to take a pay cut to gain shorter hours.[76] Corporation agents accelerated threats of firings and of blacklisting. When September 15 arrived, many mill hands struck by refusing to sign the special contracts. As many as two-thirds of the workers in some mills remained out. In Nashua the strikers held processions with music and banners. The corporations stood firm, however. Ten-hour advocates complained about "men so emphatically black-hearted, as to 'blacklist' an operative for exercising a right conferred by . . . statute," but the law was not decisively on the laborers' side. Eventually, the mills were once again filled with farmers' daughters and with an increasing number of Irish immigrants. A law passed in Maine during the next year proved no more efficacious.[77]

Pennsylvania textile workers also drew flexibly on a variety of tactics to secure shorter hours. During the years between 1845 and 1848, Pennsylvanians launched militant strikes, pressured legislators to pass a ten-hour law, and even attempted to organize a nationwide textile general strike for the ten-hour day. Pittsburgh agitation began defensively, but labor soon took the offensive. At least some of the mill workers there appear to have had relatively short hours in the early 1840s. While Lowell's mills operated until 7:30 P.M. eight months per year, Pittsburgh-area factories quit at 6:45 P.M. until 1843 when an hour per day was added with no increase in pay. A brief strike against the extension failed, but in 1845, as news of the stirrings in Massachusetts reached Pennsylvania, operatives from Allegheny City joined women from Pittsburgh in a June 16 mass meeting demanding the ten-hour system. The 5,000 demonstrators received a communication from five manufacturers who had "no hesitation in saying that they believe it entirely impracticable to adopt that system here whilst in places the twelve-hour system is continued." On September 15 thousands of laborers, mostly women, struck for shorter hours. A strike meeting, described by the *Pittsburgh Ariel* as containing "5000 of the pretty girls and bone and sinew of Allegheny [C]ity and Pittsburg[h]," elected a six-person strike committee, half-female. The meeting also organized strike support on a ward-by-ward basis.[78]

For nearly a month the strike remained solid, buoyed by nocturnal processions and ward meetings. When necessity began to cause a few—as one account has it "perhaps not two in a hundred"—of the hands to return to work, women acted to defend the strike. Their roving pickets shut down four reopened factories in a single day. The circumstances surrounding the closing of the fourth mill were vividly preserved by a *Pittsburgh Journal* reporter, describing what he called the "Battle of Blackstock's Factory":

> On their arrival, they [women pickets] saluted the enemy with three shouts of defiance, and a universal flourish of sticks and bonnets . . . they moved forward in a solid column of attack, on the principal gate of the fortress— that is, the pine gate of the yard. In a moment the gate was forced open. But the defenders were determined . . . , and the assailants were thrown back and the gate again closed. A second time the assault was made with a similar result.

With the women's third push, the last of the reopened factories fell. Male operatives only stood by as reinforcements; the police and mayor watched. However, within another week, impoverished and threatened with the arrest of male leaders, the strikers returned to work under the old system, or perhaps a slightly longer schedule.[79]

Beaten, the Pittsburgh laborers were hardly bowed. When quizzed as to whether the end of the strike spelled the end of the ten-hour demand, one of the labor leaders answered "Certainly not," citing "arrangements for continuing the warfare of meetings, associations, etc." Reacting to the employers' contention that the ten-hour system could not be established in any one area, the workers improved their contacts with "operatives eastward." Lowell's labor literature circulated in Pittsburgh while the *Voice of Industry* gave coverage to Pennsylvania's ten-hour struggles.[80]

The strategy on which organized textile workers from Pittsburgh and some New England mill laborers agreed was that advanced by John Cluer, a British immigrant weaver. Cluer, a temperance agitator, land reformer, and ten-hour advocate, brought tactics learned in the English Chartist and ten-hour movements. By the end of 1845, the year in which he arrived in America, Cluer had become a spokesperson for the New England Workingmen's Association and had developed a tripartite plan for securing a shorter day. The plan's first stage involved convening a meeting of workers and manufacturers to agree upon a program to reduce hours. If such a convention failed, the next step was the renewal of petition drives. Should neither of the first two tactics succeed, the third part of the plan was to take effect with the organization of a July 4 general strike. The Pittsburgh workers proposed July 4, 1846, as the date for such a strike to "declare . . . independence of the oppressive manufacturing power." The Manchester Labor Reform Association concurred in December 1845.[81]

The Cluer plan, like its author, curiously combined strength and weakness. Its biggest asset was the choice of July 4 as the target date. Identification with the revolutionary and republican tradition remained strong among male craftsmen. During the July 4 holidays of 1844, for example, 2,000 met at Rodman's Grove to hear speeches in favor of ten hours as a patriotic demand. One minister won the crowd's approval by observing that shorter hours were "a part of the Declaration of Independence, 'the pursuit of happiness'." A contemporaneous Boston labor meeting adopted a ten-hour resolution alongside a vow to "show the world we are not the degenerate shoots of the Liberty-sowing seed stock of '76."[82]

Male mechanics identified women ten-hour supporters as the latter-day counterparts of the Daughters of Liberty, and factory women labor leaders accepted and extended this republican designation. Bagley claimed a place alongside "the heroines of the Revolution" for the females of the movement. However, the labor women took a more leading role than had their revolutionary sisters. They broadened patriotic rhetoric to make it cover the rights of working women.[83] Octavia, a New Hampshire correspondent, measured her situation against republican values, adding a heavy dose of irony: "What a glorious privilege we enjoy in this boasted republican land, don't we? Here am I . . . bestowing just half of all my hours including Sundays upon a company for less than two cents an hour." The Cluer plan had an appeal among those female workers who took the advice of the *Voice of Industry* and questioned, "why there is so much want, dependence and misery among us, if foresooth, we are *freemen* and *freewomen*?"[84]

But problems vitiated the republican strengths of the Cluer plan. Employers showed little or no interest in attending the meetings prescribed by the plan's first stage. Moreover, many labor leaders, especially in influential Lowell, continued to prefer legislative pressure rather than a general strike. Demonstrating that legislative avenues were exhausted was difficult and disunity on this matter, along with communication problems, ethnic divisions, and the continued sway of mill paternalism, rendered a strong strike unlikely. The plan's association with Cluer also served to discredit it after William Schouler began to publicize embarrassing details concerning the English organizer's past. Early in 1846, amidst a barrage of truths, half-truths, and irrelevancies from Schouler, debate shifted from the merits of the plan to whether its author was a bigamist, liar, ex-convict, reformed alcoholic, and Chartist. Operatives who expected to be free of long hours after 1846's Independence Day were disappointed as the general strike never occurred.[85]

But Pennsylvanians continued to agitate for the ten-hour day. In 1846 Philadelphia supporters formed a "Ten-Hours Association" which called for a national transition to the shorter day. Child labor in smaller mills made long hours an issue in the Philadelphia area. In nearby Delaware County a factory-based ten-hour group, which stressed health, education, and employment, emerged during 1847. Throughout that year, spurred by the examples of ten-hour legislation in New Hampshire and Britain, the Philadelphia and Delaware County organizations joined with others in pushing for a ten-hour law. The Delaware County forces submitted petitions and acted to secure favorable publicity in both Democratic and Whig papers. By January 1848 one of the petitions had 3,500 signatures. Bipartisan support carried the law through the legislature the following April.[86]

Pennsylvania's ten-hour statute differed in particulars from New Hampshire's but contained the same loophole. A clause allowing a "special contract" for longer days circumvented the ten-hour provision and even made it possible for parents to sign agreements requiring children over fourteen to work longer hours. Greeley's *Tribune* referred to the act as a "humbug" but hoped that "Those whom it was intended to put to sleep will come back . . . and, like Oliver Twist, 'want some more'." [87]

Weeks before the July 4 date when the law was to take effect, the proprietors of the largest Pittsburgh-Allegheny City mills met to decide on a strategy to render the ten-hour provision inoperative. Arguing that they could not compete with mills in areas not requiring a ten-hour day, the owners vowed to "employ . . . machinery twelve hours per day as heretofore and to require special contracts." [88] On Independence Day, as the employers insisted on the contracts, 2,000 workers shut seven mills by refusing to sign. For eight weeks the conflict, part strike and part lockout, dragged on. As in 1845, pitched battles resulted when a few workers went back to the mills after about a month. This time the pine gate at Penn Mill had an iron backing and police actively opposed the female-led crowds. Nonetheless, amidst "Amazon vehemence" and a "hurricane of brickbats, mud and stone," the mill stopped production. The laborers kept the mills closed for another four weeks before most of the corporations acquiesced to the ten-hour day with a 10-16 percent reduction in pay. By this time the mill workers had suffered over 100 arrests on antiriot charges. The meager resources of the strikers, supplemented by aid from craftsmen and proceeds from a "Factory Operatives' Ball," had been taxed for two wageless months. Most of the mill hands accepted the wage cuts and rejoiced that "Victory No. 1" —the ten-hour day— had been won.[89]

In the Philadelphia area some factories also switched to the ten-hour system. However, a three-week strike at the largest textile mill there failed to stop wage reductions for those not "choosing" a thirteen-hour day. In Delaware County employers fired recalcitrants and ignored the law for the next five years.[90] Nevertheless, and despite the failure of a new law to close the loopholes in 1849, Pennsylvania's combination of political and direct action had made it the leader among the industrial ten-hour movement's modest successes.[91]

The achievements of the New England movement look so small when compared to the commitment of many of the workers that one must ask how the struggles there could have ended so rapidly and unsuccessfully. In 1846 all Massachusetts mills owned by the Lowell Corporation did react to pressure by adding an average of twenty minutes to the dinner break; New Hampshire's large mills followed suit the next year.[92] These gains were significant to laborers who had but about two leisure hours per day, but they fell far short of the ten-hour goal. By early 1847 the New England movement fell into disarray. The Lowell Association lived up to its motto of "Try Again" by attempting to organize on new lines. Rechristening itself as the Lowell Female Industrial Reform Association and Mutual Aid Society, it stressed "real practical" measures like the payment of sick benefits and managed to keep the *Voice of Industry* afloat until late in 1847. But by March 1848 the newspaper and the New England Labor Reform League were both defunct. When the movement reappeared in the 1850s it was preponderantly male and less strongly based on factory workers.[93]

Each of the two prevalent explanations for the sudden decline of the ten-hour struggle—misleadership and ethnic division—is only partially correct. The argument, put forward by Hannah Josephson and others, that utopians and land reformers diverted the regional labor associations from practical goals and caused working members to lose interest, applies but with strong caveats.[94] Certainly the second convention of the New England Working Men's Association represented a missed opportunity. That Lowell gathering, held in March 1845 during a crest of ten-hour agitation, was "captured" by Fourierists from Brook Farm who elected L. W. Ryckman and George Ripley as association officers. The ten-hour goal, which the Fourierist utopians usually supported but regarded as of minor import, drew little discussion as the utopians resolved to establish "a permanent Industrial Revolutionary Government" to usher in class harmony. The next meeting, in May in Boston, attracted only thirty delegates, few of whom were from mill towns outside Lowell. Among such visionaries as Albert Brisbane, William

Lloyd Garrison, Wendell Phillips, Theodore Parker, William H. Channing, Ryckman, and Ripley, there was little trade union input.[95]

Still it will not do simply to blame the utopians and other reformers. In late 1845 and 1846 (especially at the Nashua Convention), working women had put the regional association back on a ten-hour track. That no such renewed insistence on a ten-hour emphasis developed when the regional group again came under utopian influence in 1848 indicates that the working- class elements in the movement had weakened. Moreover, it should be recalled that some of the platform of the radical reformers, many of whom were themselves artisans, had a strong appeal among the working class. George Henry Evans's land reform forces, in both the National Reform and Industrial Congress movements, coupled demands for free land with calls for ten-hour laws and won support among urban workers, especially in factory towns like Lowell and Lynn. And many, including Bagley and Luther, agreed with Ryckman that the ten-hour system was "an important primary step" that would lead to "great social reform" and to far greater working-class power. Leading cooperativists and land reformers like George Henry Evans, George Lippard, Eliza Heminway, and John Commerford had long records of commitment to a shorter working day. Nor was utopian vision necessarily linked with organizational impotence. Hewitt, for example, combined practical union-building activity with a commitment to utopianism.[96] In order to place the negative impact of the utopians into context, it is necessary to admit their dedication and considerable accomplishments and to identify specific adverse influences of the reform group. Probably the major such influence was the Brook Farm emphasis on avoiding strikes.[97]

The other common explanation for the ebb in the ten-hour movement is the coming of the Irish, an analysis that stresses the role of immigration in displacing New England natives from the mills and thus dividing the labor force and removing veteran ten-hour supporters from the textile industry. In the Hamilton Company mills at Lowell, for example, Thomas Dublin's recent studies show Irish workers moving from 3.7% of the work force in 1836, to 29.4% in 1850, and to 46.9% in 1860. By 1860, 15% of the workers were also immigrants of other nationalities, chiefly Canadian and English. If it intimates that the Irish were incapable of responding to the ten-hour appeal, this argument lacks force. As early as 1846 Irish immigrants actively led shorter-hours strikes. Furthermore, as H. M. Gitelman has shown, the changes in the textile industry just after the Irish arrived were not dramatic and the drop in absolute numbers of New England workers was not precipitous.[98] The influx of immigrants made ten-hour agitation more difficult, but it did so within limits. Irish immigration, for example, brought more family and child labor to the factories. By 1850, 6.6% of the operatives in the Hamilton Company mill were less than 15 years old; another 25.6% were between 15 and 19. Men, who had made up just 14% of the labor force in 1836, accounted for nearly a fourth of the workers just fourteen years later. Irish families pieced together a family wage through the participation of adults and children in mill labor. This made work stoppages a devastating risk for the entire family. The community of women on the shop floor was divided both ethnically and by the presence of a greatly increased number of men and boys. The Irish likewise brought far less political power to the ten-hour struggle because many of their recently arrived males could not vote.[99]

The old explanations, thus refined, also need to be supplemented. The 1848-1851 period was one of serious depression in New England industry. Company repression, long implemented by blacklisting, became more fearsome during these years.[100] The threat of the removal of industry to other areas if ten-hour schedules were enforced also carried special weight at a time when a national shorter-hours law had hardly been suggested and competition from slave states remained a reality. The fight of the 1840s had always been uphill; as the incline got steeper at decade's end—as legislative loopholes, depression, black-lists, and other company threats took their toll—the women's ten-hour movement disintegrated. The period of agitation against long odds still surely requires more explanation than does the ending of the period.

4

Hours, Labor Protest, and Party Politics in the 1850s

Those interpreters of the early labor movement who focus on the conflict between industrial organization and political action as competing strategies lapse into contradiction when analyzing the ten-hour movement of the 1850s. Commons's *History of Labour* provides information on hours legislation in six states during the 1850s before announcing, "Because of the strength of trade unionism in that decade, the movement for shorter hours by legislation disappeared, except in Massachusetts, where factory conditions prevented the growth of unionism."[1] Norman Ware's *The Industrial Worker* generally assumes the same inversely proportional relationship between trade unionism and labor politics but draws opposite conclusions. Ware writes that "working-class agitation [over hours] died out," after 1848. He also characterizes the movement of the 1850s as "of a different sort . . . finding its leaders among the middle class and its field of operations the political." The issue of hours consistently embarrasses Ware's attempts to analyze both the 1840s and 1850s. For the earlier decade he argues that a weak and defensive labor movement generated a strong "industrial" ten-hour campaign. During the latter a dynamic and "aggressive" craft union movement coexisted with a weak, middle-class shorter hours movement. To complicate the situation further, Ware admits that the industrial forces of the 1840s relied mainly on political pressure in seeking to gain the ten-hour day.[2]

This chapter makes no effort to cast trade union and political action as opposites. It argues instead that the ten-hour movement of the 1850s remained strongly based in the working population and that labor's interest in the demand, as evidenced by strikes and protests, was a factor encouraging politicians to embrace shorter-hours legislation in the early 1850. Strike activity among craftsmen seeking fewer hours grew in the 1850s and factory strikes over the issue may have involved even more workers than in the previous decade.[3]

Because of labor interest and the specifics of coalition politics giving rise to the new Republican party, the ten-hour movement briefly threatened to inject an important class issue into the electoral arena. The process by which middle-class political reformers retreated from that issue merits attention, both as it presages a similar reaction during Reconstruction and as it reflects a liberalization on the part of employers, who cut hours between 1853 and 1855 to defuse the issue. In assessing this process of conflict and liberalization, comments on the relationship between free labor ideology and the issue of a shorter working day are also offered.

During the first two years of the 1850s, labor protests and ten-hour contracts proliferated in the East. In 1850 about 750 railroad laborers near Philadelphia struck for the shorter day but failed after a sheriff and posse broke up their "riotous demonstrations." Throughout 1850 and 1851 Philadelphia itself witnessed steady activity by skilled and unskilled workers sometimes demanding an eight-hour day. This agitation, the first to unite various American crafts in a struggle for the eight-hour demand, gave rise to the Philadelphia Assembly of Associated Mechanics and Workingmen but soon abated.[4] In Salem, Massachusetts, seventy-nine of ninety-eight employers of skilled workers engaged in manufacture acceded to the ten-hour demand in 1850. The same city's carpenters, Lynn's mechanics, and some of Baltimore's coopers made similar agreements during the same year.[5] In 1851 most Boston machinists won the ten-hour day. That same year, Lowell's master carpenters and masons successfully held out against a ten-hour strike by their employees.[6]

Three major textile factory strikes over the length of labor erupted in July 1851. The first, on July 7, again came in Allegheny City, where Pennsylvania's ten-hour law still did not universally apply. Although not so large or so violent as the Pittsburgh-Allegheny City strikes of 1848, this work stoppage resembled its predecessors in that women took leading roles and dismantled factory fences. Only Eagle Mills shut down, and the strike was short and unsuccessful.[7]

Also in the wake of 1851's Independence Day came turnouts in both Paterson and Gloucester, New Jersey. These strikes, which constituted a response to the failure of New Jersey's 1851 ten-hour law to provide a shorter day and a living wage, illustrate how difficult it is to separate economic and political action by antebellum labor. The statute, passed after substantial lobbying and electoral activity by working-class organizations, took effect during the first week of July. At Paterson an 8 percent to 17 percent wage cut accompanied the reduction in hours, while at Gloucester factories took advantage of the law's vagaries and adhered to old schedules, even for child laborers. A compromise pay settlement quickly ended the Paterson strike, but Gloucester's protests continued for at least a month. Conflicts in the latter city featured strike support meetings of up to 3,000 in an urban area with just 4,500 inhabitants. As the strike wore on, women leaders called for the eight-hour day in factories. Ultimately, the New Jersey law could not be enforced by strike or litigation.[8]

In New York City shorter hours became a live issue because of the efforts of carpenters to reduce their ten-hour day further and because of the agitation of other tradesmen whose daily hours still far exceeded ten daily. As early as October 1850, house carpenters left their jobs in what may have been America's first eight-hour strike, though a failing one.[9] At about the same time the city's tailors engaged in a strike that unified perhaps 2,500 men and women of Irish, German, Jewish, Scottish, English, and Yankee heritage. Though fought mainly over the price of labor, the tailors' strike reflected grievances against sporadic unemployment and increasingly subdivided, routinized labor in very small shops. Specifically, it castigated the long hours—sometimes in excess of sixteen daily—necessary to survive under the old wages. Leaders held that a higher return on labor would enable tailors to work less and thus further increase wages by removing gluts in the market. As one spokesman complained, tailors work too much:

> Instead of working eight hours in the day—all that any may of the fact of God's earth ought to work—they work sixteen hours a day. This is all a mistaken idea. If every man would throw down his tool at the extirpation [sic] of eight hours . . . there would then be work enough and pay enough for all.

After a proposal for a general strike was rejected, the tailors returned to their jobs having made substantial gains.[10]

The hours of New York City's bakers and retail clerks rivaled those of workers in the needle trades. Bakers, who worked sixteen or more hours daily, seven days a week, unionized in 1850. Their Operative Bakers' Union made the twelve-hour day (mealtime included) its primary demand. The union agitated vigorously for the next two years but enjoyed little success even after Horace Greeley editorialized in favor of ten-hour shifts. In late 1849 workers in retail establishments combined in the Dry Goods Clerks' Mutual Protective Benefit Association. At meetings described as "very large and influential," clerks complained of working days of up to fourteen hours and suggested that if night shopping could not be eliminated, stores ought to close by 8 P.M. The group wished to cooperate with employers to encourage daytime shopping. Clerks eventually elicited the support of the city's mayor and probably achieved some success. Although they distanced themselves from trade union tactics, the retail workers contributed to the new prominence of the shorter-hours issue in New York, especially since their plan for early closing implied that other jobs should end early enough that shopping could be completed by 8 P.M.[11]

Labor protests over hours continued in 1852 and peaked in 1853. Factory cities such as Chicopee, Amesbury, Lawrence, and probably Holyoke, Massachusetts, saw ten-hour agitation during the earlier year. At Chicopee records detailing the 1852 struggles have largely disappeared, but the diary of local merchant George S. Taylor uses the phrases "rebellion among the operatives" and "ten-hour furor" to describe the year's events.[12] In the case of Amesbury documentation does exist for a full recounting of the way in which the industrial idyll praised by John Greenleaf Whittier became embroiled in one of the most bitter strikes in antebellum America. In 1850 Whittier, who often supported the ten-hour movement, wrote that "Amesbury is the pattern manufacturing village in

New England," and that at the Amesbury Flannel Manufacturing Company, "the utmost harmony prevails." Two years later, both factories in the area closed when workers struck against an increase in working time.[13]

A twelve-hour day prevailed at Salisbury Manufacturing Company, a corporation employing about 250 women and 150 men and producing a diverse line of rob roy cloaking, flannels, and shawls. A few hundred feet away, at the Amesbury Flannel Mills, employees had slightly more leisure because the factory's directors had decided to discontinue artificial lighting during winter. Both companies traditionally allowed a fifteen-minute "luncheon recess" in the morning and one in the afternoon. During these breaks workers often hastened to the village's open market.[14] When a new agent at the Salisbury plant took away the breaks, laborers ignored his order. The agent then promised to fire anyone who left the mill during the working day. On June 1, 100 males, mainly spinners, machinists, and block printers, defied the order. Women weavers later joined the men, closing the mill. Parading with a band and a temperance banner, the strikers visited the home of the old agent to cheer and that of the new agent to hiss.[15]

Soon the Amesbury Flannel Mill also outlawed the luncheon breaks. By July employees of both mills were on strike and large crowds picketed the factory gates to berate strikebreakers, some of whom were Irish immigrants. Townspeople, probably including the small businessmen who lost shoppers with the end of the breaks, reacted with what a report called "sympathy and material aid for the strikers."[16] When antistrike overseers held meetings on the Sabbath, community support increased. The local paper opposed the corporations. Strikebreakers could find no rooms to rent, and the village fire company did not so much as fight a blaze that razed a building at Salisbury Mills on the day after Independence Day. But neither the workers nor the community swayed management. After six months most of the workers drifted into new jobs in other communities. Whittier placed his name at the head of Amesbury's ten-hour petition in 1853.[17]

Late in 1852 strikes briefly thrust forward the political issue of hours when the federal government attempted to begin work at the Charlestown, Massachusetts, and the Washington, D.C., navy yards an hour earlier than usual. In Charlestown, the secretary of the navy's directive caused a strike of 300 "mechanics and laborers" in the shipyard. Within two days the government relented. The Washington, D.C., work stoppage carried its demand more quickly. The diary of Michael Shiner, a worker in the yards, best records the events there:

> On the 1st of December 1852 on Wensday an order was sent down from the . . . Secretary of the Navy . . . to go to work at sun rise and on the morning of 15 the Bell rang and all the men were at the gat and out of five hundred men thare were no more than . . . twenty men that cared out that order and befor twelve o'Clock that same day an order cam down countermaning that order and all the Mechanics and laborers went to work at ther old usual hours.[18]

Federal investigators soon complained that in some navy yards the daily hours of labor in winter had fallen to seven.[19]

By 1853 the ten-hour forces in manufacturing had recovered somewhat from the 1848 depression, and among skilled tradesmen the demand was as much agitated as it had been since 1835. About 100 men and boys at Lowell's Mechanic Planing Mill won the ten-hour day after a week's strike, and a third of the city's machine shop employees also went out with at least partial success. Protest throughout Massachusetts was so rife that an 1867 legislative document recalled the "labor crisis of 1853." Trade agreements in Worchester made the ten-hour day "all but universal" there. In Boston several announcements regarding employer adoption of the shorter schedule appeared in the city's press in April, alongside news of a successful ten-hour strike by 500 cordage makers. Shipwrights in private yards in the area signed contracts reducing hours to just over eight daily on repair work and some clerks worked nearly as short a day.[20]

Nationally, wages constituted the most common issue underlying union organization in 1853, but hours struggles were also widespread and were a special bane to employers. *Hunt's Merchants' Magazine* deprecated "organizations, combinations and 'strikes'," which it saw as infecting "almost every branch of industry" in 1853. As the editors spelled out their concerns in detail, they showed an understanding of the way in which conflicts over hours raised particularly broad questions of control: "Were [trade unionism's] advocates to confine its operation simply to demands for increased wages, the system would be more tolerable . . . If workmen may dictate the hour and mode of service . . . they may also regulate other items of the business with which their labor is connected."[21]

The most dramatic of the 1853 actions centered in Cincinnati, the nation's third largest producer of manufactured goods, although many other cities also experienced agitation. In Cincinnati seventeen crafts organized to seek shorter hours, often in conjunction with higher pay. In some cases employers simply acceded, but several successful strikes are also recorded, including one by day laborers against their twelve-hour shifts. In San Francisco organizations of riggers, longshoremen, shipwrights, dray men, teamsters, carpenters, stonemasons, and steamboat firemen participated in an 1853 strike over wages and hours. Longshoremen in that labor-short city won a nine-hour day after striking.[22] Pennsylvanians working in textile factories at Media and Rockdale signed agreements providing the ten-hour day and celebrated by sending two representatives to New England to encourage unionism and shorter hours. Central New York iron molders made ten-hour agreements in 1853 and, during the first week of 1854, sawmill workers in Petersburg, Virginia, struck against an increase in hours and won after threatening to ride their employer out of town on a rail.[23]

Such trade union activity in support of shorter hour demands during the first four years of the 1850s has been little noticed by historians, but it forms a backdrop against which the subsequent political movements for the ten-hour day must be studied. During the remainder of the period before the Civil War, labor struggles over hours continued, even during the years following the 1857 depression. However, as a policy of liberalization decreased working hours in 1852, 1853, and 1854, the number of industrial conflicts ebbed.

Two points stand out in relation to trade union struggles over hours from 1854 through 1861. The first is that all three textile strikes involving time during these years were defensive ones. In 1854 conflict at an unidentified Massachusetts mill arose after employers continued "lighting up" after March 20, the customary closing date. In both the Manchester, New Hampshire, general strike of 1855 and the Chicopee strike of 1858, management attempts to add to the recently adopted eleven-hour day precipitated the work stoppages. Manchester's victorious strike involved perhaps 5,000 workers. Chicopee's turnout influenced but one mill and lost. Neither successfully raised the ten-hour issue, although some Manchester strikers signed ten-hour pledges.[24]

A second observation concerns the geographical spread of the movement in the years after 1854. In 1854 demands for an eight-hour day (five hours for children) found support in Richmond, Virginia. In 1857 ship carpenters and caulkers in New Orleans organized to win the nine-hour day, under the leadership of Richard Trevellick, a Cornish veteran of successful eight-hour struggles in Australia and New Zealand. And in 1860 workers on the Memphis and Charleston Railroad gained the ten-hour day after a series of protests.[25] Finally at the close of the decade, such familiar groups as Boston and Philadelphia machinists engaged in ten-hour struggles, but some Southern iron molders, San Franciscan laborers, and even Midwestern farm hands had also embraced the demand.[26]

The nation by no means reverberated with ten-hour appeals, but the variety of labor groups participating in the movement during the 1850s—clerks, artisans, factory workers, day laborers, and farm workers, employees from North, South, and West—frames any discussion of political conflict over hours by reminding us that the demand need not have been confined to the nation's few heavily industrialized areas. The kind of subtle changes in production and supervision which first generated the push for the ten-hour day continued to produce a range of recruits. The ten-hour demand had a chance to develop into a vital political issue in the 1850s. The political context of the campaigns for ten-hour legislation in the early 1850s included the breakdown of the second American party system and the testing of new alignments and coalitions. Both the Democrats and Whigs split and weakened largely in response to sectional issues. From 1848 until 1854 forces from both parties coalesced in each election around platforms based mainly on free soil, an opposition to the spread of slavery into the territories. By 1854 antislavery and modernizing elements from both the old parties had forged the Republican party and had begun to elaborate for it an ideology based on free labor and free soil—on opportunity for social and geographic mobility within a nation committed to capitalist expansion without the formation of a large permanent proletariat.[27]

The decline of party unity and the maturation of Republican sentiment generated opportunities for the political ten-hour movement. At the state level, divisions in the parties made pressure groups (which could deliver a bloc of votes around the issue of hours) a greater factor in the outcome of elections. Also, the various Free Soil and Republican groupings brought together many politicians who had been most receptive to the ten-hour idea within the old parties. For example, Van Buren, the single politician most identified with shorter hours because of his presidential directive on the subject, led a celebrated split of New York Democrats into the Free Soil ranks in 1848. In Massachusetts Marcus Morton, associated with the shorter hours movement since 1840, joined a Free Soil schism from the Democracy.[28]

Many Free Soil and Republican ex-Whigs were among the few members of the Whig party who had supported ten-hour reform. Most prominent was Horace Greeley, who consistently backed the reform after the mid-1840s, arguing that it but extended the concept of the protective tariff to shield workers as well. The support given by the Southern antislavery ex-Whig Cassius M. Clay for ten-hours legislation is even more striking.[29] Among the many other prominent politicians who combined support for ten hours with participation in a Free Soil party were Charles Skelton, Charles Sumner, Benjamin Butler, Nathaniel Banks, George Boutwell, William S. Robinson, Henry Wilson, and Alvan Bovay. Democrats, who had traditionally given the ten-hour measure the small support it enjoyed in politics, were still backers of the demand in some states. But Free Soil and Coalition politicians came to push ten hours more vigorously, especially in Massachusetts.[30]

In this atmosphere the spread of the political shorter-hours movement was dramatic. By 1855 legislative bodies in at least fourteen states considered the subject. New Jersey (1851), Rhode Island (1853), California (1853), and Connecticut (1855) emulated New Hampshire, Pennsylvania, and Maine by passing ineffectual ten-hour laws in the early 1850s. Georgia legally reaffirmed that the working day for whites under twenty-one years old should be "from sunrise to sunset, the usual and customary time for meals being allowed" in 1853.[31] New York rejected a ten-hour law the same year but provided a ten-hour day for public employees. In Massachusetts, where advocates of legislation to reduce hours continued to insist on a law with teeth, debate and committee hearings on the question became almost annual.[32]

This proliferation of legislative activity over the length of the working day suggests, as did the many strikes of the early 1850s, the possibility that the issue might have become significant one in national party politics. However, the middle class ideology of the political reformers meant that the debate over hours would be shorn of its more radical implications, especially those regarding control over the labor process and the realization of value for one's work. Moreover, with the liberalization of hours between 1852 and 1855, with the decline of labor action over hours, and with the heating up of North-South tensions, the reform forces lost interest in ten-hour legislation after 1855.

By no means did all of the Free Soil and proto-Republican ideologues support shorter hours, but, for the first time, the party politicians who did eclipsed radical artisans and operatives as the most prominent public spokespersons for the ten-hour idea. In their attempts to graft the struggle for legislative limits on hours onto the shared system of middle-class political precepts (which Eric Foner has termed "free labor ideology"), the reform politicians produced a limited, contradictory case for cutting the length of the working day. Republican ideology, with its emphasis on the sanctity of the wage bargain and on the absence of government intervention in that arena, clashed with the proposal for the state to regulate hours at a basic level. Specifically, the free laborites ignored two sides of the ten-hour demand. On the one hand, labor's persistent demands regarding hours suggested that many workers did not totally share a faith in social mobility. If most believed, with Republican senator Zachariah Chandler, that "A young man goes out to service—to labor if you please to call it so—for compensation . . . and soon he becomes himself an employer of labor," interest in shorter hours would have been small among those who sought only to accumulate capital and then to employ laborers efficiently.[33] Nor did the record of agitation for shorter hours support the analysis, central to free labor ideology, that all "producers," including small businessmen, farmers, and master craftsmen, belonged to a "laboring class." While this conception of class did run through both the labor movement and the larger society, ten-hour struggles undercut it by driving a wedge between employing masters and journeymen.[34]

Most of the politicians supporting hours laws confined their reforms to workplaces run by corporations and eschewed reference to class in their arguments. Unlike earlier labor spokespersons, the politicians of the 1850s saw capital and labor as in harmony. While few followed Greeley in viewing the ten-hour law as the "protective tariff" for workingmen, many argued that such legislation would redress the imbalance caused by laws allowing corporations to be chartered. This stance, characteristically Jacksonian, recurred often and sometimes sounded a bitter note against corporations not "restrained . . . by human sympathy."[35] But more revealing were the passages which repeatedly promised that shorter hours themselves "will harmonize with the true interest of the manufacturing capitalist and employer" by increasing productivity. This theme became nearly an obsession in the legislative hearings of the 1850s as example was piled upon example to show that the ten-hour standard was profitable.[36]

While the struggles in several states did open the way for professional politicians to emerge as spokesmen for the ten-hour movement, the situation was fluid. As the major parties disintegrated and factions tested new alliances, extra-party organizations, sometimes strongly based in the working class, organized political ten-hour campaigns. The weak agitation in Wisconsin stemmed from the efforts of the National Reformers, a small land reform group led by the long-time radical labor activist George Henry Evans. In New York the Industrial Congress, another Evans-influenced group with a base among craftsmen, helped keep the ten-hour demand before the legislature.[37] Far more significant were the lobbying activities of the Workingmen's Association of Trenton, New Jersey, and of the Ten-Hours State Convention in Massachusetts, which together serve as a barometer of the potential of hours to shape the new party system.

Since 1847 a Trenton organization had fought for laws to protect labor in New Jersey. Heading the list were a ten-hour law for adults, an eight-hour statute for children, and a related proposal to fund public education. After 1848, when the "Friends of the Ten-Hour System" formed a broader group known as the Workingmen's Association of Trenton, mass meetings which called for shorter-hours laws occurred regularly in that city. When the 1850 state legislature failed to act on any of its favored planks, the Workingmen's Association called for formation of workingmen's clubs throughout the state. A state convention, independent of the major parties, loomed and many debated the wisdom of a labor slate in the 1851 elections.[38]

Both the Democrats and the Whigs courted the New Jersey labor vote in 1851. The ten-hour law found expression in the Democratic platform and Charles Skelton, a shoemaker and leader of the Workingmen's Association, won the party's nomination for Congress from the Trenton area. The Whigs supported free public education and a plank "regulating the hours of labor in manufactories and protecting children working therein." The Workingmen's Association also quizzed individual candidates who overwhelmingly assented to each proposed reform. A Democratic victory sent Skelton to Congress and resulted in the enactment of much of the Workingmen's Association program by the New Jersey legislature. While the state's ten-hour law, passed in 1851, lacked provisions for enforcement, it was nonetheless one of the period's stronger statutes. Because it contained no provision for "special contracts," strikes to make the law apply, such as that at Gloucester, could therefore rally public support by arguing that employers were in violation of the law.[39]

Massachusetts, according to the historian Henry Farnam, remained "the storm center of the ten-hour movement." Party lines there shifted in response to proposals for shorter hours, as well as to debates over slavery and land policy. From 1850 until 1856 no session of the state legislature passed without debate on ten-hour legislation, and in 1850, 1852, 1853, and 1855, House committees made extensive reports on the question.[40] From 1850 until 1853 the proposed law bound Free Soilers and reform Democrats together in a Coalition party which successfully challenged Whig hegemony in the factory towns of eastern Massachusetts. In 1853 this coalition, backed by over 10,000 petition signatures, pushed a strong ten-hour bill through the House and narrowly missed winning the Senate vote. The Ten-Hour State Convention, an extra-party pressure group that included some factory women, marshaled support for the legislation with large local and statewide meetings. Only after a liberalization that brought an eleven-hour day to the largest textile mills did the ten-hour storm abate and ethnic issues come to dominate the state's urban politics.[41]

Coalition politics between Democrats and Free Soilers began in 1850 when the former party endorsed the platform of the latter at the state level. Early the next year the two parties combined with Conscience Whigs in the legislature to elect a Democratic governor, a Free Soil president of the Senate and a Democrat-*cum*-Free Soil speaker of the House. While the Free Soil revulsion against the Whigs' complicity in the proslavery Compromise of 1850 solidified cooperation between the parties, other issues were important. Antislavery Democrats such as Marcus Morton, proslavery Democrats such as Ben Butler, and Free Soilers such as William S. Robinson combined in 1851 to push through reforms, including a mechanics' lien law, a general incorporation law, a homestead law, and a measure guaranteeing the secret ballot in national elections.[42] In the industrial centers the Coalition ticket was increasingly identified as the "Ten-Hour Ticket." Elections, according to the historian Charles E. Persons, "in all the mill towns regularly turned on this issue."[43]

The Coalitionists' support of shorter hours has long seemed opportunistic to scholars. The charge, made by a mill agent, that ten-hour reformers hoped "to advance the interest of some particular political aspirant" finds an echo in historical accounts which concentrate their fire on Lowell representative Benjamin Butler's demogoguery without examining the shared assumptions of ten-hour reformers. The standard sympathetic account, meanwhile, contrasts Butler's self-seeking behavior with the humanitarian devotion to the cause shown by *Lowell American* editor Robinson and by James Stone of Charlestown.[44] In fact, differences of style aside, Butler, Robinson, and Stone shared the middle-class reformer's approach to the issue of hours—an approach that helped both to raise and to shelve ten-hour legislation. All three shared a long standing commitment to shorter-hour laws. If Butler's early activities in this regard included the discouraging of strikes in favor of exclusively political action, they differed little from Stone's, who abstained from supporting the "socialistic" New England Workingmen's Association. Indeed, Butler's commitment to shorter hours spanned more than a quarter century and quite matched Robinson's. The Coalitionists did stress ten-hour laws selectively, mainly in factory towns, but they are best described not as opportunists, but as reform politicians generally adhering to free-labor ideology.[45]

The minority reports of 1850, 1852, and 1853 in the House and the majority reports in the 1855 House and 1856 Senate best represent the thinking of Coalitionist labor reformers.[46] Their logic superficially resembles that of many of the arguments made by labor groups during the 1830s and 1840s. The 1850 report, for example, copiously quotes Dr. Josiah Curtis's "Public Hygiene of Massachusetts," a moderate 1849 presentation to the American Medical Association documenting the ill effects of long hours. Reports also frequently adverted to child labor and to the effect of long hours on education.[47] Massachusetts's legislative committees, like the activists of the 1830s and 1840s, also frequently referred to the example of Britain and even "the kingdom of Prussia, the Swiss Confederation and several of the German states" in reducing hours.[48] Proposals for a gradual transition to the ten-hour day drew directly on the British example.[49]

Missing from the reports of the reformers is any hint of the militant republicanism, class solidarity, or bursting hope for the future which characterized earlier artisan and factory appeals. Even the most passionate passages from Curtis's medical study, for instance, reflect the belief of the physician (and the Coalitionists) that the corporations were not culpable for conditions in the mills. Moreover, the internationalism of the politicians identified not with the struggles of European labor movements but with middle-class and aristocratic political reformers of other lands as Charles Persons's reference to Stone as "the Lord Ashley of the Massachusetts movement" aptly shows.[50]

With regard to child labor, to ten-hour laws, and to education, the middle-class reformers differed from earlier labor radicals. The earlier agitators often promised that shorter hours and an end to child labor would contribute to the maturation of an articulate, educated, and politically aware working population. For the pragmatic politicians of the 1850s, shorter hours represented not a first step toward social change but a holding action. They spoke as benefactors of a weak, degraded population of workers. Sympathetic lawmakers urged that if the largely Irish immigrants filling jobs in the mills were ever to escape their "unenlightened condition," statutes must give the immigrants some leisure. Alternating between decrying immigration and hoping to uplift the newcomers through shorter hours, the reform politicians, some of whom joined nativist groups, did not look forward to the day when Irish immigrants would exercise power.[51]

An index of the reformers' adherence to class harmony is the controversy that surrounded Butler when he strayed from that ideal, albeit in style more than in substance. A Jacksonian Democrat in Whiggish Lowell, Butler entered politics in the mid-1840s and cultivated an intense love-hate relationship with the corporations. Combining law and politics, he represented mill women in a series of small suits against the mills. Through skill and perhaps because of his role in discouraging ten-hour strikes, Butler became a corporate counsel. He retained a commitment to the ten-hour day, although he shared the opinion of his official biographer and most reformers that ten-hour strikes "entailed suffering upon the operatives a thousand times greater than the evils for which they sought redress." At a factory in which he acquired a large interest, Butler instituted the ten-hour system (at very low wages) and reported great increases in productivity. Despite his Jacksonian rhetoric and his ties with proslavery Democrats, Butler shared much of the emphasis on class harmony with others who preached free labor and ten hours.[52]

Rhetoric, though, was enough to brand Butler as a figure whom even his fellow Coalitionist, William S. Robinson, called "the stump orator who swayed the tumultuous mob . . . against the agents of the mills."[53] The events surrounding Lowell's November 1851 elections secured him such a title. On November 10 a Coalition slate won a narrow victory in the race for several state legislature seats from Lowell, but the following day Whig city officials used a small irregularity in voting in one ward as pretext for calling new elections. Butler, who was not on the original Coalition ticket, took the place of one of its candidates during the interim. At his insistence the Coalition made the ten-hour demand its foremost, indeed almost exclusive, issue in the second election. Agents, especially Linus Child of the Boott Corporation, reacted against the "ten-hour ticket." In addition, workers at the Hamilton Corporation complained that signs appeared at their workplaces that read:

NOTICE
Whoever, employed by this corporation,
votes the Ben Butler ten-hour ticket
on Monday next, will be discharged.[54]

With support from some of his frightened Coalitionist running mates eroding, Butler responded to the threatened firings with a verbal barrage uncharacteristic of the political advocates of a shorter day. Addressing an overflow crowd at the city hall, he pulled few punches in his speech. After reminding his audience that their "fathers fought the battles of the Revolution" to establish freedom, Butler thundered that:

> this question must be settled here and now . . . . They have their mills and machinery, their bricks and mortar . . . . You have your right arms and your torches, and by them we will blot out this accursed outrage . . . if one man is driven from his employment I will commence by applying the torch to my own house.

Butler still took care to leave the corporations a way to respond, by hinting that the notices were not authorized by top management. The notices disappeared the next day, and the election went off without incident, with all the Coalitionists but Butler victorious. Thus ended a rare burst of militant talk from one leading Coalitionist.[55]

The point of a critical examination of shorter-hours arguments of the 1850s is not to suggest, as Ware does, that political struggles replaced economic ones or that reformers diluted working-class demands beyond recognition. In fact, strike actions continued apace in the early 1850s, and reformers, though usually of much more romantic and thoroughgoing bent than the pragmatists of the 1850s, had long participated in the ten-hour movement. Of course, labor leaders of earlier years had also been influenced by free-labor ideology and the idea that all "producers" were in a single, harmonious class. What was new in the decade before the Civil War was that professional politicians supported the movement in an ongoing way and for a time emerged as its most prominent ideologues. Their arguments differed perceptibly not only from those of the earlier artisan and operative spokespersons, but also from labor leaders of the 1850s. In the Massachusetts Ten-Hours State Convention, reform politicians and labor representatives mixed, producing a hybrid set of ideas and a potent organization.

The Ten-Hours State Conventions emerged from meetings of the New England Industrial League, a small organization that supported a broad range of social reforms. The league's October 1851 meeting proposed a convention to concentrate on the single issue of hours. In January 1852 the first such convention met in Boston; seven months later a second convention drew 196 delegates from sixteen cities. Throughout 1852 and 1853 the group held large ten-hour meetings in major industrial areas. One such Lowell gathering had an audience of 1,700 persons, 200 of them female. Local branches of the convention movement distributed a standardized ten-hour petition, securing 3,500 signatures in 1852 and nearly 10,000 in 1853. Such efforts helped to force both parties' candidates for governor and lieutenant governor, and the entire Coalition ticket, to pledge support to shorter-hours legislation in 1852. These efforts also set the stage for the near passage of the law in 1853.[56] Reform politicians, mostly Coalitionists, composed the leadership of the conventions, but the organization steered a nonpartisan course and recruited working-class members. Robinson and Butler were both active in the conventions, and Stone served as the head of the State Central Committee to the convention movement.[57] The size of the movement's following, the concentration of its strength in industrial areas, and the appeals to "workingmen" help place the social base of the conventions among skilled workers. While the leadership and rank and file were not antagonistic, the agitational material distributed by the organization reflected the participation of working people and differed from the legislative reports of politicians supporting a reduction in the working day. The second convention of 1852, for example, printed a pamphlet on reasons for cutting hours. In it were passages, probably reflecting the participation of shipwrights working eight-hour days, warning that ten-hour laws must not be construed as a sanction for extending the hours of those working shorter days. The religious language common in the 1830s and 1840s also reappeared: "If it be God's will to abridge man's daily labor, we ought cheerfully submit and say—'Thy will be done'."[58]

More importantly, the pamphlet broke with the doctrine of class harmony by acknowledging that shorter hours favored employees more than employers. Under the heading "DIMINUTION OF HOURS INCREASES WAGES," the pamphlet argued that in jobs requiring only manual labor, workers would achieve the same production on a ten-hour shift as on a longer one, but in employments using machinery the reform would "be equivalent to diminishing the supply of labor" and would thus drive up wages. More jobs would also open, since "more mills and more machines" would be necessary to maintain production. "These new demands for things produced by labor," the pamphlet promised, "will . . . enhance wages still more." This new position, which one historian terms the "trade union" argument for shorter hours, evidences perception of ongoing class conflict by at least some of the convention movement's members.[59]

If other states did not share with Massachusetts the hope that an effective ten-hour law might pass in 1853, the issue was, as discussed above, popular elsewhere. The failure of any national party to embrace shorter hours and the decline of the movements in the states after 1855 therefore deserve explanation. The argument, advanced by several scholars, that antislavery and other sectional issues pushed the labor question into the wings is not a full explanation. After all, the ten-hour movement had thrived through the years of sectional division after the Compromise of 1850. However, sectional politics do help to illuminate the failure of the national Democracy to call for a federal shorter hours law covering government workers, although some in the ranks of Democracy would call for such a law after the Civil War. The Democratic emphasis on states' rights and sectional diversity would have jarred against any such attempt to imply national guidelines regarding hours.[60] Among those forces coalescing into the Republican party, the opposition of capitalist farmers—an important element in the new party's ranks—to a law that might raise prices of nonfarm goods and encourage restiveness among farm laborers helped to guarantee inaction at the national level.

Loyalty to free-labor strictures against government interference, especially among ex-Whigs, also contributed to Republican willingness to abandon the issue in the late 1850s. Again, the slavery question played a role by encouraging Republicans to mount a defense of free labor in the North and not to dwell on long hours.[61] However, a strategic liberalization of working hours by employers between 1852 and 1855 surely was as crucial in assuring that the question would be dropped in state politics and would generate no labor wing in the Republican party.

George McNeill later wrote, "In 1853 eleven hours was adopted in many parts of the country as the work day, apparently for the purpose of heading off the ten-hour movement."[62] Although his tone is too suggestive of conspiracy and his dating too precise, McNeill's statement holds in its outlines. According to computations made from figures in the Tenth Census, the average working day for reporting cotton factories fell from eleven hours and 53 minutes to eleven hours and 27 minutes between 1850 and 1855. Most of the changes came between 1852 and 1855, the years in which reforms in textile mills in Lowell, Lawrence, Chicopee, Manchester, Salem, Newburyport, Rockdale, Fall River, and other towns in New Hampshire, Connecticut, Pennsylvania, Massachusetts, Maine, Delaware, Rhode Island, and Maryland were all made.[63]

The large cotton corporations set the pattern for the Northeastern industry, and they, at least, acted in a consciously political manner. In September 1852, during the campaigns for state elections, factory machine shops in five major Massachusetts industrial towns lowered the number of daily working hours to eleven. Historian Constance McLaughlin Green observes that "voters were tossed a sop" with the reform. In those parts of the mills using mainly women, who could not vote, no lessening of hours generally took place. When hours reduction became more popular in 1853, the larger corporations again granted a pre-election concession during the next year. This time, with Lowell and Lawrence mills setting the pace, they set slightly over eleven hours as the daily schedule for all operatives and granted an early Saturday closing. As other factories fell into line, and as the ten-hour day became more common among skilled male workers, the basis for ten-hour agitation eroded.[64] Legislation on the subject was no longer as necessary to set a symbolic standard governing the hours of employed craftsmen; and to the mass of women laboring in the mills of the corporations affected by the law, the promised amelioration now was smaller than what had already been won.

5

The Civil War and the Birth
of the Eight-Hour Movement

In the mid-1860s, Ira Steward, a Boston machinist and father of the eight-hour movement, directed a letter to the Massachusetts Commission on the Hours of Labor. Steward's prose captured the extent to which some eight-hour advocates felt they had embarked on an earthshaking historical enterprise. Drawing, in a manner typical of the eight-hour movement, upon analogies from the Civil War experience, Steward posited a gulf between the old shorter-hours movement and the new:

> reasons which were given in the twelve or fourteen hour system for reducing to ten are not reasons which have much weight for the proposed eight-hour reduction. There is as much difference between the class of arguments for the two systems, ten and eight hours, as between the reasoning which is especially adapted to the movement for giving the slave his freedom, and the later one, of giving the freeman a ballot.[1]

This chapter places the transition to an eight-hour demand in the context of the Civil War, arguing that comparisons like Steward's reflect a complex relationship between the war, racial issues, and battles over hours. It explores the infusion of republicanism and class feeling, which gave the movement of the 1860s a different tenor from that of the 1850s, leading Steward to think a new day had dawned.

While instances of eight-hour agitation occurred much earlier, the emergence of a movement for the eight-hour day dates from the Civil War period. Before 1830 William Heighton had envisioned the possibility of an eight-hour day and, just a few years later, Boston's Charles Douglas proposed an eight-hour law. After 1836 most federal offices operated on eight-hour shifts during the winter. In 1842 Charlestown, Massachusetts, shipwrights became the first American artisans to win an eight-hour day. An eight-hour organization with members from several crafts met in Philadelphia in 1850 and 1851, and during the former year New York City carpenters engaged in the nation's first recorded eight-hour strike. By 1861 the national unions of iron molders, machinists, and blacksmiths had considered the demand.[2] Nonetheless, the ten-hour demand remained by far the most common rallying cry of shorter-hours advocates prior to the Civil War.

By 1866 eight-hour organizations thrived across the nation. A vigorous labor press, hundreds of local organizations, and the National Labor Union supported the demand and caused legislatures that had not even considered ten-hour bills a decade before to debate eight hours. Marx's observation from 1867, if florid, also fit the facts closely: "Out of the death of slavery a new life at once arose. The first fruit of the Civil War was the eight hours' agitation, that ran with the seven-leagued boots of the locomotive from the Atlantic to the Pacific, from New England to California."[3]

Before expanding on the way that the war against Southern slaveholders contributed to the fortunes and ideas of the eight-hour forces, two caveats are in order. One is that the rise of the eight-hour movement did not wholly end ten-hour agitation. Some labor reformers continued to regard the older demand as more practical. In Massachusetts, for example, James Stone, speaker of the House in the state legislature, and others organized Short Time Committees, taking the name from British reform groups. Although the Short Time Committees stood apart from the trade unions and criticized the Eight-Hour Leagues as counterproductive, their activities received attention in the labor press. As eight-hour prospects dimmed, the Short Time Committees even enjoyed renewed appeal, especially among women textile workers. Moreover, in many cases eight-hour activists were willing to allow for a ten-hour day on farms and in factories, at least for a transitional period.[4]

The second caveat is that the war was not the only reason for the emergence of an eight-hour movement. Such a demand would have matured as skilled workers, most of whom had the ten-hour day or worked on piece rates, came into conflict with an increasingly mechanized industrial capitalist order. While building tradesmen remained very active in the eight-hour movement, leadership passed mainly to molders and machinists.[5] These trades had, since before the 1850s, undergone substantial changes. Large increases in the capitalization of firms, increasing division of labor, and technological advances helped to transform the two industries. A few of these changes, such as the introduction of the universal milling machine in machine shops during the 1860s, grew out of wartime invention, but most simply accompanied the rise of factory production.[6] Molders and machinists were skilled workers who often exercised a good deal of independent judgment on the job, but they were not displaced artisans whose position as journeymen in a small workshop had only just eroded.[7] As early as 1850 the typical Philadelphia machine-shop worker labored in a shop that had 50 or more employees. Stove-molding factories, such as those in the highly unionized Troy area, were similarly large by the late 1850s. Moreover, many machinists worked for textile corporations or for the locomotive-producing companies.[8] By 1869 over half the nation's industry had made the transition to using steam rather than water, horse, or human power. The woodworkers, another group active in the early eight-hour movement, experienced expansion in capitalization, mechanization and size of companies during the 1850s and 1860s. Steam came into wide use in the shipyards, a continuing arena for conflict over the working day.[9]

Eight-hour leaders, maturing in this setting, often gloried, as Steward and Thomas Phillips did, in the productive potential of machinery. They conceived of leisure as a separate category from work and wanted more of it.[10] They also harbored grievances concerning the increasing alienation of labor, the threat of technological unemployment, and the direction in which profits from rising production flowed.[11] An eight-hour movement would have eventually developed out of these concerns. It crystallized rapidly and in a special shape in the setting of Civil War America.

The war, which began inauspiciously for labor organizations, generated conditions and attitudes that encouraged a dramatic renaissance of trade unionism and molded the eight-hour movement. The unions, weak in the wake of the 1857 depression, suffered through another economic downturn and heavy labor enlistments in the months after Fort Sumter. Locals collapsed in many areas, and the three existing national unions failed to meet in 1861 and 1862. One Philadelphia local adjourned after enlisting *en masse* and resolved, "this Union stands adjourned until the Union is safe or we are whipped."[12]

During the continued fighting trade unionism rebounded. The discriminatory 1863 draft laws combined with inflation and the use of troops against strikers to convince many tradesmen that organization was required to equalize patriotic sacrifice. The shortage of available labor also improved the prospects of trade unions.[13] According to notices in *Fincher's Trades' Review*, the period's leading labor paper, union strength grew from seventy-nine locals in twenty crafts in December 1863, to 270 locals in fifty-three crafts one year later. By 1864 unions claimed 200,000 members. Eight-hour agitation was strongly based in these unions, especially in large cities.[14]

The eight-hour demand first became prominent in this setting of labor resurgence during wartime. Partaking of the martial and patriotic spirit of the times, the eight-hour advocates raised arguments that differed in style and content from those of ten-hour groups of the previous decade. They claimed the right to an eight-hour day as the just reward for the performance of working people in battle and in war production. *Fincher's Trades' Review*, whose decision to append "Eight Hours: A Legal Day's Work for Freeman" to its masthead signaled a breakthrough for the new shorter-hours movement, justified the eight-hour system as the "Nation's gift to workingmen in the army." As early as 1863 it proposed a scenario for how agitation for a law on the subject of hours should proceed: "First, by agitation and action among ourselves; then secure the cooperation of the army. Let the mechanics and laborers of our armies repeat the cry until it echoes from Texas to Maryland."[15]

The labor press could also allude to the prospect that 500,000 men would enter the labor market anew upon demobilization and could argue that the eight-hour system was not just a debt owed to soldiers but a necessary brake on postwar unemployment. Eight-hour organizations in several locales built coalitions of veterans and laborers on this basis. Eight-hour rallies seldom failed to include speeches by military heroes or to feature references to workingmen as the saviors of a beleaguered republic. This republicanism, reminiscent of the 1830s, led to the renewal of the custom of holding shorter working day rallies on the Fourth of July, beginning in 1864 and 1865.[16]

Wartime advocates of the eight-hour day usually affirmed a willingness to wait until after the armistice for the system to take effect. Loyalty to the war effort tempered resistance to long hours, but there were limits on this acquiescence to the demands of war production. In one trade the federal government itself attempted to extend hours. Under a law passed in July 1862, the commandants of the federal navy yards could require as much labor as was consistent with local practice in private yards. Using this statute, the Navy Department tried to start work an hour earlier in the Boston Navy Yard in December 1862. After a two-day strike, work resumed under the old schedule. Four months later, a similar extension of hours was given up in the Washington Navy Yard after the threat of a strike. Strikes over hours were rare in private industry. New York City longshoremen did walk out seeking a nine-hour day in 1864.[17] And in San Francisco a series of shorter-hours strikes occurred among bakers, bricklayers, ship joiners, laborers constructing street railway lines, and grooms in livery stables in 1863 and 1864. However, eight-hour advocates seem to have largely followed Fincher's advice "not . . . to take advantage of the demand for labor during the hostilities" and to have foregone shorter hours strikes.[18]

For the great majority of Northern workers, the Civil War was a fight to preserve the Union; for many it was also a battle against slavery. The leaders of the emerging eight-hour movement were often committed to freedom for the slaves and sometimes merged antislavery and prolabor arguments into a general indictment of class oppression. Ira Steward, who was said to have dedicated himself to the movement for a shorter working day in 1851 at age nineteen, entered the labor movement in a period of sectional strife. Steward, a machinist, may have fought with John Brown against Kansas slaveholders during the 1850s. He supported Wendell Phillips's egalitarian Reconstruction measures and identified the postwar struggle against labor's oppression with the struggle against slavery.[19]

Indeed Steward's theoretical innovations regarding shorter hours grew out of his exposure to antislavery arguments. Steward contended, in the words of a couplet written by his wife:

Whether you work by the piece or work by the day, Decreasing the work increases the pay.[20]

But others had already made this point during the previous decade, basing their case on the fact that fewer hours meant less available labor power, which would drive wages up. Steward's contribution lay in the much more complex argument that an increase in leisure would create new wants among workers and cause them to seek higher wages. For Steward this rising desire and ability to consume would act as the key factor in encouraging more production. "New employments," according to Steward, "depend upon a more expensive style of living . . ." He added, "Wealth cannot be consumed sparingly by the masses and be produced rapidly," and predicted that machinery would help meet the demand of better-paid workers to consume. The entire economy would innovate more and produce more as a result of high wages, short hours, and increased consumption.[21]

Most studies have found this theory a radical departure from the prevailing economic thought of the period in that Steward rejected the idea of a limited wages fund and began with pleasure and consumption rather than with sacrifice and productivity. But in the American context, Steward's writings are not so surprising. Many of his criticisms of long hours and low wages paralleled the criticisms that Cassius M. Clay and others had long made against the Southern slave system. Many antislavery theorists regarded the inability of the slave labor force to consume as the chief barrier to economic growth in the South. Steward appropriated such criticisms of the slave South and applied them to the postwar economy, which according to his "Political Economy of Eight Hours," was still governed by a logic suitable to "chatel [sic] slavery."[22]

Other prominent eight-hour spokespersons shared antislavery convictions and applied them to labor struggles. George E. McNeill, second to Steward as the best-known advocate of the eight-hour system, matured in an abolitionist family in Amesbury. McNeill described the war as an attack by the "chattel labor masters upon the Republic" and equated the "Grand Army of the Republic [with] the grand army of Labor." Edward H. Rogers, Massachusetts shipwright turned state legislator, also took a strong antislavery stance and connected the issue with that of hours.[23] Wendell Phillips, abolition's leading white orator before the war and labor reform's top speaker after it, joined such reform luminaries as Charles Sumner, Karl Heinzen, William F. Channing, Gerrit Smith, Josiah Abbott, and William Lloyd Garrison in combining agitation against slavery with some support for the eight-hour day. Phillips saw the defeat of the "slave power" as clearing the way for a new prolabor campaign. "No doubt," he wrote in 1865, "the next great question for our country . . . is the rights of the laboring class . . . Eight hours to make a working day is the first rule to be observed."[24]

Such identification of the eight-hour movement with the war and with the liberation of slaves gave shorter-hours activists a sense that they were agitating a question of historical significance for the republic and the world.[25] Especially in the Boston area, where the first Eight-Hour Leagues formed, organizers saw participation as part of an ongoing assault on oppression and misery. For Steward himself, the eight-hour system "mean[t] anti-pauperism, anti-aristocracy, anti-monopoly, *anti-slavery*, anti-prostitution, want, waste, and idleness." It further presaged an end to "Speculation, . . . Woman's endless Drudgery . . . Land

Monopoly and War."[26]

Other leaders also saw the eight-hour system as a "first step" linked to broader goals. Wendell Phillips foresaw the expansion of equal educational opportunity, and for Rogers and others the decline of alcohol abuse was in view. Similarly broad claims came from supporters in other cities. Philadelphia's Fincher maintained "Labor is equality. Labor is dignity. Labor is power. It is able to regulate its hours." From Detroit, Trevellick echoed Fincher's sentiments and added, "we are about to be emancipated." Proposals for a six-and even for a four-hour day surfaced and found a hearing before the city council in Boston. The anarchist Josiah Warren soon proposed that two hours of daily labor might suffice.[27]

Nowhere was the connection between the liberating aspects of the Civil War and the feeling of high expectation among eight-hour advocates clearer than in the music surrounding the movement for a shorter day. Tunes from war songs and images from the conflict recurred in shorter hours music. E. R. Place's "A Song of Eight Hours" described the anticipated triumph of the shorter working day as a "jubilee"—the same word used by ex-slaves to describe the coming of their freedom. Another of Place's songs, "James Brown's Body," paraphrased the Civil War tune and evoked, according to McNeill, a fervor equal to that present at the revival meetings of Dwight Moody.[28]

The heritage of the war and the defeat of slavery also had more concrete effects in making possible a national movement to reduce the length of the working day. The Radical Republicans, a wing of the party that coalesced around the issues of emancipation, equality, and the use of federal power to reconstruct the defeated South, furnished many leaders of the campaigns for eight-hour laws, especially in Massachusetts, Ohio, and New York.[29] Ultimately, as David Montgomery has shown, the Radicals failed, as a group, to support the cutting of hours and to challenge "freedom of contract" as the guiding star in the relations between labor and capital. However, the importance of the Radicals lay not just in the specifics of their mixed record of backing or working against eight-hour laws in state legislatures. The existence of Radicalism as a body of political opinion which explicitly encouraged national power and a national perspective on social issues was as significant.[30]

Advocates of shorter hours, formerly hamstrung by the necessity of carrying on state-by-state agitation and answering the objection that if one state complied, it would lose industry to others, began to urge a national standard and a federal law during the Civil War period. Fincher repeatedly editorialized that state laws were insufficient, even counterproductive, and that a national statute was needed. German immigrants, some of them veterans of the revolutionary attempt to form a national republic in Germany in 1848, were in a good position to appreciate the limitations of an approach based only on the disparate actions of individual states. Often sympathetic to Radicalism, German-Americans brought a national perspective to the eight-hour movement.[31] One of them, Joseph Weydemeyer, a

Union army officer, Marxist, and Saint Louis county auditor, wrote: "[Laborers'] interests are identical throughout the country . . . and they can expect nothing essential for them from the legislatures of the different states [and] they can expect nothing from that party which advocates the breaking up of the country into small state sovereignties."[32]

Most leaders did not adopt the predominantly national political orientation urged by Fincher and Weydemeyer. The state legislature remained the locus of political conflict over hours.[33] But the issue did come before the federal Congress repeatedly between 1865 and 1868 in the form of legislation providing for an eight-hour day for mechanics and laborers in the government's employ. Such a law, according to Steward, would demonstrate the viability of the eight-hour day and have a symbolic significance equal to the legislation which had outlawed slavery in the District of Columbia. Steward also proposed a strong federal statute to deny patent protection to private manufacturers not complying with the eight-hour rule. The campaign for eight-hour legislation for federal employees proved successful in 1868, after a national petition campaign the previous year.[34]

The war and the successful struggle against slavery also made possible a national perspective by opening opportunities for agitation in the South and Midwest. For the first time, many among the formerly enslaved black workers in the South could contract for a set number of hours. Although task work prevailed in much agricultural labor after emancipation, some freed men and women demonstrated a commitment to working shorter hours.[35] Most contracts sanctioned by the Freedmen's Bureau specified a twelve-or ten-hour day, but in Louisiana the bureau prescribed nine-hour shifts in the winter. Black Radicals associated with the New Orleans *Tribune* supported a further reduction to eight hours, and in South Carolina a largely black State Labor Convention called, in 1869, for a nine-hour day for craftsmen and laborers.[36]

For white workers in the South, the abolition of slavery guaranteed that members of labor organizations could no longer be threatened with replacement by slave labor. Southern and border cities became new centers of shorter-hours agitation. Both the conventions attempting to rally national labor organizations to fight for the eight-hour day, for example, were held in former slave cities. In 1864 Louisville hosted the founding of the International Industrial Assembly of North America. Delegates there found it a "propitious time" to start a nationwide campaign to make eight hours a legal working day, but these delegates never met again. Two years later, 60 delegates from unions and eight-hour leagues met in Baltimore to convene the National Labor Union, a more durable organization that made shorter-hours legislation the center of its early program.[37] Baltimore was an appropriate site, since it had one of the most powerful local eight-hour movements in the nation. An estimated 25,000 had rallied there to support the demand in the fall of 1865, and in 1866 the city passed the country's first thoroughgoing municipal ordinance giving city workers an eight-hour day. Nearby towns in Delaware, Maryland, and Virginia also had active Eight-Hour

Leagues, as did the District of Columbia.[38]

In Saint Louis and New Orleans strong eight-hour movements also developed after the abolition of slavery. The former city, America's third largest manufacturing metropolis by 1870, witnessed rapid unionization during the war. A city central formed in 1863, and the *Daily Press*, a labor paper begun by striking printers in 1864, soon carried announcements for labor organizations in twenty-two crafts. Over 30 percent of the city's wage earners may have joined unions by the spring of 1865. The *Press* stressed the eight-hour goal during the latter months of the war, and on a bitterly cold November evening in 1865, the Trades Union League mobilized 10,000 for an eight-hour rally that prepared the ground for a local Eight-Hour League. Along with the banners of at least thirteen local unions were slogans that had double meanings for the Saint Louis workers who had fought to prevent Missouri from seceding: "Union is strength" and "None but Union men need apply."[39]

Political reconstruction and concern for a shorter working day began early in New Orleans, which came under union control in 1863. Under the military administrations of Generals Benjamin Butler and Nathaniel Banks, both of whom had long been advocates of a ten-hour day as Massachusetts politicians, New Orleans labor organized throughout 1863 and 1864 in the Working Men's Union League. When Banks convened the Louisiana Constitutional Convention in 1864, a large contingent of labor representatives sat as delegates. White New Orleans workers presented the convention with a petition whose 1,500 signatories asked that the constitution specify a nine-hour day. The convention voted to set a day's work at nine hours for laborers on the state's public works and to provide a two dollar daily minimum wage. However, the new constitution failed to provide for black suffrage and fell victim to the opposition of Radical Republicans in the U.S. Senate.[40]

Another refusal to accept black equality dogged the later efforts of New Orleans workers to obtain an eight-hour day. In 1866 the Workingmen's Central Committee, representing eleven all-white trade unions, insisted that the New Orleans *Tribune*, a Radical paper advocating the eight-hour day, should limit its demands to whites only, notwithstanding that the *Tribune* was itself a black newspaper, the first such daily in the United States. The *Tribune* persisted in coupling "EIGHT HOURS A LEGAL DAY'S WORK" with the egalitarian racial demands and in attempting to educate white workers on the need for unity. But the local Eight-Hour League, begun in 1866, rejected blacks as members and attempted a springtime eight-hour strike based on its all-white constituency. Excluded blacks helped to break the strike.[41] Boston's *Daily Evening Voice*, one of the most vigorous advocates of black civil rights among the labor press, asked after the defeat of the strike, "How many kicks like that which the workingmen of New Orleans have received will be required to give them the hint that . . . if the white will not lift the colored up, the colored will drag the white down?" While the New Orleans example indicates that emancipation did not heal the racial rifts hindering the progress of the eight-hour cause, the examples of the *Tribune* and the *Voice* were sometimes followed by the shorter-hours movement during the years after the Civil War, and instances of unity between blacks and whites who realized that progress required unity dot the history of the period.[42]

The spread of the eight-hour movement into Ohio, Illinois, Michigan, Indiana, Wisconsin, Iowa, Minnesota, and California also stemmed in part from the war. The connection was most clearly successful in California where the fighting brought trade unionism "its first far western bonanza" by cutting imports and immigration to that state simultaneously. California's local industries lacked skilled labor, and tradesmen took advantage of that shortage to organize. In November 1863 San Francisco's *Evening Bulletin* noted a "general disposition on the part of the operatives to strike." Wages were the main issue in these strikes, but during 1863 and 1864, retail clerks, bakers, bricklayers, construction laborers, and shipwrights raised the issue of the working day.[43]

The 1865 election of the printer Alexander Kenaday as president of the San Francisco Trades' Union marked the accession of the eight-hour demand to first place among the goals of organized labor there. Kenaday, impressed by the shorter-hours arguments of *Fincher's Trades' Review*, briefly tried to publish a Pacific counterpart to Fincher's paper in April 1865. His *Journal of Trades and Workingmen* survived but a month, but he managed to publicize the issue of hours through his inaugural address to the union. The city central circulated 4,000 copies of his speech, in which Kenaday referred to eight hours as a demand "which should unite every class of laboring men . . . one of the most important [reforms] within the scope of your duties." House carpenters convened a mass meeting of eight-hour supporters from the San Francisco area in December 1865. That gathering undertook a petition drive for a state eight-hour law. The petition campaign extended the agitation to other California towns. It generated 11,000 signatures, twenty-two feet of them, in three months. In 1876 the legislature passed an eight-hour statute, complete with a loophole allowing for contracts requiring a longer day.[44]

The Civil War also brought working class patriotism, labor shortages, and inflation to the Midwest and, as Eugene Roseboom observed in his study of Ohio, "made [labor] organization necessary." While the conflict probably failed to stimulate economic growth or great institutional change nationally, it had an impact on the Midwest.[45] As rural youths went to the front, farmers purchased mechanical reapers and mowers to replace their labor power. In 1864, 90,000 such machines were sold; in 1859 only 125,000 had existed.[46] The war may also have increased the rate of industrial growth in the Midwest, though this was not true for nation as a whole. Annual series of production in various industries are too inaccurate to permit the pinpointing the exact occurrence of the growth that took place between the censuses of 1860 and 1870. For the decade, the censuses show a 262% value added increment to Illinois's mining and manufacturing product, a 394% increase for Missouri (which increasingly saw itself as a part of the

West rather than the South), and an 81.5% increase in the number of Ohio wage earners. At the same time the Homestead Act of 1862 made one kind of land reform a reality and, by rendering proposals for agricultural reform less intriguing, opened the way for Midwest labor groups to concentrate on hours. Prior to 1861 only Ohio had any record of sustained *ten*-hour agitation. By 1866 scores of local *Eight*-Hour Leagues thrived in the Midwest.[47]

In Michigan and Illinois eight-hour campaigns began well before the end of the war. Richard Trevellick, whose organizing tours branched out from his Detroit base, was instrumental in spreading the movement throughout the Midwest. In 1864 he was elected as the first president of the Detroit Trades' Assembly representing 5,000 unionists. At a mass meeting in June of that year, Trevellick spoke in favor of the eight-hour system. An Eight-Hour League soon organized and entered municipal politics. In the city elections in the fall of 1865, the league supported candidates from the major parties in some aldermanic districts and slated its own candidates in others. Eight-hour men won in five of the city's wards, and in three others major party candidates endorsed by the league triumphed. The city council adopted an eight-hour day for most city employees during the next year. By then, Detroit was just one of twenty-five locals in the Grand Eight-Hour League of Michigan, which Trevellick also headed.[48]

Chicago's *Workingman's Advocate*, a labor paper founded by striking printers, initiated the eight-hour movement in Illinois in the fall of 1864. Andrew S. Cameron, the *Advocate*'s editor, quizzed candidates for the state legislature as to whether or not they agreed "to introduce and advocate the passage of a bill to *shorten the hours of labor*." The responses, ranging from the Republicans' general opposition to the Democrats' proviso that shorter hours must be accompanied by a wage cut, caused the General Trades' Assembly to warn that laborers would no longer be "dupes of . . . false statements and past hypocritical catchwords." The city central's endorsements of candidates had little effect on the election results, but the *Advocate* and the unions continued to stress the eight-hour system. Workers in retail stores also discussed the necessity of reducing hours in the Dry Goods Clerks' Early Closing Association.[49] In 1865 eight-hour advocates held a large Independence Day picnic and an autumn rally in which 4,000 marched at night by the light of Chinese lanterns. The city's Eight-Hour League had fourteen branches at the ward level and branch meetings sometimes drew audiences of several hundred. By the end of 1865 the Grand Illinois Eight-Hour League had formed, and local organizations existed in such other Illinois cities as Springfield, Peoria, Bloomington, Cairo, and Centralia. Both parties appealed for eight-hour votes in Chicago in 1866 by supporting an ordinance giving city workers the shorter day. Municipal employees in Aurora won the same concession that year. In 1867 Illinois passed the nation's first eight-hour law.[50]

Wisconsin may also have experienced some eight-hour activity during the war. Frederick Merk mentions public discussions on the subject in 1864 in Milwaukee.[51] In late summer of 1865 the issue became a prominent one. When

William Swinton, travelling deputy of the International Union of Machinists and Blacksmiths, visited Milwaukee on an organizing tour in the Midwest, he found an audience eager for his address on the hours of labor. A local Eight-Hour League came together on the early September evening of his talk. The league made endorsements in the fall elections for the Wisconsin assembly on the basis of each candidate's stance on eight-hour legislation. The backing of the Eight-Hour League probably influenced a pair of Milwaukee elections in favor of Democrats who supported such a law. The Milwaukee *Sentinel* complained that two outstate races may also have hinged on "the omnipotent aid of the eight-pointed star."[52] Early in 1866, after the movement had spread to several larger towns in the state, an eight-hour law came before the legislature. At about the same time, Milwaukee's Eight-Hour League ran a separate slate in the city's election but had little success. In 1867 the state passed an ineffective eight-hour law covering nonfarm workers. The Wisconsin movement, interestingly, tended to run ahead of trade unionism so that some workers, such as Milwaukee's carpenters, organized their crafts only after shorter-hours activity.[53]

Indiana, like Wisconsin, was a thinly unionized state and, in 1860, had no city of over 20,000. The record of its movement is a useful reminder that a high degree of urbanization was not a precondition for the growth of eight-hour sentiment. Eight-hour activities started in Evansville, Indianapolis, Fort Wayne, Richmond, Terre Haute, Laporte, Madison, and New Albany during late 1865. The scenario usually involved a visit from Swinton or Fincher at a meeting initiated by a small local chapter of the machinists and blacksmiths or by a carpenters' union. Such meetings ended with passage of eight-hour resolutions and often with the promise of members of various crafts to work together.[54] Indianapolis held the first such meeting in August under the leadership of machinist John Fehrenbatch. Three months later it was the site of the Workingmen's Convention at which, according to *Fincher's Trades' Review*, "a large number of delegates [from] most of the trades" in the state founded the Indiana Grand Eight-Hour League. Indianapolis probably was chosen to host the convention because of its central location and because it gave delegates a chance to pressure the legislature. The announcement of the statewide meeting came from Evansville, and Noyes White, a native of that city, won the convention's presidency with Fehrenbatch serving as secretary.[55]

Citing jobs and mechanization as reasons to cut hours, the league in Indiana opted to pressure the major parties rather than forming, as some delegates proposed, a labor party. By 1866 the league's lobbying caused both the state's major parties to include its demand in their platforms. Radical Republican Congressman George Julian of Indiana played a large role in securing the eight-hour law for federal workers, and Evansville passed an 1866 ordinance on the subject, but no state law won approval during the postwar period.[56]

Of the other midwestern states, only Ohio had a strong eight-hour movement, although Iowa had a statewide Eight-Hour League before the end of 1865 and the Minnesota legislature considered proposals on the subject shortly thereafter. Cincinnati's city central and particularly its German workingmen and German-language press broached the issue in July 1865. Fall elections that year saw about half the candidates pledge support for an eight-hour law. After the elections the Cincinnati labor movement chartered the state's "Eight-Hour League No. 1."[57] Salineville, Zanesville, and possibly Cleveland also sustained eight-hour activities. Columbus had an active local organization and on at least one occasion, that of an "immense meeting" to hear Fincher speak in December 1865, eight-hour advocates came there to impress legislators with a show of strength. Both houses of the legislature approved an eight-hour law in 1866, but in slightly different versions. These differences went unreconciled and the bill died, as it would again in 1867.[58] However, the importance of the early eight-hour movement, in Ohio and in the whole Midwest, lay beyond its meager legislative yield. Among its achievements must be counted the bringing together of various tradesmen into one city or state labor organization for the first time.

"From east to west, north to south," Fincher wrote in 1865, "the cry has gone forth: 'Eight hours shall be a legal day's work'."[59] This chapter has reversed Fincher's emphasis by concentrating first on the South and Midwest. Nonetheless, the Northeast remained the hub of the shorter-hours movement. With the transformations wrought by the war, the shorter-hours cause there involved unprecedented numbers of workers. If the figures given in the labor press are correct, as many as 67,000 participated in six eight-hour demonstrations near the eastern seaboard between March and December 1865.[60] As in other regions the agitation largely matured during or immediately after the war. Prior to the end of 1865, eight-hour meetings had occurred in Philadelphia, Boston, New York City, Newark, Paterson, New Brunswick, Buffalo, Albany, Rochester, Pittsburgh, Brooklyn, Fall River, Lawrence, Providence, and Jersey City and had even spread to towns like Brownsville, Pennsylvania, and Boonton, New Jersey. Massachusetts had fourteen local Eight-Hour Leagues by October.[61] Legislators in the Bay State and New York took sides on the issue and several city councils considered eight-hour ordinances. Activities in the Northeast have received a relatively full treatment from historians, but for our purposes, discussions of New York and of Massachusetts, the ideological center of the eight-hour movement, are appropriate.[62]

New York illustrated several common aspects of the eight-hour movement in the Northeast. New Yorkers initiated agitation on the subject well before Appomattox. From the start, trade unions played a key role in raising the issue and in carrying it into politics. In January 1864 the Iron Molders' International Union met in a national convention in Buffalo and, on the suggestion of William Sylvis, resolved to begin education on the eight-hour system. The following July Brooklyn unionists followed the lead of the city's carpenters and organized a group to inquire whether candidates for the state legislature supported an eight-hour law. The New York *Sun* decried the mixing of labor and politics, but the workingmen persisted, supported even by Fincher, who is generally regarded as the main advocate of an apolitical labor movement during this period.[63]

At the beginning of the next year, the National Association of Journeymen Plasterers adopted the eight-hour standard at its convention in New York City; carpenters followed suit at the same site in September.[64] A February 1865 mass rally in New York City, described as "one of the largest indoor meetings ever held in the City," concerned both wages and hours and took place in the Early Closing Association Hall, a meeting place of white-collar workers. A representative of the Dry Goods Clerks' Early Closing Association convened the rally, and the Carpet and Furniture Clerks' Association also participated along with many craft unions. Such cooperation was typical of the solidarity around the question of hours among various trades and between white-collar and manual workers in the Northeast.[65] Other New York actions continued a united willingness to combine trade unionism with political action. During the winter of 1865 the union-based New York State Workingmen's Assembly called for a nationwide convention to "devise the most eligible means to secure to the workingmen, eight hours labor as a legal day's work." That call generated no national action, but organization within the state grew. During the next nine months, Buffalo unions formed an eight-hour group, and over 6,000 turned out for an "Eight-Hour Picnic" in Rochester. Organized workers in New York City's *Arbeiter-Bund*, a German city central, overwhelmingly approved the demand. Their president shared the rostrum with the head of the Workingmen's Union, the English-speaking city central, at a large December eight-hour rally at Cooper Union. In autumn of 1865 another state labor convention passed a series of resolutions calling for an eight-hour law and began a petition campaign on the issue.[66] By the following March the petitioners had secured as many as 27,000 signatures, an unprecedented number for the shorter-hours movement in any state. The State Workingmen's Assembly, convening in Albany to pressure the legislators, entertained a proposal for a statewide general strike to force consideration of the law. This strike proposal was not carried out, however. Through the efforts of George A. Brandreth and other Radical Republican legislators, the measure did reach the House floor, where it lost by a sixty-four to fifty-three vote.[67]

Almost immediately thereafter, 10,000 Long Island area workers in the shipbuilding industry unsuccessfully attempted to gain the eight-hour day by striking. Partly as a result of the labor solidarity and public support evidenced during that six-week strike, and partly because of increased agitation and Democratic support at the state level, New York passed an eight-hour statute in 1867. Lacking provisions for enforcement and leaving open the possibility of special contracts, the law never measured up to the hopes of labor groups who lobbied for its passage.[68]

A similar pattern of activities by trade unionists with diverse skills was evident in Massachusetts. In 1863 Steward persuaded fellow members of the International Union of Machinists and Blacksmiths to endorse the eight-hour demand at its national convention in Boston. The union's resolutions identified the eight-hour system as "the most important change to us" and asked the Boston Trades' Assembly for its cooperation. The city central agreed that eight hours was "the leading point in the great problem of labor reform," and asked its constituent unions to fund agitation around the issue. During 1864, when the joint project appeared stalled, Steward withdrew from the Trades' Assembly to form an independent Boston Labor Reform Association, explicitly dedicated to the eight-hour day. The Labor Reform Association, while rooted in fewer trade unions, was still largely a labor organization.[69] The split with the Trades' Assembly probably resulted in part from Steward's growing conviction that unions by themselves were too narrow and craft-based to win the eight-hour day, and in part from his emphasis on campaigns of education around the issue. But the emergence of a second organization did not signal a loss of interest in hours by the crafts in the Trades' Assembly. On March 3, 1865, the officers of the first mass meeting favoring shorter hours held in Boston during the war included the presidents or representatives of twenty-seven different unions. During the following two weeks the heads of the city central convened eight-hour rallies in Lawrence and Charlestown.[70]

During the week following the first March demonstration, John W. Mahan, a Boston lawyer, army captain, and state legislator, moved that the Massachusetts House should appoint a committee to investigate whether legislation on hours was advisable. In May that radical committee, which included the ex-shipwright Edward H. Rogers and Charles McLean, a millwright, unanimously reported that the testimony presented favored the eight-hour system, that shorter hours would not interfere with industrial progress, and that the state should act to prevent the spread of "cringing servility and supineness" among the many workers who were being reduced to "little else than a machine."[71] The document gave respectability to the eight-hour movement and demonstrated, as Montgomery observes, how the demand might be sanctioned "in terms of the nationalist and utilitarian formulas of the Radicals themselves." Mahan, Rogers, and Martin Griffin, who chaired the committee, all spoke at the July eight-hour "Jubilee of Labor" sponsored by the Trades' Assembly. Steward inscribed the couplet: "Let all now cheer, who never cheered before. And those who always cheer, now cheer the more, " on the copy of the report he sent to *Fincher's Trades' Review.*[72]

The Boston Labor Reform Association saw its strategy of a broad public appeal outside the unions as vindicated by the legislative report and accelerated its campaign to popularize Steward's ideas. The association's 1865 publication of Steward's *A Reduction of Hours an Increase of Wages* provided the first exposition of his views. The pamphlet consisted of an attempt to convince an average worker that eight hours meant more pay. Steward supplemented the old ten-hour theory that cutting hours narrowed the labor market and thus raised wages with a more elaborate argument. Two propositions convey the crux of his position but not its complexity: "That more leisure, will create motives . . . for the common people to ask for more wages [and] that where all demand more wages, the demand cannot be resisted."[73]

As Steward later admitted, relatively few workers were converted by following the nuances of his presentation. His pamphlet was, in any event, often contradictory, at once predicting that shorter hours would revolutionize the economy by ushering in cooperative production and that the new system would have little effect on "the enterprise of capital." More important than any specifics was Steward's general insistence that the problem of hours was part of a conflict between classes and that such conflict required a political solution. "The eight-hour system," he held, "will make a coalition between ignorant labor and selfish capital on election day, impossible" and "hasten the day" that craftsmen and unskilled laborers unite in the recognition that "We march to fate abreast."[74]

In August 1865 this desire to bring the eight-hour question into politics brought the followers of Steward and the Trades' Assembly into the same organization again. First in Charlestown and then in Boston, the nation's first Grand Eight-Hour Leagues came together. Steward saw the political independence of labor as depending on a reduction in the working day. He therefore urged that eight-hour agitation use members of the existing parties to secure legislation rather than attempting to found its own labor party. Steward wrote that labor reform must "be served by men who at heart want nothing but position, power, pay and honour; for it cannot be served without them." He therefore suggested that eight-hour advocates go to all candidates and ask, "Will you . . . if elected . . . vote for this bill?"[75] Wendell Phillips, instrumental in forming the Eight-Hour Leagues, lent support to this strategy by claiming that it was the technique that had made abolitionism a success.[76] The Eight-Hour Leagues adopted Steward's stance and attracted a number of trade unionists, politicians, and middle-class reformers. Within two months after the formation of the first league, a dozen more chapters were chartered. In September a visit by four local leagues to the Republican state convention yielded an endorsement from the party's gubernatorial candidate and the writing of an eight-hour plank into the party's platform.[77]

The weeks before the November elections teemed with activity. Boston's city council passed an eight-hour ordinance for municipal office employees. In October a second House committee on hours held hearings and distributed questionnaires through the state.[78] Mill operatives in Taunton, Southbridge, New Bedford (Wamsutta Mills), and nearby Woonsocket, Rhode Island, all struck for fewer hours and in each case cut at least an hour from their official working day.[79] Rallies in Charlestown and Boston heard Phillips, Steward, Griffin, and Rogers. Trade union officials convened both gatherings. Rogers promised that the skilled workers who "were going to get this eight-hour law very soon would not abandon the factories and sewing women . . . until they get it too." By November there were eighteen local Eight-Hour Leagues in a state organization.[80]

Election results brought disillusion. Only between twenty-three and twenty-five legislators pledged to the law won office. In some districts neither party had endorsed the demand. The *Voice* drew the conclusion that "workingmen must stand out as an independent party organization." This new strategy resulted in the election of a large minority of independent eight-hour men to the Lowell and Boston city councils in late 1865. The Eight-Hour Leagues nevertheless stayed with pressure politics as a strategy in 1866, and the *Voice* returned to the fold, attempting to secure a Republican nomination to the U.S. Congress for Phillips before the abolitionist withdrew his name.[81]

But Steward's plan became less tenable as the year progressed. While ostensibly bipartisan, the league's leaders hoped that the Radical Republicans would pick up the eight-hour banner. Despite the meager results of the 1865 legislative elections, strategists could still point to the support of Republican Governor Alexander Bullock and of House Speaker James Stone and could still reread the 1865 House report produced by the Radicals.[82] In March 1866, with the release of the second House document on hours, such a hopeful view was discredited. The committee, composed of three prominent citizens with strong Radical ties, accepted most contentions of the eight-hour advocates who had testified regarding health, education, and republican ideals, but refused to recommend legislation except on child labor, and launched into a spirited defense of the free market: "Law having declined the task of establishing communism . . . it cannot invade the principle that a loyal man has a right to do as he pleases with his own, in the case of the millionaire, without damaging it in the person of the . . . laborer."[83] The *Voice*, which described itself as "RADICAL BUT INDEPENDENT," branded those who took such a position on hours as "radical only for Louisiana," but its protests, and those of the eight-hour caucuses in the Republican party, were ignored. Support of eight-hour laws by some National Unionists and Democrats who took conservative positions on Reconstruction further muddied the issue. Labor reformers with egalitarian sympathies ran a separate candidate in some cases and endorsed anti-Radicals who "opposed the elevation of Southern labor" in others.[84] The Grand Eight-Hour Leagues declined throughout the year, and the elections turned more on Reconstruction than labor issues. Despite a ten-hour strike wave among men and women in textile mills during 1867, no shorter-hours statutes passed in Massachusetts.[85]

The mixed success of the early eight-hour movement should not obscure its achievements in breaking new ground in the struggle for a shorter working day, and in recapturing much of what had been distinctive and dynamic in earlier ten-hour campaigns. Some aspects of the agitation for the eight-hour day were unprecedented. The geographical expansion of the movement and the inauguration of campaigns for federal legislation, for example, made the shorter-hours cause a national one for the first time. Steward's philosophy, with its stress on levels of consumption and on the desirability of using a reduction in the working day to force employers to create new technology, also constituted an innovation.

While Heighton, Skidmore, and other early labor leaders saw productive advances as necessitating shorter hours, Steward originated the argument that the opposite held true as well: the eight-hour day would cause productive advances.[86] Also new was the contention that the working day should allow for travel time to and from the job and that, as a Boston handbill put it, the eight-hour day contributed to "The growth of suberban [sic] towns and cities—the sensible relief from the evils of large *cities*."[87] Both the argument regarding technology and that concerning suburbanization indicate how firmly the eight-hour advocates were situated in a growing industrial order and how little they considered themselves defenders of an attacked artisan community.

Eight-hour advocates also reiterated the argument, common in the 1830s and 1840s but submerged in reform rhetoric of the 1850s, that the shorter-hours issue was part of the broader antagonism between capital and labor. Steward, always ready with a Civil War phrase, described the two groups as locked in an "irrepressible conflict."[88] Sylvis's premise was that a "collision between labor and capital . . . a war of classes" existed and had to exist in "an order of things so contrary to the dictates of justice and humanity." Fincher found labor and capital "in the nature of things opposed to each other," and Trevellick pledged, "I will pawn my coat before I yield one point to all the capitalists in Detroit."[89] Some labor reformers from outside the unions also alluded to class conflict. Wendell Phillips, whose contradictory positions have caused historians to view him as everything from a nostalgic New Englander to the American Marx, maintained that "Capital and Labor must be . . . opposing forces" but also that the two were bound together "like the Siamese whose life is one."[90] Weydemeyer, an American Marxist, consistently analyzed the eight-hour cause as part of class strife.[91]

Early advocates of the ten-hour movement had embraced Ricardian socialist ideas regarding the justice of labor's claim to the full value of its labor partly as a result of their scrutiny of how many hours the laborer worked for himself and how many for his employer. Likewise, eight-hour leaders were concerned with the rate of exploitation. Steward was specific about the relationship between cutting hours from ten to eight:

> We understand, quite as well as Employers, that four-fifths of a day's labor are not worth as much as *five*-fifths. But this is not the point. It is the *Wages* we have received, or that we may receive in the future . . . whether we can or can not [produce as much in eight hours] is not the question to ask us; it is whether we can *get* as much of what we *do* produce . . .*Our share* of what we produce is the idea.[92]

It is true that many, especially after the failure of the 1867 eight-hour laws, settled for profit-sharing schemes to rectify inequalities in the wage bargain or stressed currency reform plans designed to curb financiers and to furnish capital to set up cooperatives.[93] But at the height of the early eight-hour agitation, Sylvis and others clearly conceived of employers and financiers as part of the capitalist group whose interests opposed labor's. Steward and his followers even had a plan, which they pursued well into the 1870s, for making cooperative production possible by continually reducing hours and raising wages until corporate profits so declined that cooperatives could compete. Some of the Eight-Hour Leagues envisioned "cooperation of labor [as] the final result to be obtained" by cutting hours. Although such a strategy was as utopian as that of the currency reformers, it differed in that it concentrated its fire on industrial, rather than only on finance, capital. As in the 1830s shorter-hours agitation served to call into question the prevailing idea that all producers—employers and employed—formed a single class.[94]

Also harkening back to the early ten-hour struggles was the establishment of labor unity around the eight-hour issue. Fincher, for example, theorized that the eight-hour cause could not succeed in any one trade if it were "unsupported by the other branches of the great mechanic family." For both Steward and the *Voice*, unity of skilled and unskilled was of paramount importance. Especially in Massachusetts, eight-hour advocates included women workers and took an interest in textile factory conditions.[95] The demand united German and Irish immigrants with each other and with native American workers.[96] Most city centrals came together over wages during the Civil War, but in the Eight-Hour Leagues a variety of workers (and some farmers) united on the basis of a belief that shorter hours would be won or lost statewide. The National Labor Union announced its special emphasis on the eight-hour day in the call to its founding convention in 1866.[97]

Connected with this ability to inspire solidarity, and also reminiscent of the early ten-hour movement, was the manner in which the eight-hour demand focused diverse labor grievances on a single goal. When Boston eight-hour agitators issued handbills advocating shorter hours to stop seasonal joblessness, they were repeating an argument that ten-hour protesters had used as early as 1791.[98] Sylvis and others also took familiar ground when they presented the eight-hour system as the solution to the taking of jobs by new technology. Machinery and other productive advances, according to Sylvis, usually "emanate[d] from the brain-work and handiwork of the toiler" and ought to have led to a shorter working day rather than to less jobs.[99] By addressing the problems of seasonal and technological unemployment, and by offering the prospect of less working time to employees whose jobs were becoming more alienating, the eight-hour demand functioned as a common denominator around which workers with various concerns could unite.

But the cry "Eight hours for work, eight hours for rest, eight hours for recreation," acted as more than a common denominator. It embodied, as the ten-hour demand had for Douglas, Luther, Ferral, Bagley, Hewitt, and their followers, the highest aspirations of the working population. It expressed cherished values. To dismiss, as Norman Ware does, all eight-hour arguments but economic ones as "the old reformist grounds for short hours, 'more time for moral, intellectual, and social culture',", is to mock dreams and to miss the sense of expectation present after the Civil War.[100] In making the eight-hour system the key to equal education for children, to the continued mental development of adults, to the defense of republican virtue and class interests by an enlightened and politically active citizenry, to health, to vigor, and to social life, supporters viewed their demand as an initial step to major changes, not as a niggling reform.[101]

Leaders contended that long hours blocked broad cultural advances by denying workers access to social institutions. Sylvis, for example, nearly repeated Frances Wright's comment of four decades before when he wrote: "It is true that churches are erected, school houses are built, mechanics' institutes are founded and libraries are ready to receive us . . . but alas! we lack *the time to use them—time.*"[102] Intelligent working-class political behavior likewise, according to some eight-hour advocates, awaited the shorter day. Just as Heighton described leisure as the precondition for a labor party, Steward despaired that "laborers . . . [would] be found, every election day, in company with master Capitalists, *voting down schemes for their own emancipation,*" until the eight-hour system applied.[103]

The notion that the eight-hour day meant something as broad as "freedom" for the working population was derived from the war experience and from analogies with slavery, but acquired more meaning because it meshed so well with the Methodist faith of several of the movement's ideologues.[104] Specifically, labor leaders applied the Wesleyan doctrine of "free agency" to leisure time. The concept of free agency, which held that humans could choose salvation or sin, enriched eight-hour arguments by allowing supporters to admit that leisure might not always be used "wisely" but still to hold that labor should be free to make its own mistakes. Steward, for example, used terms which were familiar to Methodists and other Protestants who dominated the eight-hour movement, in describing leisure as "a blank—a negative—a piece of white paper." He even admitted that prior oppression would "be sure to stamp [its] humiliating record upon the first leisure hours in the Eight-Hour System." But he discounted the possibility of errors as a reason to refuse implementation of the eight-hour system. Answering such objections with a quote from Macauley, he wrote, "There is only one cure for the evils which newly acquired freedom produces—and that cure is FREEDOM."[105] The concept of free agency allowed for a long-term view of the progress that might accompany the shorter day—progress that would occur unevenly, with setbacks, and "not the first day nor first week." In calling upon employers to grant the freedom that the deity did not deny, eight-hour advocates aligned themselves with powerful Protestant religious sentiments, much as Seth Luther had done long before.[106]

Continuity between the ten-and eight-hour movements characterized the record of both issues in combining political action and strikes. Successes of labor parties that formed around the ten-or eight-hour plank were rare. But the pattern of labor unions supporting broader organizations to pressure the major parties, and of frequent consideration of the need for an independent labor party by those most active in hours agitation, held in the 1860s as well as in the previous four decades. In 1865 such political action seldom existed alongside the tactic of striking, but in 1866 and 1867 the two tactics complemented each other.[107] Only Steward, among the eight-hour movement's major leaders, opposed strikes. Much of his opposition and much of the caution of other leaders regarding strikes must be attributed to the greater possibility of uniting all crafts (and the unorganized) in a political contest than in the support of isolated job actions.[108]

The eight-hour agitation during and just after the Civil War thus showed marked affinity to the ten-hour movement preceding it. The war, the boldness of the new demand, and continuing changes in the economy made for a more passionate and popular commitment in the 1860s than had been the case in the 1850s. To that extent, Steward was right in positing a gulf between ten-and eight-hour agitation. But the larger picture was one of continuity based on the place of shorter hours as the clearest and most appealing working-class demand raised between 1825 and 1866.

6

Victory, Defeat, and New Alliances, 1867-1879

In the years following the Civil War, the apparent accomplishments of the political movement for a shorter working day were impressive. Not only did eight states pass eight-hour laws by 1868, but during that same year, Congress also approved a statute making eight hours a legal day's work for employees of the national government. However, in each instance, the laws either lacked provisions for enforcement, contained loopholes, or became objects of conflicting interpretation. In no state did workers uniformly gain an eight-hour day and only in New York City was there a general local change to that standard. The story of the eight-hour movement during Reconstruction is thus one of reaction to disappointment in the wake of the republican euphoria bred by the Civil War. At different times in different places during the late 1860s, the labor movement learned either that its forces were insufficient to secure shorter-hours laws or that the laws themselves were ineffectual.

The collapse of confidence that political action would usher in the eight-hour system gave rise to jettisoning of the shorter-hours demand by some politically inclined and cooperative-minded labor leaders, and to the search for a viable strategy by those committed to continued struggle. During Reconstruction, working-class enthusiasm for the eight-hour day remained high despite defeats and despite a major economic depression. Within labor leadership, new alliances formed among veteran followers of Steward, young socialists, and trade union leaders who still favored emphasis on the hours issue.

The frustrations of the political eight-hour movement in 1867 and 1868 are exemplified by the fate of legislation in Massachusetts, where it failed to pass, and in Illinois, where it passed in ineffective form. Most other states with eight-hour legislation, including Connecticut, Missouri, Wisconsin, and Pennsylvania, followed the pattern of practical stasis despite legislative victories.[1] Only in New York, where massive strikes both preceded and succeeded passage of the statute, did some substantial adoption of the eight-hour day take place. There, as elsewhere, the pattern that emerged was one of strikes to enforce what the law could not provide.

In Massachusetts the political thrust for an eight-hour law was blunted by 1867, but, largely independently of the leagues, factory workers took up the hours demand that year. Although the issue arose in several factory towns through the efforts of either spokespersons for the leagues or, more commonly, through lectures by political ten-hour reformers from the 1850s who helped to organize Short Time Committees, rank-and-file workers acted in several instances to mount prolonged strikes that the reformers did not counsel.[2] What began as a petition campaign, replete with educational forums on shorter hours, could quickly spill over into a work stoppage. Among the reasons for this incidence of direct action were the militancy of skilled immigrant textile workers—especially experienced British trade unionists—and the growing practice of presenting ten-hour petitions to local owners as well as sending them to the legislature.[3]

The first breakthrough for the Short Time Committees, which stressed the ten-hour demand as more realistic for textile workers than a call for eight hours, occurred in Fall River. In that textile center, with a high concentration of immigrant weavers and spinners from Lancashire and Yorkshire, a committee cited unemployment and low pay as its reasons for circulating a ten-hour petition in the fall of 1866. When employers at the city's twenty-two mills refused to consider the demand in the absence of its adoption by corporations in Lawrence and Lowell, workers shut the town's factories with a two-week strike. The settlement, negotiated with the help of Samuel A. Chase, a Republican state legislator, provided that Fall River's mills would convert to a ten-hour schedule. This transition gave spirit to ten-hour advocates throughout Massachusetts, and in Connecticut and New Hampshire as well. The capitulation of Fall River's mills also signaled a split in the position of owners regarding the working day and made it impossible for employers to argue that they were following form in adhering to the longer working day. Indeed the Fall River owners became advocates of the ten-hour system, testifying before legislative committees on its behalf and even granting paid time off to textile organizers whose touring efforts seemed likely to force competitive mills in other cities onto the same standard.[4]

In the wake of the Fall River victory, agitation in other mill towns grew. The Mule Spinners of New England, a small body of skilled workers, had already set April 1, 1867, as a target date to institute the sixty-hour week.[5] After Fall River's adoption of the system, the goal seemed well within reach. Short Time Committees met with increasing frequency, providing a forum in which the spinners and weavers could exercise leadership but also cultivate ties to the unskilled operatives and to reformers from outside the mills. In Lowell, where the mayor and other prominent local politicians supported the demand, women formed the Ladies' Short Time Committee, which, according to one historian, "practically took command of the movement" there. At their meetings, the women occupied the floor while men sat in the balconies. The Ladies' Short Time Committee voted aid to strikers in other cities and influenced the Hamilton Corporation to rehire a discharged female worker who had testified for shorter hours before the legislature.[6]

The key contest over hours took place in New Bedford, a city that grew with the whaling trade and had but two textile factories. New Bedford nurtured an active middle-class reform tradition, in which none were more prominent than the Howland family, principal stockholders in Wamsutta Mills. Rachel Howland, wife of the son of the mill's founder, delighted in touring the factory to exhibit to visitors the pleasant working and living environment it provided. Thomas Bennett, the paternalistic young agent at Wamsutta, was as reform-minded as his employers and, on January 1, 1867, took action on his own initiative to match the Fall River owners by putting his 1,050 workers on the ten-hour schedule. When Bennett reneged and announced reestablishment of the eleven-hour day beginning on February 1, Wamsutta Mills erupted in class conflict.[7]

Skilled employees responded to the increase in hours by convening a public meeting in a local church. At that gathering local ministers Isaac Knowlton and Isaac Coe—the latter doubled as a state legislator instrumental in child labor reform—helped engineer a compromise under which the ten-hour schedule would continue until March 1 and would remain in effect thereafter if other mills adopted the new timetable. The negotiating committee, dominated by weavers and spinners, also accepted a 9 percent wage cut for day laborers as part of the package. Day laborers complained of the cuts and for two weeks resignations and on-the-job discussions among workers disrupted production. One of Bennett's overseers fired a member of the committee for being absent from his workplace on February 16. A round of firings and walkouts followed, culminating with the closing of the plant.[8]

Six hundred workers, a hundred of them females, mapped out a strike strategy at Eight Hour League Hall. Their demands had by now broadened to include amnesty for fired committee members and a firm commitment to the ten-hour day at the pay rate formerly received for the longer day. With the day laborers, skilled spinners, and weavers united, the movement organized a mass rally at the city hall, and a relief committee for the strikers was formed. Aid came from likeminded workers in Fall River and from Lowell, where women led the strike support. Management, like labor, perceived that the eyes of the textile industry in the Northeast were on Wamsutta Mills. In a counterproposal to a committee of three townsmen, Bennett refused amnesty and insisted on an eleven-hour day at 1866 wages. Bennett further announced his intention to reopen on March 1.[9]

The strikers, who voted unanimously to reject Bennett's offer, built an enthusiastic rally on the eve of the projected reopening. On March 1 less than a seventh of the full work force (even by company estimates) reported to the mills. The strikers claimed that not a score of strikebreakers went to work. Strikebreaking skilled workers from Rhode Island, drawn to New Bedford by promises of $2.25 a day, generally reversed field when they confronted female strike patrols, an aroused citizenry, and the offer of a paid fare home.[10] The strike looked solid, but on March 2 the strike committee met with Bennett and suddenly put forward another compromise. This time the proposal called for a ten-hour trial period from April 1 to July 1 and an extension if Lowell, Lawrence, or the Massachusetts legislature embraced the shorter schedule. Perhaps the committee expected rejection from the increasingly vituperative Bennett and hoped to gain support by contrasting the flexibility of other mill employers with his own intransigence. Bennett did refuse the compromise but Rachel Howland, seeing the opportunity to restore harmony, forced him to reconsider.[11]

Howland's personal intervention left the committee in the awkward position of having to present to its ranks a settlement that admitted the employer's contention that Wamsutta's hours should be tied to practices elsewhere. At the ratification meeting on the evening of March 3, the committee used the technicality that Bennett had not signed the compromise to justify refusing to read its terms. Company spokespersons, including Rachel Howland, spelled out the terms at a meeting the next evening and nearly gained a vote for ratification until Joanna Maher, a women worker, persuaded the strikers to vote with their leaders. But the next morning 300 hands resumed mill operations and within a week nearly a full complement of operatives ran the mills. To hungry day laborers, the compromise proposal, which their strike committee had once endorsed, gradually began to seem enough. The spinners continued the strike alone but lost. The entire episode, as David Montgomery has suggested, not only set the pattern for defeats elsewhere but graphically illustrated the failure of the middle-class reformers to support shorter hours over the free market and high profits.[12] The events at Wamsutta Mills also predicted the specific weakness that would be fatal to the ten-hour movement in other textile cities. The spinners, organized as a craft union, determined to go it alone in Lawrence, Lowell, and Manchester, New Hampshire. They insisted on an April 1 transition to the ten-hour system despite the disillusioning impact of the defeat in New Bedford and the lack of preparation among day laborers for a strike. The division between skilled and unskilled, aggravated by the corporations' policy of applying wage reductions selectively against the unskilled, left the spinners isolated. In most mills employers locked them out before they had a chance to strike. In all mills the April 1 movement lost decisively. A few employers unexpectedly began ten-hour experiments that spring, but in late 1868 the Lowell corporations set a uniform sixty-six-hour week, which became the standard for the industry outside Fall River.[13]

It is difficult to imagine whether Massachusetts organizers and workers who failed on both the political and strike fronts felt the sting of the 1867 defeats most sharply, or whether their counterparts in states where legislative victories only revealed labor's inability to enforce the law suffered most. Indeed the whole question of what organizers, let alone the rank and file, saw as the goal of eight-hour legislation is vexed. Ira Steward, for example, advocated an assortment of laws at various times during his career: laws to fine offending firms, laws applying only to chartered corporations, laws denying patents to offenders, laws setting an example by placing government workers on the eight-hour day, local laws, state laws, and national laws.[14] William Sylvis likewise took a range of positions on what kind of legislation was required. In Illinois the Eight-Hour League was explicit in calling for a law that provided penalties for chartered corporations violating the eight-hour standard and set eight hours as a legal day's work in other jobs where no special contracts existed. Yet the eight-hour advocates rejoiced in the passage of a different law with no enforcement provisions.[15] The issue of whether or not an eight-hour day dictated a commensurate cut in pay further complicated matters.

Part of the vagary surrounding labor's goals in legislation on hours was studied and unavoidable. As Steward realized, the movement required victories and, above all, examples of successful application of the eight-hour system. Therefore, a wide variety of "experimental" legislation could be supported according to prospects for success. The failure to broach the issue of wages likewise had a pragmatic edge because the eight-hour forces included skilled workers, whose savings might allow them to withstand a short period of reduced earnings in exchange for the eight-hour day, as well as unskilled laborers who could afford no such concession.

On the other hand, the failure to spell out the exact role of the laws reflected a real confusion over what powers the state might wield in regulating the economy. Before even the formation of Bureaus of Labor Statistics at the state level, it was difficult to conceive of how workplaces might be policed and labor laws enforced. The position, common to the Boston *Voice*, the *Workingmen's Advocate*, the anarchist Ezra Heywood, and to most of the eight-hour movement, that enforcement of labor laws would fall to labor groups themselves, may also have led to a fatal lack of criticism for weak legislation, though it made sense in terms of labor's view of the power of the state.[16] Rather than split its constituency over practical and ideological questions, the eight-hour movement opted for a vague view that legislation of various sorts was a step toward the shorter day.

Thus it mattered little, at first, to Pennsylvania miners that the law passed by their state legislators in April 1868 contained virtually the same loopholes as the Pennsylvania ten-hour statute of 1848. Rather than debating the fine points of law, the anthracite miners in the Schuylkill County area built the Workingmen's Benevolent Association from an organization of twenty persons in January 1868 to a striking force of thousands in July of that year, as they tried to make July 1 the effective date of the new legislation, coincide with the real inauguration of the eight-hour system.[17] When the miners near Mahanoy City asked management, during a mid-June lunch hour, whether the eight-hour day would apply in local mines, the response sparked a wave of protest that one report called a "general strike" and another termed a "revolution." Receiving no satisfactory answer, the miners quit work and moved to the next mine and the next.[18]

The strike wave tramped from colliery to colliery gaining numbers and momentum as it went. According to the 1872-1873 Pennsylvania labor report, the work stoppage enlisted the loyalty of "nearly the whole working population of the [Mahanoy] Valley." Leaders divided the county into districts and sent squads to spread the strike into each. By early July every Schuylkill County mine was at a standstill and the strike committee turned its attention to mollifying residents who complained of thefts by the tramping miners. A rally at Mahanoy City, designed to show public support for the strike attracted as many as 20,000, remarkable in a far-flung county with a population of but 110,000.[19] The employers held out for months maintaining, as did *Hunt's Merchant's Magazine* in its discussion of the strike, that "compliance with this demand is out of the question." An attempt to extend the strike far to the northeast failed to attract support in the Pittston, Pennsylvania area. By September 1 the men returned to work. The long strike resulted in a huge increase of membership for the Workingmen's Benevolent Association. It gave the participants a feeling "that a great thing had been achieved by the gathering of all the different nationalities and clans together."[20] But it disappointed those who hoped that eight hours would become an actual, as well as a "legal," day's work.

In Illinois, where the nation's first state eight-hour law passed in March 1867, the scenario of legislation, exaltation, conflict, and defeat occurred even earlier than in Pennsylvania. Illinois's organized workers, particularly in Chicago, rejoiced at the passing of the state law with perhaps greater enthusiasm than their counterparts in Pennsylvania because, unlike the miners to the east, they had fought a long political battle to secure the legislation. The city's ward-based Eight-Hour Leagues petitioned and electioneered at the city, county, state, and federal levels for shorter-hours laws from 1865 through 1867. Led by the Scottish immigrant Andrew C. Cameron, editor of the *Workingman's Advocate*, they secured pledges to support local legislation applying to city employees from a third of the alderman elected in 1866. Despite the opposition of Mayor John B. Rice, the eight-hour advocates won a municipal law setting the hours of city employees at eight in 1866. Largely through pressure from highly unionized Chicago, the Illinois legislature approved a statute providing for the eight-hour day in "cases of labor or service by the days, except in farm employments." The law neither forbade special contracts nor banned long schedules based on hourly pay. Nonetheless, the eight-hour day, what the *Workingman's Advocate* called "the millennium toward which the workingman is looking," was to take legal effect on May 1, 1867.[21]

Neither capital nor labor saw the May 1 transition as a foregone conclusion. Over seventy employers banded together in an organization designed to forestall application of the law. Workers, especially skilled workers organized in the Illinois State Workingmen's Convention, also agitated around the issue. On March 30 they held a mass meeting in Chicago to "ratify" the new law. Republican politicians Governor Richard Ogelsby and Attorney General Robert Ingersoll attended and expressed support, with Ingersoll calling for a still shorter day. Individual unions met to set up new wage scales in accordance with the eight-hour schedule. Following the pattern set by the Machinists' and Blacksmiths' Union, most of the craft unions voted to accept reductions in pay in exchange for the shorter day.[22]

On May 1, forty-four different unions cooperated in a massive parade from the Back of the Yards on the South Side to the downtown Lake Michigan area. The procession featured floats, bands, and as many as 10,000 marchers. Mayor Rice addressed the crowd to encourage moderation and compromise, but speeches by Richard Trevellick and by local labor leaders urged insistence on strict adherence to the eight-hour day.[23] On the following day strikes in carshops, freight depots, planing mills, lumber yards, packing houses, rolling mills, machine shops, and iron molding plants paralyzed the city. In Bridgeport, an Irish working-class enclave, the work stoppage was general and at the massive McCormick reaper works, employees simply walked out after eight hours of labor. Ship carpenters quickly won the eight-hour day, as did some workers in other crafts. Crowds of eight-hour supporters in Bridgeport undertook to spread the strike by roving the city, closing down plants, and menacing strikebreakers. Antilabor papers, including the Chicago *Tribune* and New York *Times*, made much of the "riotous" behavior of the crowds, especially after May 4 when the "mob" swelled to 5,000 and battled with police. Although instances of violence were rare and minor, the press and Mayor Rice stressed law and order in justifying their opposition to the strike.[24]

The mayor did not even wait for the May 4 events to issue a stern proclamation against any protest designed to interfere with the work of non-strikers. With the city under near martial law, the eight-hour movement lost force. Strikebreakers replaced the eight-hour men at freight depots by May 5, and after a week the strikes in other industries weakened. By June only a few scattered trades persisted, and within weeks even the strongly organized ship carpenters and caulkers were back on the longer day. On March 7, 1868, the *Workingman's Advocate* reprinted an "Eight-Hour Song" possibly written months earlier. Its lyrics must have rung hollow to Chicago's workers who recalled the law of 1867:

We must rally for the fight,
Stand for justice and for right,
Till the law for work be made eight hours a day.[25]

The entire eight-hour movement felt the adverse impact of the precedent set by Illinois. A small wave of strikes and protests in Missouri, when that state's eight-hour law took effect in May 1867, paralleled the events in Chicago in time but never gained much strength except among bricklayers, whose struggle was also unsuccessful.[26] In Wisconsin the eight-hour law applied after July 4, 1867 but trade unionists there, especially the Machinists' and Blacksmiths' Union, decided not to press the issue aside from having a small parade in Milwaukee. Nor was the 1867 eight-hour law in Connecticut more productive of change.

According to the first report of that state's Bureau of Labor Statistics, the 1867 statute "had no particular effect upon previously existing relations."[27]

Labor leaders also had two other ambiguous examples to which to react during 1867 and 1868 in assessing the usefulness of state intervention regarding labor hours. The New York statute of 1867 was part of a process that led to the establishment of the eight-hour day for some craftsmen, but the small size of the gains and the role played by trade union pressure rather than the law in securing them, assured that few would conclude that such legislation per se was of great value. To those who still hoped, as Andrew Cameron did, that "the sanction of our national legislature" would accomplish what state laws had failed to do, the second example proved more troubling.[28] Not only did the 1868 federal eight-hour law for manual laborers in the national government's employ fail to generate imitation among employers in the private sector, it also gave rise to a series of problems regarding enforcement and wages.

From the first days of the New York City Workingmen's Union during the Civil War, New York witnessed strong political pressure based among trade unionists in support of an eight-hour law. From March 1866 the trade unionists also showed an awareness of the strike as a weapon for influencing government policy and for forcing accession from individual employers. As discussed above, the defeat of eight-hour legislation in 1866 came despite the threat of a statewide general strike, and preceded a long but unsuccessful strike of from 4,000 to 10,000 ship carpenters and caulkers in New York City. Like the shipwrights, Brooklyn ropemakers struck in 1866 to demand shorter hours in the absence of legislation, seeking a ten-hour day rather than the eleven to thirteen hours they had worked. A planned general strike in the building trades was also rumored.[29]

The labor activities of 1866 helped to alert Democrats to the depth of feeling regarding hours. In 1867, as Radical Republican legislators split on the issue, increasing numbers of New York Democrats rallied behind the eight-hour bill. Patrick Keady, a Brooklyn Democrat who formerly headed the New York Practical Painters' Association, introduced the measure in the state assembly. On March 27 the lower House accepted a version of the law which exempted farm labor and allowed contracts to contravene the eight-hour standard. In the Senate the bill seemed destined to die in committee until the legislature received both a new round of eight-hour petitions and news of renewed threats of massive strikes in New York City. As the strikes materialized among journeymen in April, the Senate overwhelmingly passed the eight-hour bill. However, New York's governor did not sign the law until May 9, although it was to go into effect on May 1.[30]

The delay in the signing of the bill enabled organized labor in New York to ponder the defeat of the Illinois trade unionists whose protests in early May had failed to enforce an eight-hour law. The conclusion of the New Yorkers was that tight organization would be necessary to make the law work. Meeting in June, the State Workingmen's Assembly counseled against "extreme measures" and suggested November 1, 1867, as a realistic target date. The delegates hoped that the legislature would add to the law by making the eight-hour standard binding for all unionized workers in chartered corporations. In October a delegation of workingmen urged that if no additions were to be made to the law, that the governor might at least issue a proclamation calling public attention to the unobserved statute. The governor declined and the trade unionists, who allowed the November deadline to pass, girded for a renewed struggle.[31]

With the possible exception of a strike in the New York City shipyards, eight-hour advocates concentrated on legislative action during 1867. Seeing no results, unionized crafts in the building trades returned to the tactic of work stoppages in 1868. In March New York City painters won the eight-hour day in union contracts, as did plasterers shortly thereafter. For most of the summer a fourteen-week strike idled the city's bricklayers. Backed by large contributions from the plasterers and from tradesmen in other cities, 1,800 of the bricklayers succeeded in winning the eight-hour day with a 10 percent wage cut.[32] Although even the bricklayers' strike was only a partial success and the number of workers benefiting from the new schedule represented a small proportion of New York's wage earners, the gains of 1868 engendered a different attitude in New York than in the other states. The Building Trades Leagues, which took form in New York City during the year, indicated the renewed confidence of many craftsmen that, whatever the failings of the law, shorter hours could be secured by trade union pressure and by solidarity among various crafts.[33]

If the lesson of the several states, and especially of Illinois and New York, was that eight-hour laws mattered little unless backed by trade union pressure, the protracted disillusionment with federal eight-hour legislation further discredited the idea that a legislative solution to long working hours was possible. The disillusionment also helped sour the faith in political action of a generation of young militants, many of whom would later be active in the American Federation of Labor. The federal eight-hour law of 1868 was the first victory in Congress in the realm of social legislation governing the workplace and the first object lesson in how that legislation could be emasculated by courts and federal agencies.

Congressional response to the agitation of the National Labor Union and the Eight-Hour Leagues for a federal law providing the eight-hour day for its federal employees came with surprising speed. Although such legislation came before Congress in 1865, the 1867 sessions saw the first sustained and serious debate on the proposals. During March of that year Congressman Ebon Ingersoll of Illinois introduced a measure that would have made eight hours a legal working day in the District of Columbia. That bill died for lack of quorum, but later in the month Nathaniel P. Banks, a Radical representative from Massachusetts and an ex-shoemaker, called up a proposed statute that provided an eight-hour day to federal employees in manual jobs. (Federal office workers already labored on such a schedule for six months of the year.) Banks's proposal, which had first been submitted to the Senate by George Julian, an Indiana Radical Republican, passed the House by a voice vote but stalled in the Senate where an 18 to 17 vote sent it to die in the Committee on Finance.[34] A barrage of pressure from labor groups kept the issue before Congress. The NLU, meeting in Chicago, undertook a national petition drive in October 1867. When the forms reached the Senate the following spring, they included thousands of names. New York, led by labor organizer William Jessup who advised Julian on the issue, presented a petition with 2,713 names. The NLU also sent delegations to President Andrew Johnson, who reportedly promised to establish the eight-hour day for government workers by executive order if Congress failed to act in 1868.[35] Workers in the District of Columbia engaged in a series of protests to dramatize labor support for the law. And from California, a state where trade unions representing ship caulkers, plumbers, and gas fitters had enforced the eight-hour standard in a labor-scarce economy, came a mammoth petition with nearly 5,000 signatures. The California agitation reflected the leadership of the Mechanics' State Council and the House Carpenters' Eight-Hour League and helped to cause John Conness, a Republican senator, to assume a prominent role in renewing the congressional debate over hours.[36]

Reintroduced by Banks in 1868, Julian's bill might have sailed through both houses were it not for a manuever by John Sherman, a conservative Republican senator from Ohio. After the measure cleared the House by a voice vote, Sherman attached an amendment to the Senate version. The amendment, which specified that "the rate of wages paid by the United States shall be the current rate for the same labor *for the same time* at the place of employment," would have brought a 20 percent wage reduction along with the eight-hour day. Many legislators supporting the Julian bill argued for it as a means to alleviate unemployment in the navy yards during the 1867-1868 recession by spreading the work. Sherman's amendment offered these senators an opportunity to appear as both foes of unemployment and economizers by backing eight hours *and* a pay cut. The amendment forced supporters of the original Julian bill to take a frankly prolabor stance, and it undercut labor support by raising the possibility of the substantial reduction of pay among both skilled and unskilled workers in the government yards. Sherman's amendment failed by a twenty-one to sixteen vote in which a coalition of Radical Republicans, Democrats, and Johnson conservatives prevailed over a largely Republican opposition. The Julian bill then passed by more than a two-to-one margin.[37] In each vote the decisive factor was the abstention of nineteen senators, some of whom spoke against the bill. A defeated Sherman attempted a parting shot by offering a final sardonic proposal: "The title of the bill ought to be changed, it seems to me, to read: A bill to give Government employees twenty-five percent more wages than employees in private establishments receive."[38]

Labor's triumph seemed remarkably complete. The language of the law, which pronounced its application to "all laborers, workmen and mechanics . . . employed by or on behalf of the government of the United States," implied broad coverage of not only direct employees of the government but also of those working for private business contracting with the United States. Sherman's forcing of the issue of wages had also backfired to the apparent benefit of labor. Without his intervention, the issue of pay reductions would have gone unresolved and much might have been made of Banks's statement by advocates of a pay cut during the House debates that wages would still vary with those in private yards. The failure of Sherman's amendment provided strong evidence that the intention of the Senate was not to reduce the wages of those covered by the law, however.[39]

Nonetheless, labor realized few benefits from the federal eight-hour law. Almost from the beginning, the War Department allowed arsenals to enforce a 20 percent pay reduction for day laborers securing the two-hour cut in the working day. Management at the Springfield Armory, satisfied that workers labored "harder and more faithfully" under the new system, paid the ten-hour wage rate for a month before slashing day laborers' wages.[40] Protests by Springfield armorers and a strike by workmen at the arsenal at Rock Island brought the issue before President Johnson. The president referred the matter to his attorney general, who ruled that the wartime law of 1862 still applied and linked government wages to those in private industry. The ruling raised the same threats as the Sherman amendment and robbed the eight-hour law of its appeal as a standard to be emulated by workers in all industries. Eventually President Ulysses S. Grant, under pressure from the NLU, issued an order mandating a interpretation of the law for favorable to labor on May 19, 1869, but the edict was at best irregularly enforced.[41]

In response to the poor enforcement, President Grant repeated the exact executive order of 1869 again in the election year of 1872. During that same year an attempt to repeal the federal eight-hour law failed, and Congress even voted an appropriation for retroactive pay to those workers who had lost wages because President Grant's 1869 order had been ignored. But defeat again followed seeming victory. When Ralph Ordway, a quarry owner in the Richmond, Virginia, area, maintained the ten-hour day among stonecutters producing granite for which the federal government had contracted, the quarrymen asked for Nathaniel Banks's intervention. The attorney general issued an opinion in response to Banks's plea, but his decision was that the eight-hour law did not apply to work on government contracts. In 1877, when the Supreme Court finally ruled, it unanimously supported the attorney general's stance. In so doing, the court solidified an 1869 decision that the law did not apply to laborers constructing the New York Post Office.[42] Most seriously, in the 1876 case of the *United States v. Martin*, the high court rendered the entire law an exercise in voluntarism by finding against a laborer who claimed back pay for extra hours worked in the Naval Academy's boiler room. According to Justice Ware Hunt, the eight-hour law applied only "when no special agreement was made upon the subject." By the 1880s both the chairman of the House Committee on Education and Labor and the pioneer labor historian, Richard Ely, agreed that the federal eight-hour law was a "dead letter."[43]

The defeats of 1867 and 1868 are sometimes presented as a prologue to the emergence of "greenback" currency reform as the major plank in the platform of labor organizations. The strength of such a view is that it accounts well for the timing of ideological changes within the NLU. While early NLU conventions had dwelled long on the eight-hour demand, that of 1867 featured the brief admission that while "Eight Hour laws have been passed by the legislatures of six states, . . . for all practical purposes they might as well have never been placed on the statute books, and can only be described as frauds on the labouring class." Those conventions held after 1868 relegated the issue to a small niche. Currency reform came to dominate the proceedings and to engage the sympathies of such labor leaders as William Sylvis and Richard Trevellick.[44] However, focus on greenbackism as the dominant trend in labor reform after 1868 can mislead. Alongside the currency reformers there existed another tendency that favored concentration on class demands, and specifically on hours, despite the failures of 1867 and 1868. Those who opted for such a priority came primarily from three overlapping sources: young, largely immigrant trade union leaders; the Marxist sections of the International Workingmen's Association (IWA); and the followers of Ira Steward. These three groups shared a distrust of greenbackism, a hesitancy to rush into independent labor politics, and a commitment to eight hours.

Steward's forces centered in Boston where their attempts to make the New England Labor Reform League adhere to eight hours as the centerpiece of its program failed when that organization embraced greenbackism in 1869. Steward, who seceded and formed the Boston Eight-Hour League in response, distrusted currency reform and any quick move into politics, although he kept alive some efforts to influence the course of the Massachusetts Labor Reform party.[45] Increasingly disenchanted with Republicanism, Steward hoped that workers could organize directly around the eight-hour demand, which his group still considered "the most important measure ever proposed on behalf of labor." Practically an adjunct to the Eight-Hour League was the Massachusetts Bureau of Labor Statistics, the first such state agency, founded in 1869 largely as the result of labor pressure. Henry K. Oliver, first director of the bureau, sympathized with the goals of Steward. In fact, Oliver's coworkers, George McNeill and Mary Steward, were Eight-Hour League members. Early reports focused squarely on hours. The overall strategy of the Stewardites was to lessen efforts at electoral pressure but to redouble general education around the hours issue.[46]

The IWA, founded in London in 1864, made the eight-hour day its rallying cry in several nations. There was no American section until the 1869 affiliation of Section One in New York City, but sympathizing groups like the Community Club and the General German Workingmen's Association had existed since the Civil War. These groups, in which the followers of Ferdinand Lassalle were strong, stressed cooperatives, currency reform, and political rather than trade union action. However, after 1868, when the Social party, backed by the General German Workingmen's Association, fared disastrously in New York City elections, the socialists—like the Stewardites—pulled back into a period of slower educational work. In the wake of the Social party's defeat, Marxist ideas, including an emphasis on trade unionism and the eight-hour day, gained respect inside the IWA, and leading members, such as F. A. Sorge, expressed admiration for the work of Steward as an alternative to the stance of the NLU. Although the *Arbeiter Union*, press of the German emigre socialists, continued to uphold greenback doctrines, it also included a generous sampling of eight-hour propaganda in 1868 and 1869.[47]

Receptive to the arguments of the Marxists in the IWA were young labor organizers, especially immigrants from the New York City area. The IWA-supported Economic and Sociological Club provided a forum in which socialists and trade unionists met to study Marxism and the doctrines of Steward. The participants in these sessions included such important figures as Sorge, Adolph Strasser, Peter J. McGuire, Robert Blissert, J. P. McDonnell, David Kronberg, and Samuel Gompers, whose early career was crucially shaped by eight-hour activities. For Gompers and most of the other young organizers, some of whom actually joined socialist groups and some of whom did not, the polemic of Marxists against Lassallean socialists had a special impact in that the Marxists asserted the tactical primacy of building strong unions.[48]

Other union organizers also persisted in the struggle for a shorter working day. In New York City, William Jessup, head of the New York Workingmen's Assembly, and for a time a Greenbacker, became the leading figure among craft unionists who kept up the eight-hour fight. Many labor reformers continued to hold that the eight-hour day was the "legal" standard in states having legislated on the subject and urged election of officials who would enforce the statute while emphasizing the ultimate necessity of unions for enforcement purposes.[49] In more remote areas, newly organized unions were also beginning to raise the eight-hour demand. The coalition of Stewardites, socialists, and union organizers did not blossom at once, but in various combinations and various locales the groups began to work singly and together. Rather than seeing the defeats of 1867 and 1868 as an end, they reoriented toward educational activities and trade union tactics and began anew.

With the coming of the 1870s, the movement for a shorter working day rebounded from the defeats of 1867 and 1868. In 1870 and 1871 Eight-Hour Leagues in several locals revived as the NLU weakened. By 1872 and 1873 the eight-hour movement was again cresting and involving tens of thousands of workers. The renascent agitation took many forms including the lobbying of the Boston Eight-Hour League and the political campaigning of the Equal Rights party. The latter organization, a split from the International Workingmen's Association, ran the woman's rights and free-love advocate Victoria Woodhull for president, in 1872, on a platform that featured an eight-hour plank. Trade union activities loomed large. In 1872 eight-hour strikes, many of them successful, occurred in scores of cities, including Philadelphia, Buffalo, Chicago, Jersey City and Albany. In Rhode Island the textile centers of Woonsocket and Pawtucket saw strikes, as did the Olneyville section of Providence where Irish-American women led a militant walkout and organized ten-hour picnics and parades after the strike's failure.[50] The most dramatic of these many struggles were a series of strikes and demonstrations in New York City, where the cooperation of the Marxists and trade unionists built a huge and effective movement; and the "Sawdust Wars," in which Saginaw Valley, Michigan, Jacksonville, Florida, and Lycoming County, Pennsylvania, sawmill owners clashed with their workers in the kind of direct confrontation that would increasingly characterize eight-hour campaigns.

In New York, where an 1870 state law supplemented the 1868 eight-hour statute by providing an eight-hour day for state employees, trade unionists joined socialists and followers of Steward in leading solidarity actions with eight-hour strikes among stonecutters. They also sponsored an 1871 parade to kick off a drive to demand compliance with the laws. A crowd of 20,000 or 25,000 marched in the rain during the September demonstration. A contingent of black workers and a group of 200 members of the IWA attracted press attention as did a painters' union float carrying the slogan "Peacefully if we can, forcibly if we Must. When peaceful efforts fail, then the Revolution."[51]

The next year New York City workers struck for eight hours. Taking their cue from the Brooklyn house painters who walked out in April, other building tradesmen in New York left their jobs, some of them for months. The mass strike ultimately involved some 100,000 workers and featured eight-hour rallies throughout the spring. Leadership came from both branches of the IWA, from the various German and English unions and, most importantly, from Steward's followers, organized in the North American Eight Hour League. Related crafts cooperated in such bodies as the Building Trades League, Furniture Workers' Eight Hour League, and Metal Workers' Eight Hour League—three organizations which counted 21,400 members. By early June the building tradesmen had nearly all won their demand. Later that month a New York *Sun* account estimated that 60,000 of 95,000 strikers had secured the eight-hour day. According to some accounts, victory parades drew 150,000. But the furniture workers and metal workers failed to prevail. The strength of their strikes waned, especially after Theodore Banks, a painter in the anti-Marxist faction of the IWA, issued a June 5 letter urging arson if strike demands were not met. In the backlash that followed, some unionists distanced themselves from cooperation with the IWA.[52]

Some of the gains of summer disappeared by fall, but the eight-hour movement again went on the offensive in April 1873. The IWA, whose Federal Council convened a meeting of fifteen representative unions which formed the Eight-Hour Enforcement League, played a role in the renewed agitation, but a strike among the city's gas workers focused all eyes on the issue. Some gas men, whose social power to leave a city in darkness and whose skill in relatively dangerous jobs had made them a militant and independent section of the labor force in several nations, had briefly won the eight-hour day in 1872 but saw their hours increase in 1873.[53] Because the works ran around the clock, they moved from three shifts to just two, thereby raising hours from eight per day to twelve. The New York *Times*, generally unsympathetic to labor reform of the period, found some justice in the gas men's complaints because of the large increase in hours and because "these men are employed in an atmosphere that is in the highest degree unwholesome, and are compelled to work in a temperature that is almost intolerable." Such considerations, and the bad reputation of the gas companies regarding rates, ensured that the gas workers could command substantial community support.[54]

On April 5 the gas strike began at New York Gas-Light Company, which lit the city from Grand Street to the Battery. Shortly thereafter, strikers gained some support among workers at the Manhattan Company. The strike committee demanded the eight-hour law be enforced and called for the state legislature to provide for municipalization of the offending utilities.[55] Besides dramatically reversing the old formula of legislate first, strike later, this strategy brought the issue before the community. Support came not only from trade union groups— including the pianomakers, tailors, wood carvers and the State Workingmen's Assembly—but from citizens' groups attacking the gas monopoly. Early days of the strike produced solidarity meetings and gatherings aimed at a municipal take-over of the works. Several of these protests were sponsored by the IWA and by the Citizens' Anti-Monopoly Association.[56] The strike emboldened Brooklyn carpenters and building tradesmen at one New York City firm to imitate the gas men's example. Wood carvers and streetcar conductors in the city, and painters in Brooklyn also planned job actions in pursuit of an eight-hour day.[57] After New York City headlines shrieked, "HALF THE CITY IN GLOOM," after their columns told of police battling to control crowds of hundreds outside the gas works, after New York faced a transit strike in addition to the gas strike, and after the very clock mounted in City Hall lost its illumination, the gas men's actions gradually subsided.[58] The strike fell for two reasons. Importation of foreign workmen, in some cases directly from the immigration holdover, enabled the companies to get through the first days of the strike. However, these inexperienced workmen, laboring in separate Swiss, Italian, and German gangs, produced poorly. One account estimated their efficiency to be a quarter of that of the regular workers. What ultimately saved the corporations was that the Metropolitan and the Mutual Gas Works failed to join the strike and not only produced extra gas but also loaned skilled workers to the struck enterprises. In accounting for the loyalty of the gas men at the plants not striking, it is worth noting that the press described the Mutual Works as an "open" factory. That is, employees could come and go at will, leaving briefly during lulls in labor. Such preindustrial practices, fast disappearing in American gas works of the period, may have muted the hours issue.[59] In any case, by April 18 it was clear that no serious gas shortage would occur, and shortly thereafter the strike ended in defeat. As the strike waned, the Eight-Hour Enforcement League called for a national council to unite the movements in New York, Chicago, Boston, and elsewhere, promising that ten days of national protest would ensure the eight-hour day.[60] However, by this time the defeat of the gas men and a deepening depression combined to discourage further agitation.

The sobriquet "Sawdust War" is usually reserved for the long 1872 strike in Lycoming County, Pennsylvania, lumber mills, but it applies as well to the bitter sawmill strikes in Jacksonville, Florida, and Saginaw Valley, Michigan, during the same period. Although the strikes were not connected in terms of organization, they all reflected conditions in an industry in which capitalization and use of new machinery was accelerating rapidly. Seasonal unemployment and high labor turnover among a work force with a high percentage of blacks and immigrants further characterized the industry.[61]

The Jacksonville sawyers worked from 6 A.M. until "near sunset" in spring and summer when they demanded the ten-hour day in May 1873. The strike at several area mills concentrated on improving the conditions of black day laborers by cutting hours and raising daily wages to fifty cents. Jacksonville's Labor League, a black strike support group, aided the laborers. However, white workers scabbed on the strike with police protection. After a month, the strike ended with militants drifting into new jobs. No gains were made, but the black laborers apparently had found sympathy in the community. Seven of the strikers won acquittal on charges of attacking the home of a strikebreaker when a largely black jury returned a "not guilty" verdict despite the fact that the defense did not contest the prosecution's evidence.[62]

Both the Northern lumber strikes centered around Independence Day 1872. In the Saginaw area, strike rumors circulated after mid-June throughout a valley with over fifty mills, none of them unionized. On June 28, mill hands met and set July 5 as the date on which the ten-hour system was to take effect. From the first days of July, production dwindled and by the target date a strike paralyzed virtually all the mills in Bay City, Saginaw City, East Saginaw, and Zilwaukee. As it did repeatedly throughout the nineteenth century, the shorter-hours demand proved an organizing tool among workers who previously had not only lacked experience with unions, but had seldom even met in a common place. At the first rally to support the strike, about a thousand sawyers gathered to hear speeches.[63]

From the start of the conflict, the gap in organization between the companies and the strikers was manifest. Although some societies of German workers existed, the mill workers were virtually without organization at the start. An aptly named "Strikers' Union" took shape at a July 3 meeting, but its meetings tended to be so chaotic that reporters complained that proceedings could hardly be summarized. The ad hoc union did attempt to distribute strike benefits and marshal support from such other local trade societies as the iron molders, but perhaps its greatest impact was in the discouragement of violence and arson. The owners, meanwhile, cooperated consummately, holding frequent public meetings to avow their mutual intention to hold out for a twelve-hour day and to express their joy that the strike came during weather in which conditions for processing lumber were in any case poor.[64] The owner of the Sage Mill expressed the resolve of the employers to fight to the finish: "The only remedy for the case is to let the whole laboring community feel the burden of the strike till there grows up in their midst a sense of folly . . . Collect your rents promptly—especially from strikers—They must not live on us while their conduct destroys us." Mill hands held out between two and three weeks before the strike was broken. Labor organizations that formed during the conflict did persist, however.[65]

The class violence that threatened in Michigan and Florida erupted throughout Lycoming County in north-central Pennsylvania. The county boasted an annual lumber production of over $5.3 million by the 1870s and had over 3,000 sawmill workers. In late June of 1872, a group calling itself the Labor Reform Union began to hold meetings in Williamsport, the county seat. Although county histories refer to the entire episode as the whipped-up creation of outside agitators who had no contact with mill work, the identified leaders of the Labor Reform Union were mainly local lumber workers and miners. However, some of the activists had moved to the area after participating in shorter-hours campaigns in other locales, including New Brunswick in Canada and nearby Schuylkill County, Pennsylvania.[66] The Labor Reform Union couched its early appeals as a defense of Pennsylvania's eight-hour law, but the group never actually demanded less then a ten-hour day. The group functioned as a trade union, maintaining strike solidarity and distributing strike benefits. At the same time, the leaders held that the most important asset of the mill workers was the fact that the "community favored the working man" and oriented their public meetings toward maintaining that support.[67]

After a pair of evening meetings to marshal support, the Labor Reform Union launched a strike on July 1. Upon hearing speeches at Market Square, the ten-hour supporters formed into what one local historian called a "monster parade" and moved as a roving picket line to shut down open mills working the twelve-hour day. Black laborers led the procession, which carried banners proclaiming:

Ten Hours at the Present Wages,
Our demands are Reasonable -
Our Cause is Just,
Workingmen Should Rule.

The early and implacable opposition of Mayor S. W. Starkweather to the strike made Starkweather one target of the last of the slogans. Starkweather responded by issuing a July 1 proclamation closing all saloons and warning of possible violence.[68]

The Lumbermen's Exchange, the organized body of owners, vowed to suffer no more than two days of down time due to the strike, but weeks passed without a resumption in production. Nor did the owners present a solid front. Some mills accepted the ten-hour day and one politically active employer gave support to the strikers. One mill published figures showing a 9 percent *increase* in production after changing to the shorter day.[69] The job action also spread to Watsontown and nearby Lock Haven, where over 300 men walked out and two mills quickly acceded to the ten-hour day. Solidarity messages and money came from Philadelphia and elsewhere. A labor ball—the *Gazette and Bulletin* called it a "carnival of pleasure"—at a German hall raised cash for strike benefits. Leaders reacted to the mayor's proclamations regarding threats to civic order by praising the behavior of the labor militia, which kept order during marches and by reiterating that the sawyers were winning the ten-hour day in an orderly manner. Local butchers who donated meat to the picketers typified the substantial community support for the union. When townspeople initiated a labor store during the strike, a nearby farmer gave ten acres of wheat and five of potatoes.[70] In light of such positive developments, it is difficult to accept county historian John F. Meginness's contention that the violence that erupted after July 20 resulted from a plot by leaders of the Labor Reform Union who feared that a back-to-work movement was afoot. During the days before the rioting, two changes took place. The mayor, continuing to brand the strike as dangerous, deputized scores of strike opponents as special police. Meanwhile, the Lumbermen's Exchange began recruiting strikebreakers from outside the area.[71] By July 20 a showdown was imminent. That Saturday the head of the Pennsylvania state labor union federation told a huge strike crowd to remember labor's role in the war and prepare for a patriotic labor parade on the following Monday. Early the next morning strike supporters gathered in a scheduled parade but also organized squads at various points along the railway line to dissuade incoming strikebreakers. After a short march, the main body of demonstrators diverged from the permitted line of march and neared Filbert and Otto's Mill. The deputized police, fearing an attack on the mill and on the strikebreakers, turned pistols on the crowd. Pandemonium ensued and, amidst a shower of brickbats, the police were overwhelmed. The crowd marched from mill to mill and ended production in each.[72]

Although the violence committed in the rioting probably consisted of less than a dozen minor injuries to deputies and strikebreakers, the mayor called in militia from surrounding cities. By the following morning troops from Harrisburg patrolled the city, and by that afternoon over 300 soldiers from seven cities kept order under an edict from Pennsylvania's Republican Governor John W. Geary. Keeping order meant arresting all leading strike supporters. Fifty-eight men were apprehended and twenty-one bound over for trial. Extremely high bail immobilized the Labor Reform Union, and within days the mills reopened under both the old schedules and military guard. The strike leaders received Geary's pardon after brief prison terms, but their release was conditional on their agreeing to leave Williamsport.[73]

By late 1873 trade union efforts to enforce a shorter working day had begun to wane throughout the country. The onset of the Long Depression, one of the most serious in American history, had decimated union strength.[74] While the shorter-hours forces still consisted of unionists, socialists, and Massachusetts eight-hour reformers of the Steward camp, the latter two groups would become more important in the depression years. The shorter-hours movement during the Long Depression did not involve nearly as many workers in active protest as during the preceding six years, but what activity did occur was vital in keeping the eight-hour idea alive going into the 1880s. The existing activity was important in forging alliances between socialists, radical trade unionists, and eight-hour reformers. At the start of the depression, trade union leaders embraced the shorter-day demand as a cure for the joblessness that threatened their organizations. Moreover, as soon as labor's bargaining position deteriorated, employers sought to lengthen the working day, especially in California and New York City, where the eight-hour day had gained currency. Both local unions and the Industrial Congress, a labor federation including delegates from five national unions, vigorously protested the extension of hours as contributing to still greater unemployment. A wave of demonstrations around the issue took place in May 1874. In San Francisco, where 10,000 rallied, in Rochester, in Columbus, in New York City, and elsewhere demonstrators supported the eight-hour system in private industry and demanded that the federal statute on hours be enforced. Such protests declined as the strength of unions ebbed and especially after the police violence against the 1874 demonstration against unemployment at Tompkins Square in New York City, but individual unions, such as the Cigarmakers' Union, continued to call for the eight-hour day.[75]

In the face of organized labor's declining power, the activities of Steward's supporters and of socialist organizations assumed larger importance. In 1873 the Stewardite labor statisticians McNeill and Oliver were removed from the Massachusetts Bureau of Labor Statistics after attacks by employers, who objected to their openly prolabor stance, and by greenback reformers, who complained that the bureau concentrated too much on the shortening of the working day. But the cumulative impact of the Bureau's painstaking documentation of long hours and child labor abuses, along with the testimony of William Gray, treasurer of the Atlantic Cotton Mills in Lawrence, moved the Massachusetts legislature to pass a ten-hour law for factory workers at its 1874 session.[76] Republican Governor William B. Washburn reflected the sentiments of the bureau and Gray in arguing that educational imperatives and the need to assimilate immigrant groups necessitated factory legislation. The governor also argued, as Boston's French section of the IWA had in a pamphlet of the previous year, that the law should not apply only to women. The House passed a bill providing a fifty dollar fine for each offense by a textile factory employing workers for more than ten hours daily. The Senate created obstacles to enforcement. Factory inspectors had to observe each plant for a week and had to prove intent in order to levy a small fine. Still, the legislation was effective by nineteenth-century standards, especially after a contingent of inspectors was set up by an 1876 law and "willfully" was stricken from the 1874 act in 1879.[77]

Socialists meanwhile stressed the eight-hour demand as both a cure for unemployment and a means to unify the working class. In November 1873 the Federal Council of the IWA drafted a manifesto on the depression, which demanded relief, a rent moratorium, and, first and foremost, an eight-hour day. The manifesto became the basis for the IWA's highly successful agitation among the unemployed in New York and also attracted the attention of thousands in Philadelphia; Camden and Newark, New Jersey; and elsewhere. The United Workers, a largely Irish group of labor organizers that affiliated with the IWA in 1875, also organized around the eight-hour issue. In 1878 and 1879, when Congress held hearings on the depression, socialists and labor radicals defended the eight-hour day in their testimony.[78]

Even the Lassallean faction of the socialist movement, which had left the IWA in 1874 to pursue more exclusively electoral strategies, accepted the eight-hour day as the central demand of the new Workingmen's party of the United States (WPUSA) when the Lassalleans, Marxists, and others again united in 1876.[79] The WPUSA, though short-lived, precipitated the first general strike in a major industrial city in the United States one year later by raising the eight-hour demand in Saint Louis during the nationwide railroad strike of 1877. The master tactical stroke of calling for a citywide work stoppage to end child labor and to establish the shorter day placed the WPUSA at the head of the general strike that shut down a city of 300,000. However, as the strike progressed, the all-white Saint Louis section of the WPUSA recoiled at the militancy of black workers while seeking to bargain with the mayor. Ultimately, the headquarters of the WPUSA came under siege by a deputized posse, and the strike ended in defeat.[80] In Chicago WPUSA leaders also spoke in favor of extending the railroad strike into a classwide struggle for shorter hours. The executive committee of the WPUSA issued a circular pinpointing eight hours and nationalization of the rails as key goals of the national strike—a stance later endorsed by a local meeting in Boston and implemented by the party in San Francisco.[81]

In response to the obvious popularity of the eight-hour demand in 1877, and to the failure of both legislation and pitched battles with police, leading Marxists within the WPUSA broke with the Lassallean leadership of that party in early 1878 and allied with Steward, McNeill, and George Gunton of the Boston Eight-Hour League to form an organization devoted to "Union and Eight Hours." The new group christened itself the International Labor Union (ILU). Although it lasted less than half a decade, the ILU was an important, conscious attempt to use the eight-hour demand to unify diverse groups of workers, including black workers. As McNeill, president of the ILU, put it, the goal was "to band together Jew, Greek, Irishman, American, English and German, all nationalities in a grand labor brotherhood." While the ILU hoped to organize trade unions among unorganized skilled workers, its chief focus was on enlisting the unskilled. Combining labor solidarity and a commitment to the radical reformation of society, it continued in some of the finest traditions of eight-hour agitation, though it probably also reflected an extreme distrust of politics born of post-Civil War experiences and, as Christopher Tomlins suggests, a hardening of trade union "voluntarism."[82]

The ILU concentrated on textile organizing, carrying the message "Shorter Hours and Higher Wages" to mills from Vermont to New Jersey. Between 1878 and 1880, operatives in many mill towns responded to depression wage cuts and ILU propaganda with strikes. Most spectacular were the walkouts at Cohoes, New York, and Fall River, Massachusetts. Many of the 5,000 Cohoes workers who struck in 1880 and won a 10 percent wage boost and a fifty-minute dinner break, joined the ILU.[83] At Fall River 5,000 workers had enlisted in the union at the height of the great 1878-1879 strike for a nine-hour day and restoration of a 15 percent wage cut. Over 100 strike supporters, mostly spinners, suffered arrest as the conflict dragged on for over three months. Despite a solidarity parade attended by 25,000, the demands did not carry. After rapid early growth—the ILU attracted nearly 8,000 members in thirteen states during its first year—the ILU declined rapidly in response to a series of setbacks in strikes at Fall River and elsewhere. By 1883 the ILU had ceased to exist outside Sorge's hometown of Hoboken, New Jersey.[84] Nonetheless, the organization was important not only in the struggle for a shorter working day, but in American labor history generally. Its strategy of emphasizing trade unionism reflected the lessons taught by the failure of hours legislation during Reconstruction. Its composition reflected the willingness of eight-hour reformers, union organizers, and Marxists to cooperate on the basis of a common belief in the significance of shorter hours. Its leading members and its ideas would play a vital role in the Knights of Labor, and especially in the American Federation of Labor and in the struggles of the next decades. As Kenneth Fones-Wolf has recently written:

When asked what labor wanted in the 1890s, Gompers could quickly answer—eight hours. Because of Steward and McNeill, the AFL president recognized it to be a vital first step toward reaching an American working class goal that would guarantee the worker the full product of his labor. If trade unionists felt the eight-hour workday so crucial for achieving working-class unity, it was Steward and McNeill who made it so. And it was in the ILU that Steward and McNeill firmly entrenched this traditional American issue in the thought of the heirs of Marxist trade unionism.[85]

7

Haymarket and Its Context

Albert Parsons. August Spies. Adolph Fischer. George Engel. Michael Schwab. Samuel Fielden. Oscar Neebe. Louis Lingg. The names of the victims of the governmental violence which took place after a bomb exploded in Chicago's Haymarket Square during the unprecedented strike wave of May 1886 deserve pride of place in any account of the movement for a shorter working day during the 1880s. But the very nature of the Haymarket events, with all the excitement and heroism that surround them, has somewhat overshadowed other important considerations in understanding the period and Haymarket itself. This chapter describes Haymarket and its relationship to a continuing tradition of class struggle over hours, to the interaction between skilled and unskilled workers, to ethnic interplay in the labor movement, and to the development of new organizational forms.

One point is certain: Working hours remained long throughout the early 1880s. The most complete figures, covering 552 establishments in forty industries and twenty-eight states, date from 1883 and indicate that the mean working day was still over ten hours, including Saturdays. By that year a ten-hour, six-day week had become the norm in most of the surveyed industries, but glaring exceptions to this schedule persisted.[1]

When European socialists Edward Aveling and Eleanor Marx-Aveling toured the United States in 1886, they collected data showing that street railway drivers and bakers in various locales labored more than fifteen hours daily. Complaints concerning "shaving" of time by employers arose regularly, especially in textile mills, where, operatives complained, the manipulation of clocks often added twenty to thirty minutes to the agreed-upon working day. Despite laws passed in nineteen states, women and child laborers continued to bear the brunt of the taxing workloads. One Connecticut report showed that one woman in five and one child in three working in cotton factories stayed more than ten hours per shift, while just one man in eight did so. Numerous state labor commissions, from New York to Kansas, polled workers concerning hours throughout the decade and found a nearly unanimous sentiment in favor of a reduction.[2]

Three elements brought urgency and complexity to the struggle over the working day in the 1880s. The problems of high unemployment and intensified labor posed the issue of hours forcefully while mounting immigration raised new problems and opportunities for the shorter-hours movement. Although most arguments for less labor followed Steward's theories concerning increased consumption as a result of a greater leisure, the simpler notion that a reduction of hours spread jobs became popular.[3] The economy failed to enjoy four good years between the Long Depression of 1873 to 1879 and the renewed slump of the mid-1880s. Unemployment rates neared 13 percent in 1884 and 1885.[4] A substantial population of "tramping poor" developed, an itinerant mass of tens of thousands of chronically unemployed workers. These "tramps" were a troubling phenomenon, which politicians, trade unionists, and businessmen could not ignore.[5] While the Knights of Labor and the Federation of Organized Trades and Labor Unions explicitly linked their eight-hour calls with society's desire to ease joblessness, anarcho-syndicalists headed leaflets "To Tramps" and promised that a just society would employ all, but for only two to four hours per day.[6]

Those working complained that jobs became harder. What one state labor commission described as the "hurry and push" system came to numerous industries as workers used words like "grinding" and "driving" to describe the pace prevailing in workshops and factories, especially after the introduction of steam power and new machinery. Ironically, some of the speedup in textile factories appears to have been inspired by a desire to increase production after the institution of rather effective ten-hour legislation.[7] In certain large industries, including iron and steel, mining, and tool and die production, workers retained a good deal of autonomy even as technology changed; in other industries, subdivision of labor lent truth to the bleak observations of Episcopal clergyman R. Heber Newton, who told the 1883 Senate hearings on labor and capital that the American worker suffered alienation because he "makes nothing" and "is reduced to being the tender of a steel automaton."[8] Intense, alienated labor often brought an intense desire to lessen that labor.

Rising waves of immigration, especially from French Canada, China, and East Europe, had a multifaceted impact on the shorter-hours movement. The immigrants, especially those from cultures different from the Anglo-Saxon mainstream, often drew criticism from organized labor because they were said not only to depress wages but also to enable employers to maintain or extend hours. In California, for example, labor and radical groups consistently subordinated the eight-hour demand to laws curbing oriental immigration on the racist theory that the Chinese, not the employers, constituted the gravest threat to existing working conditions.[9] French-Canadians received the blame for defeating the New England textile strikes led by the ILU resulting in a labor outcry which found expression in the 1881 report of the Massachusetts Bureau of Labor Statistics:

The third objection to ten hours is the presence of the Canadian French. Wherever they appear, their presence is urged as a reason why the hours of labor should not be reduced to ten . . . the Canadian French are the Chinese of the Eastern States . . . a horde of industrial invaders . . . not a stream of stable settlers . . . . All they ask is to be set to work, and they care little who rules them or how they are ruled.

As provocative recent works by Alexander Saxton, Gwen Mink, and Herbert Hill have shown, such early 1880s immigrant-bashings set precedents that would much favor the long-term development of conservatism and craft organization in the U.S. labor movement, aiding leaders most willing to ask much from the state in terms of immigration restriction and little in terms of labor reform, including shorter-hours legislation. It might also be added that the legislative prospects of such racist planks as Chinese exclusion had already, by the early 1880s, proven to be much better than those of effective labor reform.[10]

Despite such political division, many of the hours strikes discussed in this chapter managed to forge impressive ethnic unity and drew critically on immigrant experiences. While some immigrants from a preindustrial past expressed longings for a shorter working day by taking off to fish, hunt, or drink, many also participated in organized protests designed to cut hours.[11] The immigrant's knowledge that the working day was not a preordained length only served to sharpen his or her willingness to struggle over hours. Workers from Britain often reported that the day was substantially longer in the United States despite the fact that work was far more arduous.[12] Similarly, Michael Schwab, a German-born Haymarket martyr, described a variety of European rural and urban work schedules in his brief autobiography. Schwab, who observed that miners in Saxony worked two or three hours per day less than American miners, also produced a fine summary of the impact of mechanization on the working day. During his migration through Germany and Switzerland before coming to the United States, Schwab worked thirteen-to seventeen-hour days in various settings and concluded:

> The reader thinks it probably a horrible thing to work 14 hours a day, and it is; but . . . in out-of-the-way towns, which are still deep in the mire of the middle ages, everything goes along in a slow way . . . . It is simply impossible to work as many hours with machines as without them. Without machines the workman stops here a minute, there a minute; goes slower now and then, and is careful not to overwork himself. The machine alters this. It does not stop for a minute, or run a little slower; it takes no consideration whatever . . . . There the reduction of the hours of labor was a necessity.[13]

The movement for an eight-hour day influenced, and was profoundly influenced by, the ideas and practices of the two mass organizations of labor that grew during the 1880s. Both the Knights of Labor and the Federation of Organized Trades and Labor Unions (FOTLU, later the American Federation of

Labor) made the shorter day a cardinal point in their programs. But the two organizations differed markedly in their approaches to the issue. Ultimately, one organization built the May 1, 1886, mass strike for the eight-hour day, while the other officially abstained from that struggle. However, in understanding the different attitudes of the Knights and the Federation, as well as the distinctive positions taken by more radical groups, it is well to recall that many activists held memberships in more than one body. For example, Albert Parsons was an "anarchist," a Knight, and a typographical unionist, and even Gompers briefly held a Knights of Labor card. Moreover, members such as Peter McGuire who went from Lassalleanism to Marxism and to the Federation, and George McNeill who abandoned the Knights in favor of the Federation, often changed organizational allegiances.[14] Finally, local bodies often acted with considerable autonomy so that national directives from either the Knights or the FOTLU applied unevenly.

Throughout most of the 1880s the largest and most important American labor union was the Order of the Knights of Labor. Local assemblies of the Knights existed since 1869 as labor-oriented secret societies replete with ritual and oaths. During the Long Depression these local bodies developed a centralized organization, but until 1878 the group lacked a platform. After dropping most of its secrecy and ritualism, the Knights of Labor grew rapidly, from 9,287 members in 1878 to 51,914 in 1883, to about 100,000 in 1885 and to possibly 700,000 in 1886. Apart from its size, the order exercised a key influence in the labor movement because it organized both skilled and unskilled workers, including black and female workers, and had a truly national constituency with a base in the South.[15] On the other hand, the Knights did not limit their membership to wage-workers. The inclusion of local politicians and small businessmen strengthened the order's predisposition against strikes.[16]

From its beginnings, the Knights of Labor propagandized in favor of a shorter working day. In 1871 Uriah Stephens, founder of the Knights, advocated "a universal movement to cease work at 5 o'clock on Saturday." The first constitution adopted by the order, approved in Reading, Pennsylvania, in 1878 featured the following demand in its preamble: "The reduction of the hours of labor to eight per day, so the laborers may have more time for social enjoyment and intellectual improvement and be enabled to reap the advantages conferred by the labor-saving machinery which their brains have created." A year later, the grand master workman proposed that eight-hour laws be criminal statutes with stiff penalties for offenses.[17] After 1882, reports from the Knights' grand statistician gave detailed evidence of long hours. The first report found only 8 percent of local statisticians reporting any trades working the eight-hour day and added "26 percent report that their brothers work more than 10 hours; many among them working 12 to 16 hours per day."[18] From 1881 until 1883 the general assembly considered resolutions to set aside a particular Monday, on which "all branches of labor throughout the country shall make a demand upon employers that thereafter eight hours shall constitute a legal day's work." The resolution contemplated legislative action to enforce the demand, but was regularly defeated or tabled for fear that small demonstrations would hurt the order by exposing its size. In 1884 the Knights did decide to declare their desire "To shorten the hours of labor by a general refusal to work more than eight hours."[19]

The pronouncements of the Knights remained divorced from any general effort to win the eight-hour day. Especially under Terence V. Powderly, grand master workman after 1879, the issue was subordinated to land reform and to the cooperativism that Powderly promised would automatically solve the hours question. Powderly, who himself often worked three to four hours of overtime rather than displease his superiors when employed as a machinist, commanded all the arguments for a shorter day but never seriously addressed tactics. His articles in popular magazines linked unemployment and long hours forcefully and recapitulated Stewardism. But his writings and speeches were empty of suggestions as to how the eight-hour system could be brought into being. His main advice was negative: Strikes were to be avoided as a plague which had "done more injury to labor than they can ever make amends for."[20]

Under Powderly, as Marion Cahill has remarked, the Knights had "nothing that could be termed a policy" regarding hours. The organization drifted toward the use of legislative pressure to secure the shorter day, briefly supporting a lobbying effort designed to secure national eight-hour legislation. The impressive delegation that went to Washington, D.C., in 1880 to press for the law included Richard Trevellick, Albert Parsons, and Charles Litchman, grand secretary of the Knights. But when it came to supporting the delegation with funds, the Knights faltered. Litchman, who remained in the capital for six years, paid his own expenses.[21]

At the state level the Knights of Labor participated in several initiatives to pass shorter-hours statutes. The early 1880s featured many instances of reformers wishing to curtail the length of the working day, and, especially where women and children were concerned, some ameliorative legislation did pass. The Bureau of Labor Statistics and pioneer female labor reformers, such as the Chicago socialist Elizabeth Morgan, played vital roles in marshaling support for those small improvements that did occur, but in some areas the efforts of the Knights also proved decisive.[22] In Rhode Island the order organized successfully on the basis of its support for the ten-hour legislation before the state legislature from 1883 to 1885. In 1885 the state forbade women and children under sixteen from being employed more than ten hours daily, although the law was readily circumvented. The order also could claim partial credit for passage of Michigan's 1885 ten-hour law and for the Ohio statute passed in 1886.[23]

While Michigan and Ohio hosted strikes, supported half-heartedly by the Knights, in order to enforce recently passed statutes, the Maryland order struck first and then appealed to the legislature. The coal regions of western Maryland witnessed spectacular growth of the Knights in 1879 and 1880. When Knights District Assembly 25, representing 2,170 workers, published work rules in its

Frostburg Mining Journal in 1881, the mining companies were taken aback. Not only did the rules specify a ten-hour maximum working day, but they set ten tons as a day's production for a two-man crew. This meant that mine drivers, laborers, and mechanics—all of whom sometimes worked very long hours—achieved a standardized working day, and miners, who formerly worked by the ton on less favorable terms, could sometimes turn out a day's production in a few hours and leave the mines. Mineowners complained of the high wages but appeared even more galled by the Knights' presumption to manage work.[24]

After a year of living with the regulations, the owners provoked the Great Strike of 1882 by insisting on an eleven-hour day and a wage cut. On March 14, 3,800 mine workers walked out. The strike spread, even into West Virginia, but soon lost momentum. The employers' assault included importation of strikebreakers and eviction from company housing, but Powderly's effect on the morale of the strikers was as harmful as any of the owners' actions. The Knights' leader privately opposed the strike and lectured local leaders with aphorisms such as: "*Strike at the boss and hit yourself.*" Powderly took no note of the hours issue and pushed for an arbitrated settlement based on the wages. Such a solution was not forthcoming, and the strike was four months old before Powderly acknowledged that it might be serious enough to require a special levy for support. Substantial support never arrived, and the miners admitted defeat after five months. In 1884 a ten-hour law applying to two mining counties passed the Maryland legislature with the support of the Knights, but the enfeebled mining unions could not force compliance. Formal struggle gave way to informal limiting of production by dissatisfied workers, but the Knights found no resurgence in Maryland.[25]

The craft unions and the FOTLU, like the Knights, displayed a consistent interest in eight hours. Unlike the Knights, they made attempts to develop a meaningful strategy to implement the demand. Many individual unions, including the cigarmakers, carpenters, molders, furniture workers, and painters were on record as supporters of the eight-hour system.[26] The National Federation of Miners and Mine Laborers, founded in 1885, placed the eight-hour day high on its list of objectives. With the advent of the Bessemer converter, some members of the Amalgamated Association of Iron and Steel Workers secured the eight-hour shift, either through strikes or by agreement, and the union favored universal adoption of the system.[27]

When unionists met in the FOTLU, they immediately addressed the issue of hours. Ironically, in view of later history, they first opted for a legislative approach. The 1881 founding convention of the labor federation heard a report which advised, "Grasp one idea, *viz.* less hours and better pay," asked "How will we accomplish this?", and answered, "As the capitalists and wage-grabbers obtain their ends—by law." The following year the FOTLU delegation met with U.S. President Chester A. Arthur to lobby for enforcement of the 1868 federal eight-hour law, but Arthur reportedly brushed them aside with the comment, "I do not think the Eight-Hour Law is constitutional and no power on earth can make me enforce an unconstitutional law."[28] The 1882 and 1883 conventions raised the enforcement issue to first place among FOTLU demands. Although the latter convention directed inquiries to the two major political parties regarding hours, neither the Democrats nor the Republicans replied. By 1884 the legislative road to shorter hours came into disfavor. The convention of that year heard in its secretary's report, "This much has been determined by the National Eight-Hour Law—it is useless to wait for legislation in this matter."[29]

By 1884 the influence of Marxists and ex-socialists in the FOTLU had helped propel the organization toward trade union action to secure shorter hours. Leaders such as Gompers and Adolph Strasser of the Cigar Makers' Union, J. P. McDonnell of the New Jersey Federation, and Peter J. McGuire of the Brotherhood of the Carpenters and Joiners had long been associated in New York-New Jersey-Connecticut eight-hour struggles, socialist study groups, and various organizations allying trade unionists and socialists. McGuire, initially a Lassallean, stressed the importance of trade unionism to members of the Socialistic Labor party in the early 1880s. Although Gompers and Strasser had already begun a rightward swing, especially relating to internal matters in the Cigar Makers' Union, both retained a commitment to eight hours heavily influenced by Marx and Steward.[30] Gompers remembered that long hours stimulated his early thoughts of labor reform and considered the eight-hour day as the one demand that could produce working-class unity.[31]

At first McGuire, who espoused the eight-hour day as a "socialist" demand, failed to win Gompers's support for his proposal that workers should establish it by direct action. During the 1882 convention Gompers opposed McGuire's resolution declaring the eight-hour system to be labor's prime demand, although his opposition was mainly to the resolution's class-conscious rhetoric, not a disagreement with its thrust. However, by 1884 Gompers helped to draft the fateful resolution that set May 1, 1886, as the date on which the eight-hour system would take effect in all industry. The resolution, which passed twenty-three to two, did not specify what tactics would be used, but when the delegates approved Frank K. Foster's proposal that "a vote be taken in all labor organizations, . . . as to the feasibility of a universal strike for a working day of 8 (or) 9 hours, to take effect not later than May 1, 1886," they implied that a massive work stoppage might occur.[32]

At first the Knights seemed likely to reach an accord with the FOTLU on tactics. The former organization, asked by the FOTLU "to co-operate in the general movement to establish the eight-hour reform," had after all promised, at its 1884 convention, "to shorten the hours of labor by a general refusal to work more than eight hours." But the actions of the Knights, and especially of Powderly, remained reflexively antistrike. Powderly's approach to the eight-hour question was to oppose the FOTLU resolution and to call, instead, for Knights to write essays on the working day and to release the essays for the education of employers and the general public on Washington's Birthday 1885.[33]

Any accounting for the differences between the Knights and the FOTLU regarding eight-hour strategy must take several factors into account. The Knights, who never completely shed their secret society trappings, generally failed to attract freethinking German socialists and thereby lost contact with the most theoretically advanced section of the labor movement. Irish influence, and with it a preference for boycotts rather than strikes, was great in the Knights' officialdom although, at the local level, Knights often struck, and dramatic strike conflicts such as that of the Great Southwest Strike of 1886 led to the order's most dramatic growth. Powderly's own involvement in Irish nationalist politics may have increased his propensity to subordinate the hours issue to land questions. The greater size of Powderly's organization also meant that it had more to risk than the fledgling, faltering FOTLU which had just 50,000 members when it undertook the May 1 plan.[34] The Knights, because of their mixture of skilled and unskilled workers, also felt a variety of cross-pressures which the craft unions did not. Powderly held that the FOTLU could afford an eight-hour demand because the few workers it represented already had won working days of ten or less hours, but that an organization representing the unskilled had to call the demand unrealistic for the many laborers who still sought the ten-hour day. Moreover, to retain an appeal to the unskilled, the Knights would have had to support the eight-hour day with *no cut in pay*, since the unskilled could not afford a large slash in wages. The FOTLU largely stayed silent as to whether wage reductions might accompany reductions of working hours, but the Knights could not sidestep the issue.[35]

In a deeper sense the Knights and FOTLU represented extremes of the conclusions that workers might draw regarding the role of state power in industrial society. The Knights, strongly marked by the heritage of abolitionism, the Civil War, and parts of Stewardism, held out hope for the gradual, peaceful triumph of legislative reform if the public were enlightened and the labor movement persistent. At the same time, they warned of massive violence, like that of 1877, if the government were provoked by labor protest.[36] The FOTLU, on the other hand, molded a measure of Marxism with a long list of governmental failures to respond to labor demands with anything more than promises, bullets, and truncheons into the position that the unions would have to achieve what the state would not. In reviewing legislative attempts to reduce hours, they concluded that "organization would prove vastly more effective than the enactment of a thousand laws depending for enforcement upon the pleasure of aspiring politicians or syncophantic department officials." The very choice of May 1, the anniversary of the demonstrations which failed to implement the Illinois eight-hour law of 1867, rather than July 4 as the day on which to act, indicates how the FOTLU eschewed republicanism.[37]

During the months before May 1, 1886, yet a third current, an anarchosyndicalist trend which not only regarded the legislative struggle as useless but saw all government power as an instrument of class oppression, attained prominence in the eight-hour movement. This rising "anarchist" influence afforded Powderly yet another reason to refuse to cooperate in the eight-hour struggle. However, the presence of the anarchists did not originally motivate Powderly's actions. It was fear—fed by Powderly's own conservatism and by the ideological and organizational underpinnings of the Knights—of eight-hour strikes rather than of revolution that kept the Knights of Labor from supporting the FOTLU proposal. To understand the depth of that fear and the depth of FOTLU hopes, it is necessary to consider the largely overlooked record of labor conflict over hours which took place as the two major labor organizations deliberated during the early 1880s.

One reason that the events of May 1886 have seemed to historians such a bolt from the blue is that strikes over the length of labor in the years preceding Haymarket have received inadequate attention. Henry David's classic *The Haymarket Affair*, for example, discussed the supposed lack of legislative action on hours in the early 1880s and added, "Nor did labor, both organized and unorganized, spend its forces in strikes to secure reductions in hours." David cited figures showing that only 1.26 percent of 1883 strikes concerned hours and that the figure rose to only 2.03 percent in 1884.[38] Such figures understate the vitality of the shorter-hours movement during the years prior to Haymarket. During the period from 1881 through 1885, federal statistics list 142 strikes resulting from conflicts over hours. This number represents some 5.7 percent of all strikes. The 47,541 workers participating in the conflicts over hours account for about 7.7 percent of all strikers during the same years. Because so many wage strikes were only brief defensive actions to restore pay cuts, such statistics still underplay the importance of the working day as an issue in strikes of the early 1880s.[39] Hours sparked many of the largest, most dramatic strikes of the period and the conflicts most impinging on working-class life.

Though mounted at a time when a national market was emerging for most commodities, the hours strikes of the early 1880s concentrated in industries whose products and services were still locally produced and consumed. For this reason the strikes raised the issue of the shorter working day not only to participants and to members of allied crafts, but also to the broader working population, which felt the impact of the strikes. Drivers and laborers on street railways, for example, rebelled against a working day that often topped fourteen hours in a series of strikes that disrupted urban public transportation. Following a New York City railwayman strike in 1880 came walkouts in Boston (1881), Saint Louis (1881 and 1884), Cincinnati (1881), Chicago (1882 and 1885), New Orleans (1884), Brooklyn (1885 and 1886), and Petersburg, Virginia (1885). The Saint Louis strike of 1881 established a 72-hour week, but three years later, hours had been extended to 98 weekly. In New Orleans the "victory" of the 1884 strike established a fourteen-hour day, down from fifteen.[40] Union and radical leaders stressed such incredibly long hours in arguing for public support for the transit workers and in generally raising the question of hours in public debates.[41]

Building tradesmen, also producers of locally used commodities, continued a tradition of long, large strikes over hours. Stonecutters in Philadelphia won the nine-hour day in 1881. Carpenters in Port Chester, New York, unsuccessfully attempted to reduce their ten-hour day the following year. By 1884 large strikes gripped the building trades. Over 2,000 Chicago carpenters walked out, most of them gaining an hour more leisure per week. In New Orleans 800 carpenters and laborers, working nine-hour days, successfully resisted a cutting back of their dinner hour. Twenty strikes involving 8,389 building tradesmen in four crafts punctuated the summer in New York City, and nearly a thousand Brooklyn plumbers suffered a lockout in a dispute over time. Fourteen of the New York City strikes did shorten the working day, usually from fifty-nine hours weekly to fifty-three. In 1885 stonecutters in Saint Paul and Baltimore also struck, both victoriously, and Denver bricksetters walked out in successful defense of the forty-five-hour week.[42]

Alongside the interruptions in transportation and housing construction were strikes stopping the production of two working-class staples—bread and beer. Bakers, who often labored over a hundred hours a week, embarked on an impressive series of strikes in May 1881 in New York City. Involving over 600 shops and nearly 2,500 strikers, the strikes saw the winning of a 74-hour week for over half the participants. Some bakers in Chicago and Newark also gained huge reductions in the working day by striking in 1881, while Jersey City bakers struck unsuccessfully. Other walkouts involving bakers occurred in Chicago (1882) and New York City (1885). By the latter year, according to George McNeill's accounts, working-class communities frequently employed "Saint Boycott" to wrest reductions in hours for bakers by patronizing only shops working the shortest schedules.[43]

Workers in the brewing industry, organized in the Brewery Workers' Union, also undertook an ambitious work stoppage in New York in 1881. Demanding a twelve-hour day, six days per week, and a brief two-hour Sunday shift at the unheard of rate of fifty cents per hour, the brewers struck on June 6. The Central Labor Union of New York City boycotted scab beer. Nearly 2,000 brewers in Brooklyn, Staten Island, and New York joined the strike, but nowhere was it solid. Beer-truck drivers, ignored by the union, not only transported beer but did brewing work. Despite such weaknesses, the walkout resulted in a decrease of the working week from ninety-six to ninety hours for most brewers and gave a few a seventy-seven-hour week. In Newark the hundred-hour week survived an 1881 strike. Nor did the 500 brewery workers who struck in Cincinnati that year secure a decrease in their seventy-two-hour week. By 1885 and 1886 a combination of effective boycotts and trade union pressure began to pay stunning dividends in New York City. The brewers there, who had worked fourteen-to eighteen-hour shifts at the start of the decade, gained the ten-hour day, plus a wage increase and the abolition of Sunday labor in April 1886.[44]

Other strikes compelled attention because of their size and dynamism. For example, in 1883—the year that David cites as the nadir of strike action over hours—just eight recorded job actions involved the issue but 12,603 workers participated. Two strikes alone, a national action by telegraphers and a New York City walkout by cloak and suit makers, involved over 11,000 workers. In a month-long strike the telegraphers demanded abolition of Sunday work and the institution of an eight-hour day. Their union expected massive aid from the Knights of Labor but received less that $4,000. The Knights' leadership denounced the action of the telegraphers as precipitous and influenced the decision of the union to admit defeat in mid-August.[45]

An important precedent was set that same year when 750 Jewish immigrants joined 5,000 other workers, almost evenly divided between the sexes, in the cloak and suit makers' strike. This massive New York City action, described in the press as the "first immigrant strike," sought an 8 A.M. to 6 P.M. working day at a $2.50 wage. Supported by the Knights, the Central Labor Union, and the newly organized Dress and Cloak Makers' Union, the strike also benefited from the socialist leadership of Jacob Schoen, a Hungarian Jew, and Louis Smith, a Polish-Jewish veteran of the Paris Commune. The walkout won a wage boost although it left the twelve-hour day intact. Organizing around the issue continued, especially in the Jewish Workingmen's Union, which called for the eight-hour day in the first Yiddish labor leaflet in the United States, in 1885. A mass strike that year secured a wage boost and a cut in hours for cloak makers.[46]

The most dynamic strikes continued to occur in sawmill regions. It was there that the tramping strike, featuring roving pickets and parades, continued traditions established in the Schuylkill coal strike of 1868, the lumber strikes of the early 1870s, and the Saint Louis and Chicago actions during the 1877 railroad strike. There were four major "Sawdust Wars" in the early 1880s. Two thousand strikers participated in the Muskegon, Michigan, walkout of 1882, and over 1,200 joined the Marinette, Wisconsin, outbreaks of 1885, but the strikes at Eau Claire, Wisconsin, in 1881 and in the Saginaw-Bay City-Menominee, Michigan, region in 1885 were the most spectacular.[47]

At Eau Claire the July 1881 ten-hour strike spread to the many small mills in the area as tramping strikers visited plants. Although the only full account is a state labor report extremely hostile to the strikers, sections of the document admit that the strike enjoyed local support. So serious was the situation in Eau Claire that Wisconsin's governor, William E. Smith, came to the city and wired for the National Guard. On July 22, 376 guardsmen, each displaying twenty rounds of ammunition, faced down 2,000 strike supporters described as "men armed with guns, clubs, pistols, crow-bars and mill tools." Although the mills reopened on a twelve-hour basis, a chastened management quickly granted the eleven-hour day.[48]

In Michigan 5,210 workers entered into ten-hour strikes in sawmills in 1885 and an additional 981 millhands were locked out in order to forestall a ten-hour strike at Menominee. Although a few local strikes, such as those at Zilwaukee and Muskegon, carried the demand, the failing strikes at Bay City, Saginaw City, and East Saginaw are of most interest as case studies in labor solidarity, governmental action, and community response. They, like most of the Michigan strikes, stemmed from the passage of a state ten-hour law. Although the law allowed for special contravening contracts and did not take effect until after the height of the lumbering season, the millhands could legitimize their struggle by referring to the statute.[49]

Although the Knights of Labor had done some agitational work in the area and had 3,000 members there, the strike started spontaneously when six or seven workers at Rouse's Mill left the premises on July 6 shouting "Hurrah for Ten Hours." Improvising a pennant from a bandanna on a stick, the small group visited another mill and initiated a series of processions that spread the strike in succeeding days. From the start, solidarity prevailed. The region's mill labor force included American natives (38 percent), French Canadians (24 percent), Germans (20 percent), Poles (10 percent), Irish (4 percent), and other nationalities. At Bay City the various groups, especially unskilled Polish Catholics and more skilled German Lutherans, cooperated. An early strike meeting featured a black speaker. Most importantly, unemployed millhands, perhaps responding to appeals made by the Knights, took an active role in the processions.[50]

Bay City's strikers enjoyed local support. Early processions were accompanied by a tolerant sheriff, himself a Knights of Labor member. The sheriff lost patience on the third day when 500 men attempted to close the Rust Brothers Mill by force. Three arrests occurred, but by evening the mayor, another Knight, ordered the release of those seized. The strike then spread until it involved 2,500 workers. The Bay City press generally backed the strike, though usually with less vehemence than journalist D. C. Blinn, a strike leader and editor of the local *Labor Vindicator*. Blinn's calls for a general strike drew criticism, but the community remained prostrike. The city council reacted so strongly against the importation of Pinkertons by the largely absentee-owned companies that the detectives were withdrawn. Henry W. Sage, a leading businessman, denounced the city's capitulation to the rule of mobs. After shutting down Bay City's mills on July 10, about 1,500 protesters draped barges with banners reading "Ten Hours or No Sawdust" and journeyed to East Saginaw and Saginaw City. There they were met by another Knight, Thomas Barry, a Democratic-Greenback legislator who had introduced the state ten-hour law, and by longshoremen supporting the ten-hour day. The roving crowd closed all Saginaw-area mills, mostly without violence, but with a few incidents of clubbing and stoning. These incidents, and the feeling that Bay City "outsiders" had "invaded" the area, enabled the mayors of the two Saginaws, both sympathetic to the mill owners and one an owner himself, to deputize 100 Pinkertons. Even so, the strike in the Saginaws enjoyed some local support; the Saginaw City police chief and the militia captain of East Saginaw, both Knights, hesitated to use force to reopen the mills.[51]

While municipal authorities divided on their approach to the walkouts, the state government attacked the strike. Michigan's governor, Russell A. Alger, an owner of several mills in the northern part of the state, came to Saginaw Valley on July 14. Alger was an opponent of the ten-hour system who insisted that his employees sign contracts promising to continue longer hours. Despite the nearly total absence of conflict during his stay in the valley, Alger called out state troops in a move which, as Jeremy Kilar observes, "was part of a determined effort to reopen mills and intimidate strikers." As such it was partly successful. The five companies of militia enforced the governor's ban on parades and mass meetings. Alger called for the arrests of Barry and Blinn under the state's antilabor Baker Conspiracy Laws. While these actions broke the enthusiasm of the strikers, they did not win full community approval. With the Knights offering to protect the mills, the rationale for keeping troops in the region was suspect, and after a week the militia withdrew.[52]

But the period in which the militia occupied the region gave the initiative back to the owners. Members of the millowners' association issued statements that they would open the mills only on their own terms and held, perhaps disingenuously, that the strike benefited them by limiting lumber supply. By July 25 owners reopened a few Saginaw mills on the ten-hour system with a wage cut. When a logjam caused flooding of farmland near Saginaw City, local support for the strike eroded with the soil. Powderly, who visited the area, delivered another blow by counseling acceptance of ten hours' wages for ten hours' work. The back-to-work movement in the Saginaws grew and, when Bay City mills sent their logs to the Saginaws for processing, Bay City millhands became anxious and some mills opened. After August 6 strikers engaged in a series of battles with police and local militia at reopened mills. At Saginaw strikers suffered clubbings and in Bay City a brief gun battle left a sheriff and three strikers wounded. By late August these last violent gasps of the strike ceased, and defeated millhands returned to work in hopes of making some money before the slack season. Most mills converted to ten hours on September 15, the day prescribed by law, while cutting wages. But the Saginaw Valley strikes did not offer entirely bleak lessons for the labor movement. They again showed the capacity of the hours demand to unite a variety of laborers in a common cause. Mill owners, who pledged to refrain from employing immigrants in the future, had learned what the nation was to learn the following May—that foreign-born and unskilled workers could act on the demand for a shorter working day.[53]

Set in this context of continuing struggle over the working day, the FOTLU's decision to press on with its bold 1884 plan to enforce the eight-hour system with a mass strike on May 1, 1886, was not extravagant. The demand was well timed—raised during a depression which made unemployment an issue and maturing during a recovery which made workers readier to strike without fear for their jobs. Of the seventy-eight FOTLU unions polled in 1885, sixty-nine supported the May 1 plan. Working-class militancy meanwhile grew in early 1886 as the Knights of Labor led the Southwest strike against Jay Gould's railroad empire and attracted hundreds of thousands of new members.[54]

The FOTLU, realizing that cooperation by the larger Knights of Labor would go far toward building the mass strike, bid again for Powderly's support. Gabriel Edmonston, FOTLU secretary, wrote the Knights during the summer of 1885 to ask their aid, but received no reply. At the September 1885 Knights convention, an FOTLU request was read but, after Powderly denounced the date of the action as "not . . . suitable" and the use of a strike as "not . . . proper" the delegates passed a vague resolution in favor of the eight-hour system. Still, the press frequently linked the Knights to the May 1 movement and, to Powderly's consternation, Knights' organizers used eight-hour promises to enroll members, who passed local resolutions in support of the mass strike. On March 13, 1886 Powderly promulgated a "secret circular" which rebuked organizers for invoking the Knights' support for the May 1 strike and insisted that the time was ripe for education and not action. The lack of official Knights' support seriously hurt the movement, both by lessening its numbers and by sowing confusion, but in many locales, Knights of Labor did participate in the eight-hour strikes.[55]

If the FOTLU's plan got mixed support from the Knights, it eventually received enthusiastic backing from the trade union wing of the anarchist movement. Within the International Working People's Association (IWPA), an anarchist body of several thousand, two tendencies coexisted. The first, led by the German expatriate Johann Most and based around the *Freiheit* newspaper in New York City, advocated "propaganda by the deed" and saw individual terror as leading to a society without authority.[56] The second wing, propounding the "Chicago Idea" of anarchism, was more an anarcho-syndicalist movement. Developing mainly in Midwestern cities with a rich heritage of police and Pinkerton violence against the labor movement, the syndicalist wing drew many radicalized immigrant and American-born trade unionists into the IWPA. At the 1883 Pittsburgh IWPA convention, the two leading syndicalists, Albert Parsons and August Spies, joined Most on the platform committee and secured his acquiescence to a platform accepting trade union work as an arena for anarchist agitation. The "Pittsburgh Manifesto" also outlined the anarchist society of the future and promised "that nobody need work more than a few hours a day."[57]

The syndicalist wing of the anarchist movement produced only a loose body of theory. Its syndicalism, its belief in a future society organized around working-class organizations, was not fully developed. Leaders could, for example, enthuse about a utopia vaguely based on consent and freedom, or could pinpoint "the Granges, trade unions [and] Knights of Labor assemblies" as the "embryonic groups of the ideal anarchistic society." Similar imprecision marked the group's ideas of force. At various times the "Chicago Idea" appeared to mean advocacy of individual terror, of mass insurrection, and of working-class self-defense. Most commonly, the last mentioned function of violence was stressed, although leaders engaged in a good deal of loose "bomb-talking," as the socialist writer Floyd Dell termed it.[58] Such countenancing of violence gave the press the chance to attack the eight-hour movement through its most radical IWPA wing, but the positive aspects of the syndicalist participation outweighed such bad publicity.

The syndicalists brought a class analysis, energy, and an appeal to the unskilled and immigrant worker to the eight-hour campaign. A persistent myth regarding the syndicalists is that they entered the eight-hour movement late and as opportunists. Such a charge, raised by the prosecution during the trial, and by historians, is an over-simplification.[59] Albert Parsons, for example, had acted as the chief English-language spokesperson in Chicago for the Workingmen's party when that group demanded an eight-hour day during the 1877 railroad strike. He led in the building of the July 4 eight-hour demonstrations of 1878 and 1879—demonstrations that brought Ira Steward and George McNeill to Chicago—and held office in the Eight-Hour League. During 1879 he publicly differed with his Socialist Labor party comrades, Thomas Morgan and George Schilling. Parsons argued that eight hours was a revolutionary demand. In 1880 he joined four other labor leaders as a member of the eight-hour lobby in Washington, D.C. That same year he withdrew from active electoral activity in part because of his conviction "that the number of hours per day that wage-workers are compelled to work . . . amounted to their practical disenfranchisement."[60] Throughout the early 1880s Parsons attempted to build revolutionary unionism by consistent activity in favor of basic class demands—including shorter hours— both as a member of the International Typographical Union and as a founding leader of the Central Labor Union. Others of the Haymarket martyrs similarly noted that the length of the working day abetted their radicalization and pointed with pride to their record as activists in the shorter-hours and trade union movements.[61]

The confusion that provided slim justification for the view that the IWPA syndicalists had no sincere concern for the eight-hour day stemmed primarily from two articles that appeared in the English-language anarchist newspaper *Alarm* in 1885. The first article, an August reply to a FOTLU circular asking cooperation in the May 1 campaign, branded the FOTLU plan a "waste of precious time and effort." A month later the *Alarm* pledged not to "antagonize the eight-hour movement" but argued that eight hours meant nothing if capital still ruled. This posturing, which termed the eight-hour day "more than a compromise . . . a virtual concession that the wage system is right," came in part from a desire to placate the Most faction of the IWPA which barely countenanced revolutionary unionism and regarded all reform as anathema.[62] It also gained credence because IWPA organizers, influenced by a literal application of Marx's ideas on surplus value, had generally ceased to preach eight hours but had instead argued that justice would be served if the capitalist received just the two, three, or four hours of work that it took for labor to produce the value of its wages. But the anti-May 1 position, arrived at with Parsons traveling away from Chicago, was speedily overturned. The syndicalists came to endorse the struggle as "a class movement" from which they did not want "to stand aloof," and from January until May of

1886, threw their energies into the May 1 campaign.[63]

The syndicalists provided skilled organizers and added a sense of the dramatic to the movement. Particularly in Chicago, IWPA women such as Lucy Parsons, Lizzie Swank-Holmes, and Sarah E. Ames did vital organizing in the needle trades while Albert Parsons, Samuel Fielden, Michael Schwab, and Oscar Neebe enrolled cloakmakers, packinghouse workers, clerks, and painters into the eight-hour effort. The Chicago IWPA members had familiarity with a flair for the theatrical. In the 1879 eight-hour parade Albert Parsons' union local sent a float bearing a working press churning out shorter-hours materials, and in 1885 the IWPA captured huge publicity by protesting the opening of the Chicago Board of Trade with leaflets headed "Workmen, Bow to Your Gods!" As May 1 approached, the IWPA publicity machine again cranked up when the Central Labor Union sponsored a festive April 25 rally on the Chicago lakefront.[64]

The IWPA also made a contribution by organizing armed workers' militias ostensibly capable of defending strikes. Since the 1877 railroad strike, various socialist rifle clubs had sprung up as a response to police violence. The growth of these "Study and Defense Clubs" in Detroit, Milwaukee, Cincinnati, Saint Louis, and Chicago during 1884 and 1885 derived mainly from IWPA influence. From October 1885 until the strike, the syndicalists emphasized that strikers would have to defend themselves.[65] While these calls to arms must be described as shows of bravado by a still-tiny group, they represented an attempt to show how a mass strike might be defended. Moreover, they were the lone attempts by a labor organization to speak to what was a prime concern of prospective strikers— the possibility of attacks by private and public police.

Finally, the IWPA broached what was the main issue of the strike for the unskilled workers. At the time the FOTLU did not state that no wage cut should accompany the transition to the eight-hour system. Publications of the craft unionist Trades and Labor Assembly of Chicago openly offered to take wage cuts to win less hours, but the IWPA raised banners reading "Eight Hours Work for Ten Hours Pay."[66] This formulation was crucial in enlisting the support of lowly paid unskilled laborers who could not afford to lose wages.

As May 1 drew near, it became clear that the FOTLU did not have sufficient forces to coordinate a national campaign. Instead of a centralized effort of craft unions, strike propaganda went out under the auspices of various local coalitions. In New York City the craft unions did most of the work. In Chicago Knights of Labor leader George Schilling, a socialist, joined the IWPA at the head of organizing efforts. Knights and the craft-oriented Trades and Labor Assembly predominated in Cincinnati, while an Eight-Hour League unified the forces of the Knights and others in Milwaukee.[67]

But localism did not mean weakness. By March the campaign forced city councils in Chicago and Milwaukee to grant the eight-hour day to municipal laborers. The cigarworkers successfully demanded a nine-hour shift in January as preparation for later events. By mid-April *John Swinton's Paper*, a labor weekly, reported "eight-hour agitation everywhere." The Wisconsin commissioner of labor and industrial statistics later wrote that eight hours "was *the* topic of conversation in the shop, on the street, at the family table, at the bar, in the counting room, and the subject of numerous able sermons from the pulpit." Newspapers speculated on the size of the coming strike and bewailed the influence of "Communism, lurid and rampant" in the eight-hour ranks.[68]

Meanwhile, workers smoked "Eight-Hour Tobacco" and wore "Eight-Hour Shoes"—products already produced in shops working the shorter day—and sang hymns of the movement including:

> We want to feel the sunshine;
> we want to smell the flowers;
> We're sure that God has willed it.
> And we mean to have eight hours.
> We're summoning our forces from
> shipyard, shop and mill;
> Eight hours for work, eight hours
> for rest, eight hours for what we will.

In the warm weather of late April many workers must have followed the logic of the young immigrant Cincinnati furniture worker Oscar Ameringer and, with "buds and blue hills" beckoning, resolved to fight for more leisure. Thousands jumped the gun by striking before May 1.[69]

When May 1 arrived, a massive strike wave accompanied it. Its exact proportions remain unclear, but the number of strikers certainly far exceeded the 100,000 which some observers had predicted in April, although it fell short of the million participants predicted by Albert Parsons. The traditional estimates made by the Commons group put the number of workers involved at 340,000. Of these, 190,000 are said to have struck and 150,000 to have demonstrated or won a voluntary reduction in hours: 45,000 in New York, 32,000 in Cincinnati, 4,700 in Boston, 4,250 in Pittsburgh, 3,000 in Detroit, 2,000 in Saint Louis, 1,500 in Washington, and 13,000 in other cities.[70] These guesses err on the low side. For example, a thorough study of Milwaukee suggests between 14,000 and 20,000 strikers, and federal statistics indicate that in the strike center of Minneapolis-Saint Paul about 2,500 walked out. Government data on Saint Louis, which fail to mention several of the local strikes, nonetheless number over 4,500 participants in hours strikes in late April and May. For the District of Columbia the figures should be corrected to upwards of 2,200. Probably 400,000 and perhaps half a million workers joined in the agitation. They did so not only in urban centers, but in smaller cities and rural towns—in Montclair, New Jersey; Duluth, Minnesota; Argentine, Kansas; South Gardiner, Maine; Mobile, Alabama; Lynchburg, Virginia; Galveston, Texas; Cedarburg, Wisconsin; and a score of other localities.[71]

With perhaps 90,000 demonstrators on the streets, with 30,000 to 40,000 on strike, with 45,000 having already benefited from decreases in hours, with "every railroad in the city . . . crippled [and] most of the industries . . . paralyzed," Chicago had the most eventful May 1.[72] In New York City Samuel Gompers addressed a crowd of 10,000 in Union Square after a torchlight parade. Ameringer, carrying a piece of wood shaped into a dagger, found the May 1 demonstration in Cincinnati to be a fitting beginning to a "jolly strike" and noted the presence of "a workers' battalion of four hundred Springfield rifles." In Milwaukee, where 7,000 struck on May 1, there were picnics and parades the following day. Eleven thousand Detroiters marched and 5,000 struck in Troy, New York, where Italian railroad laborers improvised red flags by tying their handkerchiefs to pickaxes.[73]

The May 1 strike featured processions of roving pickets who spread the strike. This meant that the already large number of strikers would swell further as the strike went on. In Milwaukee, for example, the second two days of the strike yielded at least 7,000 more participants. A like pattern developed in Chicago, Saint Louis, and Cincinnati.[74] Two events, both involving police action, intervened to stem the strike's momentum. The celebrated events at Haymarket occurred three days after the strike's start, while the equally bloody Milwaukee tragedy followed one day later.

The prelude to Haymarket was a chance May 3 confrontation at the McCormick Harvester plant. Labor relations at the reaper plant had long been grim. After armed Pinkertons attacked strikers there in April 1885, the Metal Workers' Federation Union at the factory organized an armed section. Trouble flared again the following February when the company violated an agreement not to discipline union activists and locked out workers for protesting. The lockout generated a bitter strike which continued in May. The strike did not concern hours, but the factory was located near the Black Road site at which the Lumber Shovers' Union, 10,000 of whose largely immigrant members had struck for eight hours, held a rally.[75]

Six thousand lumber workers turned out for the afternoon rally at which IWPA member August Spies was scheduled to speak. As Spies's brief, tepid address neared its end, the McCormick factory bell sounded day's end for the strikebreakers manning the plant. Members of the crowd left the rally to taunt those leaving work. When the stick-and-stone-throwing protesters caused the strikebreakers to retreat toward the factory and Harvester's windows were menaced, police fired into the crowd. One demonstrator died immediately from wounds, and probably three more died later.[76]

Spies, who saw the massacre, dashed off a circular at the office of *Arbeiter-Zeitung*, the paper he edited. Printed in English and German, the circular called on workers to "rise . . . and destroy the hideous monster that seeks to destroy you," in the former language and advised "avenge this horrible murder" in the latter. Spies later testified that the heading "Revenge! Workingmen! To Arms!" was added without his knowledge and that he insisted on the excision "Arm yourselves and appear in full force" from a circular issued the following day. Nonetheless, the protest meeting set for 7:30 on May 4 promised to be tense because of the circulars, the inflammatory accounts in the newspapers, and the saber-rattling of police captain John Bonfield.[77]

Throughout the day of May 4 strikers and police clashed, but the night's meeting proved surprisingly small. With a spring storm looming and other protest meetings slated in the neighborhoods, the demonstration did not draw more than 3,000. The crowd filled only one end of the huge Haymarket area and left ample room for police informants and Mayor Carter Harrison to observe. Spies led off with a short address directed against the press. Parsons, who had just returned from Cincinnati and knew little of the Chicago events, followed with an impressive oration that argued for socialism and urged workers to arm themselves, but cautioned against individual terror. A thunderstorm interrupted Samuel Fielden's speech, the last of the evening, and sent home two-thirds of the listeners, including Harrison. Fielden was about to finish when the police issued an order to disperse. As he protested that the meeting was peaceful, 180 police waded into the crowd on Bonfield's order. Seconds later a sputtering, flickering bomb flew through the air and exploded in front of the police, killing one and wounding fifty. The police then fired at the protesters and inflicted perhaps seventy wounds, at least one of them fatal. Seven police died later, mostly from wounds received in the gunfire. "NOW," headlined the Chicago *Inter-Ocean*, "IT IS BLOOD."[78]

The wheels of injustice turned swiftly. Massive police dragnets began immediately after the bombing. Police arrested hundreds and searched scores of homes and labor organizations, usually without warrants. Arrests of IWPA members, at first with no charge and then on the charge of conspiracy, mounted. In all, thirty-one indictments came down in connection with the murder but, when informers and the wildly improbable were weeded out, eight were selected for trial. Captain Michael Schaack supervised the dragnet with, as Henry David observes, "an immoderate appetite for fame." Schaack produced a steady stream of uncovered "plots" complete with planted bombs. The press raged against anarchist "vipers" and "serpents." The New York *Tribune* and the Chicago *Inter-Ocean* editorially convicted IWPA leaders of murder on May 5; the New York *Times* waited until May 6; *Harper's Weekly* delayed conviction until May 8.[79]

Police raids and journalistic vituperation hurt more than the IWPA. The hysteria spilled over to brand socialists, eight-hour advocates, and immigrants as threats to order. No fine distinctions applied. The Chicago Furniture Manufacturers' Association listed society's enemies as "any communist, anarchist, nihilist, or socialist or any other person denying the right of private property."[80] In Chicago, center of the May 1 movement, labor was put on the defensive. Elsewhere, outlandish rumors enjoyed credence and the "anarchist threat" legitimized repression. In Cincinnati, Ameringer recalled, the strikers heard newsboys shout "Anarchist bomb-throwers kill one hundred policemen . . . in Chicago"—news which descended "like a very cold blanket." On the day the news came, the city's mayor deputized 1,000 special police. Two days later he called out the state militia.[81]

Reaction to Haymarket in Milwaukee followed a bloodier scenario than in Cincinnati. A large contingent of Polish strikers, mostly unskilled workers, led strike processions which emanated each morning from Saint Stanislaus Church. The processions succeeded in closing a large brewery, the West Milwaukee railroad shop, a stove works employing 2,500, and Reliance Works of Allis farm machine company. On May 4 three companies of militia prevented the closing of the North Chicago Rolling Mill in Bay View without violence. The next day, after Haymarket, the mayor banned "crowds upon the streets or other public places." Wisconsin's governor called in additional troops.[82]

Still the marchers went forth, but assured Milwaukee *Journal* reporters that they "had no intention of making an attack on the militia or company property, and simply wished to show that they had not been intimidated." As they neared the North Chicago Rolling Mill, the militia's commander issued a single and, according to the *Journal*, inaudible, order to stop. Then, apparently acting on orders from the governor, the troops fired directly into the crowd. Nine men, eight Poles and a German, died from their wounds.[83] In the post-Haymarket atmosphere a coroner's jury praised the militia for "ordering the firing to cease" and returned no murder indictments. Meanwhile, nearly fifty workers were indicted, and some served six-to nine-month terms for "riot and conspiracy." The local press reported, "From all parts of the State messages have come commending Governor Rusk for the promptitude with which he acted." There were only mild objections when the employers made cash gifts to the militia companies involved.[84]

Such an atmosphere devastated the eight-hour movement, and by mid-May the campaign lost its impetus. Still, it was far from a total failure. In Cincinnati strikers continued to argue that the law, a recent eight-hour statute, was on their side. According to a recent study, over 70 percent won some positive settlement of hours and/or wages, and nearly an eighth secured hours reductions with no pay cuts.[85] Nationally, nearly 200,000 workers shortened their days, some by as many as five hours. As many as 87,000 may have won the eight-or nine-hour day in New York City alone, and some trades, such as the fur workers and cigarmakers, enjoyed success in many cities. Gompers later estimated that the net effect of the 1886 action cut the working day by an hour. Federal statistics show the average working week of all those who struck over time in 1886 as going down from just less than sixty-two to less than fifty-nine hours per week.[86]

The most direct effect of the Haymarket bombing was to decimate the leadership of anarcho-syndicalist movement in the United States. That movement, personified by the Haymarket defendants, received a speedy trial and death sentence in Chicago. The trial, which began on June 21, was openly an inquisition against the IWPA rather than a murder investigation. Its judge, Joseph E. Gary, cooperated with the prosecutors to assure that the defense would have to use its preemptory challenges in jury selection against candidates whose stated biases, and even relationship to the victims, merited disqualification for cause. The result was a twelve-man jury which included no industrial workers, but was composed of managers, salesmen, contractors, and businessmen.[87]

The prosecution, led by State's Attorney Julius S. Grinnell, made some attempt to marshal evidence that the defendants had met in a "Monday might conspiracy" to plan the bombing as part of a general insurrection, but it could place only two of those on trial at the alleged planning session—an open public meeting.[88] On the opening day of the trial, Grinnell found a more promising line of argument to which he would return throughout the proceedings. Defending "our institutions" from "Anarchy," Grinnell argued that "these defendants hourly and daily for years, have been sapping [those] institutions, and that where they have cried murder, bloodshed, Anarchy and dynamite they have meant what they said." The words of the syndicalists, wrenched from context or reported by a hostile press, would convict them when evidence of their actions could not. Seven years later, in discussing the case, Gary commented that the identity of the bomb-thrower was "not an important question."[89]

Albert Parsons grasped a serious problems of the defense when he wrote in his notebook during the trial, "It can and must be shown that all this arming was for resistance and not for attack." But because of Gary's rulings, and because of past "bomb-talking" in the IWPA, such a point could not be made. On August 20 the jury recommended death for all those charged save Neebe whose sentence was set at fifteen years. The Chicago *Tribune* suggested raising a fund to reward the jurors. Headlines read, "Chicago, the Nation and the Civilized World Rejoice."[90]

Not all rejoiced. As the executions approached, a strong, international defense movement developed. After the Illinois Supreme Court upheld the verdict while acknowledging faults in the trial and after the U.S. Supreme Court denied appeals, the unions entered the defense effort in force. The newly organized American Federation of Labor, heir to the FOTLU, pled for clemency and both the United Trades of New York and the Central Labor Union of New York City called for protest meetings. Gompers and McGuire spoke and wrote on the behalf of the condemned men. Despite Powderly's continued refusal to defend the anarchists, to whom he said the labor movement owed nothing but a "debt of hatred," local assemblies of the Knights acted.[91] The Chicago Knights of Labor, after following Powderly for a time, switched to a position of support for the accused. In England the many protest meetings featured speeches by George Bernard Shaw, William Morris, and Eleanor Marx-Aveling, and in France members of the Chamber of Deputies petitioned against the executions. Distinguished Americans, including Congressmen Robert Ingersoll, Governor Benjamin Butler, Senator Lyman Trumball, entrepreneur George Francis Train, future Socialist Labor party leader Daniel DeLeon, writers William Dean Howells, John Swinton, and Henry Demarest Lloyd, and former abolitionists Moncure D. Conway and John Brown, Jr., all participated.[92]

The most outstanding figures of the defense campaign were the defendants themselves. Spies, who spoke first to the court, addressed the judge: "Now these are my ideas. They constitute a part of myself. I cannot divest myself of them, nor would I, if I could. And if you think you can crush them out . . . by sending us to the gallows . . . I will proudly and defiantly pay the costly price. Call your hangman." Neebe asked to be killed with his comrades and Parsons refused to plead for a pardon.[93] Even on the gallows where Parsons, Engel, Spies, and Fischer died on November 11, 1887, the condemned men remained unawed. Parsons demanded, "Let the voice of the people be heard!" as his own voice was stilled. Spies's last words were simply, "There will come a time when our silence will be more powerful than the voices you strangle today!"[94]

The long term effects of the Haymarket affair unfolded slowly. Certainly the labor and eight-hour movements suffered, both from repression and from the rapid decline of the Knights of Labor, a decline related to that organization's division over whether or not to back the Haymarket defendants. When the leadership of the Knights ordered Chicago packinghouse workers, on strike in October 1886 in defense of the eight-hour day they had gained in May, to return to work, the prestige of the order further plummeted.[95] On the other hand the AFL grew steadily throughout the post-Haymarket years, and the United Labor Party (ULP), an independent political group calling for the eight-hour day among other demands, grew spectacularly in 1886. The ULP took nearly a third of the votes in the New York City mayoral election, where its candidate was Henry George, the celebrated land reformer who also had a record of shorter-hours advocacy. And the ULP took more than a quarter of the votes in embattled Chicago.[96]

That the anarchists should have stimulated a brief renaissance of political action by labor is not merely supreme irony. In the wake of Haymarket, the mass strike to secure the shorter day had suffered the same fate as had the efforts at legislative reform of the late 1860s. It had been tried and found no panacea. In the space of two decades had come graphic illustrations that the state could neither be relied upon to grant eight hours, nor ignored in mounting an eight-hour struggle against employers.

8

The Rightward Drift of the AFL and the Temporary Decline of the Hours Issue, 1887-1908

During the two decades following Haymarket, numerous changes altered the character of the eight-hour movement. The *de facto* bloc of center and left trade unionists which had built eight-hour agitation in the 1870s and early 1880s split in the wake of post-Haymarket repression. The decline of the Knights of Labor decimated for a time the size of the organized labor movement and limited the enlisting of the unskilled, blacks, women, and immigrants—key elements in any classwide drive for a shorter working day. The AFL gradually adopted strategies befitting a narrow craft unionism, rejecting the mass strike as an eight-hour tactic and, especially after 1894, largely ignoring political action as means to reform working conditions. Thus the labor movement entered the twentieth century without the tactical flexibility and militancy that had characterized its nineteenth-century stance regarding the working day. The absence of ongoing political activity around the question of hours made eight-hour agitation episodic, so much so that one historian has even suggested that rank-and-file workers lacked interest in the eight-hour demand by 1890.[1]

In such a situation the increasing numbers of women in the labor force occupied a key position as the most innovative shorter-hours advocates. Both feminists and labor groups raised the issue, often in productive counterpoint. However, AFL reluctance to organize females, or even to admit that women had a place in the work force, contributed to middle-class domination of the feminist-labor coalition. In contrast to early labor leaders like Seth Luther and Sarah Bagley, who saw the shortening of hours for women as bound up with the increased leisure and power of all workers, Gompers and feminists in the National Consumers' League shared a perspective which stressed the alleged need to protect females and, as Gompers argued, to return them to the home.

Another contribution to the recasting of the hours issue as one not based on divergent class interests was the growth of a professional group of reformers, especially factory inspectors and labor statisticians. These reformers ostensibly stood outside of class conflict and generally encouraged voluntary reforms in the working day based on the arguments of efficiency and health. Combined with the partial decline of working-class cultural institutions—in the face of the crumbling of the culturally creative Knights of Labor, of the coming of professional and middle-class domination of many ethnic cultural institutions, and the growth of mass culture—this reform ideology made labor's leisure seem less a threat to some employers.[2] As recreational theorists argued that leisure could contribute to "Americanization" of immigrants and to labor discipline, and as Frederick Winslow Taylor theorized on the compatibility of reduced hours and more productivity, a tiny number of manufacturers and a larger number of Progressive liberals came to embrace a voluntary reduction in working hours. The last years of the nineteenth century and the first years of the twentieth thus saw a series of changes which softened bourgeois opinion on the working day. Suburbanization, progressive ideas regarding leisure, the early growth of scientific management, and the development of labor statistics and labor economics as professions contributed to an intellectual climate in which shortening the working day could be approached not as a class issue but as a reform worthy of consideration on the grounds of efficiency, uplift, and safety. Some sectors of management, many professionals, a few important early Progressive politicians, and a small minority of industrial enterprises came to favor abridging the length of work.

The movement of upper-and middle-class people from the central city to suburbs, a migration which accelerated in the major metropolitan areas, made working-class leisure less threatening. Neighborhoods in the physically small cities of the mid-nineteenth century often included rich and poor within a short walk or earshot of each other. With the growth of class-segregated suburbs, often with private single-family homes, elite concern over the after-hours behavior of workers took different forms. Arguments by employers that less hours meant more working-class drinking, noise, and vice were less urgent. Desire to order the lives of workers more often found expression in plans to shape the leisure of the lower classes, not in a crude determination to limit that leisure.[3]

From the 1860s and earlier, reformers had argued that control over institutions of leisure and play could help ensure class peace. Similarly, since the 1850s, society as a whole and reformers in particular had backed off slightly from a single-minded stress on the curative properties of hard work and found some value in what Herbert Spencer called the "gospel of relaxation." Daniel T. Rodgers, whose *Work Ethic in Industrial America* treats play as well, observes, "Slowly and hesitantly many middle-class Northerners abandoned the idea of a world so crimped and dangerous that social and psychological health demanded constant doing; in its place they turned their imaginations to metaphors of surplus." Such trends found expression in the 1890s in proplay movements for more parks, for school sports, and for organized childhood leisure. The Progressive Recreation Movement was one such proplay movement. Moreover, the 1890s witnessed a bicycling craze, the rise of modern baseball, a mania for college athletics (especially football), and the growth of popular cultural institutions like Coney Island.[4]

The desire to recapture the virtues of play in a hardworking, industrial, capitalist society inevitably embodied great contradictions. That Theodore Roosevelt could be seen as a playful hero suggests how deeply Puritan, masculine, and capitalist attitudes toward work influenced attitudes toward play, producing in Roosevelt the idea that "strenuous play" was best. Coney Island itself, according to one recent historian, sought to "counteract weariness and boredom . . . [by] prescrib[ing] a homeopathic remedy of intense, frenetic physical activities, without imaginative demands." The Russian writer Maxim Gorky, a visitor in 1906, described the ethos of the island as based on American workers' attitude that "Life is made for the people to work six days in the week, sin on the seventh, and pay for their sins, confess their sins and pay for the confession." Professional advocates of recreation often argued not for play per se but for play as a means to secure higher productivity, obedience to authority, and even Americanization of immigrants.[5]

Coinciding with the new emphasis on leisure came a series of changes in management which held out the possibility of dramatically increasing working time and productivity *within* the confines of a given working day. These changes are usually grouped under the heading of Taylorism but were broader than the theories of scientific management advanced by Frederick Winslow Taylor. The time clock, for example, came into common use during the early 1890s, providing an easy way to keep track of tardiness and breaks.[6] However, Taylor was the most influential innovator in management strategy and the most attentive to the idea that management control over small units of time and over the rhythm of work was central to reordering the work process.

Insisting that his system was one of "time-saving," Taylor wrote of the trebling and more of production in the same number of hours and with virtually the same technology through the wresting of the control of the pace of production from workers, recruitment of adaptive laborers, and payment of premium bonuses. Taylor himself sometimes held that to "make shorter working hours" was a goal of scientific management. Although few employers using his method agreed and Taylor hardly pressed the issue, the idea that efficiency was compatible with a shorter working day appealed to some Progressive reformers and especially to professional investigators of labor conditions. The old contention that rest led to increased productivity could now be stated with special force: long hours signified the failure to adopt scientific, efficient management methods.[7]

Such arguments found an audience among the new professionals studying labor. After an early period in which many leaders of state Bureaus of Labor Statistics openly supported labor demands (especially in states like Massachusetts, New Jersey, Wisconsin, and Missouri where labor protests brought the agencies into being and socialists headed the bureaus), a professional class neutrality came to the bureaucracies, most notably through the agency of the National Association of Factory Inspectors (NAFI), founded in 1887.[8] At NAFI's second convention Massachusetts reformer Rufus Wade set the pattern for the inspectors' arguments for shorter hours. He held that no success had come to the shorter-hours advocates until "scientific knowledge" proved long days "unprofitable to the . . . owner" and maintained that the problem "was in a fair way to settlement," now that "it was shown that a reduction of the hours of labor meant better results, both as to the amount of production and quality of it." Two years later a Maine labor statistician, L. R. Campbell, began his speech to NAFI favoring ten-hour laws by observing, "It is evident to every thinking person that it is impracticable to reduce the hours of labor in a manner whereby the world's product is curtailed or lessened in the least," but his moderate resolution still passed by just two votes over the opposition of a conservative bloc desiring to have the inspectors only "interchange views" and not make recommendations.[9]

To reform-minded inspectors like Josephine Goldmark, and reform-minded academics like John R. Commons, scientific management offered sanction for the idea of progress through harmony of capital and labor, and through greater efficiency. Seeing labor opposition to Taylorism as misguided, these reformers embraced scientific management as the key to less hours. Even as late as 1912, when evidence was in that Taylorism did not reduce the working day, Goldmark could write. "Excessive hours, . . . are marks, . . . of inefficiency. That scientific management itself has shortened the working day in fair proportion to the increased productivity of its workers, no one can justly maintain. In regard to hours and conditions, the new system still has to share its marvelous gains more equitably with labor."[10]

Those Progressive politicians who embraced shorter hours or showed some flexibility on the issue, especially Louis Brandeis and Theodore Roosevelt, shared a fascination with scientific management and labor efficiency in general.[11] The most impressive early Progressive document to feature an appeal for shorter hours was the 1902 report of the U.S. Industrial Commission. Established by Congress in 1898, the commission spent nearly four years gathering data from 700 witnesses and from state labor reports. Its conclusions included a long section on the working day, which collected evidence that a shorter day increased production and left "employer and employee . . . agreed upon the advantages of the change." The commission backed a reduction in the length of labor for those working over eight hours and directly suggested that workers trade control over their work for shorter hours:

The entire tendency for industry is in the direction of increased exertion. Any restriction on output must work to the disadvantage of American industry, and the employers are often right in their demand, usually successful, that such restrictions be abandoned. This being true, there is but one alternative . . . a reduction of the hours of labor.[12]

Such a stress on the connection between leisure and efficiency might have been expected to produce a boom in legislative restriction on hours and voluntary reductions in the working day. That it did not testifies to the continuing depth of employer opposition to reform. The Industrial Commission Report of 1901 cited only a single, minor example of voluntary reduction of hours by an employer since a similar report fifteen years earlier. The report missed a few other instances of voluntary reform before 1901: the National Cash Register Company cut hours to eight for women workers; a Fitchburg, Massachusetts, ball bearing manufacturer instituted the eight-and-one-half-hour day; Fels and Company, soapmakers in Philadelphia, granted the eight-hour day to women; the visionary, profit-sharing N. O. Nelson Company in Leclaire, Illinois, operated on nine-hour shifts making plumbing supplies; the Solvay Process Company of Syracuse adopted an eight-hour shift at its Syracuse steel mills in 1892; shoe manufacturers in Boston (1898) and Philadelphia (1901) instituted the nine-and eight-hour day respectively. After 1901 examples of voluntary action multiplied only slowly. Armour Fertilizer moved to an eight-hour schedule between 1901 and 1905. In 1904 the Sharon Steel Hoop Company reduced hours from ten to eight. The biggest Minneapolis flour mills began the eight-hour day in 1902 and the International Time Recording Company made a transition to a nine-hour day. These cases hardly balanced the aggressive record of individual capitalists and employer associations who still fought against shorter hours.[13]

The clearest barometer of business opinion was the behavior of employer associations. The employers' associations, which grew dramatically in the early Progressive Era, often in response to the hours issue, focused their ire on shorter-hours laws for women and federal employees. The Illinois Manufacturers' Association, for example, consolidated around the opposition of employers to an 1893 statute enforcing an eight-hour day for women workers and dwelled on that issue through 1913. Employer cooperation in California similarly accelerated in 1900 with the campaign against eight-hour legislation for women.[14]

Leading the antilabor offensive was the National Association of Manufacturers (NAM), whose opposition to an eight-hour bill for federal employees in 1902 signaled a change in the organization's philosophy. From its inception in 1895 until 1902, NAM had functioned as a lobby on trade and tariff policy. However, in the latter year NAM president, David M. Perry, began an uncompromising campaign against all that he saw as evil in America: "Gompersism, 8-hour laws, boycotts, anti-conspiracy laws, and the making of socialists by the A. F. of L."[15] Leading other employer groups in an "open shop drive" designed to attack union strength, NAM first entered labor lobbying with a fierce attack on a bill which sought to strengthen the 1892 federal hours law by specifying that an eight-hour provision be written into all contracts for goods bought by the federal government. After sending a barrage of telegrams to Congress, NAM claimed credit for defeating the bill. For the next fifteen years, NAM continued to battle for "the American workmen['s] right to work more than 480 minutes of a calendar day." Referring to hours laws as "arbitrary, needless, destructive [and] dangerous," NAM found ready allies in other employer associations, especially the Citizens' Industrial Alliance, the National Metal Trades' Association and the League for Industrial Rights.[16]

Another employers' association, the National Civic Federation (NCF), included labor representatives and has sometimes been portrayed as representative of an enlightened corporate capitalist strategy which, in contrast to the small manufacturer-dominated NAM, undertook farsighted programs of conciliation, welfare, and labor reform. But the NCF, founded in 1900, made small attempts to shorten the working day. While a few individual NCF leaders showed flexibility on the issue, they generally did so half-heartedly. For example, NCF leaders praised the 1900 Murray Hill Agreement which briefly brought labor peace between the International Association of Machinists and the National Metal Trades Association, and which gave the machinists the fifty-four-hour week, but watched as the pact dissolved the next year when employers refused national bargaining over wages.[17] In 1902 some top NCF members from the steel industry supported the federal eight-hour law, but they may have done so, Norman Ware suggests, in return for Gompers's conservative influence in a strike. In 1905 NCF President August Belmont seized the occasion of the Interborough Transit strike, directed against a corporation he headed, not to grant the nine-hour day workers demanded but to break the union and institute an open shop.[18]

Arguments, but not strategies, for shortening the working day found an occasional place in both NCF conventions and the organization's *Review*. Particularly popular were materials produced by the ex-follower of Ira Steward, George Gunton. By now a professor, Gunton became a leading exponent of business-labor cooperation during this period. His writings stressed the necessity of workers accepting Taylorism and unsatisfying work but held out shorter hours in return: "The exhaustion of the laborer must be avoided, but it cannot be avoided by reducing production . . . they must have relief by lessening the duration of the pressure everyday."[19]

However, such appeals to efficiency-minded employers seldom led to NCF action. The organization did not support legislation on hours, even for children. Few of the leading corporate members, despite conciliatory rhetoric, bargained with unions after 1906 and voluntary reductions of hours remained rare.[20] The new context of the hours issue did not generate any significant softening of employer attitudes and trade union action remained the dominant method of gaining concessions regarding the working day.

AFL policy concerning the working day meanwhile changed subtly, but critically, during the two decades following Haymarket. Both the rationale for the eight-hour day and plans for inaugurating it shifted to more conservative grounds. After an early period of fluidity in which the AFL encouraged hours legislation and mass strikes, the AFL came to limit its role in hours agitation to advocacy of legislation protecting special groups of workers (such as miners, bakers, railwaymen, government employees, and women) and to doing support and educational work around hours strikes by individual craft unions. AFL leaders, especially Gompers, increasingly stressed the practical aims of eliminating unemployment and of increasing productivity in eight-hour propaganda and less often emphasized the connection of hours with higher wages or with more visionary goals such as working-class self-education and labor political activity.

In reviewing the positions of the AFL, it is necessary to observe that a range of considerations shaped the federation's actions. Craft union leaders responded to pressures from other groups, including the Knights of Labor, the Socialist Labor party, Socialist party, and the Populists. They gauged the relative power of organized labor versus that of capital and often concluded that frontal assaults (like mass strikes or general legislation on hours) were unproductive in an age of vigilante violence, intervention into strikes by state and federal troops, and the courts' use of frequent, successful legal challenges to protective labor laws.[21] They appealed to public opinion with arguments designed to win a broad hearing among not just workers but also the middle classes and Progressive reform groups. Moreover, the AFL strategy was not wholly unsuccessful during these years. By one estimate, the average working week in all industries declined by 4.9 hours between 1890 and 1914.[22]

On the other hand, AFL policy was far from being solely the result of rational calculation concerning what was possible and what was best for trade unionism, and for all American workers. It reflected the distrust of politics common to Gompers and many conservative craft leaders, a distrust fuelled by an unwillingness to concede to socialist and Populist opponents in the unions that a contest over control of the state was important. It also betrayed a narrow craft consciousness that neglected the demands of unskilled workers and discouraged sympathy strikes. The idea of a craft-by-craft march to the shorter working day, led by the most powerful unions, moving alone but with some monetary aid from the AFL, reflected the notion that mass solidarity actions were counterproductive.[23]

The AFL's tactical conservatism stemmed also from a bias against immigrant labor, which, according to the conventional wisdom, could not be organized and actually favored long hours. A joke repeated by Chicago needle trades organizers, regarding a "greenhorn" who heard of the union's call for an eight-hour day and responded approvingly but added that "the organization would do even better to demand sixteen hours" is instructive.[24] Such perceptions of immigrants became self-fulfilling prophecies which excused the AFL from organizing unskilled workers around hours. Significantly, Gompers interrupted the chapter on the working day in his memoir with a racist digression on San Francisco's Chinatown and a plea for immigration restriction.[25] The mixed motives and results of AFL policy on hours are best viewed in a sustained consideration of three aspects of that policy: arguments for the shorter day; rejection of independent political action by labor; the craft-by-craft strategy of securing the eight-hour day. A later section of this chapter considers AFL sexism and the shorter hours movement among women.

152

The evolution of AFL thought on the eight-hour demand is difficult to summarize. Indeed two serious treatments of the subject diverge in their conclusions. Henry Raymond Mussey's 1927 study of eight-hour theory in the AFL found that the ideas that eight hours would cure unemployment and raise wages became less important in federation statements between 1886 and 1900. The contention that shorter hours would increase productivity bulked larger as the century neared its end and, by 1900, with the publication of George A. Schilling's "Less Hours, Increased Production—Great Progress" and Frank Foster's "Sidelights on the Shorter Workday Demand," the AFL had virtually adopted the same grounds—productivity and creation of consumer market—that Henry Ford would later use to justify granting the eight-hour day. Daniel Rodgers, on the other hand, has portrayed Gompers as fighting a holding action against turn-of-the-century overemphasis on production and as claiming leisure as the right of those "who have borne the awful strains and burdens of exacting toil."[26] Only after 1900, according to Rodgers, did Gompers "compromise the dream of lessened toil by taking up the argument that the eight-hour workers would make up production losses by more efficient work." Both authors agree that by 1910 eight-hour theory in the AFL was less creative and less passionate than it had been 1890. Mussey in particular observed a drop in the "theoretical temperature" of eight-hour appeals and, after a summary of eight-hour discussions at the 1906 convention, commented, "Verily the glory is departed from Israel!"[27]

However, a closer reading of AFL literature suggests that the lessening heat of shorter-hours appeals stemmed from causes more complex than the emphasis on productivity. From the immediate post-Haymarket period, when the AFL published three noteworthy eight-hour pamphlets, the organization had generally followed Ira Steward's arguments that less hours would lead to innovation, to increased consumer demand, and, therefore, to productive advances. George McNeill, George Gunton, and Lemuel Danryid, authors of the pamphlets, were all decisively influenced by Steward's ideas, with Gunton drawing most heavily on that side of Steward's thought which implied that shorter hours would be good for all classes.[28] Gompers himself, in an 1888 statement, followed this line of thought, defining the hours of labor as an issue "which creates the greatest revolution in the conditions of the people with the slightest frictions upon any" and commenting, in 1900, that every cut in hours leads to "the introduction of a new machine" and to more production.[29]

Thus emphasis on productivity was an ongoing theme inherited from Steward, not a new invention of turn-of-the-century theorists. However, for Steward, McNeill, and others, the productive advances came as part of a lengthy process of technological advance, not as the simple result of fresher workers, achieving in ten hours what had been done in eight. McNeill, for example, held that the "day will never come when one can do as much in eight hours as he might the day before or after in ten hours' labor," but maintained that *in the long run* shorter hours led to more demand, better technology, and more production. Similarly, for Steward and McNeill, though not Gunton, shorter hours were owed to labor as a matter of justice quite aside from the question of productivity.[30]

During periods of faith in cooperation with employers, and especially in the first years of the twentieth century when labor leaders were fascinated by arbitration plans sponsored by the NCF, the AFL verged upon subsuming the class aspect of the issue of the working day, though it never quite did so absolutely. Thus Gompers might say, "We want no friction, our aim is to avoid conflict," but in the next breath observe, "Toilers recognize, however, that there are worse evils than strife."[31]

As the rhetoric regarding productivity and class harmony changed slowly, so too did other aspects of eight-hour theory. Steward's involved ideas on the working day existed alongside simpler notions regarding the desirability of shorter hours. The most popular of these were the simple formulae that less hours meant higher wages and more jobs. Although Steward usually held that leisure created new demands for increased pay, most unionists probably understood the relationship between pay and hours in terms of shorter hours driving up wages by limiting the available workers and thus upping the demand for labor. In any case, as Mussey observes, the wage argument became less prominent after 1890. Craft leaders, anxious to demonstrate to employers that no one's interests suffered from shorter hours, shied away from stressing that wage raises would follow. Still some union organizers hammered home the slogan that "Decreasing the work, increases the pay."[32] Most dramatic was the change to the new preeminence accorded to unemployment as a reason for instituting the eight-hour day. Practical share-the-work arguments appealed during these years of frequent, serious depressions. Gompers reiterated that hours were too lengthy so long as even a single worker was out of a job. This approach, which matured during the depression of 1893, enabled the AFL to continue to maintain that the eight-hour plank was also a wage demand, since wages were seen as set partly by the minimum renumeration an unemployed worker would take for doing a job.[33] The argument for shorter hours as a jobs measure also had public appeal. However, in all the AFL agitation for adjustment of the working day to combat joblessness, the federation assumed that such changes were to result from the private actions of employers and unions.

As productivity and unemployment bulked larger in AFL arguments, vision of a working class remade and fitted for power through self-education and political discourse during leisure hours receded. In part this probably resulted from changes in cultural attitudes toward leisure discussed above, especially the growing perception of leisure as a mass activity shared by Americans of various classes. But it also reflected the limited goals of the AFL leadership and its distaste for radical visions and independent labor politics. Gompers might at times refer to the eight-hour day as a way to sharpen the perceptions of workers who were "cattle . . . whose votes are purchased on election day," but he foresaw no great political transformations as a result of this change. An 1891 AFL document had stated: "The taste for freedom grows upon that on which it feeds, and would-be oppressors of labor well know that if the wage-earner is once given time . . . to learn his own strength . . . he is thereby furnished with the weapons which shall secure for him industrial emancipation."[34] After 1900 such rhetoric gave way to more pedestrian arguments.

In the wake of Haymarket it seemed possible that the AFL would again consider political solutions to the problem of long hours. However, by 1887 Gompers and the federation had withdrawn into a refusal to become involved in partisan activity on the United Labor party's behalf. At AFL conventions direct trade union action was the only tactic discussed seriously between 1886 and 1890 as a method for reducing hours for all workers. A deep distrust of the government remained a part of the craft unionist's assumptions. "Eight-Hour Laws made by politicians," remarked the *Carpenter* in 1891, "will never be observed by the employers. The only eight-hour law that will ever have binding force in this country will be made and enforced by the workingmen."[35] No other group challenged this assessment during the seven years after Haymarket. The dwindling Knights, and especially Powderly, still favored education and voluntary action though they maintained a paper commitment to legislation; Edward Bellamy's Nationalist Clubs saw shorter hours as desirable but also as a diversion from the broader goals of their movement. Bellamy in his work, *Looking Backward*, envisioned a system under which the labor hours were much fewer and fluctuated according to the difficulty of the task. The Socialist Labor party emphasized a complex scheme of linking shorter hours to production increases or stressed the necessity of abolishing the entire wage system.[36]

In 1894 the AFL leadership did come under serious challenge from a labor-Populist-socialist alliance which, among other political issues, posed the necessity of AFL agitation for "a legal eight-hour work day." Using British labor politics as a model, the labor Populists endorsed independent political action around a broad platform and carried well over a third of the convention votes on the controversial Plank 10, advocating common ownership of the means of production and distribution, while passing ten other reform planks including that on the eight-hour day. However, Gompers and the AFL leadership were able to defeat the program as a package and thus claim that votes for individual planks were invalid; many socialists came to abandon the AFL in protest.[37] Gompers recognized the political potency of the eight-hour demand and responded by broadening the limited scope of AFL legislative activities around the issue. Thus, he added support for protective legislation for women and children at the national and state level to the existing AFL commitment to lobbying for well-enforced legislation applying to federal employees.[38]

Although the Populists' People's party did support eight-hour laws, their program was neither detailed nor their agitation energetic on the point. With the defection of socialists from the Populist ranks and with the ultimate fusion of populism with the Democratic party, any serious possibility for independent labor politics partly around the eight-hour plank disappeared.[39] The Socialist party included eight-hour demands in its platforms and fought hard in several states for hours laws, but the Socialists were handicapped in the early years by their lack of numerical strength at the polls and in most unions.[40] Moreover, some Socialists were reluctant to push the eight-hour issue because it was seen as a palliative which "in the long run . . . if adopted, will have hardly any effect upon wages, profits, the unemployed and foreign commerce."[41] Thus the AFL national policy of limited legislative action on hours persisted without serious objection for nearly two decades after 1894, although local and state federations sometimes did endorse general eight-hour laws.[42]

The record of legislative and judicial action regarding the working day during the early years of the AFL reinforced skepticism as to the possibility of political reform. Laws often contained loopholes or were unraveled by courts until such holes appeared. The pet project of the AFL, a statute applying to federal workers, is a prime example. The ineffective 1868 law providing the eight-hour day for government employees was strengthened somewhat in 1888 by specific acts requiring the Public Printer and the Post Office to observe that standard. The postal officials defied the law, which applied specifically to letter carriers, for five years, on the grounds that time working at the office should not be considered as part of the mailman's letter-carrying workday, before the courts upheld the postal employees.[43]

Later rulings on the broader, AFL-sponsored eight-hour law of 1892, which specified that the eight-hour provision obtained on work contracted for by the government, would not favor labor. The Supreme Court ruled that "public works" meant permanent, stationary structures owned by the government, and therefore, the law did not apply in such areas as privately owned shipyards and factories doing government work. Such decisions so outraged Gompers that he proposed that the AFL "insist" that "all work for the government shall be performed by the government, without . . . contractors." But the ruling stood, as did a loose interpretation of the "emergency" provision in the law which enabled contractors to claim that "permanent emergencies" existed during construction of levees and dams simply by virtue of the tendency of rivers to rise and fall.[44]

In another major political test, a 1906 battle over whether the eight-hour standard would apply to work on the Panama Canal, the AFL appeared to be winning the legal fight, having secured a favorable opinion from the attorney general, only to have Congress pass a canal appropriation bill with a rider nullifying the application of the law to Panama Canal construction. In addition, the AFL complained that federal authorities refused to enforce the law even when it did apply.[45]

Other national legislative campaigns of the AFL faced equally stiff resistance. At its 1897 convention the federation went on record as favoring "efforts to secure an amendment to the Constitution . . . so that Congress may be empowered to legislate . . . the hours of labor for women and children." No such amendment passed Congress until 1924, when it was approved only to stall for lack of ratification by state legislatures. A decade of efforts by the railway unions, supported by the AFL, to achieve federal limitation on the hours of railroad workers eventuated in 1907 in the Hours of Service Act. Though important in establishing a precedent for federal intervention, that law allowed workers "to be or remain on duty" for up to "sixteen consecutive hours."[46]

State laws also suffered in the courts. A statute that broke with tradition by not providing a loophole allowing contracts contravening the law passed the Nebraska legislature in 1891. The act, which called for overtime to be paid after eight hours, was declared unconstitutional by the state supreme court three years later. The court, in a precedent-setting decision, ruled that the law discriminated against certain trades by exempting domestic and farm laborers from its provisions and that it violated freedom of contract.[47] In many cases, especially in New York State, courts even denied that states and municipalities could constitutionally set hours and require that wages not be cut for eight-hour workers on projects for which they contracted. A landmark 1903 U.S. Supreme Court decision in *Atkin v. Kansas* reversed that trend, but on narrow grounds that specified that the rights of the state, not of workers, were being upheld.[48]

Legislation to protect laborers in jobs where special health and safety considerations applied faced intense lobbying efforts from the industries and, if passed, drew court challenges. Only New York and California enacted a law protecting the public from overworked druggists and drug clerks during this period. California set ten hours as a maximum length for a working day in pharmacies in 1901. Similar proposals surfaced in New York in 1898 and drew denunciation as a species of "state socialism" before passing the legislature in 1901.[49] State laws limiting the hours of railroad workers generally enacted mandatory rest periods, ranging from thirteen hours to a full day, between shifts. Such statutes, and the laws setting hours for street railwaymen in several states, were justified mainly in terms of public safety, a ground for legislation that the Rhode Island Supreme Court defined as constitutional in a 1902 case. However, legislation generally failed to ameliorate the long hours of street railwaymen. The transition from horse-drawn cars to electrically powered vehicles cut hours somewhat, but during and after the turn of the century, days of thirteen and even seventeen hours persisted, and the median working day for 345 surveyed companies was between ten and eleven hours. A 1905 Bureau of Labor Statistics report found over 80 percent of street railway workers required to work on Sundays.[50]

When legislation designed to protect workers in hazardous jobs came before the courts, decisions varied widely. The most significant early cases involved mining. Several western states, whose industrial economies revolved around mines and smelter, passed eight-hour laws during the 1890s and the first decade of the twentieth century. In Utah the AFL, the Western Federation of Miners, and Tom Kearns, a politically active mineowner who had begun his career as a miner, combined forces to secure the passage of an eight-hour law, which survived challenges in both the state and national supreme courts. The national decision in the landmark case of *Holden v. Hardy* explicitly recognized the disingenuousness of employers' arguments that hours laws violated the rights of workers.[51] But in Colorado, where Populists had begun agitation on the matter in the early 1890s, the state supreme court twice declared eight-hour laws for miners to be unconstitutional "class legislation." In 1895, expressing an opinion on a proposed law before the legislature, the court found the statute violated freedom of contract. Four years later it held a virtually exact copy of Utah law to be unconstitutional, declaring, "It is beyond the power of the legislature, under the guise of the police power, to prohibit an adult man from working more than eight hours . . . on the ground that working longer may . . . injure his . . . health." Despite a three to one margin in a popular vote in 1901 favoring an amendment to the state constitution allowing the legislature to fix miners' hours, no effective eight-hour law emerged till 1911.[52]

Montana, which passed an eight-hour law for miners and smelters in 1901 after narrowly failing to do so a decade before, resembled Utah in that legislation resulted from cooperation between unions and a mineowning politician. Like Utah, it also produced a law that was enforced, if tardily and unevenly. Arizona, whose 1903 territorial statute applied only to mines, made no effort to prosecute under the law and used the Arizona Rangers to attack eight-hour strikers at Morenci. A Nevada law survived some constitutional tests but not others, while a 1901 Missouri statute covering underground miners remained unenforced until it passed a 1904 court test. By 1911, with California having entered the eight-hour ranks, hardrock mining generally operated, by law, on that schedule. But the battle had been long and disillusioning. As a recent study observes, for many miners "The struggle over the eight-hour day in the century's opening years first eroded and then destroyed the links of trust and support which bound them to their government."[53]

The most significant Supreme Court defeat for labor came in a case involving New York bakers. After over a decade of trying to remedy their long hours—up to sixteen and even eighteen daily—through strikes, boycotts, and legislation, the Bakers' Progressive Union secured passage of a ten-hour law for bakers.[54] The campaign leading to passage of the law, brilliantly led by Henry Weismann, stressed both the damage to health done by laboring in hot shops and the public's interest in bread baked by healthy workers. The law was poorly enforced; in 1897 only 312 of 855 baking establishments investigated by factory inspectors complied with the ten-hour provision. However by 1899 many unionized bakers secured the ten-hour system. Master bakers, heartened by the defection of Weismann to their ranks and by the decisions of California courts that hours laws for bakers there were unconstitutional, began an offensive against the ten-hour standard by backing Joseph Lochner, a nonunion bakery owner in Utica, who refused to comply with the 1895 law. After the state supreme court found in favor of Lochner's employees in 1904, the Master Bakers' Association appealed to the U.S. Supreme Court. The high court, split five to four, rejected the argument that "wholesome bread" could best be produced by setting hours. More importantly, it held that regulation of hours in the absence of a clear health hazard violated the rights of "liberty" and "property" guaranteed by the Fourteenth Amendment.[55] This devastating decision, along with those discussed above (and below in connection with women's labor) helped to rivet the AFL to a policy accentuating trade union action to gain the eight-hour day.

After Haymarket the AFL took two years to regroup before returning to an aggressive policy of using strikes and threats of strikes to reduce hours. Local hours strikes did occur during this period, especially in New York City where an 1888 dispute involved 15,000 garment workers.[56] But it was the December 1888 AFL convention in St. Louis that renewed national agitation. That convention targeted May 1, 1890, as the date on which organized labor would enforce the eight-hour day. The resolution left open the possibility of a mass strike and inaugurated an energetic educational and organizational campaign around the issue. Four holidays—Washington's Birthday in 1889 and 1890, Labor Day in 1889, and July 4, 1889—were set aside for eight-hour rallies. Local eight-hour leagues, quite different from the craft-dominated structures usually associated with the AFL, emerged. Tens of thousands of eight-hour pamphlets went out; about a thousand meetings, with speakers like Gompers, McNeill, and Henry George, took place in hundreds of cities. Gompers, who at the time encouraged industrial federations in the AFL, saw the eight-hour demand as the key organizing tool of the labor movement, as an issue which "will wake up the millions of workers from their present lethargy."[57] The AFL president sent a message to the Paris Congress of Socialist and Labor Movements in 1889 proposing, as he later recalled, that May 1 be celebrated as "an International Labor Day" and successfully urging solidarity with the planned eight-hour demonstrations in the United States. The original of that letter has never been found but certainly a series of AFL actions, from Haymarket through 1890, were instrumental in the adoption of May Day as an international workers' holiday.[58]

The eight-hour campaign not only enabled the AFL to make positive organizational moves on its own behalf but won workers away from the Knights of Labor, whose leadership continued to oppose action on the issue. Powderly, speaking for the Knights, attempted to discredit the AFL strategy as a reckless repeat of 1886, but Gompers fended off criticisms by denying that a general strike loomed. "In the present condition of labor," he wrote, "no movement for a general strike would have my support. The end of the labor movement will not come in 1890."[59]

At the 1889 AFL convention, delegates made clear that they were not threatening a general strike by voting to follow Gompers's suggestion "that one or two trades . . . be selected . . . upon which to concentrate the whole efforts of Organized Labor to secure the Eight-Hour workday, May 1, 1890." Gompers added that inauguration of the eight-hour system without strikes remained possible.

This initial decision to pursue the eight-hour demand on a craft-by-craft basis did not coincide with a complete turn to craft conservatism by the AFL though it did reflect distrust of the mass strike as a tactic. Indeed, the convention adopted a series of progressive measures, including a decision to fund and distribute an international eight-hour journal. Gompers, in his presidential address, held that the 1886 actions had achieved much and stressed that the movement united skilled and unskilled workers.[60]

After polling the various member unions, the AFL Executive Council chose the carpenters to carry the eight-hour banner in 1890, to be followed by the miners in a subsequent year. Internationalism and cross-craft solidarity characterized the May 1 movement. The large strike fund of the Carpenters' and Joiners' Union received additional funds from an AFL assessment of other unions. Union after union resolved to aid the carpenters with cash and to march in May 1 demonstrations. Despite refusal of cooperation by the Knights, 46,000 building tradesmen gained the eight-hour day and 30,000 won nine hours, largely without long strikes. Indeed, the New York *Times* found the first of May "a quiet day throughout the country" as master builders acceded to their employees' demands.[61]

The day was hardly quiet in terms of jubilant labor demonstrations. In many cities the AFL joined the Socialist Labor party in sponsoring rallies. In Chicago 30,000 members, and in New York City members of seventy unions turned out, bearing banners with such slogans as "No More Bosses—Wage Slavery Must Go" and "The 8 Hour Day is the Next Step in the Labor Movement." The New York demonstration pointed with pride to concurrent rallies in such nations as Australia, Austria, Belgium, Chile, Cuba, Denmark, England, France, Germany, Holland, Hungary, Italy, Peru, and Switzerland and looked forward to "the reorganization of society on a socialist basis."[62] For Gompers the victories and the demonstrations of a quarter million English workers signified, "the universality of our movement . . . a ray of hope for the attainment of the poet's dream, 'The Parliament of Men, The Federation of the World'."[63]

Such gains were never repeated. After 1890 the AFL did not attempt centralized direction of another large eight-hour campaign. Most studies narrowly see this decline in emphasis on the working day as the result of the poor choice of the miners as the trade to succeed the carpenters in pressing the issue. The miners, with only one worker in ten unionized and largely led by John Rae, who sympathized with the Knights and favored wide local autonomy, became embroiled in a costly 1891 strike, partly contesting for the eight-hour day, in the Connellsville, Pennsylvania, coke area. The union had to default on its commitment to mount a May 1891 campaign for eight hours.[64] Disillusioned, the 1891 AFL convention turned down applications by the International Typographical Union and the Journeymen Bakers and Confectioners National Union to lead the shorter-hours movement next.[65]

But the choice of the miners, however unfortunate, need not have stifled eight-

hour enthusiasm. It is true that the miners' failure left bitterness among AFL delegates, especially Gompers, who regarded it an instance of Knights of Labor
duplicity and contended that the miners' union acted precipitously and improp-
erly in unilaterally calling off the wider eight-hour effort. But the action did not
end eight-hour campaigning. Building tradesmen extended their gains of the previous year in a concerted 1891 campaign. The following year, the AFL backed
the New Orleans general strike, a massive display of black-white unity forged
largely around the issue of hours. The New Orleans walkout was successful in
winning the ten-hour standard for the "Triple Alliance" of teamsters, scalesmen,
and packers.[66]

The retreat of the AFL leadership from large-scale, nationally coordinated
eight-hour campaigns stemmed mainly from the triumph, in the early 1890s, of
craft consciousness and conservatism. The alliance of Gompers with those federation leaders pressing for craft autonomy produced a hesitancy to embrace a
demand which hinged on cross-craft cooperation and on solidarity of skilled and
unskilled, and which sparked unpredictable eight-hour leagues, sympathy strikes,
and tramping strikes. The most significant action of the 1891 convention was not
the rejection of the bakers' and printers' applications, but the decision to leave
the eight-hour struggle to individual craft unions without central direction and
mass publicity. Among the convention's resolutions was a plank pledging not to
reveal which craft would strike for eight-hours until the time of the strike.
Although justified with the rationale that "no competent strategist in military
science would so prejudice any plan of operations," this decision left hours strategy in the hands of AFL executives and craft leaders. The struggles against socialists and populists inside the AFL made the radical aspects of the eight-hour
demand seem a liability to conservative unionists. Thus the 1891 AFL convention resolved to "rely for counsel, sympathy and support only upon those who
are identified with the trade union cause, and to whom the success of the . . .
short-hour movement is a matter of honest and vital concern."[67]

For the rest of the 1890s and for a time thereafter, AFL initiatives on hours
sputtered. President John McBride of the AFL asked delegates to consider the
"feasibility of inaugurating a movement to establish the eight-hour work day," in
1895 but no action eventuated. A year later Gompers proposed May 1, 1898, as
a date for either "general" or limited enforcement of the eight-hour system. Mod-
eled on the 1890 plan, the 1898 campaign included meeting on holidays and issuing pamphlets, but the Executive Committee did not pick a union willing to
strike, and the target date passed uneventfully. The National Granite Cutters'
Union did secure the eight-hour day through a coordinated campaign in 1900,
but, as Marion Cahill observes, this came through the internal strength of the
union, not the "feeble" solidarity efforts of the AFL.[68] By 1901 the AFL only recommended "discussion and commendation" of eight-hour efforts and, in 1904,
reacting to plans by the International Typographical Union to press for shorter
hours, the federation abdicated central direction by endorsing any eight-hour

campaign inaugurated by a national union. The wave of shorter-hours strikes during the active union organizing of the 1901-1904 period developed without the AFL's leadership. Even so, in 1901 one striker in five acted purely to lessen hours, and over 35 percent of all strikers had hours among the issues in their walkouts. Wage increases alone were at issue for less than 25 percent of 1901 strikers. In 1902 and 1903, a total of 588,200 strikers listed hours as a demand while 397,595 sought only higher wages.[69]

Turn-of-the-century hours strikes by miners, machinists, and printers illustrated how far the AFL had come from its positions of 1886 and 1890. Anthracite miners in the East and metal miners in the West agitated for the eight-hour day, a gain many miners of soft coal achieved despite company violence and attempts to introduce strikebreakers in 1898.[70] The anthracite miners, concentrated in eastern Pennsylvania and represented by the UMW, asked for a reduction in hours from ten to eight, among other demands. Ninety percent of area miners joined a strike in September 1900. Largely through the intervention of the National Civic Federation, whose leaders fretted about electing a Republican president in that election year, the railway executives controlling the mines were persuaded to settle with a compromise package providing higher wages but not shorter hours.

Mine owners reneged on the agreement almost immediately and continuous friction resulted in another walkout, involving 184,000 miners in May 1902. The celebrated Anthracite Strike of 1902 focused on union recognition and on the size of a projected wage increase, and also involved a demand for eight hours. The conflict lasted into the fall of 1902 and witnessed numerous attempts by NCF leaders to bring UMW leader John P. Mitchell, along with rail and mine executives, to the conference table. Mitchell and Gompers entertained repeated overtures from the NCF to moderate the strikers' demands and prevented a sympathy strike in the bituminous coalfields.[71] With socialist strength in the coalfields growing rapidly, with even the Chicago *Tribune* turning against the hard line taken by George F. Baer and his management associates, and with the development of a movement to nationalize the mines, President Theodore Roosevelt intervened. In early October he persuaded Mitchell to induce the miners to return to work with the strike issues to be settled through arbitration by a presidential commission. Five months later the arbitrators granted a nine-hour day and a wage increase but not union recognition. Throughout the conflict the union leadership minimized the hours demand and warned of threats from "radicals," sharp contrasts to the policies of the early years of the AFL.[72]

The stormy strikes of nonferrous metal miners in the West at the beginning of the twentieth century, strikes which Philip Taft and Selig Perlman have called "class war on a grand scale," usually revolved around the eight-hour issue. Those Colorado disputes at Telluride (1901), Cripple Creek (1903), Idaho Springs (1903), and at American Smelting and Refining Company in Denver, like earlier ones at Leadville (1880) and Cripple Creek (1894), centered on the hours of labor as did another in South Dakota in 1907.[73] These struggles are best considered as part of the development of western radicalism and industrial unionism and will be briefly discussed in a later chapter. It is worth noting here that the Western Federation of Miners (WFM), unaffiliated with the AFL after 1900, led these offensives, and that the AFL made few attempts to support eight-hour strikes in the West, making only tardy efforts to oppose repression against the unionists and peppering those efforts with reiterations of employers' charges that the WFM was irresponsible and violent. Most seriously, in the case of the Cripple Creek strike, the AFL-affiliated UMW called off a strike in the northern Colorado mines enabling troops and mine police to concentrate an often fatal campaign of terror on miners to the south. The nadir of this retreat from solidarity came when UMW head John Mitchell reportedly asked Colorado's governor to order the great organizer Mary "Mother" Jones to leave the state, after Jones opposed abandonment of the strike.[74]

AFL support for the International Association of Machinists' (IAM) drive for a shorter working day in 1901 was influenced by Gompers's passion for arbitration and misplaced faith in the NCF. The IAM grew rapidly from 1898 to 1900, increasing its membership fourfold to 60,000. In 1900 the national union demanded the nine-hour day in five major cities. As a result of the Murray Hill Agreement between the union and the National Metal Trades Association (NMTA) in the spring of 1900, the fifty-seven-hour week was to be established nationally in six months, to be succeeded by a fifty-four-hour week six months later.[75] Both Gompers and IAM President James O'Connell showed enthusiasm for the pact, as did NCF leaders, but when the May 10, 1901, deadline for beginning the fifty-four-hour schedule came, so did trouble. Especially in St. Louis, workers argued that their wages should not fall as a result of the change in hours. When IAM and AFL leaders asked the NMTA to reopen negotiations on the issue, the employers' association refused, counseled local adjustments, and warned shopowners to prepare for strikes on May 20. The 58,000 strikers achieved some local successes, but usually not on the hours issue, and the NMTA, formerly at the head of labor-mangement detente, became an outspoken advocate of an open shop and a bitter foe of shorter hours.[76]

In the printing trades the International Typographical Union (ITU), after a dozen years of agitation, had reached a nine-hour agreement—which also covered unionized pressmen and bookbinders—with the United Typothetae employers' association in 1899. Three days later the ITU began a campaign to extend its gains to the eight-hour day. The national union appointed an Eight-Hour Committee and advised locals to seek a fifteen-minute reduction in the working day for the next four years. The 1903 convention set January 1, 1905, as the date to achieve a transition to eight hours. In 1904 that date was moved back by a year and a hefty assessment for a strike fund was approved.[77]

In anticipation of a battle over the eight-hour day scheduled by the ITU for the following January, the large Chicago printing firm, R. R. Donnelly, brought in nonunion employees to provoke a strike in August 1905. Similar provocations took place in San Antonio, forcing the ITU to call for immediate, unified action to enforce the eight-hour system. During the two-year campaign that followed, the union collected a 10 percent assessment on its working members to bolster a strike fund for those still fighting for the shorter day. Ultimately the fund paid out $3.5 million in benefits. In Cleveland 600 printers marched in the 1905 Labor Day parade bearing shining white umbrellas emblazoned with the ITU symbol and the words "EIGHT HOURS." By 1907 the forty-eight-hour week was a reality in large unionized shops almost everywhere except Nashville and Kansas City. However, many formerly unionized employers instituted the open shop during the strike. In 1910 the ITU was still trying to "reclaim" workplaces, including the giant R. R. Donnelly, in Chicago. Other employers agreed to the forty-eight-hour week but, observing a half-holiday on Saturday, retained shifts of closer to nine hours on weekdays. The AFL levied only a penny per week assessment (and that for just a month) to support the printers' eight-hour strikes, justifying Marion Cahill's view that the parent body "did not take an active part in the struggle."[78] In printing as in other trades, the AFL no longer led and extended, but instead limited and channeled, shorter-hours campaigns. In the realm of struggles to limit the hours of women's labor, the federation would have an equally conservative impact.

The female component of the labor force significantly increased between 1880 and 1900. The figure of 2,647,000 employed women of 1880 became 4,005,500 a decade later and 5,319,500 at the turn of the century. In 1880, 15.2 percent of all employed persons were female; in 1900, just over 18 percent.[79] The presence of so many adult and child female workers attracted the sympathies of factory inspectors, middle-class reformers, and, at times, of the AFL leadership. Nonetheless, from 1895 through 1908 the number of women belonging to unions in New York, the largest and most unionized state, grew by only 596 while the number of organized men grew by 191,632; the tiny female proportion of the labor movement declined from 5.6 percent to a mere 2.9 percent. In Missouri, the other state for which reliable figures exist, between 1902 and 1908 the ranks of unionized women declined from 2,835 to 2,159, and their percentage edged downward from 3.6 percent to 2.8 percent. The figures from Chicago are more dismal. In 1903 an estimated 31,400 women belonged to all-female unions alone in Chicago; by 1909 the Women's Trade Union League found only about 10,000 Chicago women in unions of any kind.[80]

Although employer opposition, especially in small clothing manufacturing shops, accounted for part of the failure to organize women, a large share of the blame belongs with the AFL leadership. Edward O'Donnell's *American Federationist* article of 1897 summarized the feelings of many craft union heads in its title, "Women as Bread Winners—the Error of the Age." O'Donnell spoke of an "invasion of the crafts by women," "an evolutionary backslide," and "an insidious assault upon the home," while contending that women were simply being used to undermine wage scales of skilled male workers.[81] An 1898 resolution urging the confining of women to the homes received serious consideration at the AFL's national convention. Samuel Gompers himself, after earlier taking less sexist positions, echoed O'Donnell's rhetoric in 1905 articles for both the labor and popular press. Such a stance, combined with the fact that many working women were blacks and immigrants, made the AFL chronically unwilling to invest organizers and money in order to enlist women members. "From the 1880's until after World War I," as Meredith Tax writes, "efforts to organize women came less from the mainstream of the labor movement than from a series of united front efforts by socialists and feminists."[82]

AFL indifference to organizing women had a damaging impact on the entire eight-hour movement. Working women of the period were not just organizable; they were *the best* constituency for struggle over the working day. Over half of all women workers labored in either the making or washing of cloth or clothing, or in domestic service. Hours, long an explosive issue in the textile and needle trades, continued to be a grievance, especially among garment workers whose "seasonal unionism" often produced ephemeral organization, strikes over long hours, and settlements which were not honored even months after the conflicts. From the strikes of Jewish sewing tradespersons in New York City in 1888, to the use of Mary Steward's shorter hours jingle as a motto for the Chicago Cloak Makers' Union in 1896, to the fifty-five-hour week campaigns of cap and hat makers in several cities after 1903, needle trades unionism emphasized hours as a cure for seasonal unemployment and featured an ebb and flow of gains and losses on the issue.[83] In domestic service and in many laundries the absence of *any* set hours made the working day a central issue. Service workers usually expressed their dissatisfaction by looking for another job, but some joined with reform groups or radical unions promising a shorter day.[84]

Moreover, the double burden of employed women, working at home and on the job, made leisure particularly prized. Echoing a folk saying, socialist feminist Theresa Malkiel observed in 1908 that keeping a home was itself a full-time job and more: "She [the housewife] works the longest hours and gets the lowest remuneration. The average tailor's work is done when the sun is down but the housewife's work is never done." Recent research suggests that housework may have been more time-consuming in gritty early twentieth-century America than at any other time. When combined with a long shift of wage labor, housework left virtually no time for recreation and as little as four and a half hours for sleep.[85] The observations of union organizer Alice Henry suggest something of the insensitivity of AFL officials and of the tight schedules of working women:

> The girls may prefer that the meeting should begin shortly after closing time so that they do not need to go home and return, or have to loiter about for two or three hours. They like meetings to be over early. The men mostly name eight o'clock as the time of beginning, but business will

not start much before nine. Working women and factory inspectors [agree] that women work many more hours every day than men . . . . Ten hours a day to at least one third of the working women means often fifteen.

As late as 1920 the Retail Clerks' journal complained that women workers were mysteriously and unreasonably ready to shelve wage demands in order to gain "the enjoyment of more leisure hours."[86]

In addition to sharpening the focus of employed females on the length of the working day by placing such a premium on time, the combination of house and wage work may also have caused women to be sensitive to the deadening aspects of capitalist labor discipline. The findings of Herbert Gutman and others regarding resistance to industrial rules regarding time and work by peasant immigrants, rural people, and artisans reared in preindustrial cultures apply, of course, to many immigrant women workers. They may also apply in a different way to all working women who share in housework, a variety of labor neither paced by the clock nor supervised closely. Respites on the job, even if only for minutes, were cherished by women workers. Mary Kenney, a Chicago bookbinder and activist in the Illinois Women's Alliance, received adulation from other women workers when she simply began to take ten-minute breaks twice a day. At the glovemaking shop where young Agnes Nestor, later president of the Chicago Women's Trade Union League, worked early in her career, women sang on the job and "all chipped in and bought a dollar alarm clock" to hang on the wall in order to make high piece rates and still find time each hour to turn off machines and talk.[87]

Women cared more about time than the AFL cared about women, but the point runs deeper than that. As Meredith Tax has pointed out, the organizations pressing for bettering conditions for working women are best understood as "united fronts" in which women of various classes and ideologies—workers, professional reformers, middle-and upper-class feminists—cooperated on issues. In such alliances the class participating most vigorously and contributing the clearest analysis tends to shape the behavior and ideas of the entire group. Tax maintains that after an early period in the late 1880s and 1890s when socialist and working women were hegemonic inside important women's organizations, a middle-class ideology based on charity, voluntary reform, consumerism, efficiency, and protection of women became dominant in subsequent years. This analysis applies well where hours are concerned and suggests that the AFL's backwardness helped to open the way for conservative, classless, and even sexist justifications by reformers for limiting the hours of work for women.[88] The history of the Illinois Women's Alliance (IWA), of the early years of Women's Trade Union League (WTUL), and of the National Consumers' League (NCL) illustrates the promise and perils of a feminist-labor alliance and illuminates the impact of AFL inaction.

It is hard to imagine a more varied and talented group of women than those who contributed to the growth of the IWA and the passage of Illinois's precocious 1893 eight-hour law for women. Since 1878, when the Working Women's Union was organized by women socialists, the city had had a tradition of labor activity by females. The union—led by Lucy Parsons; by Alzina Stevens, a Lowell girl turned printer and member of Chicago Typographical Union No. 16; by Lizzie Swank, a cloakmaker; and by Elizabeth Rodgers, a housewife, mother of eleven, socialist, and officer of the Irish National Land League of America— defended women's suffrage as a socialist demand and pressed for a shorter day, contributing an impressive pink float to the 1879 Chicago Eight-Hour League parade. In 1881 the Knights of Labor chartered the Working Women's Union as Labor Local Assembly 1789. On the eve of the fateful May 3 when police shot down the eight-hour demonstrators at the McCormick Works, Knights' organizers Lucy Parsons and Lizzy Swank led over 300 sewing women in a march for the shorter day. The Chicago *Tribune*, which branded the demonstrators "shouting Amazons," reported that they tramped from shop to shop augmenting their ranks. But the Haymarket events rended the women's labor movement, and Local 1789 quickly disbanded.[89]

Among the women organizers who endured was Elizabeth Morgan, for a time the master workman of Local 1789. Morgan, the wife of the machinist and Socialist Labor party leader Thomas Morgan, joined Swank and a group of Chicagoans to organize Ladies' Federal Labor Union No. 2703 in June 1888 and secured its charter from the AFL. Like other federal unions in the adventurous early days of the AFL, No. 2703 contained a variety of workers: clerks, candy makers, typists, dressmakers, music teachers, bookbinders, gum makers, housewives, and others. Within four years Local 2703 had built unions in twenty-three crafts and had become the leading organization of AFL-affiliated female workers. The best of the local's organizers, Mary Kenney, described herself as "a tramp bookbinder, going from shop to shop to organize the trade." Her organizing efforts focused on hours and, in at least one instance, Kenney enlisted both male and female binders by contrasting their ten-hour day with the eight-hour shift of unionized building tradesmen.[90]

Local 2703 quickly delivered on its stated promise to build ties with "the great labor organizations of this city" and to secure the "active assistance of many women's organizations" in order to study and combat "the moral, physical and mental degradation of women and children employed." In late summer of 1888, the Chicago *Times* published a sensational series of reports on "City Slave Girls," which stressed long hours, low wages, child labor, and abysmal conditions, mainly in the needle trades. The federal union appointed an investigating committee, which confirmed the *Times* accounts and won the approval of the Chicago Trades and Labor Assembly for a reform plan that included the enforcement of factory inspection and compulsory education laws by women inspectors "responsible to women's organizations." Drawing on ties nurtured by the local's support of women's suffrage (a position shared by Gompers and the AFL), Morgan called a meeting of women's groups. The October 6, 1888, gathering marked the beginning of the IWA, in which over thirty reform groups, most of them bourgeois, united at the behest of the women trade unionists and embraced the program for factory reform approved by Local 2703 and the Trades and Labor Assembly. Suffragists, single-taxers, homeopaths, missionaries, and advocates of kindergartens joined members of ethical societies, temperance groups, religious orders, medical associations, literary circles, metaphysical clubs, and charities to press for factory inspection, compulsory schooling, sanitary regulations, and an end to harassment of women by policemen enforcing antivice laws.[91]

The sometimes sentimental propaganda of the IWA and the famous memoirs of Jane Addams lend superficial credence to the criticisms of Lizzie Swank, who withdrew from the alliance, regarding it as hydra-headed, mild-mannered, and reformist. Indeed the discussion of women's labor in conjunction with child labor did imply that working women required protection, and alliance literature did hold that immoral employers, not the class system itself, bred oppression. And criticisms of unsanitary workplaces were couched as a defense against conditions "destructive to womanly purity" and inimical to motherly virtues. But Local 2703, which initiated the alliance, stated that the protection sought for working women was "self-protection." Moreover, the emphasis on purity need not have derived from middle-class moralism. Women workers of the period (and some male unionists) emphasized the need to "protect" females from sexual harassment and to fight against prostitution, evils they saw as rooted in the class system.[92]

In practice the alliance brought a class perspective to its work, particularly on hours and acted creatively to make demands on government and to build institutions of independent female and working-class power. The campaigns against female and child labor and for compulsory education rested explicitly on the idea that the whole "sweating system" of clothing production, based on the labor of young people and powerless women working seasonally in decentralized and arbitrarily run open shops, had to be dismantled. After succeeding in 1889 in causing the Illinois legislature to pass a strong compulsory education act, the alliance attacked long hours by demanding enforcement of an 1881 Chicago ordinance specifying an eight-hour maximum working day for children under fifteen. The IWA followed the lead of the Chicago Trades and Labor Assembly in arguing that school inspectors ought to be nonsalaried volunteers who could thus remain outside the city's machine politics. Where no inspection agencies existed, or where appointments proved unsatisfactory, the alliance set up agencies of its own using the labor of women volunteers.[93]

The lobbying and statistical skills developed during the child labor fight soon found application in the investigation of conditions, particularly hours, of adult women. Labor initiative began the campaign. Abraham Bisno, socialist head of the Cloak Makers' Union, delivered an indictment of sweatshop labor before the

Trades and Labor Assembly in August 1891. The assembly set up a committee, consisting of Morgan and two women from Hull House, to elaborate on Bisno's charges, and the three led reporters, the city attorney, and a health department official through Chicago's underside, where fourteen-hour days were not uncommon. Morgan's findings, printed in *The New Slavery*, underscored the "degradation of labor" and also played on middle-class fears of disease contagion through infected garments. After the Trades' Assembly distributed 10,000 of her pamphlets, Morgan brought the issue before the Women's Alliance. Leisured women faced the human cost of their clothing and worried about the germs thereon. According to Bisno, health arguments proved best in enforcing the "economic motive" of the unionists.[94]

Although Jane Addams later disavowed any "radicalism" on the part of those lobbying for passage of an eight-hour law for women, Florence Kelley, the Hull House resident most instrumental in pressing for the legislation, wrote to Friedrich Engels at the time of the campaign that her goal was nothing short of a "systematic endeavor to clear out the sweating dens." A Marxist, Kelley viewed her role as a labor investigator in strict class terms: "The factory inspector of today, like the militiaman, is the child of the struggle of labor against capital. The factory inspector enforces the law for the worker against the capitalist, the militiaman shoots down the worker by command of the capitalist."[95]

Kelley moved to Chicago in January 1892 partly in order to obtain a divorce. She immediately urged the Illinois Bureau of Labor Statistics to undertake an investigation of Chicago sweatshops and agreed to supervise the project. By November 1892 Kelley, herself working twelve-hour days as an investigator, had completed a report on 800 shops and had joined Elizabeth Morgan in guiding U.S. Congressman Sherman Hoar on well-publicized tours of the establishments. After the 1892 election of populist Democratic Governor John Peter Altgeld, Illinois legislators appointed another committee to probe sweatshops and, with Kelley and Morgan assisting, the committee proposed legal reforms.[96]

The resulting legislation, the Factory and Workshop Inspection Act, was, even given the agitation preceding it, a bolt from the blue. It introduced into Illinois industry provisions banning child labor in manufacturing, empowering the Board of Health to seize goods from unclean shops, requiring physicians' certificates for young workers between fourteen and sixteen, and, most controversially, limiting the hours of work for women to eight. Support for the law came mainly from the Trades Assembly, the IWA, Hull House, and the General Federation of Women's Clubs whose president, the wealthy Ellen Henrotin, became a fixture in Chicago labor reform movements for decades. Those testifying for the bill ranged in their arguments from the Rev. V. P. Gifford, who held that "the men should make the money and the women remain at home," to the populist radical Henry Demarest Lloyd, who broached the subject of nationalizing the industry. The bill passed in June 1893 with surprisingly little opposition. Altgeld appointed a dozen investigators, headed by Kelley and including Bisno, Alzina

Stevens, and Mary Kenney; manufacturers counterattacked, despite less than vigorous early efforts of prosecutors to try the cases involving violations of the law.[97]

The Manufacturers' Protective Association wished to end all prosecutions under the eight-hour clause. After assessing contributions from its membership, it initiated suits to render the clause inoperative. Asking that the factory inspectors not bring suits until the Illinois Supreme Court decided the constitutionality of the issue in a test case, the association met with a rebuff from Kelley and her cohorts, who successfully pressed prosecution in thirteen consecutive cases. Kelley, writing to Engels, pointed with pride to the use of the law against "stockyard magnates" who "having been arrested until they are tired of it . . . instituted the 8 hour day for 10,000 employees, men, women, and children."[98]

But in the same December 31, 1894, letter to Engels, Kelley worried that "the SC may annul the law." Ten weeks later the Illinois Supreme Court did just that in accepting the Manufacturer's Association's argument in the landmark case of *W.C. Ritchie v. Illinois*. Ritchie, a paperbox manufacturer arraigned for violating the eight-hour clause, maintained that the law was unconstitutional. The court agreed, holding not only that gender was an insufficient reason to limit hours but that the legislature absolutely had no right to infringe on freedom of contract by setting maximum hours for either sex. The far-reaching language of the court emphasized, as Kelley put it, that "This is not a question between the day of eight hours and the day of ten [but] between an unlimited working day and one restricted by statute." Kelley reported that, in the wake of the decision, some fourteen-year-old women worked shifts of twenty hours and that "two of the best literature classes [at Hull House] were broken up because the girls who composed them were obliged to resume . . . working at the Electric Works until nine o'clock at night."[99]

The battle over enforcement of the eight-hour clause split the IWA. Its labor wing, formerly able to command a sure majority on such important issues as strike support, the use of organization and pressure rather than charity as reform strategies, and support for the passage of the Inspection Act, failed in February 1894 to pass a resolution "strongly condemning the manufacturers of this city for combining to nullify the State laws." Though the alliance reversed itself at the next meeting, some of its members and at least one of its officers had developed ties to the Manufacturers' Association. The alliance did sponsor a meeting, attended by a thousand people, to debate the bill. Morgan, Henry Demarest Lloyd, and Ellen Henrotin represented the alliance's position of support for the law; the Manufacturers' Association, which had first requested an opportunity to present its case, declined to attend. The very fact that the eight-hour clause had become an object for debate showed the tensions in the alliance. By October 1894 the Ladies' Federal Labor Union had withdrawn from the dying IWA to form its own women's labor organization, a weak group that admitted no bourgeois women, rejecting even Henrotin.[100]

Obviously a coalition like the IWA ran constant risks of internal discord between working-class and middle-class women. But it is misleading to see its demise as resulting simply from the maturation of such conflict around the eight-hour issue. Throughout the life of the alliance, labor women had confidently fought for their politics amidst opposition. That they withdrew suddenly in 1894, without ever losing on a major issue inside the alliance, reflects a loss of unity and confidence by the working women. Not only did the women unionists face splits over division between socialism and Gomperism during this period, but they also faced the failure of the AFL to support women's organizing. In 1892 Gompers appointed Mary Kenney as the first paid national AFL organizer of women. Kenney based her activities in Chicago, organizing unions of shoe workers, bookbinders, hack drivers, retail clerks, and garment workers there. In the garment trades a series of strikes resulted in the ten-hour day at many shops and "the Cloak Makers' Union gained its first important membership among . . . women." But after just six months, the AFL Executive Council, over Gompers's objection in this case, withdrew Kenney's funds, finding the expense of organizing women was not worthwhile. With the Depression of 1893, unionism in the needle trades collapsed. The very time of the early enforcement of the Inspection Act, when unionism was expected to boom, became a period of defeat for labor organizations. In this context labor women retreated from the labor-feminist coalition and the IWA dissolved. Building on the work of the alliance and that of early women labor organizers, Chicago females built the strongest women's labor movement in the nation, organizing 35,000 women workers by 1903 and mobilizing thousands of female clerks in support of early closing.[101] But no united front dominated by working-class women reemerged.

The next united front experiment, the organization of the Women's Trade Union League (WTUL), began in 1903 when both the National WTUL and the New York WTUL took shape. That year Mother Jones stirred the consciences of women and men throughout the nation by leading a celebrated "March of the Mill Children" along the East Coast in support of child labor laws and of a fruitless shorter-hours strike by 75,000 Philadelphia-area textile workers. Since from 10,000 to 16,000 of the strikers were children and most of them female, Jones's march lent urgency to the issues raised by the WTUL. Many familiar names joined the new organization: social wokers like Addams and Kelley; organizers like Mary Kenney (now Mary Kenney O'Sullivan); and the wealthy "allies" Mary Dreier, Margaret Dreier Robins, and Ellen Henrotin. New faces included the Chicago settlement house worker Mary McDowell; organizers Agnes Nestor, Rose Schneiderman; Mary Anderson, Melinda Scott, Elizabeth Maloney, Emma Stephensen and garment worker Lenora O'Reilly. The WTUL structured itself as a conscious coalition of leisured allies and workers, in which "The majority . . . shall be women who are, or have been, trade unionists . . . the minority of those well-known to be earnest sympathizers."[102]

The cooperation was fraught with tension. In theory the elite component was to educate working women to lead their own struggles, but until 1907 allies dominated the membership rolls and even afterwards their greater resources and leisure made the wealthy disproportionately influential in the league. Lenora O'Reilly's complaint, before her temporary resignation in 1905, that allies "must drop the attitude of the lady with something to give her sister," typified the suspicion of upper-class reformers by working-class members. But a network of friendships, a consciousness of sisterhood, and a general support for the AFL approach to organizing strategy united the WTUL.[103]

The WTUL, from its founding convention in 1903, supported the eight-hour day. Its anthem, written by the socialist-feminist Charlotte Perkins Gilman, proclaimed:

> For the right pay for us
> We stand as one;
> For the short day for us,
> stand as one.

Its logo, dating from 1903, linked eight hours and defense of the home. Margaret Robins, long time WTUL president, advocated a shorter working day during her employment as a Chicago settlement house worker and during her tenure as head of the league. Robins's efforts helped make the Illinois WTUL exceptionally active in legislative campaigns for a ten-hour day for women, campaigns which resulted in passage of such a state law in 1909.[104]

But the WTUL failed, in its early years, to contribute much to the cutting of the working day. Taking the AFL as its model, it regarded organization rather than legislation as its central activity and generally saw the two as counterposed. Although somewhat active in campaigns to restrict the hours of children, the WTUL generally left the dominant role in the legislative movement to restrict women's hours to the National Consumers' League.[105] Nor were the early WTUL organizing efforts successful at reducing hours. Although the AFL maintained cordial relations with the WTUL and the organizations usually held national conventions at a common site and time, the Executive Council suspected WTUL feminism and socialism, refused to commit funds and to appoint women organizers, and sometimes urged the union label rather than organizing as a panacea. International unions failed to follow up on organizational efforts by the WTUL so that gains in limiting the working day were often reversed only months after they occurred. Adherence to AFL practice meant that the WTUL attempted, inappropriately, to set up craft unions, even in industries like garment manufacture. Thus the WTUL was, between 1903 and 1909, less an organizing force than a strike support group. Its allies backed largely spontaneous strikes, mainly over wages and especially over union recognition. Occasionally, as at the New York strike at a Broadway boxmaking factory in 1904, the WTUL intervened significantly in a strike over hours, but more often, as in the larger, successful San Francisco laundry workers' hours strike of 1907, no WTUL chapter functioned.[106] The New York chapter, with Chicago's chapter being the nation's most active, probably had only a few score active members in 1907. With the later mass strikes in the garment industry and with the 1909 WTUL resolution in favor of specific shorter-hours legislation, the group had greater impact on the working day, but it did not challenge the National Consumers' League (NCL) as the chief ideological force in the movement to protect women workers.[107]

The NCL originated in New York City, largely out of contacts between Alice Woodbridge, a retail clerk, and Josephine Shaw Lowell, a Civil War widow who continued the reform spirit of her ancestors in a variety of charitable enterprises. Woodbridge, leader of the Working Women's Society, a small group founded in 1889, conducted an investigation of the clerking trade and produced an 1890 report with a list of grievances that led off with the complaint: "We find the hours are often excessive, and employees are not paid for overtime." Woodbridge's testimony so moved Lowell, the feminist physician Mary Putnam Jacobi, and Maud Nathan, a wealthy housewife, that it was decided to call a mass meeting on the subject. Woodbridge spoke before a large crowd, which included church leaders from the city. The meeting pledged support for a state eight-hour law for women and children, and resolved to appoint a committee to assist the Working Women's Society in preparing a list of shops which "deal justly with their employees." That committee imitated a similar British reform group by taking the name "Consumers' League."[108]

The New York Consumers' League adopted the basic ideas and strategy that were to characterize the leagues in various states and nationally. Both Woodbridge and her bourgeois associates despaired of organizing young, female clerks and saw reform as coming about through legislation or voluntary compliance. Consumers, not workers, constituted the key to change and, organized, could ensure that working "conditions shall be at least decent." According to Maud Nathan, consumers were in a position to exercise power "greater than either . . . labor [or] capital." Florence Kelley, longtime president of the NCL, came to agree with Nathan (and the AFL) that women's power lay at home and in the market, more so than at work. "Since the exodus of manufacture from the home," she wrote, "the one great industrial function of women has been that of purchaser." The international motto of the Consumers' Leagues of various nations summed up the reform rationale: "Vivre c'est acheter; acheter, c'est pouvoir; pouvoir, c'est devoir."[109] That is, "To live means to buy, to buy means to have power, to have power means to have duties."

The Consumers' League took a neutral stance on class issues and ultimately barred both employers and workers from membership. From the start the New York league absolved owners of blame for abuses, declaring in 1891 that "the Majority of Employers are virtually helpless to improve conditions as to hours and wages, unless sustained by public opinion, by law, and by the action of consumers."[110] Thereafter, as Nathan stressed, the league "never sentimentally put the rights of the employee above the rights of the employer." Only on occasions, most notably the 1913 New York City retail clerks' organizing drive, did the league back unionization.[111]

Such a class-neutral approach shaped league response to the length of the working day, an issue that it held to be central during the two decades after 1890. League literature vividly portrayed the demands placed on the time of retail clerks—long hours of constant standing, twenty-minute lunches often delayed till 3 P.M., the absence of breaks, and the prevalence of forced overtime especially during the holidays. The simplest league solution was to educate shoppers to shop only during a limited number of hours and to discontinue browsing, an activity which Nathan regarded as a "crime."[112] A second strategy, instituted in New York in 1891, centered on the publication of a "White List" of stores approved as having established "just conditions." The stipulations included an 8 A.M. to 6 P.M. working day, forty-five minutes for lunch, a week's paid vacation during the summer, and pay for overtime. Of 1,400 stores surveyed, eight qualified for the 1891 White List. The White List idea suffered from employer disinterest and the refusal of the press to publicize the list, but it continued to be a favorite league emphasis. Issuing of the "Consumers' Label" on garments, begun in 1898, reflected a similar voluntarism-plus-pressure approach.[113]

The failure of voluntarism encouraged the NCL to participate in legislative efforts to shorten the working day for women. In 1890 the New York league supported AFL-sponsored legislation to extend the state's hours law for factory women to cover clerks. That effort failed, but six years later, league testimony before the state Senate's Commission on Female Labor contributed to the passage of the Mercantile Inspection Act, which set sixty hours as the maximum working week for women under twenty-one and boys under sixteen in all commercial establishments in towns of 3,000 or more. Three years later, league pressure helped secure a strengthening of the law. During the first decade of the twentieth century, it was the League, more than the AFL, that fought against attempts to add loopholes and exemptions, especially for canneries, to hours legislation covering New York women. On the other hand, the league, having defined ten hours as just, moved slowly toward support for the nine-hour-day legislation advanced by the unions after 1901. The one area in which the league and the unions cooperated completely was the passage of 1907 legislation providing an eight-hour day for child laborers in New York.[114]

As the Consumers' League movement spread to ninety local chapters and twenty state organizations,' efforts to decrease women's hours through education, through use of the list and label, and through legislation proliferated. Leagues helped to pass or extend shorter hours legislation for women and or children in a dozen states and the District of Columbia between 1898 and 1922. Landmark enactments for women included the fifty-eight-hour-week law for Massachusetts women clerks (1898); the eight-hour-day law in the District of Columbia (1916); the nine-hour-day laws in Missouri (1909, 1911, and 1913), Rhode Island (1913), Pennsylvania (1913), and New York (1912); and the ten-hour statutes in Kentucky (1912), Delaware (1913), Maryland (1912), and Oregon (1903). The last mentioned of these codes, which applied to women workers in factories and laundries, was most important because it generated a key legal victory for the constitutionality of laws limiting the working day for women in the case of *Muller v. Oregon* (1907-1908).[115]

Although *Muller v. Oregon* itself only involved the question of whether Oregon's ten-hour law would apply to laundresses working for Cult Muller, the case had significant ramifications. Louis D. Brandeis, the liberal lawyer invited onto the case by Josephine Goldmark, his sister-in-law, and by Florence Kelley, both of the NCL, represented the State of Oregon by presenting a brief that broke decisively from legal tradition. Citing barely two pages of legal arguments, and only a single precedent of courts upholding the constitutionality of restricting women's hours, Brandeis devoted scores of pages to material on the history and sociology of shorter hours. Using the wording of the court's decision in *Lochner v. New York* (1905), Brandeis maintained that such evidence was relevant because it aided the court in determining whether a "direct relation" existed between the statute and the public good. When this novel line of argument was allowed, Brandeis won a victory that, as one biographer put it, changed "the development of the legal profession and the path of the law." Coming in the wake of *Ritchie v. Illinois* and *Lochner v. New York*, as well as the striking down of general eight-hour laws in Nebraska (1894), *Muller v. Oregon* offered new hope for the enforcement of hours laws, even those that infringed upon the freedom of contract.[116]

The importance of *Muller v. Oregon* and the innovation present in Brandeis's "Oregon Brief" have led many historians to regard the brief, and the NCL, which researched and published it, as radical.[117] While the brief is a creative departure in terms of legal theory, its arguments were anything but leftist. Instead they rested on a need to institute moderate reforms to forestall demands for more extreme measures, on perception of women as biologically inferior beings whose morals and capacity for motherhood needed protection, and on the view that greater efficiency in fewer hours would increase productivity and benefit employers.[118] In further briefs, especially that prepared by Goldmark for Brandeis in *Ritchie v. Wayman*, a 1910 Illinois case overturning the antilabor Ritchie decision of 1898, the themes of women's inferiority, women's place, and productivity became even more prominent. When, in 1912, the Russell Sage Foundation published Goldmark's researches on the working day, the book bore the title, *Fatigue and Efficiency* and included homage to Taylorism, which Brandeis and Goldmark both embraced as an "incentive" to reduce hours.[119]

Of course it is idle to suggest that Brandeis could have won his case before the Supreme Court with attacks on sexism and class privilege. But in a slightly different context, the judicial arguments might have changed perceptibly. With a strong contingent of organized women supporting reform, the protection argument might have centered not on woman's "biological" disadvantages but on her double oppression as a wage-worker and a homemaker, and on her subjection to sexual harassment. The contention that shorter hours contributed to the public good might have emphasized not Taylorist efficiency but the regulation of hours to ensure full employment. Outside the courts and legislatures, debates on shorter hours for working women might have included, as they did through much of the nineteenth century, discussions of surplus value and of whether employers ought to control the workplace absolutely. In such an environment a stronger labor wing of the women's suffrage movement, seeking the vote specifically to implement labor reform, might have developed. AFL conservatism, in small and large ways, touched the whole eight-hour movement.

9

Class Conflict, Reform, and War:
The Working Day from 1907 to 1918

The years before, during, and just after World War I were, as David Montgomery has written, "the decisive period in the battle for the eight-hour day."[1] From 1905 until 1920 the average working week of nonagricultural workers plummeted from 57.2 to 50.6 hours. In manufacturing it dropped from 54.5 to 48.1—the rough equivalent of an eight-hour day, six days per week. In 1910, 8 percent of the nation's workers labored 48 hours or less per week; in 1919, 48.6 percent did. The proportion of workers laboring over 54 hours weekly declined from 70 percent to 26 percent during the same decade.[2] In the wake of World War I, hundreds of thousands of trade unionists gave favorable consideration to fighting for a working day of six hours or less.[3]

This chapter describes the most productive period of shorter-hours agitation in U.S. history. It also describes a period which again features many of the same characteristics of the movement for reduced hours that had become so well established in the nineteenth century: the coexistence of political and trade union campaigns for more leisure; the tendency for workers to unite across lines of sex, skill, and ethnicity in support of eight hours; the meshing of workday demands with those calling for workers to have more control over their lives off, and especially on, the job. These features, which had somewhat declined in importance between 1891 and 1907, reappeared dramatically as battles for control on the job and for the right to leisure were joined.

Two major hours changes of this period came from outside the labor movement: the granting of the eight-hour day by Henry Ford in 1914 and the federal government's seeming embrace of eight hours, especially in the 1916 passage of the Adamson Act, and in the War Industries Board's later approval of a "basic" eight-hour day. Indeed, the combination of an easing in corporate animosity to shorter hours and a desire "to see to it that the private's uniforms of the Army of the United States (and other war goods) are not . . . made in sweat shops"[4] could provide an easy explanation for the progress in shortening the working day, were Ford not such a maverick and the commitment of the government not so brief and shaky. Both Fordism and wartime labor policy deserve emphasis as genuine innovations, but neither is understandable without sustained consideration of the deepening class conflict surrounding the length of labor.

The commitment of trade unionists and unorganized workers to the eight-hour day (or less) in the years after 1907 came from several sources. Certainly the proliferation of mass popular culture, in the form of silent movies, professional and college sports, amusement parks, inexpensive fiction, and other pastimes made leisure more prized. But the notion that corporate capital shrewdly "granted" shorter hours, knowing that workers would be drawn into the wastelands of consumer culture, cannot withstand scrutiny.[5] Usually corporations fought shorter hours. Ford, the leading figure who did not, viewed mass culture with nearly paranoid suspicion. Moreover, the motivations of many activists in the shorter-hours struggles hinged on gaining time not to pursue empty diversions, but to participate in a variety of working-class and ethnic institutions.[6]

Labor activism and self-education required time. William Z. Foster, a syndicalist active within the AFL during these years, bitterly recalled that prior to World War I his schedule as a railway worker entailed twelve-hour days and thus barred him from attending most Chicago Federation of Labor meetings. "It is obvious," wrote the Socialist activist Mary Marcy, "that men or women working from ten to sixteen hours daily will have little strength or leisure to study [for] revolutionary work."[7] Stress on study was especially vital, since this period saw a boom in workers' education, which, by early 1921, produced over two dozen labor schools. Unions, the Socialists, the IWW, and the anarchists all had schools. Colleges, including Bryn Mawr, Northwestern, and the University of Chicago offered courses for unionists, often under the auspices of the WTUL.[8] In addition, many rank-and-file workers attended night schools to learn English and new skills. A remarkable intellectual life, conducted in many languages, graced the left and labor movements and the classics along with cheaply available left-wing pamphlets circulated among activists. One of the most popular works, Paul Lafargue's *The Right to Be Lazy*, extolled proletarian leisure.[9]

A second factor making the hours demand prominent was pressure from groups outside the labor movement. As so often happened in the nineteenth century, political reform and trade union strategies coexisted in the battle for shorter hours. Reform groups such as the NCL, WTUL, and American Association for Labor Legislation agitated for shorter-hours laws, especially for women. In 1913 the WTUL in New York headed a strong movement for an eight-hour law and, in contrast to the state AFL, fought hard against exempting seasonal industries from the hours law. The WTUL also supported strike actions aimed at shorter hours, especially in the needle trades. In 1916 the WTUL initiated a Mid-Atlantic States Eight-Hour Conference, which favored the "eight-hour day through collective bargaining as well as through legislation."[10] In the steel industry a reform group centered around *Survey* magazine began a protracted attack on the twelve-hour day and the seven-day week. The broadest-based reform group to raise the eight-hour issue was the Progressive party whose 1912 platform, on which Theodore Roosevelt campaigned for the presidency, included a plank proposing eight-hour laws covering children, women, and all workers in continuous production industries like the steel industry.[11]

The Socialist party (SP) had special impact on the course of AFL strategy regarding the working day. SP platforms consistently pressed for the eight-hour day as did *International Socialist Review* and other socialist periodicals. Godfrey Ritterskamp's socialist indictment of the welfare system in Chicago and New York in 1914 proposed a more substantial cut in hours and linked such a reduction to broader issues: "What will help us now? Socialism, says somebody. Right. Lets take a step towards Socialism. Begin with the six-hour day. The six-hour day will give work to every unemployed man and woman. It will fill every empty stomach."[12]

Socialists generally proposed a legislative solution for the problem of long hours. It was on this score that they opposed the policy of AFL leadership. In 1914 the Socialists sponsored eight-hour initiatives in the November elections in Washington, Oregon, and California. Each failed, in the words of John R. Commons and John B. Andrews, "largely through the opposition of the farmer vote." At the 1915 AFL convention a Socialist-led coalition challenged the position of the Gompers leadership which held that only collective bargaining should be used to usher in the shorter day. Socialists and their allies held that tactics should be flexible. William Green, then an AFL vice-president and head of the UMW, broke with Gompers on this score. "Is there anyone here," he asked, "who believes the man who enjoys the benefit of the eight-hour day through . . . economic organization . . . enjoys it more than the man who secured it through legislation?"[13] John Fitzpatrick, head of the Chicago Federation of Labor, spoke for "the eight-hour day by legislation, both industrially and politically," a position endorsed by the Illinois Federation of Labor. Gompers and his supporters, sure that political initiatives were a "waste [of] effort" because "the courts will knock it [an eight-hour law] out," held on to win a close vote on the issue, but labor bodies continued to back eight-hour laws in some states.[14]

While the lures of mass and class leisure and the activities of reform and radical groups outside of the labor movement helped to focus attention on the hours demand, changes in labor and in the unions themselves were more critical factors. What Andre Tridon referred to in 1914 as the "New Unionism" swept the United States in the years surrounding World War I, producing not only strikes of unprecedented size, but also an upsurge of interest in workers' control and of cooperation among workers of various levels of skill and in diverse branches of industry. Underlying this labor dynamism was a collection of grievances effecting the skilled, the unskilled, and those between. The proliferation of managerial rationalizations and naked speedups undermined the traditional control over production that skilled workers had held by virtue of their expertise. Job structures featuring a multiplicity of categories of semiskilled labor made craft distinctions obscure. Semiskilled "specialists" faced unemployment during frequent recessions. Among the largely immigrant unskilled workers, speedups, layoffs, and low wages drew protest. As Montgomery observes, "the new industrial discipline had promoted a sense of raw injustice among, as well as within, the . . . ethnic communities."[15]

Reacting to these grievances, it is not surprising that workers seized upon the issue of hours. The most systematic expression of early twentieth-century changes in management, Taylorism, forced those on the shop floor to focus on the clock. It undertook studies that subjected every activity on the job to timing by stopwatch. With informal kinds of workers' autonomy under siege, claiming of the right to limit one's hours of work became a fundamental assertion of control over conditions of employment. Gompers's 1914 position suggested how bound up was the issue of the working day with the issue of control on the job: "It is not just a question of an eight-hour work day, a shorter workday, but the method our trade union movement is going to sanction that will be used to regulate and determine the conditions under which we are going to work."[16]

With craft barriers eroding, the eight-hour demand also functioned to hold together movements containing a variety of workers. Amalgamation, federation, and industrial unionism, as well as cooperation among unions in strikes, hinged upon unity around a common issue. Most often, the eight-hour day (or union recognition) was that issue. As Debs observed: "There is something in the shorter workday that appeals to every working man whether he belongs to a union or not, or whether he is class conscious or not, and it is this something which gives . . . power to the movement that . . . fights to realize it for the workers."[17]

Those labor organizations that most strongly pressed for labor unity, that sought to organize the unorganized, that addressed the need to assert job control, that attempted to unionize mass production industries, that innovated in terms of organizational forms, and that included an ethnically, sexually, or racially diverse rank and file, brought the issue of the working day to the fore during the years before 1916. The most conscious advocates of the "new unionism," the Industrial Workers of the World (IWW), made the hours question central in their organizing, but this stance was not unique to the far left wing of the labor movement. Whether influenced by the IWW or not, unionism in the heavy mass production and extractive industries, and in the female-and immigrant-dominated clothing and textile industries, stressed shortening the working day.

The IWW persistently emphasized the shorter day. A group that projected a syndicalist vision of industry and society managed by workers could hardly have ignored the struggle to provide the spare time necessary for such democratic self-management. Moreover, in organizing the unskilled, the Wobblies, as IWW members were often called, faced the issue of unemployment constantly and held up shorter hours as a palliative, though not a solution. Since poorly paid members of its unskilled constituency could hardly afford pay cuts in conjunction with shorter hours, the IWW often raised pay demands along with reductions in hours.[18] Finally, the IWW's ancestry, especially its descent from the

Western Federation of Miners (WFM), ensured that it would be sensitive to the eight-hour issue. In the four years before the IWW's 1905 founding, the WFM led a series of eight-hour strikes among miners and smeltermen in Colorado. The strikes culminated in the bloody disputes at Cripple Creek and Telluride in 1903 and 1905 respectively. These two strikes claimed 42 dead, over 1,100 wounded, and 1,300 arrested before ending in defeat at Cripple Creek and victory at Telluride. From their inception, Wobbly strikes, led by WFM veterans like Big Bill Haywood and Vincent St. John, adopted the same eight-hour goal.[19] (IWW strikes, like those of the AFL during this period, often addressed the hours question in combination with other grievances. Thus most of the conflicts described below in this chapter involved the working day as one vital issue, but not as the only issue).

In addition to striking for the shorter day in individual cases, the IWW attempted two major national agitational campaigns around the issue. At its founding convention, the group received a letter from the General Confederation of Labor in France, which promised, "FROM MAY 1, 1906, FORWARD, WE WILL WORK ONLY 8 HOURS A DAY." The U.S. group later set into motion similar campaigns with the IWW printing thousands of stickers reading:

I Won't Work More than 8 Hours After
May 1st 1912. How About You?[20]

At its September 1911 convention, the IWW dropped the May 1, 1912, target date, but the campaign gave rise to a number of local Eight-Hour Leagues, important in such major strikes as that at Paterson in 1913. In late 1913 Wobbly attempts to organize the unemployed began to feature calls for a six-hour day. Activists sometimes reverted to an eight-hour demand in unemployed organizing and in actual negotiations, as on the Philadelphia docks where an integrated IWW won shorter hours and job control. But the logic was the same: "If those who are now working would take it easy and not work so many hours a day . . . there would be plenty of work for all." Later the IWW demand would be for the "Four-Hour Day (Jobs for Everyone)."[21]

In the following description of prewar and wartime shorter-hours strikes, the IWW will loom large, more so than its size alone—always less than 200,000 and usually substantially less than 10 percent of all organized labor—would suggest. But equally remarkable was the record of many AFL unions in organizing semi-industrially, enrolling minorities, federating and amalgamating—in breaking craft barriers—to win reductions in the working day. During these years the shorter-hours activities of the IWW and AFL, despite rancor between the two groups, were similar enough to deserve discussion together.[22]

The pre-World War I years witnessed the most spectacular strike wave by women workers in U.S. history, with the walkouts centering in the textile and clothing industries. These "uprisings," as they were termed at the time, have received attention from historians, but several themes regarding their connection with the movement for a shorter working day deserve emphasis.[23] These themes include the tendency toward industrial unionism in response to speedups in production and to a long workday, the necessity of linking wage and hour demands in low-wage industries, the use of the shorter-hours demand to combat unemployment, and the attempted unity, usually under socialist leadership, of men and women of various ethnic groups seeking a reduction in hours.

Both the most famous IWW textile strikes, those at Lawrence and at Paterson, hinged on hours, though the former did so indirectly. The 1912 Lawrence strike followed the 1911 passage of a Massachusetts state law limiting the hours of women and children to fifty-four per week. In Lawrence, where about half the 30,000 textile workers were women and children, and where a third of all mill-hands earned less than $7 for a week of fifty-six or more hours, laborers could not afford the reduction of pay that would accompany the reform. The celebrated demand for "Bread and Roses," raised during the strike, bespoke a desire for leisure and for more pay, but the former issue dominated, since the reduction of hours had already come by law. A small IWW chapter led the 25,000 workers who walked off their jobs on January 13, after their first payday under the new law. The strikers, speaking forty-five different languages, stayed out for two months before winning pay boosts of up to 25 percent. Lawrence set the crucial precedent that shorter hours need not lead to less wages among unskilled workers. Throughout 1912 the textile strike wave continued. By April 1, 275,000 New England textile workers had gained higher pay as a result of the inspiration of Lawrence.[24]

In the major textile strike in which the IWW directly addressed the issue of hours, the results were not so positive. That struggle, among Paterson, New Jersey, silk workers, saw unionists demand an abolition of the four-loom system, a $12 weekly minimum wage, and, for the first time in a major textile strike, eight hours. As Bill Haywood wrote, "the demands of the workers have crystallized around a determination to have the eight-hour day." Beginning in late January 1913, after agitation by an IWW Eight-Hour League, the Paterson struggle involved over 25,000 workers, mostly women and children. The strikers shut down America's silk capital for four months by successfully forging an alliance among immigrants, especially Russian Jews and Italians. Advised by Haywood, Elizabeth Gurley Flynn, and Carlo Tresca, the workers resisted employer appeals to that brand of "Americanism" equating the national good with the open shop.[25] Why female workers, saddled with both housework and millwork, backed eight hours is suggested by a telling incident related by Flynn in her accounts of Paterson:

> Tresca made some remarks about shorter hours, people being less tired, having more time to spend together and jokingly he said: "More babies." The audience of tired working wives did not cheer this suggestion. "No,

Carlo," interrupted Haywood, "we believe in birth control—a few babies, well cared for." The women started to laugh and applaud.[26]

Ultimately, in the face of police violence, mass arrests, separate settlements with English-speaking workers, and want, the strike faltered. The defeat stopped the momentum of the IWW textile-organizing drive. Efforts continued, most significantly at Greenville, South Carolina, where Matilda Rabinowitz organized the first Wobbly textile local in the South and led an unsuccessful strike for shorter hours. The tide, however, had turned.[27]

In the needle trades the IWW and independent AFL unions led a series of struggles around wages, union recognition, and a shorter working day in industries manufacturing both men's and women's clothing. These campaigns, marked by tremendous rank-and-file activity, were often limited by the conservatism of the AFL leadership and sometimes by the leadership of the clothing trades unions themselves. Still, they enjoyed at least one advantage over those of the IWW unions. They had the support of the WTUL and other feminist organizations, a support usually denied the IWW.

In the earliest of the garment industry strikes, the 1909 "Uprising of the 20,000" in New York City, both pressure from the ranks and WTUL support were critical. The shirtwaist and dressmakers who participated in the strike, 80 percent of them young women, had the worst of both worlds. Their long hours, at least fifty-six to fifty-nine per week and up to thirteen daily, alternated with bouts of unemployment. Cuts in piece rates reduced their average weekly pay to $9-$10 in 1909. Arbitrary work rules abounded; fines and dismissals enforced labor discipline. The fragmented labor force included 35,000 to 40,000 workers in 600 separate shops. Over two thirds were Jewish immigrants, with native-born Americans (including several hundred Afro-Americans) and Italians making up most of the balance. Given these conditions, any attempt to organize had to focus on uniting workers around shorter hours at higher wages and on union recognition. But the male leadership of the tiny International Ladies' Garment Workers' Union (ILGWU) Local 25, had little confidence in the ability of the women to organize, no matter what the demands.

Influenced by Rose Schneiderman and other WTUL organizers, and by socialists from the United Hebrew Trades, the women workers mounted a series of shop-by-shop strikes in the early fall of 1909. On October 21, with 2,000 new members added to Local 25, a Cooper Union meeting convened to consider a general strike in the trade. After hearing Samuel Gompers speak guardedly about the possible necessity for such an action, the crowd listened to a rank-and-filer, a victim of a beating during one of the recent shop strikes. Young Clara Lemlich declared, "I would not have further patience for talk, as I am one of those who feels and suffers from the things pictured. I move that we go on a general strike!" The motion carried admist cheers and the 3,000 in attendance then swore a Hebrew oath of loyalty to the strike.[28]

Organizers hoped for 5,000 strikers, but got 18,000 or more on the first day. At its height, according to WTUL leader Helen Marot, the "Uprising of the 20,000" may have had as many as 30,000 participants. It was, she wrote, a "woman's strike"—80 percent were female. Nine strikers in ten were Jewish but some American-born women and 2,000 Italians also walked out. This solidarity produced speedy results, then protracted conflict. Many small shops agreed to Local 25's demands quickly, granting a fifty-two-hour week, a union shop, changes in work rules, and arbitration of wage issues. But the largest clothing concerns vowed to stand together for the open shop. In the nearly four months of picketing that followed, hundreds of strikers and several WTUL allies suffered arrest. Women's suffrage groups such as the Political Equality League worked in cooperation with socialists to build early strike support demonstrations. When the strike spread to Philadelphia in late December, Bryn Mawr students and the Pennsylvania Women's Suffrage Association rallied in support.

On December 27 the larger employers proposed a settlement that granted most of the strike demands, but preserved the open shop. The strikers overwhelmingly rejected it. For a time solidarity remained strong. A Carnegie Hall rally on January 2, in which wealthy members of what Schneiderman called the "Mink Brigade" played a prominent role, featured proposals for citywide sympathy strikes by all women workers. But support soon waned. AFL backing, measured in money and organizers, was meager. Middle-class allies became less supportive when the issue was purely union recognition. By February 1910 the strikers returned to work in open shops. But they did so with a fifty-two-hour week (fifty-two and a half in Philadelphia) and four paid holidays.[29] This pattern of granting concessions regarding hours while maintaining the open shop enabled some employers to sever the connection between a shorter working day and other union-inspired initiatives for control over work. The pattern would recur frequently, especially in packing and steel, over the next decade.

Ultimately, the "Uprising of the 20,000" bettered the lives of hundreds of thousands of workers. Strikes over hours raced through the clothing industry. In July 1910, 60,000 cloak and suit makers engaged in a general strike in New York City, demanding a forty-eight-hour week, double pay for overtime, and recognition. This "Great Revolt," as the press called it, involved Italian immigrants far more fully than the 1909 shirtwaist uprising. Its success rested on the cooperation between the Jewish majority and the Italian minority in the trade and between the 54,000 men and 6,000 women employed. Taking note of females participating in the strike, the WTUL distributed 209,000 free quarts of milk to strikers' children. After two months the cloak and shirt makers signed a compromise agreement granting the preferential union shop, a fifty-hour week, ten paid holidays, and bonus pay for overtime. This "Protocol of Peace," though replete with antilabor provisions, represented the first collective bargaining agreement in the industry and continued the shorter-hours momentum.[30]

In Chicago, despite opposition from the male-dominated and craft-oriented leadership of the United Garment Workers (UGW), women producing men's clothing at Hart, Schaffner, and Marx walked out over wages in September 1910. The wave of strikes that followed ultimately involved 40,000 workers, 10,000 of them women. The Chicago WTUL, with headquarters in the same building as the AFL, made the UGW place two WTUL members on the strike committee and policed the Chicago police on the picket lines. Nonetheless, the strike left two workers dead and brought 374 arrests. Thomas Rickert, the conservative head of the UGW, reacted to the tumult and to the rising numbers of immigrant women in his union by pressing for a quick settlement. In both early November and early December he recommended agreements leaving the open shop intact. The rank and file rejected both and eventually won a union contract which established the 54-hour week (down from 57.5), a minimum wage, overtime at time-and-a-half, and safety concessions at Hart, Schaffner, and Marx. However, the 30,000 strikers at other firms made no gains when Rickert unilaterally declared their strike over in February 1911.[31]

Socialist leadership and support was vital in the 1912 general strike of New York City furriers. Led by the United Hebrew Trades, that strike united about 7,000 Jewish fur workers with 2,000 Germans, Greeks, Italians, French-Canadians, Bohemians, Slovaks, and others. It represented the most complete victory of multiethnic, shorter-hours unionism in the prewar clothing trades. Holding out for thirteen weeks in order to force accession to the demand for a Saturday half-holiday, the furriers won a 49-hour week, ten paid holidays, and time-and-a-half overtime pay along with union recognition.[32]

In early 1913 protocols calling for a fifty-hour week came to cover 60,000 dress, shirtwaist, kimono, wrapper, white goods, and children's dress makers after WTUL sponsored strikes in New York and Boston. By 1915, when Chicago ladies' cloakmakers and some ladies' glovemakers there won the fifty-hour week, shorter hours had reached most major northern clothing manufacturing centers. Gains then radiated outward to smaller cities.[33]

For a time the men's clothing industry remained an exception to the organizational successes in the clothing trades. However, this branch of the industry, with the rise of the Amalgamated Clothing Workers (ACW), would see the fullest expression of socialist-led industrial unionism in the needle trades. Again, the working day was crucial. The discrediting of the Rickert leadership of the UGW grew from the leadership's betrayal of three major strikes, all of which involved the reduction of hours. Even before Rickert's capitulation in the Chicago walk-out of 1910 discussed above, the UGW had ordered the end of a 1907 strike of New York City tailors, who sought a fifty-three-hour week, and had expelled nine locals for defying the order. The final straw in alienating the radical, often Yiddish-speaking, tailors in the UGW from the leadership came on February 28, 1913, when Rickert called off a nine-week-old general strike among as many as 100,000 New York City men's clothing workers. The strikers, who sought a forty-eight-hour week, union recognition, and a pay boost, gained next to nothing from the settlement. Rank-and-filers stayed on strike for eleven additional days and won the gradual institution of the fifty-two-hour week (forty-eight for cutters). Partially victorious but thoroughly embittered, the union's militants would, within two years, follow the advice of the socialist writer Isaac Hourwich: "If [the tailors] are to profit by the lesson of the [1913] strike, they must rid themselves of boss rule . . . if need be, by cutting loose from the national organization." After being outmaneuvered in an attempt to take leadership of the UGW, the left-wing majority of that group seceded and joined with the Tailors' Industrial Union to form the Amalgamated Clothing Workers of America (ACW), representing 40,000 members, in December 1914.[34]

With such young socialist veterans of Chicago and New York strikes as Sidney Hillman, Joseph Schlossberg, and Bessie Abramowitz providing the leadership and with a mandate to prepare for the time when organization would "put the . . . working class in actual control of the system of production," the ACW pressed for more free time. The second resolution passed by the new organization called for "a universal eight hour day . . . to lessen the evil of unemployment." In the first major ACW strike, waged by 25,000 Chicago men and women from September until December 1915, the forty-eight-hour week headed a list of demands. Although the Chicago strike is usually considered to have been defeated, it did suceed in enlisting the support of Chicago Federation of Labor leaders, including John Fitzpatrick, and of top women reformers, including Jane Addams and Grace Abbott. During the 1915 walkout the new union grew quickly. "Workers returned to their shops not as unorganized men and women," the ACW history of the strike observes, "but as members of a union." And they returned to the prospect of shorter hours. Much of the industry "voluntarily" adopted a reduced workweek just after the end of the strike, cutting hours to forty-eight or fifty weekly. By 1919 the ACW and ILGWU would successfully engage in a joint campaign to bring about the forty-four-hour week in the needle trades. Within one decade after the 1909 uprising, clothing workers had cut a dozen or more hours from their week's work, raised their wages, and built enduring unions.[35]

The steel industry invited shorter-hours agitation. Not only did its major corporation, U.S. Steel, boast of its success in maintaining an open shop, but the whole industry had a record of lengthening the working day. In the 1880s Carnegie plants had experimented with the eight-hour day, but, after completion of mechanization, the employers held that the hard work had disappeared from most of steel production and turned to longer shifts. Forcing through the extensions during economic downturns, the employers instituted twelve-hour days in much of the industry, beginning in 1887 and culminating with the conversions at South Works and Joliet, Illinois, between 1902 and 1904. By 1910, 30 percent of all steelworkers labored on Sunday, and the working week, according to figures compiled for Illinois, was seven hours more than it had been in 1882. Once every two weeks, workers in many departments put in a twenty-four-hour "long turn."[36]

At the AFL's 1909 convention the first resolution introduced called for "thorough organization of all branches of [the steel] business." The AFL campaign to carry out that resolution in early 1910 emphasized labor's "avowed desire for a normal work day and an American wage standard." However, the AFL's craft organization served as a poor vehicle for organizing in a mass-production industry undergoing changes in the division of labor that diluted craft expertise and created a range of semiskilled job classifications. The AFL unions, also hesitant to organize immigrants, committed only six organizers to the steel effort and had lost enthusiasm for the project when an hours strike at Bethlehem, Pennsylvania, presented new opportunities.[37]

At Bethlehem Steel Company, skilled workers had a Saturday half-holiday. But they worked ten hours and twenty-five minutes each of the other six days —sixty-eight hours per week. The less skilled complained of a thirteen-hour-and-twenty-minute workday. Since 1907 the company had refused to pay time and a half for overtime. On February 3, 1910, some of the skilled machinists at Bethlehem struck, demanding overtime premiums and an end to Sunday work. Shortly thereafter, unskilled laborers and apprentices joined their ranks. With the aid of AFL and International Association of Machinist organizers, the local craft unionists pursued unity with the unskilled, mostly Hungarian immigrants. Appeals directed to ethnic clergymen drew little support outside of Hungarian Catholic parishes, but many laborers still stood by the machinists through much of the 108-day strike. The skilled workers also refused a separate settlement ignoring the unskilled. Even so, the strike never succeeded in shutting down the entire plant. Overtime and Sunday work became optional as a result of the settlement, but wages remained unchanged and so low that long hours remained a necessity.[38]

Although the Bethlehem strike lost and although a summertime ten-hour initiative at McKees Rock failed, the events of 1910 changed labor relations in the steel industry. Reformers, especially the members of the Federal Council of Churches and John Fitch of the Pittsburgh Survey group, relentlessly publicized conditions in steel factories in the wake of the Bethlehem strike. "The entire industry," according to historian David Brody, "stood implicated." The AFL and the reformers forced an investigation of the corporations and won support for requiring the eight-hour system on government-contracted steel. Moreover, the unskilled and immigrants no longer seemed beyond organization. Critically, craft lines gave way. "Semi-industrial" unionism, still fraught with problems but more apt to organize the ethnic unskilled, had come to the steel industry. When AFL organizing returned to the mills in 1913, with the goals of recognition and "the three shift system of eight hours," agitational literature was printed in thirteen languages.[39]

In the lumber industry the IWW led a six-week strike of 3,000 Oregon sawmill workers in the spring of 1907, demanding nine hours (ten to twelve hours being the rule) and higher wages. It won wage concessions and established the union in the Northwest for the first time. By 1911 the largest IWW affiliate there organized around the eight-hour day, and in March 1912 the Wobblies led a huge walkout of unorganized Greek, Austrian, and Finnish sawmill workers at Grays Harbor, Washington, seeking eight hours plus up to a 20 percent pay boost. Despite a sympathy strike among lumberjacks, the movement failed to overcome vigilantes and deportations.[40] In the South the Brotherhood of Timber Workers (BTW) grew out of a 1907 general strike among Louisiana and East Texas lumber workers protesting, among other things, a lengthening of hours. That strike failed but by December 1910, the BTW had taken shape. At first the BTW agitated for a ten-hour day, but after joining the IWW in 1912, the union raised its demand in November 1913 to an eight-hour day with time and a half for overtime. More remarkably, in a southern industry in which skill and race distinctions overlapped, the BTW abandoned segregated locals as it fought for more leisure.[41]

In extractive industries the bloodiest and most important of the period's labor disputes concerned the working day. It mattered little, in terms of the emphasis on the working day or in terms of the violence of the repression, whether the Wobblies or the UMW, the strongest industrial organization in the AFL, provided the leadership. Reduction of hours addressed the two major concerns of miners: safety and unemployment. The UMW-led strikes in West Virginia in 1912 and 1913, involving 4,000 coal miners and described by one journalist as "Civil War in the West Virginia Coal Mines," began with a series of demands featuring the nine-hour day, down from ten. The West Virginia strikes, during which IWW composer Ralph Chaplin was inspired to write the classic labor anthem "Solidarity Forever," featured mass arrests, gunplay, evictions from company housing, and a militancy that made even the socialist leader Eugene Debs the target of criticism from the left. They ended in a compromise that included a nine-hour clause.[42] In Colorado the UMW's strike of 1913 and 1914 against the Rockefeller-owned Colorado Fuel and Iron Company involved over 10,000 coal miners, many of them Greek immigrants, who sought the eight-hour day and other reforms. The strike is best known for an unprovoked April 20, 1914, attack by the Colorado National Guard on the tent city in which the strikers camped. Machine-gun fire and arson claimed as many as thirty-two lives in the "Ludlow Massacre." After federal intervention and nearly nine more months of striking, the UMW called off the strike, defeated. In another extractive industry Rockefeller interests took a less hard line, granting the eight-hour day in the California oil industry in 1917. The Oil and Gas Workers' Union, an industrially organized AFL affiliate, secured the concession from Standard Oil of California with no strike and then led a whirlwind organizing campaign that lay the basis for an award of the eight-hour day in other California oil companies in a wartime mediation decision.[43]

In the metal mines, where transportation into the pits could add as much as an hour to the working day, hours were at issue in the three major strikes between 1906 and 1916. IWW strikes at Goldfield, Nevada, in 1906 and 1907 combined the issues of eight hours and "job control" (union regulation over work and posting of schedules and wage scales) successfully. By spring of 1907 nearly every job in and around the gold mines adopted the eight-hour system at high wages. In a remarkable experiment in mass unionism, 1,500 miners united in the same union with 400 "engineers, clerks, stenographers, teamsters, dishwashers [and] waiters."[44] In the Michigan copper strike of 1913 and 1914, 16,000 miners walked out to win the eight-hour day and concessions on wages and safety. Cornishmen, Irishmen, Croats, Slovenes, Poles, Italians, and Austrians joined together under WFM auspices. The nine-month dispute established the eight-hour day, but at terrible cost. Mine owners instituted the reform as part of a back-to-work movement designed to destroy the union and, although the strategy enjoyed no immediate success, the loss of the strike did help break the union. Worse, a 1913 Christmas party of strikers at Italian Hall in Calumet ended in seventy-three deaths, sixty-two of them children, when a false cry of "Fire" caused a fatal stampede.[45] The Mesabi Range strike of 1916 began as a walkout over wages, but blossomed under Wobbly leadership into a strike of 10,000 iron miners who placed a portal-to-portal eight-hour day at the head of their demands. Repression, including an accessory-to-murder indictment against seven strike leaders, and waffling federal mediation helped ensure defeat of the strike, though wages rose as a result.[46]

A list of other important shorter-hours campaigns during the prewar years would be long, but several deserve brief mention because they exemplify the issue's tendency to promote both solidarity and repression. The 1913 Buffalo, New York, strike of 4,000 retail workers reflected a growing demand for maximum-hours laws, rather than just early closing, by clerks and salespeople who increasingly identified with trade union methods. The strikers, 80 percent female, prevented delivery of scab goods and paraded in defiance of civic authorities. Fewer than three weeks after its May Day beginning, the strike ended with the Merchants' Association agreeing to an eight-and-a-half-hour day. In Los Angeles in 1910 a strike and lockout of 12,000 iron and metal workers seeking eight hours and a raise formed the context of the celebrated prosecution of the McNamara brothers on murder charges growing out of a bombing. Six years later the equally celebrated bombing that caused the prosecution of labor organizers Thomas Mooney and Warren Billings took place amidst a long, tough, and successful strike for the eight-hour day by San Francisco's structural steel workers. At Akron, Ohio, in 1913, 14,000 to 20,000 rubber workers, responding to appeals in Serbian, English, Italian, and Hungarian, shut down the city's major factories demanding shorter hours in an unsuccessful Wobbly-led strike.[47] In short, the years before Henry Ford's labor liberalizations and United States entry into World War I witnessed massive labor activity around hours. This activity formed a part of the context for Henry Ford's decision to grant the eight-hour day.

"The manufacturers of automobiles," wrote Upton Sinclair in describing the pre-1914 period, "were confronting a problem. The more men they had working, the more time these men wasted moving from one job to the next, and getting into each other's way." Henry Ford perceived two further problems. Unions of the radical IWW variety had made inroads in organizing in the open-shop bastion of Detroit, and Ford's new Highland Park factory suffered from astronomical turnover rates while it rationalized production. In 1914 Ford addressed all of these problems as he instituted a moving belt assembly line, a five-dollar daily wage, and the eight-hour day. In summarizing the goals of his labor policies as "profit sharing and efficiency engineering," Ford neatly indicated how welfare capitalism and calculation regarding productivity mixed in his response to the problems of efficiency and labor unrest.[48]

Scholars have long debated whether humanitarian or fiscal conditions predominated, but where the eight-hour day is concerned, it is impossible to disentangle the two. Ford was thoroughly committed to capitalist efficiency and to starting, in the words of his mentor, Thomas Edison, "to make this world over" through leisure.[49] Like most Progressive reformers, but unlike most industrialists, he saw no contradiction between the two goals. His rationales were always self-interested but seldom hypocritical. Therefore, it is appropriate to discuss how Ford came to the eight-hour decision (and why few other industrialists followed) by beginning with Ford's own statements.

Ford offered several reasons for the labor liberalizations of 1914. His most direct linking of such policies with the labor crisis occurred in a statement recalled by Joseph Galamb, an official in the experimental toolroom. "Mr. Ford," according to Galamb, "said he would lick the IWW by paying the men the five-dollar day." The eight-hour day was perhaps more pointedly designed to disarm the IWW, which had led a brief, unsuccessful strike of 5,000 Studebaker workers seeking eight hours and had won the shorter day at three Detroit metal wheel factories during the previous year.[50] The Wobblies propagandized widely at Ford's factory gates, demanding eight hours. Nor was the IWW in Detroit dying in early 1914, as the historian Allan Nevins would have it. Rather, it led thousands of jobless Detroiters on a demonstration in February of that year and carried out joint work with the AFL around the question of cutting hours to cure depression in the auto industry. While the IWW had probably not organized more than a thirtieth of Detroit's 60,000 auto workers, it had shown a capacity for influencing those who were not members. Moreover, the industrially organized AFL Carriage, Wagon, and Automobile Workers' Union as well as AFL craft unions were organizing in the auto industry with some success. Thus, Ford's "lick the IWW" stance, suggested also in his boast to a Detroit periodical that there "will be no more excitement in Detroit's labor circles," deserves to be considered a serious motivation for his reforms.[51]

In a second explanation of his rationale for the five-dollar, eight-hour day,

Ford said, "We have settled on the eight-hour day . . . because it so happens that this is the length of time which we find gives the best service from men, day in and day out." This notion that the institution of the eight-hour day was a matter of "proven" efficiency, was based on no solid calculation showing the specific superiority of eight hours. Still, Ford could point to several ways in which the new schedule served the company. The switch from two nine-hour shifts to three eight-hour shifts provided for an extra six hours of production. Although Ford later moved away from a full night shift, he held that "expensive tools cannot remain idle. They ought to work 24 hours a day." In inaugurating three shifts, with only one ten-minute lunch break on each shift, Ford secured optimum use from his machinery.[52] Ford and his advisors also saw efficiency as served by the eight-hour, five-dollar day in that the new labor policy decreased turnover and absenteeism and increased labor discipline. Ford's Highland Park plant suffered problems in achieving a stable labor force between 1910 and 1913. In the latter year Ford hired over 52,000 men to maintain a complement of 14,000 workers. Six times as many employees quit as were fired. Absenteeism ran as high as 10 percent daily.[53]

The high numbers of quits and truancies reflected alienation engendered by a rapid rationalization of production. In 1903, at the Mack Avenue factory, according to Ford, workmen fetched parts and material to one central location and built a car "exactly the same way one builds a house." By 1907, at the Piquette Plant, 45 cars sat in a circle and specialized workers, or work groups, walked from one to the next performing a limited task. That same year, time and motion studies began at Ford, and foremen received orders to enforce standards based on calculations of engineers with stop watches. "If the first man does not come up to that standard," Production Supervisor Max Wollering wrote, "try another. That was Henry's scheme of things." The tendency toward calculating production by the second accelerated with the building of the Highland Park plant. There, Ford mechanized material delivery systems in the foundry in 1912 and began to produce fly-wheel magnetos on a moving assembly line in April 1913. The magneto assembly, formerly done in about twenty minutes by a single skilled mechanic working at a bench, broke down into twenty-nine separate tasks performed by twenty-nine men at the chain-driven pace of thirteen minutes ten seconds total work per assembly. Efficiency experts juggled the line's speed to give "every second necessary but not a single unnecessary second" to the assemblers. In the fall of 1913, as the eight-hour decision approached, Ford men also pondered how to put assembly functions on a moving line. They knew, in September of that year, that stationary assembly required twelve hours and twenty-eight minutes of labor time under ideal conditions. Within six months that standard was cut to one hour and thirty-three minutes on a moving line.[54] Immigrant workers referred to the Highland Park plant as the "House of Corrections" in 1913, and the IWW branded Ford the "Speed-up King."[55]

Liberal labor policies could reward a work force willing to put up with such constant changes toward more alienated and disciplined labor. During the first week of the application of the 1914 reforms, 1,000 workers, mostly Greeks and Serbs, were fired for taking off on a Greek Orthodox religious holiday. Working at Ford was to be a privilege; liberal wages and hours were "a matter for management," a gift and not a right. Dissident employees knew, as the engineers Horace Arnold and Fay Faurote put it in their 1914 study, that "the door to the street is open for any who objects in any way [by] questioning obedience to any directions whatever."[56] Such division of labor also entailed an abandonment of mental work to management. Ford, although he sometimes held that "the average worker . . . above all . . . wants a job in which he does not have to think," saw repetitive, purely physical labor as "terrifying" and compensated by encouraging an intellectual life for workers —but only during hours after work. "Man needs leisure to think," he wrote, "and the world needs thinkers." He experimented with funding a variety of night and technical schools and delighted in finding employees who had unexpected skills, unrelated to their shop jobs.[57]

The 1914 reforms, as Ford's educational activities suggest, not only compensated for alienated labor, but also sought to develop, through leisure, a more efficient work force. Italian communist philosopher Antonio Gramsci, whose commentary on "Americanism and Fordism" remains indispensable, termed Ford's goal as the creation of "a new type of worker and of man," thoroughly Americanized by night classes and utterly committed to morality, duty, and family. Leisure, Ford insisted, would be used by the worker "for the greater happiness of his family" and this orientation toward family was to ensure "proper living" among employees. The five-dollar wage was designed as a "family wage," which would function by "not only supplying [the worker's] basic need, but also in giving him a margin of comfort and enabling him to give his boys and girls their opportunity and his wife some pleasure in life." Ford refused to hire married women whose husbands had jobs and discouraged taking in boarders. Profit-sharing, a large part of the five-dollar compensation, did not extend to young males without dependents, married men living alone, or men in the process of divorcing. Functionaries in the Sociological Department, formed immediately after the labor reforms to see that money and time were wisely spent, checked to see which men were "living unworthily" by drinking excessively, smoking tobacco, or defaulting on family obligations.[58]

Efficiency meant both the creation of a stable, disciplined labor force on the job and the reproduction of that work force through family life. Public and private considerations were inseparable. Indeed, John R. Lee, Ford personnel manager and first head of the Sociological Department, recalled that not until 1912 did management begin "to realize something of the relative value of men" and that it did so after an investigation into declining production in a drop hammer operation revealed that "sickness, indebtedness, and fear and worry over things entirely related to the home had crept in and put a satisfactory human unit entirely out of harmony with the things . . . necessary for production." The company's first response, cutting hours from ten to nine and raising wages 15 percent, set precedents for 1914.[59]

Although it is difficult to judge how much family life, temperance, and education benefited from Ford's labor reforms, productive efficiency was served. Labor turnover dropped by 90 percent, and absenteeism was at least halved. According to some figures it plummeted from 10 percent to .3 percent per day. During the first week of the 1914 reforms, 14,000 job seekers descended on the Highland Park factory in search of now-desirable employment. In departments where no technological or operational changes occurred, eight-hour productivity easily exceeded that formerly accomplished in nine. Ford could report that the five-dollar, eight-hour day was "one of the finest cost-cutting moves ever made."[60]

However, Ford was after more than efficiency and the outflanking of the IWW in his 1914 actions. His further rationale for the new wage-hours system reinterpreted the role of leisure and consumption into a businessman's version of Ira Steward's philosophy. Like Steward, Ford saw less hours as generating increased demand for industrial products. Workers with more leisure, he wrote, "have time to see more, do more—and, incidentally, they buy more. This stimulates business and *increases prosperity*, and in the general economic circle the money passes through industry again and back into the workman's pocket." Low unemployment—Ford once commented that he had considered instituting the four-hour day in 1914 as a cure for joblessness—and higher wages would similarly contribute to a greater demand for goods. "Wives are released from work, little children are no longer exploited," according to Ford, "and, given more time, they both become free to go out and find new products, new merchants and new manufacturers." Not incidentally, Ford was engaged in mass marketing cars. "People who have more leisure time," Ford held, "have more clothes." They also, he added with some self-interest, "must have more transportation facilities."[61]

The key question regarding the relationship between Ford's institution of the eight-hour day and the policies of other employers is to what extent Ford's decision was idiosyncratic and to what extent it represented a "corporate capitalist" outlook shared by other employers. We argue that Ford's actions neither reflected nor sparked a broader tendency toward voluntary reduction of hours. In Detroit, where other auto makers faced concerns like Ford's, the 1914 reforms met with their opposition. As the Socialist party of Michigan expressed its appreciation of Ford in a pamphlet and as labor organizer William Z. Foster lauded the new labor policy, some among Ford's fellow auto makers branded him a "traitor to his class." John R. Lee later implied that bitterness over the 1914 reforms led to Ford's withdrawal from the Employers' Association. Detroit industry cut hours grudgingly, and in 1920 many factories still operated on a schedule of more than 48 hours per week. General business reaction to Ford in 1914 was also negative. *The Wall Street Journal* criticized the new policies as an "economic crime" and an "intrusion of *Biblical principles . . . where they do not belong.*" The New York *Times* branded Ford's actions as "distinctly Utopian and against all experience" and sent a reporter to ask Ford if he were a socialist.[62]

Marion Cahill, who conducted a close study of voluntary reductions of hours during this period, concluded that "not only did employers fail voluntarily to reduce hours but that they did not give the matter serious consideration." His survey of the welfare capitalist journal *Human Engineering's* four 1911 issues, for example, yields just one example of an employer-initiated reduction. Cahill mentions five other examples of voluntary reductions between 1907 and World War I, the most important being among employers who belonged to the National Association of Lithographers who, in 1910, introduced the eight-hour day in an effort to keep the open shop. So slow was the pace of voluntary reform that in 1916 Henry Ford proposed to Woodrow Wilson that the latter include a national eight-hour law in his presidential platform. That Ford would make such a proposal bespeaks the lack of private corporate initiative in cutting hours. That Wilson declined reflects a continued ambivalence even among Progressives toward legislative action regarding the working day.[63]

During the half century from the close of the Civil War until 1915, the federal government had played but a small role in limiting working hours. The periodic passage of legislation providing the eight-hour day for federal employees not only failed to set a precedent for private industry, but disappointed organized labor when the courts and the federal agencies administered the laws so as to limit their coverage. Even the AFL-supported eight-hour federal employee law of 1912 was eroded when its stiff penalty provision was held by the attorney general not to apply if workers engaged in labor on a mixture of federal and private contracts.[64]

However, from 1916 to 1918, the federal government made an apparent change of course and engaged in activity that challenged long hours in private industry. This federal activity took several forms, the most significant of which included the Adamson Act (1916), which provided the eight-hour day to some railroad workers; the Keating-Owen Child Labor Law (1916), which provided an eight-hour maximum working day for children aged fourteen to sixteen working in industries engaged in interstate commerce; and the activities of the War Labor Policies Board and the War Labor Board in providing for the "basic eight-hour day" on war contracts. However, all these partial reforms came largely in response to agitation or threatened agitation by labor.

The reforms of 1916-1918 began in the context of the 1916 reelection campaign of President Woodrow Wilson and of the need to ensure labor peace during war preparation and the actual fighting. Wilson and the Democrats, who had promised organized labor much and had delivered little during the president's first campaign and term, made skillful use of the hours issue in the 1916 election. Wilson, who inherited the Commission on Industrial Relations (CIR) from Taft, staffed that federal labor investigative agency with a mixture of moderate labor leaders, social reformers, and NCF members and excluded the more vociferous open-shop advocates of the National Association of Manufacturers. Led by the reform-minded Kansas City attorney Frank Walsh and S. Thruston Ballard, a Louisville miller whose winter wheat refinery was the world's largest and the first to institute the eight-hour day, the CIR's 1916 *Final Report* recommended federal and state laws enforcing a six-day work week of eight-hour days along with a child labor law. Wilson benefited from his association with this CIR policy and from his signing of the Adamson Act.[65]

Wilson did not take Henry Ford's (or the CIR's) advice and make "Out of the shops in eight hours" one of his campaign slogans in 1916.[66] Instead, he managed to identify himself as an eight-hour supporter without making any conclusive commitment to eight-hour legislation outside of the railroad industry and child labor. This he did principally by declaring in the fall of 1916 that "the eight-hour day now undoubtedly has the sanction of the judgement of society in its favor and should be adopted as a basis for wages even where the actual work to be done cannot be completed within eight hours." Wilson's statement actually applied to a limited point in the enforcement of railway labor laws, but organized labor seized it as a presidential seal of approval for eight hours. Gompers campaigned for the president's reelection and later wrote, "I have never known a man either within or without the White House with whom it was so satisfactory to cooperate upon big matters as President Wilson."[67] During the campaign and the months of war which followed, the eight-hour day was a "big matter" but one on which Wilson never took an unequivocal stand for federal action. Both the Adamson Act and the Keating-Owen Child Labor Law illustrate Wilson's political skill and the ambiguity of federal commitment to shorter hours.

The demand for an eight-hour day among operating personnel on the railroads developed with stunning speed. The Hours of Service Act, a 1907 federal measure directed mainly at rail safety, required only eight hours rest to punctuate sixteen-hour working days. Within a decade, the Adamson Act would make an eight-hour day the law of the land for railroads. After 1907 the four unions representing operators on the rails (the Brotherhood of Locomotive Engineers, Brotherhood of Locomotive Firemen and Enginemen, Brotherhood of Railroad Trainmen, and Order of Railway Conductors) began to discuss the eight-hour day at the local and division level. By 1913 the trainmen and conductors were readying joint action on the issue, and by 1915 a few southern rails had already switched to the new schedule. In 1915 the "Big Four" railway brotherhoods solidified plans for joint negotiations with the railway carriers and focused on the eight-hour day. On December 15, executives of the four unions and the executive committees of their regional committees voted to submit to their members prosposals that:

In all road service 100 miles or less, eight hours or less will constitute a day, except in passenger service . . .
On runs of 100 miles or less overtime will begin at the expiration of eight

hours [and]
All overtime to be compensated on the minute basis and paid for at time and one-half times and pro rate.

Of those polled 95 percent approved of submitting the demands to the carriers.[68]

Both sides immediately began fierce public relations campaigns. The companies insisted that the eight-hour demand was no more than a ploy to gain higher wages through overtime, and that the eight-hour day would raise rail rates, reduce safety expenditures, and necessitate cutting wages of the 1,500,000 nonoperating employees to meet the demands of the operators.[69] This last argument, however disingenuous, had the potential to divide the Big Four further from the rest of organized labor. None of the operating brotherhoods was affiliated with the AFL, and the Switchmen's Union, which represented nonoperating personnel and which was part of the AFL, opposed support for the Big Four. Only the vigorous backing of Gompers, socialist unionists, and others who believed, in Gompers's words, that "there is a big principle involved in the fight the road Brotherhoods have been making . . . . [a] principle which affects the interest and welfare of all," assured that the AFL would back the Big Four.[70]

The unions' publicity stressed, as the title of one leaflet put it, that "Long Hours Cause Death" by leading to poor health, accidents, and the crippling injuries, which had increased fourfold from 1889 to 1910. Big Four officials also observed that if the roads wished to avoid higher wage bills from overtime, they had only to schedule fewer long shifts. Far from cloaking a wage measure in shorter-hours rhetoric, workers were willing to accept less total wages in return for less hours. Reports of high profits for the major carriers buttressed the unions' contention that transition to an eight-hour day was not impractical.[71]

Negotiations on the issue began on June 1, 1916, in New York City with A. B. Garretson of the conductors speaking for the 400,000 members of the Big Four. Division chairmen of 640 brotherhood locals came to the conference where Elisha Lee of the Pennsylvania Railroad represented the National Conference Committee of Railroad Managers. Garretson proposed eight hours with no cut from the existing ten-hour pay scales and refused to entertain counterproposals for arbitration of all issues or for complex work rule changes which would have negated all pay raises stemming from overtime after eight hours. Negotiations ceased on June 16.[72]

With bargaining adjourned, the unions balloted. On August 8, the day negotiations reconvened, the Big Four announced that 94 percent of their members had opted to strike on Labor Day (September 4) for the eight-hour day. The *Literary Digest* headlined "Facing Our Greatest Labor War"; the socialist *New York Call* declared that "the greatest attack on capital . . . in all [U.S.] history" loomed. The carriers continued a hard line, with *Railway Age Gazette* starkly stating: "If the choice is between further concessions and a strike, then the strike should be allowed to come." After a brief attempt at mediation, all parties agreed that no progress was being made.[73]

President Wilson, expressing fear that "a general strike may be disastrous," asked to meet with the brotherhoods and carriers. In the midst of the 1916 election campaign, and under pressure from the AFL and a host of worried business groups, Wilson stepped into the railway dispute. He brought with him a modest record of supporting shorter hours and a suspicion of the railway corporations nutured by experience in antitrust cases and by respect for the ideas of Louis Brandeis.[74]

On August 15, the day after the White House conference on the eight-hour day on the railroads began, Wilson tipped his moderate hand. Eight hours, he advised, but with arbitration of wage issues based on an inquiry into railroad finances. Wilson's stance, which one historian has termed a "middle-of-the-road maneuver," had the effect of forcing each side to acknowledge whether the working day was the key issue or whether wages really were being discussed. It was in this context that Wilson declared, "I believe the [eight hours] concession right. The eight-hour day now undoubtedly has the sanction of the judgement of society . . . and should be adopted."[75]

As the unions debated the president's proposals, management rejected them. Without guarantees of higher rates, they argued, the carriers could not concede eight hours. Since Wilson was legally powerless to offer such guarantees, the rejection was a blanket one and the carriers added bitter denunciations of the president for playing politics and undermining arbitration. Wilson replied that no mechanism to force arbitration then existed. By August 27 the corporations had tendered a pair of counterproposals. One provided for appointing an investigating committee and for outlawing strikes during the investigation. The second envisioned an interim period in which railroads kept both "ten-hour" and "eight-hour" books while an investigation occurred. The brotherhoods rejected both suggestions and, on August 28, the labor chairmen began leaving Washington with secret orders authorizing a strike for September 4. When three chairmen leaked the strike plan to the press, Wilson summoned Garretson to the White House, where the latter confirmed the projected strike.[76]

Faced with an impending walkout of 400,000 railwaymen, Wilson turned to Congress for help. Addressing a joint session on August 29, he upheld the eight-hour day as conforming to "the whole spirit of the times and the preponderant evidence of recent economic experience" and then elaborated a complex proposal designed to placate the carriers. Alongside the eight-hour day were provisions to enlarge and reorganize the Interstate Commerce Commission, to appoint a committee to study the impact of the shorter day and make recommendations on wages and on freight rates, and, most controversially, to amend the Newlands Act so that it outlawed strikes and lockouts while an investigation of a labor dispute was in progress, and to empower the president to take over and operate the railroads, and draft personnel "in case of military necessity." The last two provisions caused the labor press to score Wilson's "Slave Act" weeks before the election.[77]

The attitude of the unions toward proposed legislation, a historic initiative for shorter hours by *political* means, was mixed. Gompers, on the spot because of his longtime opposition to eight-hour laws for adult men in the private sector, reiterated that "whatever progress has been made in reducing . . . hours . . . has been due to organized economic power." Nonetheless, the AFL had to enter the campaign for the eight-hour law both to prevent its antilabor provisions from passing and to avoid abstaining in a historic victory that it had worked hard to achieve. Moreover, Gompers had accepted legislative regulation of hours for seamen the previous year. He eventually wired AFL bodies with instruction to "telegraph both your . . . Senators and your Congressmen . . . insisting upon the eight-hour work day at present compensation, and in your telegram emphatically protest against enactment of any law imposing upon American workers involuntary servitude." Similarly, although W. S. Stone of the engineers and W. G. Lee of the trainmen *later* expressed opposition to the Adamson Act, at the time of congressional hearings on the matter, neither spoke vigorously against the bill, and Lee gave every indication of favoring it, especially as a way to head off the impending strike.[78]

Senator W. C. Adamson, chairman of the Commerce Committee, soon convinced Wilson that the rate increase and antistrike provisions could not pass. On September 2, just in time to avert the strike, a simpler bill named for Adamson cleared the Senate 43 to 28 after passing the House by a 239-to-56 vote. Wilson signed the act in his private railway car, using four pens and then presenting one to the head of each railway brotherhood. A giant victory for labor, in that it gave the eight-hour day to operating railroad employees, the law also instructed Wilson to appoint a committee to report within nine months on the fiscal impact of the measure and forbade railroads from lowering eight-hour wages below ten-hour standards in the interim. The unions canceled their strike, while Gompers's office issued a statement saying the "brotherhoods still maintain their opposition to legislative methods."[79]

The carriers resolved to fight the Adamson Act in the courts and refused to confer with the brotherhoods on its implementation. Answering management's threat "to fight to the end," W. G. Lee observed that a "strike vote is still in effect" and promised that the unions would play "their strongest card." On November 24, with no enforcement provisions made for a law slated to take effect on January 1, the carriers and government agreed to a speedy test case on the constitutionality of the law using an injunction secured by the Missouri, Oklahoma, and Gulf Railroad. In late December Wilson's "Eight-Hour Commission" reported that the Adamson Act was economically feasible and should be fully implemented.[80]

Employers continued to ignore the law in January, and a reelected Wilson renewed pleas for a ban on strikes during investigations of labor disputes. A January meeting of rail union chairmen agreed to delay a threatened strike on the matter. Socialists branded the unenforced Adamson Act the "defeat of the railroad workers." On March 10, with all signs pointing to U.S. entry into World War I, the chairmen again met. This time they resolved to have implementation by March 17 or to strike. Wilson, appealing to the patriotism of all concerned, successfully requested a two-day delay in the strike and turned the matter over to mediators from the Council of National Defense. Early in the morning of March 19, apprised by Wilson that under no circumstances would a strike be acceptable, the carriers agreed to implement the eight-hour law. Several hours later the Supreme Court declared the law constitutional in a 5-to-4 vote, treating it as a wage measure.[81]

In the wake of the Adamson Act, reformers committed to the eight-hour day burst with enthusiasm. Senator Robert Owen of Oklahoma, a child labor reformer, announced that the shorter day would "distribute happiness and property more equitably," while Frank Walsh, chairman of the Commission on Industrial Relations, rhapsodized:

1916 marks the beginning of the end of an industrial despotism which allows a few men to exercise autocratic control over the lives, mental aspirations and craving for happiness of countless . . . producers. Wilson's Eight-Hour Day Plea Will Become the Demand of the Whole World's Workers.[82]

But the impact of the Big Four's victory was far more limited than the reformers allowed. The unions had won the eight-hour day at precisely the time when they were strong enough to take it. The victory did not automatically extend to other workers. Only a small number of organized switchmen also won eight hours quickly in the wake of the Adamson Act. Ironically, the railroad shopmen, who pioneered in federated bargaining in the bitter, 45-month Harriman System strike (fought partly over eight hours between 1911 and 1915, and defeated largely because operating brotherhood employees continued to work) remained unrewarded prophets. "What next?" socialist writer Jack Phillips asked, "Will it be the shopmen next? Will the 80 percent of railroad workers outside the brotherhoods come next?" The answer was complex, as the crazy-quilt pattern of craft jurisdictions on the rails dictated that it would be, but ultimately the Adamson Act was to prove an important, but far from binding, precedent in securing the eight-hour day for nonoperating personnel in shop crafts and telegraphy through wartime actions of the Rail Wage Commission.[83]

The history of the Keating-Owen Child Labor Act is also marked by the exigencies of the 1916 election and by court challenges, which in this case set aside the law. Wilson had, between 1908 and 1912, firmly opposed federal child labor legislation. The National Child Labor Committee succeeded only in convincing Wilson not to speak against the Palmer-Owen bill on child labor in 1914. Wilson did not protest either when Democratic Senator Lee Overman of North Carolina objected to the bringing of the Palmer-Owen bill directly to the Senate floor in March 1915, thus ensuring that the bill, which had passed the House by a 5-to-1 margin, would die in committee. Nor, despite strong support for the measure from the AFL, NCL, U.S. Children's Bureau, and American Medical Association, did Wilson object when Overman again kept a child labor bill, the Keating-Owen Act, off the Senate floor on June 3, 1916.[84]

However, Wilson suddenly embraced the child labor measure and assumed a position of leadership in the campaign for reform. On June 16 the Democratic convention, worried by possible defections of progressive voters to the Roosevelt wing of the Republican party, adopted a platform plank favoring "the speedy enactment" of a federal child labor law. The Republicans did likewise, but it was Wilson who, by virtue of his refusal to accept formal renomination until the Keating-Owen Act passed, received credit for blocking Southern threats to filibuster. On September 1 Wilson signed the Keating-Owen Act into law. In accepting renomination the next day, he pointed to a record which included "the emancipation of the children of the nation from hurtful labor."[85]

The Keating-Owen Act did not end child labor. It did forbid from interstate commerce the products of mines and quarries where children under sixteen were employed and the products of mills, factories, canneries, and workshops where children under fourteen were employed or children between fourteen and sixteen worked more than eight hours a day. But such provisions covered only about one in fourteen of the nation's nearly 2 million child laborers. One federal court declared the Keating-Owen Act unconstitutional even before it took effect. In that case, *Hammer v. Dagenhart*, the southern cotton manufacturers challenged the Keating-Owen Act before Judge James E. Boyd of North Carolina. Boyd, an opponent of child labor laws, ruled on August 13, 1917, granting a permanent injunction holding the law unconstitutional. He cited no precedents and appended no written opinion, but his order barred federal district attorneys in his jurisdiction from prosecuting child labor violators. Nine months later, the U.S. Supreme Court sustained Boyd on an appeal of *Hammer v. Dagenhart*. By a 5-to-4 vote, the high court held that if the principles embodied in the child labor law were upheld, "all freedom of commerce will be at an end and the power of the states over local matters may be eliminated, and thus our system of government be practically destroyed."[86]

The activities of the War Labor Board (WLB) and War Labor Policies Board (WLPB) further brought hours, trade unions and politics together. A 1918 report of the Executive Council of the AFL began, "As might easily have been predicted, the most important issue in war production has been the application of the eight-hour law." Such a prediction could have been based not only on the exigencies of war production, which occasionally required long shifts, but on the militancy with which workers had demanded the eight-hour day before the war. In 1916, for example, more workers were on strike than in any year, save one, during the first two decades of the twentieth century.[87] Of the 2,501 strikes whose cause is enumerated in the *American Labor Year Book* covering that year, 110 (or 4.4 percent) involved only the issue of hours and an additional 490 (or 19.6 percent) involved hours in combination with other issues. Over 340,000 workers secured the eight-hour day that year. In 1917, despite wartime attempts to foster labor peace and attempts to bring voluntary compliance with the eight-hour day, comparable statistics show 4.3 percent pure hour strikes and an additional 15.1 percent partially involving hours. Over half a million workers gained the eight-hour system in the first half of 1917 alone.[88]

Labor protest around the issue centered in the most sensitive war industries. In addition to the railway agitation surrounding the Adamson Act, there was the Mesabi Range strike of Minnesota iron ore miners. Even more dramatic were the munitions strikes, which began in Bridgeport, Connecticut, in 1915 and continued there through 1918. These strikes spread to arms factories throughout Connecticut, Massachusetts, and Rhode Island as well as to the Westinghouse factories producing shells and airplane engines in the Pittsburgh area. All these strikes revolved around the eight-hour day and most were successful. The Bridgeport and Westinghouse strikes deserve attention as illustrations of the mood of labor militancy, the tendency toward industrial unionism and even workers' control, and the continuing capacity of the hours demand to generate unity.[89]

In Bridgeport, where time study and incentive pay had come to the metalworking industry by 1910, a socialist-led lodge of the International Association of Machinists, grew dramatically with the war orders of 1915. Threat of a strike caused the huge Remington Arms plant to concede the eight-hour day in August of that year, a month after a short walkout by 125 women workers at Remington won the eight-hour demand. By December 1915, as a result of a summertime citywide strike, 23,000 Bridgeport machinists won the same concession. The largest Bridgeport munitions strikes prior to American entry into the war involved wage rates rather than hours, but weeks after that entry the union began a series of brief, rolling strikes to generalize the eight-hour system and to institute an elaborate system of union control over job classifications and activities on the shop floor. Leadership by ex-Wobbly Samuel Lavit and by Edwin O'Connell engineered impressive unity between skilled and unskilled workers, between native-born Americans and immigrants, and between men and militant women strikers who joined the walkouts even though largely barred from craft union membership. The unions stressed shorter hours and a simplification of the wage structure in a campaign that culminated in massive strikes in May and June 1918. The IAM formally secured the eight-hour day, which already was established in most shops, as part of an August 28, 1918, settlement by the National War Board.[90]

The Westinghouse strike of 1916 began on April 21 when 2,000 workers at Westinghouse Electric in East Pittsburgh walked out for the eight-hour day. Organized by the locally powerful American Industrial Union, the strike reflected that organization's commitment to "organize workers in all industries in

. . . the Pittsburgh District, without regard to age, creed, race, sex or craft." By the second evening 13,000 Westinghouse workers, 3,000 of them women, had struck against Westinghouse, one of the largest fully Taylorized corporations. At a strike meeting, they sang their demands: "All we want is an eight-hour day/ With nine and one-half hours' pay."[91]

Within four days the strike spread to four Westinghouse plants in the area and involved 36,000 employees at Westinghouse Electric and Westinghouse Machine alone. The IAM, spurred on by the accomplishments of the AIU, sent in sixteen organizers. The IAM and AIU issued a joint call for a regional general strike to enforce the eight-hour day on May 1 and as many as 20,000 strikers, many of them foreign-born, marched to U.S. Steel's Edgar Thomson Works in an effort to spread the walkout. A thousand company guards fought the demonstrators, killing three and wounding three dozen. Pennsylvania's governor then ordered 1,000 National Guardsmen to the Westinghouse Electric plant, and after leaders were arrested, the strike was broken. But the 1916 eight-hour actions at Westinghouse sparked a series of other shorter-hours protests. Mediators headed off strikes in several other machinist/munitions disputes by granting concessions regarding hours.[92]

Despite these indications of resolve to win shorter hours by workers in key industries, many industrialists, not corporate liberals on this issue, remained unwilling to grant the eight-hour day, even as a war measure. *Iron Age*, a trade organ of the metal industry, proclaimed, "that the unparalleled situation which has made victory in Europe turn not only upon sheer tonnage in steel projectiles, but upon the metalcutting capacity of American mechanic tools, must not be allowed to settle for years to come so important an issue as the eight-hour machine shop day." The president of the National Founders Association decried the eight-hour day at that group's 1917 and 1918 conventions, calling for its abolition. The NAM reiterated its opposition to the shorter day. Individual manufacturers complained that the limited pro-eight-hour policies of the government caused labor strife. "The story," they argued, "came to the men and made them believe they would eventually get an eight-hour day."[93] Nor was the anti-eight-hours sentiment confined to small unenlightened producers. The National Industrial Conference Board, articulating a reform philosophy based on "cooperative action" between government, business, and labor, issued a series of research reports, arguing that maximum efficiency would be obtained with a work week of more than forty-eight hours. And U.S. Steel, in other ways a model of welfare capitalism, remained a fierce holdout against shorter hours.[94]

The first clash of a labor movement wanting shorter hours, a reluctant corporate elite, and a government bent on efficient war production came in February 1917 when, according to an AFL Executive Council report, "the forces . . . hostile to according Labor any rights—assumed it to be a propitious moment . . . to launch an agitation for repeal of the eight-hour law" of 1912.[95] In debate on the Naval Appropriations Bill, three congressmen asked whether an amendment ought not to provide the president with power to suspend the eight-hour law in emergencies. Gompers wrote House Speaker Champ Clark to argue that no amendment was needed, since existing legislation already included the proviso: "Except in case of extraordinary emergency." One month later the AFL nonetheless supported an amendment that empowered the president to suspend the eight-hour day on government work in cases of "national emergency." Wilson signed the bill on March 4 and within three weeks suspended the eight-hour law in navy yards, on "all contracts for ordnance and ordnance stores and other miliary supplies," on arsenal or fortification building, and, incredibly, among workers distributing seeds for the Department of Agriculture.[96]

Gompers regarded the March amendment as a labor victory that "completely protects the basic eight-hour day." Such a position shows the defensiveness of the AFL leadership at a time when it could have made major demands—including a national eight-hour law for all workers or, as Gompers once proposed, a seven-hour day.[97] Far from a victory, the amendment allowed the president to sweep away the actual eight-hour day in industry after industry in favor of the "basic eight-hour day." In accepting the "basic eight-hour day," the AFL implicitly accepted the idea that long hours meant greater production—an idea the organization had fought for years. The "basic eight-hour day" also opened the AFL to charges that it had no real interest in hours and merely sought higher wages through overtime. Finally, the amendment violated the wishes of many AFL members who, according to an *American Federationist* article in 1918, wanted an actual eight-hour day.[98]

In practice it proved hard to differentiate between "war labor" and the rest of industry and reformers in the government attempted to extend the basic eight-hour day to greater numbers of workers. Newton Baker, secretary of war and a supporter of the shorter-hours work of the National Consumers League, appointed the young lawyer and professor Felix Frankfurter to act on behalf of the War Labor Board in clarifying application of the eight-hour provisions. Frankfurter, a disciple of Brandeis and a backer of shorter hours mainly on the grounds of efficiency, faced a troublesome situation: "in many cases workers in the same factories engaged on different articles . . . were treated differently." He blamed this situation for "a great many labor troubles." In his position as secretary of the War Labor Policies Board (WLPB) formed in May 1918, Frankfurter attempted to remedy the situation and to serve the cause of a shorter working day by bring the "basic eight-hour day" to general application. Though the eight-hour system was by no means universally applied, progress was made. WLB estimates held that over 925,000 workers received the eight-hour day during 1917 and the first half of 1918.[99] Frankfurter soon served notice that he considered hours a part of the determination of wages and intended to move against U.S. Steel, the leading defender of the twelve-hour day.[100]

The steel industry stood as the great example of the unevenness of wartime controls on hours and, as an open shop committed to setting its own conditions of work, of industrial refusal to make concessions on hours. At its South Bethlehem plant, for example, Bethlehem Steel briefly granted the basic eight-hour day only to workers laboring exclusively on government contracts, sparking protests from machinists and electrical workers in other parts of the plant. On April 16, 1918, it suddenly reverted to the ten-and-five-twelfth-hour day it had used before the war, paying no time-and-a-half bonus for overtime beyond eight hours. Government investigators from the WLB treated the Bethlehem Steel barons harshly: "While America is sacrificing a generation of its best men, the executives of the steel company are devoting most of their attention . . . to perpetuate feudal control of labor." Bethlehem's operating head, Eugene Grace, tried to refuse compliance with WLB directives to correct abuses at the plant, but in the face of a strike WLB cochairmen William Howard Taft and Frank Walsh required his compliance on the issues of hours, wages, and the election of shop committees to represent workers.[101]

In one sense, the public contention between Frankfurter and U.S. Steel head Elbert H. Gary was unnecessary. Frankfurter, in attempting to apply the "basic eight-hour day" to the steel industry acknowledged that labor was short and an actual eight-hour day should not be implemented. The issue thus turned on wartime wages for overtime. And, as James Weinstein has written, "the cost of the increase in wages due to the adoption of the basic eight-hour day could be passed on to the government" in higher prices for war orders.[102] Still, the fact that Frankfurter saw the campaign as part of a crusade for shorter hours, and that Gary reacted as if the steel industry had been attacked, gave their differences symbolic importance.

Frankfurter first asked Gary's cooperation and invited U.S. Steel to work with the WLPB on July 9, 1918. Gary, sensing reforms to come, stalled and pleaded that he was too busy with war production to meet. After Frankfurter sent a memorandum on long hours in the steel industry, Gary opened a further breach between his company and the board by calling a meeting of 150 steel manufacturers at the Waldorf-Astoria Hotel in New York on August 26. Gary announced that steel workers favored both long hours and the open shop. Acting as the steel industry's spokesman, he evaded meeting with Frankfurter to discuss the eight-hour day until September 20, 1918. At the meeting Gary railed at eight hours as a ruse to get higher wages, but Frankfurter threatened government action, including making Henry Ford the umpire on the hours question in steel. The Iron and Steel Institute announced that the industry had adopted the "basic eight-hour day" as a war measure five days later. Gary had toed the line, happy perhaps to have kept the open shop. The war was to last just six more months. After its close, much of the steel industry returned to extremely long schedules. Despite high, and what one historian calls "naive," hopes among reformers, war policy in steel set no lasting precedents.[103]

Indeed, despite the efforts of Frankfurter, Baker, and others, the entire record of the WLB, the clearinghouse for labor disputes, remained quite mixed. Board policy on the hours of labor was that the "basic eight-hour day is recognized as applying in all cases in which existing law required it. In all other cases the question . . . shall be settled with due regard to governmental necessities and the welfare, health and proper comfort of the workers."[104] In applying this standard, umpires from the board did not, as Cahill suggests they did, "almost invariably [award] the basic eight-hour day." A Bureau of Labor Statistics report from 1921 offers the best summary of the WLB's decisions on hours with the phrase "NO GENERAL RULE ESTABLISHED." Although the basic eight-hour day was obtained as a result of more board rulings than any other system, in numerous cases the arbitrators left longer schedules intact. Longshoremen in the South Atlantic continued on ten-hour shifts. The schedule of fifty-seven and a half hours per week for night workers at American Locomotive in Richmond passed the board unscathed. Nor did the basic eight-hour day apply to street railway employees or workers in coastwise or deep-sea shipping or in harbors. Even after the adoption of a clause providing time and a half for overtime after eight hours by the WLPB in June 1918, no clear eight-hour policy was set.[105]

The biggest union success in securing shorter hours during the war, that of the packinghouse workers, shows strikingly how solidarity and organization conditioned awards. The stockyards, an open shop, had witnessed a phenomenal division of labor on, to use David Brody's pun, the "disassembly" line. As skills were undermined, jobs often became the provenance of one or more of the many ethnic groups who crowded the packing house neighborhoods. By 1909, 43 percent of the workers in the four major centers were East European born; more than one packing worker in ten in Chicago was female. By 1918 over 20 percent of the Chicago packing workers were black. The unemployed "shaped up" outside the gates in the early mornings ready to underbid each other for jobs.[106] These, clearly, were the unorganizable. And yet, in a matter of months, they were organized—the first unionized mass production industry in the United States.

Impetus for meatpacking unionization came from an unlikely alliance. William Z. Foster, working as a railway carman in Chicago, later wrote of the simple origins of the movement: "One day as I was walking to work and I remember well that it was July ll, 1917, it struck me suddenly that perhaps I could get a campaign started to organize the workers in the great Chicago packinghouses." That night Foster got the approval of the District Council of his Carmen's Union; two nights later, the Butcher Workmen, a small craft union in the yards, agreed. On July 15 the two unions secured approval from the Chicago Federation of Labor (CFL) to initiate an organizing drive. John Fitzpatrick, the head of the CFL, gave enthusiastic support. Within two weeks the Stockyards Labor Council, an experiment in federation embracing butchers, carmen, machinists, electricians, coopers, carpenters, office workers, steam fitters, engineers, firemen, and other trades with jurisdiction in the yards emerged. With black organizers supported by the Illinois Federation of Labor, with volunteers from the Chicago WTUL, and with two Polish and Lithuanian organizers supported, as it turned out, by the packers and acting as spies, the Stockyards Labor Council slowly organized, concentrating on minority and unskilled workers. The 500 recruits who signed up in six weeks seemed paltry to Foster, but Fitzpatrick continued to be enthusiastic. Eight hours, a Fitzpatrick crusade, and the right to organize were the key selling points from the earliest day.[107]

By November workers flocked to the renascent unions. Dennis Lane, craft-conscious head of the Butcher Workmen, saw this as resulting in part from his planting "recruits" at organizing meetings. The "plants," waving dues money and signing up enthusiastically, broke the ice and others followed. To Foster, the convening of a national meeting of the packinghouse trades after a series of small strikes in western cities was crucial. Those as the meeting, held on November 11, 1917, in Omaha, drew up a coherent set of demands and enabled the organizers to conjure up threats of a massive strike in Chicago papers. At the first Butcher Workmen meeting after the Omaha conference, 1,400 workers signed up. By year's end, according to the president's Mediation Commission, between a fourth and a half of all packinghouse employees had joined unions.[108]

In wake of the Omaha meeting and of the "Big Five" packers' refusal to bargain, union members overwhelmingly voted to authorize a strike. An informal national federation of stockyards unions took shape, headed by Fitzpatrick and with Foster as secretary. But before any strike plans could mature, the Wilson administration pressed for labor peace to ensure uninterrupted meat production to fill war orders. In some of his memoirs, Foster stressed that he and fellow organizer Jack Johnstone campaigned "against such government interference" and "for a strike to force the packers . . . to sign a union agreement," adding that Fitzpatrick also distrusted the government's intentions. Still the federated trades and the Big Five signed a no-strike, no-lockout pledge for the duration of the war on Christmas 1917.[109]

President Wilson requested that the two sides come together in Washington. On January 25 Secretary of Labor W. B. Wilson brought labor and management to an initial accord: no preferential union shop, no grievance committees, and no recognition of unions in return for concessions on employment and shop conditions. Wilson appointed Federal Judge Samuel B. Alschuler to arbitrate all other issues. With members flocking to the unions, Alschuler held hearings in Chicago from February 11 until March 7, 1918. Having heard Frank P. Walsh, Fitzpatrick, and rank-and-filers present the union's case, and with Fitzpatrick worrying aloud that the unions "will be unable to prevent a walkout if the decision is not announced immediately," Alschuler ruled on March 30.[110] He granted, even according to the skeptical Foster's reckoning, "85 percent of the union's demands," including the basic eight-hour day with time and a quarter for overtime and a twenty-minute paid lunch. At an Easter Sunday meeting of 40,000, Fitzpatrick announced the agreement and added, "It's a new day, and out in God's sunshine you men and you women, black and white have not only an eight-hour day but you are on an equality."[111]

One other point regarding war labor policy needs emphasis. The cooperation of the AFL with the war effort signaled brief legitimation of its place in society but also exposed those elements in the labor movement who did not support the war to fierce repression, which sometimes rebounded to victimize AFL unions as well. For example, in the Northwest lumber fields, a war industry by virtue of its production of spruce for airplanes, the IWW had organized the Lumber Workers' Industrial Union (LWIU), which had 6,000 members at the time of its 1917 founding convention, one month before American entry into the war. The Wobblies led a successful eight-hour strike in parts of Washington and Idaho that spring and planned further actions, especially in Washington's Douglas fir industry. The AFL, reacting to IWW successes, revived its moribund affiliate in the region and issued a general strike call for July 16; the Wobblies set their own general strike for July 17. The Lumbermen's Protective Association uncompromisingly defended the ten-hour day. For six weeks much of Northwest lumber production remained tied up as employers used private police, local sheriffs, attorneys, and federal officials to try to break the IWW. Sympathy strikes in Northwest shipyards proliferated. The AFL, which played little part in the strike, tried to appeal for recognition by the owners as a moderate alternative to the IWW. The president of Washington's AFL served on an investigating committee, which warned against the subversive IWW. But, as Melvyn Dubofsky has shown, the employers had as little use for negotiating with the "patriotic" AFL as with the "pro-German" IWW.[112]

The War Department and the Labor Department made repeated pleas to the lumbermen to grant the eight-hour day and to recognize AFL unions in order to undercut the IWW. When the employers proved unreceptive and when imprisonment of IWW leaders failed to restore production, the military entered the lumber labor picture with the dispatch of Lt. Col. Brice Disque to survey labor conditions in the Northwest. Gompers supported Disque's anti-IWW mission, hoping that the army would aid AFL organizers. Disque persuaded the timber owners to accept the eight-hour day in February 1918, but also broke both the IWW and AFL unions and set up a company union, the Loyal Legion of Loggers and Lumbermen, in their stead.[113]

Already in Pacific Northwest events, the policy of AFL-government cooperation had begun to unravel. In the months to follow, eight-hour (or six-hour) strikes, intimately connected to issues regarding union recognition and control over work, erupted in mining, meatpacking, the needle trades, and steel. Government repression came increasingly to concentrate on AFL unions and charges of radicalism were especially leveled at industrial unionists inside the AFL. The AFL, which had grown from 1,946,347 members in 1915 to 2,726,478 members in 1918, was in a position to press for realization of the gains promised by wartime cooperation. Corporations, meanwhile, resolved to defend the open shop and their ability to set conditions of employment, especially hours. The mood of expectancy in industrial relations was summed up in a phrase by the young Jay Lovestone, then a leftist: "Wait Till the War Is Over."[114]

10

Trade Unionism, Hours, and Workers' Control in the Postwar United States

By 1919 the AFL had for more than three decades experienced contradictory pressures regarding how to organize, whom to organize, and what to demand. In the wake of Haymarket the precarious position of the AFL, the fear of the state, and the desire for immigration restriction combined with sexism, racism, and the privileged position of skilled workers (in terms of both wages and control over work) to make for conservatism, craft organization, and susceptibility to the blandishments of "liberal" employers' organizations and of nativist politicians. But the sharp limits of corporate liberalism, the substantial militancy of rank-and-file workers, the existence of common on-the-job experiences among skilled and unskilled workers, and, at times, the strength of American socialism, made the turn to craft conservatism partial and contradictory. In the decade before World War I, with the maturation of managerial attacks on the position of skilled workers and the growth of mass production, initiatives toward amalgamated, federated, and even industrial unionism abounded. As a result, some AFL unions increasingly opened their doors to immigrant, women, and unskilled workers in strikes and organizing campaigns that emphasized workers' control and unified workers around the eight-hour day. The war itself accelerated the growth of such "new unions" but also created new opportunities for the AFL leadership to accept junior partnership in a "voluntary state" alongside and beneath corporate and governmental officials and fostered new fears of rank-and-file initiatives. Thus the labor movement, as it entered the postwar world, was pulled both toward sharply confrontational militancy and toward a government-facilitated detente with management.[1] The sharp confrontations developed quickly in 1919 and featured an explosive combination of hours and control demands; the detente took shape over the next decade and more after the 1919 strikes and witnessed both the divorce of the demand for shorter hours of work from the demand for more control over work, and the greater reliance on the class-neutral arguments of reformers for reductions in the workweek. Arguments for shorter hours and more control increasingly became the province of the far left within the labor movement.

The 1919 strike wave, involving at least 4,160,000 workers and 22.5 percent of the labor force, marked a twentieth century crest of U.S. working-class activity. Recent studies have effectively emphasized that radical demands for more control over work joined wage demands in sparking that wave of strikes. But in the most important 1919 walkouts—those in coal, steel, textiles, and clothing—control demands took the particular form of a call for shortening the hours of labor. Although other issues, including union recognition, were involved, Selig Perlman and Philip Taft were right when they referred to the 1919 strikes as being illustrative of an ongoing theme in this study, as strikes in which "shorter hours demands made for greater fellow feeling between trades and industries." In the wake of the defeat of many of the 1919 strikes, AFL unions adopted a far more defensive posture regarding the working day. After having resolved to press for a day of less than eight hours and to agitate for a five-and-a-half-day working week in 1919, the national AFL downplayed the hours issue in subsequent years. Constituent unions, with the exception of the printers and the left-wing unions in the fur and clothing industries, generally concentrated on holding gains made before 1920. AFL inaction on the working day coincided with a period of labor defeats that saw a diminution in the size of the organized labor movement by over 1.6 million members during the 1920s, a retreat from previous experiments with organization along industrial or quasi-industrial lines, and an abandonment of the struggle against scientific management in favor of emphasis on labor-management cooperation to up production. In effect, the historic connection between shorter hours struggles and those over control of work was severed in the 1920s.[2]

The ascendancy of William Green to the AFL presidency in 1924 brought on no rush toward industrial organization nor one toward shorter days, despite Green's background as chairperson of the AFL Committee on a Shorter Workday and as an official of the UMW, an industrially organized AFL affiliate that fought for the six-hour day. Under Green the AFL did publicize a five-day-week plank in the late 1920s, but so weakly that constituent unions failed to notice the demand. Green placed any lessening of labor time in the context of enhanced productivity and labor-management cooperation. During the first five years of his administration, about half the number of workers struck as had in 1919 alone, and hours-workweek walkouts were most rare. As in the early 1920s, only a few members of unions managed to reduce the working week significantly.[3]

It is doubtless true, as Louis Adamic wrote at the decade's end, that the 1920s saw "the struggle of the have-nots against the haves [go] on unceasingly and relentlessly . . . underneath the surface" despite the repression of unions and left-wing parties. Workers might "strike on the job," as Adamic put it, to gain respites during the working day. Indeed Whiting Williams' participant observations on work in the 1920s probed the relationship between informal restriction of output and explicit trade union or political action to reduce hours. Williams identified "taking easy" and "shortening the working day" as alternative working-class strategies to prevent increases in productivity from taking away jobs. In the 1920s the former was more often practicable.[4]

But informal resistance was not accompanied by a sense that industry could be transformed to provide enough free time for a flowering of workers' culture, intellect, or political power. With restrictions on immigration, with the institution of Prohibition, and with the burgeoning growth of advertising and of mass media, community-based popular culture came under attack. Left-wing cultural activities suffered from repression against foreign-language groups, the IWW, the Socialist party, and the Communist party. Given all these constraints, it is small wonder that when Helen and Robert S. Lynd studied workers in the industrial city of Muncie, Indiana, in the mid-1920s, their respondents often said they could not imagine what they would do with more leisure.[5]

Contrasting with the disorientation of the working-class movement for shorter working hours was the activity of reformers. Two distinct reform trends combined efforts, especially in the attack that culminated in success in 1923, on the twelve-hour day and the seven-day week in the steel industry. Religious reformers, energized by the report of the Interchurch World Movement on the 1919 steel strike, pressed the case against long hours and Sunday labor largely on the grounds of faith and humanitarianism. A second and ideologically dominant reform trend enlisted the efforts of engineers, efficiency experts, and management consultants interested in the demonstrable effects of leisure on productivity and, to a lesser extent, in shoring up American capitalism generally. Herbert Hoover, the Quaker engineer who served as an activist secretary of commerce during the campaign against long hours in steel, united both tendencies.

This strong reform impulse, coinciding as it did with prosperity and with the much-heralded "welfare capitalist" initiatives by employers during the 1920s, might have been expected to yield large voluntary reductions of hours. With productivity in the manufacturing sector jumping by as much as 72 percent between 1919 and 1929, there was ample room for beneficence. Indeed, the shift from a twelve-hour day in steel, achieved with little union pressure, and the voluntary granting of the five-day week by Henry Ford in 1926 secured reduced hours for more workers than any strike of the 1920s. Nonetheless, as a whole, these years of optimal conditions for voluntary reform by employers produced only meager reductions in the working week. According to the figures of the economist John D. Owens, the workweek in nonagricultural industries fell by 7.0 hours between 1906 and 1919 and by just 1.3 hours in the decade thereafter.[6]

In many ways the immediate post-World War I period resembled that following the Civil War where labor and the working day were concerned. Though democratic rhetoric and the feeling of sacrifice on labor's part were more tempered following the latter war than after the more heroic former one, the AFL nonetheless affirmed that workers had done their "utmost to win the war for democracy" and therefore deserved a shorter working day.[7] The analogy with the post-Civil War period extends to the presence after World War I, of a host of leftover grievances, particularly over hours, which accumulated through the war.

The New York harbor witnessed one of the first and most serious strikes resulting from such complaints at a time when the war was scarcely over. Harbor workers, represented by a collection of divided unions, had begun to cooperate in 1913 and by 1917 had united in the Marine Workers' Affiliation of the Port of New York (MWA). Employers refused to bargain with the MWA early in the war. In October 1917 a board of arbitrators patched together a wage settlement without ruling on the issues of union security or affiliated bargaining. By January 1918 unions had filed complaints against 200 harbor employers for failure to comply with the award. The following March's government investigation of eighty such complaints showed three in four to be justified. Railroad workers and ship carpenters in the harbor found further unity around a demand for the eight-hour day, a standard that had already been provided by the Railroad Administration to most other railwaymen nationally.[8]

As the war ended, the MWA took up the eight-hour call and a brief strike in late December 1918 brought President Wilson's intervention. Even so, only one private boat owner agreed to enter arbitration on the hours issue. The Labor Board's March 1919 settlement on the issue had but limited application. Moreover, it favored the employers on wage issues and by allowing the eight-hour day to only a handful of harbor crafts representing few workers. A second strike followed, with the result that the Railroad Administration and other agencies acceded to the shorter day while private owners not involved in government-contracted work kept the ten-hour standard. In April 1920 those who had won eight hours were forced into yet another strike, involving 15,000 marine workers, to defend their gain.[9]

The post-World War I period also held one final parallel with the post-Civil War years. In 1865 most craft workers had achieved the ten-hour day and the thrust of postbellum agitation was for a new and visionary eight-hour demand. In 1919 nearly half (48.6 percent) of all U.S. agricultural workers had attained the forty-eight-hour week, and a clear majority of organized labor had done so. Gompers had briefly called for a seven-hour day during the war. In weak industries such as mining, fear of massive unemployment upon demobilization gave force to arguments for new goals regarding the working day, including cuts to well below eight hours per day.[10]

Any study of hours in 1919 must therefore proceed from an acknowledgment of the possibilities and achievements of that year: an unprecedented strike wave, adoption of a variety of hours legislation by twenty-eight states, and passage of yet another ill-fated federal law attempting to find a constitutional way to limit the working day of child laborers.[11] The hours of labor were decidedly a public issue. Farmers in the Non-Partisan League joined labor groups in the Great Plains in calling for forty-four-hour-workweek laws at the state level. The Illinois Independent Labor party, supported by the Chicago Federation of Labor, campaigned for an eight-hour law and a forty-four-hour week. Some women's groups called for a four-hour day; the IWW made the six-hour (or less) day one of its prime demands and helped to raise the six-hour issue in the 1919 Butte general strike and elsewhere.[12] Industrial planners mulled over six-hour plans, especially in depressed industries.[13]

The AFL itself showed signs of moving toward a demand for a sharp reduction in the working day. In 1918 state AFL resolutions in Ohio and California called for days of less than eight hours. At its 1919 convention the AFL resolved that the "right of Labor to fix its hours of work must not be abrogated, abridged or interfered with." The convention backed six-hour demands by individual unions, especially the UMW, and caused the New York *Times* to headline: "LABOR WILL WORK FOR SIX-HOUR DAY." Only in 1921, when a general resolution favoring a "six-hour day with an eight-hour pay" came before its convention, did the AFL reject a general call for six hours. It was rejected as merely ill timed.[14]

The 1919 shorter-hours strikes attempted both to generalize the eight-hour day and to transcend it. The strikes fall into three categories. In the coalfields, well organized at the time but plagued by unemployment, the UMW became the first major American union to fight for the six-hour day. The unions in the clothing trades and in printing sought the forty-four-hour week. Strikes in the largely unorganized steel and textile industries attempted to enlist workers with very long hours around the demand for a working week of six, eight-hour days coupled with union recognition. The largest of these strikes were important because, in their goals and vision, they summed up so much of the possiblity to be gained by organizing around shorter hours and the "new unionism" and because, in their results, they previewed defeats and retreats to come.

The long and huge bituminous miners' strike of 1919, which brought John L. Lewis to national prominence, involved 400,000 miners who sought a six-hour day and a 60 percent pay increase to compensate for wartime erosion in purchasing power and to make possible the maintenance of piece-rate income as hours went down from forty-eight to thirty weekly. The strike illustrated the intimate connection of hours and control as well as the problems associated with labor's reliance on the "voluntary state." Coalmining, probably more than any other U.S. industry, was plagued by overproduction, mismanagement, and seasonal unemployment, and the thirty-hour plan was a union response to the chaos. In 1918, despite war orders, an average of 63 of 308 possible working days were lost in the mines; in 1919 this figure rose to 115, with no more than 29 of those attributable to strikes. As Carter Goodrich's 1925 study of miners observed, "The famous demand for the thirty-hour week was in large part based on the feeling that an industry that on the average provided little more than thirty hours work a week ought to share that work equally among those engaged in it." Mechanization did not necessarily increase efficiency, in part because loaders often waited hours for cars to arrive. Disorganization of loading especially followed double shifts, and UMW opposition to that practice was in essence an efficiency demand. In sum, the thirty-hour week without double shifts constituted a proposal to spread work and rationalize the industry.[15]

The issue of government intervention found its way into the miners' strike because mine operators insisted, nearly a year after the armistice, that wartime negotiation procedures still held. The mine owners, backed by the hysterical anticommunist "Red Scare" propaganda so much a part of 1919, maintained at one point that the miners acted on orders from the Soviet Union and, before the strike even began, secured an injunction against it and a statement from President Wilson branding the miners' plans to strike as "not only unjustifiable but unlawful."[16] The strike itself featured what one historian has called "the most sweeping injunction issued against a major union since the Pullman Boycott of 1894" as well as use of wiretaps on Lewis's phones and massive threatened deployment of federal troops.[17] Complicating strike strategy was the greater willingness of Gompers than of Lewis to cooperate with federal officials policing the strike. Lewis, then acting president of the UMW, repeatedly defied injunctions but also dropped the thirty-hour week demand during negotiations and, after five weeks of striking, decided on December 6 to "submit to the inevitable" in the face of government pressure and to accept arbitration. The final settlement won 20 to 34 percent pay increases but left the working week unchanged.[18]

After 1919 the six-hour day became an issue identified mainly with the large, anti-Lewis left-wing in the coal unions. In 1922 the full UMW convention did resolve for a six-hour day rather than the eight-hour demand proposed by the resolutions committee. A call for six hours was briefly made--and bitterly attacked by employers and legislators in congressional hearings—before being dropped in the huge 1922 strike involving over 600,000 miners. In some mines even the eight-hour day was then lost.[19] John Brophy's platform in the 1926 UMW presidential election, a vote often said to have been stolen by Lewis, raised a demand for a thirty-hour week in the same plank as nationalization.[20] Workers' (later Communist) party agitation in conjunction with Kansas miners' leader Alexander Howat and the Trade Union Educational League (TUEL), consistently stressed the six-hour (or four-hour) day during the early 1920s. In 1928 the thirty-hour week was again coupled with nationalization in the program of the "Save the Miners' Union" conferences undertaken by left-wing UMW supporters.[21]

In the largest six-hour strike of the late 1920s, the IWW led a four-month walkout in the three major Colorado coalfields. After a wildcat strike in Colorado mines in early August 1927 to protest the execution of Nicola Sacco and Bartolomeo Vanzetti, IWW organizer A. S. Embree and miner-delegates drew up a list of economic demands including a "six-hour day from bank-to-bank" and mounted an October strike. Repression by the Colorado Rangers and attacks on the strike by the Colorado State Industrial Commission marked the conflict. Planes attempted to break up the strike meetings, and the Rangers massacred strike supporters at Columbine, killing six, and at Walsenburg, where two died. The miners won raises but not the six-hour system.[22]

The shorter-workweek campaigns of the Amalgamated Clothing Workers, the International Ladies' Garment Workers, International Printing Pressmen and Assistants Union, and the International Typographical Union culminated, just after the war, in a series of strikes for the forty-four-hour week and, especially in the printing trades, for control issues. Because the strikes in these trades sought mainly a Saturday half-holiday and, later in the 1920s, Saturdays off in a forty-hour week, they are treated more fully separately in dicussion of the rise of the five-day working week.[23]

In many industries the eight-hour day was still a dream in 1919. On the street railways, among operating engineers, in the oil fields, in canneries, in textile mills and, most dramatically, in steel mills, days of ten, twelve, or more hours continued. In steel, canning, oil, municipal transportation, and domestic service, the seven-day week also persisted for hundreds of thousands of workers.[24] As Grace Hutchins wrote, "The very workers most in need of a strong union to demand shorter hours are often too exhausted at night to attend . . . meetings."[25] In 1919 workers in long-hour industries tried to remedy this situation in a series of actions centering on the working day and union recognition. These actions were so particularly concentrated among public workers and those in mass transit as to give the hours issue special prominence.

In Chicago 15,000 public transportation workers struck in late July causing what *Survey* magazine called a "complete tie-up" of elevated and surface trains there. The strikers defied the president of their international who was "howled down" by a crowd of 4,000 at a ratification meeting. The leadership then asked for a referendum on ending the strike and carried the back-to-work motion by only 386 votes among more than 12,000 cast. The surface-train employees especially opposed the settlement. Under the settlement just 60 percent of them received the eight-hour day, and working time was spread over as much as fourteen hours. Elevated train workers, whose votes gave the pact its margin of victory, did slightly better with 70 percent gaining an eight-hour day.[26] Many other public workers likewise protested against long working hours in 1919. New York City firefighters supported a Socialist-sponsored municipal resolution calling for the introduction of the "three-platoon" (eight-hour) system in the firehouses. Cleveland witnessed a firefighters' strike over the same issue. The most famous public employee strike of the year, the September walkout of Boston police, resulted from the refusal of the city government to allow the police to affiliate with the AFL and from the firings of nineteen union leaders. However, long hours figured prominently in prestrike union organizing.[27]

Other struggles similarly used shorter hours as a rallying cry. In the Pacific Northwest, lumbermen in the AFL's International Union of Timberworkers (IUT) undertook an eight-hour organizing drive concentrating on those camps in which the government-sponsored Loyal Legion of Loggers and Lumbermen had allowed the restoration of longer shifts. The IUT also attempted to extend the eight-hour system to forests throughout the nation. Orange pickers in parts of California unionized around demands for an eight-hour day at half a dollar per hour. In Kansas City Afro-American domestic workers, organized by the WTUL in 1918 and 1919, won the eight-hour day and a 67 percent raise.[28]

The most significant instances of organizing around the eight-hour day lay in the textile and steel industries. Organizational banners mattered in the fierce textile strikes of this period but so too did rank-and-file initiative and, in virtually all the shorter-hours strikes in the industry, the tendency of that demand to unite a particularly diverse working population and to raise issues of control over work applied strongly. The particularly fierce repression which had historically greeted shorter-hours struggles was also present in these textile struggles, regardless of the leadership. Competing unions attempted to capitalize on the popularity of the shorter-hours demand. With as much as half of its membership in the South following the war, the AFL-affiliated United Textile Workers (UTW) searched for a way to revitalize New England organizing. That search took on special intensity because the UTW leadership favored craft organization, but the union's southern wing was largely organized on an industrial basis. At its November 1918 convention the UTW planned a northern membership drive keyed to the achievement of the eight-hour day by February 3, 1919.[29]

At first the eight-hour drive in northern mills was very successful. In late January New York *Times* reports indicated participation by 120,000 New England workers. Conservative UTW President John Golden found many employers ready to grant forty-eight hours; he signed pacts with the management of large cotton mills in Manchester and Pawtucket, and with some silk producers in Paterson. The huge American Woolen Company in Lawrence also was ready to sign but opposition to the settlement suddenly developed among workers.[30]

Popularity of the UTW's forty-eight-hour contracts eroded as low-wage workers in textiles realized that the six-hour reduction in hours also entailed over an 11 percent pay cut, since piece rates and hourly wages were left untouched. In Paterson, where women members of UTW Local 480 struck for maintenance of wages with reduced hours, Golden responded by expelling hundreds of unionists and exposing them to blacklisting. In Lawrence 20,000 struck against UTW wishes on February 3, chanting "Fifty-four hours' pay for forty-eight hours' work," and 25,000 workers joined the walkout. Over half were women, many of them Italian or Polish immigrants, with Lawrence's thirty-one other nationalities also represented.[31]

During the Lawrence struggle a new textile union matured. Conceived by the Rev. A. J. Muste, the Amalgamated Textile Workers (ATW) patterned itself after the Amalgamated Clothing Workers and embraced socialist industrial unionism. The ATW rekindled the embers left in Lawrence, Paterson, and elsewhere by earlier IWW strikes. Affiliation with the AFL was precluded because of the opposition of the UTW. But the textile union could take heart from the advice of Joseph Schlossberg, the ACW's general secretary, who counseled, "With us the membership rules . . . . That is why we win. And that is why you will win."[32]

In Lawrence ATW tactics harkened back to the Wobbly strike of 1912 and included round-the-clock picketing and separate strike meetings for the major national groups involved. Women clashed with the police who, just four days after the strike's start, killed a Polish worker. When the strikers voted to turn down a compromise of forty-eight hours' work for fifty-one hours' pay, city officials intensified repression. Backed by police from nearby towns, the local force especially limited picketing by females. A women's delegation tried vainly to visit Massachusetts Governor Calvin Coolidge to protest suspension of civil liberties.[33]

By March 7 Lawrence Commissioner of Police Peter Carr denied the strikers' rights to assemble in either public or private places. Carr, by his own account, felt he had to suppress "Bolshevist propaganda" in a city in which "most . . . are foreign." When Muste and the ATW responded with large picket lines, a week and a half of conflict and arrests ensued. On March 18 pickets returned gunfire initiated by police and thereafter the strikers became subject to increasingly frequent clubbings by Carr's men.[34] With misery growing among mill families, with the UTW encouraging strikebreaking, and with part of its leadership driven from town at gunpoint, the Lawrence ATW ended its fifteen-week strike on May 21. Shortly thereafter, while setting up company unions, mill owners granted the forty-eight-hour week with no wage reduction. It was a voluntary concession fairly bathed in blood.[35]

The Lawrence strike publicized the ATW as an alternative to the "eight-hour day, with less pay" strategy of the UTW. In Paterson hatband weavers, ribbon weavers, and broad silk workers broke with the latter union over its cautious bargaining in a February 3, 1919, strike of as many as 27,000 workers who sought the forty-four-hour week in mills where the eight-hour day was not obtained. The UTW, negotiating with the War Labor Board, agreed to a schedule of five, eight-and-a-half-hour days with the prospect of adding a five-and-a-half-hour Saturday shift. In July the hatband weavers struck without UTW authorization to win the forty-four-hour standard. After hundreds were expelled by the UTW and after the local ribbon weavers lost their AFL charter, the Associated Silk Weavers formed to unite the two specialized trades.[36]

ATW agitation in Paterson started slowly. Before July 10 the union's organizers could find no public hall in which to meet. On July 10 the ATW managed to hold a meeting at the Sons of Italy hall. Two of its conveners suffered arrest after speeches that again stressed the working day. The charges against the two expressed the vagaries of Red-Scared American justice: "attempt by speech or writing, printing or in any other way whatsoever, to incite or abet, promote or encourage hostility or opposition to the government of the United States or of the state of New Jersey."[37]

After this unpromising start, the ATW rapidly organized silk workers in Paterson and led a large strike for the forty-four-hour week among the broad silk operatives. By August the forty-four-hour standard was established in the Paterson silk industry, though employers rescinded it over the next decade. In July 1919 the UTW had claimed 8,500 members in Paterson. In 1920 its local there disbanded.[38] The ATW grew, drawing on Wobbly traditions and on the desire for shorter hours not just in Lawrence and Paterson, but also in Passaic, where it led a successful hours strike of 10,000. By its 1920 convention the ATW had 40,000 to 50,000 members and took credit for igniting a campaign that brought the forty-eight-hour week, and even some shorter schedules, to 250,000 workers. However, the union faded with the economic downturn of the early 1920s in New England textiles.[39]

While the UTW's 48-hour campaign boomeranged in the North and ended up generating support for the ATW, the former union did get unexpected results in the South where "not much success" had been anticipated. On the appointed February 3 date for transition to eight hours in New England factories, many spontaneous strikes erupted in southern cotton mills. With support from local craft unions, over 10,000 millhands in the South left their jobs. Barely a third of the strikers in Columbus, Georgia received UTW strike benefits, but the conflict there lasted for more than two months before workers went back under the old schedules of more than ten hours daily. Shortly after their return, management granted a fifty-five-hour week, as had several other Georgia mills and the major South Carolina factories.[40]

An eight-hour strike in Macon, Georgia, in August 1919 involved 2,000 operatives from five mills and resulted in the deaths of two black strikebreakers during an attack by white picketers. The incident signaled the defeat of the strike and exposed the Achilles heel of UTW organizing in the South: the failure to enlist black workers. In North Carolina two 1919 summertime settlements in Charlotte and others in Concord and Kannapolis won the fifty-five-hour week at sixty hours' pay for over 5,000 millhands. The UTW claimed 40,000 members in North Carolina by the fall. However, little of this organization survived the depression of 1921-1922. In 1926 the average southern millhand worked fifty-five hours or more weekly in an almost unorganized industry.[41]

After 1920 both the UTW and ATW had to assume defensive postures. However, both of these organizations, along with the ephemeral, syndicalist One Big Union, did contribute to the defeat of a series of 1922 efforts by New England employers to cut wages by as much as 20 percent and to extend the working day.[42] As many as 125,000 New Englanders joined the defensive strikes of 1922, but the tide of unionism continued to ebb. The ATW disbanded shortly thereafter and UTW was virtually moribund from 1922 until 1933.[43]

The Associated Silk Workers Union was the only labor organization left in Paterson in 1924 to lead a strike for reinstitution of the eight-hour day, a wage boost, and limits on the number of looms tended by each worker. Though gaining concessions on pay, it failed to regain the eight-hour system. In 1928 the union tried again, leading 30,000 striking silk workers in Paterson in a three-month walkout for eight hours. Again defeated, the Associated Silk Workers acknowledged the difficulty of formal textile union activity in the 1920s with the pledge to continue the "struggle . . . for the eight-hour day," through "unceasing guerrilla warfare with individual bosses."[44]

With textile union membership falling during the decade by more than 75 percent from its 1920 peak, shorter-hours agitation came to be carried on in the mills largely by explicitly left-wing groups. After having been active in the Paterson strike of 1924, Workers' (Communist) party members assumed leadership, between 1926 and 1929, in a series of large and symbolic textile strikes at Passaic, New Bedford, and Gastonia.[45] In each case the hours of labor were at issue. The National Textile Workers Union (NTWU), formed with Communist leadership in 1928 during the New Bedford strike, consistently emphasized the forty-hour week. The Communist press praised the Soviet Union's announcements of the implementation of the eight-hour day and its 1927 experimentation with seven-hour shifts.[46] At the same time the Communists rejected the Taylorist strategy with which Soviet planners sought to increase productivity while cutting hours. At least for the United States, the Workers' party continued to combine demands for shorter hours with an assault on scientific management in an attempt, as James Green puts it, "to revive the 'new unionism'."[47]

Since the story of the Communist-led textile strikes of the 1920s has been told in such detail elsewhere, it is perhaps well to concentrate here on how hours and control issues combined in the most important such strike (and, perhaps, the one most expressive of Communist attempts to revive and extend "new unionism") that at Gastonia, North Carolina, in 1929. Gastonia must be placed, however, in the context of a developing campaign of hours/control strikes led by Communists at Passaic in 1926, in which 15,000 wool and silk workers walked out and at New Bedford in 1928, where nearly 30,000 largely unskilled cotton-mill workers struck. Though the long New Bedford strike failed, it saw the Communist-led NTWU enroll 6,000 new members.[48] Some of those active in New Bedford would find their way to Gastonia, where the new textile union would try to carry its pledge to enforce a five-day, forty-hour week into the South. Largely as a result of the spectacular strike at Gastonia, NTWU strategy would confront that of the AFL in the unorganized mills of Dixie. And *Labor* would prophesy, "Southern workers will be organized. If this is not done by responsible craft unions, it will be done by the Communists."[49]

The 1929 Gastonia walkout represents the fullest application of the strategy of promoting class solidarity and industrial unionism through agitation against long hours, Taylorism, and low wages.[50] The origins of the Gastonia conflict were simple. The Loray Mill, under the absentee ownership of the Manville-Jenkes Corporation of Rhode Island, instituted a set of stringent management practices in 1927. Loray workers dramatized this "stretch-out" system with a street theatrical featuring the parading of a coffin down Gastonia's main street. At intervals, an effigy of the manager popped up to lay off pairs of workers, leaving the burden to those who remained to carry the casket. "The comedy," as historian George Tindall has remarked, "masked a growing tension."[51]

In March 1928 fifty Loray workers struck unsuccessfully to protest the stretch-out and wage cuts. As the year ended, pressured by the local clergy, Manville-Jenkes replaced the superintendent in charge of the speedups. The move produced little in the way of reform at an enterprise that had already laid off more than a third of its 3,500 workers while maintaining production levels. Since it took the wages of about three persons for an average family to live, such layoffs meant not just much harder labor for those employed, but also increasing debts to the company store. Speedups raised the issue of time sharply. As one worker explained, "It used to be you could git five, ten minutes rest now and then. But now they keep a-runnin' all the time."[52]

Into this cauldron came NTWU and Communist organizer Fred Beal in January 1929. Beal, an ex-Wobbly, had helped to lead the New Bedford strike. During the weeks after his arrival in Gastonia, Beal organized a secret union local of about sixty members. When, on March 25, five of the unionists were fired after being betrayed by a company spy, Beal convened a public meeting of protest. At that meeting about 1,000 workers voted to hold a second gathering to discuss recommendations for an immediate strike. The mill management responded with a new round of firings, which helped to solidify a strike by about 90 percent of the 2,200 Loray employees.[53] In part because a working wife was often a condition of male employment at Loray, most of the strikers were women.[54]

On April 3, with the strike two days old, the unionists drew up a list of demands that reflected both the general aspirations of the workers and the special ones of the women. These included a forty-hour, five-day week (down from sixty hours weekly), ending the stretch-out, abolition of piecework, equal pay for equal work for women and children, a $20 weekly minimum wage, a 50 percent reduction in rent and light charges, sanitary improvements, and union recognition.[55]

Mass pickets and parades characterized the early strike. Injunctions kept strike activity away from the mills, but despite the presence of a howitzer company of the National Guard, protests continued. As the labor writer Tom Tippett observed, "Parades were broken up by force every day and just as consistently the strikers would form again the following day to march . . . into clubs and rifles." On April 15, with relief slow in arriving and the AFL opposing the strike, the mills partially reopened. Two days later, a relief depot opened. Strike leaders appeared unfazed by episodic returns to work, with Beal later writing:

> The scab of today was the striker of tomorrow. This, and the fact that most of the strikers were related to each other, established a unique attitude on the part of the strikers to the scabs . . . . In Gastonia the scab was

considered merely as a potential striker. I began to organize the scabs to have periodic walkouts to support the regular strike.[56]

Local commercial leaders, politicians, newspaper owners, and American Legionnaires joined in escalating attacks on the strikers. A mob of hundreds of masked, armed men descended on the relief depot and union headquarters by night on April 18. They destroyed relief supplies and union offices. Local authorities arrested ten strike supporters, victims in the incident. In May the company then undertook to break the strike by evicting participants from company housing.[57]

Although the National Guard was removed after protests, a committee of 100 ensured, as one historian has put it, "the continuance of the reign of terror on the strikers."[58] Company supporters played on the fear that blacks might enter the textile labor force in numbers for the first time as strikebreakers. Many Communist organizers and local militants, such as the twenty-nine-year-old mill worker and balladeer Ella Mae Wiggins, took Albert Weisbord's advice and countenanced "absolutely no compromise" on the "Negro question" as they organized among blacks. Their efforts met with but mixed success, and some organizers did bow to local prejudices, but the attempt to apply egalitarian policies further enraged local officials and vigilantes.[59] On June 7 a carload of police moved against the tent colony of evicted strikers. In the ensuing gun battles, Chief of Police O. F. Aderholt was fatally wounded. Seventy-five of the tent colonists suffered arrest, and grand jurors later indicted sixteen for murder and seven for assault.[60]

Throughout the summer the NTWU was more occupied with conducting a defense campaign than a strike. Eventually, charges against nine of the murder defendants were dropped. The trial saw the prosecution stress Communism, atheism, and race-mixing, while the defense emphasized the drunkenness of Aderholt and his aides and their lack of legal business at the tent colony. A mistrial eventuated on September 7 when a prosecution dramatization featuring a bloodspattered effigy of Aderholt caused an attack of insanity in a juror.[61]

Further mob violence greeted the news of the mistrial. A horde of 500 vigilantes again raided the union headquarters, kidnapping and beating strike leaders. A union rally to protest the repression met with more tragic violence on September 14. As they headed for the demonstration, a truckload of unionists encountered ten automobiles of vigilantes who blocked the road and fired into the group of strikers in broad daylight with fifty witnesses. Ella Mae Wiggins died as a result of the blasts. Those charged with her murder all won acquittals while jail sentences resulted for all seven defendants in the Aderholt case. The strike dwindled gaining none of its original demands, though it did help to bring about the adoption of a fifty-hour week at Loray and other area mills.[62]

During and after the Gastonia strike and since, a variety of journalists and historians have asked whether the local authorities and state officials opposed revolution or trade unionism. Few have differed much in their conclusions from those of *Nation* correspondent Paul Blanshard who doubted that a conservative AFL union would have been any better received during the strike in Gastonia.[63] The brutality occasioned by a large wage strike in Elizabethton, Tennessee, just before Gastonia and by a conflict over wages and hours in Marion, North Carolina, just after Gastonia support Blanshard's interpretation. UTW leadership in these instances, as Herbert Lahne observes, was "accorded no more peaceful welcome than . . . the Communist NTWU."[64]

While the coal strike was larger and more extreme in its shorter-hours demands, and the textile strikes of 1919 and the 1920s were more protracted, the 1919 steel strike was the pivotal hours conflict of the postwar period. Involving hundreds of thousands of workers in a key industry, uniting the skilled and unskilled, focusing on the eight-hour demand as a key to organizing the unorganized, and raising the issues of control over work, the steel strike summed up many of the trends of the previous decade, indeed of the previous century. It also represented a climax of repression of the labor movement and the failed leadership of the AFL. Participants on both sides recognized the steel strike as a watershed in the organization of mass production industries. Its defeat helped to signal the decline of aggressive union organizing and to set the stage for a new series of efforts to reduce the working day in steel—efforts to be more often spearheaded by reformers than by trade unionists. As befits such an epochal conflict, the 1919 steel strike is perhaps the best-studied industrial dispute in U.S. history.[65]

The shorter-hours campaign began in steel while World War I still raged. Fresh from organizing victories in the stockyards, William Z. Foster and the Chicago Federation of Labor head John Fitzpatrick turned to the almost unorganized steel industry. Foster's proposal for a national steel organizing drive won assent from the CFL and at least lukewarm support from the Amalgamated Association of Iron, Steel and Tin Workers. At the June 1918 AFL convention the CFL pressed for a conference on steel organizing and succeeded in holding three large meetings on the subject. A heady sense of possibility prevailed. Foster saw a victory in steel sparking speedy organization of 5 or 10 million workers. John Fitch asked, "If an industry so completely nonunion may become organized under the new conception of human rights as formulated at Washington, what may not be possible?"[66]

From the start the working day was a main issue in steel, with "Eight hours and the union," serving as the central organizing slogan. The demand carried special weight in an industry in which long hours of labor continued for most workers. Even according to the estimates provided by U.S. Steel head Elbert Gary, nearly one production worker in three labored twelve hours daily at that corporation in 1919. The Interchurch World Movement (IWM) *Report* suggested that a more accurate figure was over 50 percent for the whole industry.[67] The corporations, led by Gary, defended such schedules by backpedaling from one position to another. They held—despite firm evidence to the contrary—that the situation was improving, that immigrant workers wanted twelve-hour days, that economic and metallurgical necessities made reform impossible, that mechanization made twelve-hour shifts bearable.[68]

Despite high hopes and desperate grievances, the steel campaign began inauspiciously. Kicking off the organizing with a conference in Chicago on August 1 and 2, 1918, fifteen unions with jurisdiction in steel did agree, without debate, to a federated effort. But craft jealousy and disunity remained problems. Gompers presided over the Chicago conference, and nominally, over its creation, the National Committee for Organizing Iron and Steel Workers. However, busy with war and reconstruction tasks, he showed little inclination to aid in organizing work and raising funds. Fitzpatrick, as temporary chairman, and Foster, as secretary-treasurer, led the campaign. The Chicago conference rejected the specifics of Foster's plan for a six-week wartime organizing blitz in steel and funded the movement with $2,400 rather than the $500,000 he requested.[69]

The greatest obstacle to organizing was the denial of free speech to unionists by local governments. Municipal officials, particularly in western Pennsylvania, refused permits for the National Committee to hold meetings. At Duquesne the mayor, brother of a tin company president, proclaimed that "Jesus Christ himself could not speak . . . for the AFL."[70] The situation was similar in Monessen, Donora, Homestead, Clairton, Braddock, and elsewhere.[71]

Nevertheless, the organizing drive gathered force. Its leaders executed, as Philip Taft has written, "one of the great organizing feats in American labor history."[72] Beginning in the Chicago-Gary area, the National Committee built outward to Ohio, Colorado, and West Virginia. By early 1919 agitation started in the Pittsburgh region, where opposition was fierce. The unions used wartime protections of the right to organize ably, and the National Committee applied the rhetoric surrounding the war effort to labor at home.[73] And the union's case was presented in the immigrants' languages through foreign-language bulletins and the words of over two dozen multilingual organizers.[74]

The skills of the steel organizers shone most clearly in the campaign for free speech in Pennsylvania.[75] Foster and others defied bans on free speech in illegal street meetings. A "flying squadron" of organizers faced down death threats and endured arrest to restore civil liberties in city after city. On August 20, 1919, Mother Jones, nearing her ninetieth birthday, asked in a speech in Homestead whether the town "belongs to Kaiser Gary or Uncle Sam." She was arrested and then briefly released from jail to dissuade an angry crowd bent on freeing her. Another woman supporter, Fannie Sellins, was murdered in West Natoma.[76]

The National Committee enrolled 100,000 unionists by June 1919. Workers rejected Gary's concession of overtime after eight hours. One Italian helper put it succinctly when, after completing a twenty-four-hour double shift and being told that steel workers make "pretty good money," he replied, "To hell with money! No can live!" Mother Jones spoke for many immigrant workers whose wages did not reach the poverty line despite long shifts: "If Gary wants to work twelve hours a day let him go in the blooming mill and work. What we want is a little leisure, time for music, playgrounds, a decent home, books and the things that make life worthwhile."[77]

Skilled American-born workers joined the unions in a second wave after the immigrants. The skilled men worked fewer hours than the unskilled, but few totaled less than sixty hours weekly. Grievances over speedups and promotion policies energized the skilled and semiskilled operatives. The less skilled proved most loyal to the strike, but all groups shared what David Brody has called the "terrible sense of betrayal" brought about by peace without reform. Layoffs in early 1919 gave added force to shorter-hours, share-the-work arguments.[78]

Repression, in the form of firings of union leaders and refusal to bargain, heightened resistance. Corporate use of power and influence over local officials and clergymen provoked free-speech fights and split immigrant workers from pro-company community leaders. As David Saposs wrote regarding immigrants and the 1919 events in the steel industry, "For almost the first time the immigrant workers dared to defy the dominant element, the old leaders and newspapers, and followed the National Committee."[79]

Rank-and-file commitment to unionism and shorter hours grew so fast that it changed the plans of the union strategists. Local leaders began to preach the possibility of the six-hour day, though the National Committee had no such plans. On May 25, 1919, when 583 local union representatives met in Pittsburgh, they had to be reminded that only the international unions could call strikes. The delegates proposed an eight-hour day "or less."[80] On June 20 the National Committee wrote to Gary, spokesman for the steel industry, asking that he meet with a negotiations committee. No reply came and three weeks later Foster warned, "Some action must be taken . . . men are in a state of great unrest . . . great strikes are threatening." The National Committee, though reluctant to move until 60 percent of the industry was unionized, soon authorized a strike vote. It carried with 98 percent of whose polled voting to strike. Union recognition headed the list of demands, but below this were calls for an eight-hour day at an "American" wage, one day's rest in seven, and an end to twenty-four-hour shifts.[81] When the union negotiators visited Gary on August 26, he refused to meet, citing the industry's open shop policy.

Gompers, still nominal head of the National Committee, asked President Wilson to bring Gary to the bargaining table. The AFL president reported that Wilson thought Gary's intransigence misplaced, but Wilson made no public move. Wilson's emissary, Bernard Baruch, also failed to persuade Gary to bargain. The president ultimately followed Baruch's advice not to jeopardize ratification of the League of Nations treaty by pushing Gary further.[82] Wilson did pressure the unions. On September 10 labor officials learned that he had requested that Gompers postpone the steel strike, set for September 22, until after the White House Industrial Conference, which was to convene on October 6. The heads of seven participating unions stated their intention to defer striking, but Fitzpatrick, Foster, and most of local unionists involved saw delay as certain to lead to demoralization and to weak wildcat strikes. They stuck to the order: "STOP WORK SEPTEMBER 22."[83]

Few union leaders and fewer executives envisioned a large strike. Foster was almost alone in appreciating that gang labor and group loyalty among immigrants could generate a mass strike with only a minority of the workers enrolled in unions. On September 22 as many as 275,000 struck. The strike peaked early the next week with about 365,000 strikers. Plants in Chicago, Wheeling, Johnstown, Lackawanna, Cleveland, Youngstown, and Pueblo, Colorado, shut down. In the Pittsburgh area the walkout was totally effective in Monessen and Donora, somewhat less so in Homestead, Braddock, and Bethlehem. It largely failed in Duquesne and in some Pittsburgh mills. Pig iron production dropped to less than 54 percent of normal output by October 1.[84]

The steel corporations mounted a fierce counterattack. As Brody has observed, "The hard-won fruits of the free speech fight were immediately cancelled." After brief rioting in Gary, precipitated by the importation of strikebreakers in early October, repression grew. In a few cities labor did command sufficient political power to have its own men deputized to keep order, but in the key Pennsylvania centers, the strikers faced hostile local and state police and company guards. The last group killed a child, a young mother, and several men at New Castle on the first day of the strike. As many as twenty-two steelworkers and their supporters were killed during the conflict. Labor spies dogged union activities and attempted to sow ethnic and racial discord.[85]

The corporations suffered a disadvantage. As long as the twelve-hour day and Gary's refusal to bargain constituted the main strike issues, public opinion would not support the steel trust. The solution was to use anti-immigrant and antiradical propaganda to change the meaning of the strike. The sermon of a Catholic priest in Braddock, for example, became a widely broadcast antistrike pamphlet, commended by Pennsylvania's governor. Part of it read: "This strike is not being brought about by intelligent or English-speaking workmen but by men who have not interest in the community, are not an element of our community . . . . But you can't reason with these people. Don't reason with them . . . knock them down."[86]

The rhymes of popular, sentimental poet Edgar Guest drove the nativist, antiradical themes home in a factory magazine:

Said Dan McGann to a foreign man who
worked at the selfsame bench,
"Let me tell you this," and for emphasis,
he flourished a monkey wrench,
"Don't talk to me of this bourjoissee, don't
open your mouth to speak

"Of your socialists or your anarchists,
don't mention the bolshevik,
"For I've had enough of this foreign stuff,
I'm sick as a man can be
"Of the speech of hate, and I'm telling
you straight, that this is the land for me.[87]

When a reporter for the employer publication *Iron Age* rediscovered Foster's 1911 pamphlet *Syndicalism*, coauthored with Earl Ford, charges of communist influence on the strike came to focus on Foster's leadership. Though Foster appeared before a Senate committee to testify that he rejected some of his former ideas on syndicalism and on direct action, the committee found that "behind this strike is massed a considerable element of IWW's, anarchists, revolutionists and Russian soviets." It recommended deportation of alien strikers. In the atmosphere of the Palmer raids and of the postwar drive for "Americanism" by veterans' groups, such redbaiting nurtured a growing back-to-work movement among American-born, mostly skilled, workers.[88]

Victimized by a press that consistently and prematurely proclaimed that work was returning to normal and unable to overcome the animus of as many as 30,000 black strikebreakers to unions that had practiced racial exclusion, the strike also suffered from poor cooperation by the AFL leadership. Gompers, who had opposed going ahead with the walkout, staked his hopes on pressuring Gary at the White House Industrial Conference which began on October 6. Baruch, eyeing a possible detente between Gary and Gompers, added the former as a "public" spokesman at the last moment. "Then for the love of Mike," asked the *UMWA Journal*, "who will represent the employers?"[89] Gary flatly refused arbitration, and Gompers could not force him into discussion of the issues. The full conference, called to discuss broader matters, did not press Gary on the steel situation. After two weeks Gompers walked out of the meetings in protest.[90]

The AFL contributed little to the support of the strike. The twenty-four participating unions pledged a strike fund of $100,000, but raised only $46,000. All other AFL unions added just $272,000, nearly a third of which came from the radical ILGWU and furriers. The ACW, outside the AFL, was more generous than any union in it, giving $100,000. Even if all funds had been distributed, only $1.15 would have gone to each striker during the course of the fifteen-week strike. Moreover, the AFL unions often subordinated strike support to their craft interests. While significant rank-and-file unity developed, organizational differences remained. Federation proved to be an indecisive step toward industrial unionism. The Amalgamated Association sent its members who were under contract back to work during the walkout. The Operating Engineers broke with the strike leadership over jurisdictional matters.[91]

By November 24, with the strike deteriorating, the National Committee saw arbitration as its last hope for partial success. Fitzpatrick sought intervention by the Interchurch World Movement. The IWM accepted his overture, though it insisted on acting not as an arbitrator, but as a mediator. Gary refused mediation, adding that there was "absolutely no issue" to discuss. When the strike officially ended, on January 8, 1920, production had already returned to normal in all major steel centers. The twelve-hour shift was intact. The capitulation of the National Committee managed some bravado, announcing a return to work "pending preparations for the next big organization movement." But despite a flurry of activity in 1923, no such campaign would materialize until the 1930s.[92]

After the defeat of the steel strike most trade union action concerning the working day was defensive until the limited five-day-week campaigns of the late 1920s. Exceptions included the International Association of Firefighters, which led fights to gain the eight-hour day, primarily through legislation, in New York, Montana, and elsewhere during 1926 and 1927. These efforts bore fruit in the latter years when New York City instituted the eight-hour day for police and firefighters.[93] At least two unions tried to transcend the eight-hour standard in the mid-1920s. About 8,000 New England telephone operators, organized by the International Brotherhood of Electrical Workers, struck for the seven-hour day in July 1923, and hundreds of Chicago soda clerks organized for the seven-hour day in 1926.[94] But these movements were isolated and often episodic and came in the context of a general retreat among trade unions, a retreat characterized by great hesitancy to link shorter hours with workers' control.

Progress in reducing the working day in the 1920s came as much through the efforts of reformers as through those of unions. Again, steel was pivotal, with the twelve-hour day finally yielding to reformers. But in the absence of mass labor pressure the reformers adopted increasingly conservative rationales for ending long hours and soon lost interest. The AFL came also to adopt those rationales, for the first time accepting the argument that working conditions and control over work should be traded for leisure.[95] Much of the ironic story of the failure of reformers to sustain shorter-hours agitation, and the willingness of the AFL to abandon shorter hours as a demand tied to workers' control, is bound up with the beginnings of five-day workweek campaigns and is described in a separate study.[96] Within the scope of this book the eight-hour campaign among reformers in steel deserves attention, along with its antecedents and legacy.

The reform coalition supporting a shorter workweek in the early 1920s included both religious humanitarians who pressed the fight against long hours largely by appealing to the concept of justice and who often supported labor unionism, and corporate/engineering experts who emphasized productivity and profit. That the ideas of the corporate/engineering group came to dominate the coalition speaks to the weakness of the post-1919 labor movement, both in numbers and in ideas, as a pole to attract humanitarian reformers.

The religious reformers who participated in the 1919-1923 campaign against long hours in the steel industry were part of the longest tradition of protest over the working week in the United States. Spiritual opposition to Sunday labor long preceded the formation of trade unions.[97] After the Civil War, both six-day-week and eight-hour-day activism among church leaders and laity existed as important minority trends. The Christian Labor Union, founded in 1872, functioned not as a union but as a religiously based shorter-hours propaganda group in which Ira Steward and George McNeill were central figures. From the 1880s through 1907 the Church Association for the Advancement of the Interests of Labor supported shorter hours, especially for women, children, and railroad workers, and campaigned for a Saturday half-holiday. By 1889 some of the religious press, including the *Andover Review*, the *Christian Union*, and the *Independent* favored the eight-hour system.[98] Pope Leo XIII's 1891 encyclical, "On the Condition of Labor," recalled "the obligation of the cessation from work and labor on Sundays and certain festivals" and added more generally that "in all agreements between masters and work people there is always the condition, expressed or understood, that there be allowed proper rest for soul and body." At the turn of the century Gompers commented that the ministry was ceasing to be part of that "host that prayed for us one minute on Sunday and preyed on us all the rest of the week" and was showing an interest in Sunday leisure.[99]

In the early twentieth century socially concerned Protestant ministers representing a wide variety of denominations newly organized into the Federal Council of Churches (FCC), addressed the hours question in that group's 1908 "Social Creed." Drafted by the radical Methodist, the Rev. Harry F. Ward, and influenced by the Presbyterian minister, Charles Stelzle, the document resolved in favor of "a release from employment one day in seven" and for "the gradual and reasonable reduction of the hours of labor to the lowest practicable point." In 1910 an FCC committee investigated the Bethlehem steel strike and found long hours in steel "unhealthy and unsocial" and "a disgrace to civilization." It proposed a law requiring three daily shifts in all continuously operating industries. The government, it advised, should buy only steel made on a forty-eight-hour-week basis.[100]

Between 1910 and 1918 the FCC reaffirmed its commitment to the "Social Creed" and Ward, heading the Methodist Federation for Social Service, developed a brilliant case for the shorter working day. Attuned to labor's critiques of the alienation engendered by scientific management, Ward argued for less hours as part of a broader strategy to reunite "the task and the song." Concrete political stands, especially in 1916, in support of eight hours for railway workers, accompanied his theorizing. Stelzle supported hours legislation and, as field secretary for the FCC, pressured the New York State Industrial Commission to act against the twelve-hour day in the steel industry.[101]

In many ways, the contributions of churches to the shorter hours movement were weak before World War I, however. The great body of churchmen were either aloof or opposed to reform. Both the historian Richard Ely, an advocate of the social gospel, and his associate John R. Commons complained in the late nineteenth century that even the issue of Sunday labor elicited only a small response from the ministry. Ely, for example, reported contact with one bakers' union leader seeking the clergy's support for a New York law against Sunday labor. The unionist sent 500 circulars to New York City and Brooklyn ministers and received six replies. "You will have a hard time, Professor," he told Ely, "to convince the toilers of this country that the clergy will even do anything for them. There is no money in it, you know."[102]

Many religious leaders held an abstract view of labor that had little application to the modern workplace and dissipated concern over the working day. Although early twentieth-century Catholic thinkers developed an antimaterialist critique of the alienating aspects of mass production, this critique coexisted with the papal view that work, since the fall of Adam, had to be alienating. "Cursed be the earth in thy work," Leo XIII quoted Genesis, adding that labor "will have no end or cessation on this earth . . . for the consequences of sin are bitter." At the same time, and in seeming contradiction, some Catholic leaders idealized labor, with James Cardinal Gibbons seeing productive activity as the key to "gladness, health and contentment" in contrast to the "indolent life [that] breeds discontent, disease and death." This same view of labor as the source of virtue was prominent in Protestant thought and sometimes led to an evasion of the issues of the working day.[103]

Such tendencies toward an abstract view of labor often led the churchmen to formulate their positions on the working day in terms having little relevance to concrete campaigns for the universal eight-hour day. Leo XIII's position that hours should vary, indeterminately, according to the job, age, sex, and even season, for example, could hardly become the object for agitation. Nor did the FCC's advocacy of "gradual and reasonable reduction of hours" carry a concrete thrust.[104]

Finally, religious advocacy of shorter hours tended to strengthen the most conservative elements in the labor movement. Catholics and Protestants eyed each other's appeals to working-class Americans suspiciously and sought to build religiously based alliances with union leaders. Both groups blocked mainly with "pure-and-simple" craft unionists. The Catholics particularly found common cause with the Gompers leadership, especially between 1910 and 1916, on the issue of antisocialism and on a distrust of state action to reform social ills. The latter stance led to Catholic opposition to even child labor laws. This stance also dovetailed neatly with Gompers's insistence that workers would "look upon [shorter hours] as injustice or hardship" if the reforms were "forced upon them by law." Protestant reformers joined the Catholics in castigating socialism, preaching class harmony, and supporting AFL conservatives.[105]

Nonetheless, religious reformers were at times valuable allies for even the most militant shorter-hours agitators. Ward showed how Christian concepts regarding the dignity of labor could be welded in a critique of long hours and capitalist efficiency.[106] Under certain circumstances more conservative churchmen also inched toward support of industrial unionism and toward concrete proposals for a shorter workweek. The crisis years of World War I and the 1919 strike wave provided such circumstances.

Protestant denominations articulated increasingly specific postwar reform agendas, which included the eight-hour day. The Committee on the War and Religious Outlook of the Episcopal Church refused to accept the need for continuous output as a justification for long days and seven-day weeks, writing, "it is only the setting of profit above personality" that prevents adding more workers and shortening the workweek.[107] The most ambitious of the war-bred Protestant organizations, the IWM, played a leading part in shorter-hours agitation. Taking shape in 1918 largely as an organization to raise funds for missionary work, the IWM had enlisted the support of sixty denominations by January 1919. By October 2, 1919, just after the steel strike had begun, the IWM had readied a conference on industrial relations, called at the request of AFL, congressional, and cabinet officials. The steel strike and conditions in the industry dominated the conference which resolved for a "thoroughgoing investigation" of the strikes in steel.[108] A nine-person committee of the IWM investigated the conflict from the third week of the steel strike until a month after its end. Its members' views ranged from those of its chairperson, Methodist Bishop Francis McConnell, a left-liberal supporter of independent labor politics, to the apolitical fundamentalism of the Presbyterian Dr. John McDowell, and generally betrayed little sympathy for radical unionism. However, the staff investigators included David Saposs, Heber Blankenhorn, and George Soule, all among the greatest modern experts on labor and all then inclined toward socialism.[109]

The IWM *Report*, released to the press on July 28, 1920, was a prolabor document of the highest order. Along with the subsequent companion volume *Public Opinion and the Steel Strike*, it squarely took the union's side, scoring the twelve-hour day, low wages, and Gary's refusal to bargain. The *Report* castigated the complicity of local, state, and federal authorities in violating free speech for labor organizations. It consistently emphasized the working day as an issue and ridiculed the notion that the strike had been a Bolshevik plot. Few strikers, it maintained, "could put together two sentences on 'Soviets' but almost all . . . cursed 'long hours'."[110] "Americanization," the *Report* continued, "is a farce, night schools are worthless, Carnegie libraries . . . are a jest, churches and welfare institutions are ironic while the steel worker is held to the twelve-hour day . . . . Not only has he no energy left, he has literally no time."[111] A separate study by the Federal Council of Churches reinforced the same point.[112]

The investigators wrote as witnesses to an unprecedented organizing feat and to a series of events in which the steel strike, as Mary Heaton Vorse put it, "bled to death like a living thing." Their *Report* displayed a frank admiration for the possibilities of amalgamated trade unionism. When the report discussed inefficiency, it did so in the context of destroying the "petty tyrannies" of management and of expanding rank-and-file "control of the production process." Although opposed to the closed shop, the investigators saw unions as central to reform and predicted that "another strike must come."[113]

The *Report* speedily went through five printings, secured nearly a score of laudatory mentions in religious publications, and became the subject of hundreds of articles and editorials in the broader press, over 75 percent of which the IWM termed favorable. European papers carried digests of the investigation, and the city government of Glasgow, Scotland, for a time held up a large order of steel rails to protest labor conditions in the American industry. Labor papers embraced the document and purchased it in large quantities.[114]

We might measure the broad acceptance of the *Report* by the ambitious attempts of the steel corporations to discredit it. *Iron Age* denounced the document as the work of radicals. Pamphlets by F. M. Barton and the Rev. E. Victor Bigelow criticized the *Report* and enjoyed wide distribution by U.S. Steel. Marshall Olds's huge *Analysis of the IWM Report on the Steel Strike*, a wildly anti-Bolshevik tract, also drew corporation backing.[115] Members of the National Civic Federation and National Assciation of Manufacturers withdrew support from the IWM, sending its available funding down to 15 percent of its former level by 1921. By the time of the 1923 reform campaign in the steel industry, the Industrial Relations Department of the IWM had disbanded. In the 1923 events, more moderate religious forces would register their protests against long hours and register them in softer tones easily drowned out by those of a growing contingent of corporate reformers.[116]

The reformers who approached the working day from the standpoint of efficiency and profit, like their religious counterparts, had a long tradition of activity around the hours issue. That tradition was also transformed during the war years into a new set of arguments advanced with more force and urgency. Since the mid-nineteenth century a small minority of workshop and factory owners and managers had maintained that shorter hours did not necessarily lead to a decrease in production. Basing themselves on the experiences of individual firms, these capitalist reformers pointed to the payoffs—in goodwill, workers' health, longevity of machine performance, and quality of work—engendered by a shorter working day. A few, following George Gunton, connected less hours to increased markets and to technological innovations. Others saw eight hours as a way to defuse labor protest.[117]

During the prewar Progressive Era the strongest nonreligious reform arguments for reductions in hours linked national efficiency with corporate interests. Mixing biological and mechanical metaphors, Progressives considered "conservation" of "humanity" to require the construction of society as "the perfect machine." When, according to one theorist of conservation, mankind "shall have learned to apply the common sense and scientific rules of efficiency to the care of body and mind and to the labors of body and mind," the nation would "be nearing the condition of perfect."[118]

Such a view of shorter hours as productive of both industrial and social efficiency characterized the writings of the main prewar group attacking long hours, the steel industry reformers centered around *Survey* magazine and the Cabot Fund. John Fitch and Paul Kellogg, Fitch's supervising editor on the massive 1907-1908 sociological study known as the Pittsburgh Survey, identified the twelve-hour day as a source of social problems in the steel industry. From the start they cooperated in their attacks on long hours with steel company officials and stockholders. William Brown Dickson, a U.S. Steel vice president who had risen through the ranks and recalled the twelve-hour day and seven-day weeks as "twin relics of barbarism," had attacked the long-hour system as inefficient and socially destructive as early as 1907. Charles Cabot, a minority stockholder, joined Dickson in his calls for reduction of hours shortly thereafter, and the two pressed the issue at stockholders' meetings.[119]

Dickson and Cabot emphasized that the long day meant inefficiency and that financial returns could survive reform; Fitch, especially in his much-quoted 1911 article "Old Age at Forty," stressed social costs. Louis Brandeis's testimony before a House committee just after Fitch's article was published distilled Fitch's points: the steel worker was "a useless individual and a burden to his family at 40 [and transmitted] perhaps through many generations, the evil weaknesses and the degeneration which have come to him." In 1911 the reform coalition succeeded in establishing a committee, initiated by the U.S. Steel stockholders, to investigate Fitch's charges. When that committee returned its findings the following year, it allowed that the prevailing shifts led to "a decreasing of the efficiency and lessening of the vigor and virility" of workers.[120]

However, reform arguments regarding the physiological and psychological benefits of the shorter day suffered from their failure to mesh well with scientific management. Although Frederick W. Taylor and other scientific managers held out the possibility of reducing hours to provide incentive to workers, in practice they much more often used short-term pay differentials. Taylor's ideal of a "high-priced man" translated easily into managerial practice regarding wages. Cuts in hours, on the other hand, would have had to influence whole departments, producing the kind of group feeling which was anathema to Taylor. Moreover, Taylor had little concern with psychology or physiology, basing his studies mainly on mechanics. Taylorism thus undercut the older rationales for securing cooperation from a healthy, happy work force through reduction in hours. The standard guidebook of the Taylorists, published in 1911, featured a daily time clock, calibrated to the hundredth of an hour. It was a ten-hour clock.[121]

Reformers wishing to draw on Taylorism to argue for shorter hours had to make a largely negative case. Brandeis, Goldmark, and Frankfurter, in their legal documentation for statutes regulating the hours of women's labor, did hold that Taylorism lay the groundwork for shorter hours, but they stressed not so much the leisure-creating possibilities of scientifically managed productivity as the alienating aspects of newly designed jobs. Embracing both scientific management and reduced hours, they portrayed the latter as antidote for the former.[122]

After 1915, and especially during and just after World War I, many of the impediments to the development of an efficiency-based, profit-oriented reform argument for a shorter working day dropped away. With Taylor's death in 1915, the work reform movement, building on his basic framework of de-skilled labor, began to devote more attention to the problem of motivation through psychological incentives.[123] The post-1915 management experts also emphasized physiology more than Taylor had. Crucially, the new breed of efficiency experts followed Ford in seeing not just systematic loafing but also turnover and absenteeism as key management problems and in believing that these problems required a welfare capitalist strategy not hinging on wage incentives.[124]

The coming of the war and the institution of Prohibition after the war helped to solidify the trend toward a welfare capitalist management style, which could coherently attack very long working days. War production elevated the attack on waste of human resources into a national duty. The War Labor Board encouraged labor-management cooperation, often by granting shorter days to unions and concessions on implementing scientific management to employers. Such actions cemented the AFL's making of peace with a wing of the scientific management movement and culminated in Gompers's work with Morris Cooke on the 1920 treatise "Labor, Management and Productivity," a systematic defense of labor/scientific management detente.[125] Prohibition, which seemed to many executives a tremendous boon to productivity, also helped disarm the nineteenth-century objection that shorter hours led to debauchery.[126]

By 1920 John R. Commons and John B. Andrews could write, "Of the many lessons which the world war taught industry, none is more clear-cut than that long hours do not pay."[127] In addition, they could be certain that management experts and reformers would understand their point on several different levels. They could point out that in a number of wartime studies of specific industries, shorter hours had proven compatible with maintained production levels in at least some of the factories surveyed.[128] Moreover, studies emphasized that for much of the day, workers were resting or waiting for work and that increased actual work time was therefore possible within shorter shifts. Finally, the celebrated postwar *Waste in Industry* report, prepared under the direction of Herbert Hoover, so overwhelmingly concentrated on inefficiency among managers that small changes in production resulting from reductions in hours paled by comparison.[129]

Other reform arguments stressed that a third of the 2.5 million men examined for army service were rejected as physically unfit by pointing out that a long day did "not pay" in terms of national health. With both "social well-being and productive efficiency" at stake, experts considered whether long hours contributed to occupational disease. Although some early studies held out little prospect that adjusting hours fostered health or decreased accidents, by 1924 a growing body of literature linked shorter hours with decreased absenteeism due to illness or disability and enabled the economist P. Sargent Florence to argue that "about one-quarter" of the eight-hour difference between a fifty-two-hour and a sixty-hour working week, was simply given back in increased lost time due to sickness.[130]

Others emphasized that disputes at work resulted from tiredness. One management expert who worked in steel mills in order to observe them, held: "If it is true . . . that 98 percent of the disputes they were asked to solve simmered down finally to some petty dispute between a foreman and a man, then I am willing to wager that the majority of these 98 percent [came] when both the foreman and worker were just plain tired." U.S. Public Health Service researches suggested that the adoption of an eight-hour day might significantly decrease tardiness among workers.[131] Long hours were inefficient, Whiting Williams wrote, because "men are paid for energies which they simply are not able to deliver." It remained for the crusading department store owner, Edward Filene, to add that management ought not apologize for alienating jobs, but hold out increased consumption and the eventual possibility of a five-hour day as compensation.[132]

By 1920 such efficiency-based reasons for a shorter day produced a strong case against very long working days. The steel industry, the storm center in 1919 and the bastion of an eighty-four-hour week, naturally became the object of the reformers' attention. That industry's many unemployed workers gave force to the argument that shorter hours could be part of a voluntary business-labor-government plan to ease joblessness. The 1921 President's Conference on Unemployment, organized by Commerce Secretary Herbert Hoover, advised such work-sharing as well as regulation of hours to rationalize seasonal industries, at the very time that critics of the steel industry pointed to its unwillingness to abandon the twelve-hour day in order to create jobs.[133] Indeed Hoover, bringing together and towering over the other corporate reformers, became the central figure in the campaign against the long day in steel.[134]

With labor action against the steel industry stalled, humanitarian reformers who had mixed religious appeals, support for unions, and efficiency arguments increasingly concentrated on the last. *Survey* magazine allowed that the AFL was "unlikely" to change conditions in the industry soon and added "the employers are in full possession of the power" to bring about reform. Losing confidence in labor pressure, *Survey* sometimes still stressed the role of public opinion, but most often reported on the professional opinion of engineers. Even Fitch's free-wheeling and humane attacks on long hours, which drew here on religion, there on social uplift, gave way, in *Survey's* pages, to narrower descriptions of how an eight-hour day might enhance productive efficiency.[135]

Paul Kellogg, the reform editor who in 1920 persuaded his fellow Cabot Fund trustees to reopen the hours issue in steel, opted for an efficiency-engineering approach. The Cabot Fund commissioned Morris Cooke, the Taylor follower instrumental in bringing the AFL into cooperation with scientific management, to study the economic feasibility of a transition to eight hours. Cooke, working with Horace Drury of the American Engineering Council, studied a score of U.S. steel plants already working under a three-shift system, and found "no outstanding obstacle" to adoption of that system. The Cooke-Drury study, published by the Taylor Society, predicted that as little as a 3 percent rise in costs would accompany the transition. A Cooke report even found a dairy farm more profitably run under the eight-hour system and concluded, "If the cow seems able to adapt herself, it ought not be hard for some others to make the change." Reformers, emphasizing that the three-shift system was one which "practically every steel production center in the world, excepting the United States, has universally introduced," also drew on studies from abroad to show that managerial improvements "could enable. . . employees to earn more in eight hours than they previously had in twelve."[136]

Kellogg moved to commit the Cabot Fund to further action but met resistance from other trustees. Only after giving assurances that fund contributions would not be used not to undertake a publicity campaign against the steel industry but only to mobilize internal pressure, did Kellogg's designated leader for the new campaign, Columbia professor Samuel McCune Lindsay, secure necessary funding. Lindsay, a prominent Republican with ties to Hoover and to President Warren G. Harding, found in the former an especially strong ally. As president of the Federated American Engineering Societies, Hoover had initiated studies that he felt showed the long day to be "barbaric" and "uneconomic." By early 1922, cooperating with Lindsay, he initiated a Commerce Department investigation as well. Hoover wanted quick progress because he thought that high stakes were involved. Reform would forestall the spread of radical unionism, he maintained, and would give "the steel industry credit for some kind of initiative instead of waiting until they are smashed into by some kind of legisalation."[137]

Taking heart from Gary's 1921 statements that the twelve-hour day would end in "the comparatively near future," Hoover delayed asking public action of Harding until after the April 17, 1922, annual meeting of U.S. Steel in hopes that Gary might sound the death knell of the long day at that meeting. Hoover did present his findings on the question to Harding on April 8 and induce the president to send Gary a letter designed to "stir his imagination" just before the meeting. Release of the report of the American Engineering Council's Committee on Work Periods in Continuous Industry and the announcement of a new study on steel by that group also were timed to pressure Gary. The strategy failed when Gary not only failed to commit himself to reform but repeated his 1921 statement laying blame for the long day on the desire of the workers to be paid for twelve hours and adding that the work was usually "not laborious and not injurious." Gary also cited the impossibility of finding enough labor, with the closing of immigration, if eight hours were adopted.[138]

Hoover, with rare passion, persuaded Harding to call a May 18 meeting of 41 steel executives at the White House. At the meeting the commerce secretary denounced long hours in terms Gary found "unsocial and uneconomic." Harding persuaded the group to investigate the working day. Gary, who praised the president because he did not "insist unduly" on reform, was made head of the investigating committee. Hoover, "in less than a good humor," left the dinner to tell reporters that Harding "was trying to persuade the steel industry to adopt the eight-hour shift."[139]

No action came from the steel corporations through the succeeding six months. Hoover and Secretary of Labor James J. Davis meanwhile pressed for administration support for eight hours. With Gary a leading financial backer of Republican candidates, the president hesitated to act, but political considerations made him slowly move against the twelve-hour day. By November 1922, when the Federated American Engineering Society issued its *The Twelve-Hour Shift in Industry*, Harding agreed to sign an introduction praising the study. The president, in words likely drafted by Hoover, endorsed the idea that the "old order of the 12-hour day must give way to a better and wiser" system.[140]

Even as Hoover and Lindsay engineered pressure from corporate leaders inside and outside the steel industry, Gary stood his ground and delayed reporting on his much-promised study. When, on May 25, 1923, the Gary Committee did release the results of its study, they justified continuing long hours on every count. The workers wanted long shifts; the schedule did little or no harm; the system was a productive one; and change would add 15 percent to costs.[141]

Hoover attacked the Gary *Report* in a letter asking Harding "not [to] allow this matter of fundamental social importance to drop." By June 13 he wrote not just to Harding but for him, drafting a letter to Gary, which the president signed. Reiterating engineering reports and making humanitarian arguments, the letter cornered the steel leader by asking that he admit that long hours were destructive and pledge to ameliorate them when recessions cut the demand for labor in steel. With even the conservative New York *Times* implying that it would welcome legislative action on the issues and with bodies representing America's Jewish, Catholic, and Protestant clergy aroused, Gary capitulated at last. On June 27 he wired Harding that the eight-hour day would be established "at the earliest practicable time" and appended a personal note inviting Harding to make the announcement. Harding chose an Independence Day speech to tell Americans that tens of thousands of steel workers could look forward to as many as thirty-six more hours of freedom weekly. His ringing remarks, again penned by Hoover, discouraged tendencies toward delay. By August major mills in Gary, Pittsburgh, and Chicago were on the new schedule. Wage boosts of 25 percent gave back some of the lost pay. A moderate 5 percent boost in costs of steelmaking was far offset by other factors, and the months after the reform proved profitable for the steel industry.[142]

At the time of the reform both union and Communist papers predicted that Gary would again evade implementation by making use of vague language. Gompers advised all "not to expect too much." *The Worker* warned of "The 8-hour Hoax of U.S. Steel." As late as 1930 *New Republic* documented continuing twelve-hour days in steel.[143] Nonetheless, average weekly hours in the industry plummeted from 63.2 in 1922 to 54.4 in 1926. Reform had come, despite relative absence of immediate union pressure. Indeed, between 1921 and 1923, the impetus for reform came largely from those with close ties to corporate capitalism. With the steel reform under way, the question became whether or not the reform coalition would push for further reductions of hours in other industries.[144]

The question of whether such corporate reform could be harnessed to management-labor cooperation was especially vital to William Green and the embattled leadership of the AFL. As one historian has put it, with the relationship between scientific management and labor "blossoming into a love affair," at least on labor's side, Green hoped to deliver what trade union radicals promised, a forty-hour week.[145] The idea of cutting the workweek by cutting the days of labor had its earliest origins in Sabbatarianism and, more recently, in the Saturday half-holiday campaigns begun in the late nineteenth century and the actual scattered achievement of the five-day week as early as 1908.[146] But the goal remained a dream for the overwhelming majority of U.S. workers, and Green gave it a new twist. Rather than packaging the shorter workweek as a control demand to be won along with other workplace issues, he came to argue that the five-day week was compensation for acceptance of alienating labor. When the AFL went on record as favoring the five-day week at its October 1926 convention, Green's logic found echoes in those of many delegates and overshadowed older arguments stressing health, happiness, citizenship, and control.[147]

In 1925 Green had led the AFL in proposing a "social wage" tied to productivity and given in exchange for union cooperation on work rules.[148] The five-day week was, as *Labor* pointed out at the time, an extension of the same logic.[149] In the 1926 debate on the workweek, Green made it clear that labor must accept not only machinery (as the unions long had) but also increasingly alienating relations of production:

We would not go back to the old times if we could, but we are adjusting ourselves to the new, and as we look upon a modern factory with its mass production, with its specialization and with its standardization, we realize that we . . . must point the way by which we can adjust ourselves to this new industrial order.

That adjustment, he added, hinged on increased wages and increased leisure for "recuperation" and "readjustment."[150]

Other delegates reinforced this point. John Frey held that the new educational campaign was not a "continuation" of old AFL work around the issue but a new departure based on "increased per capita production." James Lynch specifically added that he did not "believe that Henry Ford himself could eliminate these processes that have grown up . . . the continuous performance by the individual of the same task." But, he continued, "the committee has indicated the remedy for the fatigue and atrophy that follows the repetitive processes in industry" by proposing a shorter week.[151]

Such logic ensured that the AFL would have to redouble efforts to eliminate radical influences in the unions. Thus, it is not quite so paradoxical as it might seem that one of Green's first actions after the passing of five-day resolution was to attempt to purge the leadership of the Furriers' Union in New York where a long strike had just won what the historian Bert Cochran has called "a spectacular left-wing victory . . . the first 40-hour, five-day week in the garment industry." Under Ben Gold, the New York furriers leadership was largely Communist and therefore seemed less a model of five-day effectiveness than a threat to AFL leaders.[152]

A more abiding paradox lies in the fact that the AFL's five-day proclamation came in the same month that one of modern America's staunchest antiunionists announced the institution of the five-day week for all but a few of the workers in his huge enterprise. Ford, eyeing increased consumption and more production from man and machine, towered over all other corporate officials in systematizing the rationale for a five-day week and in actually providing workers with the new schedule. The 270 companies identified by the National Industrial Conference Board as having the five-day week in 1928 employed just over 218,000 workers; 80 percent of them worked for just one firm: Ford. Fuller figures estimated that 400,000 wage earners had a five-day week. Over 40 percent of them were Ford workers.[153]

The very proximity of Ford's October announcement and the AFL's five-day resolution ensured that Ford and William Green's arguments would be mentioned together frequently. Some AFL leaders welcomed the comparison. But militant unionists and prounion reformers like the young minister Reinhold Niebuhr had to balance Ford's open-shop position, speedups, and institution of pay cuts, estimated by the *Christian Century* at $4 to $6 per week, against his five-day week position. Some pointed out that since Ford boasted that output in five days could equal that of the longer week, the reform was in effect a speedup paid for by lost wages among the workers. Although the labor press sometimes reported on Ford sympathetically, he was far from a perfect ally. Indeed Ford's five-day week received scathing indictment as "bunk" (a favorite Ford word) in several labor papers, although his rationale for reform differed little from that of the AFL leadership.[154]

More importantly, even with the arguments developed before and during the shorter-hours campaign in steel and with the opportunity afforded to management to lead and co-opt further a compliant labor movement, the AFL-Fordist initiative regarding a five-day week was simply a failure in the 1920s. Only a relative handful of managerial experts, and still fewer employers, embraced either the five-day week or working days of below eight hours. Indeed, once the steel reform had been partially implemented, the urgency of attacking even very long hours diminished. Hoover, who later contended his actions in the steel campaign rid all American workers of the twelve-hour and even the ten-hour day, joined most other corporate reformers in ignoring the continued existence of such long days, sometimes combined with seven-day weeks, through the 1920s. The oil industry, railroad telegraphy, and rubber manufacturing were especially notorious on these scores. Some occupations appear to have witnessed attempts to lengthen the week to seven days during the decade.[155] In the climate of reform through voluntary business-government association, even legislation providing a day's rest in seven made only slow headway.[156] The very success of the steel drive, with its plethora of specific productivity-oriented research reports in its latter stages, may have led to later inaction, both by producing an example which suggested legislation was superfluous and by making reformers hesitant to act in other industries in which comparable studies had not been prepared. The reform activities had produced precious little to motivate employers to lower hours *below* the long-sought ideal of forty-eight per week. Sober perusal of the NICB studies, for example, would have revealed that, for all their considerable animus against long hours, they consistently opposed even reductions in hours to forty-eight weekly, finding efficiency best served at just above that standard.[157]

Moreover, among humantarian reformers formerly allied with the shorter-hours movement, divisions in the mid-1920s led to weakness. This was true of feminists who split over the issue of whether or not to emphasize protective legislation (including maximum hours laws) or to stress passage of an Equal Rights Amendment, which called the logic of special protection into question.[158] The child labor movement likewise split over whether to continue to push for a federal amendment or to opt for limited statewide campaigns.[159]

Large corporations almost universally opposed the five-day week during the 1920s. Through 1927, according to NICB statistics, only three other corporations employing over 2,000 had followed Henry Ford's lead in establishing the shorter schedule. Elbert Gary, representing U.S. Steel, found the five-day system deplorable on every count and repeated as evidence against it the biblical injunction his company had until so recently defied by requiring Sunday work: "Six days shalt thou labor and do all thy work." Westinghouse's president censured Ford in strong terms which he felt "express[ed] the view of practically every manufacturer and employer in this country."[160]

Smaller manufacturers and employer associations likewise decried concessions on the workweek. John Edgerton, head of the National Association of Manufacturers and president of a Tennessee woolen mill, proclaimed it "time for America to awake from its dream of an eternal holiday" and linked extra leisure with dissipation. Particularly feared was union imposition of the shorter week. One Buffalo bronze casting manufacturer found the AFL idea that production could be maintained during a five-day week to be "unadulterated bunk," predicting that no "union man" would exert himself "one iota more per hour." NAM's 1926 article, "The Five Day WorkWeek: Can it Become Universal?" answered its title's question with a resounding "It will not!" *Iron Age, Bulletin of the National Association of Building Trades Employers, Commerce and Finance, Commercial West, Manufacturer's News, Real Estate Board and Builders' Guide,* and the Philadelphia Chamber of Commerce all viewed the five-day plan negatively as did the U.S. Chamber of Commerce.[161]

In contrast to the situation prevailing during the campaign against the long day in steel, even those companies which had adopted the five-day week often did not speak enthusiastically on its behalf. The New York *World's* mid-decade study of the five-day week in stores in fourteen large cities where Saturday closings had been adopted revealed wide divisions of opinion as to the efficiency of the system. Some mercantile leaders objected that the closings kept workers from shopping, but no sentiment for extending the system to industry found expression.[162]

Similar early studies of five-day industrial concerns found almost an even split between satisfied employers and those upset by the results. Those factories keeping hours of more than forty per week, but spreading them over five days, were happiest with the system. An ambitious NICB study, published in 1929, found greater approval for the five-day week among the 270 plants it surveyed, but over half those plants worked greater than forty-hour schedules. Of those plants reducing hours 6.4 percent reported "substantially less" production and 25.4 percent saw no increase in per-hour output under the five-day format.[163]

Nor did many efficiency, management, economics, or engineering experts embrace the five-day week in the 1920s. The AFL, though anxious to show the reform as part of a strategy to increase production and consumption, could cite only a handful of experts who directly supported its theories.[164] AFL president William Green so cast about for corporate reform supporters that he strained the facts with a 1926 claim that Secretary of Treasury Andrew Mellon supported the five-day week, when Mellon did so only to the extent that he commented, "if a man can accomplish his work in five days, there is no reason why he should work six days."[165] *Labor Age* and other magazines of the socialist labor movement often published articles by efficiency engineers, most of whom only generally criticized the waste associated with long days and others of whom eschewed specifics concerning what schedule should apply by asking "Is a Shorter Work-Day Enough?" The *American Labor Legislation Review* greeted the call for a five-day week with lukewarm interest, using it as an occasion to call for abolition of the seven-day week. The Society of Industrial Engineers published criticisms of the reform.[166] Those rare employers who supported the five-day week usually engaged in the production or sale of consumer goods or services. Richard Feiss, whose 1920 article recounted the positive impact of a five-day system, pointed to increased productivity, less turnover (especially among women workers whom his firm more easily attracted), and a "speeding up" of "the slower workers." Feiss, a Clevelander, manufactured clothing in a nonunion shop. Edward Filene, who saw the shorter week as part of a plan to "Fordize America," was among the nation's largest department store owners.[167] W. Burke Harmon, a leading New York realtor, welcomed the five-day week as likely to spur home ownership. The National Amusement Parks Association listened to descriptions of the reform with lively interest.[168]

Just as few employers followed Ford to voluntary concessions regarding the five-day week, few unions secured that goal through bargaining. At its 1928 convention the AFL boasted of about 165,000 members working five-day, 40-hour weeks. While this represented an increase of about 75,000 since 1926, about 70 percent of the total came from just five extremely well-organized building trades unions. The painters' union alone furnished 38 percent of the total with bricklayers, carpenters, electrical workers, and plasterers accounting together for about one unionized five-day worker in three. At least a fifth of those unionists benefiting from the reform, and perhaps nearly 30 percent, came from Communist-influenced unions in the fur and clothing industries.[169] Conservative AFL leaders could hardly take much comfort from these figures, nor from the fact that more manufacturing establishments adopted the new system in the year before AFL agitation began than in the year after.[170] Nonetheless the AFL leadership maintained that "steady progress" was being made and held out hope that "public demand" would bring the five-day week.[171]

Even in the building trades the adoption of the five-day system came slowly, outside of the painters' union, before 1929. During that year the number of five-day building tradesmen more than doubled in a single stroke when the Building Trades' Employers Association of New York granted the reform for 125,000 to 150,000 workers.[172] That action came despite the fact that most of the unions involved had earlier agreed not to bargain over the working week until 1930. However, the reform leadership of the Brotherhood of Electrical Workers won the five-day week and a 10 percent pay hike effective February 1, 1929. Other building trades responded by seeking the same schedule, citing language in their contracts "stipulating that basic improvements won by any other trade in the industry" would apply.[173] The New York Building Trades Council won the new system on May 4 and, in late May, defended it from an employer attempt to break up craft solidarity by locking out those unionists who refused to work with nonunion electricians. The reform quickly spread to Chicago, Saint Louis, and other cities.[174] But the brief contagion of five-day fever in the building trades in 1929 did not signal a further spread until the deepening Depression made easily justifiable "share-the-work" plans lively issues.

In the 1920s the shorter-week initiative of the AFL leadership and of Ford failed. Its greatest shortcoming was that it presumed the existence of corporate reform support which simply did not exist. Its weaknesses included a continuing AFL commitment to voluntarism which made the organization disdain legislation on the working week even as its leaders spoke of the power of "public demand." Throughout the decade labor lobbying for federal hours legislation remained confined to laws extending a forty-four-hour week to more government employees and remained unsuccessful.[175] The fact that many workers, including some unionists, had not approached even the forty-eight-hour week and that some still worked seven days, also complicated the agitation. This forced the AFL to defend the six-day week at eight hours daily instead of the forty-hour week.[176] Many unions ignored the five-day-week call. Even the machinists, considered prominent in five-day agitation, continued throughout 1928 to print preambles in their journal calling for a forty-four-hour week with a Saturday *half*-holiday.[177] At least one union leader, George L. Berry of the pressmen, openly opposed the five-day week in the name of "promoting the spirit of cooperation" with employers.[178]

In the period from 1906-1919, when strikes and labor protest carried forward the movement for shorter hours and when the demand came in tandem with attacks on Taylorism, the workweek in nonagricultural industries fell by an average of 7.0 hours. In the decade thereafter, with Fordist ideas in full flower in an ideal setting of prosperity and with little labor opposition to a partially Fordized Taylorism, the workweek fell by just 1.3 hours, a figure buoyed mainly by Ford's 1926 reforms, the attack on the twelve-hour day in steel, left-wing union campaigns, and some 1919 settlements borne of militant organizing and strikes.[179] The AFL/Fordist initiative for a five-day week was virtually stillborn. If the new unionism had suffered critical defeats in its efforts to link hours, control, and militant labor action in 1919, so too had conservative AFL efforts to disentangle the workweek and control issues during the 1920s.

11

The Great Depression, the New Deal, and Shorter Hours

"In 1929," writes Irving Bernstein, "the hours of work in American industry were long. Only 19 percent of the wage earners in manufacturing were scheduled for fewer than 48 hours per week; 26.5 percent were at 48; 31.1 percent were scheduled between 49 and 54; 15 percent between 55 and 59; and 7.4 percent worked a schedule of 60 hours or longer." At this time, by way of contrast, "virtually all the industrialized nations of Europe and Australia enjoyed the eight-hour day" while the Soviet Union had introduced the seven-hour principle. In this regard, the United States lagged behind every other industrialized nation in the world. "A shortening of the workweek in American industry was to be expected," according to Bernstein, "even if there had been no depression. Unemployment added a note of urgency."[1]

While unemployment statistics during the Great Depression were inadequate, we can chart the disaster on the basis of what we do have.[2] In October 1929 fewer that 1 million people were out of work. In January 1930 the unemployment figure passed 4 million. It reached 9 million in October 1931 and passed 10 million in December. The number of jobless went over 11 million in January 1932, crossed 12 million in March, and surpassed 13 million in June. In January 1933 there were more than 14 million persons out of work. The bottom was reached in March 1933—15,071,000 were unemployed. Moreover, immense numbers of employed persons were on short time.[3]

The seriousness of the situation was not at first appreciated. In the months following the financial crash, both business and labor leaders urged a policy of patience concurring in the belief that the depression would be short. Just as President Hoover and the leaders of big business believed that the stock market crash was merely a temporary decline, so the leadership of the AFL was convinced that "within a few months, industrial conditions will become normal, confidence and stability in industry and finance will be restored, and labor, strong and aggressive, will be prepared to demand and secure higher wages and greater degree of leisure." In the meantime, it was imperative that "no movement beyond that already in negotiations should be initiated for increase of wages and every cooperation should be given by labor to industry in the handling of its problems."[4]

In November 1929 the AFL leadership had already promised President Hoover, who had exacted a pledge from business tycoons to maintain the 1929 wage levels, that it would not seek wage increases nor strike during the economic crisis. At the 1930 convention the AFL Executive Council reported that the affiliates were cooperating "by not raising issues that might embarrass or interrupt efforts to turn the tide upward." Such inaction proved futile either to overcome business stagnation, prevent wage cuts and the lengthening of working hours, or to stem the rising tide of unemployment.[5]

Meanwhile, early in the Great Depression the Communist party and the newly formed Trade Union Unity League began to organize the jobless into groups known as Unemployed Councils. Under the slogan "Starve or Fight," the Unemployed Councils issued calls for nationwide demonstrations for passage of an Unemployment Insurance Bill, an end to evictions, improved relief in cash and in kind, state and federal aid, a seven-hour day and a five-day week, with a six-hour day for harmful and strenuous occupations, without reduction in pay.[6]

Until 1932 the AFL refused even to consider the demand for passage of an Unemployment Insurance Bill, labeling it as the "dole," but it was ready to raise the demand for shorter hours as its sole plan to increase employment. The advocates of shorter hours in the labor movement reasoned that the depression had been caused by the rate of technological advance, which exceeded that of either wage increases or hours reduction. The inevitable result was technological unemployment, the displacement of workers by machines. The solution was to cut the hours of work with no loss in earnings, thereby increasing the number of jobs. This would lead to expanding purchasing power and the recovery of the system.[7] The Railway Employees Department of the AFL, representing the nonoperating crafts, advocated a forty-hour week as the solution to joblessness as early as March 1930. In November the train-service brotherhoods began a drive for the six-hour day while the AFL Metal Trades Department endorsed the five-hour day.[8]

The demand for shorter hours dominated the AFL Convention in Boston in October 1930. Even the metal trades' radical proposal for the five-hour day was given a hearing before the convention voted to refer it to the Executive Council for "immediate and thorough consideration." However, most of the discussion centered around the five-day week. "We have arrived at the period in our history of our nation and our industrial progress," declared President William Green, "when the institution of the five-day week in all industries out of the service industries should be immediately inaugurated."[9]

The demand for the five-day week also loomed large in the labor press in the months following the convention. Special attention was paid to the statement of Sidney Hillman of the Amalgamated Clothing Workers that "the universal adoption of the five-day week would put all of the unemployed to work."[10] But apart from John J. Raskob, chairman of the Democratic National Committee, who had made his wealth in General Motors, few members of the capitalist class endorsed the call for a five-day week. To be sure, the Government Printing Office instituted the five-day week, and the Snow Baking Powder Company went on five days. But these were exceptions. A Bureau of Labor Statistics survey in 1932 revealed that "only 5.4 percent of 44,025 establishments" had adopted the five-day week for all or some of their employees.[11]

The unions lacked strength to enforce the demand for shorter hours. The idea of strikes for shorter hours was judged to be hopeless. But at a meeting of 3,500 fur workers on June 17, 1931, union leader Ben Gold rejected the argument that the crisis made it impossible to obtain higher wages and shorter hours. "This is a bosses' theory," he cried, "which the agents of the bosses use in order to beat the workers into submission, into forcing them to accept hunger wages and conditions of slavery." The fur workers proved Gold correct by winning strikes for the forty-hour, five-day week along with wage increases.[12] But the AFL leadership took no heed and intensified its efforts to destroy the left-wing fur workers' leadership.[13]

During the early years of the Great Depression, Green was an advocate of the practice of sharing work as a means of reducing unemployment: "The principle of relating the number needing jobs to the total number of man- hours of work available should be permanently incorporated in national policy and business procedure."[14] By the summer of 1932 work-sharing was receiving such enthusiastic support among employers that the movement crystallized into a national enterprise, and a share-the-work committee was appointed by President Hoover with Walter C. Teagle, president of Jersey Standard Oil, as its chairman and William Green an enthusiastic supporter.[15]

Green, however, did not represent the dominant response to work-sharing in the labor movement. To be sure, a few unions, especially in the needle and printing trades, did adopt work-sharing. But most unions opposed the idea. They pointed out that work-sharing was quite different from a reduction in working hours. The consequence of spreading the shrinking number of actual working hours over a larger number of people with no advance in the hourly wage rates was lower earnings for the employed. Moreover, with most workers already at the subsistence level, work-sharing could not increase jobs because it did not increase purchasing power. "Work-sharing," declared President A. F. Whitney of the Railroad Trainmen, "is a device which tends to remove the burden of charity from the backs of the rich by giving all workers a wage which will barely remove the need for charitable assistance."[16] Whitney explained the support for "share-the-work" by some labor leaders as a result of their naive belief that "this plan is a *bona fide* movement toward permanent shorter work hours, with the ultimate increased hourly rates of pay." But he noted that "share-the-work" had won support among many employers and the endorsement of the National Association of Manufacturers because it reduced incomes for workers enabling employers to get the same work done at a lower cost.[17]

The AFL Executive Council, meeting in Atlantic City on July 20, 1932, issued a statement indicting industry for persisting in support of work-sharing but refusing to introduce a shorter workweek. It urged President Hoover to call a conference of labor and industrial leaders to devise means looking to the early adoption of the five-day week and the six-hour day for the nation's wage earners as the basic means "of creating work opportunities for millions of idle men and women."[18] Green conveyed the Executive Council's request to Hoover in person. The president's only response was to urge the AFL to support share-the-work and the Teagle Committee.[19]

A double break with tradition came in 1932. The New York *Times* reported the first departure as follows:

> Unable to withstand the rapidly mounting tide of sentiment for compulsory unemployment insurance, evidence by a flood of communications from local unions, city central labor bodies and State Federations of Labor, the executive council of the American Federation of Labor abandoned today [May 15] its traditional opposition to the proposal, which has been denounced by labor leaders since the days of Samuel Gompers as "the dole."

Green was directed by the Executive Council to formulate a compulsory unemployment insurance plan to be enacted by Congress.[20]

The second departure took place at the AFL convention held in Cincinnati in November. After both Green and the Committee on the Shorter Workday called for the five-day week and the six-hour day with no reduction in weekly wages, the convention unanimously adopted a shorter-hours resolution that included the following language: "That we instruct our Executive Council to take all necessary steps toward having proper legislation . . . presented to the incoming session of congress."[21] In calling for the aid of the state in regulating the hours of work for men, the AFL had reversed the Gompers tradition of voluntarism.

On December 21, 1932, less than three weeks after the Cincinnati convention, Senator Hugo L. Black of Alabama introduced a simple bill for shorter hours. The measure called for a thirty-hour week as the "only practical and possible method of dealing with unemployment." It proposed to deny the channels of interstate and foreign commerce to articles produced in establishments "in which any person was employed or permitted to work more than five days in any week or more than six hours in any day."[22]

Speaking on a coast-to-coast radio hookup, Senator Black stressed that his bill could pass and called on all Americans to support it. "Hunger in the midst of plenty is the great problem," he declared, adding that the prompt enactment of his measure, which was known as the "30-Hour Work-Week Bill," would bring about the quick employment of about 6.5 million jobless Americans, and at the same time benefit legitimate industry and languishing agriculture by increasing purchasing power.[23]

Hearings on Black's bill ran from January 5 to February 11, 1933. Testifying for the bill, William Green held, "I am firmly convinced that the shorter workday and the shorter work-week must be applied generally and universally if we are to provide and create work opportunity for the millions of workmen who are idle and who are willing and anxious to work." He stated that a thirty-hour week in manufacturing industries would create jobs for 1,800,000 while a universal thirty-hour week in industry and government, except agriculture, would create 4,500,000 jobs.[24]

The belief that technological improvements were the chief cause of unemployment and that a reduction in the length of the working week was almost the only way to offset these technological displacements was common to all the labor witnesses in favor of the Black bill. Green insisted that industry had become so mechanized that it was utterly impossible to provide work opportunities for all workers. Unless the length of the working day came down, the United States would have to be prepared to maintain a permanent army of unemployed.[25]

However, labor split on the question of what wages should be paid for a thirty-hour week. One group demanded legislation that would guarantee that the same wage should be paid for thirty hours as was paid for a longer workweek. Another group only asked for a law providing a thirty-hour week. Speaking for this group, Green said:

We are dealing with a five-day work week and a six-hour day for private industry, for the purpose of taking up the slack incident to unemployment . . . our official position is that the standard rates of wages should be maintained, but pass your bill and let us handle the question of wages.[26]

Green felt that the wage for thirty hours could be made equal to the forty-eight-hour wage because the workers' efficiency would be so increased and improved that they would do practically the same amount of work. In keeping with traditional AFL policy, he opposed legislative interference with the wages of men.[27]

On the other hand, those unions which were industrial unions and which included large numbers of semiskilled and unskilled workers, favored inclusion of minimum wage provisions for all workers in the thirty-hour bill, as did some in the craft unions. Sidney Hillman testified that he favored "a minimum wage for men and women, and, of course, children," and the UMW announced it favored the Black bill with a minimum wage provision.[28] Louis Weinstock, a Communist activist in the Painters' Union and leader of the campaign for unemployment insurance legislation in the AFL, insisted in his testimony that Green did not speak for the federation's membership. The rank and file, he argued, were opposed to the thirty-hour bill unless it provided for no cut in wages and for a minimum wage. Dr. John A. Ryan, a veteran supporter of minimum wage legislation, also charged that Green spoke only for the selfish craft interests of the skilled workers: "In other words, he is more concerned with the better paid minority than with the underpaid majority."[29]

For his part, Senator Black made it clear that, although it did not include wage provisions, if his bill did not ultimately result in increasing wages, it would not serve its purpose. He argued that too much profit was going to capital and that by raising wages the bill would redress the balance between wages and profits.[30] In short, most labor groups and the sponsor of the thirty-hour bill viewed it as a plan to reduce unemployment and increase the total wage payments so that the aggregate purchasing power of the masses would be increased sufficiently to increase the demand for goods and thus start the wheels of recovery.[31]

On March 30, 1933, the Judiciary Committee reported the thirty-hour bill favorably and urged the Senate to adopt it. In its report, the committee stated that the unemployed could not be put to work without reducing hours, that this reduction had not been and could not be accomplished by voluntary action on the part of the employers, that it had not been done by state laws, and that it could not be done by the states with sufficient rapidity to meet the emergency facing millions of destitute and unemployed citizens.[32] The debate on the Senate floor was concerned chiefly with the scope of the law itself and with the question of whether or not Congress had the constitutional power to pass such a law. Many senators representing various geographical and economic regions sought to have the dominant industries of their states exempted from the bill's provisions. These related mostly to seasonal industries and to agriculture, and amendments exempting such industries were accepted.[33]

On April 6, 1933, the Senate passed the amended thirty-hour-week bill by a vote of 53 to 30. "GREAT VICTORY," exulted *Labor* as it noted:

If labor leaders of past generations would have sat in the Senate gallery last week, they would have thought themselves dreaming. When they fought for the 10-hour day and then for the eight-hour day, the whole conservative population around them blew up in their faces. Last week, Senator Black brought out his bill to restrict working time to 30 hours per week in establishments producing articles used in interstate commerce. Ten years ago, such a bill would have been smothered in committee. Last week a tremendous majority of Senators, progressives and conservatives alike, were in favor of it . . . . This marks the most amazing change in public opinion in recent American history.[34]

The bill went to the House on April 17, 1933, where Congressman William P. Connery, Jr., of Massachusetts, chairman of the Labor Committee, assured the labor movement he would push for its passage. And the thirty-hour bill did receive favorable action in the House Labor Committee which urged the House to pass the measure.[35] At this point, however, the bill met with opposition that it could not overcome.

On January 31, 1933, *Labor* had commented that "a gratifying development at the [Senate] hearings on the Black six-hour bill has been its strong advocacy by enlightened employers." But Black conceded that most of industry, led by the National Association of Manufacturers, vigorously opposed the bill as both a poor way to achieve recovery and as unconstitutional.[36] While this opposition could not effectively counter Black's argument that only by reducing the hours of work could idle hands and idle machines be put to productive use, in the House it received a tremendous boost from the newly inaugurated administration of Franklin D. Roosevelt. Roosevelt opposed the thirty-hour bill as economically unworkable and unconstitutional, and joined with big business in opposing its passage. Spokespersons for the administration, including Secretary of Labor Frances Perkins, suggested that the National Industrial Recovery Act, then pending before the special session of Congress, would reduce hours more rapidly and, in addition, would boost wages. As a result of administration pressure, the House Rules Committee buried the thirty-hour bill.[37]

In discussing the defeat of the thirty-hour bill, *Labor* took some comfort from the report making the rounds in Washington that workers were given a trade off for the defeat of the Black-Connery bill in the form of Section 7(a) of the National Industrial Recovery Act (NIRA) which declared that every industrial code must provide, among other things, that "employees shall have the right to organize and bargain collectively through representatives of their own choosing, and shall be free from interference, restraint, or coercion of employees . . . in the designation of such representatives."[38]

Although Black had been skeptical of obtaining shorter hours through the National Industrial Relations Act, which turned over the writing of codes to representatives of the industries whom he considered the chief offenders, he indicated a willingness to go along with the Roosevelt administration. Connery had hoped to substitute the thirty-hour bill for Title I of the NIRA. But when nothing came of this idea, he went along with Black. The NIRA bill was introduced in the House on May 23, 1933. It was given special order privileges, taking precedence over the thirty-hour bill. Despite lobbying by much of industry against inclusion of Section 7(a), the National Industrial Recovery Act became law on June 16, 1933, with the section included.[39]

The thirty-hour week did not entirely disappear with the defeat of the Black-Connery bill. Under the National Industrial Recovery Act, hours on public projects, commonly known as the W.P.A. (Works Progress Administration), were to be limited to thirty a week "so far as practicable and feasible."[40] In the main, however, the champions of the thirty-hour week were doomed to disappointment by the NRA codes. The codes covered 22,022,000 workers, and in general, the workweek averaged forty hours per week, but longer hours also prevailed, up to forty-eight hours. The forty-hour week was a proviso in 85 percent of the codes which covered 50 per cent of all workers. Less than forty hours a week was provided for in 7.2 percent of the codes and 12 percent of all workers were covered by these codes. More than forty hours a week was provided for in the remaining 7.3 percent of the codes, which applied to 38 percent of all workers covered.[41] The fur workers compelled employers to grant a thirty-five-hour week with no reduction in pay in the code governing their industry.[42]

On March 30, 1934, the New York *Times* reported a miners' victory as a "milestone in American labor history." That day the UMW obtained the thirty-five-hour week, along with a wage increase, for the majority of the 350,000 bituminous coal miners of the Appalachian area, thereby becoming "the first labor organization to obtain the seven-hour day and five-day week." The new pact came as a result of direct negotiations between the coal operators of Appalachia and representatives of the UMW. The victory was marked by a "wake" in the Washington hotel at which the new agreement was signed. A mock coffin, with candles burning at both ends, was set up in the hotel. An inscription on its base read: "Eight-hour day. Born April 1, 1898. Died March 26, 1934/Rest in peace."[43]

October 4, 1934, marked another milestone in American labor history. The International Union of Elevator Constructors announced it had reached an agreement with employers for a five-year contract under which the 19,000 members of the union would enjoy a thirty-hour week (five-day week, six-hour day). "This," the New York *Times* reported, "is the first major unit of the [American] Federation [of Labor] to be within sight of the goal of labor." It was especially significant, since the Union of Elevator Constructors had been chosen at the 1932 AFL Convention "to act as a spearhead in organized labor's fight for the shorter workweek."[44]

But the Union of Elevator Constructors set no real bargaining precedent, and a new effort was made to achieve a thirty-hour law at the next session of Congress. Hearings were held on three new bills which sought to have the thirty-hour week provisions incorporated into existing codes. H. R. 8492, one of these bills, provided a five-day week and a six-hour day for industry with the proviso that no person should evade these provisions by working thirty hours for one employer and then working for another. It provided further that the same wages must be paid for the thirty hours as for the hours previously worked under the codes where the hours were more than thirty.[45] Witnesses testified at the hearings that the NIRA codes had failed to reduce substantially the weekly hours of labor so that more of the unemployed could be reemployed. "We asked for the thirty-hour week in order to relieve the terrible ravages of unemployment among employees of the steel industry," witnesses for steel workers complained, "That was rejected." Once again the thirty-hour bills died in committee.[46]

In February 1935 the original Black bill, considerably revised, was also revived. The 1933 bill had provided that all employers of labor engaged in interstate commerce must work their employees not more than six hours per day, five days per week. The 1935 Black bill added to this provision one stating that the government may not purchase any supplies from manufacturers who work employees more than thirty hours a week; that contractors on public works projects may buy only from employers complying with the thirty-hour law; that the Reconstruction Finance Corporation and other government lending agencies may not make or extend loans to industries that did not obey the law; and that all NIRA codes should "be amended so as to include these provisions for a thirty-hour week and six-hour day."[47] But in April 1935 the Senate, by a vote of 56 to 21, refused to act on Black's thirty-hour bill. Black thereupon declared, "I could, of course, remind the Senate that we are still feeding 20,000,000 people, and that the only way to put them to work in private industry, seemingly, is through the adoption of shorter hours."[48]

With the AFL and many of its affiliates depending on the NIRA codes and on the possibility of the Black bill becoming law, it is perhaps not too surprising that the issue did not loom very large in the labor uprising of 1933-1934 when a wave of strikes broke out all over the country. In 1933, 1,168,000 workers went out on strike, a number far exceeding that for the combined four years of the economic crisis from 1929 until 1932. In 1934 the number of strikers rose to 1,467,000 workers.[49]

In most of these strikes the demand for shorter hours was present, but as a tangential issue, and usually took a back seat to union recognition, higher wages, or, in the case of the San Francisco general strike of 1934 where a demand was raised for a seven-hour day, to the union hiring hall. In the bloody Toledo Auto-Lite strike of 1934, shorter hours was mentioned, but the main emphasis was placed on "a general wage increase of 20 percent, recognition of the union, and seniority rights for union members."[50] Involving 450,000 textile workers, many of them women, the textile strike was the biggest strike of 1934. The strike demands included one for the thirty-hour week, but it was acknowledged that the more important issues were union recognition, wage increases, and abolition of the stretch-out system.[51]

But the situation soon changed. In May 1935, in a unanimous decision, the Supreme Court declared the National Industrial Recovery Act unconstitutional. Following the demise of the NIRA codes there was an immediate reversion in private industries to the lower wages and longer hours that prevailed before the codes were put into operation. The Bureau of Labor Statistics made a study of sixteen important industries to see what happened to wages and hours over the period of twelve months following the Schechter decision voiding the NIRA. The bureau found that in all sixteen industries weekly hours had increased substantially during the post-National Industrial Recovery Act period. In the steel industry, for example, only 3 percent of the workers had been working between forty-one and forty-eight hours a week prior to the demise of the NIRA. A year later 67 percent of the steel workers worked these hours. In the hardware industry no workers worked over 40 hours per week in May 1935; one year later 56 percent were working between forty-one and forty-eight hours per week.[52] A study by a special board of investigation set up by President Roosevelt to gather information on what had happened to wages and hours under the codes since the Supreme Court decision, reported that in hotels, restaurants and service industries generally, "the twelve hour day and seven-day week abolished in the codes, have again returned."[53]

Hardly had the ink dried on the Schechter decision before a number of unions went into action to retain the standards that were now threatened. The Amalgamated Clothing Workers of America, the International Ladies' Garment Workers' Union, and the International Fur Workers' Union called strikes to resist the lowering of wages and the increase of hours. The coal miners let it be known that they would strike if the operators increased the workweek. Surveying the situation at the end of 1936, Louis Stark of the New York *Times*, the most knowledgeable labor reporter in the field, observed:

Today there appears to be considerable industrial unrest because of the lengthening of work hours since the NRA was invalidated in May, 1935. In some industries hours are already over forty a week and instances where the extension of the work period has not been accompanied by pay increases there are serious threats of strikes.[54]

"An unusual aspect of this situation," Stark continued, "is that a large proportion of the workers affected are affiliated with unions that have membership in the Congress of Industrial Organizations (CIO), headed by John L. Lewis."[55]

A year later Lewis claimed that these unions had not only stopped the lengthening of work hours that followed the invalidation of the NIRA, but also that at least 2 million workers who had affiliated with the (CIO) since its formation in 1935 had won a shorter week. Of these nearly a million had achieved the thirty-five-or thirty-six-hour week under their agreements. He added:

What amounts to a universal maximum of forty hours a week has been secured in all industries organized by the C.I.O. A six-hour day has been won for C.I.O. members in several industries including flat glass workers and some of the rubber workers. Noteworthy reductions in working hours have been secured in the petroleum and textile dustries.[56]

The Roosevelt administration had also voiced concern over the lengthening of the workweek after the Supreme Court decision in the Schechter case. In October 1935 *Labor* reported "that the President had voiced regret that he did not get behind the Black-Connery Thirty-Hour Week Bill and push it through Congress."[57] Although no thirty-hour law was enacted during the Roosevelt administration, there was legislation that did reduce working hours. This included the Motor Carriers Act of 1935, which set the maximum hours of service of employees engaged in interstate transportation in order to insure safety of operation and equipment; the Postal Act of 1935, which fixed the hours of all postal employees except charwomen and part-time employees at forty hours per week; the National Bituminous Coal Conservation Act of 1935, which included a regulation of labor hours for coal miners; the Maritime Hours Law of 1936 which placed licensed officers, coal passers, and sailors of vessels under the Maritime Commission on a three-watch basis, or an eight-hour day in place of the previous nine-hour day. In addition, the Sugar Act of 1937 stipulated that children between fourteen and sixteen years of age must not be employed more than eight hours a day in the beet-sugar industry except where the family of the child owned the crop.

But the two leading laws passed under the New Deal after the NIRA was declared unconstitutional were the Public Contracts Act of 1936 and the Fair Labor Standards Act of 1938. Passed June 30, 1936, the Public Contracts Act, popularly known as the Walsh-Healey Act, required, among other things, that all contractors, and/or subcontractors, working for the government on contracts of $10,000 of more to establish a maximum eight-hour day, forty-hour week for their employees.[58] Section 1(c) of the act read:

> That no person employed by the contractor in the manufacture or furnishing of the materials, supplies, articles or equipment used in the performance of the contract shall be permitted to work in excess of eight hours in any one day, or in excess of 40 hours in any one week.

Employees covered by the act might be employed in excess of eight hours in any one day or in excess of forty hours in any one week, provided that such persons were paid for any such overtime work at one and one-half times the basic hourly rate or piece rate at which the employee was actually paid. Where abiding by the law would "impair operations of government business, work an injustice, or cause hardships," the secretary of labor was permitted to modify wages and hours.[59]

In the Democratic party platform on which Roosevelt ran for reelection in 1936, emphasis was placed on pledges to seek shorter hours and higher wages for all workers, especially the lower third of the working class. The overwhelming vote of confidence given Roosevelt in his reelection, in which the AFL and especially the newly organized CIO played important roles, was taken as an indication that the majority of the voters supported this objective.[60] In his annual message to Congress in January 1937, Roosevelt made no proposal in favor of wage-and-hour legislation. But in a special message to Congress on May 24, 1937, the president declared: "Legislation may, I hope, be passed at this session of Congress to help those who toil in factory and on farm. We have promised it. We cannot stand still."[61]

Still no legislation was passed. However, the recession of 1937 set in after the end of the first session of the 75th Congress, and Roosevelt, pressured by organized labor and the unemployed, and feeling the need for immediate action to halt the economic decline, called a special session of Congress to consider labor and farm legislation. In his message to the special session, Roosevelt asked a question that has lost none of its significance: "What does the country ultimately gain if we encourage businessmen to enlarge the capacity of American industry to produce, unless we see that the income of our working population actually expands to create markets to absorb that increased production?" It was high time, the president told Congress, "that we had legislation relating to goods moving in interstate commerce" that would accomplish two immediate purposes: "Banish child labor and protect workers unable to protect themselves from excessively low wages and excessively long hours."[62]

On May 24, 1937, the same day on which Roosevelt in his special message urged the passage of a wage-and-hour law, Senator Black and Representative Connery introduced bills that had been drafted by the administration. In its main features the new Black-Connery bill provided for federal regulation of minimum wages and maximum hours, the prohibition of child labor, and the elimination of certain labor practices such as the hiring of labor spies and professional strikebreakers. These latter provisions were dropped from the bills early because it was felt that a simple wage-hour law would have the most chance of passage.[63]

Actually, no firm standards were set for wages and hours in the proposed legislation. In his message to Congress on May 24, 1937, President Roosevelt lamented, "One third of our population, the overwhelming majority of which is in agriculture or industry, is ill-nourished, ill-clad, and ill-housed." To remedy this situation he urged that some means be devised to ensure "to all our able-bodied working men and women a fair day's pay for a fair day's work" through establishment of minimum wage and maximum hour standards and the elimination of child labor. There was much talk of "40 cents and 40 hours" as the "fair" standards, but the administration did not insist on these. The bill left a blank for the exact standards to be established.[64]

Three weeks of public hearings were held before the Senate Committee on Education and Labor. After leading employers and economists had voiced opposition to the bill, Senator Black read into the record the fact that in his history of regulation of hours in England, published in 1875, Dr. L. Brentano had observed that the movement "to curtail hours enjoyed the sympathy of all men except the manufacturers and political economists of that day."[65] On July 6, 1937, the Senate Committee on Education and Labor reported out favorably an amended bill which was passed by the Senate on July 31 by a vote of 56 to 28.[66] The House Committee on Labor immediately took the bill under consideration and on August 6 reported it favorably to the House. But the Rules Committee, dominated by a coalition of Southern Democrats and Northern Republicans, refused to permit the bill to be brought out onto the floor, preventing any vote before the session of Congress closed.[67]

Having placed a wage-and-hour law on his "must" legislation list, Roosevelt called a special session of Congress for November 15, 1937, and urged that the administration bill be passed. But the same process was to be repeated as had occurred in the previous session of Congress. The Rules Committee again refused to permit the bill to come to the floor of the House. In December, however, the required 218 signatures on the petition to discharge the Rules Committee from further consideration of the bill were obtained, and the measure was placed on the floor of the House for consideration. At this point, the main opposition to the bill arose from the AFL which feared that the CIO would be favored in the administration of the law. Accordingly, the bill was recommitted to committee.[68]

Ordinarily, recommittal meant death to a proposed bill, and it appeared that the bill had been killed, both for the remainder of the special session and for the regular session, which began in January 1938. But a number of important developments changed the picture. In the Democratic primary election in Alabama, a senator who had supported the measure won a decisive and symbolic victory over a prominent anti-New Dealer. Then the poll of the Institute of Public Opinion was announced, and it showed that a big majority of the voters favored the measure, and that this was true of every section of the country with the exception of the West Central, where sentiment was evenly divided. Finally, on May 3, 1938, came the victory of Senator Claude Pepper in the Democratic senatorial primary in Florida. Pepper had been an ardent supporter of the wages-and-hours bill, while his opponent had as ardently opposed it.[69] After the Florida primary a petition to discharge the Rules Committee from further consideration of the bill and to bring it out on the floor of the House obtained the needed 218 signatures in less than two and a half hours.[70]

The bill, after having been modified to meet AFL objections, passed the House on May 24, 1938, by a vote of 314 to 97. A Joint Conference Committee was then appointed to reconcile the differences between the House and Senate. On June 12 the committee presented a unanimous report, which was accepted in the House by a 291-to-89 vote, and in the Senate on a voice vote. President Roosevelt signed the Fair Labor Standards Act on June 25, 1938, and it became effective the following October 24.[71] The last significant piece of New Deal social legislation had thus been debated in Congress for more than a year, had been rewritten several times, and forced out of the Rules Committee on two occasions. But as one contemporary report noted, "organized labor's persistent campaign for this legislation, despite reactionary opposition, was finally victorious."[72]

Not that the legislation was a radical new departure. "It embodied," observes Jeremy P. Felt, "in a constitutionally successful federal statute ideas on minimum wages, maximum hours, and child labor which had been the common currency of debate among social reformers for at least thirty years."[73] The Fair Labor Standards Act provided that in employment affecting interstate commerce, workers should be paid not less than twenty-five cents per hour during the first year; thirty cents per hour during the next six years; and forty cents per hour thereafter. Less than minimum wages might be paid to learners, apprentices, messengers, or aged and physically handicapped workers. Hours of work were limited to a maximum of forty-four per week during the first year, forty-two the second year, and forty weekly thereafter except when overtime was paid for at the rate of time and one half. Higher maximum hours provided in *bona fide* collective bargaining agreements were permitted provided that no one work more than 1,000 hours in twenty-six or 2,000 hours in fifty-two consecutive weeks. In seasonal industries a twelve-hour day, fifty-six-hour week was permitted for a maximum of twelve weeks per year. Food-processing industries were exempted from hour standards for fourteen weeks per year. Wholly exempted from the provisions of the act were employees in administrative, professional, or executive work; in retail establishments; in the fishing, packing, marketing, and processing of aquatic products; seamen, transport, farm, and agricultural cannery workers; and workers engaged in making cheese and butter. Willful violations of the law were punishable by a maximum fine of $10,000 or imprisonment for six months, or both, imprisonment applying only to the second offense. In the U.S. Department of Labor the act created a Wage and Hour Division with an administrator appointed by the president.[74]

Organized labor took satisfaction in the fact that the Fair Labor Standards Act (the Wages and Hours Law as it was popularly called) applied to the largest number of workers of any federal law passed. Nevertheless, it criticized the law for fixing the initial level of the maximum weekly hours too high, for being silent on the limit for daily hours of work, for failing to provide a specific and enforceable provision to ensure that the same weekly wages were maintained when weekly hours were shortened, for vagueness of the language of section 7(b) relating to maximum hours and overtime pay, and for weaknesses in the language concerning child labor.[75]

Labor's criticism of the law was mild compared to the attack launched by employers' groups. The act was denounced by the Cotton Textile Association as not "indigenous to America," and by the National Association of Manufacturers as "a step in the direction of Communism, bolshevism, fascism, and Nazism."[76] Big business also attacked the act in the federal courts on constitutional grounds. But in two important 1941 cases the Supreme Court affirmed the constitutionality of the Fair Labor Standards Act and the machinery by which it was administered.[77]

The federal government had moved vigorously, if belatedly, into the field of hours legislation during the years from 1933 to 1938. None of the laws made up for the defeat of the Black-Connery thirty-hour week bills. But each one marked, as Elmer F. Andrews, Administrator of the Fair Labor Standards Act, put it, "another step out of the jungle."[78]

12

The Hours Stalemate since 1939

During the early years of the twentieth century, eight-hour advocates often held that the schedule they proposed was not a "recent innovation" but a return to practices which had prevailed four centuries before. Following the research of historian Thorold Rogers, they argued that until the very late Middle Ages frequent holidays and breaks made an eight-hour (or at most, nine-hour) day the European average before post-Reformation and industrial capitalist forces combined to lengthen the working day. Though a comforting thought insofar as it helped establish eight hours as a traditional and "natural" shift, such a long view was also unsettling in that nearly half a millennium had yielded little progress and perhaps even regression. After 1938 those who accepted Rogers's view needed not to have been so disconcerted. The Fair Labor Standards Act of that year made the eight-hour day and forty-hour week the law of the land beginning October 24, 1940. But today the observer of long-term trends who accepted the reality of an eight-hour day in 1500 would again be troubled by lack of progress in shortening the length of labor. Not only, according to such a view, would it have taken four centuries to regain the eight-hour day, but also, in nearly a half-century since 1938, there has been little or no increase in leisure.[1]

Although the picture is complicated by to postwar trends toward earlier retirement, longer vacations, overtime patterns, and a host of other factors, there is no question that the increase in leisure time has slowed greatly in the last 45 years; there is a serious possibility that negligible or negative changes in the amount of free time available to American workers have occurred. Bureau of Labor Statistics figures show a drop in average weekly working hours from 40.4 in 1947 to 40.2 in 1949, for example, but a comparison of 1949 and 1978 shows a 1.3 hour *increase* in average weekly working time.[2] John D. Owen's studies, which adjust basic weekly hours to account for increased holidays and vacations, demonstrate "no net change" of consequence for the 1948-1975 period. In 1976 Owen observed that, had historical trends from the pre-World War II period continued, the working week would have been more than half a day less than it actually was. The workweek, according to Owen, declined "from 58.4 hours per week in 1901 to 42.0 hours in 1948." It experienced "little or no change since."

Peter Henle's somewhat earlier research revealed that the proportion of full-time, nonagricultural workers, waged and salaried, who labored forty-nine or more hours weekly *rose* from 12.9 percent in 1948 to 18.2 percent in 1965.[3] A *Special Labor Force Report* treating May 1973 and May 1974 found over 16 million Americans working over forty hours per week during both months and noted that half of these workers received no premium overtime pay. Between 1956 and 1978 about one worker in twenty also "moonlighted" in a second job, with the rate staying relatively constant.[4]

Moreover, the trend toward earlier retirement has been offset by increased female participation in the labor force, especially by married women. In 1900 about 12 percent of an average woman's life (in years) was spent in marketed labor. By 1970 that figure was 31 percent. This more than compensates for a decrease among men, whose work years represented 67 percent of their life expectancy on the average in 1900 and 60 percent in 1970. In terms of hours of paid labor for total hours of life of the entire population, the ratio remained nearly constant from 1900 to 1948 and has since *increased* significantly.[5] The recent work of Ivan Illich argues that this trend in female labor, combined with increased consumption of time in socially necessary activities not remunerated by wages (for example, shopping, waiting in lines, getting to work, filling out forms) translates into a society of lessening leisure.[6]

Meanwhile, forty hours appear to have become almost sacrosanct as a lower limit for the workweek. Most plans to readjust hours ask, "How many days make a workweek?" while assuming a forty-*hour* standard. "Flexitime" schedules, options allowing some employee decision making about when to work, join plans for four-day weeks in assuming that innovations ought not challenge the established parameters for the number of hours in a week's work.[7] Trade unions have generally opted for what Juanita Kreps called "lumps of leisure" —in the form of added vacations, three-day weekends, and earlier retirement —rather than agitating against the forty-hour week, let alone the eight-hour day.[8] Perhaps the best index of the ebb of labor efforts in this area comes when newscasters tell of declines in the average workweek. The changes are not labor news but "economic indicators." Dips in the number of hours are seen not as labor victories but as omens of a deteriorating economy.[9]

Benjamin Kline Hunnicutt's valuable study of recent changes in the workweek is thus significantly titled: "The End of Shorter Hours." It proclaims, and with some reason, that the "shorter-hour movement stopped after the Depression."[10] This chapter argues that the picture of shorter-hours progress since 1938 is not so unrelievedly bleak as Hunnicutt's provocative work implies, and that the prospects for future gains are not bleak at all. Nonetheless, Hunnicutt and others are right in pointing to a marked decline in the struggle to reduce hours. In examining why the shorter-hours movement has been so long moribund, and then in arguing that it has still not died, this chapter proceeds chronologically. But it also lingers over points that help account for the paucity of postwar progress—the legacy of depression and war, the demography of the postwar working class, labor law, alienated leisure, alienated work, the purging of union radicals, consumerism, and the strategies of labor's leadership.

During the months between the 1938 passage of the Fair Labor Standards Act and the December 1941 entry of the United States into World War II, there was substantial headway in reducing hours. Not only did the forty-hour provision of the Fair Labor Standards Act give about 2 million workers that schedule when it took effect on October 24, 1940, but many unions fought for and won weeks of below forty hours. In particular, the hours issue continued to be a rallying point for AFL militancy during a period in which that organization opposed CIO organizing efforts. Craft union leaders, especially those of the carpenters, photo-engravers, electrical workers, and others in the building trades, legitimated themselves to their memberships by extending reductions in the working day, even as they mounted a destructive campaign against the CIO as a "Communist" organization. The October 1938 *Carpenter*, for example, counted seven cities, mainly in the Northwest, with contracts for six-hour days; eight more, including New York City, reported a seven-hour standard. The *American Photo-Engraver* listed Youngstown, Akron, Philadelphia, Chicago, Rochester, Washington, D.C., Davenport, Rock Island, New York City, Boston, Cleveland, Providence, Baltimore, Detroit, and San Diego as sites of 37 1/2-hour or thirty-five-hour week successes in 1939 and 1940.[11] The AFL consistently "reaffirmed its endorsement of the six-hour work day without any reduction in . . . pay" and argued that both cyclically and technologically-caused unemployment necessitated such a change. At its 1940 convention, the AFL even entertained, and referred to the Executive Council, a six-hour shift resolution applying to defense industries. In 1940, despite large increases of hours in the defense sector, and decreases in part-time employment, no appreciable rise in average working hours occurred.[12]

However, with U.S. entry into the war, labor's position became more defensive where the working day was concerned. Pearl Harbor had hardly been bombed before many industrialists launched a drive to abandon the forty-hour week. Linking the fall of France to the shortening of working hours there, World War I aviation hero Captain Eddie Rickenbacker, by the second war an aviation executive, toured the nation speaking against forty hours. Senator Harry F. Byrd of Virginia even held, in late 1942, that shorter hours had contributed to American military defeats. This came despite a 1942 rise in the average workweek in manufacturing industries from 40.6 to 43.1 hours, the second biggest annual increase in the twentieth century. Indeed, by February 1942, more than half of all war materiel plants worked over 48 hours weekly; in machine shops, the average was fifty-five hours, with seventy hours per worker per week not uncommon. Nor did the fact that the workweek rose by 7.1 hours in manufacturing industries between 1940 and 1944 disarm labor's critics. Similarly, although women war plant workers normally worked forty-eight-hour weekly schedules by 1942, protective legislation governing the schedules of females came under attack.[13]

Confronting this campaign and supporting a war more prolonged and more noble in its aims than World War I, labor made concessions regarding the working day. Early in the war, for example, double time for Sunday and holiday work came to be abandoned in most industries, often with union consent, upon a request from War Production Board Chairman Donald M. Nelson. In some instances AFL unions were more zealous in defending hours standards than their CIO counterparts. In the auto industry, for example, the UAW leadership moved forcefully to end overtime premiums and subsequently lost a series of representation elections to the AFL's International Association of Machinists over the premium pay issue.[14] In its conventions the AFL was more active than the CIO in pillorying "anti-labor interests seeking to abolish the forty-hour week," and more persistent in raising thirty hours as an ultimate goal. The AFL, joined by the railway labor paper, *Labor*, also insisted early in the war that overtime not be greatly increased while large numbers of Americans remained out of work. In no case, according to the AFL, was a workweek of more than forty-eight hours efficient. In particular, the AFL protested, at its 1942 convention, against war production plants which "even at this late hour are not operating . . . around the clock" but which instead depended "on overtime work . . . long hours per day and sometimes 7 days per week."[15]

The wartime issues of wages and hours proved inseparable, much to the detriment of any campaign to reduce the latter. The Roosevelt administration applied the "Little Steel Formula" after July 16, 1942, in computing wage increases permissible in War Labor Board decisions. It also increasingly limited the board's power to correct wage inequalities by granting pay boosts. Since the labor movement argued that the Little Steel guidelines did not nearly permit wages to keep pace with prices, let alone with profits, both the AFL and CIO had serious wage grievances during the war.[16] An administration policy which partly compensated for conservative wage guidelines was to increase hours. After brief defenses of the eight-hour day, and of no more than eight hours overtime weekly, by a host of government agencies in 1942, Roosevelt instituted a *minimum* forty-eight-hour workweek with Executive Order No. 9301 on February 9, 1943. The order, applying wherever the War Manpower Commission deemed it necessary, came just a day after an extremely unfavorable wage decision in the "Big Four" meatpacking cases. The forty-eight-hour decree, *Monthly Labor Review* promised, "is expected to result in substantial increases in the weekly earnings of a large number of workers."[17] With the overtime provision of the Fair Labor Standards Act intact, unions generally did not oppose the fourty-eight-hour order, though many employers, reluctant to pay overtime premiums and to yield control over scheduling, did offer opposition. *Labor* noted that corporate leaders had "CRIED FOR LONG HOURS AND CONTINUED TO YELL WHEN THEY GOT THEM."[18]

Just as extra work smoothed over wage problems for the unions supporting a no-strike pledge and government-industry-labor cooperation during the war, it ultimately helped to do so also for John L. Lewis and the UMW who challenged the terms of that cooperation. Lewis's long, controversial, and finally successful campaign to secure wage increases for miners in excess of the Little Steel guidelines generated a series of work stoppages and truces between January and November 1943. The UMW began with a thirty-five-hour workweek as part of its negotiating package but eventually accepted slight increases in working time as part of a War Labor Board decision granting a 21 percent pay boost.[19]

Besides contributing to a tendency to sacrifice shorter hours for overtime pay, the war had two other effects on the movement to reduce the hours of labor. The less important of these was to remultiply the tremendous volume of litigation and hearings stemming from the Fair Labor Standards Act, particularly from employer attempts to evade the hours and overtime provisions of that law. The war witnessed a vigorous and mostly successful drive by employers to exclude canneries from the Fair Labor Standards Act. It saw also the major judicial defeat for labor in *Walling v. A.H. Belo Corporation*, a Supreme Court decision on the law's overtime provisions, an unfavorable executive order on premium pay, and a morass of War Labor Board hearings and decisions, often productive of contradictory precedents regarding hours and overtime. After the war the Labor Board would lapse, but the great volume of complex litigation would not.[20]

The final important impact of the war, and of the period of relatively full employment under a no-strike pledge concommitant with it, was to encourage informal, extra-union protests against long hours and forced overtime. Such protests included slowdowns, wildcat strikes, absenteeism, and high turnover. Women workers, burdened with household as well as wage labor, and poorly supported by social services, proved especially likely to quit jobs and to take time off from six-day weeks. One study concluded that, in Detroit alone, as many as 100,000 worker/hours per month were lost to the necessity of women workers staying home to do laundry. Turnover was great among both sexes, especially before War Manpower Commission curbs on job changes began in September 1943.[21] Some will find in the many wartime quits, absences, and wildcats, evidence of a working-class assertiveness against overwork even when formal channels of protest are blocked or when workers do not wish to undertake formal protests. Others will note that such informal and individual styles of opposition to long hours, strengthened by the war and strong since, have not succeeded in reducing the length of the working day.

With the close of the war, fears of massive unemployment as troops returned gave urgency to shorter hours arguments. Again it was the AFL which responded with particular energy. At its 1944 convention the AFL called for enactment of a six-hour day, thirty-hour week law to take effect "immediately upon the cessation of the fighting." On September 30, 1946, the AFL's weekly news service proclaimed, "The forty-hour week, once labor's proudest boast, is doomed to be discarded within the foreseeable future. The thirty-hour week is bound to come."[22] The CIO did not include shorter hours in its "Re-employment Plan" of 1944, or in resolutions thereafter, but confined itself to calls for elimination of overtime and for longer vacations and more holidays. Nonetheless, important CIO unions, including the United Auto Workers (UAW) and the United Steel Workers (USW), resolved in favor of "30 for 40" (a thirty-hour week for forty hours' pay) between 1943 and 1947.[23]

The AFL, UAW, and USW all kept their shorter-hours commitments largely confined to paper, however. For the craft unionists in the AFL, the reduction of hours demand found justification almost entirely on the grounds of spreading work. When high unemployment did not occur after the war, the shorter work-week campaign in the AFL lost steam. After interest in the demand revived amidst signs of economic slowdown in 1948 and 1949, the AFL's Committee on a Shorter Work Day acknowledged that its work had lapsed during the previous years.[24] For the top leadership in auto and steel, shorter hours was a distant goal. The guaranteed annual wage and alliances with liberal Democrats in support of Keynesian economic policies were much preferred as antirecession, antiunemployment measures by the UAW and USW leaders. So committed was the UAW's Walter Reuther to these priorities that he often attacked "30 for 40" as an ill-timed and even subversive demand in the early and middle 1950s.[25] The logic of the labor/liberal Democrat coalition was best displayed in the lobbying to pass the Full Employment Act of 1946. Both labor leaders and the Democrats agreed then that fiscal policy, military spending, and overseas expansion of markets, not trade union action or legislation for less hours, would be used to fulfill the goals of the law.[26]

The decision of union leaders to concentrate on issues other than the reduction of hours reflected the demands of the rank and file to some extent, though the question is by no means a simple one. The great postwar labor initiatives for "rounds" of wage increases, in industry after industry through 1949—and especially in the huge and extended strike wave of 1945 and 1946—expressed pent-up consumer demands, deferred through depression and war. For many workers shorter hours may have suffered by association with the poorly remunerated work-sharing years of the 1930s. Returning veterans—marrying, buying homes on credit and starting families—needed wages. They continued to do so during the "baby boom" of the postwar years. Prosperity and consumer credit also made it possible for workers to buy leisure goods, such as cabins, fishing boats, outboards, and skis, better used in large "lumps of leisure" such as vacations and holidays. More wages made for more such purchases. The tasks of home maintenance also made vacations (which had grown to effect 85 percent of all workers covered in collective bargaining agreements by 1944 after covering just one in four in 1940) an appealing option.[27]

Nonetheless, it will not do to portray American workers as driven by demography and pent-up demand or as seduced by consumer-oriented leisure in explaining the decline of postwar shorter hours activity. As sociologist Alvin Gouldner emphasized at the time and as historian George Lipsitz has recently reiterated, control and dignity were often important issues even in strikes ostensibly fought over wages.[28] Moreover, despite blowing hot and cold by the major unions, the immediate postwar years did witness some substantial progress in reducing the workweek, at the very time when we might expect wage consciousness to have been at its zenith. Between 1948 and 1957 the proportion of full-time wage and salaried workers laboring less than forty hours weekly rose from 4.8 percent to 7.5 percent while that of those working more than forty hours plummeted from 43.4 percent to 33.1 percent.[29] Some of the most important challenges to government wage-price policies during reconversion involved the hours of labor.

Among the industrial unions, the mine and rubber workers blazed trails where the workweek was concerned. Lewis led the miners, in anthracite and bituminous fields, in a series of strikes and negotiations in 1945 and 1946. These conflicts featured a government takeover and operation of mines in the bituminous fields beginning on May 22, 1946, and then sharp conflict between Lewis and the government over wages and work rules. The result of these mine battles was a succession of contracts preserving the prewar standard of a basic seven-hour day with wage increases in part provided by full "portal-to-portal" pay.[30] Rubber workers at the Goodyear and Firestone plants in Akron struck in September 1945 to regain the six-hour day (with a six-day week) which had prevailed before the war. Some Detroit rubber factories and a few in Los Angeles also adopted that schedule.[31]

Several industrial unions feared that large amounts of overtime obscured poor basic wage rates and therefore called for "40 for 48" or some variation of that demand, seeking a return to the actual forty-hour week at wages equal to the then-current weekly rates. This was a bargaining position of the National Federation of Telephone Workers (later to evolve into the Communications Workers of America) in December 1945 and was proposed by a conference of UAW local officers representing 400,000 members in June 1945. The Oil Workers' International Union fought for a "52 for 40" plank in a huge strike beginning in September 1945 and secured wage boosts despite government seizure and reopening of refineries.[32] The UMW's 1946 bituminous strike tried, but failed, to reduce the actual nine-hour day. In 1947 the UMW did secure a normal eight-hour day in the bituminous fields, but at the cost of having overtime computed on the basis of a forty-hour (not 35) week. President Harry Truman's Executive Order 9651, issued on October 30, 1945, specifically opposed "40 for 48" and in the auto, coal, and other negotiations after the war, and the president adhered to that opposition.[33]

Among the craft unions, the most active advocates of reductions below forty hours weekly were in the printing trades. In 1946 the Amalgamated Lithographers of America (ALA) Local One in New York negotiated for a thirty-five-hour week with two weeks vacation annually and won a 36 1/4-hour schedule without a strike, despite withholding of support by the international union. Thereafter, the less-than-forty-hour week spread rapidly among lithographers. After a breakthrough in Chicago in 1953, the national trend was toward a thirty-five-hour week for lithographers. Such a standard applied to 85 percent of ALA members by 1957.[34] Chicago was likewise the pacesetter in the International Typographical Union's postwar fight for shorter hours. The printers stressed not just the creation of jobs but also health when arguing for reductions in the workweek. In October 1945, 3,000 of the union's job printers in Chicago struck for three weeks and gained a 36 1/4-hour week, setting a precedent for similar gains by over 100,000 print workers over the next few months. By 1956 the printing trades outdistanced all other segments of American labor in their proportion of workers on normal schedules of less than forty hours weekly.[35]

Most productive of shorter-hours progress, and of rancor from the Truman administration, in the immediate postwar years were a series of strikes and threatened strikes in the transportation industry, particularly among rail and maritime workers. In the "wages and rules" campaigns, undertaken by twenty railway unions in 1945 and continuing through 1949, among the most vital of the rules disputes were those over the working day. Shop craftsmen in seven unions joined railroad dispatchers in agitating for a 36-hour week in 1945. Other unions, such as that of the trainmen, fought for complex hours and overtime demands, usually centering on making the five-day, forty-hour week apply throughout the railroad industry. The Brotherhood of Railway Signalmen's postwar demands included "40 for 48."[36]

In May 1946 all but two of the rail unions agreed to defer to Truman and drop rules demands while submitting wage issues to arbitration. When the defiant Trainmen and Engineers tested the President with a May 23, 1946, strike, the former union specifically cited hours grievances as causing the walkout. Truman broke the strike by appealing to Congress for a law granting him the power to fire and draft strikers in a "national emergency." The two striking unions had to give up the rule changes they had sought when they were forced to return to work. A. F. Whitney, head of the trainmen, continually protested against Truman's intervention and defended proposed rule changes shortening the working day. He met with some success in such rules negotiations by November 1947.[37]

Among the many railway unionists not involved in actual operation of the trains, the forty-hour week had not yet been achieved. Telegraphers still regularly worked seven-day weeks. On May 30, 1945, their leader, V. O. Gardner, left negotiations with employers pledging "We'll not take less," than reduction to a six-day week. By July 18, 1945, the telegraphers had made this basic reform a reality through most of the industry, though five railway carriers held out for a time thereafter.[38]

From May through July 1948, as the U.S. Army ran railroads seized in the face of a "wages and rules" strike threat by engineers, firemen, and switchmen, the sixteen railway unions representing nonoperating rail employees came together in a campaign which the *Railway Clerk* was later to praise as leading to "the most notable advance made in many years" in wages and working conditions. The unions demanded "48 for 40," overtime pay on Saturdays and Sundays, and wage increases. When a September 8 to 17, 1948, conference failed to settle the disputes between the carriers and nonoperating unions, a strike vote was slated for September 18. It passed overwhelmingly but negotiations continued until October 13. Truman appointed an Emergency Board as a strike loomed. The board's recommendations, given to Truman on December 17, 1948, gave the unions "48 for 40" and an additional hourly pay raise of seven cents. After further delays, an agreement based on the board's recommendations was signed on March 19, 1949. The head of the Brotherhood of Maintenance of Way Employees termed the pact the second "revolutionary change" in railroad labor relations, ranking its forty-hour week provision with the achievement of the eight-hour day four decades before.[39]

Strikes and cooperation among unions also brought changes in the workweek in the maritime industry. An October 1945 strike by New York longshoremen, submitted to arbitration after eight days, resulted in a decrease of weekly hours from forty-four to forty, a 20 percent pay boost and a week of paid vacation annually. The Great Lakes strike among National Maritime Union seamen in August 1946 demanded shorter hours and won a forty-eight-hour week at sea, and forty-four in port. In May 1946 seven maritime unions began cooperation under CIO auspices in the Committee for Maritime Unity (CMU), which called for a forty-hour week at sea as one of its major goals. A month later, with most offshore vessels still under federal control and with the CMU threatening a June 15 strike, Truman made plans to use the armed forces to break any such work stoppage. On June 14 the various unions involved settled without a strike. In addition to wage gains, licensed seamen and radio operators won a basic forty-eight-hour week at sea and forty in port, decreases of eight and four hours respectively. Engineers secured a forty-hour week in port and overtime for Sunday work. After several wage strikes in early September 1946 licensed deck officers and engine officers struck for shorter hours, more pay, and union security on September 30. That strike, supported by the International Longshoremen's and Warehousemen's Union, won a forty-eight-hour week and a 15 percent pay increase.[40]

The impetus for shorter hours action did not quickly dissipate after the war. In 1953 and 1954, for example, UAW-GM Sub-Council No. 7, Ford Local 600, Flint Chevrolet Local 659, the CIO state convention in California, the Pennsylvania CIO, and the CIO's textile, packinghouse, clothing, and woodworkers' unions all adopted shorter-workweek resolutions, mostly of the "30 for 40" variety. By the time the merged AFL-CIO held its Conference on Shorter Hours of Work in September 1956, the International Ladies' Garment Workers' Union had won a thirty-five-hour week, as had bakers in San Francisco, Los Angeles,

San Diego, Seattle, and other West Coast cities. Nearly a third of all American Newspaper Guild members had a thirty-five-hour week and almost half of organized brewery workers were on a 37 1/2-hour weekly schedule. About one building tradesman in eight had a seven-hour day and a large proportion of office and municipal employees had less than forty hour workweeks. For segments of the labor force in iron and steel forging, a thirty-hour week was obtained, as it was for some union plasterers.[41]

The progress of the shorter-hours movement between 1945 and 1956 was not great by comparison to pre-World War II standards, but it was substantial by comparison to the stasis and retreat of the post-1956 years. In accounting for the limits of this mixed postwar success, more than the attitudes of union leaders and rank-and-file workers deserve mention. Other factors, particularly what David Ziskind has called the "countermarch of labor legislation," in the postwar years and the rise of intense anti-Communism also merit emphasis.[42]

Changes in the Fair Labor Standards Act and in the National Labor Relations (Wagner) Act in 1947 badly hurt labor efforts for shorter hours. The alteration of the former law came with the passage of the Portal-to-Portal Act. In June 1946 the Supreme Court decreed, in the Mount Clemens Pottery Company Case, that employees could sue for recovery of back pay for time spent walking to the job on plant premises and spend in preliminary activities "such as putting on aprons and overalls, removing shirts, taping or greasing arms, putting on finger cots, preparing equipment," and so on. By January 1947, workers had won nearly $6 billion in over 1,500 such cases with 398 cases still outstanding. The cases came at a time when many unions were agitating for full portal-to-portal pay and appeared to be an important labor victory. However, congressional reaction to the Supreme Court's decision produced the Portal-to-Portal Act in 1947, a law which forbade compensation on claims not based on contracts for the period before May 14, 1947, permitted compromises on compensation due, and set a two-year statute of limitations on claims. The act also provided that employers could escape liability for past *or future* offenses if they could show they acted "in good faith" or "in reliance on" a government administrator's guidelines. As Department of Labor officials Harry Weiss and Robert Gronewald observed, the act institutionalized a significant "loosening of standards" for the measurement of working hours.[43]

Far more damaging than the Portal-to-Portal Act, though less direct in its impact upon the working day, was the Taft-Hartley revision of the National Labor Relations Act. Passed over a Truman veto on June 23, 1947, Taft-Hartley represented the triumph of big and small business and manufacturing interests attempting to blunt labor militancy. The Taft-Hartley amendments, though they reflected previous precedents in labor law and National Labor Relations Board (NLRB) practice, constitute the most important piece of antilabor legislation in U.S. history.[44] Taft-Hartley's provisions included the outlawing of secondary boycotts and jurisdictional strikes and the granting to employers of the right to sue when such actions did occur. The law outlawed the closed shop and gave state legislatures the right to ban the union shop. It set into motion a series of legal decisions circumscribing sympathy strikes, setting severe limits on a tactic that had historically been most significant in extending shorter hours protest. (Ironically, the Fair Labor Standards Act, a far more positive piece of labor legislation, had earlier limited the number of organizational strikes for shorter hours by providing the forty-hour week in many unorganized workplaces.) Taft-Hartley limited picketing rights. It gave the president the power to declare that a strike will "imperil national health or safety," then to appoint a fact-finding board, and to institute a sixty-day "cooling-off" period during which strikers would be forced to return to work and during which the NLRB would supervise a referendum on the employer's last offer. The law forbade unions from proceeding in unfair labor practice cases unless their officers and the "officers of any national or international labor organization of which it is an affiliate or constituent unit" filed affidavits certifying that they were not associated with the Communist party. It declared illegal, and specified stiff penalties for, strikes by public employees. Labor lawyer and historian Staughton Lynd's comment on one provision of Taft-Hartley, that its "thrust . . . is to outlaw working class solidarity," applied well to the whole act. Taft-Hartley made effective trade union activity, and thus also shorter-hours initiatives, far more difficult.[45]

Indeed, perhaps the least appreciated part of Taft-Hartley, a section in Title 3 of the law, contributed most to the decline of protest over the length of labor. That section facilitated the legal enforcement of collective bargaining agreements by making unions liable for violations. It codified the employer's decisive remedy for wildcat strikes and slowdowns through lawsuits against the entire union. This effective attack on informal protests over conditions encouraged shop stewards and paid union officials to participate in causing rank-and-file workers to accept what David Brody has called the "workplace rule of law." It reinforced wartime tendencies among workers to see unions as cooperating with management in maintaining shopfloor discipline and solidified the accompanying tendencies to not press control issues or to press them outside of union channels.[46]

This weakening and reorienting of control struggles had an effect on the quality of leisure. Studies from the 1950s and early 1960s, though tending to blame "mass culture" for what was perceived as an increasingly debased and conformist life off the job among most Americans, occasionally illuminated the relationship between unfulfilling work and unsatisfying play. Sociologist David Riesman's preface to the 1961 edition of *The Lonely Crowd*, for example, corrected the emphasis of the original edition of that classic study by castigating "the burden put on leisure by the disintegration of work." Riesman added, "leisure itself cannot rescue work, but fails with it, and can only be meaningful for most men if work is meaningful." Empirical research meanwhile showed those with the most decision-making opportunities on the job to be the best able to use time away from the job. A few critics, most notably Herbert Marcuse, joined Riesman in affirming what we could have learned from the history of hours struggles in the early twentieth century: that is, the treasuring of leisure best coexists with the treasuring of meaningful work.[47] With Taft-Hartley limiting control initiatives on the job, and with much of the labor movement holding the position it first articulated in the 1920s—that shorter hours could be won by trading off control prerogatives—the movement for leisure withered.[48] Leisure came to be viewed, by social critics from both the left and right, as a "problem." A 1963 Gallup Poll which found just 42 percent of union members in favor of a thirty-five-hour workweek suggests that many workers may have shared the critics' views.[49]

The most serious consequences for the shorter-hours movement stemming from the Cold War and from the expulsion of the Communist-influenced unions from the CIO in 1949 and 1950 were indirect ones. If the Communist-influenced unionists and unions displayed more concern with the working day in the immediate postwar period than did non-and anti-Communists in the unions, the differences were less than dramatic. Communist influence in some of the maritime unions, especially the International Longshoremen's and Warehousemen's Union (ILWU), coincided with emphasis on achieving shorter hours but opponents of the Communists also stressed that issue. Harry Bridges, the ILWU head indicted in 1949 for swearing in a naturalization affidavit that he was not a Communist, was a staunch opponent of overtime work and, in 1959 and 1960, negotiated a widely publicized West Coast longshore agreement providing a guaranteed thirty-five-hour week and lowering retirement from sixty-five to sixty-two. The left-led Food, Tobacco, Agricultural and Allied Workers' Union gained a forty-hour week (down from fifty) for Reynolds Tobacco Company workers in Winston-Salem between 1943 and 1947 before falling victim to redbaiting and racebaiting. The United Electrical Workers also vigorously agitated for a shorter workweek.[50] However, on the whole, Communist-influenced trade union leaders, like their adversaries in the unions, emphasized wages and, to a lesser extent, vacations after the war. At times, the Communists' antiracist emphasis even put them in a position of having to warn against viewing a thirty-hour week as a panacea. For example, in 1950 Hal Simon wrote in the Communist journal *Political Affairs*, "The general struggle for jobs for workers as a whole should not be permitted to submerge the special struggle for jobs that must be conducted in relation to Negro workers." He added, "The achievement of the thirty-hour week will not end discrimination."[51]

But anticommunism must nonetheless be counted as a factor of importance in any weighing of the reasons for the limited progress of the postwar shorter-hours movement. Redbaiting contributed, of course, to the passage of Taft-Hartley; it decimated union membership, particularly CIO membership; it dissipated organizing energies in raids and jurisdictional battles; it helped to cause the failure of the Operation Dixie campaign to organize the South after the war; and it stalled white-collar organization. In short, it weakened the labor movement as a whole.[52]

Where hours were more specifically concerned, anticommunism split trade unions, especially in the maritime industry, at a critical time in struggles over the workweek. Furthermore, Communists in many localities and industries resisted labor-management cooperation and, in shopfloor struggles, defended workers' rights on day-to-day control issues. Their removal helped to solidify among workers the idea that the pursuit of dignity and control on the job would take place largely outside union channels. Moreover, unions repeatedly connected their acceptance of long hours with Cold War preparedness, as *The Machinist* did in 1957 when it headlined the question: "Will Soviets Cut THEIR Overtime?"[53]

The 1955 reunification of the labor movement promised, with the formation of the AFL-CIO, a renewal of labor strength and trade union unity and thus greater possibiliites for the reduction of working hours. Indeed on September 11, 1956, George Meany convened the merged organization's Conference on Shorter Hours of Work with a sense of history and of hope. "It is significant," he said, "that this is the first conference on a collective bargaining subject to be held under the auspices of the AFL-CIO."[54]

But if Meany's hardhitting opening address, and the very existence of the conference, suggested major AFL-CIO initiatives to come, the actual proceedings of the 1956 meeting showed deep division in the labor movement regarding the hours of work, and presaged the unsteady, start-and-stop course of future AFL-CIO actions. George Brooks, the research director of the Pulp, Sulphite, and Paper Mill Union, followed Meany to the rostrum, ostensibly to provide historical background regarding the working day. But Brooks also treated the present, holding that the "evidence is all on the other side" from the contention that American workers wanted shorter hours. "Workers," according to Brooks, "are eager to increase their income, not to work fewer hours." The conference, Brooks maintained, needed to avoid "any ethical judgments about the morality or desirability of shorter hours." Brooks added that, in any case, reduction of hours would not effectively control mass unemployment.[55] Of the sixteen union officials commenting on Brooks's speech, only a handful questioned his conclusions regarding "overtime hunger," the preference among workers for wages rather than leisure and the inefficacy of work-sharing as an unemployment cure.[56] Other speakers complained (with, as Sylvia Gottlieb of the Communications Workers of America keenly observed, little evidence beyond allegations) that a six-hour day merely fueled moonlighting. Otto Pragan of the International Chemical Workers' Union held that "labor productivity has lost its importance as an argument for shortening the hours of work."[57] A corporate spokesperson might easily have pirated much of the proceedings to show labor denying in turn the major reasons for a shorter workweek.

Two penetrating conference comments cut to the core of AFL-CIO problems in developing an hour strategy. Pragan pointed out that the movement to reduce hours below forty did not enjoy the support from reformers nor the union solidarity which earlier campaigns for a shorter day had elicited:

> The movement for the eight-hour day was a social movement spear-
> headed by the whole labor movement and the liberal forces in the United
> States. The movement was based on economic as well as moral grounds.
> Today the drive for shorter hours is not a nationwide movement . . . .
> Changing the standard . . . workweek is [an economic] problem in a few
> selected industries.

Pragan might have added that, in contrast to the eight-hour campaigns of the
World War I era, few reform economists and even fewer employers were willing
to vouch for the efficiency of further shortening hours.[58]

Moreover, having lost its emphasis on "moral" (let alone, class-conscious) reasons to reduce hours, the labor movement rested its shorter-week case on two
props which, as UAW speaker Nat Weinberg's shrewd comments made clear,
did not always stand well together. That is, the arguments that shorter hours led
to increased productivity and to decreased unemployment caused a quandary in
which, according to Weinberg, "We can contradict ourselves," because high productivity would erode the job-producing aspects of shorter hours. Weinberg advocated large cuts in the workweek, "to offset . . . the potential advanced in productivity that will flow not only from normal technological innovations but also . . .
from the impact of the reduction of the workweek itself." But almost all the
other speakers predicted slow reform at best.[59]

Such slow projected changes created yet another problem in hours strategy. If
only fifteen or thirty minutes per day could be cut for working time, how should
such reductions be packaged? To add to breaks or lunch hours did not reduce
the time required in a shift. To make a small cut every day might hardly seem
worthwhile, especially since travel and preparation time remained the same. A
four-day week of eight-hour days was thought to be practically precluded. But a
four-and-a-half-day week was probably not efficient. To work four days of
nine-or nine-plus hours violated long insistence on the eight-hour day. The result
was further union emphasis on vacations and, for a time, even the sabbatical
leave, as the most practical ways to accumulate and apportion small doses of
leisure.[60]

Given these problems, it is not surprising that in his 1957 keynote address to
the AFL-CIO convention Meany ignored shorter hours. Indeed the pattern suggested by the 1956 conference and the lack of followup at the 1957 convention
became the hallmark of trade union action and inaction on the working day. It
was not a useful strategy, this blowing hot and not at all on the hours issue.
Between 1957 and 1978 the proportion of workers putting in fewer than forty
hours per week increased only from 7.5 percent to 9.4 percent; meanwhile, those
working 49 or more hours rose from 14.3 percent to 20.6 percent of all full-time
wage and salaried workers.[61] Such figures, dismal as they are, do not reflect
union inattention to the reduction of hours, but rather ineffective, episodic
attention.

The AFL-CIO felt increasing pressure from its constituent unions for shorter-hours action in the late 1950s. In 1957 the machinists and the International Union of Electrical Workers called for a shorter workweek. Walter Reuther of the UAW, though subordinating the issue to a guaranteed annual wage, advocated a four-day week. David McDonald, leader of the steel workers, proposed either a four-day week or a three-to-four month sabbatical every five years, and his union went into its 1959 bargaining session with the shorter workweek as a central demand.[62]

Although the tendency was to drop these demands in bargaining, the AFL-CIO took note of interest in them, especially in periods of higher-than-usual unemployment. In 1959 the AFL-CIO convention heard thirty-five-hour week proposals (30 hours having been dropped) from the International Jewelry Workers' Union, the New York AFL-CIO, and the Metal Trades Department, and resolved to press for such a reform through "public education and an active militant collective bargaining program." Two years later Reuther himself introduced a resolution for "Creating Job Opportunities by Reducing Work Time." After noting that International Brotherhood of Electrical Workers (IBEW) Local 3 in New York City had demanded a four-hour day and that Meany's Plumbers' Union worked a six-hour schedule, the convention linked shorter hours with a forthcoming conference on unemployment. The 1963 convention reaffirmed an AFL-CIO goal to amend the Fair Labor Standards Act "to provide for a standard thirty-five-hour workweek without reduction in take-home pay" and heard nine shorter-workweek resolutions.[63]

These resolutions produced few concrete results. Although McDonald pressured John F. Kennedy to declare that he favored a thirty-two-hour workweek during the 1960 election, he later recalled that Kennedy "wouldn't buy it and refused to say anything . . . kind about it," even privately.[64] Kennedy's secretary of labor, Willard Wirtz, did advocate "a thirty-five-hour week or less now and later on, God knows only how short it will be," at the 1963 AFL-CIO convention but no serious Democratic or Republican support for amending the Fair Labor Standards Act materialized during a period in which Kennedy referred to unemployment as the "major domestic challenge of the sixties." Indeed, the Kennedy administration opposed Congressman Adam Clayton Powell's 1961 bill for a phased-in thirty-five-hour week. The AFL-CIO continued to show ambivalence on the hours issue, with McDonald grudgingly admiring Kennedy's refusal to yield to thirty-two-hour pressure and with top unionists, as Dan Wakefield observed in 1963, often portraying less hours as a regrettable measure to cure joblessness.[65] Scattered breakthroughs in bargaining included the steel workers' 1963 negotiation of the first sabbaticals for industrial workers included in an industrial collective bargaining agreement, and shorter-hours pacts for white-collar workers negotiated by the Office and Professional Employees International Union, which went on record for a four-day, 32-hour week in 1962.[66]

By far the most significant advance occurred when IBEW Local 3 in New

York City followed up its 1961 demand for a four-hour day to eliminate unemployment with a solid strike over the issue in January and February 1962. Local 3, part of a union that had pioneered in shorter hours since the late 1930s and led brilliantly by Harry Van Arsdale, Jr., saw the employers' negotiators at first refuse to discuss the hours issue. But the strike, authorized by a 5,000 to 3 vote, forced bargaining and generated a compromise of a five-hour day and twenty-five-hour week. The agreement drew a large volume of publicity, but little emulation.[67]

During the relatively full employment coincident with American involvement in Vietnam, the AFL-CIO paid little attention to the reduction of hours. A 1967 resolution on the subject stressed "socially desirable job-creating fiscal and monetary policies" as the major cure for joblessness but added that a thirty-five-hour week was necessary "as fast as practicable." Shorter hours also found justification as one of several "efforts to share productivity gains." The most interesting aspect of the 1967 hours resolutions was a call for punitive overtime pay at the rate of double-time to discourage forced, regularly scheduled overtime. In 1969 the AFL-CIO's shorter-hours demands were embedded in a resolution that merely mandated the AFL-CIO "to investigate the feasibility of introducing federal legislation . . . for a thirty-five-hour workweek."[68]

The movement for shorter hours during the Vietnam War largely took place in small campaigns against overtime (sometimes under union auspices, more often informally) and in the decisions of countless, especially young, workers to absent themselves from work, sometimes on a regular basis. The latter phenomenon, particularly observed by sociologists and lamented by managers at the model General Motors factory at Lordstown, Ohio, helped to spawn a huge literature concerning absenteeism, turnover, and the "revolt against work." But it generated little from management, social scientists, the unions, or the rank and file in the way of sustained calls for more leisure.[69]

With few shorter-hours efforts forthcoming from most unions or party politicians, the shorter-hours activities of left-wing groups became more important. The Communist party, League of Revolutionary Black Workers, and Progressive Labor party (PL) were especially active in this regard.[70] The League, based in Detroit, and its offshoot, the Black Workers Congress (BWC), effectively linked hours with control over work and fought vigorously against the UAW's acceptance of virtually forced overtime in its 1973 negotiations, branding the contract of that year a "54-hour week" pact and agitating for a twenty-hour workweek. PL meanwhile made "30-for-40" a familiar demand in the Students for a Democratic Society and in some union locals. In 1973 PL organizer William Gilbreth led a wildcat sitdown strike at the Mack Avenue Chrysler plant. The strike raised the "30-for-40" demand before being broken by police, UAW officials, and management. Although both the BWC and PL suffered from a tendency to disparage the importance of existing unions, these groups gave the hours issue some prominence.[71]

In 1975 a new momentum for a shorter workweek developed, especially among unionists at the local and state level. Three hundred delegates to the Illinois AFL-CIO convention signed a "30-for-40" resolution that year and the Coalition of Black Trade Unionists endorsed such a demand. The 1975 AFL-CIO national convention resolved to strive for a thirty-five-hour week. The following year Sar Levitan and Richard Belous of George Washington University's Center for Social Policy Studies predicted, "If stickiness in unemployment continues much longer . . . pressures for shortening worktimes will mount and become heavier than during any time since the dawn of the post-World War II era."[72] In 1976 the *National Steelworkers Rank-and-File Report* endorsed "30-for-40" and termed a shorter workweek the "No. 1 Need" of American steelworkers. Ed Sadlowski, the reform candidate for the Steelworkers' presidency, emphasized a six-hour day. The Committee for Trade Union Action and Democracy made shorter hours a major part of its agitational activities, bringing together a variety of unionists around the issue. At the 1976 Illinois AFL-CIO convention, a "massive petition campaign" aimed at shorter hours with no pay reduction won unanimous endorsement.[73]

In the fall of 1976 the UAW, under pressure from the Auto Workers Action Caucus and other rank-and-file groups to make a shorter workweek a priority demand, negotiated a series of contracts with twelve extra holidays over a two-year period. Although UAW President Leonard Woodcock sometimes opposed the thirty-two-hour week as encouraging moonlighting, the UAW advertised the agreements as "the opening wedge in its drive to make the four-day, 32-hour week standard" in the auto and farm equipment industries. Union dissidents, on the other hand, argued that little real increase in leisure had been achieved.[74]

Early in 1977 over fifty local steel union presidents endorsed a thirty-two-hour week just before the Sadlowski reform forces squared off with those led by Lloyd McBride in a hardfought USW election. The New York Central Labor Council, with Harry Van Arsdale playing a prominent role, passed a thirty-five-hour resolution in February, just as the AFL-CIO Executive Committee reaffirmed its support of that goal.[75] The Auto Workers Action Caucus meanwhile reemphasized its commitment to "30-for-40," kicking off a series of UAW resolutions for shorter hours prior to the union's May convention. At that convention, 300 delegates signed petitions supporting Michigan Congressman John Conyers's proposal, advanced in April 1977, for a law providing a thirty-five-hour workweek, double time for overtime, a ban on compulsory overtime, and "35-for-40" in government-contract-related employment. New UAW President Douglas Fraser told the convention that the four-day week was "inevitable" and said he "would be delighted" if the Conyers proposal passed.[76]

Throughout the rest of 1977 shorter-hours activity accelerated. In July over sixty representatives of Iowa unions met in the Iowa Union Conference for Shorter Hours, demanding "35-for-40." The Illinois International Women's Year Conference adopted a similar resolution.[77] By October, when fifty local union officials from eleven states met in Detroit to launch the All Unions' Committee to Shorten the Workweek (AUCSW), the Machinists, Fur Workers and United Electrical Workers had assumed particularly instrumental roles with steel, auto, longshore, retail clerks, mine, and government employee union officials also active. Frank Runnels, president of UAW Local 22, won the presidency of the new group, which launched plans for a broad April 1978 shorter-hours conference.[78]

The April conference drew 700 delegates from 200 locals and twenty-five international unions. It heard such labor luminaries as Fraser, Runnels, Frank Rosen, and Jim Balanoff address the hours issue, with Fraser promising, "As sure as I'm standing here, the American worker is going to have a four-day work-week without a cut in pay." The conferees also heard John Conyers explain the provisions of his H. R. 1784, a thirty-five-hour-workweek bill. They pledged support for H. R. 1784 (over some opposition from Fraser and Steel Workers' Union officials), for abolition of all compulsory overtime, and for introduction of shorter hours with no pay reduction as a priority in bargaining for every international union. The AUCSW argued that each hour chopped from the forty-hour week translated into 1.4 million new jobs.[79]

The campaign to make the thirty-five-hour week a mass issue made slow gains after the April 1978 conference. In Illinois over two dozen union leaders from a dozen unions joined the Illinois Labor History Society endorsing a shorter-hours rally to commemorate Haymarket. Iowa unionists were again especially active, initiating a summertime campaign on behalf of the Conyers bill. The United Electrical Workers' national convention gave top priority to the struggle to reduce hours, resolving, "We have to be prepared to wage a serious, determined and unrelenting campaign" for legislation on the issue.[80]

By 1979 such a campaign had developed enough to force hearings on Conyers's thirty-five-hour amendments to the Fair Labor Standards Act before the Subcommittee on Labor Standards of the House Committee on Education and Labor. Although the bill never reached the House floor, the hearings gathered labor and reform support, much of it coordinated by the AUCSW. Nine trade unionists as well as prominent economists and historians joined Detroit Mayor Coleman Young and other municipal officials in supporting the bill. The absence of top-level AFL-CIO leaders at the hearings meanwhile suggested the limits of AUCSW progress at mobilizing shorter-hours support.[81]

In the atmosphere of "givebacks" surrounding bargaining in the post-1981 recession, little hours progress has occurred. Jane Slaughter's assessment, that "union gains on shortening work time have been among the first to go during the concessions offensive," may be an overstatement, although several unions have yielded to longer hours, sometimes in order to keep current weekly wages. Cutbacks in public spending have also led to lengthening hours for the thinned ranks of government employees in many areas.[82] However, at the same time some unionists have argued that recession makes the antiunemployment arguments for shorter hours more compelling and that shorter hours ought to be a concession demanded *from* employers. The Oil, Chemical, and Atomic Workers' Union has led in making shorter hours union policy. Dissident steelworkers, leaders of the UAW Skilled Trades Council, unemployed groups, and activists grouped around the *Labor Today* newspaper have taken the same position.[83]

The Professional Air Traffic Controllers' Organization strike, begun in June 1981 and broken at length by the U.S. government's use of strikebreakers and heavy fines on the union, illustrates many of the contradictory tendencies in contemporary hours struggles. The controllers' persistence in calling for a thirty-two-hour week as a health-and-safety demand, the way that demand was lost in press treatments emphasizing wages, and the record of AFL-CIO unions in solidarity with the strike suggest the promise of both future action and inaction on the issue.[84]

A lack of progress in the last four decades, and particularly in the last three, raises the question of whether or not the shorter working day is an issue belonging to the dead past. For several reasons, we think that it is not and that possibilities of a renaissance are real. Among the hopeful signs are the growth of religious-labor cooperation on the working day. Another possible constituency lies among family farmers, long opposed to a reduction in hours, but today among the Americans most likely to moonlight in a second job for wages. The demand can also appeal to young and minority workers, victims of massive unemployment. Moreover, recent Department of Labor studies show the *average* U.S. worker willing to forego 4.7 percent of his/her earnings in exchange for more leisure.[85]

Employers also are likely to ensure that consciousness of the hours issue remains alive because of their insistence on rolling back existing hours gains and on denying privileges regarding breaks during the working day. In the 1979 organizing campaign at Sanderson Chicken Farms in Laurel, Mississippi, for example, among union demands were toilet breaks and two, fifteen-minute rest periods daily.[86] A major issue in the 110-day miners' strike of 1978 was management's resolve to deny Saturday overtime pay and to change other aspects of scheduling. In the 1981 cannery negotiations, a main concern of United Steel Workers' negotiators was still abolition of the twelve-hour day. The continuing presence of long hours coexists, as the Nobel Prize-winning economist Wassily Leontief has pointed out, with rapid mechanization creating a situation of ever-growing rates of structural unemployment not yet dented by policies other than a reduced workweek.[87]

Finally, a reduction in working hours is a women's demand, or rather a human demand especially important to women because of their shouldering of child-rearing and household responsibilities. In 1956 Elizabeth Lawson wrote:

While the labor movement fights for a working week of less than forty hours . . . , a large section of our population regularly, without vacations and with no days off, puts in 100 hours a week or more—a longer working day than that against which American workers revolted more than a century ago. These are not sharecroppers or migratory workers . . . . They are housewives.[88]

Since 1940 the labor force participation rate of such housewives has risen from about 15 percent to just over 50 percent—the most spectacular recent demographic change in the work force. The hours such women spend in housework have declined, but only marginally.[89]

Women workers' sacrifices have heretofore functioned to smooth family problems regarding time as well as money. Female workers in 1975, for example, worked full time for a full year in only 41.8 percent of all cases. Part-time workers comprised 32 percent; 26.3 percent were off full-time jobs much of the year.[90] In part these figures reflect sexist employment and layoff policies. But they also reflect pressured choices by women workers with family responsibilities. For such women to participate fully in the labor force, to avoid poorly paying part-time jobs, and to win promotions according to merit, a shorter work schedule enabling consistent labor is necessary. Or, to envision a different scenario, if men begin to share child-rearing and household responsibilities more equally, the issue of shorter hours will be increasingly important to their wage-earning and career potentials. In Norway and Sweden, where a resurgent thirty-hour week movement has joined the shorter-hours campaigns of German metal workers in bringing working time to the fore as an issue in labor negotiations, specifically feminist arguments for a reduction in the workweek have found sophisticated expression.[91]

Scholarly researchers and labor organizers have agreed that women workers are most receptive to shorter-hours arguments.[92] In the recent past of inaction on reducing hours, much of this interest has been translated into concern with such partial solutions as job-sharing, flexitime, and providing full benefits for part-time workers.[93] Even so, unions with high percentages of women workers have made some of the major gains in negotiating shorter full-time workweeks. In healthcare, for example, the Service Employees' International Union, the Communications Workers of America, and Retail, Wholesale, and Department Store Union Local 1199 have all won schedules of substantially less than forty hours.[94] If, as numerous observers of American labor have held, the organization of women is the key task determining the future of U.S. unions, it may be that shorter hours hold the key to such organization. It may even be that women workers, used to self-paced work at home and responsibilities with children, will again inject control issues into struggles over the working day.[95]

For all these reasons and in light of the rich past of workers' efforts to gain leisure, there is little cause to quarrel with Andre Gorz's recent assessment:

Nowhere is the line separating left and right clearer than on the question of time: the politics of time. According to whether it is a politics (and policy) of the right or left, it may lead either to a society based on unemployment or one based on free time. Of all the levers available to change the social order and the quality of life, this is one of the most powerful.[96]

Notes

Preface

1. The most explicit use of the supposed Gompers's quotation to structure research is Malcolm Keir, *Labor's Search for More* (New York, 1937), esp. xi, which sets Gompers's response in the context of an exchange with the Socialist leader, Morris Hillquit, before the U.S. Commission on Industrial Relations. But in the recorded testimony of the hearings, Gompers merely assents to Hillquit's question as to whether the AFL "demands more now." See Morris Hillquit, Samuel Gompers, and Max J. Hayes, *The Double Edge of Labor's Sword* (Chicago, 1914), 119-24. For an allusion to recent study by the Samuel Gompers Papers Project (University of Maryland), which suggests Gompers may never have used a simple "more" to describe AFL goals, see Lane Kirkland, "A Few Words from Lane Kirkland," *Dissent* (Spring 1983), 145.

2. John R. Commons and Associates, *History of Labour in the United States*, 4 vols. (New York, 1918-1935); Keir, *More*, esp. v; F. T. Carlton, "Ephemeral Labor Movements, 1866-1889," *Popular Science Monthly* 85 (November 1914), 503. Marion Cahill's otherwise valuable *Shorter Hours: A Study of the Movement Since the Civil War* (New York, 1932) does not manage to transcend this approach. In addition, the pre-Civil War shorter-hours movement is nowhere systematically treated. It is slighted in Cahill, in Horace A. Davenport, "The Regulation of Hours" (Unpublished M.A. thesis, University of Pennsylvania, 1947), and in John E. Robinson, "The History of the Reduction of Working Hours" (unpublished M.A. thesis, University of Pennsylvania, 1933). Gustav A. Kleene, "History of the Ten-Hour Day in the U.S." (n.p., n.d.) has useful information but is brief and sometimes unreliable. Other short accounts of the history of shorter-hours agitation are found in William McGaughey, Jr., *A Shorter Workweek in the 1980s* (White Bear Lake, Minn., 1981) and Labor Research Association, *The History of the Shorter Working Day* (Newark, N. J., 1942).

3. See Paul F. McGouldrick and Michael Tannen, "Did American Manufacturers Discriminate Against Immigrants Before 1914?" *Journal of Economic History* 37 (September 1977), 723-46; Edward Greer, "Racism and U.S. Steel," *Radical America* 10 (September-October 1976), 45-68; Paul Brissenden, *Earnings of Factory Workers, 1899-1927* (Washington, D.C., 1929), 29-30, 85, 103.

4. Saint Louis *Daily Press* (August 8, 1866); AFL, *Proceedings, 1895* (Washington D.C., 1895), 5; Frank Runnels, "Shorter Hours Can End Unemployment," *Labor Today* (November 1977). On race and ethnicity and U.S. labor, see Mike Davis, *Prisoners of the American Dream* (London, 1986).

5. Commons and Associates, *Labour in the United States*, esp. Vol. 1; Norman Ware, *The Industrial Worker, 1840-1860* (Chicago, 1964), esp. 125; and *The Labor Movement in the United States, 1860-1895* (New York, 1929); Cahill, *Shorter Hours*, 139.

6. See below, ch. 9-12.

7. Montgomery in *Beyond Equality: Labor and the Radical Republicans, 1862-1872* (New York, 1967), 238ff. Cf. Frederick Engels, "Preface to the Fourth German Edition of the *Communist Manifesto*," cited in Alexander Trachtenberg, *History of May Day* (New York, 1947), 19-21; V. I. Lenin, "May Days in Kharkov (1900)," in Lenin, *Collected Works*, 40 vols. (New York, 1927), 4:357-65; John Foster, *Class Struggle and the Industrial Revolution* (London, 1974), 108.

8. Trevellick, quoted in George McNeill, ed., *The Labor Movement: The Problem of Today* (Boston and New York, 1887), 344-45. See also esp. the second and fourth chapters below.

9. See below, esp. ch. 9. For a fuller discussion of hours and workers' control, see David Roediger, "The Movement for a Shorter Working Day in the United States Before 1866" (unpublished Ph.D. dissertation, Northwestern University, 1980), 271-73. A pair of recent studies briefly suggest that shorter hours may have been traded for lost control. See Paul Johnson, *A Shopkeepers' Millennium: Society and Revivals in Rochester, 1815-1837* (New York, 1978), 42; and esp. Roy Rosenzweig, *'Eight Hours for What We Will': Workers and Leisure in an Industrial*

City, 1870-1920 (Cambridge, England 1983), 38-39.

10. Ibid.; Montgomery, "The 'New Unionism' and the Transformation of Workers' Consciousness in America, 1909-1922," *Journal of Social History* 12 (Summer 1974), esp. 514-15; McNeill, ed., *Labor Movement*, 340; Labor Research Association, *Shorter Working Day*, 6.

11. Richard Price, *Masters, Unions and Men: Work Control in Building and the Rise of Labor, 1830-1914* (Cambridge, 1980). Conversations with Price and with Walter Licht of the University of Pennsylvania sharpened this analysis of the relationship between hours and control.

12. Table 1-A is from T. S. Adams and Helen Sumner, *Labor Problems* (New York, 1905), 517-19. Table 1-B is from data in McGaughey, *Shorter Workweek*, 189-97.

13. Herbert Gutman, *Work, Culture and Society in Industrializing America* (New York, 1977), esp. 3-78, is the seminal work on these questions in the United States. It in turn owes much to E. P. Thompson, "Time, Work- Discipline and Industrial Capitalism," *Past and Present* 38 (December 1967), 56-97.

14. Kenneth Stampp, *The Peculiar Institution* (New York, 1956), 74-80 and 97-190; Alice Bauer and Raymond Bauer, "Day-to-Day Resistance to Slavery," in John H. Bracey, August Meier, and Elliott Rudwick, eds., *American Slavery: The Question of Resistance* (Belmont, Calif., 1971), 39-54; Eugene D. Genovese, *Roll, Jordan Roll: The World the Slaves Made* (New York, 1976), 285-324; and R. Keith Aufhauser, "Slavery and Scientific Management," *Journal of Economic History* 33 (December 1973), 811-24.

15. Benjamin Kline Hunnicutt, "Monsignor John A. Ryan and the Shorter Hours of Labor: A Forgotten Vision of 'Genuine' Progress," *Catholic Historical Review* 69 (July 1983), 385-86.

Time, Republicanism, and Merchant Capitalism: Consciousness of Hours before 1830

1.   Thompson, "Time, Work-Discipline and Industrial Capitalism," 56-97, is a masterful treatment of changing perceptions of time but must be modified by an analysis of American conditions.

2.   For the distinction between merchant and industrial capitalists, see Louis M. Hacker, *The Course of American Economic Growth and Development* (New York, 1970), 140-42. Thompson, working from the British example, sometimes links time-discipline too directly with "the coming of large-scale, machine- powered industry," but at times he also is sensitive to ambiguities in the terms "preindustrial" and "industrial." See "Time, Work-Discipline and Industrial Capitalism," 71, 79-81, 96.

3.   For the Philadelphia strike, see ch. 2 below. The figures are from Bruce Laurie, "'Nothing on Compulsion': Life Styles of Philadelphia Artisans, 1820-1860," *Labor History* 15 (Summer 1974), 339.

4.   Cited in Mary Rays Baker, "Anglo-Massachusetts Trade Union Roots, 1130- 1790," *Labor History* 14 (Summer 1973), 359. Middle English "noon" was at 3 P.M.

5.   Henry Gavens, *Shorter Hours—How? When?* (Washington, D.C., 1938), 2; A. L. Morton, *A People's History of England* (New York, 1974), 118, 121-26, 137, 170. See also Edmund Morgan, *American Slavery—American Freedom* (New York, 1975), 62; Winton Solberg, *Redeem the Time: The Puritan Sabbath in Early America* (Cambridge, Mass., 1977), esp. 40-46; and Philip S. Foner, *History of the Labor Movement in the United States*, 8 vols. (New York, 1947), 1: 15-16.

6.   Baker, "Anglo-Massachusetts Trade Union Roots," 359; Thompson, "Time, Work-Discipline and Industrial Capitalism," 85; John Rae, *Eight Hours for Work* (New York, 1894), 1-13; M. A. Bienefield, *Working Hours in British Industry: An Economic History* (London, 1972), ch. 1 and 2.

7.   Richard B. Morris, *Government and Labor in Early America* (New York, 1946), 59, 65, 78-79, 81; Paul Zankowich, "The Craftsmen of Colonial New York City" (unpublished Ph.D. dissertation, New York University, 1956), 46; Baker, "Anglo-Massachusetts Trade Union Roots," 359-60. John E. Robinson, "The History of the Reduction of Working Hours," (unpublished M.A. thesis, University of Pennsylvania, 1933), 5, suggests, on weak evidence, that much longer hours, up to 15 per day, were typical.

8.   Morris, *Government and Labor*, 72, 87; Solomon Lincoln, Jr., *History of the Town of Hingham* (Hingham, Mass., 1827), 52; and Morgan, *American Slavery*, 88, for indications that a four-hour day may have prevailed at Jamestown in the early years. For an example of a 1633 Massachusetts law implying that day-long labor was required, see Solberg, *Redeem the Time*, 163.

9.   William H. Whitmore, ed., *The Colonial Laws of Massachusetts, Reprinted from the Edition of 1672, with the Supplements through 1686* (Boston, 1887), 104-5; Baker, "Anglo-Massachusetts Trade Union Roots," 360. Baker adds, on the same page, that the inmates of the Boston Work House, built in 1739, received the customary three hours daily for rest and worship.

10.   Morris, *Government and Labor*, 64, 84, 86; *Duke of York's Book of Laws of the Province of Pennsylvania Passed Between 1682 and 1700* (Harrisburg, 1879), 37.

11.   Morgan, *American Slavery*, esp. 59-68.

12.   *New York Weekly Herald* (January 7, 1733); Max Weber, *The Protestant Ethic and the Spirit of Capitalism* (London, 1930), and R. H. Tawney, *Religion and the Rise of Capitalism* (London, 1926), ch. 1 and 2; Morgan, *American Slavery*, esp. 59-68. Franklin is quoted in Thompson, "Time, Work-Discipline and Industrial Capitalism," 89. See also Alfred Young's forthcoming book on colonial and revolutionary artisans and Ian M.G. Quimby, "Apprenticeship in Colonial Philadelphia" (unpublished M.A. thesis, University of Delaware, 1963), 60-63. See also Gary B. Nash, "Up from the Bottom in Franklin's Philadelphia," *Past and Present* 77 (November

1977), 57-83.

An important unpublished study by Margaret Bohn Alexander, "Apprize the People of the Time': Clocks and Watches in Preindustrial America" in the possession of its author at Northern Illinois University discusses bells and public clocks in the colonies in terms of the timing of civic events. Alexander finds the number of privately owned clocks and watches small through the Revolution, by which time she estimates 30,000 clocks and 42,000 watches existed in the United States.

13. *New England Courant* (December 7, 1724); Baker, "Anglo-Massachusetts Trade Union Roots," 359; McNeill, ed., *The Labor Movement*, 70; Solberg, *Redeem the Time*, esp. 40-46, 92, and 158-240.

14. Garry Wills, *Inventing America: Jefferson's Declaration of Independence* (New York, 1979), 93-110. Quotes are from 101.

15. Edmund Morgan, "The Puritan Ethic and the American Revolution," *William and Mary Quarterly* 3rd Series, 24 (January 1967), 3-43; Ronald Takaki, *Iron Cages: Race and Culture in Nineteenth Century America* (New York, 1979), 3-65, includes quotes from Rush (22) and Jefferson (40).

16. Benjamin Franklin, *The Autobiography of Benjamin Franklin* (New York, 1962), 51-53, 83, 86; McGaughey, Jr., *Shorter Workweek*, back cover.

17. Morris, *Government and Labor*, 200.

18. Steven J. Erlanger, *The Colonial Laborer in Boston, 1775* (Boston, 1975), 20-21; Foner, "Tom Paine's Republic: Radical Ideology and Social Change," in Alfred E. Young, ed., *The American Revolution: Explorations in the History of American Radicalism* (DeKalb, Ill., 1975), 195-96. Other important works in this area include Young, *The Democratic Republicans of New York: The Origins, 1763-1797* (Chapel Hill, N.C., 1967); Richard Walsh, *Charleston's Sons of Liberty: A Study of the Artisans* (Columbia, S.C., 1959).

19. *Philadelphia Independent Gazetteer* (October 9, 1784). *New York Packet* (January 20, 1785) contains an announcement from a master builder who complains of "many disputes between (the) employer and the different artificers" over what should constitute a day's work. It may be that this meant disputes over *how much* work was to be done in a day. The watchmakers' slogan is from Edward Countryman, *The American Revolution* (New York, 1985), 215.

20. "An Address of the Journeymen Carpenters of the City and Liberties of Philadelphia," *Dunlap's Daily Advertiser* (May 11, 1791); Foner, *Labor Movement*, 1: 102, 117; Commons and Associates, *Labour in the United States*, 1: 69, 110, 158. Emphasis in original.

21. Jonathan Prude, *The Coming of Industrial Order: Town and Factory Life in Rural Massachusetts, 1810-1860* (Cambridge, 1983), 3-64; W. R. Bagnall, *Samuel Slater and the Early Development of Cotton Manufacture in the United States* (Middletown, Conn., 1890), 44; Caroline F. Ware, *The Early New England Cotton Manufacture* (Boston, 1911), 21, 64; Foner, *Labor Movement*, 1: 54; Rosalyn Baxandall, Linda Gordon, and Susan Reverdy, eds., *America's Working Women: A Documentary History* (New York, 1976), 41. Figures from Helen Sumner, *History of Women in Industry in the United States* (New York, 1974), 55.

22. Commons and Associates, *Labour in the United States*, 1: 103ff. See also Commons and Associates, *A Documentary History of American Industrial Society*, 10 vols. (Cleveland, 1910), 3: 42-43; Alan Dawley, *Class and Community: The Industrial Revolution in Lynn* (Cambridge, 1976), 20-32; and Alexander Hamilton's comments on the relationship between the division of labor and the inculcating of time-discipline, excerpted from the "Report on Manufactures," in *American Issues, Volume One: The Social Record*, Williard Thorp, Merle Curti, and Carlos Baker, eds. (Chicago, 1955), 399. Before 1825, however, the trend toward reorganized production based on the penetration of merchant capital was only beginning and many journeymen remained relatively prosperous and secure members of a still cohesive artisan community. See David Montgomery, "The Working Classes of the Preindustrial American City," *Labor History* 9 (Winter 1968).

23. Commons and Associates, *Documentary History*, 5: 330-334, 57-66. See also Gary Kulik, "Pawtucket Village and the Strike of 1824: The Origins of Class Conflict in Rhode Island," *Radical History Review* 17 (Spring 1978), 20; William Sullivan, *The Industrial Worker in Pennsylvania* (Harrisburg, 1955), 38-39; Kleene, "Ten-Hour Day," 2-5; Ralph Waldo Emerson, "Farming," in Edward Waldo Emerson, ed., *The Complete Works of Ralph Waldo Emerson*, 12

vols. (Boston and New York, 1903), 7: 138.

24.   See Sean Wilentz, *Chants Democratic: New York City and the Rise of the American Working Class, 1788-1850* (New York, 1984), 24-35. Commons and Associates, *Documentary History*, 3: 118; Bradford, *The Political Vagaries of a Knight of the Folding Stick of Paste Castle* (New York, 1813), 50, as cited in Howard Rock, "The Independent Mechanic: Tradesmen of New York City in Labor and Politics During the Jeffersonian Era" (unpublished Ph.D. dissertation, New York University, 1974); Foner, *Labor Movement*, 1: 68.

25.   Commons and Associates, *Labour in the United States*, 1: 103; Ware, *Cotton Manufacture*, 210; Hamilton is quoted in David F. Selvin, "The First Efforts Were Feeble," *Viewpoint* 6 (First Quarter 1976), 2. See also *American State Papers, Finance*, 3: 82.

26.   *Baltimore American and Commercial Daily Advertiser* (June 8, 1799). I am indebted to Charles Steffen for references to early Baltimore.

27.   Commons and Associates, *Documentary History*, 5: 57-66. A less ambitious investigation, in Pennsylvania one year earlier, also centered on child labor. See Charles F. Persons, Mabel Parton, and Mabelle Moses, *Labor Laws and Their Enforcement* (New York, 1911), 4-9. The Massachusetts Senate appointed committees on the issue in 1814 and 1816, but no reports are extant; see Ware, *Cotton Manufacture*, 283.

28.   John D. Hicks, *A Short History of American Democracy* (Cambridge, 1946), 277.

29.   Broadside, "To Journeymen Carpenters and Masons" (March 11, 1805), New York Historical Society. Cited in Rock, "Independent Mechanic," 35. See also Rock, 37-40. The immensely important history of clock and watch usage and production in early America is well-begun in Margaret Alexander, "'Apprize the People of the Time': Clocks and Watches in Preindustrial America" (Seminar paper, Northern Illinois University, 1979?), passim. Alexander dates the proliferation of wooden clocks particularly between 1810 and 1830, when prices fell dramatically.

30.   Ethelbert Stewart, "A Documentary History of Early Organization of Printers," *Bulletin of the Bureau of Labor* 61 (November 1905), 883; George A. Stevens, *New York City Typographical Union Number Six* (Albany, 1913), 55- 58; *Baltimore American and Commercial Daily Advertiser* (January 1, 1811); Thompson, "Time, Work-Discipline and Industrial Capitalism," 60, 78. See also E. J. Hobsbawm, "Custom, Wages and Workload," in *Labouring Men* (London, 1976), 349, for the view that piece rates and other incentives replaced working a "customary" pace more quickly in the United States than in Britain.

31.   Kleene, "Ten-Hour Day," 5; Friedrich A. Sorge, *Labor Movement in the United States*, Philip S. Foner and Brewster Chamberlin, eds. (Westport, Conn., 1977), 51; McNeill, ed., *The Labor Movement*, 341-42; Paul Faler, "Cultural Aspects of the Industrial Revolution: Lynn, Massachusetts, Shoemakers and Industrial Morality, 1826-1860," *Labor History* 15 (Summer 1974), 379, n. 20.

32.   *Providence Patriot* (May 29, 1824); Kulik, "Pawtucket Village," 20; Commons and Associates, *Labour Movement in the United States*, 1: 156, 418; Foner, *Labor Movement*, 1: 105; Grace Hutchins, *Labor and Silk* (New York, 1927), 129-31.

33.   Stewart, "Two Forgotten Decades in the History of Labor Organizations, 1820-1840," *American Federationist* 20 (July 1913), 518, 521-22.

34.   John B. McMasters, *A History of the People of the Unites States from the Revolution to the Civil War*, 8 vols. (New York and London, 1883-1913), 5: 84; James Lerner and Fred Wright, *Too Many Hours: Labor's Struggle to Shorten the Work Day* (New York, n.d.), 5.

35.   Thompson, "Time, Work-Discipline and Industrial Capitalism," 85, 93.

36.   Philip S. Foner, "An Early Trades Union and Its Fate," *Labor History* 14 (Summer 1973), 423-24. See also Commons and Associates, *Labour in the United States*, 1: 158-59 and *Columbian Centinel* (April 20 and 27, 1825).

37.   The masters' resolutions, passed on April 15, 1825, appeared in the *Columbian Centinel* (April 20, 1825).

38.   Ibid.; Edward Pessen, "Boston Labor During the Jackson Era" (unpublished M.A. thesis, Columbia University, 1950), 30; and Johnson, *Shopkeepers' Millennium*, ch. 2 and 3.

39. *Columbian Centinel* (April 20, 1825).

40. The "Resolutions of the 'Capitalists'" first appeared in the *Columbian Centinel* (April 23, 1825); Commons and Associates, *Documentary History*, 6: 73 and 79-81; Foner, "Early Trades Union," 424.

41. *Columbian Centinel* (April 23, 1825); Pessen, "Boston Labor," 31-32; Joseph Brennan, *Social Conditions in Industrial Rhode Island, 1820-1860* (Washington, D.C., 1940), 53; John K. Towles, "Factory Legislation in Rhode Island," *American Economic Association Quarterly* Third Series, 9 (October 1908), 59.

42. Heighton published "An Address to the Members of Trade Societies and to the Working Classes Generally" (Philadelphia, 1827) under the pseudonym of "A Fellow Labourer." It is this April 1827 address which helped inspire the carpenters' strike that year. He used the name "Unlettered Mechanic" for "An Address, Delivered Before the Mechanics and Working Classes Generally, of the City and County of Philadelphia. At the Universalist Church, on Wednesday Evening, November 21, 1827" (Philadelphia, n.d.). His third published address uses the pen name "An Operative Citizen" and is titled "The Principles of Aristocratic Legislation" (Philadelphia, 1828). Copies of the first two are in the Historical Society of Pennsylvania, and the third is in Newberry Library in Chicago. More available are excerpts of the first address in *Mechanics' Free Press* (June 21, 1828) and excerpts of the second in *Labor's Heritage: An Address by the Unlettered Mechanic—1827*, a pamphlet by the Amalgamated Meat Cutters and Butcher Workmen of North America (n.p., 1976).

43. On the roots of Heighton's thought, see Louis H. Arky, "The Mechanics' Union of Trade Associations and the Formation of the Philadelphia Workingmen's Movement," *Pennsylvania Magazine of History and Biography* 76 (April 1952), 145-51, and David J. Harris, *Socialist Origins in the United States: American Forerunners of Marx, 1817-1832* (Assen, Netherlands, 1966), 82-90. The Ricardian socialist premise—that labor deserved to realize the full value of the time it put into production—reappears in much of radical Jacksonian labor ideology and provides an important theoretical support for hours agitation of the period. Even in its more utopian expressions, those of the builders of cooperatives and communes, the injustice of workers laboring several hours per day to benefit their employer is implied. The Cincinnati "labour-for-labour" store, for example, justified its plan to replace money with labor notes by observing." Time is above all things most valuable . . . the real and natural standard of value." (Commons and Associates, *Documentary History*, 5: 124-28). See also McNeill, ed., *The Labor Movement*, 72; Maurice F. Neufeld, "Realms of Thought and Organized Labor in the Age of Jackson," *Labor History* 10 (Winter 1969), 18-20, 30-32; Harris, *Socialist Origins*, 5, 140-42.

The most famous of Philadelphia's artisans, Benjamin Franklin, had clearly ("so clearly," Marx later wrote in commenting on Franklin's work, "as to almost be trite") argued that labor is the source of value in his *A Modest Inquiry into the Nature and Necessity of a Paper Currency* (1731). Other possible Philadelphia sources for Heighton's conceptions include two more works by Philadelphia printers: John McIlvaine, "Address to the Journeymen Cordwainer L.B. of Philadelphia" (Philadelphia, 1802) and Langdon Byllesby, *Observations on the Sources and Effects of Unequal Wealth* (New York, 1826). See Marx, *A Contribution to the Critique of Political Economy* (New York, 1970), 52-57; Jared Sparks, ed., *The Works of Benjamin Franklin* (Boston, 1836), 2:265-67; Mark Lause, "'Fellow-Craft-Men! Arouse',", forthcoming; Bruce Laurie, *The Working People of Philadelphia, 1800-1850* (Philadelphia, 1980), 75-78.

44. Heighton excerpted in *Labor's Heritage*, 3-4, and "Before the Mechanics and Working Classes," 8-9. Cf. Marx, "Wage Labor and Capital," *Karl Marx and Frederick Engels: Selected Works* (London, 1968), 71-93.

45. Heighton, *Labor's Heritage*, 4.

46. Heighton, *Labor's Heritage*, 8, 11; *Mechanics' Free Press* (June 21, 1828); Arky, "Mechanics' Union," 144, 149-51.

47. Bernstein, "The Working People of Philadelphia from Colonial Times to the General Strike of 1835," *Pennsylvania Magazine of History and Biography* 76 (1950), 329.

48. Heighton, "Address to the Members of Trade Societies," 19, 44-45; Sam Bass Warner, *The Private City: Philadelphia in Three Periods of Its Growth* (Philadelphia, 1968), 64-76; Arky,

"Mechanics' Union," 149; Commons and Associates, *Labour in the United States*, 1: 186, citing *Mechanics' Free Press* (June 21, 1828).

49. Commons and Associates, *Documentary History*, 5: 80, reprints the ten- hour demand from Philadelphia's *Democratic Press* (June 14, 1827). See also Bernstein, "Working People of Philadelphia," 328-30; Arky, "Mechanics' Union," 152; Commons and Associates, *Labour in the United States*, 1: 186-89.

50. Commons and Associates, *Documentary History*, 5: 81.

51. Commons and Associates, *Documentary History*, 5: 82, and *Labour in the United States*, 1: 186, 188-89. Evidence that some gains were made in 1827 may be found in the *Mechanics' Free Press* (June 7, 1828).

52. Democratic Press (June 20, 1827).

53. Commons and Associates, *Labour in the United States*, 1: 189; Arky, "Mechanics' Union," 153 and n.23.

54. Sullivan, "Philadelphia Labor During the Jackson Era," 315; Commons and Associates, *Documentary History*, 5: 76, and *Labour in the United States*, 1: 189.

55. Sumner writes in Commons and Associates, *Labour in the United States*, 1: 189-90. The "Preamble" was published about a year after it was drafted and is included in Commons and Associates, *Documentary History*, 5: 84-90. *Mechanics' Free Press* (October 25, 1828). For a summary of the constitution, located by Arky in issues of the *Mechanics' Gazette*, see his "Mechanics' Union," 155-56.

56. *Mechanics' Free Press* (April 19, 1828). Sullivan, "Philadelphia Labor During the Jackson Era," 319. The several "workingmen's" parties developing during the Jackson era have become the object of intense debate by historians. The class composition of both the leaders and the supporters of such parties has been questioned, as has the relationship between the "labor" parties and one or the other of the major parties. See Walter Hugins, *Jacksonian Democracy and the Working Class* (Stanford, Calif., 1960); Edward Pessen, *Most Uncommon Jacksonians: The Radical Leaders of the Early Labor Movement* (Albany, N.Y., 1967). The point here is that the Philadelphia and the New York parties, whatever their subsequent courses, arose from labor struggles over hours.

57. Arky, "Mechanics' Union," 160-61; *Mechanics' Gazette* (February 23, 1828); "An Address to the Journeymen House Carpenters of the City and County of Philadelphia," *Mechanics' Free Press* (June 14, 1828); and Arky, "Mechanics' Union," 161.

58. Sullivan, "Philadelphia Labor During the Jackson Era," 314; *The Cooperator* (April 17, 1832); Commons and Associates, *Documentary History*, 5: 76 and 6: 215; *Philadelphia Inquirer* (May 11, 1831).

59. Foner, *Labor Movement*, 1: 127-28; *Mechanics' Free Press* (October 18, 1828); Commons and Associates, *Labour in the United States*, 1: 195-99.

60. This kind of law was introduced during the 1835 events in Philadelphia and comports with the respect for individual contracts displayed by Boston carpenters in 1825. See *Columbian Centinel* (April 20 and 27, 1825). See also (New York) *Working Man's Advocate* (March 12, 1831).

61. Foner, *Labor Movement*, 1: 128-29; Bernstein, "Working People of Philadelphia," 333.

62. Oscar Handlin, *Boston's Immigrants: A Study in Acculturation* (Cambridge, Mass., 1959), 9, 63, 83, 239; Laurie, "'Nothing on Compulsion', 344-50. Warner, *Private City*, 67-75; David Montgomery, "The Shuttle and the Cross: Weavers and Artisans in the Kensington Riots of 1844," *Journal of Social History* 6 (Summer 1972), 417; Commons and Associates, *Documentary History*, 5: 23-24.

63. Warner, *Private City*, 66-69; Laurie, "'Nothing on Compulsion'," 340- 44.

64. See Faler's "Cultural Aspects of the Industrial Revolution," 367-94, esp. 390-94; Faler and Alan Dawley, "Working-Class Culture and Politics in the Industrial Revolution: Sources of Loyalism and Rebellion," *Journal of Social History* 9: 4 (June 1976), 466-80, and Susan E. Hirsch, *The Roots of the American Working Class: The Industrialization of Crafts in Newark, 1800- 1860* (Philadelphia, 1978), 9-11.

65. Young, *Democratic-Republicans of New York*, and Rock, "The Independent Mechanic," describe the political activities of the artisans. See Rock, 35, for early evidence of the ten-hour day in New York. Conversations with Rock, correspondence with Sean Wilentz of Princeton, and further research have failed to illuminate how many New Yorkers had the ten-hour day and just when and how they won it.

66. Pessen, *Uncommon Jacksonians*, 15-16; Foner, *Labor Movement*, 1: 130- 31. On Skidmore, see Harris, *Socialist Origins*, 91-139.

67. New York *Morning Courier* (April 25, 1829), reprinted in Commons and Associates, *Documentary History*, 5: 147-48.

68. Commons and Associates, *Labour in the United States*, 1: 234-36, and *Documentary History*, 5: 147-48; Wilentz, *Chants Democratic*, 190-216; Hugins, *Jacksonian Democracy and the Working Class*, 11; and Pessen, *Uncommon Jacksonians*, 16.

Shorter Hours and the Transformation
of American Labor, 1830-1842

1. Montgomery, "Preindustrial City," 21-22.

2. David Grimsted, "Rioting in Its Jacksonian Setting," *American Historical Review* 77 (April 1972).

3. Commons and Associates, *Labour in the United States*, 1: 478-84. Two strikes over hours and wages are counted in both columns.

4. Anita Gorochow, "Baltimore Labor in the Age of Jackson" (unpublished M.A. thesis, Columbia University, 1949), 44ff; Pessen, "Boston Labor," 30; Sullivan, "Philadelphia Labor During the Jackson Era," 312; and *The Industrial Worker in Pennsylvania, 1800-1840* 222-27. In the last source, two strikes involving wages and hours are counted twice.

5. Kleene, "Ten-Hour Day," 11-12; and Bureau of Statistics of Labor of Massachusetts, *Eleventh Annual Report* (1880), 3.

6. Commons and Associates, *Documentary History*, 5: 65, 196-97; Seth Luther, "An Address to the Working-men of New England" (Boston, 1832), 19-20, reprinted in *Religion, Reform and Revolution: Labor Panaceas of the Nineteenth Century*, Leon Stein and Philip Taft, eds. (New York, 1969); Ware, *Cotton Manufacture*, 250; John K. Towles, "Factory Legislation in Rhode Island, "*American Economic Association Quarterly* Third Series, 9 (October 1908), 59.

7. In McNeill, ed., *Labor Movement*, 342. See Samuel Eliot Morison, *Maritime History of Massachusetts* (Boston, 1921), 254-56, on capital investment and growing tonnages in shipping.

8. Kulik, "Pawtucket Village," 28; *Free Engineer* (June 14, 1832).

9. McNeill, ed., *The Labor Movement*, 345-48.

10. The most prominent revisionist study is Michael Katz, *The Irony of Early School Reform: Educational Innovation in Mid-Nineteenth Century Massachusetts* (Cambridge, Mass., 1968). For suggestive comments on the role of upper-class reformers in two cities, see Montgomery, "Shuttle and Cross," 423-24 and Faler, "Cultural Aspects of the Industrial Revolution," 384-87.

11. Mittelman, in Commons and Associates, *Labour in the United States*, 1: 321. In the same work see 1: 181ff., 217, 224, 299. See also F. T. Carlton, "The Workingmen's Party of New York City: 1829-1831," *Political Science Quarterly* 22 (1907), 405-8, 414-15; Thomas R. Dew, "Delaware's First Labor Party: A History of the Association of Working People of Newcastle County, 1829-1832" (unpublished M.A. thesis, University of Delaware, 1959), 20; Foner, *Labor Movement*, 1: 115 and 123; F. T. Carlton, "Economic Influences Upon Educational Progress in the United States, 1820-1850" (Ph.D. dissertation, University of Wisconsin, 1906).

12. *New York Daily Sentinel* (November 17, 1831); Kleene, "Ten-Hour Day," 8-9.

13. Foner, *Labor Movement*, 1: 123; Frances Wright, "Sketch of the Plan of National Education," in *Religion, Reform and Revolution*, Taft and Stein, eds., 7; Warner, *The Private City*, 66.

14. Robert Owen, "Oration: Containing a Declaration of Mental Independence, Delivered . . . At the Celebration of the Fourth of July, 1826," appended to *Robert Owen in the United States*, Oakley C. Johnson, ed. (New York, 1970), 65-75; Wright, "National Education," 7; Seth Luther, "Address to the Working-men of New England on the State of Education," in *Religion, Reform and Revolution*, Taft and Stein, eds., 3. The very words "Knowledge is power" recur frequently. See William McClure, *Opinions on Various Subjects, Dedicated, to the Industrious Producers*, 2 vols. (New Harmony, Indiana, 1831), 1: 4. See also An American Citizen, "An Appeal to the Working Men of the United States" (Norwich, Conn. 1833), 10.

15. "Address," by George R. McFarlane, appended to Dew, "Delaware's First Labor Party," 127-35; Wright, "Of Existing Evils and Their Remedies," reprinted in *American Issues*, Thorp, Curti, and Baker, eds., 1: 446-47; *Daily Sentinel* (May 19, 1832); Luther, "Address," 6-32.

16. *Daily Sentinel* (July 13, 1830). Cf. Montgomery, "Shuttle and Cross," 423.

17. Commons and Associates, *Documentary History*, 5: 107-14. Cf. Anthony F.C. Wallace, *Rockdale: The Growth of an American Village During the Early Industrial Revolution* (New York, 1978), 356-59.

18. Towles, "Rhode Island," 60; *Mechanics' Free Press* (August 21, 1830). See also *Mechanics' Free Press* (June 19, 1830).

19. Commons and Associates, *Documentary History*, 5: 62-66, 195-99, 332- 34. See also Luther, "Address," 29, and the testimony of J. Kempton of Norwich, Connecticut, in the *British Parliamentary Papers* (1833), 6: 165.

20. Wright, "National Education," 7. Also see *Mechanics' Free Press* (August 21, 1830), wherein the operatives argue, "we may establish schools and academies, and devise every means for the instruction of youth in vain, unless we also give time," and Dennis Clark, "Babes in Bondage: Indentured Irish Children in Philadelphia in the Nineteenth Century," *Pennsylvania Magazine of History and Biography* 101 (October 1977), 475-86.

21. Sullivan, *Industrial Worker in Pennsylvania*, 131-33, 223-24; James Morris, "The Road to Trade Unionism: Organized Labor in Cincinnati to 1893" (unpublished Ph.D. dissertation, University of Cincinnati, 1969), 21.

22. *Daily Sentinel* (July 6, 1831); McNeill, ed., *The Labor Movement*, 345-47, indicated brief strikes took place over hours throughout the early 1830's in New York shipyards. The first successes appear to have come in 1832 or 1833. Luther, "Address," 37, suggests that the Buffalo action may have succeeded; *Working Man's Advocate* (March 12, April 7, May 7 and 20, 1831).

23. *Working Man's Advocate* (March 12, 1831 and April 7, 1832); *New England Artisan* (June 21, 1834). On the impact of skilled British immigrants, see Rowland Berthoff, *British Immigrants in Industrial America* (Cambridge, Mass. 1953).

24. Sullivan, *Industrial Worker in Pennsylvania*, 48-49, assembles information on this point. See also Luther, "Address," 20. Travelers from Europe similarly reached the conclusion that work was longer and/or harder in America than in Europe. See Harriet Martineau, *Society and Manners in America*, 2 vols. (New York, 1837), 2: 251-52, and the observations of Michel Chevalier and Anthony Trollope in Kleene, "Ten-Hour Day," 7.

25. The fullest account of the strikes is in the *Working Man's Advocate* (April 7, 1832). See also Sorge, *Labor Movement*, 43-44; Pessen, "Boston Labor," 31; and Brennan, *Rhode Island*, 55. Luther, "Address," 37, suggests that successes also occurred in Detroit, Michigan, and Utica, New York, by 1832; *Sentinel* (June 9, 1832) lists Louisville and Charles E. Persons, Mabel Parton, and Mabelle Moses, in *Labor Laws*, 13, document widespread New England agitation.

26. Sorge, *Labor Movement*, 43-44; McNeill, ed., *The Labor Movement*, 80; *Working Man's Advocate* (April 7 and May 19, 1832); Luther, "Address," 37. Herbert Gutman has made similar arguments regarding labor support in smaller cities during the post-Civil War period. See esp. his "The Worker's Search for Power: Labor in the Gilded Age," in H. Wayne Morgan, ed., *The Gilded Age: A Reappraisal* (Syracuse, N.Y. 1963).

27. Commons and Associates, *Labour in the United States*, 1: 310-12; Pessen, "Boston Labor," 31-32; *Working Man's Advocate* (April 7, 1832); United States Commissioner of Labor, *Third Annual Report* (1887), 1032ff.

28. Commons and Associates, *Documentary History*, 6: 81-86; Pessen, "Boston Labor," 32.

29. A copy of the letter is appended to Luther, "Address," 33-34.

30. Sumner in Commons and Associates, *Labour in the United States*, 1: 312; Luther, "Address," 37; and Pessen, "Boston Labor," give evidence on the results of the strike. On Luther, see Louis Hartz, "Seth Luther: The Story of a Working Class Rebel," *New England Quarterly* 8 (September 1940), 401-18.

31. Luther, "Address," 31-32, 37; Foner, *Labor Movement*, 1: 106-7; *Working Man's Advocate* (June 2, 1832) for George Henry Evans's seconding of Luther's arguments.

32. Commons and Associates, *Labour in the United States*, 1: 306-10 and *Documentary History*, 5: 192-95; *New England Artisan* (February 2, 1832); Brennan, *Rhode Island*, 53. We have yet to find evidence of ten-hour agitation among farm laborers during this period. While David Schob's *Hired Hands and Plowboys: Farm Labor in the Midwest, 1815-1860* (Urbana, Ill., 1975),

255, indicates that some farmhands in Pennsylvania and New York had secured the ten-hour day by 1829, his source is ambiguous on this point and more likely means that sunrise-to-sunset labor prevailed. Cf. James Stuart, *Three Years in North America*, 2 vols. (Edinburgh, 1833), 1: 271. Arthur B. Darling, "The Workingmen's Party in Massachusetts," *American Historical Review* 29 (October 1923) mentions support from farmers for ten-hour demands.

33. Foner, *Labor Movement*, 1: 105; Commons and Associates, *Labour in the United States*, 1: 306-15 and *Documentary History*, 5: 195-99.

34. Commons and Associates, *Labour in the United States*, 1: 358-59, 386- 87, 478; Kleene, "Ten-Hour Day," 16; Gorochow, "Baltimore Labor," 45-46; and Frederick Shipp Deibler, "The Amalgamated Wood Workers' International Union of America," *Bulletin of the University of Wisconsin*, n. 511 (Madison, 1912), 278.

35. On Exeter, see Kleene, "Ten-Hour Day," 16; Evans Woollen, "Labor Troubles Between 1834 and 1837," *Yale Review* 1 (May 1892), 92. Woollen places the strike in 1834. On Philadelphia, see Commons and Associates, *Documentary History*, 5: 323, 328-41; Bernstein, "Working People of Philadelphia," 333-36.

36. Commons and Associates, *Labour in the United States*, 1: 348, 382, 478-79; Paul Johnson, *A Shopkeeper's Millennium*, 42; Commons and Associates, *Documentary History*, 5: 303-8. The unionists also linked long hours and poor health. On Sabbatarianism, a wing of which raised the demand for Sunday closings at bakeries, stores, taverns, docks, and offices, as well as the cessation of Sabbath labor for federal postmen and for milk deliverers, see Bertram Wyatt-Brown, "Sabbatarian Politics and the Rise of the Second Party System," *Journal of American History* 58: 2 (September 1971), passim. At least one Sabbatarian, Justin Edwards, referred to Sunday leisure as a "right" of the "laborer." Edwards is quoted in Charles C. Cole, *The Social Ideas of the Northern Evangelists, 1826-1869* (New York, 1966), 105; Arthur Schlesinger, *The Age of Jackson* (Boston, 1953), 138-39, shows that Sabbatarians and labor reformers were as often opposed as united, however.

37. Pessen, "Boston Labor," 34-41; Commons and Associates, *Documentary History*, 6: 87-94; Schlesinger, *Age of Jackson*, 165; Hartz, "Seth Luther," 405; Pessen, *Most Uncommon Jacksonians*, 42.

38. Robinson, *Oration Before the Trades' Union of Boston* (Boston, 1834), 12, 25-29, 32; Persons, Parton, and Moses, *Labor Laws*, 13-15; *Massachusetts House Document*, Number 44 (1867), 51-53

39. Douglas as quoted in *The Man* (March 26, 1834).

40. Ibid.; Hartz, "Seth Luther," 413-15; Commons and Associates, *Documentary History*, 6: 94-99; Bernard A. Wesiberger, *They Gathered at the River* (Chicago, 1958), 130. Horkheimer is quoted in William A. Williams, *Roots of the Modern American Empire* (New York, 1969), 448.

41. Commons and Associates, *Documentary History*, 6: 201-3 and *Labour in the United States*, 1: 424-28.

42. Commons and Associates, *Documentary History*, 6: 208 and 217-24.

43. Cf. Commons, "Labor Organization and Labor Politics, 1827-1837," *Quarterly Journal of Economics* 21: 2 (February 1907), 324-25, with Commons and Associates, *Labour in the United States*, 1: 426, 429, 438, and Commons and Associates, *Documentary History*, 6: 192. Ely Moore, head of both the NTU and New York City's central labor union, had ceased to be a wage-earning printer after his marriage in about 1825 and made his living as a politician and a land speculator. See Walter Hugins, "Ely Moore: Case History of a Jacksonian Labor Leader," *Political Science Quarterly* 65: 1 (March 1950), 108.

44. Commons and Associates, *Documentary History*, 6: 199, 201-16.

45. Ibid. William English, a Philadelphia cordwainer, particularly objected to the NTU's sponsoring the formation of a labor party, arguing that such a course had doomed the Mechanics' Union in his city. English, hardly apolitical, was elected state senator as a Democrat in 1835. See Foner, *Labor Movement*, 1: 562.

46. Commons and Associates, *Documentary History*, 6: 217ff. Samuel Yellen, *American Labor Struggles* (New York, 1974), 39, mentions a proposal for shorter hours legislation in New York state in 1829, however. A possible allusion to the New York case is Illinois Bureau of Labor

Statistics, *Fourth Biennial Report* (1886), 466. On Luther's pressuring the Rhode Island governor and legislature in 1832, see Carl Gersuny, "A Biographical Note on Seth Luther," *Labor History* 18: 2 (Spring 1977), 242.

47. Commons and Associates, *Labour in the United States*, 1: 429, and *Documentary History*, 6: 196-97 and 220-21; Hugins, "Ely Moore," 121-22.

48. Foner, *Labor Movement*, 1: 561; Commons and Associates, *Documentary History*, 6: 196-97, 221-23. Clay, a congressman from Kentucky, and many others in the Whig party advocated an "American System" under which tariff revenues would be used to finance internal improvements.

49. Commons and Associates, *Labour in the United States*, 1: 196, 223-24. Cf. Alexis de Tocqueville, *Democracy in America*, 2 vols. (New York, 1904), 2: ch. 20.

50. Hugins, "Ely Moore," 123-24; Commons and Associates, *Labour in the United States*, 1: 429-30 and *Documentary History*, 6: 223-24.

51. Commons and Associates, *Labour in the United States*, 1: 388.

52. *Working Man's Advocate* (May 14, 1835); Commons and Associates, *Documentary History*, 6: 94-99. Another Boston worker, quoted in the *Boston Post* of April 17, 1835, was more succinct and as class-conscious: "By the old system we have not time for mental cultivation—and that is the policy of the big bugs—they endeavor to keep people ignorant by keeping them always at work." The quoted passage demonstrates the hesitancy, even among militant artisans, to lump laboring master craftsmen with merchant capitalists. At the same time, it shows the tendency of differences within the "productive classes" to be bared by ten-hour struggles. On the issue, see David Roediger's "Liberty of Leisure," delivered at the June 1987 Conference of the Centre de Recherches sur L' Histoire des Etats-Unis of University of Paris. Forthcoming in 1988.

53. Commons and Associates, *Documentary History*, 6: 94-99. Cf. Persons, Parton, and Moses, *Labor Laws*, 9.

54. Pessen, "Boston Labor," 41-42, and *Most Uncommon Jacksonians*, 42. In the course of the strike, labor editor Theophilus Fisk issued a pioneer call for the eight-hour day. See *Working Man's Advocate* (July 25, 1835).

55. Commons and Associates, *Documentary History*, 5: 280, and *Labour in the United States*, 1: 389.

56. Only the Boston plasterers appear to have been a major exception. For evidence of their success in winning the ten-hour day in 1835, see Commons and Associates, *Labour in the United States*, 1: 389, n.30; Pessen, *Most Uncommon Jacksonians*, 43.

57. Foner, *Labor Movement*, 1: 116 and 118; Pessen, "Boston Labor," 42.

58. Ferral's letter was reprinted in *The Man* (New York) on June 29, 1835. See also Seth Luther, *An Address Before the Mechanics and Working Men of the City of Brooklyn, on the Celebration of the Sixtieth Anniversary of American Independence* (Brooklyn, 1836), 18-20.

59. Sullivan, *Industrial Worker*, 152-54; *Niles' Register* (June 6, 1835); Bernstein, "Working People of Philadelphia," 337. Emphasis in original.

60. *National Trades' Union* (June 6, 1835). The heavers won a compromise settlement—sunrise-to-sunset labor with three hours in breaks. See Bureau of Industrial Statistics of Pennsylvania, *Report*, (1880-1881), 263.

61. Bernstein, "Working People of Philadelphia," 337-38; *United States Gazette* (June 3, 1835); Sullivan, *Industrial Worker*, 135; Commons and Associates, *Labour in the United States*, 1: 390, and *Documentary History*, 6: 40-41.

62. United States Gazette (June 3, 1835); Commons and Associates, *Documentary History*, 6: 41, and *Labour in the United States*, 1: 390; Woollen, "Labor Troubles," 96-97; *Proceedings of the Government and Citizens of Philadelphia on the Reduction of Hours of Labor* (Boston, 1835), 9; Philip S. Foner, *The Fur and Leather Workers Union* (Newark, N.Y., 1950), 3-4; Bureau of Industrial Statistics of Pennsylvania, *Report* (1880-1881), 263-64.

63. *Saturday Evening Post* (June 10, 1835); *Gazette* article quoted from *Journal of Commerce* (June 8, 1835); Chevalier as quoted in Woollen, "Labor Troubles," 96; *The Man* (June 29, 1835).

64. Mittelman, *Labour in the United States*, 1: 389-91; Woollen, "Labor Troubles," 96-97; *United States Gazette* (June 3-5, 1835).

65. United States Gazette (June 4 and 5, 1835); Sullivan, *Industrial Worker*, 136; *Pennsylvanian* (June 6, 1835); Commons and Associates, *Documentary History*, 6: 41-46 and *Labour in the United States*, 1: 390-91.

66. Sullivan, *Industrial Worker*, 135-37. But the moderation was short- lived. See *Journal of Commerce* (June 8, 1835), and Commons and Associates, *Documentary History*, 6: 47-49.

67. Commons and Associates, *Documentary History*, 6: 41; Feldberg, *The Philadelphia Riots of 1844* (Westport, Conn., 1975), 47. See also Bernstein, "Working People of Philadelphia," 339, and Woollen, "Labor Troubles," 97.

68. Commons and Associates, *Labour in the United States*, 1: 390; Estey, "Early Closing: Employer Organized Origin of the Retail Labor Movement," *Labor History* 13: 4 (Fall 1972), 560-70. The next major white-collar protest for shorter hours was apparently sponsored in part by the Democratic party. See *Schenectady Reflector and Democrat* (September 24, 1841). Thanks to Carol Steinsapir for the Schenectady reference.

69. Commons and Associates, *Documentary History*, 6: 43; Sullivan, *Industrial Worker*, 226.

70. Gorochow, "Baltimore Labor," 46-47; Commons and Associates, *Documentary History*, 6: 255; Richard T. Ely, *The Labor Movement* (New York, 1886), 56; Woollen, "Labor Troubles," 96; Commons and Associates, *Labour in the United States*, 1: 479-80.

71. Commons and Associates, *Labour in the United States*, 1: 393 and 479- 81; *National Trades' Union* (October 24, 1835); Hirsch, *American Working Class*, 33-34, 111.

72. *Working Man's Advocate* (September 5 and 12, 1835); *National Trades' Union* (September 26, 1835). See also Foner, *Labor Movement*, 1: 118-20 and McNeill, ed., *Labor Movement*, 87.

73. Commons and Associates, *Labour in the United States*, 1: 393 and Commons and Associates, *Documentary History*, 6: 116-19; see also 6: 337-39; *National Laborer* (November 19 and December 10, 1836); Gary M. Fink, "Saint Louis Labor During the Depression of 1837," *Bulletin of the Missouri Historical Society* 26 (October 1969), 59-61; Ware, *Industrial Worker*, 161-62.

74. Commons and Associates, *Documentary History*, 6: 47, 154-55, 321-22 and *Labour in the United States*, 1: 393; *Working Man's Advocate* (January 31, 1835).

75. Sullivan, *Industrial Worker*, 148, 155, 226; McNeill, ed., *Labor Movement*, 84; Woollen, "Labor Troubles," 92-93; Sullivan, *Industrial Worker*, 157, 230; Kleene, "Ten-Hour Day," 34; Bureau of Statistics of Labor of Massachusetts, *Eleventh Annual Report*, 5; *Report of the Bureau of Industrial Statistics of Pennsylvania* (1880-1), 266; and United States Commissioner of Labor, *Report* (1887), 1036.

76. Foner, *Labor Movement*, 1: 111; the third edition of Seth Luther's "An Address to Working Men of New England" (Philadelphia, 1836), 42-46; Commons and Associates, *Labour in the United States*, 1: 420-22; *Paterson Intelligencer* (July 29, 1835); *Newark Daily Advertiser* (July 28-30, 1835); Hirsch, *American Working Class*, 87; and *Report of the Bureau of Statistics of New Jersey* (1885), 273.

77. Commons and Associates, *Labour in the United States*, 1: 420-22; *Working Man's Advocate* (September 26, 1835).

78. *National Laborer* (November 19, 1836).

79. Based on price indices given by Mittelman in *Labour in the United States*, 1: 396 and n. 58, and Pessen, *Most Uncommon Jacksonians*, 44 and n. 29.

80. Commons and Associates, *Labour in the United States*, 1: 397, 479-84; *National Laborer* (November 5, 1836); *The Man* (June 17, 1835). Cf. Karl Marx, *Capital*, 3 vols. (New York, 1967), 1: 546-50.

81. Sullivan, *Industrial Worker*, 228-29; *National Laborer* (July 23 and November 5, 1836); *National Trades' Union* (March 19, 1836); Commons and Associates, *Labour in the United States*, 1: 481-84; McNeill, ed., *Labor Movement*, 83-85; Wallace, *Rockdale*, 356-59.

82. Sullivan, *Industrial Worker*, 229; Commons and Associates, *Labour in the United States*, 1: 483; *National Trades' Union* (March 19, 1836).

83. Sullivan, *Industrial Worker*, 143; Fink, "Saint Louis Labor," 59-61; Bettina Aptheker, ed., *The Unfolding Drama: Studies of U.S. History by Herbert Aptheker* (New York, 1978), 37. See also *Niles' Register* (July 8, 1837).

84. Commons and Associates, *Labour in the United States*, 1: 401-4, 457, and *Documentary History*, 6: 47-49; *New Yorker* (January 20, 1838); *Journal of Commerce* as quoted in *Cincinnati Daily Gazette* (May 23, 1837) and *Missouri Republican* (May 30, 1837).

85. *Public Ledger* (May 16, 1837); Fink, "Saint Louis Labor," 61ff.

86. Samuel Rezneck, "The Social History of an American Depression, 1837- 43," *American Historical Review* 40 (July 1935), 676-77.

87. Particularly noteworthy is the absence of attempts to blame the economic crisis on the introduction of shorter hours.

88. Persons, Parton, and Moses, *Labor Laws*, 8-9, 17-20, and *Massachusetts House Document*, Number 49 (1836). Rhode Island passed a child labor law comparable to Massachusett's 1836 statute in 1840. See Ware, *Cotton Manufacture*, 287. See also Mary McDougall Gordon, "Patriots and Christians: A Reassessment of Nineteenth Century School Reformers," *Journal of Social History* 11: 4 (Summer 1978), 554-74.

89. *National Laborer* (February 6, 1837); "Third Grand Rally of the Workingmen of Charlestown, Massachusetts, Held October 23, 1840," in Stein and Taft, eds., *Labor Politics*, 1: 16; see also *Boston Daily Times* (July 13, 16, 18, 20, 23, 25, 27 and 30, 1839); Ware, *Industrial Worker*, 80-88; McNeill, ed., *Labor Movement*, 91; Illinois Bureau of Labor Statistics, *Fourth Biennial Report*, 466; and Lemuel Danyrid, *History and Philosophy of the Eight-Hour Movement* (New York, 1889), 5.

90. Report of the Select Committee Appointed to Visit the Manufacturing Districts of the Commonwealth for the Purpose of Investigating the Employment of Children in Manufactories—Mr. Petty, Chairman, Senate of the Commonwealth of Pennsylvania (Harrisburg, 1838), 6-42; *Pennsylvania Senate Journal*, 2 (1837-1838), 313, 317-18, 325, 349; Sullivan, *Industrial Worker*, 46-48; J. Lynn Barnard, *Factory Legislation in Pennsylvania: Its History and Administration* (Philadelphia, 1907), 7-17.

91. Commons and Associates, *Documentary History*, 6: 232; O. L. Harvey, "The 10-Hour Day in the Philadelphia Navy Yard, 1835-36," *Monthly Labor Review* 85: 3 (March, 1962), 258-60.

92. Harvey, "Philadelphia Navy Yard," 258-60 and especially the table on 259.

93. Commons and Associates, *Documentary History*, 6: 232-35, 46-48, and 300; Hugins, "Ely Moore," 118, 123-24; *National Laborer* (August 27, 1836); *National Trades' Union* (March 5, 1836).

94. Commons and Associates, *Documentary History*, 6: 300-1.

95. *National Laborer* (August 27, 1836); Commons and Associates, *Documentary History*, 6: 301.

96. Harvey, "Philadelphia Navy Yard," 258-60; *National Laborer* (October 1, 1836); William Maxwell Burke, *History and Function of Central Labor Unions* (New York, 1899), 30.

97. Commons and Associates, *Documentary History*, 6: 246-48, 301-4; "Statement of Working Hours in the Different Navy Yards, Taken from the Correspondence of the Navy Commissioners," (March 27, 1840), Martin Van Buren Papers, Library of Congress; *National Laborer* (October 1 and 29, 1836).

98. Matthew A. Kelly, "Early Federal Regulation of Hours of Labor in the United States," *Industrial and Labor Relations Review* 3: 3 (April 1950), 362-66. The text of the order is in James D. Richardson, *A Compilation of the Messages and Papers of the Presidents, 1789-1907*, 3: 602. McNeill is quoted from his *Labor Movement*, 90; Beard, *American Labor Movement* (New York, 1928), 39; Sullivan, *Industrial Worker*, 213.

99. See also McNeill, ed., *Labor Movement*, 348; *Massachusetts House Document*, Number 44 (1867), 56; and Sterling Spero, *Government as Employer* (New York, 1948), 77-83.

100. Kelly, "Early Regulation," 365, n. 18; "Letter of Mr. Van Buren on Wages," in *Niles' National Register* (September 26, 1840).

101. Kelly, "Early Regulation," 366-67; manuscript copy of Shiner's diary in Library of Congress, 77. See also Sorge, *Labor Movement*, 45-46, 56-57; McNeill, ed., *Labor Movement*, 90-91; and the rather confused comments of Terence Powderly in *Thirty Years of Labor* (Columbus, Ohio, 1889), 472, on the significant later impact of the order.

102. This exclusion of masters from unions argues against the prevailing view, which describes the Jacksonian labor movement as possessing "an essential social outlook which harked back to the Paineite distinction between the 'producing' and 'nonproducing' classes." Such a view does not account for the complexity of the movement's consciousness. The central activity of the organized craftsmen—ten-hour agitation—placed the "productive" masters on the other side of the line. The quote is from Eric Foner, *Tom Paine and Revolutionary America* (New York, 1976), 264-65.

103. Cf. Hugins, "Ely Moore," 121-23, and Schlesinger, *Age of Jackson*, 167ff. with Pessen, "Boston Labor," 42-43, and Hartz, "Seth Luther," 412.

104. McNeill, ed., *Labor Movement*, 342-43.

Mill Women and the Working Day, 1842-1850

1. Philip S. Foner, ed., "Journal of an Early Labor Organizer," *Labor History* 10:2 (Spring 1969), 210 and 224.

2. Hannah Josephson, *The Golden Threads: New England's Mill Girls and Magnates* (New York, 1949), 274; Foner, *Labor Movement*, 1: 203-7; *Voice of Industry* (January 15, 1845). Among many examples of language use designed to include both sexes equally, see *Voice of Industry* (April 24, 1846) and "Petition to the Massachusetts Legislature" as reprinted in *Voice of Industry* (January 15, 1845).

3. Foner, ed., "Organizer," 205; McNeill, ed., *Labor Movement*, 111-15; *The Harbinger* (May 27, 1848).

4. Persons et al., *Labor Laws*, 29; McNeill, ed., *Labor Movement*, 104-5; Foner, ed., "Organizer," 217-19; W.D.P. Bliss and John B. Andrews, *History of Women in Trade Unions* (New York, 1974), 76. Bliss and Andrews originally published as Volume 10 of *Report on Condition of Woman and Child Wage-Earners in the United States*, Senate Document 645 (Washington, D.C., 1911). On the shipyards see McNeill, ed., *Labor Movement*, 96; Davenport, "Regulation," 55- 56; and Charles Morgan, manuscript diary, Mystic Seaport Museum, April 19-May 6, 1841. Thanks to Joel Shufro for the last reference.

5. Persons, *Labor Laws*, 24-26; Thomas Russell Smith, *The Cotton Textile Industry of Fall River, Massachusetts* (New York, 1944), 1-39; Vera Shlakman, *Economic History of a Factory Town: A Study of Chicopee, Massachusetts* (Northampton, Mass., 1934-1935), 123; *The Factory Girl* (March 1, 1843); Foner, *Labor Movement*, 1: 202-3.

6. *The Mechanic* (July 6 and August 8, 1844); Foner, *Labor Movement*, 1: 203.

7. Foner, ed., *American Labor Songs*, 104-5.   8.   *The Mechanic* (July 13, 1844); Merle Curti, *The Learned Blacksmith: The Letters and Journals of Elihu Burritt* (New York, 1937).

9. *New York Evening Post* (April 5, 1847). Aptheker, ed., *Unfolding Drama*, 37, discusses ten-hour campaigns in Louisville crafts during the 1840's; Alan H. Gleason, "The History of Labor in Rochester, 1820-1880" (unpublished M.A. thesis, University of Rochester, 1941), 63.

10. George White, *Memoir of Samuel Slater* (Philadelphia, 1836), 130; Luther, "Address," 31-32, 37; McNeill, ed., *Labor Movement*, 109 and 122.

11. Sumner, *History of Women in Industry*, 55-58. See also Edith Abbott, *Women in Industry* (New York, 1910), 102-3; Ware, *Cotton Manufacture*, 208-9; Thomas Dublin, *Women at Work: The Transformation of Work and Community in Lowell, Massachusetts, 1826-1860* (New York, 1979), 141-42; Dublin, "Women, Work and the Family: Female Operatives in the Lowell Mills, 1830-1860," *Feminist Studies* 3: 1/2 (Fall 1975), 30. From 1830 to 1850 the proportion of men in the textile industry as a whole *rose* from 32 percent of the labor force to 38 percent. See Edward C. Kirkland, *A History of American Economic Life* (New York, 1939), 337.

12. Constance McLaughlin Green, *Holyoke, Massachusetts: A Case Study of the Industrial Revolution in America* (New Haven, Conn., 1939), 46; Thomas M. Leavitt, ed., *The Hollingsworth Letters: Technical Change in the Textile Industry, 1826-1837* (Cambridge 1969), 22-23; Nancy P. Norton, "Labor in the Early New England Carpet Industry," *Bulletin of the Business Historical Society* 26:1 (March 1952), 21.

13. John F. Kasson, *Civilizing the Machine: Technology and Republican Values in America, 1776-1900* (New York, 1976), 53-106, sees the early owners as reformers. See also Josephson, *Golden Threads*, 204-5 and passim. Allen McDonald, "Lowell: A Commercial Utopia," *New England Quarterly* 10 (March 1937); Ware, *Industrial Worker*, 73-74, and esp. 94; and Thomas Dublin, "Women, Work and Protest in the Early Lowell Mills: 'The Oppressing Hand of Avarice Would Enslave Us'," *Labor History* 16:1 (Winter 1975), 99-100. Dublin sees an earlier transition; quote from Sumner, *Women*, 111.

14. Steve Dunwell, *The Run of the Mill* (Boston, 1978), 15, 52, and 66-67. See also

Ware, *Cotton Manufacture*, 210; Commons and Associates, *Documentary History*, 6: 196-98; Brennan, *Rhode Island*, 40ff.; Mary Alice Feldblum, "The Formation of the First Factory Labor Force in the New England Textile Industry, 1800-1848" (unpublished Ph.D. dissertation, New School for Social Research, 1977); and Ware, *Cotton Manufacture*, 200.

15. Jonathan Prude, *The Coming of Industrial Order: Town and Factory Life in Rural Massachusetts, 1810-1860* (Cambridge, England, 1983), 106-07. Brennan, *Rhode Island*, 47; Luther, "Address," 19-21, 29, 38. Commons and Associates, *Documentary History*, 5: 57-66; Sumner, *Women*, 62-64; Abbott, *Women in Industry*, 127; Leavitt, ed., *Hollingsworth Letters*, 22; Ware, *Cotton Manufacture*, 292; George White, *Memoir*, 125-29; Agnes Hanney, *A Chronicle of Industry on the Mill River* (Northampton, Mass., 1935-1936), 40 and 67; Jonathan Prude, "The Social System of Early New England Textile Mills," in Michael H. Frisch and Daniel J. Walkowitz, eds., *Working Class America: Essays on Labor, Community and American Society* (Urbana, Ill., 1982), 17-18.

16. Dunwell, *Run of Mill*, 52; Ware, *Industrial Worker*, 72; Ware, *Cotton Manufacture*, 199ff. Among the laudatory accounts are Michel Chevalier, *Society, Manners and Politics in the United States* (New York, 1961), 130-42; Harriet Martineau, *Society in America*, 2 vols. (New York, 1837), 2: 57-58; and James S. Buckingham, *The Eastern and Western States of America*, 2 vols. (London, 1842), 1: 296-301.

17. Gitelman, "The Waltham System and the Coming of the Irish," *Labor History* 8: 3 (Fall 1967), esp. 230-34. See also Dublin, *Women at Work*, 27 and 140-41 and Harriet H. Robinson, *Loom and Spindle, or Life Among the Early Mill Girls* (New York, 1898), 25-39 on the continued use of child labor in the Waltham-type mills. John Hayes, *American Textile Machinery* (Cambridge, Mass., 1877), 32, discusses the relationship between work discipline and the new technology, as does Wallace, *Rockdale*, 193. See also Hannay, *Mill River*, 39-41; Leavitt, ed., *Hollingsworth Letters*, 66.

18. Ware, *Industrial Worker*, 95 and 108; Re vols. William Scoresby, *American Factories and Their Female Operatives* (London, 1845), 87-88; Gitelman, "Coming," 231-32; *Mechanics' Free Press* (January 17, 1829); Ware, *Cotton Manufacture*, 201-2.

19. *Lowell Offering* (December 1845); Dublin, "Women, Work and Protest," 108; Ware, *Industrial Worker*, 101-5. The Lawrence Company rules are in Baker Library of Harvard University and are accessible in Dunwell, *Run of Mill*, 44. See also Barbara M. Tucker, "Our Good Methodists: The Church, the Factory and the Working Class in Antebellum Webster, Massachusetts," *Maryland Historian* 8: 2 (Fall 1977), 23-33.

20. James Montgomery, *A Practical Detail of Cotton Manufacture of the United States of America* (Glasgow, 1840), 173-76; Sumner, *Women*, 67; Lucy Larcom, "Among Lowell Mill Girls, A Reminiscence," *Atlantic Monthly* 48 (November 1881), 599; Ware, *Cotton Manufacture*, 249; Martineau, *Society*, 2: 57-58; Towles, "Rhode Island," 58.

21. Sumner, *Women*, 99-100; Josephson, *Golden Threads*, 219; Luther, "Ad dress" (third edition), 17; Montgomery, *Practical Detail*, 174. The song is cited in Foner, *Labor Movement*, 1: 110, as current in 1836.

22. Montgomery, *Practical Detail*, 173. Note that 45 minutes were allowed for dinner during May, June, July, and August. Luther's remark is cited in Josephson, *Golden Threads*, 222-23; see also Ware, *Cotton Manufacture*, 266-67; Luther, "Address" (third edition), 36, 40-42; Sumner, *Women*, 94-97; Josephson, *Golden Threads*, 230; *British Parliamentary Papers* (1833), 6: 169.

23. On early paired work, see Dublin's figures for Lowell in 1836 in "Women, Work and Protest," 102, and in *Women at Work*, 74, and Larcom, "Reminiscence," 602. Josephson, *Golden Threads*, 87, discusses shared work and reading on the job. See also Robinson, *Loom and Spindle*, 30, 43, 46, 74; Shlakman, *Economic History*, 54. The best account of antebellum factories is Herman Melville, "The Paradise of Bachelors and the Tartarus of Maids," *Harpers* 10 (April 1855), 675, which comments on working in pairs. The situation in smaller mills is discussed in Norton, "Carpet Industry," 52 and Wallace, *Rockdale*, 177-85, 212, and 380-83.

24. Smith, *Harpers Ferry Armory and the New Technology* (Ithaca, N.Y., 1977), 65-68, 151-52, 256-57, 270-75; see also Edward Wieck, *The American Miners' Association* (New York, 1940), 75-77.

25. Prude, *Industrial Order*, 144-56 and 227-35; Ware, *Cotton Manufacture*, 202; Feldblum, "First Labor Force," ch. 2 and 3; Ware, *Industrial Worker*, 75; Samuel Batchelder, *Introduction and Early Progress of Cotton Manufacture in the United States* (Boston, 1863), 74-76; Dunwell, *Run*, 52; Ware, *Cotton Manufacture*, 225-26.

26. As late as 1841 the average employee in the Boott Mills in Lowell lived but 70 miles from the mill. See *Massachusetts House Document*, Number 50 (1845), Appendix A, 19. On trips home and their role, see Lise Vogel, "Hearts to Feel and Tongues to Speak: New England Mill Women in the Early Nineteenth Century," in Milton Cantor and Bruce Laurie, ed., *Class, Sex and the Woman Worker* (Westport, Conn., 1977), 66-67.

27. Ware, *Cotton Manufacture*, 214; Sumner, *Women*, 88-89, 103-6; H. A. Miles, *Lowell as It Is and as It Was* (Lowell, 1845), 194. Commons and Associates, *Documentary History*, 8: 147.

28. Ware, *Cotton Manufacture*, 266-67. For a complete statistical account of the Hamilton Company firings, see Carl Gersuny, "'A Devil in Petti-Coats' and Just Cause: Patterns of Punishment in Two New England Textile Mills," *Business History Review* 50:2 (Summer 1976), 136-42.

29. Employers trumpeted this feature of American factory life. See Freeman Hunt, ed., *Lives of American Merchants*, 2 vols. (New York, 1856- 1858), 1: 564-65.

30. Ware, *Industrial Worker*, 74 and 98; Foner, *Labor Movement*, 1: 193; Ware, *Cotton Manufacture*, 224-25; Miles, *Was and Is*, 161ff. and·194; Sumner, *Women*, 104; Ray Ginger, "Labor in a Massachusetts Cotton Mill, 1853-1860," *Business History Review* 28: 1 (March 1954), 85-87; Gitelman, "Coming," 250- 51; Evelyn Knowlton, *Pepperell's Progress* (Cambridge, 1948), 59; Commons and Associates, *Documentary History*, 8: 146; Curtis, "Public Hygiene of Massachusetts: But More Particularly of the Cities of Boston and Lowell," *Transactions of the American Medical Association* 2 (1849), 512; see also Dublin, *Women at Work*, 184-89.

31. The 12 percent figure, based on eight mills and on 1,520 girls, is cited in Ware, *Cotton Manufacture*, 220. The quote is from the *Cabotville Chronicle* (December 6, 1845) and is reprinted in the *Voice of Industry* (January 2, 1846).

32. Ware, *Cotton Manufacture*, 217. Cf. Ware's own comments on 198 and 200 and *Lowell Offering* 5 (December 1845), 281; Robinson, *Loom*, 76; Ware, *Industrial Worker*, 96; Feldblum, "Labor Force," ch. 2 and 3. On the decline of family farms see Percy Bidwell, "The Agricultural Revolution in New England," *American Historical Review* 26 (1921).

33. *Voice of Industry* (June 3 and September 18, 1845); *Young America* (October 18, 1845); *Factory Girl's Album* (September 12, 1846); *Lowell Offering* 5 (December 1845), 281; Gitelman, "Coming," 238 and Table 1. For a different interpretation, useful in its cautions on certain kinds of evidence, but not fully convincing in its reassertion of Ware's position regarding need *not* accounting for mill work, see Dublin, *Women at Work*, 33- 39.

34. "The Factory Bell," in Lise Vogel, "Their Own Work: Two Documents from the Nineteenth Century Labor Movement," *Signs* 1: 3 (Spring 1976), 793- 94; see also *Voice of Industry* (February 20, 1846); Gutman, "Work," 26-29.

35. Ginger, "Massachusetts Mill," 91; Abbott, *Women in Industry*, 129-31; *Massachusetts House Document*, Number 50 (1845), 1-6 and 15-17; Robinson in *Loom and Spindle*, 90. Labor papers often featured watch ads. See, for example, *Factory Girl* (March 1, 1843).

36. Citizen of Lowell, *Corporations and Operatives* (Lowell, 1843), 43 and 72; Ware, *Industrial Worker*, 84; Josephson, *Golden Threads*, 219; Sumner, *Women*, 63. The evidence on hours is scattered for the 1840s. Montgomery's figures for 1839, as given in *Practical Detail*, 173-74, were most often quoted by procorporation spokesmen. (See Miles, *Was and Is*, 101). Montgomery's data indicate that twelve hours and thirteen minutes exclusive of meals was the average working day. Other accounts refer to a somewhat longer day, nearer to thirteen hours after meals were subtracted. See Citizen of Lowell, *Corporations*, 15 and 18; Commons and Associates, *Documentary History*, 7: 134; *Factory Girl's Album* (June 20, 1846); *Voice of Industry* (June 26 and September 11, 1845; January 16 and 23, 1846); John Greenleaf Whittier, *Stranger in Lowell* (Boston, 1845), 117. A few operatives doing very strenuous work (for example, warpers) were allowed to leave early. See Miles, *Was and Is*, 82.

37. *Voice of Industry* (July 10, 1845; January 8 and March 26, 1847); Sumner, *Women*, 65.

38. *Voice of Industry* (September 11, 1845, and January 16, 1846); *Lowell Offering*, 5 *(October, 1845), 217.*

39. McNeill, ed., *Labor Movement*, 107. On "lighting up" useful sources are Sumner, *Women*, 102; Shlakman, *Economic History*, 55; Whittier, *Stranger*, 116ff; Bliss and Andrews, *Women in Unions*, 66; Green, *Holyoke*, 44; *Voice of Industry* (November 13, 1846); *Working Man's Advocate* (October 5, 1844); and those sources cited in notes 40-42 below.

40. *Factory Girls' Garland*, cited in Ware, *Industrial Worker*, 134. Also see *The Awl* (October 2, 1844), and Prude, *Industrial Order*, 226.

41. Josephson, *Golden Threads*, 218-19; *Massachusetts House Document*, Number 50 (1845), 3.

42. *Voice of Industry* (March 26, 1847); Brennan, *Rhode Island*, 48 and below. Overtime excited similar complaints. See Abbott, *Women in Industry*, 127, and *Factory Girl* (March 1, 1843).

43. Benita Eisler, *The Lowell Offering*: Writings by New England Mill Women (Philadelphia, 1971), 30-31; Commons and Associates, *Documentary History*, 7: 133ff.; Sumner, *Women*, 94-100. Typical timetables are reprinted in Dunwell, *Run of Mill*, 94.

44. Cf. Lucy Larcom, *An Idyl of Work* (Boston, 1875), 129, with Ware, *Cotton Manufacture*, 255, on reading, and Vogel, "Hearts to Feel," 80. Cf. *Lowell Offering* 1 (December 1840) and Ware, *Industrial Worker*, 121, on plants and flowers; see also Josephson, *Golden Threads*, 221-23; Gutman, "Work," 27; Sumner, *Women*, 97; and Foner, ed., *Factory Girls*, 89ff.

45. The best account of this aspect of the "speedup and stretch-out" in larger cotton mills is Dublin, *Women at Work*, 109-12. In woolen mills some operatives tended just one loom in the early years according to Sumner, *Women*, 109. On the cotton industry, see also Scoresby, *American Factories*, 30-31, 59-60; *British Parliamentary Papers* (1833), 6: 167; *Massachusetts House Document*, Number 50 (1845), 1-6, 15-17; *Voice of Industry* (June 25, 1847); T. Throstle, "Factory Life in New England," *Knickerbocker* 30 (December 1847), 517.

46. Amelia, "Some Beauties of Our Factory System—Otherwise—Lowell slavery," in *Factory Life as It Is* (Lowell, 1845). Reprinted in Vogel, "Their Own Work," 799. Sumner, *Women*, 108-11, recounts conflicts over the number of looms. There were, of course, technological changes which in some cases made tending more looms possible. But even in the absence of major technological innovation, there was a significant speedup of production. See Dublin, *Women at Work*, 110-11 and McGouldrick, *New England Textiles*, 223-30. But also note Paul A. David, *Technical Choice, Innovation and Economic Growth* (London, 1975), 175-91.

47. For the role of piece rates in the transition to industrial capitalism, see Hobsbawm's seminal "Custom, Wages and Workload," in *Labouring Men*, esp. 349. Also see Marx, *Capital*, 1: 551-58.

48. Dublin, *Women at Work*, 110-11; Foner, *Labor Movement*, 1:196. The definition is from *Factory Girl* (January 15, 1845). Norman Ware's figures, based on Abbott's data, show a steady decline in the wages of spinners and weavers from 1842 through 1850, but the sample is tiny. See *Industrial Worker*, 119. Gitelman, "Coming," 238, argues for a slight increase in factory women's wages during the 1840s. Dublin, *Women at Work*, 111, finds wages "basically unchanged" in two job categories in the Hamilton Company mills from 1840 through 1854, a period of significant speedup. Ware, *Cotton Manufacture*, 307, compiles the increases in productivity. For reactions to cuts in piece rates see Robinson, *Loom and Spindle*, 86, and *Voice of Industry* (December 27, 1845, and May 15, 1846). The strikes of 1842 and 1843 are discussed in the *New York Daily Tribune* (January 3, 1843) and Shlakman, *Economic History*, 121-26.

49. *Lowell Offering* 5 (May 1845), 98-99.

50. The best accounts are Foner, *Labor Movement*, 1: ch. 11; Ware, *Industrial Worker*, ch. 8; and Josephson, *Golden Threads*, ch. 11 and 12.

51. Commons and Associates, *Documentary History*, 8: 91-97 and 133-34; Foner, *Labor Movement*, 1: 206; Persons, *Labor Laws*, 30-32; Dublin, "Women, Work and Protest," 144. The figures are those of the House committee; more than 2,000 signers in Lowell were claimed in the *Voice of Industry* (January 15, 1845) Cf. *The Factory Girl* (March 1, 1843).

52. *The Awl* (April 12, 1845) and *Voice of Industry* (June 12, 1845).

53. Foner, *Labor Movement*, 1: 197; *Voice of Industry* (December 19, 1845); Bliss and

Andrews, *Women in Trade Unions*, 79.

54. Foner, *Labor Movement*, 1: 198-99, and Foner, ed., *Factory Girls*, 159- 77. *Voice of Industry* (May 15, 1846); *Lowell Offering* 1 (1840), 25-26 (first series).

55. Robinson, *Loom and Spindle*, 43-46; Katz, *School Reform*, 88; Ware, *Cotton Manufacture*, 201; and *Lowell Offering* 3 (June 1843).

56. Beecher is quoted in Josephson, *Golden Threads*, 226. See also Shlakman, *Economic History*, 59; Larcom, "Among Lowell Mill Girls," 602-3; Foner, *Labor Movement*, 1: 197.

57. See William R. Taylor and Christopher Lasch, "Two 'Kindred Spirits': Sorority and Family in New England, 1839-1846," *New England Quarterly* 36 (March 1963), 23-41; Bertha Monica Stearns, "Early Factory Magazines in New England," *Journal of Economic and Business History* (August 1930), 687-90. See *Lowell Offering* 1 (1840), 25-26 (first series), for the Bagley article and *Lowell Offering* 2 (1842), 380, for Abel Thomas's editorial comment against long hours. Farley did little or no mill work after 1840. See Ware, *Industrial Worker*, 90; Farley, *Operatives Reply to the Honorable Jere. Clemens* (Lowell, 1850), 20-21; and *Voice of Industry* (September 25, 1845). On the exclusion of Bagley's articles, see Bagley and Farley in *Voice of Industry* (July 10 and September 17 and 25, 1845) and the *Lowell Advertiser* (July 15 and 26, 1845).

58. *Lowell Offering* 3 (1843), 48, and 5 (1845), 99; Ware, *Industrial Worker*, 92; Dublin, *Women at Work*, 123-24. The *Offering* 3 (1843), 214, did contain a protest against long hours on the grounds of health and education.

59. Stearns, "Magazines," 698-702; Foner, *Labor Movement*, 1: 197-99; Foner, ed., *Factory Girls*, 178-93.

60. *Voice of Industry* (July 10, 1845, and January 2, 1846).

61. Persons, *Labor Laws*, 32; Stearns, "Magazines," 702-4; Cole, *Immigrant City*, 120-21; Foner, ed., *Factory Girls*, 178-79; *Voice of Industry* (April 23 and July 30, 1847).

62. On the antislavery petitions and political action by women, see Carrie Chapman Catt and Nettie Rogers Shuler, *Woman Suffrage and Politics* (Seattle, 1969), 14. Eleanor Flexner, *Century of Struggle: The Woman's Rights Movement in the United States* (New York, 1971), discusses antislavery and labor agitation as roots of the movement for women's rights. Of course, the labor reform and antislavery movements overlapped.

63. Harriet Robinson did come to advocate woman's suffrage, but her influence on the ten-hour movement was only slight and exercised through her husband, prolabor editor William S. Robinson. See *Loom and Spindle*, 132 and 175. See also Eisler, ed., *Lowell Offering*, 209; *Voice of Industry* (June 5 and December 19, 1845); and esp. Foner, ed., *Factory Girls*, 295-321.

64. *Voice of Industry* (November 13, 1846); *Manchester Democrat* (August 25, 1847).

65. *Voice of Industry* (February 12 and June 5, 1845); Foner, ed., *Factory Girls*, 236; Commons and Associates, *Documentary History*, 8: 134.

66. Commons and Associates, *Documentary History*, 3: 133; *Voice of Indus try* (January 15, 1845). See Commons and Associates, *Documentary History*, 8: 134; Dublin, "Women, Work and Protest," 114. A recent study of health records suggests that lack of time for "mastication" may have caused chronic gastrointestinal ailments among the women. See Ron LaBreque, "New Industry for Mill City, USA," *Historic Preservation* 32 (July-August 1980), 37.

67. Commons and Associates, *Documentary History*, 8: 133-51. See also Sumner, *Women*, 101ff.; Ware, *Industrial Worker*, 116; *Factory Girl's Album* (September 12, 1846).

68. Commons and Associates, *Documentary History*, 8: 135-38, 142-47; Dublin, *Women at Work*, 114-15. See Marx, *Capital*, 1: 283ff. on the British laws. After (and before) Britain passed a ten-hour bill in 1847, American laborers compared their hours to those of the British. See Foner, ed., *Factory Girls*, xxii and 219; and *Voice of Industry* (July 9, 1847).

69. Eisler, ed., *Lowell Offering*, 201-2; *Voice of Industry* (January 9 and April 17, 1846); *Lowell Advertiser* (September 2, 1845). The report is *Senate Document*, Number 81 (1846).

70. Eisler, ed., *Lowell Offering*, 201; *Voice of Industry* (April 17 and May 15, 1846); Ware, *Industrial Worker*, 139; *Voice of Industry* (May 15, 1846). There were about 7,000 women workers in Lowell during these years. See Sumner, *Women*, 53, and Commons and Associates, *Documentary History*, 8: 144- 45. Dublin, *Women at Work*, 122, calculates that at its 1846 peak, the petition campaign secured signatures from a maximum of 36% of Lowell's female mill

operatives.

71. Dublin, *Women at Work*, 114-18; Foner, ed., *Factory Girls*, 243; *Voice of Industry* (November 28, 1845, and April 17, 1846); Josephson, *Golden Threads*, 261-62; McNeill, ed., *Labor Movement*, 155, reports a ten-hour law introduced before the House in 1848.

72. *Factory Girl's Album* (February 14 and September 2, 1846); *Voice of Industry* (February 13, 1846, and June 30, 1847).

73. Vogel, "Their Own Work," 787-88. On Eastman, see Josephson, *Golden Threads*, 275, and Foner, ed., *Factory Girls*, 194-208.

74. Josephson, *Golden Threads, 274-75; Commons and Associates, Documentary History*, 8: 125-26; *Voice of Industry* (October 2 and 9, 1846); Foner, ed., *Factory Girls*, 260-61; Josephson, *Golden Threads*, 276-77. A Manchester protest over Sunday labor ended in police violence shortly after the Nashua strike. See Barbara Mayer Wertheimer, *We Were There: The Story of Working Women in America* (New York, 1977), 77.

75. Commons and Associates, *Documentary History*, 8: 188-99. The *Voice*'s article (July 9, 1847) reiterated the insistence of Massachusetts ten-hour advocates that any such law must ban special contracts.

76. Sumner, *Women*, 69-70; Foner, ed., *Factory Girls*, 263-66; *Manchester Democrat* (August 25 and September 1, 1847); *Voice of Industry* (August 27 and October 23, 1847).

77. Bliss and Andrews, *Women in Trade Unions*, 66, reports a large number of firings three days before the law was to take effect. See also *Voice of Industry* (September 17 and October 1, 1847); Sumner, *Women*, 69; and *Maine Senate Document*, Number 19 (1848).

78. Ware, *Industrial Worker*, 141, and Sumner, *Women*, 69-70; Bliss and Andrews, *Women in Trade Unions*, 61-63; *Young America* (October 18, 1845); McNeill, ed., *Labor Movement*, 103-4; *Voice of Industry* (October 2, 1845).

79. *Young America* (October 18, 1845); Bliss and Andrews, *Women in Trade Unions*, 62-63; Foner, *Labor Movement*, 1: 207-9; *Voice of Industry* (October 2 and 9, 1845); *Report of Bureau of Industrial Statistics of Pennsylvania* (1880-1881), 271.

80. *Voice of Industry* (November 7 and December 19, 1845); Ware, *Industrial Worker*, 142.

81. Foner, *Labor Movement*, 1: 202; Ware, *Industrial Worker*, 139-41; *Voice of Industry* (December 19, 1845).

82. *The Mechanic* (July 13 and 20, 1844); *Voice of Industry* (July 10 and 17, 1845).

83. *The Mechanic* (August 3, 1844); Foner, *Labor Movement*, 1: 203; *Voice of Industry* (June 5, 1845); Foner, ed., *Factory Girls*, 226-27; Josephson, *Golden Threads*, 246.

84. *The Factory Girl* (March 1, 1843); *Voice of Industry* (July 10, 1845). Emphases original.

85. Ware, *Industrial Worker*, 140-43; *Voice of Industry* (January 30 and February 13, 1846).

86. Wallace, *Rockdale*, 388-94; Bernard, *Factory Legislation in Pennsylvania*, 18-20; McNeill, ed., *Labor Movement*, 112.

87. Commons and Associates, *Documentary History*, 8: 200-1.

88. *Ibid.*, 8: 202-5 and *Pittsburgh Morning Post* (July 6, 1848). The fullest account is a pamphlet written by the owners, reprinted as "The Factory Riots in Allegheny City," *Western Pennsylvania Historical Magazine* 5: 4 (January 1922), 203-11.

89. Commons and Associates, *Documentary History*, 8: 200; Bliss and Andrews, *Women in Trade Unions*, 63-65; *Daily Tribune* (August 1, 1848); *Pittsburgh Morning Post* (August 1, 2, 7, 15, 26 and 29, 1848). Some workers did hold out for full wages; see the *Post* (August 26, 1848).

90. *Pittsburgh Morning Post* (August 8, 1848); Laurie, *Working People*, 143- 47 and 237; Wallace, *Rockdale*, 392-94; Bernard, *Factory Legislation in Pennsylvania*, 20; United States Commissioner of Labor, *Third Annual Report*, 1040.

91. *Pittsburgh Morning Post* (August 11 and 25, 1848). See Commonwealth of Pennsylvania, *Legislative Documents* (1882), 3: 101-2, and Bernard, *Factory legislation*, 20-22.

92. Ware, *Industrial Worker*, 147; Wertheimer, *We Were There*, 75.

93. Wertheimer, *We Were There*, 73; Foner, *Labor Movement*, 1: 211-12; Josephson, *Golden Threads*, 278-79.

94. Josephson, *Golden Threads*, 264ff.; Foner, *Labor Movement*, 1: 206-7.

95. Commons and Associates, *Documentary History*, 8: 99-113.

96. Josephson, *Golden Threads*, 268-81; *Voice of Industry* (January 23, 1846); *The Harbinger* 1 (1845), 22; Helen Sara Zahler, *Eastern Workingmen and National Land Policy, 1829-1862* (New York, 1941), 63-87 and 183-8. Organization of the Industrial Congress was proposed by the New England Workingmen's Association. David Reynolds, *Selected Writings of George Lippard* (New York, forthcoming), introduction; Mark Lause, "The Brotherhood of the Union," a working paper in the possession of its author at University of Illinois—Chicago Circle; Dublin, *Women at Work, 121-22; Working Man's Advocate* (June 2, 1832) and *Sentinel* (April 14, 1832); Ryckman, as quoted in Persons, *Labor Laws*, 39; Foner, ed., "Early Labor Organizer," 206-7; Foner, *Labor Movement*, 1: 200; *Voice of Industry* (April 3 and 10, 1846); Alice Felt Tyler, *Freedom's Ferment* (New York, 1944), 178; Commons and Associates, *Documentary History*, 8: 21.

97. Foner, *Labor Movement*, 1: 206; Ware, *Industrial Worker*, 210-11; Wertheimer, *We Were There*, 75.

98. Gitelman, "Coming of the Irish," 227-53; Dublin, *Women at Work*, 138- 39; Ware, *Industrial Worker*, 80-88. In the 1846 strike mentioned, Germans took the jobs of striking Irish laborers in Brooklyn. See Commons and Associates, *Documentary History*, 8: 225-26, and also Frank Murray, "The Irish and Afro-American in U.S. History," *Freedomways* 22 (First Quarter 1982), 26.

99. Dublin, "Women, Work and the Family," 34-37; Dublin, *Women at Work*, 138-64; Gitelman, "Coming of the Irish," 227-53.

100. Ware, *Industrial Worker*, 127 and 152; Vogel, "Hearts to Feel," 80.

Hours, Labor Protest, and Party Politics
in the 1850s

1. Commons and Associates, *History of Labour*, 1: 544-45.

2. Ware, *Industrial Worker*, ch. 8 and 10, esp. 154.

3. See below.

4. Laurie, *Working People*, 184 and 185-94. United States Commission of Labor, *Report of the Commissioner of Labor* (Washington, D.C., 1887), 1041; Edgar Barclay Cale, "The Organization of Labor in Philadelphia, 1850-1870" (unpublished Ph.D. dissertation, University of Pennsylvania, 1940), 37-38.

5. Persons, *Labor Laws*, 75-76; Commons and Associates, *Labour in the United States*, 1: 602.

6. Persons, *Labor Laws*, 75-76; *Massachusetts House Document*, Number 22 (1853), 6; McNeill, ed., *Labor Movement*, 117.

7. *New York Daily Tribune* (July 9, 1851).

8. Bliss and Andrews, *Women in Trade Unions*, 68; *New York Daily Tribune* (July 11, 14-15, and August 12, 1851); Foner, *Labor Movement*, 1: 216-17; Henry Farnam, *ch.s in the History of Social Legislation in the United States* (Washington, D.C., 1938), 267.

9. *New York Daily Tribune* (October 19, 1850); *Hunt's Merchants Magazine* 41 (1860), 750; *New York Herald* (February 7, 1852).

10. George A. Stevens, *New York Typographical Union Number Six* (Albany, 1913), 10-14; Robert Ernst, *Immigrant Life in New York City, 1825-1863* (New York, 1949), 109-10. For a fine later defense of the nine-hour system for women in the needle trades in New York, see "Miss E. M. Powell to Editor," *New York Daily Tribune* (July 9, 1858).

11. Stevens, *Typographical Union*, 24ff.; Ernst, *Immigrant Life*, 109; McNeill, ed., *Labor Movement*, 117.

12. Shlakman, *Economic History*, 142-44, quotes Taylor on Chicopee; Cole, *Immigrant City*, 120-21; Green, *Holyoke*, 46.

13. Whittier's comments on Amesbury are in Harriet Farley, *Operatives Reply to Hon. Jere Clemens*, 10-11; John A. Pollard, "Whittier on Labor Unions," *New England Quarterly* 12 (1939); and Thomas F. Currier, "Whittier and the Amesbury-Salisbury Strike," *New England Quarterly* 8 (1935), 105-12.

14. Farley, *Clemens*, 10-11; McNeill, ed., *Labor Movement*, 118-20; U.S. Commission of Labor, *Report* (1887), 1042; Persons, *Labor Laws*, 57 and 65; *Massachusetts House Document*, Number 122 (1853), 4.

15. McNeill, ed., *Labor Movement*, 118-20; U.S. Commission of Labor, *Report* (1887), 1042. Some accounts suggest that it was several days before the women left the mills. Cf. Sara Redford, *History of Amesbury* (Amesbury, Mass., 1968), 43, and Currier and Gerish, "A Succinct Account of the Late Difficulties on the Salisbury Corporation," (Salisbury, Mass., 1852), 5.

16. U.S. Commission of Labor, *Report* (1887), 1042; McNeill, ed., *Labor Movement*, 118-20; *Massachusetts House Document, Number 122 (1853), 4.*

17. McNeill, ed., *Labor Movement*, 119-21; U.S. Commission of Labor, *Report* (1887), 1042; *Massachusetts House Document*, Number 122, 4.

18. Bureau of Statistics of Labor of Massachusetts, *Eleventh Annual Report* (1880), 14, and G. H. Preble, *History of Boston Navy Yard* (Washington, D.C., 1947), 316; Shiner Diary, Library of Congress, 116.

19. See Thirty-Sixth Congress (First Session), *House Executive Document 71* (Series Number 1056), especially the April 13, 1859, testimony of B. F. Delano of Brooklyn Navy Yard.

20. Bureau of Statistics of Labor of Massachusetts, *Eleventh Annual Report*, 14 and 58; *Massachusetts House Document*, Number 44 (1867), 56-59; Persons, *Labor Laws*, 76 and 88; Ernst,

Immigrant Workers, 110.

21. Commons and Associates, *Documentary History*, 8: 335-36, and *Labour in the United States*, 1: 607-12.

22. Eugene H. Roseboom, *The Civil War Era, 1850-1873*, vol. 4 in Carl Wittke, ed., *The History of the State of Ohio* (Columbus, 1944), 34: Ira Cross, *A History of the Labor Movement in California* (Berkeley, 1935), 300, n. 18. Cross mentions the broader range of crafts in his letter to John R. Commons, dated November 15, 1906, and in the Commons Papers at the State Historical Society of Wisconsin.

23. Commons and Associates, *Documentary History*, 8: 208-9; Foner, *Labor Movement*, 1: 213; Wallace, *Rockdale*, 393-94; Persons, *Labor Laws*, 65; Henry Graham Ashmead, *History of Delaware County, Pennsylvania* (Philadelphia, 1884), 109-12; Jonathan Grossman, *William Sylvis: Pioneer of American Labor* (New York, 1945), 130; Edward A. Wyatt, "Rise of Industry in Antebellum Petersburg," *William and Mary Quarterly* 17: 1 (January 1937), 20; Aptheker, ed., *Unfolding Drama*, 39.

24. U.S. Commission of Labor, *Report* (1887), 1043-44; Persons, *Labor Laws*, 88; Shlakman, *Economic History*, 144-45; James P. Hanlan, *The Working Population of Manchester, New Hampshire, 1840-1886* (Ann Arbor, 1981), 71-77.

25. Clifton Yearley, "Richard Trevellick: Labor Agitator," *Michigan History* 34 (December 1955), 425-27; Obediah Hicks, *Life of Richard Trevellick* (Joliet, Ill., 1896), ch. 4; biographical material on Trevellick is filed with the United States Manuscripts, 12A (Box 1) at the State Historical Society of Wisconsin; Aptheker, ed., *Unfolding Drama*, 40.

26. McNeill, ed., *Labor Movement*, 109 and 122; Henry E. Hoagland, "Rise of the Iron Molders Union," *American Economic Review* 3 (June 1913), 302; Cross, *California*, 303, n.5; Commonwealth of Pennsylvania, *Legislative Documents*, 3 (1882), 278-79; Bureau of Labor Statistics of Illinois, *Fourth Biennial Report (1886), 468; New York Daily Tribune* (May 5, 1860); Schob, *Hired Hands*, 254-55.

27. Eric Foner, *Free Soil, Free Labor, Free Men: The Ideology of the Republican Party Before the Civil War* (New York, 1970), esp. ch. 2; Roy Nichols, *The Democratic Machine, 1850-1854* (New York, 1923).

28. Herbert D.A. Donavan, *The Barnburners* (New York, 1925); Handlin, *Boston's Immigrants*, 193; Arthur Darling, "Jacksonian Democracy in Massachusetts, 1824-1848," *American Historical Review* 24 (January 1924), 282ff.

29. Commons, "Horace Greeley and the Working Class Origins of the Republican Party," *Political Science Quarterly* 24 (1909), 485-86; *New York Weekly Tribune* (August 14, 1847); McNeill, ed., *Labor Movement*, 105; Illinois Bureau of Labor Statistics, *Fourth Biennial Report* (1886), 466. See J. Parton, *The Life of Horace Greeley* (New York, 1855), 338-40; Greeley, *The Autobiography of Horace Greeley* (New York, 1872), 511ff.; L. D. Ingersoll, *The Life of Horace Greeley* (Chicago, 1873), 628-30. In one extended reference to hours in 1850, Greeley did countenance laws allowing special contracts. See his "The Emancipation of Labor," in Stein and Taft, eds., *Labor Politics*, 1: 28-32.

30. Montgomery, *Beyond Equality*, 119; Commons, "Greeley," 484; Zahler, *National Land Policy*, 147; "Third Grand Rally," in Stein and Taft, eds., *Labor Politics*, 14-18; Commons, "Greeley," 486-87; Commons and Associates, *Documentary History*, 8: 188-99; Towles, "Rhode Island," 60.

31. Farnam, *Social Legislation*, 265-67; Towles, "Rhode Island," 63-65; Roseboom, *Civil War Era*, 40; Commons and Associates, *Labour in the United States*, 1: 543-46. Other states debating the issue were Massachusetts, Wisconsin, Maryland, Delaware, and New York. See below and Thomas Gavett, *The Development of the Labor Movement in Milwaukee* (Madison, 1965), 14; McNeill, ed., *Labor Movement*, 117; *Massachusetts House Document*, Number 80 (1855), 2; Sorge, *Labor Movement*, 85.

32. See below and Commons and Associates, *Labour in the United States*, 1: 542-43.

33. See Laura E. Richards, ed., *Letters and Journals of Samuel Gridley Howe*, 2 vols. (Boston, 1909), 2: 285, for an anti-shorter-hours statement by a famous Republican and note that Schouler, the Whiggish bane of the ten-hour movement of the 1840s, became a Republican. See

Foner, *Free Soil*, 17.

34. See above and Foner, *Free Soil*, 15.

35. Commons and Associates, *Documentary History*, 8: 176-80.

36. Ibid., 8: 182; *Massachusetts House Document*, Number 185 (1852), 8 and passim; *Massachusetts House Document*, Number 122 (1853), 6 and 8; *Massachusetts House Document*, Number 80 (1855), 4.

37. Zahler, *National Land Policy*, 84-85, and Gavett, *Milwaukee*, 14. On Evans, and on the considerable extent to which antebellum labor reformers felt and articulated working class concerns, see Franklin Rosemont, "Working Men's Parties," in Paul Buhle and Alan Dawley, eds. *Working for Democracy* (Urbana, Ill., 1985), 11-20.

38. Foner, *Labor Movement*, 1: 216-17; *Trenton Daily State Gazette* (September 15-17, 1850).

39. Foner, *Labor Movement*, 1: 216-17. For the text of the law, see *Acts of New Jersey, 1851; Approved March 18*, 321.

40. Farnam, *Social Legislation*, 265; Persons, *Labor Laws*, ch. 3.

41. See below; Montgomery, *Beyond Equality*, 117-20; Persons, *Labor Laws*, 63-76.

42. Handlin, *Boston's Immigrants*, 193-97; Montgomery, *Beyond Equality*, 117-20.

43. Persons, in *Labor Laws*, 63-76; *Massachusetts House Document*, Number 185 (1852), 3.

44. From Massachusetts Bureau of the Statistics of Labor, *Report of the Bureau of Statistics of Labor* (1870), 125-26. The standard account is Persons, in *Labor Laws*, esp. 59ff. Typical of the negative ones is Robert Werlich, *"Beast" Butler* (Washington, D.C., 1962), 10-11.

45. Persons, in *Labor Laws*, 59-62. James Parton, *General Butler in New Orleans* (New York, 1864), 25-27 and 36-39; Benjamin Butler, *Private and Official Correspondence of Benjamin F. Butler*, 5 vols. (1917), 5: 572; Butler, *Butler's Book* (Boston, 1892), 91-93; Howard P. Nash, *Stormy Petrel: The Life and Times of General Benjamin F. Butler, 1818-1893* (Rutherford, N.J., 1969), 40.

46. *Massachusetts House Document*, Number 153 (1850); Number 185 (1852); Number 230 (1852); Number 122 (1853); Number 107 (1856).

47. Curtis, "Public Hygiene in Massachusetts," esp. 504-19; Commons and Associates, *Documentary History*, 8: 161-69.

48. *Massachusetts House Document*, Number 80 (1855), 3-5.

49. Ibid., 2. 50. Curtis, "Public Hygiene," 516; *Massachusetts House Document*, Number 185 (1852), 20-21 and passim; Persons, in *Labor Laws*, 60-61. Anthony Cooper Ashley, Earl of Shaftesbury, was the leading parliamentary spokesperson for shorter hours and an advocate of the idea that the shorter day would increase production. See Marx, *Capital*, 1: 412-13.

51. *Massachusetts House Document*, Number 185 (1852), 9; Commons and Associates, *Documentary History*, 8: 170.

52. The quote is from Parton, *Butler*, 26. For Butler's early career, see the works in note 45 above and Hans L. Trefousse, *Ben Butler: The South Called Him Beast* (New York, 1957), ch. 3.

53. Nash, *Stormy Petrel*, 44, quotes William S. Robinson.

54. Butler, *Butler's Book*, 97-107; Nash, *Stormy Petrel*, 41-42; Parton, *Butler*, 36-37; *Massachusetts House Document*, Number 230 (1852), passim; Persons, in *Labor Laws*, 71-74.

55. Ibid. and Robert S. Holzman, *Stormy Ben Butler* (New York, 1954), 13.

56. Persons, in *Labor Laws*, 65-88, esp. 65-70 and 87.

57. Ibid., 63-65.

58. Commons and Associates, *Documentary History*, 8: 127-32.

59. Ibid., 8: 129-32, and *Labour in the United States*, 1: 544-45.

60. Farnam, *Social Legislation*, 267; Persons, in *Labor Laws*, 89; Montgomery, *Beyond Equality*, 317.

61. Montgomery, *Beyond Equality*, 117 and 246-57. On the long-standing farm opposition

to shorter hours, see Ira Steward, "Hours of Labor on Farms," Ira Steward Papers, State Historical Society of Wisconsin, (1875?); George A. Brandreth, "Speech of Hon. Geo. A. Brandreth in Favor of the 'Eight Hours Bill'," (n.p., 1866), 13; Frederick Merk, "The Labor Movement in Wisconsin during the Civil War," *Proceedings of the State Historical Society of Wisconsin at Its Sixty-Second Annual Meeting* (Madison, 1915), 185. National party platforms of the period all ignore hours. See Kirk H. Porter and Donald Bruce Johnson, eds., *National Party Platforms, 1840-1964* (Urbana, Ill., 1966), 16-33. For an example of the way antislavery advocates of free labor ignored the issue of hours in responding to southern criticisms of female factory labor, see Farley, *Clemens*, passim., but especially the testimony of Whittier, 10-11.

62. McNeill, ed., *Labor Movement*, 121. Cf. Sorge, *Labor Movement*, 85.

63. Computations based on table in *Tenth Census* (1880), vol. 20: 328. For figures in all industries, see vol. 20: xviii; *Tenth Census*, vol. 20: 331, 340, 346, 352, 359, 390, 397, 406; Persons, in *Labor Laws*, 408; Green, *Holyoke*, 48.

64. Green, *Holyoke*, 46-48; Farnam, *Social Legislation*, 266; Foner, *Labor Movement*, 1: 215; Persons, in *Labor Laws*, 88-89; Shlakman, *Economic History*, 142-44; *Tenth Census*, vol. 20: 192, ch. 3.

The Civil War and the Birth of the Eight-Hour Movement

1. Steward, as quoted in *Massachusetts House Document*, Number 44 (1867), 67. He makes the same point in *Poverty* (Boston, 1873), 2. For a fuller treatment of Steward's relationship to antislavery thought and practice, see David Roediger, "Ira Steward and the Antislavery Origins of American Eight- Hour Theory," *Labor History* 27 (Summer 1986).

2. *Mechanics' Free Press* (June 21, 1828); *The Man* (March 26, 1834); *National Laborer* (November 5, 1836); Kelly, "Early Regulation," 366-67; Robinson, "Reduction of Working Hours," 38-39; Foner, *Labor Movement*, 1: 363; *New York Daily Tribune* (October 19, 1850).

3. Marx, *Capital*, 1: 301; Cf. McNeill, ed., *Labor Movement*, 124.

4. Persons, in *Labor Laws*, ch. 4; Foner, *Labor Movement*, 1: 369; Wendell Phillips, *The Foundation of the Labor Movement* (n.p., 1871?) as reprinted in Stein and Taft, eds., *Religion, Reform and Revolution*, 153; James C. Sylvis, ed., *The Life, Speeches, Labor and Essays of William H. Sylvis* (Philadelphia, 1872), 208.

5. Fincher, Powderly, Steward, and Midwest organizer William Swinton, were all machinists, and it was their union which first went on record on the issue. See Robinson, "Reduction of Hours," 41-43; Commons and Associates, *Documentary History*, 9: 279-83. The molders held discussions on the demand in 1861. See Frank T. Stockton, *The International Molders Union of North America* (Baltimore, 1921), 159-62; Grossman, *Sylvis*, 129-31; Thomas Farley, "The Molders' Union and the Eight-Hour Day," *International Molders' Journal* (August 1920), 598. For the continued leadership of building tradesmen, see Cross, *California*, 38; *Saint Louis Daily Press* (September 8 and 15, 1865); *Fincher's Trades' Review* (January 28, 1865).

6. See D. L. Burn, "The Genesis of American Engineering Competition," and Nathan Rosenberg, "Technological Changes in the Machine Tool Industry, 1840- 1910," both in A. W. Coats and Ross M. Robertson, eds., *Essays in American Economic History* (London, 1969), 150-64 and 165-86; David T. Gilchrist and W. David Lewis, eds., *Economic Change in the Civil War Era* (Greenville, Del., 1965), 135.

7. Harry Braverman, *Labor and Monopoly Capital* (New York, 1974), 110-11. On the extent to which labor leaders of the period were rooted in industrial life, see Montgomery, *Beyond Equality*, 205-7.

8. Bruce Laurie, Theodore Hershberg, and George Alter, "Immigrants and Industry: The Philadelphia Experience," *Journal of Social History* (Winter 1975), 225 (Table 4); Rosenberg, "Machine Tool Industry," 169; Grossman, *Sylvis*, 24.

9. Montgomery, *Beyond Equality*, 4; Leland Sage, *A History of Iowa* (Ames, 1974), 98; Anita Shafer Goodstein, "Labor Relations in the Saginaw Valley Lumber Industry, 1865-1885," *Business History Review* 27 (December 1953), 193- 221; Deibler, *Wood Workers*, 20-23, 26-27, 30-32; Storey, *Frameup*, 2, 6, 23, 26; J.C.B. Hutchings, *American Maritime Industry and Public Policy* (New York, 1969), 18-19. On steam and changes in shipbuilding technology, see Hutchins, *Maritime Industry*, 18-19. This period also marks the beginnings of a concern over hours in the industries of railroad transportation and mining. See *Fincher's Trades' Review* (January 23, 1864; March 25 and October 21, 1865); *Saint Louis Daily Press* (June 30, 1865); Edward A. Wieck, *The American Miners' Association: A Record of the Origins of Coal Miners' Unions in the United States* (New York, 1940), 76-77.

10. On the embrace of new technology, see esp. Ira Steward's unpublished "Subdivision of Labor," in which he writes, "The seven year apprentiship [sic] system cannot [make shoes]. It is too slow. The machine system is not yet perfect . . . but perfection will come that will drive all the 'custom work' out of existence." (Steward Papers, State Historical Society of Wisconsin, Madison, hereafter SHSW). See also the letter from Phillips, a Philadelphia shoemaker, to Steward (n.d.), SHSW.

11. See Steward, "Meaning of Eight Hours" (unpublished manuscript, Steward Papers, SHSW, 1869), 6-7.

12. Foner, *Labor Movement*, 1: 306-10, esp. 308, and 338; Montgomery, *Beyond Equality*, ch. 3 and 172 for a correction on the number of national unions. Punning with the word "union" occurs frequently. See *Fincher's Trades' Review* (October 1, 1864) and *Saint Louis Daily Press* (November 5, 1865).

13. Commons and Associates, *Labour in the United States*, 2: 14-15; McNeill, ed., *Labor Movement*, 126; Foner, *Labor Movement*, 1: 328-29; Roediger, "Racism, Reconstruction and the Labor Press: The Rise and Fall of the *Saint Louis Daily Press*, 1864-1866," *Science and Society* 42:2 (Summer 1978), 158.

14. Commons and Associates, *Labour in the United States*, 2: 18-19, 22; James S. Allen, *Reconstruction: The Battle for Democracy, 1865-1876* (New York, 1937), 145; *Saint Louis Daily Press* (December 5, 1865); *Boston Daily Evening Voice* (hereafter *BDEV*) (March 4, 1865).

15. *Fincher's Trades' Review* (June 17, 1863, and May 20, 1865). On Fincher's central role in initiating the spread of the eight-hour movement, see the letter from Thomas Phillips to U. S. Stephens (October 12, 1879), in the Phillips Papers, SHSW.

16. *Fincher's Trades' Review* (June 27, 1863); *BDEV* (March 17 and November 3, 1865); Foner, *Labor Movement*, 1: 369; "The Result of Shorter Hours," Boston Eight-Hour League Handbill (1865?), filed as U.S. manuscript 9A, Box 3, Folder 5, SHSW; Albert Blum and Dan Georgakas, *Michigan Labor and the Civil War* (East Lansing, Mass., 1964), 24-25; McNeill, *Labor Movement*, 128.

17. Preble, *Boston Navy Yard*, 360; *Fincher's Trades' Review* (December 12, 1863). On the 1862 law, which amended a less workable 1861 act, see Kelly, "Early Regulation," 367-69; Taylor Peck, *Roundshot to Rockets: A History of the Washington Navy Yard and U.S. Naval Gun Factory* (Annapolis, Md., 1949), 127-28; McNeill, ed., *Labor Movement*, 127.

18. Cross, *California*, 45 and 304; *Fincher's Trades' Review* (June 27, 1863). As the war wound down, labor leaders began to lose patience with those who "say it's not time." See *BDEV* (March 17, 1865).

19. Hyman Kuritz, "Ira Steward and the Eight-Hour Day," *Science and Society* 20:2 (Spring 1956), 118-19 and 122; Dorothy W. Douglas, "Ira Steward on Consumption and Unemployment," *Journal of Political Economy* 40 (August 1932), 532-33; *Massachusetts House Document*, Number 44 (1867), 67; *BDEV* (May 4, 1865); Steward, *Poverty*, 4; Roediger, "Antislavery Origins."

20. *Labor Standard* (March 3, 1877).

21. The quotes are from Douglas, "Consumption," 536-37.

22. Douglas, "Consumption," 534ff.; Kuritz, "Steward," 120; Montgomery, *Beyond Equality*, 253-59; Eugene D. Genovese, *The Political Economy of Slavery* (New York, 1967), 159-73, esp. 161; Roediger, "Antislavery Origins."

23. Commons and Associates, *Labour in the United States*, 2: 93, n.13; McNeill, ed., *Labor Movement*, 122, 124, and 127; see Rogers' unpublished *Autobiography* at SHSW, esp. ch. 5; Foner, *Labor Movement*, 1: 279; Montgomery, *Beyond Equality*, 200-10. See also "Biography of Thomas Phillips," 2, in the Labor Collection (Biographies and Papers) at SHSW.

24. *BDEV* (October 12, 1865); Montgomery, *Beyond Equality*, 123-43. Steward's relationship with Phillips is interestingly explored in Marvin Perelman, "Wendell Phillips and the Turn Toward Reformist Unionism," in the author's possession.

25. See esp., Powderly, *Thirty Years*, 31-32.

26. Commons and Associates, *Documentary History*, 9: 279-83 and 301; Steward, "Meaning of the Eight-Hour Movement," (unpublished manuscript dated 1869 at SHSW), 2. Even Steward saw eight hours not as a panacea but as an "indispensable *first step*" for all further reform in the North. Cf. "Meaning," 3-4 and *Poverty*, 2-3.

27. *BDEV* (November 3, 1865). On temperance and hours, see Montgomery, *Beyond Equality*, 203; *Fincher's Trades' Review* (January 21 and March 18, 1865); Trevellick, as quoted in Blum and Georgakas, *Michigan Labor*, 24; Steward, "Meaning," 12; Josiah Warren, *Response to the Call of the National Labor Union* (Boston, 1871), 4. The last document is in the Warren Papers in the Labadie Collection at the University of Michigan.

28.   Philip S. Foner, ed., "Songs of the Eight-Hour Movement," *Labor History* 13: 4 (Fall 1972), 571, 574-80; McNeill, "The Labor Movement of 1878 in Chicago" (unpublished paper at SHSW, 1878?).

29.   Montgomery, *Beyond Equality*, 72-89 and 264-77; Morris, "Road to Trade Unionism," 212-15; James C. Mohr, *The Radical Republicans and Reform in New York during Reconstruction* (Ithaca, N.Y., 1973), 123ff.

30.   Montgomery, *Beyond Equality*, 78-85 and 230-334, esp. ch. 6.

31.   Fincher's Trades' Review (September 17, 1864); Roediger, "Racism, Reconstruction and the Labor Press," 164; Thomas Barclay, *The Liberal Republican Movement in Missouri, 1865-1871* (Columbia, Mo., 1926), 28 and 126; *Westliche Post* (July 1866); *Saint Louis Daily Press* (July 25, 1865); Cale, *Philadelphia*, 79-80; Morris, "Road to Trade Unionism," 212-13; Montgomery, *Beyond Equality*, 123 and 165; *Fincher's Trades' Review* (December 16, 1865, on New York City). See Obermann, *Weydemeyer*, 57 and 64; Sorge, *Labor Movement*, 93; and Bruce Carlen Levine, "In the Crucible of Two Revolutions: German-American Workers, 1840-1865" (Paper delivered to Organization of American Historians, Cincinnati, April 18, 1983) for earlier German-American shorter-hours actions.

32.   *Saint Louis Daily Press* (August 19, 1866). See also Obermann, *Weydemeyer*, 124-40.

33.   Montgomery, *Beyond Equality*, 312.

34.   Steward, "Meaning," 8-12; *Workingman's Advocate* (August 17, 1867); Montgomery, *Beyond Equality*, 311-18; Commons and Associates, *Documentary History*, 9: 303; Kelly, "Early Regulation," 369-75.

35.   See Willie Lee Rose, *Rehearsals for Reconstruction: The Port Royal Experiment* (New York, 1964), 225; Leon Litwack, *Been in the Storm So Long: The Aftermath of Slavery* (New York, 1979), 410.

36.   Litwack, *Storm*, 346, contains a striking instance of informal protest; see also *New Orleans Tribune* (December 17, 1865); *Appleton's Annual Cyclopedia, 1869* (New York, 1870), 635-36.

37.   Commons and Associates, *Documentary History*, 9: 120-25; Foner, *Labor Movement*, 1: 361-63; Norman J. Ware, *The Labor Movement in the United States, 1860-1895* (New York, 1929), 6-11; Commons and Associates, *Labour in the United States*, 2: 96ff.

38.   *Fincher's Trades' Review* (September 23, 30, and October 14, 1865); Commons and Associates, *Documentary History*, 9: 278; *Fincher's Trades' Review* (September 30, October 14, and December 23, 1865); Ibid. (November 11, 1865). See also *Montgomery Daily Advertiser* (March 27, 1866) for an eight-hour resolution among shipyard workers in Mobile.

39.   Roediger, "Racism, Reconstruction and the Labor Press," 156-70, esp. 156-57 and 166-67; *Saint Louis Daily Press* (February 23, March 2, and November 5, 1865); William Parrish, *Missouri Under Radical Rule* (Columbia, Mo., 1965), 222-23.

40.   Roger W. Shugg, *Origins of Class Struggle in Louisiana: A Social History of White Farmers and Laborers during Slavery and After, 1840-1875* (Baton Rouge, La., 1972), 184-88 and 198-211; Montgomery, *Beyond Equality*, 114-15.

41.   Philip S. Foner, *Organized Labor and the Black Worker* (New York, 1976), 17-19; *New Orleans Tribune* (August 30, September 2, and November 1, 1866); W.E.B. DuBois, *Black Reconstruction in America* (New York, 1935), 456ff.

42.   *BDEV* (May 7 and 21, 1866); Foner, *Black Worker*, 18-19; *Fincher's Trades' Review* (April 21, 1866); *New Orleans Tribune* (November 1, 1866); Philip S. Foner, "A Labor Voice for Black Equality: The *Boston Daily Evening Voice*, 1864-1867," *Science and Society* 38: 3 (Fall 1974), 304-25; the South Carolina State Labor Convention, as discussed in *Appleton's Annual Cyclopedia, 1869*, 635-36; and the partial opening of the National Labor Union to blacks, as discussed in Allen, *Reconstruction*, 153-58; Foner, *Labor Movement*, 1: 416-17.

43.   Alexander Saxton, *The Indispensable Enemy: Labor and the Anti-Chinese Movement in California* (Berkeley, 1971), 68-69; Philip Taft, *Labor Politics American Style: The California State Federation of Labor* (Cambridge, Mass., 1968), 14; Cross, *California*, 34-37 and 304, n.17. The *Evening Bulletin* is quoted in Cross, 34.

44. Cross, *California*, 37-41 and 304-5, n.22; Montgomery, *Beyond Equality, 302; Fincher's Trades' Review* (February 10, 1866).

45. Roseboom, *Civil War Era*, 37. Gavett, *Milwaukee*, 9, and Arthur C. Cole, *The Era of the Civil War* (Springfield, Ill., 1919), 369-70; Thomas Cochran, "Did the Civil War Retard Industrialization?" *Mississippi Valley Historical Review* 46 (September 1961), 197-210.

46. Cole, *Era*, 381-82; Cf. Cochran, "Industrialization?" 202-3.

47. Montgomery, *Beyond Equality*, 5-6; William F. Gephart, *Transportation and Industrial Development in the Middle West* (New York, 1909), 251; Roseboom, *Civil War Era*, 6; Ware, *Labor Movement*, 4.

48. Yearley, "Trevellick," 428-32; McLaughlin, *Michigan Labor*, 13-19; "Trevellick Memorandum" at SHSW, 4; Blum and Georgakas, *Michigan Labor*, 23-25 and 28-29; *Fincher's Trades' Review* (January 20, 1866).

49. Bessie Louise Pierce, *A History of Chicago*, 3 vols. (Chicago, 1940), 2: 169-73; *Workingman's Advocate* (November 4, 1864, and September 17, 1865); Montgomery, *Beyond Equality*, 161-62.

50. *Fincher's Trades' Review* (July 22, August 26, September 23 and 30, December 2, 11, and 23, 1865; January 6, 1866); Cole, *Era*, 370; Commons and Associates, *Documentary History*, 9: 278; Montgomery, *Beyond Equality*, 307ff.

51. Merk, "The Labor Movement in Wisconsin during the Civil War," 186.

52. *Fincher's Trades' Review* (September 23 and 30, 1865); Merk, "Civil War," 186; Gavett, *Milwaukee*, 14-15; *Milwaukee Sentinel* (March 31, 1866).

53. Montgomery, *Beyond Equality*, 307 and n.6 corrects the often repeated error that the Wisconsin law applied only to minors and women; *Fincher's Trades' Review* (October 14, 1865).

54. Emma Thornbrough, *Indiana in the Civil War Era, 1850-1880* (Indianapolis, 1965), 445-46 and 555-61; *Fincher's Trades' Review* (September 2, 23, and 30, October 14, 21, and 28, November 5 and December 16, 1865; January 6, 13, and February 10, 1866).

55. *Fincher's Trades' Review* (September 2, 23, and December 11, 1865); Thornbrough, *Indiana*, 446; *Workingman's Advocate* (November 15, 1873).

56. *Fincher's Trades' Review* (October 28 and December 16, 1865); Thornbrough, *Indiana*, 446-47; Montgomery, *Beyond Equality*, 242 and 313; Commons and Associates, *Documentary History*, 9: 278.

57. *Fincher's Trades' Review* (January 6, 1866); Commons and Associates, *Labour in the United States*, 1: 109; Morris, "Road to Unionism," 212-15; *Fincher's Trades' Review* (September 30, 1865); *Saint Louis Daily Press* (July 25, 1865).

58. *Fincher's Trades' Review* (September 2 and 30, December 2 and 9, 1865); Roseboom, *Civil War Era*, 40-41; Commons and Associates, *Labour in the United States*, 2: 107-8.

59. *Fincher's Trades' Review* (December 9, 1865).

60. The cities are Baltimore (25,000), Philadelphia (15,000-20,000), Rochester (6,000-8,000), Paterson (7,000), Boston (4,000-5,000) and Lawrence (3,000) as cited in *Fincher's Trades' Review* (October 14, September 2, October 7, and August 19, 1865) and in *BDEV* (July 25 and March 19, 1865).

61. See n. 60 above; *Fincher's Trades' Review* (October 21, November 11, December 2, 9, and 16, 1865); *BDEV* (March 17, May 24, and July 24, 1865).

62. General treatments are Persons, in *Labor Laws*, ch. 4; Montgomery, *Beyond Equality*, chs. 2, 6-8; Mohr, *New York*, 123-39; Commons and Associates, *Labour in the United States*, 2: 88-93; Kuritz, "Ira Steward," 118-34. On city council actions, see Commons and Associates, *Documentary History*, 9: 278; *Fincher's Trades' Review* (November 11, 1865); and *Saint Louis Daily Press* (November 1, 1865).

63. Stockton, *Molders*, 160-61; *Fincher's Trades' Review* (June 18, July 30, and August 6, 1864); Commons and Associates, *Labour in the United States*, 2: 93.

64. *Fincher's Trades' Review* (January 28, 1865); *Saint Louis Daily Press* (September 15, 1865).

65. *Fincher's Trades' Review* (March 4, 1865); for similar examples in Paterson and Newark, see Ibid. (August 19 and December 16, 1865).

66. Ware, *Labor Movement*, 5; *Fincher's Trades' Review* (October 7, 1865); Montgomery, *Beyond Equality*, 164-65; *Saint Louis Daily Press* (October 3, 1865).

67. Mohr, *New York*, 123-29; George Brandreth, "Speech". The latter pamphlet, which concentrates on increased productivity but includes a number of other arguments concerning health, republicanism, and other issues, is available in the Labadie Collection at the University of Michigan.

68. United States Commissioner of Labor, *Third Annual Report*, 1050; McNeill, ed., *Labor Movement*, 350-53; Montgomery, *Beyond Equality*, 242-43; Mohr, *New York*, 132-39. New York City passed an eight-hour law for city workers in 1866. See Commons and Associates, *Documentary History*, 9: 278.

69. Commons and Associates, *Documentary History*, 9: 279-83; Kuritz, "Steward," 122; Robinson, "Reduction of Hours," 42.

70. Kuritz, "Steward," 121; Commons and Associates, *Labour in the United States*, 2: 96; Ware, *Labor Movement*, 6-7; *BDEV* (March 4, 17, and 19, 1865).

71. Sorge, *Labor Movement*, 104-6; *Massachusetts House Document*, Number 259 (1865); Montgomery, *Beyond Equality*, 124-25.

72. Montgomery, *Beyond Equality*, 125; *BDEV* (June 24 and July 27, 1865); *Fincher's Trades' Review* (May 13, 1865).

73. Commons and Associates, *Documentary History*, 9: 289, 284-301, and passim.

74. Ibid., 9: 289, 292, and 300-1; Steward, "Less Hours" (unpublished manuscript at SHSW, n.d.), 1; Sorge, *Labor Movement*, 100; Montgomery, *Beyond Equality*, 254-59; Perelman, "Phillips," 3-6; Commons and Associates, *Labour in the United States*, 2: 89-91, and below.

75. *Fincher's Trades' Review* (May 13 and August 26, 1865).

76. *BDEV* (October 12 and November 3, 1865).

77. Ibid. (November 3, 1865); Montgomery, *Beyond Equality*, 136; Commons and Associates, *Labour in the United States*, 2: 93; *Fincher's Trades' Review* (October 21, 1865).

78. Commons and Associates, *Documentary History*, 9: 278; *BDEV* (October 20 and November 3, 1865); *Massachusetts House Document*, Number 98 (1866), 3-4.

79. Persons, in *Labor Laws*, 99; United States Commissioner of Labor, *Third Annual Report*, 1049; *Fincher's Trades' Review* (October 7, 1865).

80. *BDEV (October 12 and November 3, 1865); Fincher's Trades' Review* (November 25, 1865).

81. Commons and Associates, *Labour in the United States*, 2: 92-93; *Fincher's Trades' Review* (November 25, 1865). The quote is from the *Voice* (November 15, 1865). On the aborted Phillips "campaign," see *BDEV* (September 19 and 25, 1865); Montgomery, *Beyond Equality*, 269-70.

82. Persons, in *Labor Laws*, ch. 3 and 4; *BDEV* (October 12, 1865); Montgomery, *Beyond Equality*, 124, 245, 265, and 292. On Radical proclivities among leaders of the Eight-Hour Leagues, see Foner, "Labor Voice," 311-23 and n. 31; Irving H. Bartlett, *Wendell Phillips: Brahmin Radical* (Boston, 1961), 268-72; Montgomery, *Beyond Equality*, 252.

83. Massachusetts House Document, Number 98 (1866), 30 and passim. On the three committee members (Elizur Wright, Franklin B. Sanborn, and Henry I. Bowditch), see Montgomery, *Beyond Equality*, 266.

84. Montgomery, *Beyond Equality*, 270-76. The *Voice*, Montgomery notes, ended up supporting the democracy.

85. Ibid., 277-95 and 302, esp. 293-94; Persons, in *Labor Laws*, 101-2 and 111-13.

86. Cf. 62 and 96, n. 46, above with Steward, "Meaning" and "Subdivision of Labor," passim.

87. See the handbill, "The Result of Short Hours," issued by the Boston Labor Reform Association (1865?) and filed with the U.S. Manuscripts, 9A, Box 3, Folder 5 at SHSW (emphasis original); Cahill, *Shorter Hours*, 31; Sylvis, ed., *Life of William Sylvis*, 208-9.

88. Steward as quoted in Perelman, "Phillips," 13; Steward, "Less Hours," 1 (in Steward Papers at SHSW); Kuritz, "Steward," 129-30. For the continued stress on class harmony and productivity by politicians, see *Massachusetts House Document*, Number 44 (1867), 86, 130, 139, and Brandreth, "Speech," passim.

89. Sylvis, ed., *Life of William Sylvis*, 101, 130-31, 154, 158-59; *Fincher's Trades' Review* (June 20, 1863 and April 23, 1864); Yearley, "Trevellick," 428-29.

90. Cf. Perelman, "Phillips," 22-23, and *Fincher's Trades' Review* (Decem ber 30, 1865). Important among historians' widely diverging views of Phillips's perception on class are Vernon L. Parrington, *Main Currents in American Thought*, vol. 3 (New York, 1930), 141-47; Richard Hofstadter, *American Politican Tradition* (New York, 1948); and Samuel Bernstein, "Wendell Phillips: Labor Advocate," *Science and Society* 20 (Fall 1956), 344-57.

91. *Saint Louis Daily Press* (August 8, 9, 16, and 19, 1865).

92. Steward, "Meaning," 6 and passim. See also Montgomery, *Beyond Equality*, 445, and *Massachusetts House Document*, Number 44 (1867), 122.

93. Montgomery, *Beyond Equality*, ch. 11 and esp. 444-46; Robert P. Sharkey, *Money, Class and Party: An Economic Study of Civil War and Reconstruction* (Baltimore, 1959), 202-220.

94. For example, see Sylvis, ed., *Life of William Sylvis*, 208. For the comparison to the 1830s, see ch. 2 above. On plans to achieve cooperation through less hours and more wages, see Steward, "Meaning," 12; McNeill, "Chicago," passim; and John Curl, *Work Cooperation in America* (Berkeley, 1980), 29.

95. *Fincher's Trades' Review* (June 18, 1864); Steward, "Less Hours," 4; *Voice* (November 15, 1865) under the heading "The Hod-Carriers' Strike." On women and textiles, see *BDEV* (March 17, May 24, July 25, and October 12, 1865); Persons, in *Labor Laws*, ch. 4. See also Sylvis, ed., *Life of William Sylvis*, 208.

96. See n. 31 above; *Saint Louis Daily Press* (November 5, 1865); *BDEV* (March 4, 1865); and Montgomery, *Beyond Equality*, 126-34, 271-73, and 309.

97. Commons and Associates, *Documentary History*, 9: 126-29; Foner, *Labor Movement*, 1: 367 and 371.

98. Compare the handbill "Result of Short Hours" and the 1791 events described above.

99. Sylvis, ed., *Life of William Sylvis*, 206-7; see also *Fincher's Trades' Review* (October 10, 1863) and *Saint Louis Daily Press* (August 9, 1866).

100. The slogan is as given in the *Saint Louis Daily Press* (November 5, 1865); Ware, *Labor Movement*, 7.

101. For republicanism, see, for example, *BDEV* (March 19, 1865); Steward, "Less Hours," 7; and the handbill "Result of Short Hours." On education, see *BDEV* (May 24, 1865). A remarkably full exposition of the relation of the eight-hour demand to child labor, education, and social life is Sylvis, ed., *Life of William Sylvis*, 199-210.

102. Cf. Sylvis, ed., *Life of William Sylvis, 199, with Wright as cited in ch. 2, n. 20.*

103. Cf. Commons and Associates, *Documentary History*, 9: 292 (emphasis is in Steward's draft of his 1865 speech "A Reduction of Hours an Increase of Wages," at SHSW but not in the pamphlet of the same title reprinted by Commons) with n. 43 above.

104. Yearley, "Trevellick," 425; Sylvis, ed., *Life of William Sylvis*, 88 and 173; Montgomery, *Beyond Equality*, 202-3. Both Sylvis and Trevellick also applied their Methodism in temperance crusades.

105. Commons and Associates, *Documentary History*, 9: 288; Montgomery, *Beyond Equality*, 202-3.

106. Commons and Associates, *Documentary History*, 9: 287. See also Rogers's comments in Massachusetts House Document, Number 44 (1867), 92-95.

107. Especially important were the large strikes in the New York City shipyards (1866) and the strikes and demonstrations designed to enforce Illinois's eight-hour law (1867). See McNeill, ed., *Labor Movement*, 350-53; Cole, *Era of Civil War*, 417-18; Montgomery, *Beyond Equality*, 306-11. See below for more on these strikes and the ten-hour factory strikes at Fall River (1866) and at the Wamsutta Mills in New Bedford.

108. Kuritz, "Steward," 121; Fincher cautions against actions by separate crafts in *Fincher's Trades' Review* (June 18, 1864) and Weydemeyer's preference for political action rather than craft strikes is reflected in *Saint Louis Daily Press* (August 19, 1866). For Sylvis and Trevellick on the utility of strikes see *Fincher's Trades Review* (June 6, 1863, and September 30, 1865).

Victory, Defeat, and New Alliances, 1867-1879

1. Montgomery, *Beyond Equality*, 302-11.

2. *BDEV* (March 4, 17, 19, and October 12, 1865); Montgomery, *Beyond Equality*, 279.

3. *BDEV* (December 6, 1866, and April 9, 1867); Montgomery, *Beyond Equality*, 277-80.

4. Persons, in *Labor Laws*, 109ff; Montgomery, *Beyond Equality*, 278-80; M. F. Dickinson, Jr., "Argument of M. F. Dickinson, Jr. Before the Joint Special Committee of the Massachusetts Legislature Upon the Hours of Labor, in Behalf of the Remonstrants, Wednesday, March 15, 1871" (Boston, 1871), 11 and 14.

5. *BDEV* (April 19, 1867).

6. David Montgomery, "Labor and the Radical Republicans: A Case Study of the Revival of the American Labor Movement, 1864-1868" (unpublished Ph. D. dissertation, University of Minnesota, 1961), 322-30. Montgomery also mentions a victorious eight-hour strike led by women workers in Lockport in January 1867. See *BDEV* (February 9, 1867). For important evidence that women of the period chose jobs with shorter hours, even at a sacrifice in wages, see Judith A. McGaw, "'A Good Place to Work': Industrial Workers and Occupational Choice: The Case of Berkshire Women," *Journal of Interdisciplinary History* 10 (Autumn 1979), 242-45.

7. Persons, in *Labor Laws*, 55-59; Montgomery, *Beyond Equality*, 283-92; Montgomery, "Labor," 323-26; *BDEV* (February 13-March 14, 1867).

8. Ibid., esp. *BDEV* (February 18-20, 1867).

9. Montgomery, *Beyond Equality*, 286-88, and "Labor," 323-24.

10. *BDEV* (March 2, 1867).

11. Montgomery, "Labor," 325-26, and *Beyond Equality*, 288-90. The possibility that the strike committee expected Bennett to reject all compromise is a conjecture based upon our own reading of the situation.

12. Montgomery, *Beyond Equality*, 289-90, and "Labor," 326.

13. Persons, in *Labor Laws*, 111-12; U.S. Commission of Labor, *Report* (1887), 1050; *BDEV* (April 1, 3, 5, 9, and 13, 1867).

14. Foner, *Labor Movement*, 1: 380; Montgomery, *Beyond Equality*, 305 and 354; Kuritz, "Steward," 129, and ch. 5 above.

15. Montgomery, *Beyond Equality*, 305; *Workingman's Advocate* (May 5, 1866); Pierce, *Chicago*, 2: 176.

16. Montgomery, *Beyond Equality*, 304-5.

17. Foner, *Labor Movement*, 1: 380-81; Pennsylvania Bureau of Statistics of Labor and Agriculture, *First Annual Report* (1872-1873) (Harrisburg, 1873), 331-35; Chris Evans, *History of the United Mine Workers in America from the Year 1860 to 1890*, 2 vols. (Indianapolis, 1918-1920), 1: 13-15; William J. Walsh, "The United Mine Workers of America as an Economic Force in the Anthracite Industry" (unpublished Ph.D. dissertation, Catholic University, 1931), 49.

18. Pennsylvania Bureau of Statistics of Labor and Agriculture, *Report* (1872-1873), 332; Walsh, "Force," 49.

19. Pennsylvania Bureau of Statistics of Labor and Agriculture, *Report* (1872-1873), 332-35; Foner, *Labor Movement*, 1: 380-81, estimates participation in the strikes and protests at about 25,000. *Statistics of the Population, Ninth Census of the United States* (Washington, D.C., 1872), 58.

20. "The Eight Hour Strikes," *Hunt's Merchants' Magazine* 59 (August 1868), 94; (Philadelphia) *Public Ledger* (August 4, 1868); Pennsylvania Bureau of Statistics of Labor and Agriculture, *Report* (1872-1873), 332-35; Walsh, "Force," 49.

21. Pierce, *Chicago*, 2: 170-77; Montgomery, *Beyond Equality*, 161-62 and 306-7;

Montgomery, "Labor," 350ff; *Workingman's Advocate* as quoted in Kenneth Kann, "Working-Class Culture and the Labor Movement in Chicago" (unpublished Ph.D. dissertation, University of California-Berkeley, 1977), 54.

22. *BDEV* (March 19 and April 6, 1867); Pierce, *Chicago*, 2: 175-76; Montgomery, *Beyond Equality*, 307-8.

23. Cole, *Era*, 417-18; Pierce, *Chicago*, 2: 177; *BDEV* (May 2 and 4, 1867).

24. Pierce, *Chicago*, 2: 178-79; Montgomery, *Beyond Equality*, 309-10; *New York Times* (May 7, 1867) and *Chicago Tribune* (May 3, 1867).

25. *BDEV* (May 28 and August 10, 1867); Pierce, *Chicago*, 2: 179. Thus later accounts suggest the Journeymen Stone Cutters were the first Chicago unionists to gain eight hours, doing so in 1868. See Royal E. Montgomery, *Industrial Relations in the Chicago Building Trades* (Chicago, 1927), 14; *Workingman's Advocate* (March 7, 1868).

26. Montgomery, *Beyond Equality*, 219.

27. Gavett, *Milwaukee*, 17-18; Merk, "Labor Movement in Wisconsin," 185-88; Connecticut Bureau of Labor Statistics, *First Annual Report* (1874), (New Haven, 1874), 52. Montgomery, "Labor," 338-49, describes the political eight-hour agitation in Connecticut.

28. *Workingman's Advocate* (April 17, 1867).

29. *BDEV* (June 20, 1866); McNeill, ed., *Labor Movement*, 350ff.; Mohr, *Radical Republicans*, 124 and 135, n.47.

30. Mohr, *Radical Republicans*, 124-37, confirms the view that Republicans, including Radicals, vacillated on hours as they weighed conflicting claims of reform and the "free market."

31. Ibid., 137-38; Montgomery, *Beyond Equality*, 324-26; *New York Times* (May 13, 1867); *Workingman's Advocate* (October 12, 1867, and October 2, 1869).

32. McNeill, ed., *Labor Movement*, 350ff, probably misdates an 1866 shipyard strike as occurring in 1867; Mohr, *Radical Republicans*, 139; Foner, *Labor Movement*, 1: 381.

33. *Workingman's Advocate* (August 22, 1868); Montgomery, *Beyond Equality*, 169-70.

34. Sorge, *Labor Movement*, 88; Cahill, *Shorter Hours*, 69; Kelly, "Early Regulation of Hours," 366-70; Montgomery, *Beyond Equality*, 313ff. On Julian and labor reform see Patrick Riddleberger, *George Washington Julian: Radical Republican* (n.p., 1966), 231-32.

35. Foner, *Labor Movement*, 1: 374-77; *Workingman's Advocate* (January 25, 1868, and September 1, 1866); Montgomery, *Beyond Equality*, 314-15; *BDEV* (August 27, 1866); Commons and Associates, *Documentary History*, 9: 183-85, 199.

36. *Fincher's Trades' Review* (November 11, 1865); Cross, *California*, 50-51; *Workingman's Advocate* (February 20, 1869); Foner, *Labor Movement*, 1: 379; Montgomery, *Beyond Equality*, 315; *Congressional Globe*, 40th Congress, 2nd Session, 334-36, 3424.

37. . *Congressional Globe, 40th Congress, 2nd Session, 3424-429.*

38. Ibid., 3429.

39. Ibid., 3424-28.

40. Felicia Johnson Deyrup, *Arms Makers of the Connecticut Valley* (Northampton, Mass., 1948), 206-7; Ohio Bureau of Labor Statistics, *Second Annual Report* (Columbus, 1879), 269-70.

41. Kelly, "Early Regulation of Hours," 370-71; Montgomery, *Beyond Equality*, 319-20. On Grant's decision, see Sylvis, ed., *Life*, 326-28; Cahill, *Shorter Hours*, 70; Ohio Bureau of Labor Statistics, *Second Annual Report*, 267, reprints the proclamation by Grant.

42. Foner, *Labor Movement*, 1: 378; Montgomery, *Beyond Equality*, 321-22; Cahill, *Shorter Hours*, 70; Kelly,"Early Regulation of Hours," 371.

43. Cahill, *Shorter Hours*, 70-71; *United States v. Martin*, 94 U.S. 400; Ohio Bureau of Labor Statistics, *Second Annual Report*, 269-70; Montgomery, *Beyond Equality*, 323; Ely quoted in Sorge, *Labor Movement*, 88.

44. See Montgomery, *Beyond Equality*, 334-35; Sylvis, ed., *Life*, 76-77; Yearley, "Trevellick," 432ff.; George Brooks, "Historical Background" in *The Shorter Work Week: Papers Delivered at the Conference on Shorter Hours of Work, Sponsored by the AFL and CIO*

(Washington, D.C., 1957), 10-11. Montgomery discusses, with considerable insight, the greenback-labor movement as, in part, an attempt by labor leaders to broaden their base by appealing to middle-class elements. Nonetheless, and despite Montgomery's impressive listings of trade union greenbackers, it is still possible to argue, as Marxists of the period did, that the turn to currency reform coincided with a decline of labor participation in the NLU. Cf. Montgomery, *Beyond Equality*, 387-456, esp. 442-43, with The General Council of the First International, *Minutes*, 1870-71 (Moscow, n.d.), 146; Foner, *Labor Movement*, 1: 420-32; Allen, *Reconstruction*, 151-53.

45. Many historians have failed to take Steward's activities after 1867 seriously. See Sharkey, *Money, Class and Party*, 199-206, for the view that Steward and McNeill enjoyed little support outside New England as they pursued a "fanatical advocacy of eight hours." Useful material is in Perelman, "Phillips," passim; Montgomery, *Beyond Equality*, 413-14; Kuritz, "Steward," 126-32. For the rejection of greenbackism as class collaborationist by Steward and his followers, see *BDEV* (August 1, 1867); McNeill, ed., *Labor Movement*, 140-41.

46. Sorge, *Labor Movement*, 88-93; Kuritz, "Steward," 127. See also the annual reports of the Massachusetts Bureau of Statistics of Labor for 1870, 1871, 1872, and 1873, and *Workingman's Advocate* (March 11, 1871).

47. General Council of the First International, *Minutes*, 1864-66, 342-43; *Minutes, 1866-68*, 227, 231-34, 244, 309; *Minutes, 1868-70*, illustration facing 96, illustrations facing 176, 252, 286, 296, 415; Howard H. Quint, *The Forging of American Socialism* (Indianapolis, 1953), 3-10; Samuel Bernstein, *The First International in America* (New York, 1962), ch. 1; Herman Schluter, *Die Internationale in Amerika* (Chicago, 1918), 417-21; Montgomery, *Beyond Equality*, 168-69 and 188-89; Sorge, *Labor Movement*, 95.

48. Samuel Gompers, *Seventy Years of Life and Labor*, 2 vols. (New York, 1967), 1: 207-11, and Stuart B. Kaufman, *Samuel Gompers and the American Federation of Labor, 1848-1896*, (Westport, Conn., 1973), 16-115.

49. Montgomery, *Beyond Equality*, esp. 326-27, 395, 443. A typescript biography in the Labor Collection at SHSW treats the career of Jessup, who combined an early commitment to greenbackism, eight-hour agitation, and friendly relations with Marxists in the IWA. See also below and A. Cameron, *The Eight-Hour Question* (n.p., n.d.), 8; *Workingman's Advocate* (June 1, 1872).

50. Allen, *Reconstruction*, 170; Kuritz, "Steward," 128; Foner, *Labor Movement*, 1: 381; Ely, *Labor Movement*, 71; Paul Buhle, "The Knights of Labor in Rhode Island," *Radical History Review* 17 (Spring 1978), 46. This agitation coincided with a massive Canadian campaign for the nine-hour day--a campaign that the U.S. labor press followed with interest and supported. See *Toronto Mail* (April 16, 1872) and *Workingman's Advocate* (April 27, 1872).

51. *Workingman's Advocate* (September 23, 1871); Foner, *Labor Movement*, 1: 381; Commons and Associates, *Documentary History*, 9: 367-68; Montgomery, *Beyond Equality*, 327; *New York Times* (September 14 and 15, 1871); *New York World* (September 14 and 23, 1871). See also *Documents of the First International, The General Council, 1870-71* (Moscow, n.d.), 200.

52. *New York Sun* (June 24, 1872); McNeill, ed., *Labor Movement*, 146; *New York World* (April 18, 1872); *Woodhull and Claflin's Weekly* (June 15, 1872); Bernstein, *First International*, 128-32; Montgomery, *Beyond Equality*, 326-32.

53. For IWA (Spring Street) activities in support of the gas workers and in convening the Enforcement League, see *New York Herald* (April 18 and 22, 1873); *New York World* (April 7 and 14, 1873); *New York Sun* (April 11, 1873); Samuel Bernstein, ed., *Papers of the General Council of the IWA, New York (1872-1876)*, 65-66 and 71; *Arbeiter-Zeitung* (April 12, 1873). On gas workers, see E. J. Hobsbawm, *Labouring Men* (London, 1964), esp. 140-203.

54. *New York Times* (April 6, 1873); *New York Herald* (April 8 and 18, 1873).

55. *New York Times* (April 6, 1873); *New York Sun* (April 9-11, 1873); *New York Evening Post* (April 7, 1873). The Manhattan Works kept operating, however. See *New York Times* (April 19, 1873).

56. *New York Times* (April 12, 1873); *New York Sun* (April 11, 1873); *New York Herald* (April 18, 1873). The IWA was active in the Citizen's Anti-Monopoly Association. See *New York Times* (February 3-6, 1872).

57. *New York World* (April 7-11, 1873); *New York Times* (April 17, 1873); *New York Tribune* (April 9 and 10, 1873).

58. *New York World* (April 18, 1873); *New York Herald* (April 8, 1873); *New York Evening Post* (April 7, 1873).

59. *New York World* (April 8 and 9, 1873); *New York Herald* (April 8 and 18, 1873); *New York Times* (April 18, 1873).

60. *New York Herald* (April 18 and 23, 1873).

61. See George B. Engberg, "Lumber and Labor in the Lake States," *Minnesota History* 36 (March 1959), 153-66.

62. The Jacksonville strike may be followed in the *Jacksonville Republican* (June 5, 1873); *Tallahassee Weekly Floridian* (June 10 and 24, 1873) and *Savannah* (Ga.) *Morning News* (June 27, 1873). All are reprinted in Philip S. Foner and Ronald Lewis, eds., *The Black Worker During the Era of the National Labor Union*, 2 vols. (Philadelphia, 1978), 2: 144-48.

63. Anita Shafer Goodstein, "Labor Relations in the Saginaw Lumber Valley, 1865-1885," *Bulletin of the Business Historical Society* 27 (December 1953), 205-11. The previous month a two-week hours strike among Carrollton, Michigan, sawyers had failed. See U.S. Commission of Labor, *Report* (1887), 1058.

64. Goodstein, "Saginaw Valley," 208-10; *Bay City Daily Journal* (July 9, 1872); *Saginaw Daily Courier* (July 3, 4, 7, and 9, 1872).

65. Goodstein, "Saginaw Valley," 209-12; and *Saginaw Daily Courier* (July 9-11, 1872). Although there was no evidence of IWA involvement, strike opponents raised the spectre of communism. See *Saginaw Daily Courier* (July 11, 1872).

66. John F. Meginness, ed., *History of Lycoming County, Pennsylvania* (Chicago, 1892), 362; Thomas W. Lloyd, *History of Lycoming County*, Pennsylvania, 2 vols. (Indianapolis and Topeka, 1929), 1: 215-35. The present account is based on the *Williamsport Sun* and the *Daily Lycoming Gazette and West Branch Bulletin*, esp. the July 1-16 issues. The latter paper is hereafter referred to as the *Lycoming Gazette*.

67. *Lycoming Gazette* (June 29, July 1, 3, 5, 6, 10, and September 17, 1872).

68. Ibid. (July 1, 1872); Lloyd, *Lycoming County*, 1: 215ff.

69. *Lycoming Gazette* (July 2, 3, and 5, 1872); *Williamsport Sun* (July 11, 1872).

70. *Lycoming Gazette* (July 1, 3, 5, 6, 8, 10, 13, 16, 17, 18, and August 9, 1872); *Williamsport Sun* (July 18, 1872).

71. Meginness, ed., *Lycoming*, 362; *Lycoming Gazette* (July 18-23, 1872). Not all the local constabulary opposed the strike. The mayor cited disobedience by many local police in asking the governor for troops. See *Williamsport Sun* (July 25 and August 1, 1872).

72. *Lycoming Gazette* (July 22 and 23, 1872).

73. Ibid. (July 23-August 1, and September 16 and 23, 1872); Montgomery, *Beyond Equality*, 188, 372, and 407.

74. Foner, *Labor Movement*, 1: 439-40. On hours during the depression, see Herbert Gutman, "Social and Economic Structure and Depression: American Labor in 1873 and 1874" (unpublished Ph.D. dissertation, University of Wisconsin, 1959), 301-5.

75. *Workingman's Advocate* (May 30, 1874); Stockton, *Molders' Union*, 168; *Constitution of the Cigarmakers' International Union of America* (n.p., 1877), preamble.

76. Sorge, *Labor Movement*, 129-31; Gray, "Argument of Hon. William Gray on Petitions for the Ten-Hour Law Before the Committee on Labor, February 13, 1873" (Boston, 1873); Ewan Clague, *The Bureau of Labor Statistics* (New York and Washington, D.C., 1968), 5. Some later labor greenbackers returned to aggressive eight-hour advocacy. See *National Labor Tribune* (December 2, 1876, and February 17, 1877).

77. Persons, *Labor Laws*, 122-25; "Address to the Delegates of the Working People's International Association, Made to the New England Labor Reform League" (Princeton, Mass., 1873), 9-10.

78. See above, n. 48 and Bernstein, *First International*, 223-24. On the hearings see

Samuel Rezneck, "Distress, Relief and Discontent in the United States During the Depression of 1873-78," *Journal of Political Economy* 58 (December 1950), 503. The editor of Chicago's *Vorbote* called for a six-hour working day during the depression. See *Labor Standard* (December 2, 1877).

79. Philip S. Foner, ed., *The Formation of the Workingman's Party of the United States: Proceedings of the Union Congress Held at Philadelphia, July 19-26, 1876* (New York, 1976); *National Labor Tribune* (July 7, 1877).

80. David Burbank, *Reign of the Rabble* (New York, 1966); Philip S. Foner, *The Great Labor Uprising of 1877* (New York, 1977), 157-88; David Roediger, "Not Only the Ruling Classes: Class, Skill and Community in the St. Louis General Strike," *Journal of Social History* 19 (Winter 1985), 213-39.

81. Foner, *Great Labor Uprising*, 115-56; Robert V. Bruce, *1877: Year of Violence* (Chicago, 1970), 249 and 267-68.

82. Labor Standard (December 23, 1877; March 24 and July 24, 1878); Foner, *Labor Movement*, 1: 501-4; Kuritz, "Steward," 133-34; Sorge, *Labor Movement*, 166; *Labor Standard* (February 10, 1877; February 10 and 17, 1878); Christopher L. Tomlins, *The State and the Unions: Labor Relations, Law and the Organized Labor Movement in America, 1880-1960* (Cambridge, England, 1985), 44-59.

Haymarket and Its Context

1. United States Commissioner of Labor, *First Annual Report* (Washington, D.C., 1886), 226; Edward Aveling and Eleanor Marx-Aveling, *The Working-Class Movement in America* (London, 1891), 67-77.

2. Aveling and Marx-Aveling, *Movement*, 67-77, 223-34; Buhle, "Rhode Island," 53-54; New York Bureau of Statistics of Labor, *Eighth Annual Report* (1890).

3. Henry Raymond Mussey, "Eight-Hour Theory in the American Federation of Labor," in Jacob E. Hollander, ed., *Economic Essays Contributed in Honor of John Bates Clark* (New York, 1927), 237ff.; Terence Powderly, "The Army of the Discontented," *North American Review* 140 (April 1885), 369-77.

4. Samuel Rezneck, "Patterns of Thought and Action in an American Depression, 1882-1886," *American Historical Review* 61 (January 1956), 286-87.

5. John Garraty, *Unemployment in History: Economic Thought and Public Policy* (New York, 1978), 117.

6. See the leaflet, "To Tramps," by Lucy Parsons, in *Alarm* (October 1884). A copy of the leaflet is reprinted in Carolyn Ashbaugh, *Lucy Parsons: American Revolutionary* (Chicago, 1976), 144. See also Ely, *Labor Movement*, 361.

7. Marx-Aveling, *Movement*, 76-77; Oscar Ameringer, *If You Don't Weaken* (New York, 1940), 44; Ashbaugh, *Parsons*, 144.

8. Montgomery, "Workers' Control of Machine Production," passim; Newton, as quoted in John A. Garraty, ed., *Labor and Capital in the Gilded Age* (Boston, 1968), 37.

9. Saxton, *Indispensable Enemy*, 129-30. See also Gompers, "The Eight-Hour Workday" (Washington, n.d.), 10, for a linkage of the Chinese with long hours.

10. Sorge, *Labor Movement*, 172; Saxton, *Indispensable Enemy*; First name? Mink, *Old Labor and New Immigrants* (Ithaca, N. Y., 1986); Herbert Hill, "Race, Ethnicity, and Organized Labor," *New Politics* 1:2 (New Series) (Winter 1987), 31-82.

11. See Hareven, "Manchester," passim, on the adjustment and resistance of French-Canadians in the textile industry. For Gompers's interesting argument that a shorter day could help end preindustrial practices like Monday absences from work, see his "The Eight-Hour Workday," 6.

12. Aveling and Marx-Aveling, *Movement*, 68-69 and 225.

13. Philip S. Foner, ed., *The Autobiographies of the Haymarket Martyrs* (New York, 1969), 114-22.

14. See Lucy Parsons, *Life of Albert Parsons* (Chicago, 1903), 12-94; Grob, *Workers and Utopia*, 107, n.36; Gary M. Fink and Associates, eds., *Biographical Dictionary of American Labor Leaders* rev. ed. (Westport, Conn., 1984), 222-25; David Roediger, "Albert R. Parsons: The Anarchist as Trade Unionist," in Roediger and Franklin Rosemont, eds. *Haymarket Scrapbook* (Chicago, 1986), 31-35, and Roediger, "What Was the Labor Movement? Organization and the St. Louis General Strike," *Mid-America* 67 (January 1985), 37-51.

15. The fullest accounts of the Knights remain Grob, *Workers and Utopia*, and Ware, *Labor Movement*. Membership figures are provided in Foner, *Labor Movement*, 1: 509 and 2: 47. See also Foner, *Black Worker*, 47-63; Melton McLaurin, *The Knights of Labor in the South* (Westport, Conn., 1978); and the papers on women and the Knights presented at the 1979 Conference on the Knights of Labor sponsored by Chicago's Newberry Library, especially that of Susan Levine. Levine, Foner, and others point out that the egalitarianism of the Knights was sometimes compromised and, in the case of women, confused by a desire to have working women return ultimately to the home.

16. Foner, *Labor Movement*, 2: 55.

17. Powderly, *Thirty Years*, 85-86; Ware, *Labor Movement*, 300; "Constitution of the General Assembly, District Assembly and Local Assembly, Adopted at Reading, January 1-4, 1878"; "Record of the Proceeding of the Third Regular Session of the General Assembly in Chicago September 2-6, 1877." Both the latter two documents are in the Powderly Papers, Catholic University, Washington, D.C.

18. "First Annual Report of the Grand Statistician, Sixth Session of the General Assembly, 1882" in Powderly Papers, Catholic University.

19. Cahill, *Shorter Hours*, 41-43.

20. Grob, *Workers and Utopia*, 75; Cahill, *Shorter Hours*, 47; Samuel Walker, "Terence V. Powderly, Machinist, 1866-1877," *Labor History* 19 (Spring 1978), 170-72; Powderly, "The Plea for Eight Hours," *North American Review* 150 (April 1890), 465-69; "Records of the Proceedings of the Sixth Regular Session of the General Assembly," in Powderly Papers, Catholic University.

21. Cahill, *Shorter Hours*, 43 and 40-44; Ware, *Labor Movement*, 303; Powderly, *Thirty Years*, 480-83; Grob, *Workers and Utopia*, 75.

22. Sorge, *Labor Movement*, 196; Ralph Scharnau, "Elizabeth Morgan, Crusader for Labor Reform," *Labor History* 14 (1973), passim.

23. Buhle, "Rhode Island," 49-50; Towles, "Rhode Island," 69-72; Steven J. Ross, "Strikes, Knights, and Political Fights: The May Day Strikes, the Knights of Labor, and the Rise of the United Labor Party in Nineteenth- Century Cincinnati," Knights of Labor Conference, Newberry Library, Chicago (May 1979), and below; on Michigan, see Anita Shafer Goodstein, *Biography of a Businessman: Henry W. Sage, 1814-1897* (Ithaca, N. Y., 1961), 88.

24. Katherine A. Harvey, *The Best-Dressed Miners: Life and Labor in the Maryland Coal Region, 1835-1910* (Ithaca, N. Y., 1969), 71 and 228-61.

25. "Powderly to Robert Layton" (May 17, 1882), in Powderly Papers, Catholic University, emphasis original; Harvey, *Miners*, 237-60.

26. *Constitution of the Cigarmakers' International Union of America* (n.p., 1877), preamble; Stockton, *Molders' Union*, 168; McNeill, ed., *Labor Movement*, 376-77 and 386-87; Foner, *Labor Movement*, 2: 98-99.

27. McNeill, ed., *Labor Movement*, 255, 291, 297; Gavett, *Milwaukee*, 36; exceptional was P. M. Arthur, grand chief of the Brotherhood of Locomotive Engineers, who opposed eight hours because "two hours less work means two hours more loafing . . . two hours more for drink." Charles E. Endicott, "Capital and Labor: Address Before the Central Trades Union . . . at Boston, March 28, 1886" (Boston, n.d.), 11.

28. FOTLU, *Proceedings, 1881 Convention*; FOTLU, *Proceedings, 1882 Convention*, 2 and 18.

29. FOTLU, *Proceedings, 1883 Convention*, 16; Cahill, *Shorter Hours*, 48-49; Kaufman, *Gompers*, 122-24 and 151-52; FOTLU, *Proceedings, 1884 Convention*, 10- 11.

30. Gutman, *Work, Culture and Society*, 248-72; Gompers, *Seventy Years*, 1: 72; Kaufman, *Gompers*, 51-52 and 151; Bernard Mandel, *Samuel Gompers: A Biography* (Yellow Springs, Ohio, 1963), 52-53; Philip S. Foner, "Marx's *Capital* in the United States," *Science and Society* 31 (Fall 1967), 461-66.

31. Grob, *Workers and Utopia*, 74; Gompers, *Seventy Years*, 1: 54, 104, 122, and 171; Mussey, "Eight Hour Theory," 232.

32. FOTLU, *Proceedings, 1882 Convention*, 19; FOTLU, *Proceedings, 1884 Convention*, 10-14; Foner, *Labor Movement*, 2: 99-100. After the passing of the 1884 resolution, the FOTLU legislative committee drew up forms for voluntary eight-hour agreements between workers and employers, but the threat of a strike lay behind the distribution of these forms. The text of the form is found in Gompers, *Seventy Years*, 173.

33. Grob, *Workers and Utopia*, 74; Powderly argued that the 1884 resolution, a change in the preamble of the Knights' constitution, was ill considered and mattered little, since delegates saw the preamble as so many "glittering generalities." See Powderly, *Thirty Years*, 482-85.

34. Michael A. Gordon, "The Labor Boycott in New York City, 1880-1886," *Labor History* 16 (Spring 1975), 184-229; Michael Funchion, *Chicago's Irish Nationalists, 1881-1890* (New York, 1976), 38: Foner, *Labor Movement*, 2: 95.

35. Cahill, *Shorter Hours*, 44. Powderly later made much of a resolution approved at the 1885 FOTLU convention. The resolution, speaking of the May 1 demand, promised that the unions would "not ask for an increase of wages" in conjunction "with the reduction of the hours of labor." Powderly took this to mean that national FOTLU policy was to accept wage cuts in exchange for hours gains. But the resolution, like the FOTLU stand on the matter, was vague, in a studied way. See Powderly, *Thirty Years*, 500-1.

36. The tensions in Knights of Labor thought are brilliantly explored in Alan Dawley, "Anarchists, Knights of Labor and Class Consciousness in the 1880's," Knights of Labor Conference, Newberry Library, Chicago (May 1979).

37. *John Swinton's Paper* (October 16, 1884); Labor Day, proposed in the early 1880's, also became a day of eight-hour agitation. See Foner, *Labor Movement*, 2: 96-98. The older tradition of agitation on July 4 did not disappear, but the Chicago eight-hour demonstrations in 1879 were probably among the last mass eight-hour rallies on that date. See *Chicago Tribune* (July 5-6, 1879), (Fall River) *Labor Standard* (July 9, 1881), and Philip Foner, ed., *We, the Other People* (Urbana, Ill., 1976), 115-19.

38. Henry David, *History of the Haymarket Affair* (New York, 1936), 161.

39. Calculations are based on United States Commissioner of Labor, *Third Annual Report* (Washington, D.C., 1887).

40. All the discussed strikes are described in United States Commissioner of Labor, *Third Annual Report* save that at Petersburg, which is reported in the *Saginaw Courier* (May 15, 1885) and those in Brooklyn, which are in Sorge, *Labor Movement*, 230 and 235, and Chicago (1885) in William Adelman, *Haymarket Revisited* (Chicago, 1976), 10.

41. See Samuel Gompers's testimony before the 1883 hearings of the Senate Committee upon the Relations between Labor and Capital, in Garraty, ed., *Gilded Age*, 14-15.

42. All the building trades strikes are described in United States Commissioner of Labor, *Third Annual Report*. See also New York Bureau of the Statistics of Labor, *Eighth Annual Report*, 384 and 389.

43. United States Commissioner of Labor, *Third Annual Report*; McNeill, ed., *Labor Movement*, 368; New Jersey Bureau of Statistics of Labor and Industries, *Sixth Annual Report* (Trenton, 1883), 154.

44. Herman Schluter, *The Brewing Industry and the Brewery Workers' Movement in America* (Cincinnati, 1910), 105ff.; United States Commissioner of Labor, *Third Annual Report*; New Jersey Bureau of Statistics of Labor and Industries, *Sixth Annual Report*, 154.

45. United States Commissioner of Labor, *Third Annual Report*; Grob, *Workers and Utopia*, 61-63.

46. Morris U. Schappes, "The 1880's—Beginning of Jewish Trade Unionism," *Jewish Life* (September 1954), 21-23; Foner, *Labor Movement*, 2: 62; Louis Levine, *The Women's Garment Workers: A History of the ILGWU* (New York, 1924), 37-39.

47. See United States Commissioner of Labor, *Third Annual Report*.

48. Wisconsin Bureau of Labor Statistics, *First Biennial Report, 1883 and 1884* (Madison, 1884), 151-53; Albert R. Parsons, ed., *Anarchism: Its Philosophy and Scientific Basis* (Chicago, 1887), 51-52.

49. The Michigan strikes are described in Michigan Bureau of Labor and Industrial Statistics, *Third Annual Report* (Lansing, 1886), and United States Commissioner of Labor, *Third Annual Report*. The best secondary account of the strikes is Jeremy Kilar, "Community and Authority Response to the Saginaw Valley Lumber Strikes of 1885," *Journal of Forest History* (April 1976), 67- 79. See also Doris B. McLaughlin, *Michigan Labor: A Brief History from 1818 to the Present* (Ann Arbor, 1970), 29-49; Goodstein, *Sage*, 87ff.

50. Kilar, "Community," 67-71; Michigan Bureau of Labor and Industrial Statistics, *Third Annual Report*, 93, 105, and 125; (Detroit) *Labor Leaf* (July 8, 1885); Goodstein, *Sage*, 88.

51.   Kilar, "Community," 70-75; Goodstein, *Sage*, 88-90; *Bay City Evening Press* (July 12 and 13, 1885).

52.   Kilar, "Community," 74-75; McLaughlin, *Michigan*, 42-45.

53.   *Saginaw Evening News* (July 23-25, 1885); McLaughlin, *Michigan*, 46-47; Kilar, "Community," 75-79.

54.   Grob, *Workers and Utopia*, 66-73.

55.   Ibid., 75; Ware, *Labor Movement*, 303-13; "Record of the Proceedings of the Ninth Regular Session of the General Assembly, Held at Hamilton, Ont., October 5-13, 1885," in Powderly Papers, Catholic University; Foner, *Labor Movement*, 2: 99-101; Powderly, *Thirty Years*, 253 and 495-96; Brotherhood of Carpenters and Joiners to Powderly, November 21, 1885, in Powderly Papers; Gavett, *Milwaukee*, 57-69; David, *Haymarket*, 165.

56.   Paul Avrich, *The Haymarket Tragedy* (Princeton, N. J., 1984), 55-119; Alan Dawley, "The International Working People's Association," in Roediger and Rosemont, eds. *Haymarket Scrapbook*, 84-86, (infroms our whole analysis of the IWPA.)

57.   Michael R. Johnson, "Albert R. Parsons: An American Architect of Syndicalism," *Midwest Quarterly* (Winter 1968), 195-206, and Rod Estvan, "The Political Thought of Albert R. Parsons" (unpublished ms., Chicago Historical Society), 129-33, successfully challenge the view that the "Chicago idea" was not syndicalist—a view found in David, *Haymarket*, 137-42. The Pittsburgh platform is reprinted in Ely, *Labor Movement*, 358-64.

58.   Albert R. Parsons, ed., *Anarchism*, 110; cf. 140; Estvan, "Parsons," 86-87 and passim. See also Dawley, "Class Consciousness"; Foner, ed., *Autobiographies*, 5; and Floyd Dell, "Socialism and Anarchism in Chicago," in J. Seymour Currey, ed., *Chicago: Its History and Builders* (Chicago, 1912), 2: 391ff.

59.   Cf. Morris Hillquit, *History of Socialism in the United States* (New York, 1965), 222; David, *Haymarket*, 167-70, esp. 169; Lucy Parsons, ed., *Life*, 25 and 145; Lucy Parsons, ed., *Twenty-Fifth Anniversary Eleventh of November Memorial Edition* (Chicago, 1912), 73-74.

60.   Lucy Parsons, ed., *Life*, 21-22; Dell, "Chicago," 371-75; Ashbaugh, *Parsons*, 35-36; *The Socialist* (July 5, 1879); Estvan, "Parsons," 85; Foner, ed., *Autobiographies*, 37.

61.   Foner, ed., *Autobiographies*, 47, 76, 122, 132, and 162; David, *Haymarket*, 150-51; Ashbaugh, *Parsons*, 55; Albert Parsons, ed., *Anarchism*, 72; Bruce Nelson, "Culture and Conspiracy: A Social History of Chicago Anarchism, 1870-1900" (unpublished Ph.D. dissertation, Northern Illinois University, 1985).

62.   *Alarm* (August 5, September 5, and December 12, 1885). Most specifically denounced the May 1 actions as of no consequence. See David, *Haymarket*, 168.

63.   Avrich, *Haymarket Tragedy*, 182-83; Lucy Parsons, ed., *Life*, 123; Albert Parsons, ed., *Anarchism*, 68; Alan Calmer, *Labor Agitator: The Story of Albert R. Parsons* (New York, 1937), 78; Foner, ed., *Autobiographies*, 47; David, *Haymarket*, 170.

64.   Avrich, *Haymarket Tragedy*, 181-96; Ashbaugh, *Parsons*, 35-36, 70-71 and 144. Both Dawley, "Class Consciousness," 13, and David, *Haymarket*, 167, hold that the participation of the IWPA was crucial to the success of the May 1 movement. See also Bruce Nelson, "Dancing and Picnicking Anarchists," in Roediger and Rosemont, eds. *Haymarket Scrapbook*, 76-79.

65.   Dawley, "Class Consciousness," 2-4; Ameringer, *Weaken*, 44-45; David, *Haymarket*, 149-51; *Alarm* (November 14, 1885); Avrich, *Haymarket Tragedy*, 45- 46 and 160-62; Morris, "Road to Trade Unionism," 258; Ashbaugh, *Parsons*, 68; Roediger, "Chicago Lehr-und-Wehr Verein," in Roediger and Rosemont, eds. *Haymarket Scrapbook*, 86.

66.   Ashbaugh, *Parsons*, 70; David, *Haymarket*, 171-72; John J. Flinn, *History of the Chicago Police, from the Settlement of the Community to the Present Time* (Chicago, 1887), 258-68; Illinois Bureau of Labor Statistics, *Fourth Biennial Report*, 474.

67.   David, *Haymarket*, 166-67; Mandel, *Gompers*, 52-53; Ross, "Knights," passim.; Ameringer, *Weaken*, 44-47; Gavett, *Milwaukee*, 57-69; Jeremy Brecher, *Strike!* (Greenwich, Conn., 1974), 68-70; David, *Haymarket*, 182-97; Jama Lazerow, "The Workingmen's Hour: The 1886 Labor Uprising in Boston," *Labor History* 21 (Spring 1980), 200-220; Elizabeth and Kenneth Fones-Wolf, "Knights Versus Trade Unionists," *Labor History* 22 (Spring 1981), 201; Richard

Schneirov, "An Injury to One Is the Concern of All: The Knights of Labor in Chicago," in Roediger and Rosemont, eds. *Haymarket Scrapbook*, 81-84.

68. Philip S. Foner, "The Polish-American Martyrs of the First May Day," unpublished manuscript in its author's possession; Ashbaugh, *Parsons*, 70; *John Swinton's Paper* (April 18, 1886); Wisconsin Bureau of Labor and Industrial Statistics, *Biennial Reports for 1885-1886*, 319; Foner, *Labor Movement*, 2: 97.

69. Foner, *Labor Movement*, 2: 97; Foner, ed., *Labor Songs*, 581-82; Ameringer, *Weaken*, 44; Brecher, *Strike!*, 66-67.

70. Morris, "Road to Trade Unionism," 258; Brecher, *Strike!*, 66-67; Commons and Associates, *History of Labour*, 2: 385. The estimates are based on *Bradstreet's* (May 8 and 15, 1886).

71. Gavett, *Milwaukee*, 57-69; Brecher, *Strike!*, 69. Lazerow, "Hours," corrects the number of Boston strikers upwards to 7,000. Figures based on U.S. Commissioner of Labor, *Third Annual Report*. For an indication of how incomplete the report may be, compare its listings on Saint Louis with *Saint Louis Post-Dispatch* (May 1-8, 1886).

72. *John Swinton's Paper* (May 2, 1886); Cahill, *Shorter Hours*, 159; Foner, *Labor Movement*, 2: 103-4.

73. Mandel, *Gompers*, 52-53; Gompers, *Seventy Years*, 1: 174; *New York Sun* (May 2, 1886); Foner, *Fur and Leather Workers*, 13-14; Ameringer, *Weaken*, 44- 47; Morris, "Road to Trade Unionism," 258ff.; Gavett, *Milwaukee*, 57-69; Foner, "Martyrs," 7-8; *New York Times* (May 11, 1886) as cited in Brecher, *Strike!*, 73. Leon Fink's *Workingmen's Democracy* (Urbana, Ill., 1984) is strong on details regarding the Knights and the eight-hour movement in Milwaukee, although its emphasis on conflict between skilled workers and unskilled immigrant labor obscures cooperation between the two groups.

74. Gavett, *Milwaukee*, 57-69; *Saint Louis Post-Dispatch* (May 1-4, 1886); Ross, "Knights," 8; Brecher, *Strike!*, 69-76.

75. David, *Haymarket*, 187-91; Brecher, *Strike!*, 76.

76. Avrich, *Haymarket Tragedy*, 188-92; David, *Haymarket*, 189-91; Foner, *Labor Movement*, 2: 105.

77. See David, *Haymarket*, 191-92, 194, and 196, for texts of the circulars and for Spies's testimony concerning his attempts to moderate their contents; *Chicago Inter-Ocean* (May 4, 1886); Flinn, *Police*, 278.

78. Foner, *Labor Movement*, 2: 106-7; David, *Haymarket*, 198-205 and 279; Brecher, *Strike!*, 76, places the attendance at just 1,200; *Chicago Inter- Ocean* (May 5, 1886). Avrich, *Haymarket Tragedy*, 199 and 208-09.

79. David, *Haymarket*, 206-32; Foner, *Labor Movement*, 2: 107. Avrich, *Haymarket Tragedy*, 215-39.

80. Quoted in David, *Haymarket*, 212.

81. Ameringer, *Weaken*, 46; Ross, "Knights," 11-14.

82. *Milwaukee Journal* (May 3-5, 1886); Gavett, *Milwaukee*, 63-64; Wisconsin Bureau of Labor and Industrial Statistics, *Report, 1885-1886*, 332; Foner, "Martyrs," 6-11; Brecher, *Strike!*, 69-70.

83. *Milwaukee Journal* (May 5-6, 1886); Foner, "Martyrs," 11-13.

84. *Milwaukee Journal* (May 7, 1886); Wisconsin Bureau of Labor and Industrial Statistics, *Report, 1885-1886*, 341-42; Foner, "Martyrs," 13-17; Rezneck, "Patterns," 305.

85. Ross, "Knights," 11-15.

86. Brecher, *Strike!*, 67 and 71-72; David, *Haymarket*, 539; Mandel, *Gompers*, 52-53; Foner, *Fur and Leather Workers*, 13-14; Cahill, *Shorter Hours*, 159; Gompers, as quoted in *Report of the Industrial Commission on the Relations of Capital and Labor Employed in Manufactures and General Business* (Washington, D.C., 1901), 7: 623.

87. Accounts of the trial are based primarily on Avrich, *Haymarket Tragedy*, 260ff; David, *Haymarket*, 236-346 (249 for composition of the jury); Foner, *Labor Movement*, 2: 108-12;

Ray Ginger, *Altgeld's America: The Lincoln Ideal Versus Changing Realities* (Chicago, 1958), 49-55.

88. David, *Haymarket*, 253-85.

89. Quoted in David, *Haymarket*, 253-54; see also 297ff and Ginger, *Altgeld's America*, 52; Gary, "The Chicago Anarchists of 1886," *Century Magazine 45* (April 1893).

90. Manuscript notebook of Albert R. Parsons, in Parsons Papers, SHSW; *Chicago Tribune* (August 21, 1886) and David, *Haymarket*, 315-27.

91. Powderly, as quoted in Ginger, *Altgeld's America*, 49; Powderly, *Thirty Years*, 544ff; Foner, *Labor Movement*, 2: 111-14; and David, *Haymarket*, 393- 421.

92. Foner, *Labor Movement*, 2: 110-14; David, *Haymarket*, 393-421; Sender Garlin, *John Swinton: American Radical* (New York, 1976), 13; Lucy Parsons, ed., *Life*, 261-63; Albert Parsons, ed., *Anarchism*, 193-94; David, *Haymarket*, 486-87.

93. Lucy Parsons, ed., *Twenty-Fifth Anniversary*, 24; Lucy Parsons, ed., *Life*, 128-59, reprints part of his remarkable eight-hour speech before the court; Albert Parsons, ed., *Anarchism*, 74 and 185-86, for Parsons' October 13, 1887, letter to Governor Richard Oglesby demanding full freedom or execution, and for Neebe's remarks.

94. Albert Parsons, ed., *Anarchism*, 200. Neebe, Fielden, and Schwab were ultimately pardoned on June 26, 1893, by Illinois Governor John Peter Altgeld. See Avrich, *Haymarket Tragedy*, 415-27; Ginger, *Altgeld's America*, 61-88; David, *Haymarket*, 479-507; and Harvey Wish, "Governor Altgeld Pardons the Anarchists," *Journal of the Illinois State Historical Society* 31:4 (December 1938), 425-48.

95. David, *Haymarket*, 532-40; Foner, *Labor Movement*, 2: 86-88.

96. Foner, *Labor Movement*, 2: 115-31; Harry F. Ward, *The Gospel for a Working World* (New York, 1918), 41-42.

The Rightward Drift of the AFL and the
Temporary Decline of the Hours Issue, 1887-1908

1. Irwin Yellowitz, *Industrialization and the American Labor Movement* (Port Washington, N.Y., 1977), 125. We disagree with Yellowitz on this point. See below and New York Bureau of Statistics of Labor, *Eighth Annual Report, 1890* (Albany, 1890).

2. John T. Cumbler, "Labor, Capital and Community: The Struggle for Power," *Labor History* 15: 3 (Summer 1974), 395-415; Jonathan E. Garlock, "A Structural Analysis of the Knights of Labor: A Prolegomenon to the History of the Producing Classes," (unpublished Ph.D. dissertation, University of Rochester, 1974); and below.

3. See Johnson, *Shopkeeper's Millennium*, 36-61, on the relationship between proximity and upper-class fears of working-class leisure. Sam B. Warner, Jr., *Streetcar Suburbs: The Process of Growth in Boston, 1870-1900* (New York, 1969) remains the classic work on suburbanization.

4. Olmsted, as quoted in Roy Rosenzweig, "Middle-Class Parks and Working- Class Play: The Struggle Over Recreational Space in Worcester, Massachusetts, 1870-1910," *Radical History Review* 21 (March 1980), 31; Spencer as quoted in Daniel T. Rodgers, *The Work Ethic in Industrial America, 1850-1920* (Chicago, 1978), 94-95; John Higham, "American Culture in the 1890's," in *Writing American History: Essays on Modern Scholarship* (Bloomington, Ind., 1972), 3-102; John Kasson, *Amusing the Millions: Coney Island at the Turn of the Century* (New York, 1978), esp. 98-109. See also Rosenzweig, "Parks"; Lawrence A. Finfer, "Leisure as Social Work in the Urban Community," (unpublished Ph.D. dissertation, Michigan State University, 1974); Joel Spring, "Mass Culture and School Sports," *History of Education Quarterly* 14 (Winter 1974).

5. Quoted from Kasson, *Amusing*, 108-09.

6. "Recording Time of Employees," *Scientific American*, 69 (August 12, 1893), 101; Harry Braverman, *Labor and Monopoly Capitalism: The Degradation of Work in the Twentieth Century* (New York, 1974), brilliantly places Taylorism within the tradition of capitalist management while capturing its innovative power.

7. Taylor, *The Principles of Scientific Management* (New York, 1967), 15, 43, and passim, and "Shop Management," *Transactions of the American Society of Mechanical Engineers* 24 (1903), 1337-1456; Josephine Goldmark, *Fatigue and Efficiency: A Study in Industry* (New York, 1912), 192-203. For a fuller treatment of Taylorism and the working day see David Roediger, "Fordism, Labor and the Hours of Work," forthcoming in Gary Cross, ed. *Worktime and Industrialization: An International History.*

8. Gavett, *Labor Movement*, 89; Gutman, *Work, Culture and Society*, 254; Foner, *Labor Movement*, 1: appendix.

9. NAFI, *Second Annual Convention* (1888), 10-11, and *Fourth Annual Convention* (1890), 43-49; Goldmark, *Fatigue and Efficiency*, 370.

10. On professionalization among labor academicians, see Bari J. Watkins, "The Professors and the Unions: American Academic Social Theory and Labor Reform, 1883-1915," (unpublished Ph.D. dissertation, Yale University, 1976); Commons, "Organized Labor's Attitude Toward Industrial Efficiency," *American Economic Review* 1 (September 1911), 472 and passim; Goldmark, quoted in *Fatigue and Efficiency*, 210.

11. Samuel Haber, *Efficiency and Uplift: Scientific Management in the Progressive Era, 1890-1920* (Chicago, 1964), 14, 106; Taylor, *Principles*, 5; "Brandeis to Ray Stannard Baker" (December 31, 1910), in Melvin I. Urofsky and David W. Levy, eds., *Letters of Louis D. Brandeis* (Albany, N.Y., 1972), 2: 390-91; "Brandeis to H. C. DeRan" (February 12, 1912), *Letters*, 2: 542-43; Brandeis, *Scientific Management and the Railroads* (New York, 1912); Alfred Lef, ed., *The Social and Economic Views of Mr. Justice Brandeis* (New York, 1930), 381, 386, 391-94, 410.

12. *Report of the Industrial Commission, Final Report* (1902), 12: 764; and Goldmark, *Fatigue and Efficiency*, 169-70.

13. Cahill, *Shorter Hours*, 232-40; Goldmark, *Fatigue and Efficiency*, 168n. and 370-74

(part two); Edward Berkowitz and Kim McQuaid, *Creating the Welfare State* (New York, 1980), 1-8.

14. Cahill, *Shorter Hours*, 60ff.

15. Foner, *Labor Movement*, 3: 36-39; Albion G. Taylor, *Labor Policies of the National Association of Manufacturers* (Urbana, Ill., 1927), 8-25, esp. 13; *Cincinnati Enquirer* (April 15, 1903).

16. Taylor, *Labor Policies*, 121-22. NAM, *Eight Hours by Act of Congress: Arbitrary, Needless, Destructive, Dangerous, NAM Bulletin* (1904); Cahill, *Shorter Hours*, 63-65; Foner, *Labor Movement*, 3: 39-42; Robert Knight, *Industrial Relations in the San Francisco Bay Area, 1900-1918* (Berkeley, 1960), 66-70, 226-27.

17. David Montgomery, "Machinists, the Civic Federation and the Socialist Party," in *Workers' Control in America* (Cambridge, Eng., 1979), 48-82. For "new left" views of the NCF as an important corporate liberal force coopting labor, see James Weinstein, *The Corporate Ideal in the Liberal State, 1900-1918* (Boston, 1968), and Ronald Radosh, "The Corporate Ideology of American Labor Leaders from Gompers to Hillman," *Studies on the Left* 6 (November-December 1966), 66-88.

18. Norman Ware, *Labor in Modern Industrial Society* (New York, 1935), 323; Foner, *Labor Movement*, 3: 76-86; James J. McGinley, *Labor Relations in the New York Rapid Transit Systems, 1904-1944* (New York, 1949), 258-59. Mandel, *Gompers*, 246-49; Commons and Associates, *Labour in the U.S.*, 4: 125-27.

19. Gunton is quoted in Goldmark, *Fatigue and Efficiency*, 328 (part 2) from his remarks at the NCF Industrial Conference of 1902. See also "The First Annual Meeting of the New England Civic Federation, Boston, January 11, 1906," *NCF Review* 2 (January-February 1906), 8, and esp. "Will Labor Make Concessions in Return for a Shorter Work-Day?" *NCF Review* 1 (September 1904), 7; Cf. Gunton's eloquent "Shall an Eight-Hour System Be Adopted?" *Forum* 1 (1886), 136ff, and Jack Blicksilver, "George Gunton: Pioneer Spokesman for Labor-Big Business Entente," *Business History Review* 21 (Spring 1957). Gunton's fullest statement on hours is *Wealth and Progress* (New York, 1887).

20. William I. Trattner, *Crusade for the Children: A History of the National Child Labor Committee and Child Labor Reform in America* (Chicago, 1970), 103-05; Montgomery, "Machinists," in *Worker's Control*, 82-83; Foner, *Labor Movement*, 3: 75-77.

21. On injunctions, note that the famous Bucks' Stove and Range Company decision limiting the right to publicize secondary boycotts grew out of a dispute involving the hours of labor. See Foner, *Labor Movement*, 3: 338-42. See also "The Real Panacea," *Iron Molders' Journal* 42 (February 1906), 86.

22. Figures are from Joseph M. Viau, *Hours and Wages in American Organized Labor* (New York, 1939), 55.

23. Montgomery, "Machinists," 53; Montgomery, "Workers Control of Machine Production in the Nineteenth Century," in *Workers' Control*, 18-27; and Marguerite Green, *The National Civic Federation and the American Labor Movement* (Washington, D.C., 1956), 43-50.

24. Retold in Wilfred Carsel, *A History of the Chicago Ladies' Garment Workers' Union* (Chicago, 1940), 42.

25. Gompers, *Seventy Years*, 1: 304-05 and 309-10; New York Bureau of Statistics of Labor, *Eighth Annual Report*, 705ff.

26. Mussey, "Eight-Hour Theory," 234-41; Rodgers, *Work Ethic*, 178-79.

27. Rodgers, *Work Ethic*, 178; Mussey, "Eight-Hour Theory," 241. A recent study, valuable for its review of the AFL literature on hours, technology, and production but overreaching in its conclusion that the turn of the century saw a sharp turn toward AFL emphasis on productivity, is Irwin Yellowitz, "The AFL and Technological Change" (Paper delivered at AHA Convention, Los Angeles, December 1981).

28. L. Danryid, *History and Philosophy of the Eight-Hour Movement* (New York, 1889); George Gunton, *The Economic and Social Importance of the Eight-Hour Movement* (Washington, D.C., 1889); George E. McNeill, *The Eight-Hour Primer* (New York, 1889). All the pamphlets are in the Labadie Collection, University of Michigan, Ann Arbor. See also, Mussey, "Eight-Hour

Theory," 238.

29. AFL, *Proceedings* (1888), 9 quoted in Mussey, "Eight-Hour Theory," 239.

30. McNeill, *Eight-Hour Primer*, 15-18; Gunton, *Eight-Hour Movement*, passim; his statements in Goldmark, *Fatigue and Efficiency*, 40, 308, 328, and *Wealth and Progress*, 226-29.

31. Gompers, *Eight-Hour Work Day* (Washington, D.C., n.d.), 11.

32. Carsel, *Chicago Ladies' Garment Workers*, 33, and above.

33. AFL, *Proceedings, 1895*, 15; Foner, *Labor Movement*, 2: 243.

34. Robinson, "Working Hours," 68; AFL, *Proceedings, 1891*, 46; AFL, *Proceedings, 1892*, 14.

35. Mandel, *Gompers*, 177; Foner, *Labor Movement*, 2: 115-56; *Carpenter* (January 20, 1891).

36. Cahill, *Shorter Hours*, esp. 46-47; Powderly, *Thirty Years*, 515ff; Bellamy, *Looking Backward* (New York, 1960), 130; Cyrus F. Willard, "News of the Movement," *Nationalist* 2 (December 1889), 76; "The Eight Hour Movement," *Nationalist* 2 (December 1889), 82. But by 1890, the Nationalists supported a national eight-hour law, arguing against the AFL's nonpolitical approach in "Current Topics," *Nationalist* 3 (August 1890), 33-34; see Rev. H. H. Brown, "How Many Hours Per Day Shall We Labor?" *Nationalist* 3 (January 1891), 367- 72, for a charming visionary call for a four- to five-hour day. See also L. Glen Seretan, *Daniel DeLeon: The Odyssey of an American Marxist* (Cambridge, Mass., 1979), 246, n. 13.

37. *AFL Proceedings, 1894*, 36-37; Foner, *Labor Movement*, 2: 290-99.

38. Cahill, *Shorter Hours*, 50.

39. The Cincinnati Platform of the Populists in 1891 called for extension of the eight-hour law for federal employees to "apply to all corporations employing labor in the different states of the Union." The Saint Louis Platform of February 1892 ignored the issue, and the famous Omaha Platform of July 1892 called for strengthening enforcement of the law applying to federal workers and resolved to "cordially sympathize with the efforts of organized workingmen to shorten the hours of labor."

40. *National Convention of the Socialist Party* (Chicago, 1904), 76, 308. See also Henry F. Bedford, *Socialism and the Workers in Massachusetts, 1886- 1912* (Amherst, 1966), 50, 85, 89, 104-05, and note that the Socialists often agitated for eight-hour laws covering city employees, not all workers. The Social Democratic party in Massachusetts, a Socialist predecessor, did agitate for state eight-hour laws. See Howard H. Quint, *The Forging of American Socialism* (Indianapolis, 1953), 325.

41. A. Hirschfield, "The Social Effects of the Eight-Hour Day," *International Socialist Review* (ISB) 3 (April 1903), 610-14. But see also the visionary "How Much Work Is Necessary?" *ISR* 1 (December 1900), 347-58.

42. *Spokane Labor World* (June 18, 1909); Ruth Allen, *Chapters in the History of Organized Labor in Texas* (n.p., 1941), 23.

43. Cahill, *Shorter Hours*, 72.

44. Gompers in AFL, *Proceedings, 1894*, 15; Cahill, *Shorter Hours*, 72-75.

45. Cahill, *Shorter Hours*, 76. Efforts to strengthen the federal legislation continued throughout the period, with little effect. See "Eight Hour Bill Considered," *American Federationist* 11 (June 1904), 494-505. Robinson, "Working Hours," 63ff, gives a full account of these efforts.

46. AFL, *Proceedings, 1897*, 85. Yellowitz, *Industrialization*, 113-14; Viau, *Hours and Wages*, 64; Trattner, *Crusade*, 167ff; Robinson, "Working Hours," 71-72; Cahill, *Shorter Hours*, 84.

47. Cahill, *Shorter Hours*, 97.

48. Ibid., 100-104; Felix Frankfurter, "Hours of Labor and Realism in Constitutional Law," *Harvard Law Review* 29 (1916), 354-62.

49. Sidney G. Tarrow, "Lochner versus New York: A Political Analysis," *Labor History* 5 (Fall 1914), 281; *New York Sun* (May 4, 1898); Cahill, *Shorter Hours*, 116.

50. Cahill, *Shorter Hours*, 118-19; Frankfurter, "Realism," 359. Walter Weyl, "Street

Railway Employment in the U.S.," *Bulletin of the Bureau of Labor Statistics* No. 57 (March 1905), 592-616. The Rhode Island law, defied by the biggest transit lines, was important only as a precedent. A long 1902 strike in Providence and Pawtucket failed to enforce the law and that December the legislature repealed the ten-hour statute. See Scott Malloy, "Rhode Island Communities and the 1902 Carmen's Strike," *Radical History Review* 17 (Spring 1978), 75-98.

51. Vernon H. Jensen, *Heritage of Conflict: Labor Relations in the Nonferrous Metals Industry Up to 1930* (Ithaca, N.Y., 1950), 97-100; Cahill, *Shorter Hours*, 119-22. See also Federal Writers Project, *Labor History of Oklahoma* (Oklahoma City, 1939), 16.

52. Quote from *In Re Morgan*, 26 Colorado 427-28 (1899); Cahill, *Shorter Hours*, 122-24; Jensen, *Heritage of Conflict*, 101-04. David Lonsdale, "The Fight for an Eight-Hour Day," *Colorado Magazine* 43 (1966), 339.

53. Jensen, *Heritage of Conflict*, 100-101 and 117; Richard E. Lingenfelter, *The Hardrock Miners: A History of the Mining Labor Movement in the American West, 1863-1893* (Berkeley, 1974), 190-93; Cahill, *Shorter Hours*, 124; Mark Wyman, *Hard Rock Epic: Western Miners and the Industrial Revolution* (Berkeley, 1979), 225 and 201-24 passim.

54. Tarrow, "Lochner," 282-89; Morris Hillquit, *Loose Leaves from a Busy Life* (New York, 1971), 26-27.

55. Tarrow, "Lochner," 289-312.

56. Morris Hillquit, *History of Socialism in the United States* (New York, 1903), 288; see also Rhode Island Commissioner of Industrial Statistics, *Second Annual Report* (Providence, 1889), 102-03, for a series of building trades' strikes.

57. AFL, *Proceedings, 1888*, 8-25; Foner, *Labor Movement*, 2: 178-79; Robinson, "Working Hours," 60-61; AFL, *Proceedings, 1889*, 14; Gompers, *Seventy Years*, 1: 294-97; "A Ringing Eight-hour Call, Practical Suggestions by President Gompers," AFL Correspondence; "Gompers to H. J. Skeffington" (January 3, 1889); "Gompers to John O'Brien" (February 7, 1889), Gompers Letter Books, Library of Congress; Cahill, *Shorter Hours*, 160-61.

58. Philip S. Foner, *May Day: A Short History of the International Workers' Holiday* (New York, 1988), 40-43; Foner, *Labor Movement*, 2: 179-80; Gompers, *Seventy Years*, 1: 296-97. The May 1 date harkened back, of course, to the 1886 demonstrations which had been influenced in setting the national strike for May 1 by the Illinois eight-hour strike of May 1, 1867. Traditions of popular May 1 celebrations extend far back in European history and traditions of labor protest associated with that date began as early as 1517 when officials in London seized 400 strikers and executed nine. See Hugh Archibald, *The Four-Hour Day in Coal* (London, 1922), 10. See also Sidney Fine, "Is May Day American in Origin?" *Historian* 16 (Spring 1954), 121-34.

59. Gompers, *Seventy Years*, 1: 296; Grob, *Workers and Utopia*, 76-79; Foner, *Labor Movement*, 2: 179; Robinson, "Working Hours," 61.

60. AFL, *Proceedings, 1889*, 14-15, 29-31, 42-43, and passim. Gompers's report to the convention (13-15) clearly countenanced industrial unionism.

61. Foner, *May Day*, 45; Gompers, *Seventy Years*, 1: 296-97; "Gompers to P. J. McGuire" (May 8, 1890), Gompers Letter Books, Library of Congress; *New York Times* (May 2, 1890). However, many small and brief strikes did occur— so many, that *Bradstreet's* maintained that on no previous day in history had more individual American strikes begun. See Foner, *Labor Movement*, 2:183n, and Walter Galenson, *The United Brotherhood of Carpenters: The First Hundred Years* (Cambridge, Mass., 1983), 60.

62. *Chicago Tribune* (May 2, 1890); *New York Tribune* (May 2, 1890); *New York Sun* (May 2, 1890); Foner, *Labor Movement*, 2: 181-83.

63. "Gompers to August Keufer" (May 9, 1890), Gompers Letter Books.

64. Sidney Fine, "The Eight-Hour Day Movement in the United States, 1888- 1891," *Mississippi Valley Historical Review* 40 (December 1953), 455; Foner, *Labor Movement*, 2: 183; Robinson, "Working Hours," 62; Gompers as quoted in Grob, *Workers and Utopia*, 150.

65. Robinson, "Working Hours," 62; Grob, *Workers and Utopia*, 151; Cahill, *Shorter Hours*, 162; AFL, *Proceedings, 1891*, 47; McAlister Coleman, *Men and Coal* (New York, 1943), 54-55.

66. Gompers, *Seventy Years*, 1: 307-09; AFL, *Proceedings, 1891*, 12-13, 47; Robinson, "Working Hours," 62. Foner, *Labor Movement*, 1: 200-204 and Roger W. Shugg, "The New Orleans General Strikes of 1892," *Louisiana Historical Quarterly* 21 (April 1938), 547ff.

67. Mandel, *Gompers*, 88-106; Gompers, *Seventy Years*, 1: 310; AFL, *Proceedings, 1891*, 46-47; Foner, *Labor Movement*, 2: 279-368.

68. AFL, *Proceedings, 1895*, 15, 30; AFL, *Proceedings, 1896*, 22-23; AFL, *Proceedings, 1898*, 21; AFL, *Proceedings, 1901*; Cahill, *Shorter Hours*, 186.

69. Cahill, *Shorter Hours*, 165. Florence Peterson, "Strikes in the United States, 1880-1936," U.S. Bureau of Labor Statistics, *Bulletin No. 65* (August 1937), 39.

70. The gains of 1898 came after bargaining resulting from an 1897 national strike of 150,000 miners. Commons and Associates, *Labour in the U.S.*, 4: 25-30; Andrew Roy, *A History of the Coal Miners of the United States* (Columbus, Ohio, 1907), 323-50; John H. M. Laslett, *Labor and the Left: A Study of Socialist and Radical Influences in the American Labor Movement, 1881-1924* (New York, 1970), 198-99; Colemen, *Men and Coal*, 62-63.

71. Foner, *Labor Movement*, 3: 86-102; Robert J. Cornell, *The Anthracite Strike of 1902* (Washington, D.C., 1957), 59.

72. Ibid.; Laslett, *Labor and the Left*, 204; William Mailly, "The Antracite Coal Strike," *ISR* 3 (August 1902), 79-85.

73. Commons and Associates, *Labour in the U.S.*, 4: 189; Jensen, *Heritage of Conflict*, ch. 9; George Suggs, *Colorado's War on Militant Unionism* (Detroit, 1972).

74. Foner, *Labor Movement*, 3: 407-12; Jones, *Autobiography*, 94-113; Elsie Gluck, *John Mitchell, Miner* (New York, 1929), 171.

75. *AFL Proceedings, 1898*, 21; Commons and Associates, *Labour in the U.S.*, 4: 115; Perlman, *The Machinists*, 52-82.

76. Montgomery, "Machinists," in *Workers' Control in America*, 52-82; "The 490 Minute Crime," *NMTA Bulletin* 2 (February 1903), 93; "No Half-Holidays," *NMTA Bulletin* 3 (February 1904), 96; "An Eight-Hour Benefit," *Open Shop* 6 (August 1907), 364-54.

77. Commons and Associates, *Labour in the U.S.*, 4: 54-55; Cahill, *Shorter Hours*, 174-77; George A. Tracy, *History of the Typographical Union* (Indianapolis, 1913), 563-64; George E. Barnett, *The Printers* (Cambridge, Mass., 1909), 157-376; Jacob Loft, *The Printing Trades* (New York, 1944), 86- 89.

78. Cahill, *Shorter Hours*, 177-80, with the quote from 180; Commons and Associates, *Labour in the U.S.*, 4: 55-60; material on Chicago and Cleveland comes from Chicago Typographical Union No. 16, *Report of John C. Harding* (Chicago, 1910), 7-16; Chicago Typographical Union No. 16, *Facts and Figures: The Contest for the Eight-Hour Day* (Chicago, 1907?), 3-18, and, for the quoted material, *Typographical Journal* (October 1907), 427.

79. Abbott, *Women in Industry*, 4-6; Grace Abbott, *The Child and the State*, (Chicago, 1938), 1:266; Eleanor Flexner, *Century of Struggle: The Women's Movement in the United States* (New York, 1973), 193. Figures rounded to nearest 500.

80. Bliss and Andrews, *Women in Trade Unions*, 146-48.

81. Ibid., 150; O'Donnell, "Women as Bread Winners—the Error of the Age," *American Federationist* 4 (October 1897).

82. *AFL Proceedings, 1898*, 45; James Keneally, "Women and Trade Unions, 1870-1920," *Labor History* (Winter 1973), 44-45; Philip Foner, *Women and the American Labor Movement*, 2 vols. (New York, 1980), vol. 1; Bliss and Andrews, *Women in Trade Unions*, 152; Meredith Tax, *The Rising of the Women: Feminist Solidarity and Class Conflict, 1880-1917* (New York, 1980), 17-18.

83. Abbott, *Women in Industry*, 5, 360. Elizabeth Beardsley Butler, *Women and the Trades, Pittsburgh, 1907-1908* (Pittsburgh, 1984; originally 1909), 351-57 and passim. On "seasonal unionism" see Carsel, *Chicago*, 41-47, and Abraham Bisno, *Union Pioneer* (Madison, Wisc., 1967); Hillquit, *History of Socialism*, 288; Donald P. Robinson, *Spotlight on a Union: The Story of the United Hatters, Cap and Millinery Workers International Union* (New York, 1948), 79; Foner, *Women and the American Labor Movement*, 2:256.

84. Susan M. Strasser, "Mistress and Maid, Employer and Employee: Domestic Service Reform in the United States, 1897-1920," *Marxist Perspectives* 4 (Winter 1978), 55; David Katzman, *Seven Days a Week* (New York, 1978), 110-15; Inez Goodman, "A Nine-Hour Day for Domestic Servants," *Independent* 54 (February 13, 1902), 397-99. Faye Dudden, *Serving Women: Household Service in Nineteenth-Century America* (Middletown, Conn., 1983), 179-81; Daniel E. Sutherland, *Americans and Their Servants* (Baton Rouge, La., 1981), 97-99.

85. Malkiel, "The Lowest Paid Workers," *Socialist Woman* 2 (September 1908); Susan J. Kleinberg, "Technology and Women's Work," *Labor History* (Winter 1976), 58-72; Susan M. Strasser, "Never Done: The Ideology and Technology of Household Work, 1850-1930," (unpublished Ph.D. dissertation, State University of New York—Stony Brook, 1977).

86. Henry, "The Woman Organizer" quoted in Baxandall and Associates, *America's Working Women*, 170. "Vital Need of the Salespeople Today," *Retail Clerks' International Advocate* 27 (August 1920), 16. Thanks to Susan Porter Benson for this reference. See Nancy Schrom Dye, "Feminism or Unionism?: The New Women's Trade Union League and the Labor Movement," *Feminist Studies* 3 (Fall 1975), 120, for a similar comment.

87. Tax, *Rising*, 57; Agnes Nestor, *Woman's Labor Leader* (Rockford, Ill., 1954).

88. Tax develops this point throughout *Rising* but especially in the final chapter.

89. Ashbaugh, *Parsons*, 33-36 and 73-74; Tax, *Rising*, 38-53; Flexner, *Century of Struggle*, 196; Funchion, *Chicago's Irish Nationalists*, 38; *Chicago Tribune* (May 3, 1886); Lizzie Swank Holmes, "Women Workers of Chicago," *American Federationist* 12 (August 1905), 510.

90. Ralph Scharnau, "Elizabeth Morgan: Crusader for Labor Reform," *Labor History* 141 (Summer 1973), 340-43; Ann Doubilet, "The Illinois Women's Alliance, 1888-1894" (unpublished seminar paper, Northern Illinois University, 1973), 2; Tax, *Rising*, 54-58.

91. "Mrs. Thomas J. Morgan to Gompers" (August 20, 1891) and "Aims and Objects of Ladies' Federal Labor Union, No. 2703" in Thomas Morgan Collection (Illinois Historical Survey, University of Illinois—Champaign), Book 2; *Chicago Times* (July 30-August 17, 1888); Doubilet, "Alliance," 3-7; Tax, *Rising*, 67-69; Scharnau, "Morgan," 342-43.

92. Holmes wrote in *Alarm* (August 11, 1888); Tax, *Rising*, 68-71 and 302- 03; n. 40; Jane Addams, *Twenty Years at Hull House* (New York, 1960), 148-68. "Aims and Objects," Morgan Collection (University of Illinois) on "self- protection." Matthew Josephson, *Union House, Union Bar: The History of the Hotel and Restaurant Employees and Bartenders International Union, AFL-CIO* (New York, 1956), 51.

93. Scharnau, "Morgan," 345-46; Tax, *Rising*, 77ff.

94. Tax, *Rising*, 77-82; Bisno, *Union Pioneer*, 147-148; Doubilet, "Alliance," 11-13; Elizabeth Morgan and others, for Chicago Trades and Labor Assembly, *The New Slavery* (Chicago, 1891); Scharnau, "Morgan," 345-48.

95. Addams, *Twenty Years*, 148-68, esp. 148-54; quotes from Dorothy Rose Blumberg, *Florence Kelley, Making of a Social Pioneer* (New York, 1966), 112, 127. See also Joan Waush, "Florence Kelley and the Anti-Sweatshop Campaign of 1892-1893," *UCLA Historical Journal* 3 (1982), esp. 24.

96. Blumberg, *Kelley*, 102-04, 121-28; Scharnau, "Morgan," 347; Tax, *Rising*, 81-83, and esp. the introduction to K. Sklar, ed. *The Autobiography of Florence Kelley* (Chicago, 1985).

97. Tax, *Rising*, 83-86; Scharnau, "Morgan," 347-48; Doubilet, "Alliance," 14-15. Kelley responded to the lack of enforcement by entering law school. See Blumberg, *Kelley*, 146; Ginger, *Altgeld's America*, 134; and Earl Beckner, *A History of Labor Legislation in Illinois* (Chicago, 1929), 254-59.

98. Blumberg, *Kelley*, 146-47; Beckner, *Labor Legislation*, 189-90.

99. Kelley, as quoted in Blumberg, *Kelley*, 147; Beckner, *Labor Legislation*, 189-90; Florence Kelley, "Hull House," *New England Magazine* 18 (July 1898), 561.

100. Scharnau, "Morgan," 348-49; Tax, *Rising*, 84-89.

101. Carsel, *Chicago*, 26-28; Tax, *Rising*, 61-64 and 86-89; Foner, *Labor Movement*, 2:193-94; Wertheimer, *We Were There*, 242-43.

102. Flexner, *Century of Struggle*, 212-13; Foner, *Women and the American Labor*

Movement, 1:290-302; Tax, *Rising*, 95-97; Gladys Boone, *The Women's Trade Union League in Great Britain and the United States of America* (New York, 1942), 20ff; Dye, "Feminism or Unionism?" 111; Allen Davis, "The WTUL: Origins and Organization," *Labor History* 5:1 (Winter 1964), 3-17; Jones, *Autobiography*, xviii-xx and 71-83; *Constitution of the National Women's Trade Union League of America, Adopted in Fanueil Hall, Boston, November 17-19, 1903*, Article III.

103. O'Reilly quoted by Tax, *Rising*, 116-17; Dye, "Feminism or Unionism," passim; "Creating a Feminist Alliance: Sisterhood and Class Conflict in the New York Women's Trade Union League, 1903-1914," *Feminist Studies* 2 (1975), 24-38.

104. Tax, *Rising*, 95-96; Robin Miller Jacoby, "The Women's Trade Union League and American Feminism," *Feminist Studies* 3 (Fall 1975), 132; *Life and Labor* 2 (April 1912), 99.

105. Irwin Yellowitz, *Labor and the Progressive Movement in New York State* (Ithaca, N.Y., 1965), 67.

106. Dye, "Feminism or Unionism?" 112-20; Tax, *Rising*, 101-108; Foner, *Women and the American Labor Movement*, 1: 308-22; Alice Henry, *The Trade Union Woman* (New York, 1915), 45-50.

107. On membership, see Dye, "Feminist Alliance," 37, n. 8, for the estimate that twenty women formed the core of the early New York group.

108. Allis Rosenberg Wolfe, "Women, Consumerism, and the National Consumers' League in the Progressive Era, 1900-1923," *Labor History* 16 (Summer 1975) 383; Tax, *Rising*, 98-99; Maud Nathan, *The Story of an Epoch- Making Movement* (New York, 1926), 15-23 (quoted from 22); Flexner, *Century of Struggle*, 208-9.

109. Nathan, *Epoch-Making Movement*, 25, quoting the constitution of the New York group, 89 and 125; Florence Kelley, *Modern Industry in Relation to the Family, Health, Education, Morality* (New York, 1914), 298.

110. Nathan, *Epoch-Making Movement*, 25 (from constitution of New York League).

111. Nathan, *Epoch-Making Movement*, 59, 62; Wertheimer, *We Were There*, 241ff.

112. Nathan, *Epoch-Making Movement*, 1-2, 13-14, 30-49; Wolfe, "Consumerism," 384-86; Extracts from "Report of Alice Woodbridge," Appendix A in *Epoch-Making Movement*, 129-30; and Goldmark, *Fatigue and Efficiency*, 182- 84.

113. Nathan, *Epoch-Making Movement*, 25-32, 35-36, 67, 70, 384-86.

114. Yellowitz, *Progressive Movement*, 102, 126; Wolfe, "Consumerism," 393- 94; Tax, *Rising*, 98-99; Nathan, *Epoch-Making Movement*, 46-59, esp. 50.

115. Nathan, *Epoch-Making Movement*, appendices, 144, 147-48, 152, 156, 158, 161, 162, 167-169, 173, 178-79, 184, 198, 206, 216, 223; Wolfe, "Consumerism," 386; for details of the various acts, see "*Anna Hawley v. Joseph Walker*, In the Supreme Court of the United States, October Term, 1913; No. 217, To Replace Pages 1 to 18 in Brief Filed by Louis D. Brandeis, and Josephine Goldmark," 1-18; Jacob Andres Lieberman, "Their Sisters' Keepers: The Women's Hours and Wages Movement in the United States, 1890-1902," (unpublished Ph.D. dissertation, Columbia University, 1971), 136.

116. "*Hawley v. Walker*," 9; Melvin I. Urofsky, *A Mind of One Piece: Brandeis and American Reform* (New York, 1971), 39-42; Cahill, *Shorter Hours*, 112-13.

117. Flexner, *Century of Struggle*, 215; Frankfurter, "Realism," 354; Urofsky, *One Piece*, 39.

118. *Women in Industry, Decision of the United States Supreme Court in Cult Muller vs. State of Oregon Upholding the Constitutionality of the Oregon Ten-Hour Law for Women and Brief for the State of Oregon by Louis D. Brandeis, Assisted by Josephine Goldmark, Publication of the National Consumer's League* (New York, n.d.), 18, 47ff, and 65; Bettina Eileen Berch, "Industrialization and Working Women in the Nineteenth Century: England, France and the United States," (unpublished Ph.D. dissertation, University of Wisconsin-Madison, 1976), 300-302.

119. Beckner, *Labor Legislation*, 190-206, esp. 206; Goldmark, *Fatigue and Efficiency*, esp. ch. 7; see also the NCL publication, *The Case Against Nightwork for Women, Revised with New Introduction to March 1, 1918* (New York, 1918), esp. 224-62.

Class Conflict, Reform, and War:
The Working Day from 1907 to 1918

1. Montgomery, "New Unionism," in *Workers' Control in America*, 96.

2. Thomas Kniesner, "The Full-Time Workweek in the United States, 1900- 1972," *Industrial and Labor Relations Review* 30 (October 1976), 4, Table 1. The 46.3 hours/week figure for manufacturing in 1919 is as computed in "Hours of Work in the Two World Wars," *Monthly Labor Review* (October 1945), 621. See also Montgomery, "New Unionism," 96.

3. "Hours of Work in the Two World Wars," 621 and Table 6; Montgomery, "New Unionism," 96; George G. Groat, "Hours of Labor," in Trachtenberg, ed., *The American Labor Yearbook, 1917-1918*, 86. On the more visionary proposals, see *The Worker* (February 23, 1907), and *The People* (October 9, 1915), the latter in the Debs Scrapbooks, Book 18, Eugene V. Debs Archives, Terre Haute, Indiana.

4. Alexander M. Bing, *Wartime Strikes and Their Adjustment* (New York, 1921), 60-61 and 178. The quote is from Newton Baker, the secretary of war and a supporter of the NCL, as in Cahill, *Shorter Hours*, 195.

5. Stuart Ewen, *Captains of Consciousness: Advertising and the Social Roots of the Consumer Culture* (New York, 1976), esp. 23-30.

6. Charles Leinenweber, "Socialists in the Streets: The New York City Socialist Party in Working Class Neighborhoods," *Science and Society* 41 (Summer 1977), 152-71; Judith Smith, "Our Own Kind: Family and Community Networks in Providence," *Radical History Review* 17 (Spring 1978), 99-120.

7. William Z. Foster, *American Trade Unionism* (New York, 1947), 21; Mary Marcy, "Beginners' Course in Socialism and the Economics of Karl Marx: Lesson VIII—Shorter Hours of Labor," *International Socialist Review* 12 (July 1911).

8. Workers' Education Bureau of America, *Workers' Education in the United States: Report of Proceedings, First National Conference on Workers' Education in the United States* (New York, 1921), esp. 133-41; Tax, *Rising*, 113; James J. Kenneally, *Women and American Trade Unions* (St. Albans, Vt., 1978), 83-85; George Sirola, "The Finnish Working People's College," *International Socialist Review* 14 (August 1913), 102-4; Paul Avrich, *The Modern School Movement: Anarchism and Education in the United States* (Princeton, N.J., 1980).

9. Howe, *World of Our Fathers* (New York, 1976). Lafargue, Marx's son-in- law, wrote *The Right to Be Lazy* in 1880, but it was first available in English to U.S. readers in 1907. See Fred Thompson's preface to the 1975 Kerr edition, published in Chicago. See also Anzia Yezierska, *Bread Givers* (New York, 1975), esp. 163; Oakley C. Johnson, *Marxism in United States History Before the Russian Revolution* (New York, 1974), esp. 115-28.

10. Nancy Schrom Dye, *As Equals and As Sisters: Feminism, the Labor Movement and the Women's Trade Union League of New York* (Columbia, Mo., 1980), 145-56; National Women's Trade Union League, *Fifth Biennial Convention* (New York, 1915), 41-44; Foner, *Women and the American Labor Movement*, 1: 316-17 and 499; *Seattle Union Record* (December 23, 1916).

11. Charles Hill, "Fighting the Twelve-Hour Day in the American Steel Industry," *Labor History* 15 (Winter 1974), 19; Gerald G. Eggert, "Fight for the Eight-Hour Day," *American History Illustrated* (May 1972), 36ff.; Clarke A. Chambers, *Paul V. Kellogg and the Survey: Voices for Social Welfare and Social Justice* (Minneapolis, 1971); Theodore Roosevelt, *Progressive Principles* (New York, 1913), appendix, reprints the platform.

12. Marcy, "Beginners' Course," passim, and Eugene V. Debs, "The Eight- Hour Work Day," *ISR* 12 (May 1911), 100-101; Ritterskamp, "Unemployment and the Six-Hour Day," *ISR* 14 (January 1914), 407-9.

13. John R. Commons and John B. Andrews, *Principles of Labor Legislation* (New York, 1920), 253, n. 1; Marc Karson, *American Labor Unions and Politics, 1900-1918* (Carbondale, Ill.,

1958), 128-30, is a good summary containing the Green quote. See also Foner, *Labor Movement*, 6:178 and 178n. For Gompers's position, see Mollie Ray Carroll, *Labor and Politics: The Attitude of the AFL Toward Legislation and Politics* (Boston and New York, 1923), 63-66, and "Gompers to Mr. Edgar Wallace, Editor *UMW Journal*" (October 28, 1915), AFL Papers, SHSW; Gompers, Hillquit, and Hayes, *Labor's Sword*, 100-106. See also "Gompers to Joe Roebuck" (February 17, 1915), AFL Papers, for his explicit linking of AFL voluntarism on these matters to the failure of 1867 and 1868 hours laws.

14. John Howard Keiser, "John Fitzpatrick and Progressive Unionism, 1915- 1925," (Unpublished Ph.D. dissertation, Northwestern University, 1965), 109- 11; AFL, *Proceedings, 1915*, 492; Gary M. Fink, *Labor's Search for Political Order: The Political Behavior of the Missouri Labor Movement, 1890-1940* (Columbia, Mass., 1973), 174. The speaker is Andrew Furuseth of the Seamen's Union; *Terre Haute Tribune* (November 24, 1915); William Z. Foster, *From Bryan to Stalin* (New York, 1937), 83-84.

15. Tridon as quoted in Montgomery, "New Unionism," 91. This paragraph and the next are based on "New Unionism," passim and 104 for the final quote. See also the same author's "Whose Standards? Workers and the Reorganization of Production in the United States, 1900-1920," also in *Workers' Control*, 113-38; Mike Davis, "The Stop Watch and the Wooden Shoe: Scientific Management and the Industrial Workers of the World," *Radical America* 8 (January-February 1975), 69-96.

16. In Carroll, *Labor and Politics*, 66n.

17. Debs, "Eight-Hour Work Day," 100.

18. *Industrial Union Bulletin* (November 7 and September 19, 1908) and below.

19. Melvyn Dubofsky, *We Shall Be All: A History of the IWW* (New York, 1969), 42-43. Dubofsky errs in stating that "the relationship of the eight-hour movement to class conflict in Colorado's mining districts is tenuous." See William D. Haywood, *Bill Haywood's Book: The Autobiography of William D. Haywood* (New York, 1929), 90-155; Jensen, *Heritage of Conflict*, 96-159; Foner, *Labor Movement*, 3: 393-400; Wyman, *Hard Rock Epic*, 201-25.

20. "General Confederation of Labor to Comrade Wm. G. Trautmann, Secretary of Industrial Labor Union" (May 29, 1905), in *Proceedings of the First Convention of the IWW, Founded at Chicago, June 27-July 8, 1905* (New York, 1905), 289-90; "Committee for Local Union #163 to GEB" (November 15, 1907), and "Plan and Details of the Eight-Hour Movement" both in IWW Papers, Box 7, Folder 1, at Reuther Library, Wayne State University, Detroit; Foner, *Labor Movement*, 4: 139; *Industrial Worker* (July 27, 1911); *Solidarity* (May 27, June 3, and August 5, 1911); *Industrial Worker* (January 19 and 26, 1911).

21. *Industrial Worker* (October 12, 1911); Foner, *Labor Movement*, 4: 139-40 and 436-38. On the five- and four-hour demands, see "Our Immediate Needs," *One Big Union Monthly* 1 (March 1919), 1, and Ibid., Second Series, 2 (June 1938), back cover. On shorter-hours campaigns among farm workers, see *Industrial Worker* (January 12, 1911), and Kornbluh, ed., *Rebel Voices*, 227-50. On Philadelphia, see Theodore Kornweibel, Jr., *No Crystal Stair: Black Life and the Messenger* (Westport, Conn., 1975), 180.

22. Foster, *Trade Unionism: The Road to Freedom* (Chicago, 1916?), 18 and passim. Foster's Syndicalist League of North America advocated the six-hour day as part of agitation inside the AFL. See Foster, *Bryan to Stalin*, 61. Cf. Helen Marot, *American Labor Unions* (New York, 1914), esp. ch. 4 and 5.

23. Joel Seidman, *The Needle Trades* (New York, 1942), 102-14; Levine, *Women's Garment Workers*, 144-294; Foner, *Labor Movement*, 4: 306-72 and 5: 226-64, and *Women and the Labor Movement*, 1: 322-499; Dubofsky, *We Shall Be All*, 227-85; Tax, *Rising*, 205-75.

24. Dubofsky, *We Shall Be All*, 227-62; Foner, *Women and the Labor Movement*, 1: 426-28, and *Labor Movement*, 4: 306-50.

25. Haywood in Kornbluh, ed., *Rebel Voices*, 205 and 216; *New York Call* (March 14, 1913); Foner, *Labor Movement*, 4: 356-72; Dubofsky, *We Shall Be All*, 266-85.

26. Elizabeth Gurley Flynn, *The Rebel Girl: An Autobiography, My First Life 1906-1926* (New York, 1979), 166, and *I Speak My Own Piece* (New York, 1955), 152.

27. See n. 25 above; *Pageant of the Paterson Strike* (New York, 1913); Matilda

(Rabinowitz) Robbins, "My Story," in the Robbins Papers, Wayne State University; Foner, *Women and the Labor Movement*, 1: 454-56; and George Sinclair Mitchell, *Textile Unionism and the South* (Chapel Hill, N.Y., 1931), 35.

28. Lemlich as quoted in Leon Stein, ed., *Out of the Sweatshops: The Struggle for Industrial Democracy* (New York, 1977), 70; *New York Call* (November 23, 1909); *New York World* (November 23, 1909); Levine, *Garment Workers*, 153-54; Foner, *Labor Movement*, 5: 226-40, and *Women and the Labor Movement*, 1: 324-45; *New York Evening Journal* (November 28, 1909); Carolyn Daniel McCreesh, "On the Picket Lines: Militant Women Campaign to Organize Garment Workers 1882-1917" (unpublished Ph.D. dissertation, University of Maryland, 1975), 162-71; and Dubofsky, *When Workers Organize*, 40-101.

29. Marot, "A Woman's Strike," *Proceedings of the Academy of Political Science, City of New York* 1 (1910), 122; Tax, *Rising*, 205-40; Dye, *Equals and Sisters*, 88-95; John A. Dyche, *The State of the Ladies' Waist Makers of New York* (New York, 1910); Therese Malkiel, *Dairy of a Shirtwaist Striker* (New York, 1910).

30. Hyman Berman, "Era of the Protocol: A Chapter in the History of the ILGWU, 1910-1916" (unpublished Ph.D. dissertation, Columbia University, 1956), esp. 152ff.

31. Seidman, *Needle Trades*, 119ff; Foner, *Labor Movement*, 5: 246-51; J. M. Budish and George Soule, *The New Unionism in the Clothing Industry* (New York, 1920), 73-76; Levine, *Garment Workers*, 208-17.

32. Foner, *Fur and Leather Workers*, 39-50, and *Women and the Labor Movement*, 1: 361-65. The fur workers did not receive an official AFL charter until July 1, 1913.

33. Levine, *Garment Workers*, 229, 292, and 297-98; Carsel, *Chicago Ladies' Garment Workers' Union*, 73 and 88-91.

34. Isaac Hourwich, "The Garment Workers' Strike," *New Review* 1 (March 15, 1913), 426-27; Seidman, *Needle Trades*, 117; Foner, *Labor Movement*, 5: 259-64, and *Women and the Labor Movement*, 1: 365-81; Charles Elbert Zaretz, *The Amalgamated Clothing Workers of America* (New York, 1934), 73-102; Charles Jacob Stowell, "The Journeymen's Tailors' Union of America" (unpublished M.A. thesis, University of Illinois, 1917), 35-38.

35. *Documentary History of the Amalgamated Clothing Workers of America, 1914-1916* (New York, 1922), 75, 92, 156-57, and 172-73; AGW, *The Clothing Workers of Chicago* (Chicago, 1922), 104, 95-108 passim, and 143; Foner, *Women and the Labor Movement*, 1: 380-83; Seidman, *Needle Trades*, 141-45; McCreesh, "On the Picket Lines," 251.

36. David Brody, *Steelworkers in America: The Nonunion Era* (Cambridge, Mass., 1960), 33-40; Eggert, "Eight-Hour Day," 40-42.

37. "Gompers to Organized Labor of America—Greeting" (January 1, 1910), Gompers Papers; Brody, *Steelworkers*, 132-35, esp. 133; Katherine Stone, "The Origins of the Job Structure in Steel," *Review of Radical Political Economics* 6 (Spring 1974).

38. Brody, *Steelworkers*, 134; Robert Hessen, "The Bethlehem Steel Strike of 1910," *Labor History* 15 (Winter 1974), 3-18; "Jacob Tazelaar to John Mitchel [sic]" (February 4, 1910).

39. *Solidarity* (August 26, 1910); Hessen, "Bethlehem," 17-18; Hill, "Twelve-Hour Day," 19ff; Brody quoted from *Steelworkers*, 161 and 134-35; "Gompers to Executive Council, AFL" (February 4, 1913), Gompers Letter Books. The AFL's chief organizer in Bethlehem had complained early in the strike: "To establish twenty different craft unions in a plant so hostile . . . is no bed of roses." See the copy of the letter "Jacob Tazelaar to Frank Morrison" (February 27, 1910), circulated as "Morrison to Executive Council, AFL" (March 1, 1910), Gompers Papers.

40. Brissenden, *IWW*, 205-7; Foner, *Labor Movement*, 4: 89-92 and 214-32.

41. Merl E. Reed, "Lumberjacks and Longshoremen: The IWW in Louisiana," *Louisiana History* 13 (Winter 1972), 45 and passim; Dubofsky, *We Shall Be All*, 212-15; Foner, *Labor Movement*, 4: 233-45; James R. Green, *Grass Roots Socialism: Radical Movements in the Southwest, 1895-1943* (Baton Rouge, La., 1978), 179-80 and 204-22, and "The Brotherhood of Timber Workers, 1910-1913," *Past and Present* 60 (1973), 161-200; *New Orleans Times-Democrat* (July 20, 1911); *Industrial Worker* (December 26, 1912); *Voice of the People* (November 6 and 20, 1913); Jensen, *Lumber and Labor*, 76; Ruth A. Allen, *East Texas Lumber Workers: An Economic and Social Picture* (Austin, Tex., 1961), 54 and 58, and Hall's unpublished "Labor Struggles in the

Deep South" copies of which are at Wayne State and Tulane universities.

42. H. E. West, "Civil War in the West Virginia Coal Mines," *Survey* 30 (April 5, 1913), 45-47; Stuart S. Sprague, "Unionization Struggles in the Paint and Cabin Creeks, 1912-1913," *West Virginia History* (April 1977), passim; Foner, *Labor Movement*, 5: 182-85; David A. Corbin, "Betrayal in the West Virginia Coal Fields: Eugene V. Debs and the Socialist Party of America, 1912-1914," *Journal of American History* 64 (March 1978).

43. George S. McGovern, "The Colorado Strike, 1913-1914" (unpublished Ph.D. dissertation, Northwestern University, 1953); Foner, *Labor Movement*, 5: 196-213; Billie Barnes Jensen, "Woodrow Wilson's Intervention in the Coal Strike of 1914," *Labor History* 15 (Winter 1974), 63-77; Jones, *Autobiography*, 178-94. Rapid, though uneven, changes in technology and division of labor in soft-coal mines underlay much of the class conflict in the mines. See Keith Dix, "Work Relations in the Coal Industry: The Handloading Era, 1880-1930," in Andrew Zimbalist, ed., *Case Studies on the Labor Process* (New York, 1979), 156-69. On oil, see Gerald T. White, *Formative Years in the Far West: A History of Standard Oil Company of California and Its Predecessors Through 1919* (New York, 1962), 534-37.

44. Trades listed in *Industrial Union Bulletin* (March 30, 1907). Valuable accounts include Brissenden, *IWW*, 191-201; Jensen, *Heritage of Conflict*, 219- 35; Dubofsky, *We Whall Be All*, 120-26; Foner, *Labor Movement*, 4: 93-98.

45. Jensen, *Heritage of Conflict*, 272-88; William A. Sullivan, "The 1913 Revolt of the Michigan Copper Miners," *Michigan History* 43 (September 1959), 307-10; McLaughlin, *Michigan Labor*, 80-90.

46. Foner, *Labor Movement*, 4: 486-517; Dubofsky, *We Shall Be All*, 319-33; Flynn, *Rebel Girl*, 207-12. Just after the Mesabi Range strike the IWW also led and lost an eight-hour strike among 4,000 lumber workers in the same region. See Foner, *Labor Movement*, 4: 520-22.

47. George G. Kirstein, *Stores and Unions: A Study of the Growth of Unionism in Dry Goods and Department Stores* (New York, 1950), 15-43, esp. 42- 43; Cross, *California*, 282-84; Mandel, *Gompers*, 309-18; Steven C. Levi, "The Battle for the Eight-Hour Day in San Francisco," *California History* 57 (1978), 343-53; Dubofsky, *We Shall Be All*, 286-87; Fred Thompson and Patrick Murfin, *IWW: First Seventy Years* (Chicago, 1976), 70-74; Foner, *Labor Movement*, 4: 373-83.

48. Sinclair, *The Flivver King: A Story of Ford-America* (Detroit, 1937), 26; Ford, as quoted in Allan Nevins with Frank Ernest Hill, *Ford: The Times, the Man, the Company* (New York, 1954), 534. See also David Gartman, "Origins of the Assembly Line and Capitalist Control of Work at Ford," in Zimbalist, ed., *Case Studies*, 193-205, esp. 197, and Roediger, "Fordism, Labor and the Hours of Work," forthcoming in Gary Cross, ed. *Worktime and Industrialization: An International History*.

49. Edison as quoted in Nevins, *Ford*, 532.

50. Galamb's *Reminiscences*, in the Ford Archives in Dearborn, are cited by Nevins, *Ford*, 536. Both Keith Sward, *The Legend of Henry Ford* (New York, 1948), 50ff and Jack Russell, "The Coming of the Line: The Ford Highland Park Plant, 1910-1914," *Radical America* 12 (May-June 1978), 39-42, link fear of the IWW with the 1914 reforms. Nevins, *Ford*, 537, disagrees. On the IWW in Detroit, see Thompson and Murfin, *IWW*, 74-75; Dubofsky, *We Shall Be All*, 74- 75.

51. Nevins, *Ford*, 515, 522, and 537; Sward, *Legend*, 51; Thompson and Murfin, *IWW*, 74-75 and 90-91; Foner, *Labor Movement*, 4: 389; Russell, "Coming of the Line," 32-33 and 42, for the quote from Russell; Nevins, *Ford*, 515; Ford as quoted in Sward, *Legend*, 56. A recent study which is acute on the labor crisis and Ford's response, is Stephen Meyer, *The Five-Dollar Day: Labor Management and Social Control in the Ford Motor Company, 1908-1921* (Albany, N.Y., 1981), esp. 91-121.

52. Ford, *Today and Tomorrow* (Garden City, N.Y., 1926), 158; "The Five-Day Week in the Ford Plants," *Monthly Labor Review* 23 (December 1926), 1162; Nevins, *Ford*, 544n.

53. John R. Lee, "The So-Called Profit Sharing System in the Ford Plant," *Annals of the American Academy of Political and Social Science* 65 (May 1916), 299-308; Russell, "Coming of the Line," 39-42.

54. Russell, "Coming of the Line," 33-42; Nevins, *Ford*, 447-80; Ford, *My Life and Work*

(Garden City, N.Y., 1923), 81-82 and 83; Lee, "Profit Sharing," 299-308; Horace L. Arnold and Fay L. Faurote, *Ford Methods and the Ford Shops* (New York, 1915), 129-40.

55. Nevins, *Ford*, 549; Sward, *Legend*, 50; Sinclair, *Flivver King*, 26.

56. Sward, *Legend*, 57; Russell, "Coming of the Line," 43-44.

57. Ford, *Life and Work*, 103; Ford, *My Philosophy of Industry* (New York, 1929), 50-51; Ford, *Today and Tomorrow*, 159; Nevins, *Ford*, 549-60.

58. Antonio Gramsci, *Selections from the Prison Notebooks* (New York, 1971), 278-322; Ford, *Philosophy*, 50, and *Life and Work*, 120; Meyer, *Five- Dollar Day*, 122-68; Loren Baritz, *The Servants of Power: A History of the Uses of Social Science in American Industry* (Middletown, Conn., 1960), 32-35; Nevins, *Ford*, 551ff. Ford, *Philosophy*, 14-19, discusses leisure and Prohibition, and the authorized biography by James Martin Miller, *The Amazing Story of Henry Ford* (Chicago, 1922), suggests the range of Ford's concerns about the adverse impact of tendencies in popular culture—from baseball to movies—on workers.

59. Lee, "Profit Sharing," 299-308.

60. Ibid.; Nevins, *Ford*, 544 and 550. The Ford quote is from *Life and Work*, 147. Ford, *Philosophy*, 17. Emphasis original.

61. Ford, *Philosophy*, 17-18, and "Five-Day Week in the Ford Plants," 1166. On the four-hour day, see William Adams Simonds, *Henry Ford: His Life, His Work, His Genius* (Indianapolis, 1943), 137.

62. Quotes from Nevins, *Ford*, 536-50; Sward, *Legend*, 54. See also Sinclair, *Flivver King*, 28-29; *Butcher Workman* (September 1916). The thesis that corporate capitalists as a group engaged in labor and other social reforms to disarm radicalism and to create a docile, consumption-oriented labor force during the Progressive Era appears in the work of many New Left historians. See James Weinstein, *The Corporate Ideal in the Liberal State* (New York, 1968), and Ewen, *Captains of Consciousness*, 23-30, the latter applied specifically to reform of hours. Such studies, at least where the working day is concerned, attribute to the corporate elite far more liberality, unanimity, and foresight than the facts warrant.

63. Cahill, *Shorter Hours*, 236-48; McGaughey, *Shorter Workweek*, 240.

64. Cahill, *Shorter Hours*, 78.

65. Foner, *Labor Movement*, 5: 111-42; Weinstein, *Corporate Ideal*, 213 and 172-213, passim.

66. McGaughey, *Shorter Workweek*, 240.

67. *Butcher Workman* (September 1916), and Groat, "Hours of Labor," 87; Gompers, *Seventy Years*, 1: 547.

68. For background regarding the eight-hour struggle on the railways, see Foner *Labor Movement*, 6:143-63, and Walter Licht, *Working for the Railroad* (Princeton, N.J., 1983), 174-80; *Locomotive Firemen and Enginemen Magazine* 54 (March 1913), 278-79; Marot, *American Labor Unions*, 29-47; *Railroad Trainman* 30 (May 1913), 581; Commons and Associates, *History of Labour*, 4: 380; *New York Call* (December 22, 1915).

69. *New York Sun*, reprinted in *Literary Digest* (February 5, 1916), 275; Edwin Clyde Robbins, "The Trainmen's Eight-Hour Law," *Political Science Quarterly* 31 (December 1916), 545-46; Foner, *Labor Movement*, 6:150 ff; *New York Call* (July 4, 1916).

70. *New York Call* (August 14, 1916); "Samuel Gompers to E. L. Marcellus" (August 30, 1916), Gompers Letter Books; Foner, *Labor Movement*, 6:161-63.

71. "Long Hours Cause Death" is reprinted in *New York Call* (July 4, 1916); *Railway Conductor* 33 (March 1916), 205-9; *New York Call* (August 9, 1916); "The Railroad Man's Right to a Shorter Day," *Railroad Trainman* 33 (April 1916), 349-50; "The Eight-Hour Day and Safety First, "*Railroad Trainman* 33 (April 1916). On profits, see *Literary Digest* (February 5, 1916), 275-76.

72. *New York Times* (June 2, 16, and 17, 1916); Robbins, "Trainmen's Eight- Hour Law," 551-56; Dallas M. Jones, "The Wilson Administration and Organized Labor, 1912-1919" (unpublished Ph.D. dissertation, Cornell University, 1956), 251-52; Commons and Associates, *History of Labour*, 4: 381; Allen LaVerne Shepherd, "Federal Railway Labor Policy, 1913-1926"

340

(unpublished Ph.D. dissertation, University of Nebraska, 1971), 78-79; Walter F. McCaleb, *Brotherhood of Railroad Trainmen* (New York, 1936), 86.

73. *Literary Gazette* (August 1916), 392, reprints the *Call* article; *New York Times* (August 9, 1916); Foner, *Labor Movement*, 6: esp. 156-57; forthcoming; *Literary Digest* (August 1916), 392, reprints *Railway Age Gazette.*

74. "Wilson to W. G. Lee, W. S. Carter, W. S. Stone, A. S. Garretson, and Elisha Lee" (August 13, 1916), Woodrow Wilson Papers, Library of Congress; *New York Times* (August 14, 1916); Shepherd, "Railway Labor Policy," 82-83; Foner, *Labor Movement*, 5: 112-15; Charles Smith, "Woodrow Wilson and Organized Labor," (unpublished Ph.D. dissertation, Catholic University, 1963), 485-86; Carter, "The Eight-Hour Day As a Political Campaign Issue," *Brotherhood of Locomotive Firemen and Enginemen's Magazine* 60 (October 1916), 388-98, esp. 397.

75. Shepherd, "Railway Labor Policy," 85-86; Jones, "Wilson Administration," 253; "Wilson to Senator Newlands" (August 19, 1916), Wilson Papers, Library of Congress.

76. Commons and Associates, *History of Labour*, 4: 383; *New York Times* (August 16-26, 1916); Foner, *Labor Movement*, 6:172-76; Shepherd, "Railway Labor Policy," 87; Jones, "Wilson Administration," 244-45.

77. Wilson, "Address to Congress, August 29, 1916" in Ray Stannard Baker, ed., *The Public and Private Papers of Woodrow Wilson* (New York, 1928), 2: 267-72; *Congressional Record*, 64th Congress, 1st Session, 1336-63; *New York Times* (August 30, 1916); Jones, "Wilson Administration," 252-53; and Shepherd, "Railway Labor Policy," 89-90.

78. *New York Call* (August 27 and September 27, 1916); Carroll, *Labor and Politics*, 64; Foner, *Labor Movement*, 6:178-79; Samuel Gompers, *Labor and the Common Welfare* (New York, 1919), 168-69; U.S. Congress, Committee on Interstate Commerce, *Hearings on the Threatened Strike of Railway Engineers*, 64th Congress, 1st Session, 41-42.

79. *New York Times* (September 3, 1916); *New York Call* (September 2, 1916); Commons and Associates, *History of Labour*, 4: 384; "R. Guard for Gompers to Grant Hamilton" (September 2, 1916), Gompers Letter Books.

80. *Literary Digest* (December 2, 1916), 1447; *New York Times* (October 6, 1916); *Report of the Eight-Hour Commission* (Washington, D.C., 1918), 7-23.

81. *New York Times* (December 12, 1916, and March 15-20, 1917); Commons and Associates, *History of Labour*, 4: 384; *National Rip-Saw* (February 1917); "Wilson to Elisha Lee" (March 16, 1917) and "Wilson to Chiefs of the Four Brotherhoods" (March 16, 1917), Wilson Papers; *Wilson v. New*, 243 U.S. 32; "A Statesmanlike Decision," *New Republic* 10 (March 24, 1917), 217-18.

82. *New York Call* (August 27 and September 3, 1916).

83. Jack Phillips, "The Eight-Hour Rail Drive," *IRS* 17 (April 1917), 603; *New York Times* (September 20, 1916); Jones, "Wilson Administration," 262; Foner, *Labor Movement*, 5: 164-81; Montgomery, "New Unionism," 107-8; Leonard Painter, *Through Fifty Years with the Brotherhood of Railway Carmen of America* (Kansas City, Mo., 1941), 145-51; Walker D. Hines, *War History of American Railroads* (New Haven, Conn., 1928), 160ff; Archibald M. McIsaac, *The Order of Railroad Telegraphers: A Study of Trade Unionism and Collective Bargaining* (Princeton, N.J., 1933), 29-38 and 195-97; Bing, *Wartime Strikes*, 260ff; Brotherhood of Maintenance of Way Employees, *Milestones of Progress* (Detroit, 1969), 7.

84. Quoted in Trattner, *Crusade for the Children*, 122; see also 123-29.

85. Ibid., 129-32. See also Elizabeth H. Davidson, *Child Labor Legislation in the Southern Textile States* (Chapel Hill, N.C., 1939), 170ff.

86. Owen Lovejoy, "The Federal Child Labor Law," in Trachtenberg, ed., *American Labor Yearbook, 1917-1918*, 120-24; Trattner, *Crusade for the Children*, 132-42.

87. AFL, *Proceedings, 1918*, 75. For strike figures see Montgomery, "New Unionism," 97. National figures for some years are not available.

88. Computations based on figures in Trachtenberg, *American Labor Yearbook, 1917-1918*, 71-72, and *American Labor Yearbook, 1919-1920*, 163; Bing, *Wartime Strikes*, 178;

National Industrial Conference Board, Research Report Number Three, *Strikes in American Industry in Wartime, April 6 to October 6, 1917* (Boston, 1918), 9.

89. Florence Peterson, "Strikes in the United States, 1880-1936," U.S. Department of Labor, *Bulletin Number 651* (Washington, D.C., 1938), 21.

90. Montgomery, "New Unionism," 103-4, and "Whose Standards?" 127-32; *New York Call* (December 5, 1915); Foner, *Labor Movement,* 4: 84ff; Paul Buhle, "Italian-American Radicals in the Labor Movement," *Radical History Review* 17 (Spring 1978), 139-40; U.S. Secretary of Labor, *Report, 1916,* 20; Bing, *Wartime Strikes,* 74-79; Foner, *Labor Movement,* 6:194-96.

91. The song is from the *Pittsburgh Leader* (April 24, 1916). This account of the strikes relies on the *Pittsburgh Leader, Daily Dispatch, Post, Gazette-Times,* and Dianne Kanitra, "The Westinghouse Strike of 1916," (unpublished M.A. thesis, University of Pittsburgh, 1917); Foner, *Women and the Labor Movement,* 1: 491-94; also see Richard Edwards, *Contested Terrain: The Transformation of the Workplace in the Twentieth Century* (New York, 1979), 101.

92. Ibid. On the 1916 strike wave, see Montgomery, "New Unionism," 98; U.S. Secretary of Labor, *Report, 1916,* 17-26, and *Report, 1917,* 45ff; *Machinists' Monthly Journal* (February-July 1916), 120-21 and 694-97. We are indebted to Robert Rodden of the IAM here.

93. *Iron Age* 96 (October 1915), 884-85; Cahill, *Shorter Hours,* 248; National Industrial Conference Board, *Strikes in Wartime,* 16; Taylor, *Labor Policies,* 122-23.

94. The reports on specific industries are summarized in National Industrial Conference Board, Research Report Number 27, *The Hours of Work Problem in Five Major Industries* (Boston, 1920). For a shorter summary, see Cahill, *Shorter Hours,* 248ff. See also Research Report Number 2 in the same series, *Analysis of British Wartime Reports on Hours of Work* (Boston, 1917), passim; David Brody, *Labor in Crisis: The Steel Strike of 1919* (Philadelphia, 1965), 24; Cahill, *Shorter Hours,* 241-47.

95. AFL, *Proceedings, 1917,* 107-10.

96. Ibid.

97. Ibid., 110. On Gompers's proposal for a wartime seven-hour day as a fuel and traffic measure, see Gordon W. Watkins, *Labor Problems and Labor Administration in the United States During the World War* (Urbana, Ill., 1919), 103.

98. AFL, *Proceedings, 1917,* 107-10; Melvin I. Urofsky, *Big Steel and the Wilson Administration: A Study in Business-Government Relations* (Columbus, Ohio, 1969), 275; Cahill, *Shorter Hours,* 80-81; *American Federationist* 25 (1918), 999.

99. National War Labor Board, *Memorandum on the Eight-Hour Day* (Washington, D.C., 1918), 6, 11, 25, and esp. 27-28; Daniel R. Beaver, *Newton D. Baker and the American War Effort* (Lincoln, Neb., 1966); Baker's "Foreward" to Maud Nathan, *Story of an Epoch-Making Movement,* xi-xiv. For Frankfurter's advocacy of shorter hours, see his "Hours of Labor" and, with Josephine Goldmark, *The Case for a Shorter Working Day,* 2 vols. (New York, n.d.).

100. Urofsky, *Big Steel,* 272.

101. Brody, *Steelworkers,* 209; Urofsky, *Big Steel,* 266-69.

102. Weinstein, *Corporate Ideal,* 228-29.

103. Urofsky, *Big Steel,* 278 and 269-77, passim; Eggert, "Eight-Hour Day," 43. Brody, *Steelworkers,* 212-13, and *Labor in Crisis,* 58ff, convincingly portray defense of the open shop as the crux of big steel's wartime labor strategy and see the temporary and partial concession on hours as secondary.

104. "Principles and Policies to Govern Relations Between Workers and Employers in War Industries for the Duration of the War," appended to Bing, *Wartime Strikes,* 310. See also, Jean Tripp McKelvey, *AFL Attitudes Toward Production, 1900-1932* (Ithaca, N.Y., 1952), 33.

105. Cahill, *Shorter Hours,* 81. Cf. Bing, *Wartime Strikes,* 178-79; *National War Labor Board,* Bureau of Labor Statistics, Bulletin Number 287 (Washington, D.C., 1921), 71-86; Trachtenberg, ed., *American Labor Year Book, 1919-1920,* 42-57 and 168-69; Bing, *Wartime Strikes,* 180 and 316. Valerie Jean Conner's *The National War Labor Board: Stability, Social Justice and the Voluntary State in World War One* (Chapel Hill, N.C., 1983) is a useful recent summary of the board's motivations and performance on hours and on other matters. It regards the

WLB as a precursor of later wages and hours legislation and is correct in doing so. However, the precedents set were by no means simple or unambiguous.

106.   David Brody, *The Butcher Workmen: A Study of Unionization* (Cambridge, Mass., 1964), 1-13 and 85-86.

107.   Foster, *Bryan to Stalin*, 91-96; Brody, *Butcher Workmen*, 76; Foster, *American Trade Unionism*, 25 n.; Keiser, "Fitzpatrick," 38ff; Alma Herbst, *The Negro in the Slaughtering and Meatpacking Industry in Chicago* (Boston, 1932), 29-43.

108.   Brody, *Butcher Workmen*, 76-78; Foster, *Bryan to Stalin*, 94-96.

109.   Cf. Foster, *Bryan to Stalin*, 96-98, and the more restrained remarks in his *American Trade Unionism*, 153; Brody, *Butcher Workmen*, 79.

110.   Brody, *Butcher Workmen*, 79-82; Foster, *Bryan to Stalin*, 100; Brody, *Butcher Workmen*, 80-82. Fitzpatrick's warning comes in a letter to Walsh, dated March 26, 1918, and cited in Brody, 81.

111.   Foster, *Bryan to Stalin*, 99, adds that the award was made "with an eye on our militant movement and on the certainty of a national . . . strike in case of an unsatisfactory decision." See also Keiser, "Fitzpatrick," 40- 41.

112.   Dubofsky, *We Shall Be All*, 360-65; Jensen, *Lumber and Labor*, 125-26, overemphasizes AFL initiative. See also Thompson and Murfin, *IWW*, 115-17;

Trade Unionism, Hours, and Workers' Control in the Postwar United States

1. See ch. 7-9 above and Roediger, "Fordism, Labor and the Working Day," forthcoming in Gary Cross, ed., *Working and Industrialization: An International History.*

2. Brecher, *Strike!,* 133-80; Montgomery, "New Unionism," 91-112, including strike figures on 97; Foner, *Women and the Labor Movement,* 2: 99; Perlman and Taft, in Commons and Associates, *History of Labour,* 4: 460. AFL, *Proceedings, 1919,* 72-73, and *Proceeding,* 1921, 122, and below.

3. Irving Bernstein, *The Lean Years: A History of the American Worker, 1920-1933* (Baltimore, 1970), 84; Max Danish, *William Green* (New York, 1952); Charles Madison, *American Labor Leaders* (New York, 1950), 108-35; AFL, *Proceedings, 1918,* 225, and below. Strike figures from Peterson, *Strikes in the U.S.,* 21ff.

4. Louis Adamic, *Dynamite: The Story of Class Violence in America* (New York, 1931), 392-93; Whiting Williams, *Mainsprings of Men* (New York, 1925), 83; Susan Porter Benson, "'The Customers Ain't God': The Work Culture of Department-Store Saleswomen, 1890-1940," in Frisch and Walkowitz, eds., *Working Class America,* 185-211.

5. Robert S. Lynd and Helen M. Lynd, *Middletown: A Study of Modern American Culture* (New York, 1929), 251-312; Paul Buhle, "The Twenties," *Cultural Correspondence* 6-7 (Spring 1978), 78ff.

6. Bernstein, *Lean Years,* 54; McGaughey, *Shorter Workweek,* 200. The year 1919 had already accounted for as much as a .9 hour/week drop in the workweek before the coming of the new decade.

7. AFL, *Proceedings, 1918,* 220.

8. *Butcher Workman* (December 1917); Bing, *Wartime Strikes,* 45-49; Christie, *Empire in Wood,* 226ff.

9. Bing, *Wartime Strikes,* 48-52; *New York Call* (April 10, 1920).

10. J. C. Bowen, "The 48-Hour Week in Industry," *Monthly Labor Review* 17 (December 1923), 82-85; Watkins, *Labor Problems During the World War,* 103.

11. "Review of Labor Legislation of 1919," *American Labor Legislation Review* 9 (December 1919), 425-33 and 453; Trattner, *Crusade for the Children, 140-42;* Florence Kelley, "Changing Labor Conditions in Wartime," *The Class Struggle* 2 (March-April 1918), 133-37.

12. *Non-Partisan Leader* (August 4, 1919); Keiser, "Fitzpatrick," 120ff; "Butte in the Hands of the IWW," *One Big Union Monthly* 1 (March 1919), 36; D. C. Masters, *The Winnipeg General Strike* (Toronto, 1950), 93; Roger Horowitz, "The Failure of Independent Political Action: The Labor Party of Cook County," (unpublished B.A. essay, University of Chicago, 1982), 27; W.E.B. DuBois, *Darkwater: Voices from Within the Veil* (New York, 1920), 104, and above.

13. See Jonathan Norton Leonard, *Loki: The Life of Charles Proteus Steinmetz* (Garden City, N.Y., 1932), 238-39; Lord Leverhulme, *The Six-Hour Day and Other Industrial Questions* (London, 1918), esp. 14-35; *Labor* (October 11, 1919); Walton Hamilton and Helen R. Wright, *A Way of Order for Coal* (New York, 1928), 105; Simonds, *Ford,* 137.

14. AFL, *Proceedings, 1919,* 72-73; California AFL, *Proceedings, 1918,* 41- 46; Ohio AFL, *Proceedings, 1918,* 66-67; *New York Times* (June 24, 1919); AFL, *Proceedings, 1921,* 420; Viau, *Hours and Wages,* 78-79.

15. Sylvia Kopald, "Behind the Miners' Strike," *Nation* 109 (November 22, 1919), 658; Robert K. Murray, *Red Scare: A Study in National Hysteria, 1919- 1920* (Minneapolis, 1955), 154; Hugh Archibald, *The Four-Hour Day in Coal* (New York, 1922), 53-68; Carter Goodrich, *The Miner's Freedom* (Boston, 1925), 89- 90. Events of the strike are well covered in Melvin Dubofsky and Warren Van Tine, *John L. Lewis,* ch. 3-4, and in Saul Alinsky, *John L. Lewis: An Unauthorized Biography* (New York, 1949), Ch. 2-3.

16. Lovestone, *Government—Strikebreaker,* 13, quoting Wilson, and 14; Dubofsky and

344

Van Tine, *Lewis*, 53-57; Murray, *Red Scare*, 156; Stanley Coben, *A. Mitchell Palmer* (New York, 1963), 177-78. Cecil Carnes, *John L. Lewis: A Leader of Labor* (New York, 1936), 31; Alinsky, *Lewis*, 30-35; Gompers, "The Broken Pledge," *American Federationist* (January 1920); Murray, *Red Scare*, 155 and 157.

17. Carnes, *Lewis*, 34-35; Dubofsky and Van Tine, *Lewis*, 57; McAlister Coleman, *Men and Coal* (New York, 1943), 97.

18. James A. Wechsler, *Labor Baron* (New York, 1944), 24; Alinsky. *Lewis*, 32-35; Dubofsky and Van Tine, *Lewis*, 58-59; Carnes, *Lewis*, 44-46; *Cincinnati Enquirer* (November 12, 1919).

19. Carnes, *Lewis*, 90; "Comment," *Open Shop Review* 19 (October 1922), 456; Dubofsky and Van Tine, *Lewis*, 81; Foner, *Women and the Labor Movement*, 2: 245; "Bankrupt Leadership of the Miners," *Labor Herald* (July 1923), 28. Anthracite miners, striking at the same time as the bituminous miners called only for an eight-hour day. See *UMWA Journal* 38 (February 1, 1922), 8; (April 1, 1922), 8; (March 15, 1922), 8; and (August 15, 1922), 1-3.

20. Brophy, "Miners' Program," *New Republic* 26 (August 9, 1922), 297-98; David M. Schneider, "The Workers' (Communist) Party and American Trade Unions, (unpublished Ph.D. dissertation, Johns Hopkins University, 1928), 55-57; Bert Cochran, *Labor and Communism* (Princeton, N.J., 1977), 49.

21. *Daily Worker* (May 15 and 27, 1924); "Save the Miners' Union Call," *Communist* 7 (March 1928), 175-80; William Z. Foster, "Tasks and Lessons of the Miners' Struggle," *Communist* 7 (April 1928), 195-200; Arne Swabeck, "The National Miners' Union: A New Conception of Unionism," *Communist* 7 (October 1928), 625.

22. Donald J. McClurg, "The Colorado Coal Strike of 1927: Tactical Leadership of the IWW," *Labor History* 4 (Winter 1963), 68-92; Ronald L. Mc Mahan, "'Rang-U-Tang': The IWW and the 1927 Colorado Coal Strike," in Joseph Conlin, ed., *At the Point of Production: The Local History of the IWW* (Westport, Conn., 1981), 191-212.

23. Roediger, "Fordism, Labor and the Hours of Work," forthcoming. ACW, *Documentary History, 1918-1920*, esp. 4-35; Seidman, *Needle Trades*, 141-65; Foner, *Women and the Labor Movement*, 2: 162-70; Foner, *Fur Workers*, 234-45; Elizabeth F. Baker, *Printers and Technology: A History of the International Printing Pressmen and Assistants* (New York, 1957), 302-6; ITU, *A Study of the History of the ITU, 1852-1966* (Colorado Springs, 1967), 2: 173-74.

24. See below and Herbert Lahne, *The Cotton Mill Worker* (New York and Toronto, 1944), 137-38; Robert S. Lynd, "Done in Oil," *Survey* 48 (November 1, 1922), 137-46; "One Day's Rest in Seven," *Social Service Bulletin* 13 (November 1923); *Wages and Hours of Labor in Cotton-Goods Manufacturing, 1919-1930*, Bulletin of the Bureau of Labor Statistics, Number 539 (Washington, D.C., 1931), esp. 2-9; "Hours of Labor in the Iron and Steel Industry," *Monthly Labor Review* 30 (June 1930), 182-87; Garth L. Mangum, *The Operating Engineers: The Economic History of a Trade Union* (Cambridge, Mass., 1964), 120.

25. Hutchins, *Labor and Silk*, 120.

26. "Chicago Afoot," *Survey* 42 (August 9, 1919), 703-4;

27. Brecher, *Strike!*, 151; Murray, *Red Scare*, 122-34; "The Boston Police Strike" *Survey* 42 (September 20, 1919), 882.

28. *Timberworker Department* (March 15, 1919); *Seattle Union Record* (April 5, 1919); "IWW Headquarters Bulletin," *One Big Union Monthly* 1 (March 1919), 63; *Seattle Union Record* (March 3, 1917 and March 9, 1918); *WTUL Proceedings, Seventh Biennial Convention* (1919), 96-97.

29. Lahne, *Cotton Mill Worker*, 42-43 and 204, estimates UTW membership at one-quarter southern in 1920, but Robert R. Brooks, "The United Textile Workers of America," (unpublished Ph.D. dissertation, Yale University, 1935), 70-71, places postwar membership at one-half southern. On the textile industry and the working day after 1919, see also David Goldberg, "Immigrants, Intellectuals and Industrial Unions," (Ph.D. dissertation, Columbia University, 1983).

30. *New York Times* (January 27, 1919); Foner, *Women and the Labor Movement*, 2: 116ff.

31. *New York Times* (February 5 and August 11, 1919); Hutchins, *Labor and Silk*, 144; *Lawrence Evening Tribune* (February 5, 1919, and January 27- February 5, 1919).

32. *Advance* (April 11, 18, and 25, 1919); "Independent Textile Union," *Survey* 42 (April 19, 1919), 113.

33. Based on Foner, *Women and the Labor Movement*, 2: 119-20, and running accounts in three Lawrence papers—the *Evening Tribune, Telegram*, and *Sun and American*. See also *New York Times* (March 18, 1919).

34. *New York Times* (May 25, 1919); *Lawrence Evening Tribune* (April 23-24, 1919); "Help Lawrence Workers Win Fight for Shorter Hours," issued by Eight Hour Work Day Conference of Paterson (circa April 1, 1919) and in David J. Saposs Papers, SHSW; John A. Fitch, "Lawrence: A Strike for Wages or for Bolshevism?" *Survey* 42 (April 5, 1919), 42-46.

35. *New York Times* (May 25-28, 1919); *Lawrence Evening Tribune* (May 23, 1919); Nat Hentoff, ed., *Essays of A. J. Muste* (Indianapolis, 1967), 72-73.

36. Hutchins, *Labor and Silk*, 143-45; "IWW Headquarters Bulletin," *One Big Union Monthly* 1 (March 1919), 63.

37. "Paterson," *Survey* 42 (July 19, 1919), 602-3.

38. Hutchins, *Labor and Silk*, 118 and 144-47; "Correction," *Survey* 42 (July 26, 1919), 638; Brooks, "UTWA," 232-45.

39. Henry, *Women and the Labor Movement*, 73; Robert Dunn and Jack Hardy, *Labor and Textiles* (New York, 1931), 203-4; Marion Dutton Savage, "Industrial Unionism in America," (unpublished Ph.D. dissertation, Columbia University, 1922), 261 and 250-70; ACW, *Documentary History, 1918-1920*, 263; Brecher, *Strike!*, 150; "Textile Strike," *One Big Union Monthly* 1 (March 1919), 48.

40. Mitchell, *Textile Unionism*, 43-45; Lahne, *Cotton Mill Worker*, 205-6.

41. Mitchell, *Textile Unionism*, 45-53; Harley E. Tolley, "The Labor Movement in North Carolina, 1880-1920," *North Carolina Historical Review* 30 (July 1953), 354-75; Lahne, *Cotton Mill Worker*, 208; Foner, *Women and the Labor Movement*, 2: 226.

42. Lahne, *Cotton Mill Worker*, 208-11; Dunn and Hardy, *Labor and Textiles*, 204; Hutchins, *Labor and Silk*, 153-54; George L. Collins, "54 or 48," *Labor Age* 16 (July 1927), 4-5.

43. Brooks, "UTWA," 349; Dunn and Hardy, *Labor and Textiles*, 204.

44. Martha Glaser, "Paterson, 1924: The ACLU and Labor," *New Jersey History* 94 (Winter 1976), 155-72; Hutchins, *Labor and Silk*, 147-50 and 157- 59.

45. *Daily Worker* (August 14 and November 15, 1924).

46. Foster, *Strike Strategy* (Chicago, 1926), 19 and 36; Hutchins, *Labor and Silk*, 163-73. The Soviet example is also emphasized in *Daily Worker* (June 5, 1924; October 17, 1927; and December 18, 1929). The labor press followed shorter-hours progress abroad, and especially the 1926 International Labor Conference's agreement on an eight-hour day—an agreement ratified by most Western industrial nations but not by the United States. See *Labor* (July 16, 1917; July 4, 1925; April 17, 1926; July 31, 1926; and June 22, 1929).

47. Green, *World of the Worker*, 131; Schneider, "Workers' Party," 34; "Resolution on Trade Union Work," *Communist* 7 (July 1928), 398. Cf. Lenin on Taylorism in *Pravda* (April 26, 1918), and William Z. Foster, "Capitalist Efficiency Socialism," *Communist* 7 (March 1928), 169-74.

48. Useful accounts of the Passaic and New Bedford strikes include Mary Heaton Vorse, *The Passaic Textile Strike, 1925-27* (Passaic, N.J., 1927); Albert Weisbord, *Passaic: The Story of a Struggle Against Starvation Wages and for the Right to Organize* (Chicago, 1926); Paul L. Murphy, Kermit Hall, and David Klaasen, *The Passaic General Strike of 1926* (Belmont, Calif., 1974); Morton Siegel, "The Passaic Textile Strike of 1926," (unpublished Ph.D. dissertation, Columbia University, 1926); treatments, see Foner, *Women and the Labor Movement*, 2: 202-24; and Anne Fishel, "Women in Textile Organizing: An Interview with Sophie Melvin Gerson," *Radical History Review* 4 (Summer 1977), 113.

49. *Labor* (October 26, 1929); Sam Wiseman, "The Textile Workers Organize Their Union," *Labor Unity* (October 1928), 10-12; Cochran, *Labor and Communism*, 43-46; Foner, *Women and the Labor Movement*, 2: 221-24; Marshall, *Labor in the South*, 105; Hutchins, *Labor and Silk*, 173, reprints the NTWU program.

50. Tom Tippett, *When Southern Labor Stirs* (New York, 1931), 60-72; Liston Pope, *Millhands and Preachers: A Study of Gastonia* (New Haven, Conn., 1942); Bernstein, *Lean Years*, 20-32; Robin Hood, "The Loray Mill Strike," (unpublished M.A. thesis, University of North Carolina, 1932); Beal, *Proletarian Journey*, esp. 111-35; Lahne, *Cotton Mill Worker*, 216-19; Mitchell, *Textile Unionism in the South*, 70-75; Cochran, *Labor and Communism*, 34-36; Theodore Draper, "Gastonia Revisited," *Social Research* 38 (Spring 1971); Foner, *Women and the Labor Movement*, 2: 230-39; Dorsett Edmunds, Laurie Graybeal, Eileen Hanson, Ann Horne, Charlie Thomas, and Judith Vaughan, *Let's Stand Together: The Story of Ella Mae Wiggins* (Charlotte, N.C., 1979); Bill Dunne, "Gastonia: The Center of Class Struggle in the New South," *Communist* 8 (July 1929); Paul Blanshard, "Communism in Southern Mills," *Nation* (April 24, 1928) and "One Hundred Percent Americans on Strike," *Nation* (May 8, 1928).

51. Bernstein, *Lean Years*, 20-21; George Brown Tindall, *The Emergence of the New South, 1913-1945* (Baton Rouge, La., 1967), 344.

52. *Daily Worker* (March 29 and April 30, 1929); Cochran, *Labor and Communism*, 34; Margaret Larkin, "Tragedy in North Carolina," *North American Review* 218 (December 1929), 687; Pope, *Millhands and Preachers*, 230; Bernstein, *Lean Years*, 20-26; Dunne, *Gastonia: Citadel of Class Struggle*, 19- 21.

53. Mitchell, *Textile Unionism*, 71; Pope, *Millhands and Preachers*, 257; Beal, *Proletarian Journey*, 111-35; Foner, *Women and the Labor Movement*, 2: 232n; Dunne, *Gastonia: Citadel of Class Struggle*, 20-23.

54. Bernstein, *Lean Years*, 22; *Daily Worker* (April 1, 1929); Foner, *Women and the Labor Movement*, 2: 232. The trend toward work by married women was an important factor in making the working week a vital issue in the late 1920s in both northern and southern textile strikes. By 1930 only 46.9 percent of all cotton-mill women workers were single, down from 65.7 percent in 1907-1908. About 22 percent of all mill workers in 1930 were married (or divorced or widowed) women suffering the double oppression of household work and long mill labor. Recent feminist scholarship suggests that such a trend toward work, for reasons of necessity and desire for increased consumption, by married women went far beyond the textile industry in the years before the Great Depression. See Herbert J. Lahne, *The Cotton Mill Worker* (New York, 1944), 290; Winifred D. Wandersee, *Women's Work and Family Values, 1920-1940* (Cambridge, 1981), 7-26 and 65-68; and Heidi I. Hartmann, "Capitalism and Women's Work in the Home, 1900-1930" (Unpublished Ph.D. diss., Yale University, 1974), 227-53.

55. *Daily Worker* (April 10, 1929); Lahne, *Cotton Mill Worker*, 217.

56. Tippett, *Southern Labor Stirs*, 87; Pope, *Millhands and Preachers*, 258; *Daily Worker* (April 10, 12, and May 28, 1929); Beal, *Proletarian Journey*, 159-60; Lahne, *Cotton Mill Worker*, 217; Bernstein, *Lean Years*, 22-23.

57. *Daily Worker* (April 1, 1929); Dunne, *Gastonia: Citadel of Class Struggle*, 23-26; Foner, *Women and the Labor Movement*, 2: 233-35; Lahne, *Cotton Mill Worker*, 217.

58. Lahne, *Cotton Mill Worker*, 218.

59. Edmunds and others, *Stand Together*, 9; Dunne, *Gastonia: Citadel of Class Struggle*, 29; Cyril Briggs, "The Negro Question in the Southern Textile Strikes," *Communist* 8 (June 1929), esp. 325; Foner, *Women and the Labor Movement*, 2: 234-35; Weisbord, *Radical Life*, 260.

60. Bernstein, *Lean Years*, 24-25; Lahne, *Cotton Mill Worker*, 218; *New York Times* (June 8, 1929).

61. Foner, *Women and the Labor Movement*, 2: 235-39.

62. Lahne, *Cotton Mill Worker*, 218-19; Mitchell, *Textile Unionism*, 71-74.

63 Blanshard, "Communism," 122-24; Cochran, *Labor and Communism*, 36; Lahne, *Cotton Mill Worker*, 219; Foner, *Women and the Labor Movement*, 2: 239.

64. Foner, *Women and the Labor Movement*, 2: 228-30 and 239-41; Lahne, *Cotton Mill Worker*, 219-21; Mitchell, *Textile Unionism*, 76.

65. Brody, *Steelworkers in America*, 214-62, and *Labor in Crisis*, 61-174; Yellen, *American Labor Struggles*, 251-91; Murray, *Red Scare*, 132-52; Commission of Inquiry, Interchurch World Movement (IWM), *Report on the Steel Strike of 1919* (New York, 1920); and Keiser, "Fitzpatrick," 41-52, inform our account.

66. Brody, *Steelworkers*, 214; Fitzpatrick quoted in Brody, *Labor in Crisis*, 130; Foster, *Bryan to Stalin*, 112; Zipser, *Workingclass Giant*, 51-52.

67. Charles R. Walker, *Steel: The Diary of a Furnace Worker* (Boston, 1922), 76-77; "The Steel Industry," *Social Service Bulletin* 10 (October 1920), 1; IWM, *Report*, 44-84; William Z. Foster, *The Great Steel Strike and Its Lessons* (New York, 1920), 14.

68. Ida Tarbell, *The Life of Elbert H. Gary* (New York, 1925), 291; Brody, *Steelworkers*, 170-71; IWM, *Report*, 54ff; Marshall Olds, *Analysis of the Interchurch World Movement Report on the Steel Strike* (New York, 1923), 74- 139.

69. Foster, *Bryan to Stalin*, 108-12; Brody, *Steelworkers*, 214-16, and *Labor in Crisis*, 75.

70. George Soule, "Civil Rights in Western Pennsylvania," in IWM, *Public Opinion and the Steel Strike* (New York, 1921), 188 and passim.

71. Soule, "Civil Rights," 200-201; Brody, *Labor in Crisis*, 89-92.

72. Taft, *AFL in the Time of Gompers*, 386.

73. Brody, *Labor in Crisis*, 73ff; Foster, *Bryan to Stalin*, 112, writes that the first organizational meeting in Gary drew 15,000.

74. Brody, *Steelworkers*, 223, and *Labor in Crisis*, 73. The task was monumental. In one Homestead mill alone 54 nationalities labored. See IWM, *Report*, 132-33.

75. Brody, *Steelworkers*, 231-35.

76. Foster, *Pages from a Worker's Life*, 162-69; Brody, *Labor in Crisis*, 92-95; Jones, *Autobiography*, 211-12; *New Majority* (September 4, 1919); Foster, *Great Steel Strike*, 16.

77. Brody, *Labor in Crisis*, 98; Jones, *Autobiography*, 211-12.

78. Brody, *Steelworkers*, 233 and 223-24; IWM, *Report*, 52 and 119-43; Foster, *Great Steel Strike*, 196-97.

79. IWM, *Report*, 148; Saposs, "The Mind of Immigrant Communities in the Pittsbrugh District," in IWM, *Public Opinion*, 239 and passim; Brody, *Labor in Crisis*, 81ff.

80. Williams, *Mainsprings of Men*, 83; Brody, *Labor in Crisis*, 97-98.

81. Brody, *Steelworkers*, 237, and *Labor in Crisis*, 99-101; Foster, *Great Steel Strike*, 76-78.

82. Urofsky, *Big Steel and the Wilson Administration*, 285-89; Brody, *Labor in Crisis*, 101-2.

83. Brody, *Labor in Crisis*, 105, 106, and 111; Foster, *Great Steel Strike*, 89, and *Bryan to Stalin*, 115 and 119.

84. Saposs, "Immigrant Communities," esp. 239; Brody, *Labor in Crisis*, 112-15, and *Steelworkers*, 241-42.

85. Brody, *Steelworkers*, 250; Soule, "Civil Rights," 163-219; Brody, *Labor in Crisis*, 134-35 and 147-53; Foster, *Bryan to Stalin*, 117-18; Yellen, *American Labor Struggles*, 275; Robert Littell, "Under-Cover Men," in IWM, *Public Opinion*, 1-86; Mary Heaton Vorse, "Civil Liberties in the Steel Strike," *Nation* (November 15, 1919), 833-35; Foster, *Pages from a Worker's Life*, 219-23.

86. Quoted in Yellen, *American Labor Struggles*, 271-72; Foster, *Great Steel Strike*, 199.

87. Quoted in Brody, *Labor in Crisis*, 132.

88. Yellen, *American Labor Struggles*, 273; Murray, *Red Scare*, 139; Brody, *Labor in Crisis*, 136-59; Foster, *Bryan to Stalin*, 126-29, and *Great Steel Strike*, 196ff; Zipser, *Workingclass Giant*, 55; Edward Greer, *Big Steel* (New York, 1979), 115.

89. Foster, *Great Steel Strike*, 209ff; Brody, *Labor in Crisis*, 162-63; Urofsky, *Big Steel and the Wilson Administration*, 326-28, quote on 327.

90. Murray, *Red Scare*, 149; Urofsky, *Big Steel and the Wilson Administration*, 328-31; Foster, *Great Steel Strike*, 142; Robert R.R. Brooks, *As Steel Goes, Unionism in a Basic Industry* (New Haven, Conn., 1940), 31-32.

91. Taft, *AFL in the Time of Gompers*, 392-93; Brody, *Labor in Crisis*, 166- 71 and *Steelworkers*, 256-57; Foster, *Bryan to Stalin*, 115-16, and *Great Steel Strike*, 220-36.

92. "Addendum: The Commission's Mediation Effort," in IWM, *Public Opinion*, 338 and 331-41, passim; Brody, *Labor in Crisis*, 171-76.

93. *Daily Worker* (May 7, 1927); *Labor* (April 30, 1927).

94. *Labor* (July 7, 1923); *Daily Worker* (July 3, 1926); Eugene Lyons, "Fighting the 54-Hour Week," *Labor Age* (April 1922). Although wages were the primary issue in the massive railway shop crafts strike of 1922, Railway Labor Board withdrawals of overtime premiums after ten hours for, at various times, signalmen, stationary firemen, oilers, telegraphers, railway clerks, freight handlers, and maintenance-of-way employees constituted a major grievance uniting railroad workers. Also at issue in the 1922 strike was payment of Sunday and holiday overtime in the shop crafts. See Commons and Associates, *History of Labour*, 4: 515; McIsaac, *The Order of Railroad Telegraphers*, 197ff; Lovestone, *Government—Strikebreaker*, 143; Painter, *Through Fifty Years with the Brotherhood of Railway Carmen of America*, 158; *Labor* (December 24, 1921; February 18, 1922; April 2, 1921; March 10, 1923).

95. Milton J. Nadworny, *Scientific Management and the Unions* (Cambridge, Mass., 1955), ch. 7-8; Jean McKelvey, *AFL Attitudes Toward Production, 1900- 1932* (Ithaca, N.Y., 1952), ch. 4-5.

96. See Roediger, "Fordism, Labor and the Working Day," forthcoming.

97. See above, ch. 1; Roy Zebulon Chamlee, "The Sabbath Crusade, 1810- 1920," (unpublished Ph.D. dissertation, George Washington University, 1968).

98. Robert C. Reinders, "T. Wharton Collens and the Christian Labor Union," *Labor History* 8 (Spring 1967), 58; Clyde Griffen, "Christian Socialism Instructed by Gompers," *Labor History* 12 (Spring 1971), esp. 203 and 213; Fred Woodrow, "Side-Lights on the Labor Problem," in William E. Barns, ed., *The Labor Problem* (New York, 1886), 325; Henry F. May, *Protestant Churches and Industrial America* (New York, 1949), 104.

99. Leo XIII, *"Rerum Novarum,"* in Anne Freemantle, ed., *The Papal Encyclicals in Their Historical Context* (New York, 1956), 174-75 and 185-86; Samuel Gompers, *Labor and the Common Welfare*, Hayes Robbins, ed. (New York, 1919), 31.

100. Henry F. Ward., ed., *Social Creed of the Churches* (New York and Cincinnati, 1912), 3; Charles Howard Hopkins, *The Rise of the Social Gospel in American Protestantism, 1865-1915* (New Haven, Conn., 1940), 316-17. See also Robert F. Coyle, *Workingmen and the Church* (Winona Lake, Ind., 1903), 6- 8; Foner, *Labor Movement*, 3: 128-34; Hill, "Fighting the Twelve-Hour Day," 23; Hopkins, *Social Gospel*, 314-15.

101. Henry F. Ward, *The Gospel for a Working World* (New York, 1918), 35 and 36-64, passim; Ward, ed., *Social Creed*, 55-76; [Ward], "What 'Leisure for All' Means," *The Social Service Bulletin* 6 (July 1916), 1; Henry F. Ward, *The Labor Movement from the Standpoint of Religious Values* (New York, 1917), 19- 21; *Seattle Union Record* (November 11, 1916); George H. Nash, "Charles Stelzle: Apostle to Labor," *Labor History* 11 (Spring 1970), 159 and 163-64.

102. Cole, *Social Ideas*, 105; May, *Protestant Churches*, 56; Ely, *Social Aspects of Christianity* (New York, 1889), 44-45; Commons, *Social Reform and the Church* (New York, 1894), 38-39.

103. Leo XIII, *"Rerum Novarum,"* in Freemantle, ed., *Encyclicals*, 185-86; Gibbons, "Organized Labor," (n.p., n.d.) in Stein and Taft, eds., *Wages, Hours and Strikes*, 22-23; Viau, *Hours and Wages*, 187-97.

104. Earp, *The Social Engineer* (New York, 1911), 248; Montgomery, "Machinists," in *Workers' Control*, 77; Leo XIII, *"Rerum Novarum,"* in Freemantle, ed., *Encyclicals*, 173-75; Hopkins, *Social Gospel*, 291; Nash, "Stelzle," 163-64. As late as 1919 the "Bishops' Program" for postwar social reconstruction ignored concrete proposals on the working day. See Msgr. John A. Ryan, *Social Reconstruction*, 216-38.

105. Gompers, *Labor and the Common Welfare*, 46; Montgomery, "Machinists," 76-79; Foner, *Labor Movement*, 3: 111-35; Marc Karson, "The Catholic Church and the Labor Movement," *Industrial and Labor Relations Review* 4 (July 1951), 527-42; David Saposs, "The Catholic Church and the Labor Movement," *Modern Monthly* 7 (May-June 1933); Elizabeth and Kenneth Fones-Wolf, "Trade Union Evangelism: Religion and the AFL in the Labor Movement, 1912-1916," in Frisch and Walkowitz, eds., *Working Class in America*, 153-84.

106. See below, n. 123, and Robert E. Doherty, "Thomas J. Haggerty, the Church and Socialism," *Labor History* 3 (Winter 1962).

107. Committee on the War and the Religious Outlook, *The Church and Industrial Reconstruction*, 46-50; Olds, *Analysis*, 394-95; Philip C. Ensley, "The Interchurch World Movement and the Steel Strike of 1919," *Labor History* 13 (Spring 1972), 217-18.

108. Ensley, "IWM," 217-19; IWM, "The Commission's Mediation Effort," in *Public Opinion and the Steel Strike*, 332; IWM, *Report*, 6; Olds, *Analysis*, 400-407.

109. Ensley, "IWM," 220-22; Olds, *Analysis*, 408-32, is sometimes useful for the publications and organizational affiliations of the staffers, though his inflamed account equates any support for the left or the strike with disloyalty and Bolshevism.

110. IWM, *Report* and *Public Opinion on the Steel Strike*, 54 and passim.

111. IWM, *Report*, 82.

112. Robert Moats Miller, *American Protestantism and Social Issues, 1919- 1939* (Chapel Hill, N.C., 1958), 215.

113. Vorse, in Miller, *Protestantism*, 210; IWM, *Report*, 156ff; 241 and 249-51.

114. Blankenhorn, "The Steel Report and Public Opinion," in *Public Opinion and the Steel Strike*, 306-26; Miller, *Protestantism*, 213-16; Ensley, "IWM," 225.

115. Miller, *Protestantism*, 212; Ensley, "IWM," 225-27; Olds, *Analysis*, esp. part two and 427; Blankenhorn, "The Steel Report," 308-16 and 320.

116. Ensley, "IWM," 228; Hill, "Fighting the Twelve-Hour Day," 25.

117. See above and Foner, *1877*, 216.

118. Quoted in Samuel P. Hays, *Conservation and the Gospel of Efficiency* (New York, 1979), 124-25. Goldmark, *Fatigue and Inefficiency*, passim; William C. Redfield, *The New Industrial Day* (New York, 1913), 8-10.

119. Dickson quoted in Eggert, "Fight for the Eight-Hour Day," 38; Hill, "Fighting the Twelve-Hour Day," 21-23; William T. Moye, "The End of the 12- Hour Day in the Steel Industry," *Monthly Labor Review* 100 (September 1977), 22-23.

120. Eggert, "Fight for the Eight-Hour Day," 43 and 38-42; Brandeis, as quoted in Moye, "End of the 12-Hour Day," 22.

121. Braverman, *Labor and Monopoly Capital*, 103-8; Frederick S. Lee, *The Human Machine and Industrial Efficiency* (Easton, Pa., 1974, originally 1918), 10-23 and 90-99; P. S. Florence, *Economics of Fatigue and Unrest* (New York, 1924), 87-95; Bryan Palmer, "Class, Conception and Conflict: The Thrust for Efficiency, Managerial Views of Labor and Working Class Rebellion, 1903-1922," *Review of Radical Political Economics* 7 (Summer 1975), 38-39; H. L. Gantt and others, *How Scientific Management Is Applied* (Easton, Pa., 1974, originally 1911), 73.

122. See especially Frankfurter, *The Case for the Shorter Work Day*, 1: 193-226.

123. Palmer, "Class, Conception and Conflict," 34-40; Braverman, *Labor and Monopoly Capital*, 139-51; Cf. Frank B. Copley, "Frederick W. Taylor— Revolutionist," *The Outlook* 111 (September 1915), 42.

124. Palmer, "Class, Conception and Conflict," 38ff, and Foster, "Capitalist Efficiency 'Socialism'," 94-95; Sumner H. Slichter, *The Turnover of Factory Labor* (New York), 257-58.

125. Nadworny, *Scientific Management and the Unions*, 122-41; Morris Cooke, Samuel Gompers, and Fred J. Miller, eds., "Labor, Management and Productivity," *Annals of the American Academy of Political and Social Science* 91 (September 1920), passim; Gompers, "Organized Labor and Industrial Engineers," *American Federationist* 28 (January 1921).

126. Herman Feldman, *Prohibition: Its Economic and Industrial Aspects* (New York, 1927), 242-50.

127. John R. Commons and John B. Andrews, *Principles of American Labor Legislation* (New York, 1920), 221.

128 NICB,. *Hours of Work as Related to Output and Health of Workers: Boot and Shoe Industry*, Research Report Number 7 (Boston, 1918), 42 and 50-52; NICB, *Hours of Work as Related to Output and Health of Workers: Wool Manufacturing*, Research Report Number 12

(Boston, 1918), 18 and 28-29; NICB, *Analysis of British Wartime Reports on Hours of Work*, Research Report Number 2 (Boston, 1917), passim; Josephine Goldmark and Mary D. Hopkins, "Comparison of an Eight-Hour Plant and a Ten-Hour Plant," *Public Health Bulletin*, Number 106 (Washington, D.C., 1920); Slichter, *Turnover*, 261-64.

129. See NICB, *Wartime Employment of Women in the Metal Trades*, Research Report Number 8 (Boston, 1918), 63-64; William L. Chenery, "Waste in Industry," *Survey* 44 (August 1, 1920), 545; *Waste in Industry* (New York, 1921); Herbert Hoover, *The Memoirs of Herbert Hoover*, 3 vols. (New York, 1952), 2: 31.

130. See the NICB reports cited in n.151 above and for the quotes, Florence, *Economics of Fatigue*, 188, 302-46, esp. 328-331; Walker, *Diary of a Furnace Worker*, 151-52.

131. Slichter, *Turnover*, 226, 234, 239, and 258-63; Florence, *Economics of Fatigue*, 137-78 and 189; quoted passages from Whiting Williams, *What's on the Worker's Mind* (New York, 1920), 287.

132. Florence, *Economics of Fatigue*, 212-73, esp. 226-28, 236-37, and 266- 70; Williams, *Mind*, 287; Walker, *Diary of a Furnace Worker*, 151; Filene, *The Way Out* (Garden City, N.Y., 1925), 218-23.

133. Hoover, *Memoirs*, 2: 44-46; Joan Hoff Wilson, *Herbert Hoover: Forgotten Progressive* (Boston, 1975), 90-93; Robert H. Zeiger, *Republicans and Labor, 1919-1929* (Lexington, Ky., 1969), 88-89 and 99; Ordway Tead, "The U.S. Employment Service and the Prevention of Unemployment," *American Labor Legislation Review* 9 (March 1919), 97-98; Hill, "Fighting the Twelve-Hour Day," 27.

134. Eggert, "Fight for the Eight-Hour Day," strikes the proper emphasis on this score.

135. Fitch, "The Long Day," *Survey* 45 (March 5, 1921), 795-96; Hill, "Fighting the Twelve-Hour Day," 25; Fitch, *The Causes of Industrial Unrest* (New York, 1924), 11-17.

136. Horace Drury, "The Three-Shift System in the Steel Industry," *Bulletin of the Taylor Society* (February 1921); Cahill, *Shorter Hours*, 213- 14; "Engineers on Hours," *Survey* 45 (October 39, 1920), 151; "Three Shifts in Steel," *Survey* 45 (December 11, 1920), 387-88; "Shorter Work Day Increases Output," *Labor* (October 30, 1920); "Three Shifts in Foreign Countries," *Survey* 45 (March 5, 1921), 810; Thomas Blaisdell, Jr., "Fatigue and the Steel Worker," *Survey* 46 (June 4, 1921), 312.

137. Hill, "Fighting the Twelve-Hour Day," 27; Hoover, *Memoirs*, 2: 103; Gart Dean Best, *The Politics of American Individualism: Herbert Hoover in Transition, 1918-1921* (Westport, Conn., 1975), 45; Zeiger, "Wage Earner," 94- 95; quotes from Ibid.; Zeiger, *Republicans and Labor*, 100, and Kirby Page, *Industrial Facts* (New York, 1921), 11-12.

138. Zeiger, *Republicans and Labor*, 100; Eggert, "Fight for the Eight-Hour Day," 44; *Survey* 46 (April 23, 1921), 101, and (April 22, 1922), 101; "Three Shifts Versus Two Shifts," *Survey* 48 (April 8, 1922), 38-39; Gary as quoted in Hill, "Fighting the Twelve-Hour Day," 28.

139. Zeiger, *Republicans and Labor*, 101-2. Quote from Hoover, *Memoirs*, 2: 103-4; Moye, "Twelve-Hour Day," 24.

140. Moye, "End of the Twelve-Hour Day," 24; Hill, "Fighting the Twelve- Hour Day," 27-28; Zeiger, *Republicans and Labor*, 46 and 98; Andrew Sinclair, *The Available Man: The Life Behind the Masks of Warren Gamaliel Harding* (New York, 1965), 255-56; FAES, *The Twelve-Hour Shift in Industry* (New York, 1922), xii and passim; Hoover, *Memoirs*, 2: 104.

141. Quoted in Hill, "Fighting the Twelve-Hour Day," 31; Hoover, *Memoirs*, 2: 104; Zeiger, *Republicans and Labor*, 104-5; John Fitch, "A Confession of Helplessness," *Survey* 50 (June 15, 1923), 320-21; *Labor* (June 2, 1923); Hill, "Fighting the Twelve-Hour Day," 32.

142. Zeiger, *Republicans and Labor*, 104-6; Hill, "Fighting the Twelve-Hour Day," 31-35; Hoover, *Memoirs*, 2: 104; Frederick W. MacKenzie, "Steel Abandons the Twelve-Hour Day," *American Labor Legislation Review* 13 (September 1923), esp. 183-86; James W. Murphy, comp., *President Harding's Last Speeches* (n.p., 1923), 290-95; Brody, *Steelworkers*, 274-75; Eggert, "Fight for the Eight-Hour Day," 44; Moye, "End of the 12-Hour Day," 25; Charles L. Walker, "The Twelve- Hour Day in Steel," *American Labor Legislation Review* 13 (June 1923), 113-17; *Iron Age* (September 20 and 27, 1923; January 3, 1924); *Labor* (May 11, 1929).

143.   *Labor* (July 14 and August 18, 1923); *Worker* (August 11 and 25, 1923); *Daily Worker* (June 16, 1925); Emil M. Hartl and Edward G. Ernst, "The Steel Mills Today," *New Republic* (February 19, 1930); Horace B. Davis, *Labor and Steel* (New York, 1933), 74-80.

144.   See above n. 142 and *Labor* (December 29, 1923); "Hours of Labor and the 7-Day Week in the Iron and Steel Industry," *Monthly Labor Review* 23 (October 1926), 182-87; *Labor Age* (November 1926), 13; MacKenzie, "Steel Abandons," 186.

145.   Bernstein, *Lean Years*, 102-03.

146.   NICB, *Five-Day Week*, 17, finds the first five-day schedule in a New England spinning mill in 1908 and links it to a desire to observe the Jewish Sabbath; Richard Schneirov and Thomas Suhrbur, *The Chicago Carpenters*, forthcoming, and "The Carpenters of Chicago and the Uniform Agreement, 1900- 1929" (paper presented to Chicago Labor History Group, Newberry Library, January 15, 1982). See also *Seattle Union Record* (May 10, 1919); Thomas L. Norton, *Trade Union Policy in the Massachusetts Shoe Industry, 1919-1929* (New York, 1932), 199-200, for early labor protests leading to the five-day week; Fred Landon, "The Knights of Labor: Predecessors of the CIO," *Quarterly Journal of Commerce* (Summer-Autumn 1937), 1-7.

147.   James Lynch, "Shorter Working Day Urged as Alleviation for Depression Cycles," *American Labor World* (November 1926), 28-29; AFL, *Proceedings, 1926*, 200-207 and 199-202; AFL, *Proceedings, 1927*, 400. See also James Lynch, "The Shorter Workday: The Complete Argument," *American Federationist* 33 (March 1926); *New York Times* (October 17, 1926); AFL, *Proceedings, 1927*, 198 and below.Of course adverse working conditions, standardized tasks, and speedups had long been associated with the desire for shorter hours. But never before had the struggle over one set of issues (time) been so explicitly posed as a *substitute* for struggle over another (control over work). David Brody's provocative, though overstated, comments on the divorce between shopfloor actions and trade unionism in the Great Depression ought to be set partly in the context of the AFL's separation of control over work and control over leisure in the 1920s. For Brody's remarks, see his "The CIO After 50 Years," *Dissent* (Fall 1985), 469ff.

148.   Bernstein, *Lean Years*, 102-3; Nadworny, *Scientific Management and the Unions*, ch. 7-8.

149.   *Labor* (October 16, 1926); Sister J. M. Viau, *Hours and Wages in American Organized Labor* (New York, 1939), 81-85.

150.   AFL, *Proceedings, 1926*, 206.

151.   Ibid., 200-201.

152.   Cochran, *Labor and Communism*, 41-42; Foner, *Fur Workers*, 210-44; Schneider, "Workers' Party," 86; Foner, *Women and the Labor Movement*, 2:192- 97.

153.   Roediger, "Fordism, Labor and the Working Day," forthcoming; John B. Andrews, "One-Day-of-Rest-in-Seven Legislation," *American Labor Legislation Review* 13 (September 1923), 175-76; NICB, *The Five-Day Week in Manufacturing Industries* (New York, 1929), 11. See also Benjamin Kline Hunnicutt, "The End of Shorter Hours," *Labor History* 25 (Summer 1984), 377. *Labor* (April 1, 1922); Crowther, "Henry Ford," 613-16; Crowther, "What Is Henry Ford Going to Do?" *Review of Reviews* 75 (February 1927), 147-53.

154.   Reinhold Niebuhr, "Ford's Five Day Week Shrinks," *Christian Century* 44 (June 1927), 713-17; NAM, "Five Day Week," 2-12; *New York Times* (October 5, 1926); *Cleveland Employer* (June 1, 1927); Sward, *Legend of Henry Ford*, 201-4. Niebuhr, "Five-Day Week Shrinks," 713-17; "Editorial," *Christian Century* 43 (November 4, 1926), 1354; Irving Weinzweig, "Ford's Five-Day Work Week," *Advance* (October 22, 1926), 10; "Debunking Ford's Five-Day Week," *Advance* (November 19, 1926); *Union Reporter* (Canton, Ohio) 25 (October 1926); *Labor* (January 1-3, 1927); T. P. Headen, "Debunking the Ford Five-Day Week," *The Haldeman-Julius Monthly* 5 (April 1, 1927), 67-72. "Labor Now Out for Five-Day Week," 9-11; AFL, *Proceedings, 1926*, 201. For a radical critique of "Fordist" managerial reform, see William Z. Foster, "Capitalist Efficiency 'Socialism'," *Communist* 7 (March 1928), 169-74.

155.   *Labor* (October 14, 1929); "Legislative Notes," *American Labor Legislation Review* 13 (September 1923); Harvey O'Connor, *History of the Oil Workers International Union—CIO* (Denver, 1950), 27-29; Leon Platt, "The World Struggle for Rubber," *The Communist* 6 (May 1927), 176; "Launching the Five-Day Week," *American Labor Legislation Review* 16 (December 1926), 290- 291.

156. Andrews, "Day-of-Rest," 175-76.

157. See above and esp. William L. Chenery, "48 Hours of Less," *Survey* 46 (April 23, 1921), 118-19, and "Eight and Ten-Hour Work Day," *Survey* 45 (October 9, 1920).

158. WTUL, *Tenth Biennial Convention* (New York, 1926), 47; Foner, *Women and the Labor Movement*, 2:124-51; Lieberman, "Sisters' Keepers," esp. 405-30. WTUL, *Ninth Biennial Convention* (New York, 1924), 124; *Eleventh Bienniel Convention (First Triennial)* (New York, 1929), inside front cover, 32, 61-70, and 107; Brinson, "Shorter Day," passim.

159. Trattner, *Crusade for the Children*, 140-42, 176-83, and 287; Richard B. Sherman, "Rejection of the Child Labor Amendment," *Mid-America* 45 (January 1963).

160. NICB, *Five-Day Week*, 22; *New York Times* (October 5-6, 1926); "Attitude of Certain Employers to 5-Day Week," *Monthly Labor Review* 23 (December 1926), 16-17; National Association of Manufacturers, "The Five-Day Week: Can It Become Universal?" *Pocket Bulletin* 27 (October 1926), 2-12; "Labor Now Out for Five-Day Week," *Literary Digest* 91 (October 16, 1926), 11. See also W. H. Grimes, "Curse of Leisure," *Atlantic Monthly* 142 (April 1928), 355-60; Hunnicutt, "End of Shorter Hours," 386.

161. NAM, "Five-Day Week," 2-12; "Attitude of Certain Employers," 17; J. Charles Laue, "The Five-Day Week Is Now a Vivid Issue," *New York Times* (October 17 and 25, 1926). William Boyd Craig, "Business Views in Review," *Nation's Business* 14 (December 1926), 72-75; "Business Attitudes Toward the Five-Day Work Week," *Nation's Business* 15 (April 1927), 32; Lamar T. Beman, comp., *Five Day Week, The Reference Shelf* 5 (New York, 1928), 38-41; *Coal Age* (October 28, 1926), 592; Bernstein, *Lean Years*, 180-81.

162. "How the Five-Day Work Week Works," *Literary Digest* 86 (August 15, 1925), 10-11.

163. "Industry Tries the Five-Day Week," *Michigan Manufacturer and Financial Record* (June 30, 1923), 1-2; NICB, *Five-Day Week* 25-39, 41-42, 64- 66; "The Five-Day Week in Industry," *Monthly Labor Review* 17 (September 1923), 652-53.

164. See William Green, "The Five Day Week," *North American Review* 223 (December 1926), 566-74; John Frey, "Labor's Movement for a Five-Day Week," *Current History* 25 (December 1926), 369-72; James Lynch, "Shorter Working Day Urged as Alleviation for Depression Cycles," *American Labor World* (November 1926), 28-29; and esp. Beman, comp., *Five-Day Week*, 86.

165. Cf. *Trade Union News* (Philadelphia) (October 14, 1926), and *Labor* (August 8, 1928). The latter was able to report that C. W. Barron of the *Wall Street Journal* did favor a five-day week.

166. See Rex B. Hersey, "Is Shorter Work-Day Enough?" *Labor Age* (October 1925); "Launching the Five-Day Week," 228-89; Beman, comp., *Five-Day Week*, 41. For a different reading stressing evidence of reformers' support for shorter hours in the late 1920s, and the view that such support was significant, see Hunnicutt, "End of Shorter Hours," passim. Many of the consumption-oriented reform proposals were extremely vague, but Hunnicutt is persuasive in arguing that labor's claims to leisure, at least in the abstract, had strong support in recreational reform publications. See Matthew Woll, "Leisure and Labor," *Playground* 19 (1925), 322-23.

167. "A Five-Day Week That Pays Both Employer and Employees," *Literary Digest* 67 (October 2, 1920), 80-82; Feiss, "Why It Paid," 523-25; Amalgamated Clothing Workers of America, *Seventh Annual Report of the GEB* (Montreal, 1926), 122; Filene, *The Way Out*, 218-23; *New York Times* (October 17, 1926); *Labor* (November 29, 1926).

168. Ethelbert Stewart, "Five-Day Week Used in Several Industries," *United States Daily* (December 2, 1926); NICB, *Five-Day Week*, 22-54; Beman, comp., *Five-Day Week*, 19; *New York Times* (December 13, 1926); "Launching the Five- Day Week," 289; Frey, "Labor's Movement," 370.

169. NICB, *Five-Day Week*, 15-16. The lower figure assumes the AFL figure of 15,800 ILGWU members on the new schedule is correct. But see "Progress of the Five-Day Week," *Labor* (May 18, 1928), for much higher figures. On the painters, see *Labor* (June 12, 1925); George F. Hedrick, "The Five-Day Week," *Painter and Decorator* 40 (November 1926); Brotherhood of Painters, Decorators, and Paperhangers of America, *Reports of the General Officers to the Twelfth*

General Assembly (Lafayette, Ind., 1921), 39.

170. NICB, *Five-Day Week*, 18.

171. *Labor* (August 18 and September 22, 1928); AFL, *Proceedings, 1929*, 388. See also Cahill, *Shorter Hours*, 168.

172. NICB, *Five-Day Week*, 16.

173. *Labor* (January 19, 1929).

174. *Labor* (May 25, July 27, and September 14, 1929).

175. AFL, *Proceedings, 1926*, 196-97; AFL, *Proceedings, 1929*, 388; *Labor* (March 31 and September 22, 1928).

176. *Labor* (October 14, 1929); "Why the Six-Day Week?" *American Federationist* (September 1929); "Forty-Eight Hour Week," *American Federationist* (March 1927).

177. See *Machinists' Monthly Journal* 40:12 (December 1928), cover, and *Labor* (August 18, 1928).

178. "Labor and the Five-Day Week," *New York Times* (February 6, 1927); George L. Berry, "The Five Day Week," *American Pressman* (February 1927).

179. McGaughey, Jr., *Shorter Workweek*, 200.

The Great Depression, the New Deal, and Shorter Hours

1. Bernstein, *Lean Years*, 476.

2. Before the introduction of regular censuses of unemployed during the first Franklin D. Roosevelt administration, the task of making accurate estimates of the unemployed was formidable. Most of the statistics that economists offered during the Great Depression were informed estimates, and many were arbitrarily chosen. See Bertram Gross and Stanley Moses, "Measuring the Real Work Force: 25 Million Unemployed," *Social Policy* 3 (1962), 120-38. See also Foner, *Women and the Labor Movement*, 2: 260-63.

3. These figures are based on the monthly unemployment series that Robert R. Nation worked up for the Committee on Economic Security, which drafted the Social Security Act in 1934-1935.

4. William Green in *New York Times* (November 22, 1929).

5. AFL, *Proceedings, 1930*, 44.

6. "The Trade Union League: Its Program, Structure, Methods and History," (New York, n.d.), 26-27; *Daily Worker* (September 6 and October 9, 1929); Albert Prago, "The Organization of the Unemployed and the Role of the Radicals, 1929-1935" (unpublished Ph.D. dissertation, American University, 1976), 32-35; *New York Times* (March 7, 1930).

7. AFL, *Proceedings, 1931*, 122-23 and 144-46.

8. Bernstein, *Lean Years*, 477.

9. AFL, *Proceedings, 1930*, 18.

10. *Labor* (November 4 and December 16, 1930).

11. Bernstein, *Lean Years*, 477.

12. Foner, *Fur Workers*, 350-55.

13. Ibid.; AFL, *Proceedings, 1931*, 45.

14. *New York Times* (February 17, 1932).

15. Roy H. Bergerson, "Work Sharing in Industry: History, Methods and Extent of the Movement in the United States, 1929-1933" (unpublished Ph.D. dissertation, University of Pennsylvania, 1933), 80-91.

16. Ibid., 108.

17. Ibid., 109.

18. Ibid., 7-8.

19. Bernstein, *Lean Years*, 481.

20. *New York Times* (May 16, 1932).

21. AFL, *Proceedings, 1932*, 284-96; Bernstein, *Lean Years*, 482.

22. *Labor* (December 22, 1932).

23. Ibid., (January 10, 1933); *Congresssional Record*, 72nd Congress, 2nd Session, vol. 76, part 3, 4304.

24. *Thirty-Hour Week Bill*, Hearings on S.5267, 72nd Congress, 2nd Session, 13-14. Christopher Tomlins, *The State and the Unions: Labor Relations, Law; The Organized Labor Movement in America, 1880-1960* (Cambridge, England 1985), 129-30, sees AFL support of the thirty-hour cause as narrowly pitched at defending the interests of employed, unionized, workers, but he does so on the basis of a quite one-sided reading of the evidence. See below for the grains of truth in Tomlins's charge, especially as regards Green's position.

25. *Thirty-Hour Week Bill*, 2.

26. Ibid., 22.

27. Ibid.

28. Ibid., 22, 884, and 957.

29. Ibid., 444 and 814.

30. Ibid., 112.

31. *New York Times* (March 28, 1933).

32. *Senate Report No. 14*, 73rd Congress, 1st Session, vol. 77:9769.

33. *New York Times* (April 3-5, 1933).

34. *Labor* (April 11, 1933).

35. *Congressional Record*, 73rd Congress, 1st Session, vol. 77, part 6, 5805.

36. *Labor* (January 31, 1933). Probably referring to the testimony of Louis Weinstock; Black also referred to Communist opposition to the bill.

37. *Labor* (May 2, 1933); Irving Bernstein, *Turbulent Years: A History of the American Worker, 1933-1941* (Boston, 1970), 26-30.

38. *Labor* (June 5, 1933).

39. *Congressional Record*, 73rd Congress, 1st Session, vol. 77, part 6, 5843.

40. National Recovery Administration, *Tabulation of Labor Provisions in Codes Approved by August 8, 1934* (Washington, D.C., 1935), 31. Evidently WPA administrators did little to carry out this directive, for in July 1935, David Lasser, National Chairman of the Workers Alliance of America announced that WPA workers would soon launch a series of demonstrations throughout the country "for the thirty-hour week." See *New York Times* (July 7, 1935).

41. Leverett S. Lyons, et al., *The National Recovery Administration: An Analysis and Appraisal* (Washington, D.C., 1935), 369-70.

42. Foner, *Fur Workers*, 380.

43. *New York Times* (March 30, 1934); *Labor* (April 3, 1934).

44. *New York Times* (October 5, 1934).

45. *Labor* (April 17 and 24, 1934).

46. *Thirty-Hour Week Bill*, Hearings on H.R.7202, H.R.4116, H.R.8492, 73rd Congress, 2nd Session, 177-278; *New York Times* (May 31, 1934).

47. *Labor* (February 12, 1935).

48. Ibid. (April 16, 1935).

49. *New York Times* (February 17, 1935).

50. Ibid. (May 25 and June 17, 1934).

51. Ibid. (June 3, September 5, and October 17, 1934); Foner, *Women and the American Labor Movement*, 2: 284-88; David Milton, *The Politics of U.S. Labor from the Depression to the New Deal* (New York, 1982), 62-65.

52. Witt Bowden, "Hours and Earnings Before and After the N.R.A.," *Monthly Labor Review* (January 1937), 13-16.

53. *New York Times* (July 21, 1935).

54. Ibid. (December 20, 1936).

55. Ibid.

56. Ibid. (October 11, 1937).

57. *Labor* (October 8, 1935).

58. Other provisions of the law required these companies to (1) pay minimum wages determined by the Department of Labor; (2) employ no males under 16, females under 18, or convict labor; and (3) maintain working conditions free from hazards to health and safety of workers.

59. Act of June 30, 1936, C.881, 74th Congress, 2nd Session, 49 Stat. 2036-2039, *41 U.S. Code, Sec. 40 (Supp. 1940) as amended.*

60. *Labor* (December 8, 1936).

61. *Congressional Record*, 75th Congress, 1st Session, vol. 81, part 1, 86.

62. *Congressional Record*, 75th Congress, 2nd Session, vol. 82, part 1, 6.

63. *Congressional Record*, 75th Congress, 2nd Session, vol. 83, part 6, 11.

64. Paul H. Douglas and James Hackman, "The Fair Labor Standards Act of 1938," *Political Science Quarterly* 53 (December 1938), 502-3 and 512-13.

65. *Fair Labor Standards Act of 1937, Joint Hearings on S.2475 and H.R. 7200*, 75th Congress, 1st Session, before the Senate Committee on Education and Labor and the House Committee on Labor, June 2-22, 1937, 1078-79.

66. *New York Times* (August 1, 1937).

67. Ibid. (August 7-15, 1937).

68. *Congressional Record*, 75th Congress, 2nd Session, vol. 82, Part 1, 6; O. W. Phelps, "The Legislative Background of the Fair Labor Standards Act," *Journal of Business of the University of Chicago* 12 (April 1939), 21-22 and passim.

69. Ibid., 23-24.

70. Douglas and Hackman, "Fair Labor Standards Act," 514-15.

71. Phelps, "Legislative Background," 75.

72. Labor Research Association, *Labor Fact Book*, IV (New York, 1938), 50.

73. Jeremy P. Felt, "The Child Labor Provisions of the Fair Labor Standards Act," *Labor History* 11 (Fall 1970), 462.

74. Public Law No. 718, 75th Congress, 3rd Session, ch. 676.S.2475.

75. Boris Shishkin, "Wage-Hour Law from Labor's Viewpoint," *Monthly Labor Research Review* (June, 1939), 63-72.

76. Quoted in Felt, "Child Labor," 468-69.

77. *United States v. F. W. Darby Lumber Co.*, 312 U.S.; 61 Sup. Ct. 451; 85 L.Ed. 395 (1941); *Opp Cotton Mills v. Administrator* 312 U.S.; 61 Sup. Ct. 524; 85 L. Ed. 407 (1941).

78. Elmer F. Andrews, "History of Labor Cause," *American Labor Legislation Review* (June 1939), 86.

The Hours Stalemate since 1939

1. See Charles Edward Russell, "Eight-Hour Day Is 400 Years Old," (Cleveland) *Citizen* (January 19, 1917). For a very recent expression of the same idea by an IWW organizer active during the period in which Russell wrote, see Fred Thompson, "Introductory Notes," to Paul Lafargue, *The Right to Be Lazy* (Chicago, 1975), 23; see also Foster, *Trade Unionism*, 6ff; Thorold Rogers, *Six Centuries of Work and Wages* (London, 1886), 542-43.

2. McGaughey, *Shorter Workweek*, 35. Evidence on recent workweek trends is well summarized in Benjamin Kline Hunnicutt, "The End of Shorter Hours," *Labor History* 25 (Summer 1984); see also Ed Andrew, *Closing the Iron Cage: The Scientific Management of Work and Leisure* (Montreal, 1981), 53.

3. John D. Owen, "Workweeks and Leisure: An Analysis of Trends," *Monthly Labor Review* (August 1976), 3-8; Owen, *The Price of Leisure* (Montreal, 1970), 62ff; Peter Henle, "Leisure and the Long Workweek," *Monthly Labor Review* (July 1966), 727.

4. Diane N. Westcott, "Trends in Overtime Hours and Pay, 1969-74," *Monthly Labor Review* (February 1975), 45; Howard V. Hayghe and Kapp Michelott, "Multiple Jobholding in 1970 and 1971," *Monthly Labor Review* (October 1971), 38-45; Harvey R. Hamel, "Moonlighting—An Economic Phenomenon," *Monthly Labor Review* (October 1967), 17-22; McGaughey, *Shorter Workweek*, 124.

5. Gabriel Kolko, "Working Wives: Their Effects on the Structure of the Working Class," *Science and Society* 42 (Fall 1978), 266-67.

6. Ivan Illich, *Shadow Work* (Boston, 1981) and *Gender* (New York, 1982).

7. Janice Neipert Hedges, "How Many Days Make a Workweek?" *Monthly Labor Review* (April 1975), 29-36; Hedges, "A Look at the 4-Day Workweek," *Monthly Labor Review* (October 1971), 33-37; *Wall Street Journal* (February 16, 1977); *New York Times* (August 20, 1976); Kenneth E. Wheeler, Richard Gurman, and Dale Tarnowieski, *The Four-Day Week* (New York, 1972); Riva Poor, ed., *4 Days, 40 Hours and Other Forms of the Rearranged Workweek* (New York, 1973). Minor exceptions are Neil A. Martin, "Can a Four-Day Week Work?" *Dun's Review and Modern Industry* (July 1971), 39-42, which worries that four-day schedule will breed 32-hour weeks and Kenneth E. Wheeler, "Small Business Eyes the Four-Day Workweek," *Harvard Business Review* (May-June 1970), 141-47, which apparently projects a 36-hour week. The literature on flexitime is vast with the best bibliography in Pam Silverstein and Jozette H. Srb, *Flexitime: Where, When and How?* (Ithaca, N.Y., 1979).

8. Kreps, "Time for Leisure, Time for Work," *Monthly Labor Review* 92 (April 1969), 60-61; John Zalusky, "Shorter Work Year—Early Retirement," *American Federationist* 84 (August 1977), 4-8; John Zalusky, "Vacations— Holidays: Tools in Cutting Work Time," *American Federationist* 84 (February 1977). For perspicacious discussion of shorter hours and retirement as competing antiunemployment stratagies, though one unfortunately limited to the depression years, see William Graebner, *A History of Retirement* (New Haven, Conn., 1980), 153-80. See also H. S. Person, "The Work-Week or the Work-Life?" *Bulletin of the Taylor Society* 13 (October 1928), 230-48.

9. Hazel M. Willacy, "Changes in Factory Workweek as an Economic Indicator," *Monthly Labor Review* (October 1970), 25-32.

10. Hunnicutt, "End of Shorter Hours," esp. 374.

11. Frank Duffy, "Valuable Information," *Carpenter* 58 (October 1938), 35- 52. Information on the photo-engravers is from Edward J. Volz's "President's Message" column in *American Photo-Engraver* 31-32 (February 1939-September 1940). See also Fred C. Munson, *History of the Lithographers Union* (Cambridge, Mass., 1963), 268-69; AFL, *Proceedings, 1938*, 108 and 535, and *Proceedings, 1948*, 1127.

12. AFL, *History, Encyclopedia, Reference Book*, 1112-21; AFL Executive Council, *Report, 1939*, 133-38, *Report, 1940*, 61-65, and *Report, 1941*, 65-66.

13. Joel Seidman, *American Labor from Defense to Reconversion* (Chicago, 1953), 155-56; AFL, *Proceedings, 1942*, 685; McGaughey, *Shorter Workweek*, 192; "Working Hours in War Production Plants," *Monthly Labor Review* (May 1942), 1061; Judith Anne Scalander, "The Women's Bureau, 1920-1950: Federal Reaction to Female Wage Earning" (unpublished Ph.D. dissertation, Duke University, 1977), 230-38.

14. Seidman, *American Labor*, 155-56; Martin Glaberman, *Wartime Strikes* (Detroit, 1980), 4-15; Nelson Lichtenstein, "Defending the No-Strike Pledge: CIO Politics During World War II," *Radical America* 9 (July-August 1975), 55.

15. AFL, *History, Encyclopedia, Reference Book*, 1123 and 1120-25, passim; *Hours Administration as Influenced by the Defense Program* (Princeton, N.J., 1940), 28-29; *Labor* (August 11 and November 11, 1941, and July 16, 1943); "New Survey Debunks Propaganda to Repeal 40-Hour Standard," *Cigar Makers Official Journal* 67 (January 1943), 3. For an exceptional and relatively inconsequential mention of hours just prior to American entry into the war, see CIO, *Proceedings, 1944*, 275.

16. Seidman, *American Labor*, 113-30.

17. "Recommended Optimum Hours for Maximum Production," *Monthly Labor Review* (September 1942), 459-60; "Establishment of Minimum 48-Hour Week," *Monthly Labor Review* (March 1943), 471-72; Seidman, *American Labor*, 118. Richard O. Boyer and Herbert M. Morais, *Labor's Untold Story* (New York, 1955), 334, err in saying the decree was for a "basic 48-hour week." Overtime was protected.

18. *Labor* (February 24, 1943). The best account of wartime labor policy regarding wages and hours is the recent Nelson Lichtenstein, *Labor's War at Home: The CIO in World War Two* (New York, 1983), 96-108. Lichtenstein, 108, notes National War Labor Board decisions which helped defuse overtime/premium pay issue with compensatory wage boosts.

19. Art Preis, *Labor's Giant Step* (New York, 1974), 174-97; U.S. Department of Labor, *The American Worker*, Richard B. Morris, ed., (Washington, D.C., 1976), 224; Coleman, *Men and Coal*, 313.

20. AFL, *History, Encyclopedia, Reference Book*, 821-28 and 25-70; AFL Executive Council, *Report, 1949*, 62-63. The incredible volume of hearings and litigation may be followed in *Wage and Hour Reporter*, 9 vols. (1938- 1946); Bureau of National Affairs, *War Labor Reports* (Washington, D.C., 1945- 1946); Bureau of National Affairs, *Wage and Hours Cases* (Washington, D.C., 1942-); *Wage and Hour Manual*, 8 vols. (Washington, D.C., 1940-1947). See also Mike Davis, *Prisoners of the American Dream* (London, 1986), 111, on the war and development of a "'common law' for plant-level labor relations."

21. *Labor* (October 28, 1941) reports labor turnover the "highest in history." Glaberman, *Wartime Strikes*, 54-57 and passim; Seidman, *American Labor*; Karen Anderson, *Wartime Women: Sex Roles, Family Relations and the Status of Women During World War II* (Westport, Conn., 1981), 49-51

22. AFL, *History, Encyclopedia, Reference Book*, 1124-25; McGaughey, *Short Workweek*, 44. See also "Establishment of the 30-Hour Week a Necessity," *Boilermakers' Journal* 57 (March 1945); "Green Foresees 30-Hour Week Soon," *The Bricklayer, Mason and Plasterer* (May 1946), 79.

23. CIO, *Proceedings, 1944*, 261-65; Preis, *Labor's Giant Step*, 215-16, 258, and 488; McGaughey, *Shorter Workweek*, 44.

24. AFL, *History, Encyclopedia, Reference Book*, 1126-33; Preis, *Labor's Giant Step*, 378-79. Note also the absence of hours discussions in the AFL's *Labor's Monthly Survey* for 1946 and 1947.

25. Victor G. Reuther, *The Brothers' Reuther and the Story of the UAW* (Boston, 1979), 312-18; "Guaranteed Wage," *Steel Labor* 12 (June 1947), 6-7; Preis, *Labor's Giant Step*, 379, 440-41, and 484-96.

26. George Lipsitz, *Class and Culture in Cold War America* (South Hadley, Mass., 1982), 120-23; Allen Wolfe, *America's Impasse* (New York, 1981), 49-79 and 52-53; CIO, *Proceedings, 1949*, 114-15.

27. Clyde E. Dankert, *Contemporary Unionism in the United States* (New York, 1948),

332-34; Richard L. Rowen, "The Influence of Collective Bargaining on Hours," in Clyde Dankert, Floyd Mann, and Herbert R. Northrup, eds., *Hours of Work* (New York, 1965), esp. 30-32; Hunnicutt, "End of Shorter Hours," esp. n.4 and 6; Owen, "Leisure," passim.

28.   Gouldner, *Wildcat Strike* (New York, 1954), 23; Lipsitz, *Class and Culture*, 36-113.

29.   Calculated from figures in McGaughey, *Shorter Workweek*, 38.

30.   *UMW Journal* 16 (June 1 and 15, 1945), 16-17 and 5; *UMW Journal*, 17 (May 1, 1946), 8-9 and 17, and (June 15, 1946), 3; Colston E. Warne and others, ed., *Yearbook of American Labor* (New York, 1945), 278-303, esp. 294; Wyndham Mortimer, *Organize: My Life as a Union Man* (Boston, 1971), 260.

31.   Lipsitz, *Class and Culture*, 38; Public Affairs Press, *The Shorter Work Week, Papers Delivered at the Conference on Shorter Hours of Work Sponsored by the American Federation of Labor and Congress of Industrial Organization* (Washington, D.C., 1957), 37-39.

32.   Jack Barbash, *Unions and Telephones: The Story of the Communications Workers of America* (New York, 1952), 54-61; Preis, *Labor's Giant Step*, 258; O'Connor, *Oil Workers*, 52-57; *Labor* (October 13, 1945).

33.   *UMW Journal* 17 (June 1, 1946), 3. Colston E. Warne, "Industrial Relations in Coal," in Warne and others, eds., *Labor in Postwar America* (Brooklyn, 1949), 367-86; Bruce R. Morris, "Industrial Relations in the Automobile Industry," in Warne and others, eds., *Labor in Postwar America*, 406.

34.   Munson, *Lithographers Union*, 268-73.

35.   *Labor* (December 1, 1942); *Chicago Progressive* (Organ of ITU Progressive Party) 11 (May 1951); (Chicago Typographical Union No. 16) *Reporter* (November 1945), 1; Robert K. Burns, "Industrial Relations in Printing," in Warne and others, eds., *Labor In Postwar America*, 421-22; Public Affairs Press, *Shorter Work Week*, 66-67 and 77-79.

36.   *Labor* (September 29 and October 13, 1945) and below.

37.   Seidman, *American Labor*, 235-36; Herbert Northrup, "Industrial Relations on the Railroads," in Warne and others, eds., *Labor in Postwar America*, 449-52; Whitney, "President's Department" column in the *Railroad Trainmen*, 63-64 (1946-1947) rarely strays from the dispute. See, "Memorandum of Understanding," *Railroad Trainmen* 64 (December 1947), 396, for a limited gain.

38.   *Labor* (June 2, July 21, and 22, 1945).

39.   Hertel, *Maintenance of Way Employees*, 207-9; "Forty-Hour, 5-Day Week Comes to Railroads Sept. 1," *Railway Clerk* 48 (January 1949), 3-8; "Railroads' Insistence on Splitting Rest Days," *Railway Clerk* 48 (March 1949), 139.

40.   Herman M. Sturm, "Postwar Labor Relations in the Maritime Industry," in Warne and others, eds., *Labor in Postwar America*, 477-81; "Maritime Workers Secure Gains," *Railroad Trainmen* 63 (July 1946), 230; *Daily Worker* (June 7, 1946).

41.   Preis, *Labor's Giant Step*, 488; Public Affairs Press, *Shorter Work Week*, 25 and 67-79.

42.   Ziskind, "Countermarch in Labor Legislation," in Warne and others, eds., *Labor in Postwar America*, 661.

43.   Weiss and Gronewald, "Wages and Hour Laws," in Warne and others, eds., *Labor in Postwar America*, 239 and 246-52; William S. Tyson, "The Portal to Portal Act of 1947," in Emanuel Stein, ed., *Proceedings of New York University First Annual Conference on Labor* (Albany and New York City, 1948), 541-73. On union portal-to-portal efforts just after the war, see above on miners; *Steel Labor* (October 1946), 3 and 12, and (January, 1947), 1; Edwin E. Witte, "Industrial Relations in Meat Packing," in Warne and others, eds., *Labor in Postwar America*, 500. On union opposition to the 1947 law, see AFL, *Proceedings, 1947*, 237 and 562, and CIO, *Proceedings, 1947*, 91-92.

44.   Lipsitz, *Class and Culture*, 112-34. On the precedents, see Tomlins, *The State and the Unions*, esp. 252-81.

45.   Emanuel Stein, "Digest of the Taft-Hartley Act," in Warne and others, eds., *Labor in Postwar America*, 707-15; Lynd, *Labor Law for the Rank and Filer* (San Pedro, Calif., 1978),

21-23, quote from 22; Tomlins, *The State and the Unions*, 282-316.

46. Lynd, *Labor Law*, 22; Lipsitz, *Class and Culture*, 127-31; Brody, *Workers in Industrial America*, 208-11. Barring of the extension of NLRB protections to foremen similarly undermined workers' control.

47. Reisman, with Nathan Glazer and R. Denney, *The Lonely Crowd* (New Haven, 1961), xliv-xlv. The literature on leisure, mass culture, and alienation is vast. For a provocative criticism, see Andrew, *Closing the Iron Cage*, esp. 130-52. See also Andrew Zimbalist, "The Limits of Work Humanization," *Review of Radical Political Economics* 7 (Summer 1975), 53. Marcuse's emphasis, contrary to the perceptions of many of his critics and admirers, was never wholly rooted in consumption. See *One Dimensional Man* (Boston, 1964).

48. AFL, *History, Encyclopedia, Reference Book*, 1128-29.

49. Andrew, *Iron Cage*, 130-52; Fred Thompson, "Introductory Notes," to Lafargue, *Right to Be Lazy*, 29; Dan Wakefield, "Labor Shudders at Leisure," in Walter Fogel and Archie Kleingartner, eds., *Contemporary Labor Issues* (Belmont, Calif., 1966), 177-81; Stanley Aronowitz, *False Promises: The Shaping of American Working-Class Consciousness* (New York, 1973), 51-134. Sidney Lens, *The Crisis of American Labor* (New York, 1959), 286-87, is somewhat exceptional as are a pair of articles by Harvey Swados, "A Note on Cultural Exploitation," in Cochran, ed., *American Labor at Midpassage*, 75-82, and "Less Work, Less Leisure," *Nation* 186 (February 22, 1958), 153-58.

50. F. S. O'Brien, "The Communist-Dominated Unions in the United States Since 1950," *Labor History* 9 (Spring 1968), esp. 200-201; Charles P. Larrowe, *Harry Bridges: The Rise and Fall of Radical Labor in the United States* (Westport, Conn., 1972), 353-54; Jack Barbash, *Labor Unions in Action* (New York, 1948), 78; Herman M. Sturm, "Postwar Labor Relations in the Maritime Industry," in Warne and others, eds., *Labor in Postwar America*, 461-88; Foner, *Women and the Labor Movement*, 2: 381 and 402-3; Wright and Lerner, *Too Many Hours*, 4 and 19.

51. See James J. Matles and James Higgins, *Them and Us: Struggles of a Rank-and-File Union* (Boston, 1974), 140ff; Foner, *Fur and Leather Workers*, 633-80; Hal Simon, "The Struggle for Jobs and for Negro Rights in the Train Unions," *Political Affairs* 29 (February 1950), 37.

52. Foner, *Women and the Labor Movement*, 2: 408, 394, 416, passim; Foner, *Fur and Leather Workers*, 657-84; Mark McCullouch, "White-Collar Unionism, 1940-1950," *Science and Society* 44 (Winter 1982-1983), 405-19; Bert Cochran, "American Labor in Midpassage," in Bert Cochran, ed., *American Labor in Midpassage* (New York, 1959), 44-51.

53. Max M. Kampelman, *The Communist Party vs. the CIO* (New York, 1957), 81 and 92, n. 43; Lipsitz, *Class and Culture*, 149-50 and 153-72; *Machinist* (August 1, 1957); Preis, *Labor's Giant Step*, 487; AFL, *History, Encyclopedia, Reference Book*, 1127-28.

54. Public Affairs Press, *Shorter Work Week*, 1.

55. Ibid., 7-19, quotes from 18-19, and 35.

56. Ibid., 20-35.

57. Ibid., 37ff, 88, and 94.

58. Ibid., 60; Marcia Greenbaum, *The Shorter Workweek* (Ithaca, N.Y., 1963), 9ff; Ernest M. DeCicco, "The Four-Day Week," *The New Leader* (July 29, 1957), 3-4; Dankert, Mann, and Northrup, eds., *Hours of Work*, 152; Charles D. Stewart, "A Shorter Workweek As a Factor in Economic Growth," *Monthly Labor Review* (February 1956), 157-60; Max D. Kossoris, "Hours of Work and Output," *Monthly Labor Review* (July 1947), 5-14.

59. Public Affairs Press, *Shorter Work Week*, 62, 53, 73-74, and 82.

60. See Peter Henle, "Which Way to Greater Leisure?" in Public Affairs Press, *Shorter Work Week*, 80-88, and the discussion, 89-96; Dankert, Mann, and Northrup, eds., *Hours of Work*, 7; Joseph A. Beirne, *New Horizons for American Labor* (Washington D.C., 1962), 57.

61. Dankert, Mann, and Northrup, eds., *Hours of Work*, 24; figures calcu lated from McGaughey, *Shorter Workweek*, 38.

62. DeCicco, "Four-Day Week," passim; McGaughey, *Shorter Workweek*, 45; Dankert, Mann, and Northrup, eds., *Hours of Work*, 24-25; David J. McDonald, *Union Man* (New York, 1969), 287; *Daily World* (May 7, 1957).

63. AFL-CIO, *Proceedings, 1959*, 638-43; *Proceedings, 1961*, 559-75; and *Proceedings, 1963*, 440-52.

64. McDonald, *Union Man*, 287-90.

65. AFL-CIO, *Proceedings, 1963*, 33; McDonald, *Union Man*, 287-90; Wakefield, "Labor Shudders," passim; "Shorter Work Week," *Electrical Workers' Journal* 61 (February 1962), 18; *The Worker* (March 29, 1961).

66. Dankert, Mann, and Northrup, *Hours of Work*, 7; Joseph E. Finley, *White Collar Union: The Story of the OPEIU and Its People* (New York, 1975), 268.

67. "Shorter Work Week," *Electrical Workers' Journal* 61 (February 1962), 18; "L. U. Three Strikes for Shorter Work Week," *Electrical Workers' Journal* 61 (March 1962), 37-39; "Shorter Work Week," *Electrical Workers' Journal* 61 (July-August 1962), 13; Public Affairs Press, *Shorter Work Week*, 94.

68. AFL, *Proceedings, 1967*, 483-85, *Proceedings, 1969*, 386-87, and *Proceedings, 1973*, 344-45.

69. A summary of the vast literature on labor during the period and on Lordstown is in Aronowitz, *False Promises*, 21-50, esp. 24-26.

70. *People's World* (August 30, 1955); George Morris, *American Labor: Which Way?* (New York, 1961), 75 and 140-43; *Daily World* (October 13-14, 1976); "30 for 40," *PL* 8 (March 1972), 10-27; Dan Georgakas and Marvin Surkin, *Detroit: I Do Mind Dying* (New York, 1975), esp. 227-41. See also *Industrial Worker* (May 23, 1960) and, more recently, *Daily World* (April 28 and June 29, 1978), and (April 26, 1979); *Guardian* (June 8, 1977); Henry Foner, "Labor's Struggle for a Shorter Workweek," *International Socialist Review* (May 1978); *Militant* (March 31 and June 30, 1978); *Challenge* (December 22, 1982); *Rebel Voices* 2 (Winter 1982-1983), 37.

71. Georgakas and Surkin, *Detroit*, 227-41, esp. 230-33; "Black Workers Congress," *Radical America* 5 (November-December 1971), 91; Foner, *Black Worker*, 415-22.

72. Charles Wilson, "The Struggle for the Shorter Work Week Today," *Political Affairs* 55 (May 1976), 7; Sar Levitan and Richard Belous, *Is There a Future for Shorter Hours?* (Washington, D.C., 1976), 12.

73. *Labor Today* (May 1976), 4-5; *Daily World* (October 1 and 7, 1976); *National Steelworkers Rank-and-File Report* (August 1975), 1-23.

74. *Wall Street Journal* (February 16, 1977); *New York Times* (October 11, 1976); *Daily World* (October 13, 1976); Wilson, "Work Week Today," 2-10.

75. *Daily World* (January 20 and February 18, 1977).

76. *Labor Today* (May, 1977), 1-6; *Daily World* (February 18, April 7, May 18, 20, and 24, 1977).

77. *Daily World* (June 21 and July 29, 1977); *Labor Today* (September 1977), 1.

78. Paul Rosensteil, "The Unions' New Tune," *Nation* (December 31, 1977), 720-22; *In These Times* (November 9-15, 1977); *Daily World* (October 27, 1977).

79. *Labor Today* (May 1978), 3-6; *In These Times* (April 19-25, 1978); *Guardian* (April 26, 1978); *Daily World* (April 6 and 13, 1978); *UE News* (April 17, 1978); Fraser quoted in *Daily World* (September 7, 1978); "A Call to the First National All Unions' Conference to Shorten the Work Week." The leaflets cited here and below are in Professor Roediger's possession.

80 *Daily World* (July 29, September 7, and 16, 1978); "1886 May Day 1978" (Call for planning meeting for the Chicago 1978 Haymarket/Shorter Hours Rally).

81. *Hearings Before the Subcommittee on Labor Standards of the Committee on Education and Labor, House of Representatives, Sixty-Ninth Congress, First Session on H.R. 1784* (Washington, D.C., 1980), 74 and passim.

82. Jane Slaughter, *Concessions and How to Beat Them* (Detroit, 1983), 114; *St. Louis Labor Tribune* (December 1, 1982).

83. *In These Times* (December 8-14, 1982), 7; *Chicago Tribune* (May 30, 1983); *Labor Today* (June 1983), 3, and (July 1983), 3-5; Pete Kelley, "Strategy for Labor in the 80s," in Linda Unger and Kathleen Schultz, eds., *Seeds of a People's Church* (Detroit, 1981), 33-38.

84. R. W. Hurd, "How PATCO Was Led into a Trap." *Nation* 233 (December 26, 1981), 696-98; "Striking Air Controllers Fired by President Reagan," *Monthly Labor Review* 104 (October 1981).

85. Unger and Schultz, eds., *People's Church*, 33-48; Foner, *Women and the Labor Movement*, 2: 451-55; Doug Jenness, "American Agriculture and the Working Farmer," *Education for Socialists* (November 1979), 5-13; Wassily Leontief, "The Distribution of Work and Income." *Scientific American* 247 (September 1982), 192. Cf. Ronald G. Ehrenberg and Paul L. Schumann, *Longer Hours or More Jobs?* (Ithaca, N.Y., 1982).

86. David Moberg, "Puttin' Down Ol' Massa: Laurel, Mississippi, 1979," in Marc Miller, ed., *Working Lives: The Southern Exposure History of the South* (New York, 1980).

87. Kim Moody and Jim Woodward, *Battle Line: The Coal Strike of '78* (Detroit, 1978), 14-15; *Daily World* (January 19, 1980); Leontief, "Work and Income," 188-204.

88. *The Worker* (April 29, 1956).

89. Joan Wallach Scott, "The Mechanization of Women's Work," *Scientific American* 247 (September 1982), 175; Kolko, "Working Wives," 259; Louise Kapp Howe, *Pink Collar Workers: Inside the World of Women's Work* (New York, 1978), 186-88. For appraisal of the quality and quantity of modern housework, see Susan Strasser, *Never Done: A History of American Housework* (New York, 1982), 300-312.

90. Howe, *Pink Collar*, 255; Kolko, "Working Wives," passim.

91. Ralph E. Smith, "Hours Rigidity: Effects of the Labor-Market Status of Women," in Karen Wolk Feinstein, ed., *Working Women and Families* (Beverly Hills and London, 1979), 211-12; Howe, *Pink Collar*, 256; "Working Time a la Carte," *ILO Information* 22 (December 1986).

92. Public Affairs Press, *Shorter Work Week*, 20; *Wall Street Journal* (December 7, 1976).

93. Much of Feinstein, ed., *Working Women*, concerns these trends. See esp. Denise F. Polit, "Nontraditional Work Schedules for Women," 195-210, and William Arkin and Lynne R. Dobrofsky, "Job-Sharing Couples," 159-76. See also *New Women's Times* (June 1983), 4; Barbara Moorman, ed., *Job Sharing Through Collective Bargaining* (San Francisco, 1982). For acute theoretical commentary on part-time women's work, see Veronica Beechey, *Unequal Work* (London: Verso Books, 1987).

94. Foner, *Women and the Labor Movement*, 2: 424 and 436; *CWA News* (August 1983), 7; *Hearings Before the Subcommittee . . . on 1784*, 39.

95. See Selma James, *Women, Unions and Work* (London, 1976), 15.

96. Gorz as quoted in Hilary Rose and Sue Ward, "Time, Gentlemen, Please," (Great Britain) *New Socialist* (May-June 1984), 18. See also Irwin E. Klass, "Eight-Hour Day: Labor's Historic Matter of Time," (Chicago) *Federation News* (February 1986).

Bibliographical Essay

Because this study covers so long a period, because it addresses both work and leisure, and because it seeks to integrate the approaches of the "old" and the "new" labor history, it uses a vast number of sources, primary and secondary. Full citations to those sources are found in the notes. This brief essay identifies collections and publications which especially informed the arguments of the book.

Outstanding among previous treatments of the working day in the U.S. are Marion C. Cahill, *Shorter Hours: A Study of the Movement Since the Civil War* (New York: Columbia University Press, 1932); Horace A. Davenport, "The Regulation of Hours" (unpublished M.A. thesis, University of Pennsylvania, 1947); and John E. Robinson, "The History of the Reduction of Working Hours" (unpublished M.A. thesis, University of Pennsylvania, 1933). Especially useful for the recent past are William McGaughey, Jr., *A Shorter Workweek for the 1980s* (White Bear Lake, Minn.: Thistlerose Publications, 1981); Clyde E. Dankert, Floyd C. Mann, and Herbert R. Northrup, eds., *Hours of Work* (New York Harper and Row, 1965); and Benjamin Kline Hunnicutt, "The End of Shorter Hours," *Labor History* 25 (Summer 1984).

Our theoretical approach to the working day and labor history critically draws on the essay by E. P. Thompson, "Time, Work Discipline and Industrial Capitalism," *Past and Present* 38 (December 1967) and the title essay in Herbert Gutman's *Work, Culture and Society in Industrializing America* (New York: Vintage, 1977). Also vital is the chapter titled "The Working-Day" in Karl Marx, *Capital*, 3 v. (New York: International Publishers, 1967), I:231- 302. The emphasis on the interaction of control issues and the reduction of hours stems from an appreciation of David Montgomery, *Workers Control in America* (Cambridge: Cambridge University Press, 1979) and of Harry Braverman, *Labor and Monopoly Capitalism* (New York: Monthly Review Press, 1974). Montgomery's *Beyond Equality: Labor and the Radical Republicans* (New York: Knopf, 1967) guided our approach to the origins of the eight-hour movement. Meridith Tax's *The Rising of the Women* (New York: Monthly Review Press, 1980) also provided analytical ideas, as did Alan Dawley and Paul Faler, "Working-Class Culture and Politics in the Industrial Revolution: Sources of Loyalism and Rebellion," *Journal of Social History* 9 (June 1976), 466-81, and Louis Hartz, "Seth Luther: The Story of a Working Class Rebel," *New England Quarterly* 13 (September 1940), 401-18.

Among the multiplicity of primary sources, the pamphlet literature has been especially important. For the antebellum period, see William Heighton, "An Address Delivered Before the Mechanics and Working Classes Generally" (Philadelphia: *Mechanics' Gazette* Office, 1827?) and "Address to the Members of Trades' Societies and to the Working Classes Generally," (Philadelphia: Author, 1827); Seth Luther, "An Address Before the Mechanics and Working Men of Brooklyn" (Brooklyn: Author, 1836) and "An Address to the Working Men of New England" (Boston: Author, 1832). Important later pamphlets include Lemuel Danryrid, "History and Philosophy of the Eight-Hour Movement" (New York: American Federation of Labor Eight-Hour Series, 1889) and George Gunton, "Economic and Social Importance of the Eight-Hour Movement" (New York: American Federation of Labor Eight-Hour Series, 1889). Key labor pamphlets, almost all bearing on the issues addressed in this book, are collected in Leon Stein and Philip Taft, eds., *Labor Politics*, 2 v. (New York: Arno, 1971) and *Religion, Reform and Revolution: Labor Panaceas of the Nineteenth Century* (New York: Arno, 1971). Philip S. Foner, ed. *American Labor Songs of the Nineteenth Century* (Urbana: University of Illinois Press, 1977) and *We, The Other People* (Urbana: University of Illinois Press, 1976) were of special value, as was the unsurpassed John R. Commons and others, eds. *A Documentary History of American Industrial Society*, 10 vols. (Cleveland: A.H. Clark, 1910-11).

Government documents are particularly useful in studying the hours of labor. In the period before 1865 the various reports of legislative committees studying child labor, female labor, and factory work, especially for Massachusetts and Pennsylvania, are exceedingly rich. See especially, *Report of the Select Committee Appointed to Visit the Manufacturing Districts of the*

366

Commonwealth for the Purpose of Investigating the Employment of Children in Manufactories of the Commonwealth of Pennsylvania (Harrisburg, Pa., 1838). For later years, the reports of state Bureaus of Labor Statistics are excellent sources, especially in the late nineteenth century when shorter-hours activists helped to develop labor statistics as a profession. Also particularly noteworthy is W.D.P. Bliss and John B. Andrews, *History of Women in Trade Unions*, vol. 10 of *Report on Condition of Women and Child Wage Earners in the United States*, Senate Document 645 (Washington, D.C., 1911).

Critical among archival collections are those at the Library of Congress in Washington, D.C., (Benjamin F. Butler Papers, Martin Van Buren Papers, Woodrow Wilson Papers, and Michael Shiner Diary); at the Labadie Collection at University of Michigan in Ann Arbor (Richard Trevellick Papers, Josiah Warren Papers, Ezra Heywood Papers, and Knights of Labor Scrapbooks); at State Historical Society of Wisconsin in Madison (Ira Steward Papers, Thomas Phillips Papers, John R. Commons Papers, Edward H. Rogers Papers, Albert Parsons Papers, Samuel Gompers Papers, John Samuel Papers); and at Reuther Library at Wayne State University in Detroit (Industrial Workers of the World Collection).

Index

A

Abramowitz, Bessie, 186

Adamic, Louis, 210

Adamson, W.C., 198

Adamson Act, 194-99

Addams, Jane, 167-68, 186

Alger, Russell A., 135

All Unions' Committee to Shorten the Workweek, 274

Alschuler, Samuel B., 206

Altgeld, John Peter, 168

Amalgamated Association of Iron, Steel and Tin Workers, 222

Amalgamated Clothing Workers, 186, 226, 252

Amalgamated Lithographers of America, 263-64

Amalgamated Textile Workers, 216-17

American Association for Labor Legislation, 178

American Federation of Labor: arguments for shorter hours, 152-54, 227, 237-38; conservatism of, 152-54, 158-60, 163-65, 170, 210, 241-44; defends Haymarket prisoners, 143; and immigrant workers, 151; and the "new unionism," 179-80, 183, 209; and political action, 150, 154-55, 158, 175, 179, 198, 246-47; post-World War Two deemphasis on hours, 262; six-hour day and, 213, 246-48, 259; steel organizing, 187, 222- 23, 226; strategy of, 158-59, 163; Taylorism and, 227, 232- 33; trading control for leisure, 227, 237-38; women workers and, 145, 163-65, 170; World War One and, 202-203, 207; World War Two and, 260-61. *See also* Federation of Organized Trades and Labor Unions; Voluntarism

American Federation of Labor—

Congress of Industrial Organizations, 269; vacillation on the working day, 271-74

American Federation of Labor—Congress of Industrial Organizations Conference on Shorter Hours of Work, 269

American Revolution, and the working day, 5-8. *See also* Independence Day; Republicanism

Ameringer, Oscar, 139-41

Andrews, Elmer F., 256

Anticommunism, 214, 217, 221-22, 230-31, 268-69

Antislavery, and the working day, 81, 85-86, 305-306n.61

Arthur, Chester A., 128-29

Artificial lighting, 51-52, 57-58, 70

Artisans: colonial, 3-5; developing consciousness of hours, 8- 10; leadership of ten-hour movement, 11, 17, 44-45

Association of Workingmen, 22

Atkin v. Kansas, 156

Auto Workers Action Caucus, 273

B

Baer, George F., 161

Bagley, Sarah, 51, 54-57

Baker, Newton, 203-204

Bakers, 11, 67, 132, 157-58

Balanoff, James, 274

Baltimore, 10, 34, 87

Banks, Nathaniel P., 107, 109

Banks, Theodore, 114

Barbers, 4

Barry, Thomas, 134-35

Beal, Fred, 220-21

Bellamy, 154

Bells, 4, 20-21, 50-51

Bennett, Thomas, 103-104

Berry, George L., 242

Billings, Warren, 189

Bisno, Abraham, 167-68

Black, Hugo, 246-52, 254. *See also* Thirty-Hour Workweek Legislation

Black-Connery Bill. *See* Thirty-Hour Workweek Legislation

Black workers, in working day struggles, 87-88, 160, 188, 205-206, 216, 221 racism and, 4, 88-89, 268; in steel strike of 1919, 226

Black Workers Congress, 272

Blacklisting, 58, 64, 216

Blankenhorn, Heber, 230

Blinn, D.C., 134-35

Bonfield, John, 141

Boston, 5, 11-12, 23, 26-27, 29-31, 94, 112

Boston Labor Reform Association, 94

Boston Eight-Hour League, 112

Boycotts, 130, 132, 173

Brandeis, Louis D., 14, 174-203, 232

Brandreth, George, 93

Breaks, in the working day, 2, 3, 6, 10-11, 38, 56, 147, 165, 270, 275

Brewery workers, 132

Bridgeport, 201

Bridges, Harry, 268

Brooks, George, 269

Brophy, John, 214

Brotherhood of Locomotive Engineers, 195

Brotherhood of Locomotive Firemen and Enginemen, 195

Brotherhood of Maintenance of Way Employees, 265

Brotherhood of Railroad Trainmen, 195

Brotherhood of Railway Signalmen, 264

Brotherhood of Timber Workers, 188

Building trades, 241, 259; leading role in nineteenth century hours struggles, 16-7, 24-25, 45, 109-110, 132. *See also* Carpenters; Plumbers

Bureaus of Labor Statistics, 147-48

Burritt, Elihu, 44-45

Butcher Workmen, 205-206

Butler, Benjamin, 74-77, 143

Byrd, Harry F., 259

C

Cabot, Charles, 232

Cabot Fund, 232, 234-35

Campbell, L.R., 148

Cameron, Andrew C., 106, 108

Canada, 317, n.50

Carpenters, 110, 132; ten-hour initiatives of, 7, 10-12, 14, 22, 24-25; victory in eight-hour campaign, 159

Catholic Church, 225, 227-29

Chandler, Zachariah, 72

Chartism, 61

Chase, Samuel, 102

Chicago: eight-hour struggles, 106-107, 136-44, 205-206; women workers in, 165-70

"Chicago Idea," 136-37, 324n.57

Child labor: growth of, and ten-hour movement, 9, 11, 20-21, 28, 37-38, 74-75; legislation against, 37-38, 155-56, 158, 173, 199-200, 253-56; in textiles, 11, 35, 46, 63-64, 182

Chinese exculsion, 124-25

Christian Labor Union, 228

"Citizenship time," 7. *See also* Republicanism

Civil War, and eight-hour movement, 81-100

Clark, Daniel, 57

Class consciousness: in eight-hour campaigns, 97, 137-38, 160, 168, 180, 182-86, 206, 217-24; growth of, in early ten-hour movement, 12-13, 15, 25, 30-31, 35-36; lessening of, in hours struggles of 1850s, 72; and working day, 290n.52, 293n.102

Clay, Cassius M., 71, 85

Clockmakers, 7

Clocks, 5-6, 10, 282n.12; manipulation of, by employers, 20, 47, 51, 123

Clothing trades, 66-67, 164-70, 183-86, 241, 252. *See also under names of unions in the industry*

Cluer, John, 60

Coalition movement, 73-78

Coalition of Black Trade Unionists, 273

Commerford, John, 30

Commission on Industrial Relations, 194-95

Committee for Trade Union Action and Democracy, 273

Commons, John R., 12, 28-29, 148

Communication Workers of America, 276

Communist party: five-day workweek campaigns, 219-22, 238, 241; in Great Depression, 244, 247; and the workweek, after World War Two, 268, 272

Community support: for shorter hours campaigns, 18, 20, 22-23, 116, 118, 133-35

Concessions, 274

Coney Island, 146-47

Congress of Industrial Organizations; and the working day: during the Great Depression, 252-53, 255; in World War Two, 260-61; after World War Two, 262, 265, 268

Connery, William P., Jr., 248

Conyers, John, 273-74

Conyers Bill (H.R. 1784), 274

Cooke, Morris, 233-35

Coolidge, Calvin, 217

Curtis, Harriet, 54-55

Curtis, Dr. Josiah, 49, 74

D

Danyrid, Lemuel, 152

Davis, James, J., 236

Debs, Eugene V., 180

DeLeon, Daniel, 143

Democratic party and the working day, 38-42, 61, 70-78, 108, 244- 45, 253, 262. See also Jacksonian Democracy

Depressions, 36-37, 64, 119, 243-46

Dickson, William Brown, 232

Disque, Brice, 207

Division of labor, 8-9, 124, 205

Douglas, Charles, 26-27, 44

Drinking, breaks for, 6, 10-11, 17, 32; feared by employers, 31, 233

E

Early closing. See Retail Clerks

Eastman, Mehitabel, 57

Economic and Sociological Club, 113

Economic growth, and reduction of hours, 85, 94-95, 193

Edison, Thomas, 190

Edmonston, Gabriel, 136

Education: child labor and, 9, 21-22, 99; emphasis on, by ten- hour activists, 9, 13, 21-22, 41, 54, 74; Steward on, 86; twentieth century interest in, 178, 224; women workers and, 54, 166, 169

Eight-hour day: arguments for, 81-86, 96-98, 119, 153-54; campaigns for, in 1880s, 126-31, 135-42, 158-59. Civil War and, 81-90; comparisons to ten-hour day demand, 81, 97-100; demand for, origins of 36, 44, 66, 81-82, 93-94; Fair Labor Standards Act establishes, 255-56, 259; Henry Ford and, 189- 94, mass demand arises for, 81-100; political failures to establish after Civil War, 101-12; railroad workers and, 194-99; in steel, 186-87, 203-204, 222-27, 230-32, 234-38; strikes for, during Reconstruction, 114-16; in textiles, 182-83, 216-22; widely adopted by 1920, 177; won by printers and miners, 161-63; won by shipwrights, 44; in World War One years, 172-83, 186, 188-91, 194-208. See also Legislation; Republican Party; Democratic Party, Strikes

Eight-Hour Leagues, 88-100, 103, 113-14

Ely, Richard, 228-29

Emerson, Ralph Waldo, 8

Employer associations, 149-50, 193, 202, 239-40, 256

Engel, George, 123, 144

English, William, 31

Evans, George Henry, 53, 63, 72-73

Executive Order 9301, 260

Executive Order 9651, 264

F

Factory workers, and ten-hour day, 8, 26-27, 33, 35-36, 45-46, 49-64, passim, 102-104

Fair Labor Standards Act, 253-56, 259, 261, 267

Farley, Harriet, 54-55

Farmers, 25, 46, 50-51, 179, 212, 275, 306n.61

Fatigue, and the critique of long hours, 174, 234, 237

Federal Council of Churches, 187, 228-29

Federal employees and the hours of work, 38-42, 68-69, 84, 128- 29, 109-12, 155, 194, 253

Federated American Engineering Societies, 235-36

Federation of Organized Trades and Labor Unions, and May 1, 1886 strikes, 124-26, 128-31, 135-38, 143

Fehrenbatch, John, 91

Feiss, Richard, 240

Ferral, John, 30-31, 44

Fielden, Samuel, 123, 138, 141

Filene, Edward, 234, 240

Fincher, Jonathan, 86-87, 97

Fincher's Trades Review, 83

Firefighters, 215, 227

Fischer, Adolph, 123, 144

Fitch, John, 187, 222, 232, 234

Fitzpatrick, John, 179, 205-206, 222-23, 225

Five-day workweek, 220, 237-42, 244-47; See also Forty-Hour Workweek; Thirty-Hour Workweek

Five-hour day, 244, 272

Flexitime, 258, 276

Flynn, Elizabeth Gurley, 182-83

Food, Tobacco, Agricultural and Allied Workers Union, 268

Ford, Henry, 177-78, 204, 211, 339n.58; eight-hour reform, 190- 94; introduces five-day workweek, 237-42

Forty for forty-eight, 263-65

Forty-four hour workweek, 182, 215, 242

Forty-hour workweek: won by fur workers, 238; phased in by Fair Labor Standards Act, 256, 259; standard today, 258. *See also* Five-Day Workweek

Foster, Frank K., 129, 152

Foster, William Z., 178, 193, 205-206, 222-26

Four-hour day, 6, 181

Frankfurter, Felix, 203-204

Franklin, Benjamin, 4-6, 284n.43

Fraser, Douglas, 273-74

Free labor ideology, and shorter hours, 30-31, 72-78

Free Soil party, 71-73

Frey, John, 237

Full Employment Act, 262

Fur workers, 185, 238, 245

G

Gardner, V.O., 264

Garretson, A.B., 196-97

Gary, Elbert H., leads resistance to shorter hours in steel, 204, 222-27, 235-36, 239

Gary, Joseph E., 142-43

Gates, Thomas, 3

Geary, John W., 118-19

Gender, and the workday, 43-62, 163-75, 275-76. *See also* Women Workers

George, Henry, 144, 158

Gibbons, James Cardinal, 229

Gifford, V.P., 168

Gilman, Charlotte Perkins, 171

Gold, Ben, 245

Golden, John, 216

Goldmark, Josephine, 148, 174

Gompers, Samuel, 160, 162; and Adamson Act, 196, 198; anti-statism of, 129, 151, 179, 198; arguments for shorter day, 152-53; defense of Haymarket prisoners, 143; on eight- hour gains of 1886, 142, 159; goals, 279n.1; and immigration, 151; leadership of 1890 eight-hour drive, 158- 59; Marx's influence on, 129; and May Day, 158; an May 1, 1886 strikes, 140, 142-43; opposition to labor populism and socialism, 154, 170, 179; and scientific management, 233; and steel strike of 1919, 223-26; on unemployment and the workday, 153; and women workers, 164, 170, 183; on workers' control and hours, 180; in World War One, 203, 207. *See also* American Federation of Labor

Gorz, Andre, 227

Gottlieb, Sylvia, 269

Grant, Ulysses S., 111

Great Britain, 23-24, 60, 75, 154, 172, 231, 305n.49

Greeley, Horace, 58, 61, 72, 304n.29

Green, William: background of, 210; five-day workweek and, 237- 38, 240, 244-47; justifications for shorter hours, efficiency and, 237-38, 247; political action, support for, 179, 244, 247; thirty-hour workweek, 246-47; unemployment insurance and, 246; on wages, efficiency and shorter hours, 237, 247; on worksharing, 24.

Greenback movement, 112, 316-17n.44

Grinnell, Julius S., 143

Guest, Edgar, 225

Gunton, George, 120, 150, 152, 231

H

Hamilton, Alexander, 9, 282n.22

Hamilton Company, 48-49

Hammer v. Dagenhart, 200

Harding, Warren G., 235-36

Harpers Ferry arsenal, 48

Harrison, Carter, 141

Hartz, Louis, 27

Haymarket police riot and bombing, 123, 140-44

Haywood, William, 181-82

Health, and the working day, 27, 38, 51-52, 55-56, 74, 168, 196, 233-34, 264, 275

Heighton, William, 13-14, 284n.43

Henrotin, Ellen, 168-70

Hewitt, S.C., 43-44

Heywood, Ezra, 105

Hillman, Sidney, 186, 247

Hoar, Sherman, 168

Holden v. Hardy, 157

Holidays, 3, 5, 184

Hoover, Herbert, 238; arguments against long hours, 233-34; pressures steel to reduce hours, 211, 233-35; on worksharing, 245

Hours of labor, 45, 82, 297n.36; in Britain, 2-3; in American colonies, 2-5; in New York City (1831), 23; after 1835 strikes, 34-35; in antebellum textile mills, 46- 48, 59, 78-79; reduced in 1850s, 78-79; in early 1880s, 123- 24; after 1886 strikes, 142; among street railwaymen, *circa* 1900, 156; reductions in 1905-1920, 177; in steel, be for World War One, 186-87; nationally in 1919, 212, 215; in steel, after World War One, 222-23, 227, 236-37; early failures of five-day workweek, 238, 241-42; in 1929, 243; extent of five-day workweek in 1932, 245, under the National Industrial Recovery Administration, 249-50; after the Schechter decision, 251-52; from Middle Ages to 1938, 257; over last fifty years, 257-58; and World War Two, 259-60; from 1948-1957, 263; from 1957 to 1978, 270. *See also under individual trades*

Hourwich, Isaac, 186

Housework, 164-65, 182-83, 275-76

Howat, Alexander, 214

Howland, Rachel, 103-104

Hunnicutt, Benjamin Kline, 258

I

Idleness, fear of, 6, 13, 37

Illinois Bureau of Labor Statistics, 168
Illinois Women's Alliance, 165-70
Immigrant workers: bias against, 124-25,
        151, 217, 225-26; consciousness
        of hours among, 32, 63-64,
        66-67, 93, 143, 179-80, 191,
        223-24; reformers and, 75; in
        textiles, 58, 63- 64, 102, 217;
        and unity across ethnic lines, 32,
        63, 66-67, 93, 98, 102, 120-21,
        133-34, 142, 184-90, 205, 217,
        223-26
Independence Day, and shorter hours
        actions, 21, 61, 66, 90, 116, 130,
        236, 323n.37. See also
        Republicanism
Indians, 4
Industrial Workers of the World,
        180-83, 190, 207, 213-15
Informal resistance to long hours,
        6, 10-11, 32, 48-49, 210, 272
Ingersoll, Ebon, 109
Interchurch World Movement, and the
        working day in steel, 222, 227,
        230-31
International Association of Machinists,
        162, 201-202, 269
International Brotherhood of Electrical
        Workers, 241, 271; Local 3,
        271-72
International Labor Day. See May Day
International Labor Union, 120-21
International Ladies' Garment Workers'
        Union, 183-84, 252
International Longshoremen's and
        Warehousemen's Union, 265, 268
International Typographical Union, 137,
        159-63, 264
International Union of Machinists and
        Blacksmiths, 93-94
International Union of Timberworkers,
        215-16
International Workingmen's Association,
        112-14, 119-20, 136-44
Iowa Union Conference for Shorter
        Hours, 273
Irish immigrants, and the hours of work,
        63-64, 75

J

Jackson, Andrew, 39
Jacksonian Democracy, 18, 21, 33,
        38-42
Jacobi, Mary Putnam, 172
Jefferson, Thomas, 5-6
Jessup, William, 110
Jewish workers, 133, 183-84
Johnson, Andrew, 110-11
Johnson, Paul, 12
Johnstone, Jack, 206
Jones, Mary "Mother," 170, 223-24
Julian, George, 91, 109-10

K

Keady, Patrick, 108
Kellogg, Paul, 232
Kenaday, Alexander, 89
Kelley, 168-70, 172, 174
Kennedy, John F., 271
Kenney, Mary, 165-66, 169-71
Knights of Labor, 143, 158, 166; early
        support of eight hours, 124-29;
        leadership abstains from
        supporting 1886 eight-hour strike,
        129-31; 134-36, 138; locals
        support 1886 strikes, 136, 138;
        loses members, after 1886, 144

L

Labor parties, and ten-hour day, 16-18,
        36, 285n.56
Labor recruitment, 49-50
Lafargue, Paul, 178
Land reform, 53, 305n.37
Lassalle, Ferdinand, 112-13
League of Revolutionary Black Workers,
        272
Lee, Elisha, 196
Lee, John R., 192-93
Lee, W.G., 198
Lemlich, Clara, 183
Legislation, on the working day:

colonial, 3-4; Philadelphia (1835), 33; Massachusetts child labor (1836 and 1842), 37- 38; Pennsylvania (1848), 61-62; New Hampshire (1847), 58; New Jersey (1851), 73; Maine (1851), Rhode Island (1853), Connecticut (1855), 71; federal, for shipyard workers (1862), 84; Illinois (1867), 90; Wisconsin (1867), 91; New York (1867), 93; in 1867 and 1868, 101, 104-105; federal (1868), 109-112; Massachusetts (1874), 119-20; California (1876), 89; Maryland mining (1884), 128; Rhode Island women and children (1885), 127; Michigan (1885), 127; Ohio (1886), 127; federal (1892), 155; Illinois women and children (1893), 168-69; from 1892-1922, covering women, 173-74; Adamson Act (1916), 194-99; Keating-Owen Act (1916), 194, 199-200; Motor Carriers Act (1935), 252; Postal Act (1935), 252; Maritime Hours Law (1936), 253; Walsh-Healey Act (1936), 253; Fair Labor Standards Act (1938), 253-56. *See also* Bakers; Child Labor; Miners, Women Workers

Leisure, 223-24; consumption, mass culture and, 178, 262-63, 268, 362n.41; desire for, 275; feared, 211, 271; Henry Ford on, 192-93; in Progressive Era, 146-47, 178; and self-education, 21-22, 74, 178

Leo XXIII, Pope, 228-29

Leontief, Wassily, 275

Lewis, John L., in coal strike of 1919, 213-14; summarizes Congress of Industrial Organizations' record, on workday, 252; in World War Two era, challenges national hours policy, 261, 263

"Lighting up." *See* Artificial Lighting

Lindsay, Samuel M., 235-36

Lingg, Louis, 122, 138

Litchman, Charles, 127

"Little Steel Formula," 260

Lloyd, Henry Demarest, 143, 169

Local 2703 (Chicago), 160-67

Lochner, Joseph, 157-58

Lordstown, 272

Louisiana, 87-89

Lovestone, Jay, 208

Lowell, Francis, 46-47

Lowell, Josephine Shaw, 172

Lowell, Massachusetts, 53-62; 75-76

Lowell Female Labor Reform Association, 51, 53-62

Lowell Offering, 50-51, 53-57, 62

Loyal Legion of Loggers and Lumbermen, 207, 215-16

Ludlow Massacre, 188

Lumber Workers' Industrial Union, 207

Luther, Seth, 24-25, 27, 30, 44, 47. *See also* Ten-Hour Circular

Lynch, James, 237

M

Machinists, 150, 127, 162, 269, 274; central role in early eight- hour movement, 81-82, 91, 93-94; munitions strikes, 201-202. *See also* International Association of Machinists

Malkiel, Theresa, 164

Marcuse, Herbert, 267-68

Marcy, Mary, 178

Marine Workers Affiliation, 212

Marot, Helen, 184

Marx, Karl, 82, 129, 137, 284n.43

Marx-Aveling, Eleanor, 123, 143

Marxists, 112-14, 317nn.44, 49. *See also* Communist Party; International Workingmen's Association; International Working People's Association; Socialist Labor Party; Socialist Party

Massachusetts, 73-77, 93-96, 112

Massachusetts Bureau of Labor Statistics, 112

Master craftsmen, 8, 293n.102; oppose shorter hours, 12-14, 34

May Day, 158, 330n.58

McBride, John, 160

McDonald, David, 271

McDonnell, J.P., 129

McDowell, John, 230

McGuire, Peter J., 113, 120

McNamara brothers, 189

McNeill, George, 20, 126, 158; abolitionism of, 85-86; and International Labor Union, 119-21, and Massachusetts Bureau of Labor Statistics, 112

Meany, George, 269-71

Mellon, Andrew, 240

Mechanics Union, 15

Merchant capital: opposition to ten-hour day, 12-13, 24, 130; and the transformation of work, 8-9, 12-13, Methodism, 99

Milwaukee, 141-42

Miners: failure to undertake 1891 eight-hour drive, 159; protective legislation for, 156-57; strikes, 161-62, 188-89, 213-15, 275; World War Two era, 261, 263

Mitchell, John, 161

Molders, active in early eight-hour campaigns, 82, 92

Montgomery, David, 86, 177

Moonlighting, 258, 269

Mooney, Thomas, 189

Moore, Ely, 39, 289n.43

Morgan, Edmund, 4

Morgan, Elizabeth, 127, 166, 168

Morgan, Thomas, 137

Morris, Gouverneur, 7

Morris, Richard B., 3, 6

Morton, Marcus, 38, 71, 74

Most, Johann, 136

Muller, Cult, 174

Muller v. Oregon, 174-75

Music, and shorter hours, 44, 47, 86, 107, 139, 171

Muste, A.J., 216-17

245; opposition to shorter hours, 149-50, 202, 231, 239, 256

National Civic Federation, arguments for shorter hours, 150; general opposition to shorter hours, 150, 231; Gompers and, 153, 162; in mine and machinists' disputes, 161-62; withdraws support from Interchurch World Movement, 231

National Consumers' League, 145, 172-75

National Industrial Conference Board, 202, 239-40

National Industrial Recovery Act, 249-52

National Labor Relations Act, 266

National Labor Union, 87, 110-13

National Maritime Union, 265

National Textile Workers Union, 219-21

National Trades' Union, 28-30, 38-39

National War Labor Board. *See* War Labor Board

Nationalist clubs, 154

Neebe, Oscar, 123, 138, 144

Nelson, Donald M., 260

Nestor, Agnes, 165, 170

New England Association of Farmers, Mechanics, and Other Working Men, 25

New England Industrial League, 77

New England Workingmen's Association, 43, 53

The New Slavery, 168

Newspaper Guild, 266

"New Unionism," 179-80, 219

New York, 92-93, 157-58

New York City, 4, 10-11, 17-18, 22-23, 107-108

Niebuhr, Reinhold, 238

Non-Partisan League, 212

N

Nathan, Maud, 172-73

National Amusement Parks Association, backs five-day workweek, 240

National Association of Factory Inspectors, 147-48

National Association of Manufacturers: endorsement of worksharing,

O

O'Donnell, Edward, 163

Office and Professional Employees' International Union, 271

Oil, Chemical and Atomic Workers' Union, 275

Oil workers, 188, 263, 275

Oliver, Henry K., 112

Operation Dixie, 268

Order of Railway Conductors, 195

O'Reilly, Lenora, 170

O'Sullivan, Mary Kenney. *See* Mary Kenney

Overman, Lee, 199

Overtime, 187, 188; Adamson Act and, 196; Fair Labor Standards Act and, 256; forced, 261, 272; in recent past, 269-75; Walsh-Healy Act and, 253; World War One labor policies and, 204-205; World War Two controversies over, 260-61

Owen, Robert, 199

P

Packing industry, 205-206

Paine, Thomas, 7

Panama Canal, 155

Parsons, Albert, 123; Knights of Labor eight-hour lobbyist, 127; organization of May 1, 1886 strikes, 137-39; Stewardism and 137; trial and execution, 143-44

Parsons, Lucy, 138, 166

Paterson, strikes in, 11, 35, 217-19

Pennsylvania, 4, 37-38

Pepper, Claude, 255

Perkins, Frances, 249

Perry, David M., 149

Philadelphia, and ten-hour movement, 7, 11, 31-34, 62

Phillips, Thomas, 83

Phillips, Wendell, 95

Photo-engravers, 259

Piece rates, and the work day, 10, 23, 32, 52-53

Pittsburgh Manifesto, 136

Place, E.R., 86

Play, redefined, 146-47

Political action to reduce hours: American Federation of Labor, during Great Depression, 246-49, 253-56; American Federation of Labor, opposes general hours law, 155, 179, 244; withdrawal from United Labor party, 154;

coexistence with economic stategies, 65; Civil War and, 86-100; Eight- Hour Leagues and, 88-100, 103, 113-14; Federation of Organized Trades and Labor Unions, early support for political action, 128-29; Knights of Labor and, 127-28; National Trades' Union and, 27-30, 38-40; in Reconstruction, 102-104-109. *See also* American Federation of Labor, Democratic Party, Legislation on the Working Day; Republican party; Socialist party; Voluntarism

Populism, 154-55, 329n.39

Portal-to-portal pay, 189, 203, 266

Portal-to-Portal Act, 266

Powderly, Terence, 158, 323n.35; arguments for eight hours, 5, 127; opposition to strikes, in 1880s, 127-28, 130-31, 136; refusal to defend Haymarket prisoners, 143; and Secret Circular, 136

Powell, Adam Clayton, 271

Pragan, Otto, 269-70

Preindustrial styles of work, 1-4, 50, 52

Printing trades, 10, 162-63, 215, 242, 259, 263-64

Productivity: increases in, tied to reduction of hours, 72, 97, 146-48, 150, 152-53, 190-92, 231-35, 247

R

Rabinowitz, Matilda, 183

Racism, 4, 88-89, 124-25, 266

Railroad workers, 194-200, 264-65, 348n.94

Raskob, John J., 244-45

Reformers: arguments for shorter hours by, 74-78, 145-47, 165-75, 178, 184, 211, 230-36; domination of movement in 1850s, 74- 77; hesitancy to embrace five-day demand, 238-40; in steel, 230-36; and women workers, 145-47, 165-75, 178, 184. *See also* Child Labor, Productivity; Relgion

Religion, 5, 77, 192, 289n.36;

Methodism, 99; mixed response to shorter hours, before 1920s, 225, 227-30; shorter hours campaign in steel and, 230-32; ten-hour movement and, 26-28, 51. *See also* Sabbath

Republicanism: Civil War and resurgence of, 81, 85, 99; and class, 30-31, 72; growth of ten-hour demand and, 6-7, 9-11, 13-14; in Heighton's writings, 13-14; partial decline of, 130; in ten-hour strikes of 1830s, 23, 30-32; and women workers, 55, 60. *See also* Independence Day

Republican party: formation of, and the hours of work, 72-78; Radical wing, mixed impact on eight-hour movement, 86-100, 108-10, 112; and steel industry reforms, 235. *See also* Political Action

Retail clerks: and origins of the early closing movement, 33, 67; and support for shorter hours, 33, 67, 90, 93, 156, 165, 173, 189, 276. *See also* National Consumers' League; Women Workers

Retirement, 258, 359n.8

Reuther, Walter, 262, 271

Rhode Island System, in textiles, 46

Rickenbacker, Eddie, 259

Rickert, Thomas, 185

Riesman, David, 267

Ripley, George, 53, 62

Ritchie v. Illinois, 169

Rittenhouse, David, 5-6

Robinson, Frederick, 27

Robinson, William S., 74-77

Rodgers, Elizabeth, 166

Rodgers, John, 38

Rogers, Edward H., 85, 94

Roosevelt, Franklin D., 249, 251-54, 260

Roosevelt, Theodore, 147, 161, 179

Rosen, Frank, 274

Runnels, Frank, 274

Rubber workers, 252, 263

Rush, Benjamin, 6

Ryan, John A., 247

Ryckman, L.W., 62

S

Sabbath, as a day of rest, 3, 5, 11, 26, 28, 227-29, 239, 289n.36

Sadlowski, Ed, 273

Safety, and hours of work, 188, 196, 275

Sage, Henry W., 134

St. John, Vincent, 181

St. Louis, 36-37, 88

St. Monday, 6

Saposs, David T., 8

Saturday half-holiday, 185, 187, 215, 228, 237, 242

Schaack, Michael, 141

Schechter decision, 251-52

Schilling, George, 138, 152

Schlossberg, Joseph, 186, 217

Schouler, William, 56-57, 61

Schwab, Michael, 123, 125, 138

Scientific management, and the hours of labor, 146-48, 174-75, 202, 232-33. *See also* Taylor, Frederick Winslow

Sellins, Fannie, 223

"Secret Circular," 136

Service Employees' International Union, 276

Seven-hour day, 203, 244, 250, 271-74

Sherman, John, 110-11

Shiner, Michael, 41, 68

Shipyard workers: early struggles for shorter hours, 20-23; federal government and hours of, 38-42, 68-69, 84; win eight-hour day, 44, 77

Silk workers, 217-18

Sinclair, Upton, 190

Six-Hour day, 213-15, 263, 319n.78. *See also* Thirty-Hour Workweek

Skidmore, Thomas, 18

Skill, differences among workers in, and cooperation in shorter workday campaigns, 31-34, 45, 98, 102-104, 121, 135, 159, 179-80, 185-87, 224. *See also* Class Consciousness; Wages

Slater, Samuel, 8

Slavery, 44

Socialist Labor party, 137, 154

Socialist party, 179, 193, 329n.40

Socialists, and the workday, 120, 129, 179, 185, 193, 230, 329n.40. *See also under names of various socialist organizations and under* Marxism

Solberg, Winton, 4

Sorge, F.A., 113, 121

Soule, George, 230

Soviet Union, 243, 345n.46

Speedups, and the desire to reduce hours, 8-9, 51-52, 124, 182, 191-92, 219-20, 240

Spies, August, 123, 140

Starkweather, S.W., 117-18

Statutes of Labourers (Artificers) in 1350, 2; in 1495, 2; in 1563, 2-3.

Steel industry, 270-71; hours of labor in, 128, 186-87, 222-23, 227, 236-37; strikes in, 186-87, 222-27; twelve-hour day ended in, 230-36; working day in, during World War One, 203-204

Stelze, Charles, 228

Stephens, Uriah, 126

Stevens, Alzina, 166, 168-69

Steward, Ira, 119, 228, 317n.45; advocate of diverse strategies, 104-105; allies with Marxists, 101, 112, 120; arguments for eight-hours, 84-86, 94-95, 97-99; on class and exploitation, 97, 152-53; compares eight-hour and ten-hour demands, 81, 97; influenced by antislavery, 81, 84-85; influences Albert Parsons, 137; influences American Federation of Labor, 120- 21, 129;in Massachusetts eight-hour campaign, 93-96, 103, 112; opposition to greenbackism, 112; and Radical Republicanism, 95-96; on unity between skilled and unskilled, 98

Steward, Mary, 164

Stockyards Labor Council, 205-206

Stone, James, 74-75, 96

Strasser, Adolph, 129

Strikes: Philadelphia (1791), 7; Pawtucket (1824), 11; Boston (1825), 12; Paterson (1828), 11; Philadelphia (1827), 13-14; Pittsburgh (1831), 22; early 1830s, 19-20; Cincinnati (1831), 23; New Bedford (1832), 23; Boston (1832), 24; Baltimore (1833 and 1835), 25, 34; Boston (1835), 30-32; Philadelphia (1835), 31-34; Pittsburgh (1845), 57-58; Nashua (1846), 57-58; Pittsburgh (1848), 58-60; New York City (1850), 66-67; New Jersey (1851), 56; textile (1850s), 66- 68, 70; in Civil War, 84; Wamsutta Mills (1866), 103-104; Chicago (1867), 106-107; Pennsylvania coal (1868), 105-106; New York City (1871), 114; New York City gas workers (1873), 114-16; lumber (1872-1873) 116-19; St. Louis (1877), 120; Maryland miners (1882), 127-28; telegraphers (1883), 132-33; Michigan lumber (1885), 133-35; May 1 (1886), 139-42; carpenters (1890), 159; in metal mining, 161, 180-81; coal (1902), 161; Oregon sawmills (1907), 187; Uprising of the 20,000 (1909), 183-84; steel (1910), 187; Hart, Schaffer and Marx (1910), 185; New York City furriers (1912), 185; Lawrence (1912), 183; Paterson (1913), 183-84; in men's clothing industry (1913), 185-86; mining (1906-1917), 188- 89; Buffalo clerks (1913), 189; munitions (1915-1918), 201- 202; New York harbor (1918-1919), 212; coal (1919), 213-14; steel (1919-1920), 222-27; Colorado coal (1927), 214-15; Lawrence (1919), 216-17; Southern textiles (1919), 218; Paterson (1920s), 218-19; Gastonia (1929), 219-22; increase of (1933-1934), 251; Chicago printers (1945), 264; railroads (1946), 265; maritime (1946), 265, coal (1946-1947), 263; railroads (1948), 264-65; Professional Air Traffic Controllers (1981), 275. *See also under names of individual trades, cities in which strikes occurred and corporations struck*

Study and Defense Clubs, 138

Suburbanization, 146

Sunday labor. *See* Sabbath

Sunrise to sunset labor, 2-4, 14

Surplus value, 13, 137; 284n.43

Survey, 178, 232, 234

Survey group, 187

Swank-Holmes, Lizzie, 138, 166-67

Sweatshops, 167-68. *See also* Clothing Trades

Switchmen's Union, 196

Sylvis, William, 93, 97-98, 105, 112

T

Taft, William Howard, 204

Taft-Hartley amendments, impact on workday, 266-68

Taylor, Frederick Winslow, 146-47, 232. *See also* Scientific Management

Taylor Society, 235

Teagle, Walter C., 245

Teagle Committee, on worksharing, 245-26

Technological change, 237, 298n.46, 307nn.9-10; accepted by shorter hours advocates, 114, 83; American Federation of Labor and, 237, 244, 247, 259, at Ford, 190-92; in mining, 213-14; peripheral to early ten-hour campaigns, 1-2, 14; Steward and, 85; in textiles, 52; in trades embracing early eight-hour demand, 82-83; unemployment and, 244, 247, 259, 275

Telegraphers, 133, 264

Telephone workers, 227, 263, 276

Temperance, 193. *See also* Drinking; Prohibition

Ten-Hour Circular: content of, 30-31; impact in Philadelphia, 31-32

Ten-Hour day: arguments for, 7-8, 13-15, 21-22, 27, 31, 44-45, 50, 52, 54, 74-78; in factories, 8, 26-27, 33, 35-36, 45-46, 49-64, 102-104; first demand for, 7-8; mass movements by artisans for, in 1820s and 1830s, 11-17, 20-35, 38-40; republicanism and, 6-7, 9-11, 13-14; strikes for, 7, 12, 14- 15, 22-25, 30-36, 57-60, 68, 102-104, 116-19;

unemployment and, 7-8, 15, 31; working women and, 43-44, 52-63, 74-78. *See also* Education; Health; Ten-Hour Petitions

Ten-Hour petitions, 33, 39-40, 44, 51, 54-57, 61, 68, 73

Ten-Hour Republican Association, 73-78

Textile industry, 8, 11, 33-34, 45-64, 68-69, 102-104; 182-83, 216-22, 251

Thirty-five hour workweek, 203, 244; legislation proposed for, 271-74; miners win, 250

Thirty-for-Forty, 262, 265, 272-73

Thirty-hour workweek, 244, 355n.24; considered after World War One, 212-14; legislation for, 246-52, 254; pursued after World War Two, 262, 265, 272-73; won by elevator constructors, 250. *See also* Six-Hour Day

Thompson, Edward P., 1-2, 11

Time, perceptions of, 1-3, 8, 10-11, 50. *See also* Clocks

Townsend, Robert, 29

Trade Union Unity League, 244

Tramping, 124

Transport workers, 131, 156, 215

Tresca, Carlo, 182

Trevellick, Richard, 70, 97, 107, 127

Truman, Harry S., 26-65

Turnover, 49-50, 191, 193, 360n.21

U

Unskilled workers. *See* Skill.

Unemployed Councils, 244

Unemployment, 224, 234, 261, 355n.2; and Ford, 193; in Great Depression, 245-46, 251; in Long Depression, 119-20; in recent past, 269-70, 274, 276; seasonal and intermittent, 7- 8, 15, 31, 164, 213-14; shorter hours, as a cure for, 7-8, 31, 119-20; 152, 181, 193, 224, 234, 245-46, 251, 269-70, 274, 276; ten-hour day and, 7-8, 15, 31. *See also* Depressions; Technological Change

Unemployment insurance, 244, 246
United Auto Workers, 260, 262, 265, 272
United Hebrew Trades, 185
United Labor party, 144
United Mine Workers, 161, 213-14, 250, 261, 263
United Steel Workers, 262, 273, 275
United States Chamber of Commerce, opposes five-day workweek, 240
United States Industrial Commission, 148
United States Public Health Service, 234
United States v. Martin, 111
United Textile Workers, 216, 218
United Workers, 120
Utopian socialists, 52, 62-63

V

Vacations, 258, 262, 270, 271, 273. *See also* Holidays
Van Arsdale, Harry, 272-73
Van Buren, Martin, 40-42, 71
Voice of Industry, 50, 55-56, 58, 60
Voluntarism, and trade union distrust of the state, 121, 130, 137, 158, 179, 198, 241, 246
Voluntary reductions of hours, 103, 149, 173, 186, 190-94, 245

W

Wages, 9-10, 52-53, 236; central issue after World War Two, 262; cuts in, coincident with reduced hours, 62, 138, 182, 247; increases in, tied to reduction in hours, 33, 36, 77, 95, 138, 153, 181-82, 213; Steward on, 95; strikes over, as compared to those over hours, 19, 20, 131-33, 160-61, 181, 209-10, 251, 262. *See also* Piece Rates
Walling v. A.H. Belo Corporation, 261
Walsh, Frank, 195, 199, 204, 206
Ward, Harry F., 228
Ware, Norman, 65, 98-99
War Labor Board, 203, 203-204, 217, 341n.105. *See also* War Labor Policies Board

War Labor Policies Board, 200, 203-205
War Production Board, 260-61
Weinberg, Nat, 270
Weisbord, Albert, 221
Western Federation of Miners, 156, 180-81
Westinghouse strike, 201-202
Weydemeyer, Joseph, 86, 97
Whig party, 38-42, 61
Whitney, A.F., 245, 264
White-collar workers, 33, 271, 291n.68. *See also* Retail Clerks
White House Industrial Conference, 224-26
Whittier, John Greenleaf, 67-68
Wiggins, Ella Mae, 221
Wilkinson, David, 8
Wills, Garry, 5
Wilson, W.B., 206
Wilson, Woodrow, 194-200, 206, 212, 224
Wirtz, Willard, 271
Women's suffrage, 55, 166-67
Women's Trade Union League, 170-72, 178, 183-85
Women workers, 9, 346n.54; American Federation of Labor and, 145, 150, 163-66, 170-72, 175; in clothing trades, 164-70, 183-86, 241; female reformers and, 163-75, 178, 183-85, 216; Industrial Workers of the World and, 182-83; protective legislation and, 27-28, 127, 145, 150, 168-69, 173-75, 239; sexism and, 145, 163-64, 170, 175; special arguments for shorter hours among, 54, 61, 145, 164, 182-83, 261, 276-77; ten-hour struggles by, 11, 34-35, 53-64, 68, 102-104; in textile mills, 34-35, 43-64, 68, 102-104, 182-83, 216-22; unity with men, seeking shorter hours, 11, 35, 43-45, 68, 102-104; 184-86, 216-22. *See also* Gender; Women's Suffrage
Woodbridge, Alice, 172
Woodcock, Leonard, 273
Work discipline, 6, 9, 47
Workers' control: and shorter hours, sought as complimentary goals, 115-16, 124, 177, 183-84,

201-202, 209, 213-14, 279n.9;
trade unions and the
disconnection of workday
demands from, 237-38, 241-42,
262-65, 267, 351n.147. *See also*
Scientific Management; Speedups

Workers' party, 214. *See also*
Communist Party

Workingmen's Association of Trenton,
73

Workingmen's party, 120, 285n.56

Working Men's Party: New York City,
17-18; Philadelphia, 15-16

Working Women's Union, 166

Worksharing, 245-46

Works Progress Administration, 249-50

World War One, and the working day,
195-208, 211-12, 222. *See also*
War Labor Board; War Labor
Policies Board

World War Two, and the working day,
259-61

Wright, Frances, 22

Y

Young, Coleman, 274

Young, W.F., 55

About the Authors

DAVID ROEDIGER teaches labor history at the University of Missouri. He is the coeditor, with Franklin Rosemont, of *Haymarket Scrapbook* and the author of recent articles in *History Workshop Journal, Labor History, Journal of Social History,* and *Labour/Le Travail.*

PHILIP S. FONER is Professor Emeritus of History at Lincoln University. His many books include *Organized Labor and the Black Worker, 1619-1973* and the two-volume *Women and the American Labor Movement.*

Ohmer